FALSE SECURITY

FALSE SECURITY

THE RADICALIZATION OF CANADIAN ANTI-TERRORISM

Craig Forcese and Kent Roach

Published in 2015 by

Irwin Law Inc.
14 Duncan Street
Suite 206
Toronto, ON
M5H 3G8

www.irwinlaw.com

ISBN: 978-1-55221-410-7
e-book ISBN: 978-1-55221-411-4

Cataloguing in Publication available from Library and Archives Canada

Printed and bound in Canada.

1 2 3 4 5   19 18 17 16 15

Contents

Preface

This is a book we never expected to write. In October 2014, we were both happily working on other research projects during our academic sabbaticals from teaching at law school. In the wake of the two October terrorist attacks, we knew things would change in Canada. We hoped they would change for the better. We feared they would not.

In the immediate aftermath, we wrote "if the attack on Parliament and on Canadian Armed Forces members constituted a failure by the state to exercise its fundamental 'night watchman' function, it was probably not a failure of law."[1]

But we feared a legal overreaction based on the false idea that "legal fixes" would prevent reoccurrences. The *Criminal Code*, we argued, grows in girth "not because the evil of humans is ever mutable, but because high-profile manifestations of that evil demand a new political response of some sort . . . . It will be next to impossible for parliamentarians to resist the lure of new legal enactments, some responsive to these recent events and some more distantly related."

We endorsed the need to learn lessons from the attacks, especially answers as to why there was enough evidence to keep Martin Couture-Rouleau off flights (or more specifically, revoke his passport) but not to prosecute him. We predicted a reawakening of government interest in the 2010 Air India Commission report that had examined Canada's most deadly act of terrorism.

We urged that any new "law project or proposed power must be evaluated on its own merits. This requires time for deliberation." We hoped that new legislation would "recognize (as was not done in the post 9/11 legislation) that oversight and review of security in Canada is in disarray and that public confidence requires effective accountability that can keep pace with increased and integrated security activities." We also warned that we

cannot prosecute or detain our way out of the radicalization problem. Although this truth has become surprisingly politically contentious, the sociology of anti-terrorism cannot be ignored. Outreach and partnerships in Canada's diverse Muslim community is necessary. We should also be aware that heavy handed approaches, especially those focusing on speech, might have the unintended consequence of being counter-productive.

But we expressed confidence that lawmakers would appreciate the need to build restraint into the foundation of new powers.

Boy, were we wrong. In its content, the bill the government tabled on 30 January 2015 — Bill C-51 — was the most radical Canadian national security law ever legislated during our career as scholars and analysts of such things. And that means it was the most radical national security law ever enacted in the post-*Canadian Charter of Rights and Freedoms*[2] period. In a dubious accomplishment, it managed to raise acute rights issues that already are being challenged under the *Charter*, while rejecting security improvements that the Air India Commission recommended were urgently needed.

We were wrong also that our government and Parliament would exhibit careful deliberation, of the sort witnessed during the immediate post-9/11 period for Canada's original 2001 anti-terrorism law. For the first time in our careers, and perhaps ever, the government chose national security as a political wedge issue with an eye on an upcoming election — in this case, the one that would take place in October 2015. The government made sure that the law was rushed through Parliament with minimal amendments. The politics around the bill became polarized, and at times, toxic. Complex issues were, on both sides, too often reduced to slogans and talking points. The debate was — to paraphrase Thomas Hobbes — nasty, brutish, and short.

And we were wrong that there would be lessons-learned exercises flowing from the October attacks. To be sure, the police investigated the Ottawa attack and redacted versions of their investigation were eventually released, but there was no public, broader effort to piece together how things were *not* pieced together before the attack. This stood in stark contrast to what occurred in the aftermath of another recent attack in another democracy — Australia.

Canada was, in other words, getting it wrong. We decided, therefore, to set aside other projects and just start writing. We never set out to be protagonists in a political drama. Rather, we are two academics who, by dint of expensive educations and even more expensive careers financed by taxpayers and tuition-paying students, have spent years trying to understand national security law. One of us (Roach) spent six years working on both the Arar and Air India Commissions of Inquiry. The other (Forcese) wrote the leading (okay, the only) text on Canadian national security law.

Our approach to national security law — and every other area we work in — reflects a commitment to academic engagement and a belief that no society that protects academic freedom should tolerate academic silence when points of subject-matter expertise are at issue.

We were also cognizant that, unlike our colleagues in the United Kingdom and the United States, we do not enjoy the company of large numbers of other law professors with a national security focus, and we do not live in a country whose security agencies have invested regular and sustained effort to develop and cultivate understanding outside of their silos. And unlike the United Kingdom and Australia, we do not benefit from the role of an "independent reviewer" of terrorism laws — someone who is given access to government secrets and is charged with reporting publicly on the use and development of anti-terror law.

We first saw Bill C-51 on its release on January 30 and were astonished at the evident disconnect between its radical content and that of the short and misleading "backgrounders" issued by the government. Right away we committed to offering whatever insight we had to help fill Canada's awkward gap in anti-terror policy deliberations with what we called "real time scholarship." With the assistance of our publisher, we set up www.antiterrorlaw.ca and, during what we dimly recall as a busy and very cold February 2015, began posting lengthy "backgrounders" — legal analyses — on various aspects of Bill C-51. They were (and remain) free to download at www.antiterrorlaw.ca. We wrote many op-eds and essays for popular media[3] and fielded more press calls than we could count. And we appeared in front of parliamentary committees, when invited to do so. Since we began in January 2015, we haven't really stopped, and this book is the culmination of our deliberations.

Given its genesis, it is not your typical academic enterprise. Yes, we have poured as much detail and substance into it as we thought our readers could bear. But we want — need — there to be many readers, and not just lawyers working in the obscure, underpopulated area of national security law. We have, therefore, focused as much on policy as on law. And we have done our best to make both understandable to people who have not spent a career navigating the proverbial weeds in this obscure area of law, policy, and practice.

Although perhaps unusual for an academic work, we have been pointed in our criticism where pointed criticism is warranted. Our opinions are part of this book, and we make no attempt to hide them. It is probably inevitable that our criticisms will irk and perhaps wound officials inside executive government, hard pressed daily to protect Canada while we have the luxury of writing overlong critiques. We may also annoy those who review these security agencies, and disgruntle parliamentarians who act in complete good faith, but not always on the basis of good information.

If we do displease any of these people, it is with considerable regret. Our purpose is not to condemn their hard work — quite the contrary. Our purpose is to acknowledge how much of that hard work takes places in a security system much more dysfunctional than it should or could be. When fingers are pointed, we wish them directed at those with the power to fix this unsatisfactory situation; and in our system, ministers are ultimately responsible for the conduct of government.

There are also those who will criticize us for the very existence of our critique. Some in Canada's increasingly polarized political world will imagine partisanship lies behind it — especially our willingness to address the language and conduct of Prime Minister Stephen Harper and his ministers. But that accusation only has merits if you conflate non-partisanship with neutrality on the issues. If our focus is on the Harper government, it is because it was on that government's watch that the events of October 2014 occurred. We supported the Harper government's 2013 enactment of four terrorism offences aimed at foreign terrorist fighting and we opposed the 2015 reforms in part because of our belief that they will make such offences more difficult to prosecute.

The Harper government is the only government that has had a chance to respond to the 2006 Arar Commission's recommendations about the need to modernize the independent review of national security or the 2010 Air India Commission's recommendations (affirmed in 2011 by a unanimous Senate committee chaired by Senator Hugh Segal) about the urgent need to improve how Canada investigates and prosecutes terrorism. The fact that the Harper government failed to respond to the warnings of these and many other reform proposals is what steers our criticisms, not the colour of our (non-existent) lawn signs. It is also a government that has chosen political messaging we believe to be inimical to both security and rights, and that too gets the treatment it deserves.

Some will see in our critique the caterwauling of two former research directors of, and advisors to, ignored commissions of inquiry (albeit not all of them on national security). In this last respect, we are guilty of the view that when a government finances, at great expense, serious, comprehensive and transparent policy-thinking of the sort that now seems rarely to be done inside government, it should listen. And when it rejects the recommendations of such reports (as it is free to do), it should do so at least for rational reasons because it has a better solution, and not out of inertia or political calculation.

We make no claim to omniscience. A professor of national security and anti-terrorism law romps over terrain populated by hundreds of micro-specialists in government. And unlike our colleagues working in other areas, we are obliged to spend a career focused on the tip of an iceberg whose better part is obscured by fierce (and often excessive) secrecy. As students of history, we know that it makes us all fools. In the end, history will judge how much we have erred in the predictions and fears expressed in this book.

To save the usual disclaimers throughout the book, we note that one of us (Roach) previously served on the board of directors of the British Columbia Civil Liberties Association and acted as its counsel in *R v Khawaja* (2012 SCC 69) where he (unsuccessfully) argued that parts of the definition of "terrorist activity," specifically the political and religious motive requirement, violated the *Charter*. We both have been consulted by the Canadian Civil Liberties Association on its challenge to Bill C-51 filed in the Ontario Superior Court in July 2015, and one of us (Roach) serves on its board of directors. Additionally, we have participated in one way or another in considering all the national security laws proposed since 9/11, and our work has sometimes been on the periphery of some of the lawsuits that followed. Indeed, we have rarely opposed such laws, although often urged refinements and improvements. And even with Bill C-51 and the earlier 2015 law, Bill C-44, we did not dispute their purported objectives, merely their means and omissions. Our focus has always been on repairing 2015's security laws, not burying them, something that has put some distance between us and some rights groups that we work with and admire.

We have spoken to all and any who would speak to us — a category that includes members of each official political party (and one that is not), and a handful of government officials, mostly at academic outreach events. We have benefitted from the even more helpful input of retired senior mandarins and Canadian and non-Canadian security practitioners with considerable relevant experience who have shared their insight, although not (of course) their operational knowledge. We single out: Mel Cappe, former clerk of the Privy Council, and now professor at the University of Toronto, for special thanks in reviewing some of this book; Joe Fogarty, a former UK security liaison to Canada who generously shared many ideas with us and also came out of the shadows to testify before the Senate committee examining Bill C-51; and Professor Lorne Dawson of the University of Waterloo who generously read and commented on our chapter that deals with programs to counter violent extremism. We also thank the individuals who reviewed this book and provided comments flagged on its cover.

We have filed dozens of access to information requests and depended on others filed by journalists or researchers. Some of these requests generated useful information. Even more useful information might have been found if requests had been processed more quickly and if less material had been redacted. We have pored over the reporting of Canada's small — but tenacious — band of national security journalists. This book would not have been possible without them, and Canadians should appreciate the value provided by these determined reporters, willing to do the hard work of scratching below the surface of a secretive Canadian government's most secretive sector. Their editors deserve thanks for allowing them to pursue these stories in an industry whose modern challenges make subject-matter specialization and time-consuming investigations increasingly rare.

We have conducted much additional research beyond that which went into our original backgrounders prepared during February 2015, particularly with respect to historical approaches to terrorism, the evolving nature of the terrorist threat and response, and evolving practices with respect to countering violent extremism. And of course, we have puzzled over the government's often brief rationales and explanations for the new laws and have reviewed the findings of Canada's judges, generally publicly reported in unredacted decisions, who have the unenviable job of adjudicating right from wrong where both are sometimes obscured by a fog of secrecy. All of this is to say that we have done our best to find facts and ground our opinions in them. If we are incorrect in some of our assertions, it is not for lack of considerable effort to be as truthful as possible. This is as intellectually honest a book as we are capable of writing based on the facts we have, and it is as open a book as we can make. While we have resisted the law professor temptation to resort to overlong "essays within an essay" footnotes, we have populated this work with extensive endnoting pointing to the sources of our facts.

We have also benefitted from excellent assistance. A team of students worked assiduously in the winter to assemble an informal legislative history of Bill C-51 in the Commons, still posted at www.antiterrorlaw.ca. But we flag, in particular, the superb research assistance provided by Leah Sherriff during the crammed winter months of debate on Bill C-51, and in the lead up to this book. We rely in places very heavily on her research memoranda, especially in Chapters 3 and 13. Leah is a recent JD graduate of the University of Toronto's Faculty of Law. She has served her country courageously in the past and we predict that she will have a bright legal career, hopefully in national security law. At times in the book, we also rely on past research done in collaboration with other research partners, and acknowledge that work in the endnotes.

We underscore, however, that the opinions expressed in this book are our own, as are any errors. They should not be ascribed to others whose work assisted our endeavours. Our opinions truly do represent a blend of both of our perspectives. The order of our names on the cover reflects nothing more than alphabetical coincidence, not relative contributions: there is no "first author" to this book. It was a partnership of overlapping but also distinct specialties. And while we will not go so far as one Twitter wag and fuse our names into a shared identity — Roachese — there is no part of this book that does not bear both our sets of fingerprints.

As will be true for any project of this scale, there are many other people who deserve sincere acknowledgement. We thank the many colleagues — in academia and elsewhere — who encouraged our work in this area, and regularly spoke with or wrote to us with expressions of encouragement and gems of wisdom. We also extend sincere thanks to Jeff Miller, Alisa Posesorski, John Sawicki, Lesley Steeve, Anita Levin, Gillian Buckley, Britanie Wilson, Carey Roach, and Carmen Siu in the Irwin Law team who supported this project from the time it was a gleam in the eye right through to a fast-paced publication schedule, designed to produce this book while the issue remained ripe. Law is not a nimble creature, but legal publishers can be. Jeff Miller especially deserves praise for supporting this project as an exercise in active citizenship.

One of us (Roach) gratefully acknowledges the generous financial assistance provided by the Pierre Trudeau Foundation, which awarded him a fellowship in 2013 to conduct other research but cheerfully supported a change in direction and provided necessary funding for his sabbatical and Leah Sherriff's invaluable research assistance. We thank in particular the Trudeau Foundation's president, Morris Rosenberg, and Jennifer Petrela who also organized an important off the record meeting with retired and current security officials in early February 2014. Again, in these overheated times, we note that the Pierre Trudeau Foundation is a non-partisan charitable organization and the views expressed in this book are only our own.

Finally, we must thank our families. In fact, we must beg our families for their forgiveness. Photoshop may be able to repair our absence from family albums for the period from January to July 2015. But much more is required to thank Jan, Sandra, Madeleine, Erin, and Carey for their support and patience through long hours of physical absence, and even longer hours of mental preoccupation and our bouts of outright mental fatigue. We dedicate this book to our children, who must continue to enjoy security in this peaceable federation. And so we direct this book at those who would make Canada a safer place, while honouring our successes as an open, tolerant, peaceful, and rights-observing state.

There will always be tension in balancing security with rights and Canada is not alone in facing the challenges of evolving and serious terrorist threats. We fear that Canada is lagging behind other democracies. We must do better — both in understanding and responding. We do not have all of the answers. But we think we are asking the right questions and pointing to the right problems. We hope that at least one of our readers will be in a position, now or someday, to ask similar questions and actually do something in response to the answers.

Kent Roach & Craig Forcese

August 2015

Abbreviations

ATA	*Anti-terrorism Act* (2001)
CBSA	Canada Border Services Agency
CIA	Central Intelligence Agency (US)
CSE	Communications Security Establishment
CSE Commissioner	Communications Security Establishment's review body
CSIS	Canadian Security Intelligence Service
CSIS Act	*Canadian Security Intelligence Service Act*
CVE	counter–violent extremism
FBI	Federal Bureau of Investigation (US)
FISA	*Foreign Intelligence Surveillance Act of 1978* (US)
FLQ	Front de libération du Québec
ISIS	Islamic State of Iraq and Syria, also known as the Islamic State of Iraq and the Levant or ISIL
MI5	Security Service (UK)
NATO	North Atlantic Treaty Organization
PCO	Privy Council Office
RCMP	Royal Canadian Mounted Police
SIRC	Security Intelligence Review Committee, the Canadian Security Intelligence Service's review body
SoCIS Act	*Security of Canada Information Sharing Act*, part of Bill C-51

TPIM	terrorism prevention and investigation measures (UK)
TPP	Terrorism Prevention Program (RCMP CVE program)
TSAS	Canadian Network for Research on Terrorism, Security and Society

CHAPTER ONE

Introduction

I. THE ATTACKS AND THEIR AFTERMATH

The October 2014 Attacks

On 20 October 2014, Martin Couture-Rouleau drove his car into two uniformed members of the Canadian Armed Forces, killing Warrant Officer Patrice Vincent. Authorities had seized Couture-Rouleau's passport that summer, in order to stop the recent convert to Islam from leaving Canada to fight with the Islamic State of Iraq and Syria (ISIS). Nevertheless, he had not been arrested or charged under new terrorism offences that Canada enacted in 2013 to penalize those who attempted to leave Canada to participate in foreign terrorist groups. Nor did authorities restrict his liberties with an anti-terror peace bond (a form of restraining order).

Two days later, Michael Zehaf-Bibeau — whose passport application had also been delayed within the government for reasons that remain unclear — murdered Corporal Nathan Cirillo, a soldier who was standing ceremonial guard at the National War Memorial. Zehaf-Bibeau fired three shots from his long gun into the back of the defenseless Corporal Cirillo. Incredibly, and despite intelligence issued a few days before about increased threats of terrorism, Zehaf-Bibeau was then able to enter the Centre Block of the Parliament building where the prime minister, the leader of the opposition, and some 230 members of Parliament were in caucus meetings. He wounded the unarmed parliamentary guard who had tried to disarm him before he was killed by Sergeant-at-Arms Kevin Vickers and RCMP officers.[1]

1

Legislating in Fearful and Politicized Times

Canadians and their political representatives were united in their shock and grief at these attacks. But only for a time. Prime Minister Harper introduced Bill C-51 in an election-style rally on 30 January 2015. He defended the legislation on the basis that "violent jihadism is not a human right. It is an act of war, and our government's new legislation fully understands the difference."[2] The bill made the most far-reaching changes to Canadian security laws since 9/11. Bill C-51 was introduced not only in response to the October 2014 attacks, but also as a political reaction to terrorist attacks in January 2015 in Paris and Copenhagen. Those attacks targeted the Jewish community and those perceived to have insulted Islam, most famously the French satirical newspaper *Charlie Hebdo*.

The cold Canadian winter of 2015 was then beset by security fears. Police charged two people with conspiracy to commit murder on Valentine's Day and alleged that they had planned to shoot people in a Halifax mall. Minister of Justice MacKay stated that this was not an act of terrorism because of the absence of a "cultural" element, a peculiar turn of phrase given the absence of such a concept in the law. For some, it was a coded phrase suggesting a double standard for Islamic-related terrorism,[3] but the arrests aroused more fear. A week later, al-Shabaab, the al-Qaida-linked Somali terrorist group, issued threats to shopping malls, including the West Edmonton Mall. This led to thirty-five teams withdrawing from a cheerleading competition, one that was fortunately still held without incident and with 2,700 competitors.[4] This al-Shabaab threat was cited by government politicians as an indication of the need to enact Bill C-51 in a hurry and was reproduced in part in a Conservative party fundraising video.[5]

In March 2015, Jahanzeb Malik, a permanent resident, was arrested and held in immigration detention pending his subsequent deportation to Pakistan. He had allegedly told an undercover officer of plans to bomb the American consulate in Toronto and that he had trained in Libya and was interested in joining ISIS. He reportedly told the undercover officer that it was legitimate to attack taxpaying Canadians because of Canada's role in bombing ISIS.[6] Other developments included a mysterious tunnel near a Toronto Pan Am Games venue that turned out to be a "man cave" and a white powder sent to federal ministers from Quebec that turned out to be innocuous. Nevertheless, these incidents also raised the fear level. As a result, Bill C-51 was debated and enacted in a fearful and politicized environment. Public opinion polls suggested that over 80 percent of Canadians supported Bill C-51 in February 2015. This support declined as Canadians debated the bill, with a slim majority of those who closely followed the debate actually opposing the bill.[7] But Canadians were scared and they wanted to be safe.

In a transparent effort to capitalize on a "security bump" in public opinion and a cascade of foreign and domestic threats, government politicians legislated aggressively and quickly, deploying unusually heated terminology and rhetoric. They were not deterred by — and perhaps, they welcomed — criticisms that Bill C-51 violated the *Charter* — Canada's constitutionalized bill of rights — and transformed the role of the judiciary from a protector of *Charter* rights into a pre-authorizer of *Charter* violations. With the October 2015 election closing in, the debate about the law became partisan. At times, ministers and parliamentarians disparaged those who had concerns about the proposed law, implying that these people were uncommitted to security or even, in one egregious case, that they had ties with terrorists.[8]

Legislating without Evidence

The government made no transparent attempt to learn from the security failures that might have led to the two October 2014 attacks. In June 2015, it did eventually release narrowly framed police and parliamentary reports on the shootings and security responses at Parliament.[9] In contrast, the Australian government published a seventy-five-page report detailing all government dealings (and there were many) with a terrorist who launched an attack in Sydney in December 2014. The report was public one month after the attack.[10]

Nothing like this report has emerged in Canada. We still do not know the full story about why Couture-Rouleau's passport was seized in the summer of 2014 to stop him from leaving for Syria, but there was no subsequent peace bond or prosecution. Disturbing information emerged in June 2015 about how siloed security allowed Zehaf-Bibeau to enter the Parliament buildings, but none of the laws enacted as a result of the attacks were responsive to these security flaws, and many questions remain about how such a stunning security breach was possible in the face of previous recommendations and intelligence warnings.

When enacting its 2015 security laws, the government consistently rejected the outside policy advice it received, whether that advice related to rights or security. It radically ramped up information sharing about even marginal security threats, but disregarded advice it had received from the Privacy Commissioner and the judicial inquiry into Maher Arar's mistreatment that Canada's system of independent review was partial, stuck in silos, and manifestly inadequate. The government also disregarded the advice it received from four former prime ministers and a score of other former officials urging that increased review and oversight of national security activities were necessary and could improve rather than detract from security.[11]

The new 2015 legislation ignored the Air India Commission's 2010 recommendations that CSIS be *obliged* to share intelligence about possible terrorism offences and that its human sources not be given a veto on whether they can be compelled to be witnesses in prosecutions, a recommendation that was echoed in a unanimous 2011 report of a Senate committee chaired by Senator Hugh Segal. In the final analysis, the 2015 "reforms" were long on rhetoric about a war against "violent jihadis" and attempts to secure partisan advantage, but woefully short on evidence and deliberation.

II. THE GOVERNMENT'S NEW TERROR LAWS

Used in relation to change, "radical" means "affecting the fundamental nature of something; far-reaching or thorough."[12] It is our contention that the government's response to the October 2014 terrorist attacks were radical in (1) changing CSIS's mandate to include illegal and *Charter*-violating disruptions; (2) reversing the judicial role from preventing violations of *Charter* rights to authorizing them; (3) going far beyond existing definitions of Canada's security interests in authorizing a massive new information sharing regime; and (4) creating a speech offence for advocacy or promotion of "terrorism offences in general" that has no defences designed to protect free speech.

The full extent of the government's radical overhaul of security laws is cumulative. Bills C-44 and C-51, along with the passport measures contained in the budget bill, Bill C-59, produced the most drastic amendments to the *CSIS Act*[13] since its creation in 1984. The government amended fifteen other laws and created three new security laws: the *Security of Canada Information Sharing Act*,[14] the *Secure Air Travel Act*,[15] and the *Prevention of Terrorist Travel Act*.[16] These new laws are difficult to read and even more difficult to understand. Even with a professional lifetime in this business, we found them mind numbingly complex and attempting to understand them to be a full-time occupation. Bill C-51 in particular was drafted in a novel and provocative manner that departed from long-standing definitions of "threats to the security of Canada" or the more *Charter*-compliant pattern of past, similar laws — such as hate speech laws, immigration security certificate provisions, and the 2001 *Anti-terrorism Act*.

The Existing Security Architecture

The new laws are difficult to understand because most of them are not freestanding; most amend existing laws with their own history and purposes. The most extensive amendments were made to the *CSIS Act*, originally enacted in response to concerns about RCMP illegalities in the wake of the October Crisis. The 1984 *CSIS Act* created CSIS as a civilian and largely domestic intelligence agency that would obey the law and whose mandate was limited to intelligence collection. But in denial of this history, the new laws radically expand CSIS's role. They allow CSIS to be more muscular, breaking the law — Canadian, foreign, and international — and the *Charter* if necessary.

The new laws also changed the *Criminal Code*, an instrument that shortly after 9/11 was overhauled to create new terrorism offences and special powers such as "preventive" arrests and detention and peace bonds to restrain the actions of suspected terrorists. And the 2015 legislation amended, in a complex manner, Canada's immigration laws, which have often been used since 9/11 as a problematic form of anti-terrorism law. Also of note, the new laws established a statutory footing to facilitate no-fly lists and passport revocation without providing for adversarial challenge to the secret evidence used to justify these actions.

The new laws are also notable for what they did not do. Indeed, our sternest indictment will come in examining the government's astonishing passivity, faced with real problems that make Canadians both less secure and less free. Here, we will point to the government's inaction on recommendations made by the Arar Commission about the need for enhanced review. Additionally, we will criticize its rejection of recommendations made by the Air India Commission about both the urgent need to repair Canada's dysfunctional system of converting intelligence into evidence for criminal prosecutions and the need for enhanced oversight and co-ordination of how Canada uses its growing anti-terrorism toolkit.

Bill C-44

The first piece of legislation (Bill C-44) was slated for introduction prior to the October events. Its tabling in Parliament was delayed, and the bill was introduced a month after the attacks, on the day that wreaths were laid at the War Memorial to honour the two murdered soldiers. The bill was almost entirely designed to roll back ground lost by the government in court contests over the past several years. The government defended the legislation as common sense and gave it the reassuring name of the *Protection of Canada from Terrorists Act*.[17]

Bill C-44 gave CSIS statutory powers to conduct intelligence investigations outside of Canada, and now permits the Federal Court to issue warrants for such conduct even when such investigations violate foreign or international law. Contrary to the Air India Commission's warning that this would compromise terrorism prosecutions, it provided that those who provided CSIS with information on the basis of a promise of confidentiality would not have any identifying information about them disclosed in court or other proceedings, unless the innocence of the accused in a criminal trial was at stake. The new law also sped along the implementation of the 2014 *Strengthening Canadian Citizenship Act*,[18] allowing dual citizens convicted of terrorism to be deprived of Canada citizenship. The government has subsequently started to use these provisions, producing the inevitable *Charter* challenges.

Bill C-51

Bill C-44 passed unnoticed by most Canadians and was dispensed without much serious debate or scrutiny in Parliament. In contrast, Bill C-51, the *Anti-terrorism Act, 2015*,[19] became a lighting rod for public dispute. It was significant, complex legislation that created two new security laws to facilitate information sharing and codify the no-fly list. It also amended fifteen other laws, including the *CSIS Act* and the *Criminal Code*. In some respects, it may have been an "omnibus too far" for a government particularly fond of bundling sweeping changes into massive bills that most people (including parliamentarians) do not have the time or inclination to pick apart thoroughly. In Bill C-51's many moving parts there was bound to be something that someone did not like, regardless of political orientation.

Bill C-51 fundamentally changed the role of CSIS by giving it a new mandate to take physical — or what we called "kinetic" steps — to reduce threats to the security of Canada, so long as it thinks the measures are proportional to the risk and do not intentionally or negligently cause bodily harm, invade sexual integrity, or obstruct justice. Moreover, CSIS can now break the law and violate *Charter* rights when taking these measures, so long as they obtain a warrant from a Federal Court judge in a secret, one-sided proceeding authorizing such measures as reasonable and proportionate. The idea that judges can authorize limits on *Charter* rights — as opposed to protecting *Charter* rights — is a radical change to the role of judges, one that ignited opposition from legal academics, practising lawyers, and organizations representing the legal profession, among others.

The *Criminal Code* amendments increased the maximum period for preventive detention under pre-existing rules from three to seven days, and made it easier for the police to resort to this tool and also impose peace bonds — restraining orders — on feared terrorists. The Bill C-51 amendments also created a fifteenth terrorism offence of "knowingly promoting or advocating terrorism offences in general," while (at a minimum) being reckless as to whether someone may commit a terrorism offence. We will suggest that this offence goes beyond existing offences in the extent to which it criminalizes speech and it is vulnerable to *Charter* challenge.

The new *Security of Canada Information Sharing Act* enacted in Bill C-51 codified a radically expansive definition of national security, now billed as activities that "undermine the security of Canada." In enacting the broadest definition of security in Canada's statute book, the government urged that its reach was mitigated because "lawful" protest, advocacy, dissent, and artistic expression were exempted. In response to arguments that much protest can be technically unlawful under Canada's many municipal, provincial, and federal laws — even while being peaceful — the government simply deleted the word "lawful," one of a very few number of amendments made in a largely fruitless parliamentary vetting of the bill. The end result is an overbroad definition of national security countered with an overbroad exemption, one that on paper guts the purpose of the new law. After all, a lot of security risks are, in fact, a form of dissent. This may seem hypertechnical, but it also constituted a picture-perfect example of how Bill C-51, in many aspects, amounted to sloppy policy making on the fly. We may never know how each government department works around this unworkable exemption because of the absence of an adequate whole-of-government independent review of the information sharing done under the banner of Bill C-51.

Bill C-51 also replaced a poorly defined law and practice relating to no-fly lists with a clearer and more transparent law — a welcome development. But the details matter, and the bill codified low evidentiary burdens on the state, increasing the potential scale and risk of false positives; that is, treating people as terrorists when they are not. And the new measure failed to incorporate past lessons about the importance of real adversarial challenge when evidence is used to impose legal consequences on people from whom that evidence is kept secret.

Bill C-59

A quiet denouement to the Bill C-51 spectacle was the inclusion of the *Prevention of Terrorist Travel Act*[20] in the government's omnibus "Economic Action" budget bill. This new law, together with related amendments to the order governing passports, followed the approach taken to the no-fly list in Bill C-51: it made it easier to deny travel to terrorist suspects, but allowed the government to use secret evidence without authorizing an adversarial system for challenging the content of this information in court appeals.

III. OUR CONCERNS

We regard many features of these new laws as unwise, and some as unconstitutional. But in all the debate over these laws, we have never called for them to be abandoned. Our concerns revolved not around the ends, but rather, the means.

We accept the government's general objectives for legislating. ISIS is a new terrorist threat, one that is somewhat different from al-Qaida. The United Nations Security Council has labelled the foreign terrorist fighting inspired by ISIS and others a threat to international peace.[21] We think government politicians have overstated (and probably inflated) the risk through their political rhetoric, but the government has a responsibility to protect Canadians from terrorism, and to stop Canadians from participating in terrorism in foreign lands.

We supported a 2013 law that added four new terrorism offences applicable to those who attempt to leave Canada to participate in foreign terrorist fights. We also accept that some speech related to terrorism and some material on the Internet can be criminalized — it already is and has been since 2001. Like the Arar Commission, we recognize that enhanced security information sharing is necessary, and we agree with the Air India Commission that CSIS should share intelligence about possible terrorism acts and offences — in fact, we think it must share this information.

Our concerns are not with these objectives, but with how the new laws purport to achieve these important goals. The means matter; the details matter; proportionality matters. We are concerned that in their design and manner of addressing their legitimate objectives, the new laws make us less free, and will also likely fail to make us safer from real terrorist threats.

Our critique of Canada's new terror laws is not one that can easily be captured in a slogan or a catchphrase. Indeed our search for a title was one of the more difficult parts of writing this book. We are concerned that the new laws ignore the hard lessons of how Canada has both over- and underreacted to terrorism in the past, and also ignores the considerable informed advice the government has received about how to avoid these dangers in the future. We are concerned that under Bill C-51, Canada may be repeating past mistakes of institutionalized illegality in the name of security. We are also concerned that the new laws ignore warnings about dysfunctions in how Canada investigates and prosecutes terrorism. For these reasons, we think these 2015 laws make a false promise of security, even as they present a radical challenge to established rights and freedoms in a free and democratic society.

We briefly outline here themes that recur and will be developed throughout this book.

The Limits and Dangers of Disruption

As noted, Canada's radical new laws change the mandate of CSIS to include threat reduction measures capable of violating both the *Charter* and other laws. The police are also given enhanced powers to disrupt terrorists through preventive arrests and peace bonds. We will argue that these new powers of disruption are, at best, temporary and problematic solutions.

CSIS will act in secret, and its warrants (where actually required) will be obtained from the Federal Court in secret hearings that could be completely one-sided. Some might be willing to let CSIS engage in illegalities and dirty tricks if these acts were to make Canada safer. But we fear they won't — they may just disrupt other security agencies with the real power to put bad guys behind bars. As the new law itself confirms, CSIS is not a law enforcement agency that will arrest terrorists for criminal trials. Rather, the risk we spell out in this book is of sidelined or impaired police criminal investigations, as CSIS engages in perhaps endless surveillance and disruption of security threats — until its resources run out and a disrupted terrorist slips through the cracks.

Under their new Bill C-51 powers, the police must act more transparently than CSIS, but many suspected terrorism supporters have already agreed to peace bonds, in part to avoid additional adverse publicity. Peace bonds risk sacrificing the clear moral focus of criminal trials. They also risk posing a Goldilocks dilemma: too strong and perhaps counterproductive when applied to those who engage in mere threatening babble; too weak when applied to determined terrorists.

As a back-end and temporary solution to terrorist threats, CSIS and police disruptions are no substitute for efficient terrorism investigations and prosecutions leading to convictions and lengthy prison terms. They are also no substitute at the front end for multi-disciplinary and community-based programs attempting to curb radicalization to violent extremism. Indeed, to the extent that Bill C-51 sets us on the path of otherwise illegal, covert conduct by a secret security service, it risks creating communities of perpetual suspicion, surveillance, and disruption — a development that may well be counterproductive and likely to fuel the very extremism it seeks to stamp out.

Bill C-51's extreme whack-a-mole response may just produce more moles while managing to whack a lot of things that are not moles. It may also undermine what some call (often contemptuously) the "softer" side of anti-terrorism, a dimension that Canada has not seriously explored compared to other democracies, notably Australia, much of Europe, the United Kingdom, and even the United States.

"Less is More": The Distant and Dysfunctional CSIS-Police Relationship

Bill C-51's focus on disruption needs to be understood in the context of the troubled relationship between intelligence and evidence in Canadian anti-terrorism law and practice. It is first necessary to understand the imperfect CSIS-police relationship. The way this relationship has been described by insiders is summarized by the phrase "less is more." This term describes the standard information sharing arrangement from CSIS to the police.

CSIS is often the first agency investigating a threat — its mandate is broader and reaches pre-criminal conduct. When and if the matters it examines do cross the criminal boundary, Canadians might reasonably expect that CSIS will then share the full fruits of its investigations with police. This is not, however, Canadian practice. Rather than sharing full information, CSIS gives the police the bare bones — just enough to spark an independent police investigation of the matter. The "less is more" system is not about malice and jealous agencies, at least not any more. CSIS gives, and the police receive, sparse information so that CSIS may protect its sources and methods from disclosure under Canada's broad constitutional disclosure rules in criminal trials. Both CSIS and the police fear that if CSIS discloses more, prosecutions will be burdened with risky and perhaps unsuccessful attempts to keep the intelligence secret. And "less is more" is a rational, albeit bureaucratic, response to this secrecy preoccupation. It is, however, a dangerous security practice.

The government bills its "less is more" system of information sharing between CSIS and the RCMP as "One Vision."[22] We think it would be better labelled as "Blurred Vision." It is a system condemned in 2010 by the Air India inquiry, and it is one that knowledgeable security insiders consider reckless in a dynamic security environment, where Canadians might expect the state to deploy all the tools at its disposal. Bill C-51 makes no effort to cure this problem, and instead tempts CSIS to circumvent the dilemmas associated with keeping its secrets secret by charting its own course of disruption. Bill C-44 also enhances CSIS's abilities to keep secrets — in this case, the identity of any informer who the intelligence agency has promised confidentiality. CSIS is the big winner with these laws, but we fear this is occurring at the price of making terrorism trials even more infrequent and complex than they already are. This may mean that Canada will come to depend increasingly on the deeply imperfect whack-a-mole disruption strategies noted above.

Chilling Free Expression and Outreach

Another part of Bill C-51 that draws our gaze is an uncertain and broad new speech offence against advocating or promoting "terrorism offences in general." We are not free speech absolutists. As it is, our criminal law is replete with existing restrictions on speech sufficiently tied to violence or threats of violence — matters that the Supreme Court has ruled do not infringe freedom of expression.[23] But we fear that this new Bill C-51 offence is so carelessly and sweepingly drafted that it embraces all sorts of speech only very distantly linked to (and in no meaningful way correlated with) violence. We note later in this book how some of the passages we reproduce from radical (but very far from marginal) writers could run afoul of this new law, as might we for reproducing them.

All of these concerns would have been mitigated by careful wordsmithing attentive to the standards established in Canadian law and *Charter* jurisprudence, with no peril to the government's stated objectives. But the government chose a more radical and reckless course of action, one that will chill both freedom of expression, and the necessary efforts to engage with Muslim communities in an effort to counter the appeal of the brutal practices of ISIS to some Canadians. This new offence and other aspects of the new laws will be challenged under the *Charter* — most likely successfully. It is not clear how they fit into a balanced, evidence-based, and effective anti-terrorism strategy going forward. Instead, they simply constitute damaging anti-terror theatre, attractive only in a politically charged atmosphere, and make the mistake of equating radical and extreme ideas and ideology with violence.

Anti-Terror Overreach

Some of the 2015 laws concern us because they are not confined to anti-terrorism. Once limited to gathering information, CSIS now will be able to take physical or kinetic actions and violate laws and the *Charter* to reduce not only the terrorist threat, but also other threats CSIS has historically been authorized to investigate: espionage, sabotage, domestic sedition, and "foreign influenced" activities. Some of these broad concepts require no actual connection to violence, and can reach even lawful protest if carried out in conjunction with any of the investigated activities. This is exactly the sort of breadth that alarms environmental, Indigenous, diaspora, and other activists. The defenders of such overbreadth typically point to internal safeguards, a hard-pressed CSIS accountability regime, and resourcing limitations to suggest that we need not worry about overreaching formal legal powers. This is not, in our view, the appropriate approach to national security law, something that should always be crafted to constrain the practices of its worst purvey-ors, not dependent on the endless good judgment of the virtuous.

The government has similarly used the October terrorist incidents and the threat presented by ISIS to justify information sharing within govern-ment about almost anything. To be sure, there are the exemptions for protest, but as we imply above, these exemptions are themselves unworkable. In any event, they will not be policed by an adequate whole-of-government account-ability review system.

Despite its title, much of the *Anti-terrorism Act, 2015* (Bill C-51) reflects a new visioning of national security, one that depends on fear generated by ter-rorism to justify a march toward vaguer and broader "security" where more and more people can be defined as security risks and threats. Pursuing this sweeping and radical new concept of security will chill our democracy. It may also come with a price in the courts. The Supreme Court has been rela-tively deferential to anti-terrorism law because of concrete concerns about terrorism, but it should be less deferential to broader, vaguer security object-ives, especially given its post-9/11 warnings against falling "prey to the rhet-orical urgency of a perceived emergency or an altered security paradigm."[24]

A Large, Unfinished Reform Agenda

In 2015, the government grew its arsenal of anti-terrorism and security tools, but a bevy of tactics do not equal an anti-terror strategy. In this book, we lay out concerns that several key pieces of such a strategy are still missing and that existing pieces may not fit together in a co-ordinated manner.

The most obvious missing piece is the lack of an effective and multi-disciplinary program to prevent radicalization to violent extremism. Canada appears to be inching toward a counter–violent extremism program, with the RCMP and now perhaps CSIS in the vanguard. In other countries, teachers, social workers, health care professionals, and community leaders are playing a more significant role.

A structural challenge for Canada is that coherent counter–violent ex-tremism requires co-operation and co-ordination between federal and prov-incial levels of government. It is not clear to us that this is happening, as Quebec embarks on its own controversial path and other provinces seem to have demonstrated little movement. Another challenge is that the govern-ment seems not to regard "soft" or "sociological" pre-emption tools to be a priority. Indeed, such tools are sometimes treated as a form of appeasement. The government has insisted on hard-nosed but shortsighted political rhet-oric and actions that have strained its relations with segments of Canada's diverse Muslim communities.

Even more critically, the government has yet to demonstrate much commitment to ensuring that whatever strategy it has is subject to effective oversight and review to ensure it works properly. Here the government demonstrates a disturbing complacency in light of the security failures that allowed a terrorist so close to the seat of power. The government has insisted that existing mechanisms are more than adequate. And yet, an unedifying aspect of the Bill C-51 debate was the failure to engage this issue with attention to proper understandings or existing but unimplemented reform proposals. The term "oversight" refers to advance or real-time command and control of agencies. It is the province of the executive government, through ministers, and ultimately, the prime minister.

But in Canada, it is not clear who is in charge of the anti-terror arsenal in performing an overarching oversight function. The traditional answer has been the responsible minister. The minister of public safety already has a vast ministry but has assumed new duties under the 2015 legislation. Ministers of public safety in the past have failed to co-ordinate CSIS and the RCMP, let alone a much vaster array of anti-terrorism tools, including no-fly listings and passport revocation. The public safety department is ill-positioned to make the call on all of Canadian anti-terrorism. We will return again to one of the clear calls of the Air India Commission: someone at the centre of government — most plausibly, the prime minister's national security advisor — needs to have clear responsibilities (and not just discretionary and undefined influence) to perform a centralized anti-terror role that other democracies are finding to be necessary.

But even with enhanced oversight — that is, better command, control, and co-ordination of security agencies — the other side of the unfinished reform agendas is modernizing our antiquated and weak review system. Review, in Canadian practice, is after-the-fact auditing of agency performance. The government's repeated description during the Bill C-51 debate of Canada's existing review structure as the "envy of the world" is astonishing. For almost a decade, the government has ignored the Arar Commission's warnings that Canada's review structure was inadequate and the many candid statements by reviewers that they do not have the necessary information, powers, and resources to do their jobs properly.

IV. THE OUTLINE OF THE BOOK

Our chapters go well beyond the mostly legal analysis we prepared and posted online during the Bill C-51 debate. We include a detailed account of the history of Canadian anti-terrorism, starting with another October Crisis — the one in 1970. We mine the Air India debacle to better understand how the new powers will affect terrorism investigations and prosecutions. We lay out more information about the evolving and serious threat of al-Qaida and ISIS-inspired terrorism, and devote a chapter to examining how Canada is lagging behind other democracies in responding to the challenge of violent extremism.

Basic Constitutional Law Terminology 101

We also do not ignore the law. Non-legal readers may wish simply to skim our more detailed constitutional law analysis. But for those who wish to join us in the legal weeds, we flag here basic terminology. We speak often of *Charter* rights, in reference to the many codified rights appearing in the *Canadian Charter of Rights and Freedoms*. Rights that figure prominently in our analysis are:

- section 2 (and especially its promise of freedom of expression);
- section 6 ("Every citizen of Canada has the right to enter, remain in and leave Canada");
- section 7 ("Everyone has the right to life, liberty and security of the person and the right not to be deprived thereof except in accordance with the principles of fundamental justice"); and
- section 8 ("Everyone has the right to be secure against unreasonable search or seizure").

We also mention, from time to time, section 9's guarantee against arbitrary detention and section 15's guarantee of equality before and under the law, without discrimination.

Superimposed over these rights is the *Charter*'s section 1: "The *Canadian Charter of Rights and Freedoms* guarantees the rights and freedoms set out in it subject only to such reasonable limits prescribed by law as can be demonstrably justified in a free and democratic society." This clause amounts to a caveat on *Charter* rights, permitting constraints on them in limited circumstances.

Exactly what the words of these sections mean and how they apply is a matter decided, in practice, by the courts though their cases. In this book, we do not spend a great deal of time teasing out all of the nuance in this caselaw. From time to time we do, however, spell out significant legal holdings and conclusions, and also offer our views on whether the government's new laws meet the standards set out in them.

There are also occasions where we use other important legal phrases in describing the 2015 laws and their impact. To ease the reader's task in navigating these concepts, we include definitions of five recurring legal concepts in Table 1.1, appended as an annex to this chapter.

14

The Order of Our Chapters

Chapter 2 sets our stage. In it, we examine how Canadian history has been marred by the extremes of over- and underreacting to terrorism. We have devoted considerable effort and space to telling this history of repeated mistakes. We do so not so much for its own sake, but because we believe that it is highly relevant and was too often ignored in the Bill C-51 debate (including in our initial "real-time" analysis crafted during the debate). One pointed lesson of history is the harmful effects of state illegalities and "noble cause corruption" in the aftermath of the October Crisis. This led to the creation of CSIS, but that history is apparently only dimly remembered today. Some may be tempted to dismiss this legacy as ancient and quaint storytelling in the face of greater security threats, but we also trace a trail of CSIS post-9/11 illegalities and *Charter* violations that may help explain why someone, somewhere in government (most likely in CSIS) concluded that CSIS required the cover of warrants that purport to authorize it to violate *Charter* rights, even if this required a radical inversion of the judicial role in protecting such rights.

The other concern expressed in Chapter 2 focuses on underreaction, and specifically the continued failure to deal with the legacy of the botched Air India bombings investigation. Again, the government will claim this is ancient history. The 2010 Air India Commission did not agree, and neither do we.

Chapter 3 examines the evolving terrorist threat to which the government is responding. We begin by situating that inquiry in a broader study of national security and terrorism relating to Canada, warning about the dangers of ignoring political terrorism that is not perpetuated by Muslims. But we also note that ISIS and the challenges posed by the broader, related concept of foreign terrorist fighting were the concerns animating the politics of Bill C-51. And they run deep in the preoccupations of the security services. They deserve, therefore, especially close examination. ISIS is, in fact, a different kind of threat even from al-Qaida because it aims at mass mobilization, targets the young, has a geographic base, and has pretensions of statehood. Its challenge should not be ignored, and we trace its footprint through the data available to us.

Chapter 3 also introduces the concept of a "threat escalator," one that attempts to match different types of threats with the appropriate policy instrument. The threat escalator is particularly relevant to the ISIS threat, especially to the extent that it targets recruitment and attempts to interdict people from travelling to join ISIS or from returning to Canada. The threat escalator also analytically breaks down the broad range of "disruption" measures authorized in the new laws. Each of these policy tools is affixed with a label that then guides the name (and mostly the logical and temporal order) of the chapters that follow. We then begin to examine the new instruments that were added to the government's anti-terrorist toolkit in 2015, in light of what is known about the past experience and current practice.

Chapter 4 examines the use of surveillance as an anti-terror tool, while Chapter 5 examines the state's swelling ability to share information, including the new *Security of Canada Information Sharing Act* enacted under Bill C-51.

We then examine an escalating series of interventions that involve restrictions of movement through interdiction (Chapter 6), including new provisions for passport denial and being placed on the no-fly list; restraining terrorist threats (Chapter 7), including easier access to peace bonds and analogues of peace bonds under immigration law; and interruption when all else fails (Chapter 8), including preventive arrest. In Chapter 8, we also closely scrutinize the new CSIS "threat reduction" powers and query how and if they can be constitutionally deployed as an effective tool in our anti-terror strategy.

We question, in particular, whether these new CSIS tools may undermine prosecutions, the core criminal law device that we explore in considerable detail in Chapter 9. In that chapter we review statistical data on Canada's prosecution record and point to the structural aspects of our law and "less is more" practice of CSIS-police co-operation that make prosecutions less effective as an anti-terror tool — a problem we fear Bill C-51 will acerbate.

In Chapter 10, we look at a criminal law that has gone too far: Bill C-51's new speech offence, which is also coupled with new powers that allow "terrorist propaganda" to be deleted from the Internet. We predict that prosecutions for violating the new speech offence and related deletion orders will be rare, but that they will still have counterproductive effects both for free expression and for outreach involving Muslim communities (or any other in the speech crime's obvious crosshairs) in counter–violent extremism programs.

We have been critical of the new laws since they were introduced, but we have always intended to be constructive. In the last three chapters, we make concrete suggestions on how to improve Canadian anti-terrorism law and policy. In doing so, we draw extensively on existing research and reform proposals.

In Chapter 11, we suggest that better oversight of security activities within government is essential and that much of the Bill C-51 debate misconceived this critical issue. In this chapter, we stress that someone needs to be in charge of the growing anti-terrorist toolkit to avoid the type of inadequate and siloed response that characterized the Air India bombings investigation, and may also have allowed an armed terrorist to enter the Parliament buildings on 22 October 2014.

The better understood topic of "review" is discussed in Chapter 12 in terms of the role of parliamentary committees, independent executive watchdog reviewers, and the courts. Review is conceptually distinct from oversight because it only produces retrospective findings and recommendations and does not intrude into command, control, and co-ordination. That said, both processes are challenged by the reality of increasingly integrated whole-of-government security responses and both can contribute to more effective and balanced security responses in the future.

Finally, in Chapter 13, we examine a key tool that we think is underdeveloped in Canada's growing anti-terrorist toolkit: multi-disciplinary and community-based programs designed to dissuade people from being radicalized to violent extremism. We lay out many of the challenges that stand in the way of such an approach. Some, such as the constitutional division of powers between federal and provincial governments, cannot be changed; others, such as messaging and outreach to affected communities, can be.

In our conclusion, we suggest that Canada cannot rely on its new and problematic terror laws to accomplish the difficult task of responding to the new ISIS threat, or indeed, most other terrorist concerns. We lay out a specific action plan for Canada to improve its security game and to stop falling behind responses in other democracies. We think such a plan can better prevent terrorism while avoiding some of excesses and possible *Charter* violations in the 2015 laws.

Despite the two terrorist attacks in 2014, Canada has been comparatively lucky since the 1985 Air India attacks. We cannot continue to rely on that luck. We need a new approach, one that rejects the radicalism of the 2015 laws, learns from past mistakes, and, ultimately, makes Canada both more secure and more free.

Table 1.1: Legal Concepts

Concept	Legal Meaning
"Believe on reasonable grounds"	Sometimes called "reasonable and probable grounds" in the constitutional caselaw, this standard of proof is much lower than the criminal trial standard of "beyond a reasonable doubt." Instead, it is defined as a "credibly-based probability" or "reasonable probability." *R v Debot*, [1989] 2 SCR 1140. In the administrative law context, courts have described it as a bona fide belief of a serious possibility, based on credible evidence. *Chiau v Canada (Minister of Citizenship and Immigration)*, [2001] 2 FC 297 (FCA).
"Suspects on reasonable grounds"	A lower standard than "believe on reasonable grounds," "suspects on reasonable grounds" is a suspicion based on objectively articulable grounds that may be lower in quantity or content than the requirement of reasonable belief but must be more than a subjective hunch. *R v Kang-Brown*, 2008 SCC 18. Put another way, "reasonable suspicion is a lower standard, as it engages the reasonable possibility, rather than probability, of crime." *R v Chehil*, 2013 SCC 49 at para 27.
"Terrorist activity"	A defined concept found in s 83.01 of the *Criminal Code* and that includes listed acts — such as several terrorist crimes (e.g., hostage taking) — but also has a more open-ended definition: enumerated physical acts, usually of violence, committed "in whole or in part for a political, religious or ideological purpose, objective or cause" for the purpose of "intimidating the public, or a segment of the public, with regard to its security, including its economic security, or compelling a person, a government or a domestic or an international organization to do or to refrain from doing any act, whether the public or the person, government or organization is inside or outside Canada." It also includes a conspiracy, attempt, or threat to do one of these acts, or counselling or inciting such an act.

Concept	Legal Meaning
"Terrorist group"	A defined concept found in s 83.01 of the *Criminal Code* and that means "an entity that has as one of its purposes or activities facilitating or carrying out any terrorist activity" *or* an entity listed by the government under s 83.05 because there are reasonable grounds to believe that "the entity has knowingly carried out, attempted to carry out, participated in or facilitated a terrorist activity" (or acted in association with an entity that has done these things).
"Terrorism offence"	A defined concept found in s 2 of the *Criminal Code* and that means one of the special terrorist crimes such as facilitation, participation, terrorist travel, or terrorism financing. It also includes any "indictable" (generally, serious) offence committed "for the benefit of, at the direction of or in association with a terrorist group." It also includes indictable offences "where the act or omission constituting the offence also constitutes a terrorist activity." Finally, it includes "a conspiracy or an attempt to commit, or being an accessory after the fact in relation to, or any counselling in relation to" any of these things.

CHAPTER TWO
History: A Short History of Canada's Over- and Underreaction to Terrorism

I. INTRODUCTION

No one can seriously think that Canada is immune from terrorism or that it has ever been.

Aspiring ISIS (Islamic State of Iraq and Syria) recruit Martin Couture-Rouleau killed Warrant Officer Patrice Vincent in Saint-Jean-sur-Richelieu on 20 October 2014. Angered by the Canadian military presence in Afghanistan and Iraq, Michael Zehaf-Bibeau murdered Corporal Nathan Cirillo at Ottawa's war memorial on 22 October 2014.[1] He then stormed Parliament's Centre Block, before being shot and killed in the chaotic security response.

These events galvanized a horrified public. But that same downtown precinct of Ottawa had seen this sort of thing before. Zehaf-Bibeau shot Corporal Cirillo three times in the back, steps from the Sparks Street boarding house where Thomas D'Arcy McGee was assassinated a year after Confederation. McGee had been an Irish nationalist but turned against the violence of the Fenian Brotherhood. Patrick James Whelan, a suspected Fenian sympathizer, was convicted of the murder in a (procedurally doubtful) trial. He was hanged before 5,000 spectators in Ottawa.

The 22 October 2014 terrorist attack was not even the first time that terrorists had targeted Canada's grand Parliament buildings. A recent database created by the Canadian Network for Research on Terrorism, Security and Society (TSAS) records eighty "terrorist or extremist attacks" in downtown Ottawa between 1963 and 2013.[2] Twenty-one targeted the Parliament buildings, with most instances involving letters containing white powder delivered in 2003. But other, more serious, incidents involved attempted bombings or other physical assaults.

In 1966, officials declined Paul Joseph Chartier's request to give a speech on political matters in the House of Commons. In response, he prepared a bomb to be tossed into the chamber from the visitors' gallery. The bomb detonated prematurely in a Commons washroom, killing Chartier. Police found another six sticks of dynamite and notebooks full of anti-parliamentarian polemics in the terrorist's Toronto residence. Another plan to bomb the House of Commons was foiled by police, after a tipoff, in 1981. The perpetrator intended to express his anger at the prime minister during the constitutional repatriation debates. Then, in 1997, a man screaming "devil worshipers" drove his vehicle up the stairs leading to the front door of Parliament, ran into the lobby, and struggled with security officers before being overcome.

Also of note, given the parallels to the 20 and 22 October 2014 attacks, is a 20 May 1980 assault, occurring on the day of Quebec's first sovereignty referendum, in which a Quebec man stabbed a Canadian Forces colonel very near downtown Ottawa's national defence headquarters. To publicize his views that Quebec's language law was discriminatory, the man had declared his intent to attack Prime Minister Pierre Elliott Trudeau. Foiled in those efforts, he instead "decided to become a terrorist and attack the military leadership that morally represents the policies of the Federal Government."[3]

And these Ottawa events are not unique. The TSAS database records 1,405 terrorist or extremist incidents and 469 deaths in Canada during the period between 1960 and 2014. This latter figure includes the largest mass murder in Canadian history: the 329 deaths on Air India Flight 182, en route from Toronto to London, England.

Given these data, no one can seriously think that Canada is insulated from terrorism, that it has ever been, or that October 2014 marked some rupture between a bucolic state of innocence and a more dangerous present world.

But What Is Terrorism?

With the distance of time, we do not always know what motivated the perpetrators of all of these attacks. But we do know in many cases. Many of these incidents meet the definition of "terrorist activity" in Canada's contemporary *Criminal Code*. Under that law, terrorist activity includes most acts of violence done for political, religious, or ideological motives with the intention of intimidating the public "with regard to its security, including its economic security, or compelling a person, a government, or a domestic or an international organization to do or to refrain from doing any act."[4]

Of course, this definition did not exist until 2001, and so terrorism was more a colloquial expression than a legal concept before that time. But our law has now long since evolved past treating terrorism as a disputed definitional question, inviting endless inquiries into whether mentally ill people can be terrorists or whether certain political justifications somehow make the label improper.

There is, therefore, no purpose in endlessly disputing whether someone is a terrorist, something that consumed much oxygen after the October 2014 events. A mentally ill person can commit a terrorism offence — so long as that person is capable of forming the requisite intent. The criteria for that intent are fixed and indeed have survived constitutional challenge.[5] All that remains, then, is unearthing the facts.

Nor should we waste effort imagining that terrorism is conduct confined to one particular form of ideology — in modern practice, that inspired by ISIS or al-Qaida. In law, there is no such thing as "noble cause" terrorism. The rule of law applies to all. It does not pick sides. Our law does not, in any form, exonerate terrorist activity because the political, religious, or ideological motivation is appealing or the cause worthy. At most, the *Criminal Code* makes a modest effort to exclude from the reach of the terrorist activity definition things done during an armed conflict, in compliance with applicable international law. This is as close as Canada comes in recognizing a "freedom fighter" exception, and it is an exception very few insurgencies could satisfy in practice. It is instructive to note, moreover, that the TSAS database records a dizzying array of motivations. These historical data suggest that over the last fifteen years, al-Qaida- or ISIS-inspired "lone wolf" terrorism is less common than other forms of terrorism, especially that perpetrated by white supremacists.[6]

The truth that terrorism is a tactic is often lost in political discussion, and in the way our law is used. In January 2015, Justice Minister Peter MacKay refused to consider a plot by three youths to shoot people in a Halifax mall to be terrorism because there was not "a cultural component."[7] And yet "culture" is not a prerequisite of terrorist activity in Canadian law — indeed, the term appears nowhere in it. We suspect that if three young Muslims had hatched an equivalent plot with press reports revealing a similar nihilist ideology, the plot would probably have been labelled as terrorism.[8] And such a plot might well have attracted terrorism charges if that ideology had been confirmed by police investigations.

As we describe in Chapter 9, it is striking that all but one of the terrorism prosecutions under post-9/11 law have involved persons inspired by al-Qaida or ISIS. This is not just about the threat environment — there have been other acts of political violence by others propounding different ideologies, but these have been prosecuted using more conventional legal tools.

Reacting to Terrorism

All of this is to say that terrorism is a politically fraught issue and that the label is contested even when it really should not be. Terrorism also galvanizes strong emotions and a demand for action. After October 2014, and especially during the Bill C-51[9] debates, many Canadians wondered at the reaction. A particularly resonant (and very Canadian) objection to overreaction was that Canadians were more likely to be killed by a moose than terrorists. If measured by comparing the data in the TSAS database with the carnage caused by car crashes with wildlife, this is true.[10] It also happens to be true that more Americans died in automobile accidents in 2001 than in the 9/11 attacks.[11] But like deadly moose, that is a statistic with limited significance: car crashes are tragic background noise in the pattern of human mortality. Their risks can be mitigated and are generally well understood.

In comparison, terrorist attacks are overt acts of political violence whose scope and lethality are limited only by the capacity and imagination of their perpetrators. Terrorist attacks are unpredictable and designed to make us do things, or at the very least fear things. They are a conscious assault on freedom, in a way that is dramatically different from the accidental perils of living. Such conduct demands a response from the state. In our system, the one assumption we seem all to share about the state's function is that it must act as the proverbial night watchman, protecting us from our foes. And that is, in some important respects, the state's historical (and Hobbesian) raison d'être.

As for statistics, the TSAS database provides some comfort: it is hard to see in its numbers anything other than a low-level challenge. Terrorism is not an existential crisis. But at the same time, we must all appreciate that in terrorism, the future is an unknown country — our security services cannot simply extrapolate from the past in anticipating that future.

Bottom line: no one should be scoring political points on the question of whether Canada is, has been, or will be a terrorist target. Again, we underscore that no person should reasonably believe that Canada is insulated from this form of violence. Rather, we should focus on the much more difficult issue of how we should gauge, and respond to, the actual risk of terrorism.

Shortly before he introduced Bill C-51, Prime Minister Stephen Harper promised that Canada would not overreact to the October terrorist attacks, but that neither would it underreact.[12] We find this to be a helpful way to characterize the dilemma lying at the heart of anti-terrorism: reconciling security with liberty. If we overreact, we will harm ourselves with new laws that will not make us safer but will alienate communities, chill expression, threaten privacy, and lead to false positives — black listings, disruptions, and preventive arrests of those who are not terrorists. Overreaction to terrorism threatens human rights and harms our democracy.

Underreaction is also a danger. It may lead us to discount intelligence reports suggesting that scores of Canadians have left Canada to join ISIS and similar foreign terrorist groups, despite their manifest brutality. It may lead us to assume that we know the full consequences of this new, largely unprecedented, phenomenon and can rest easy. It may also deter us from using comprehensive and multi-disciplinary programs to understand and respond to the causes of such radicalization to violence. Instead, we may favour the blunt and temporary solutions of disruptions, preventive arrests, and peace bonds. Underreaction may also mean that we will allow a troubled and structurally dysfunctional relationship between CSIS and the RCMP to continue while also ignoring other reforms that an inquiry into the Air India bombings indicated in 2010 were required to make terrorism investigations and prosecutions more effective.

Living History

We live in an instant age dominated by sound bites and slogans. We too often forget even recent history at the cost of repeating similar mistakes over and over again. This chapter is an unapologetic exercise in present-minded history, whose purpose is to explore how Canada's new terror laws have repeated some of the mistakes of the past. That history creates a long legacy of over- and underreactions to terrorism whose cumulative impact is to make Canadian anti-terrorism, with few known exceptions, a history of failures. William Faulkner might have been talking about Canadian anti-terror law and practice when he famously reminded us that "the past is never dead. It's not even the past."[13] We need to understand this past to understand how 2015's new terrorism laws[14] reflect a form of path dependence, one that will make us less free while not making us safer.

II. OVERREACTING: THE OCTOBER CRISIS OF 1970

Introduction

October 2014 was not the first time that Canada was rocked by successive acts of terrorism. It was not even the first October. The October Crisis of 1970 and its aftermath are still very much with us. They reveal much about the dangers of anti-terrorism practices that are illegal and infringe fundamental rights and freedoms. The police illegalities committed in the aftermath of the October Crisis — including thefts, break-ins, and most famously the burning of a barn to disrupt a meeting — were all illegalities that may now be authorized under Bill C-51. In the 1970s, this conduct harmed democracy and the rule of law. It led, in 1984, to the creation of CSIS, whose mandate was strictly limited to the collection of intelligence. Now, thirty years on, Bill C-51 makes CSIS a "kinetic" service, able to do things to people to "reduce," "disrupt," or what used to be called "counter" broadly defined security threats (and not just from terrorism). The lessons of a past October have been forgotten.

CSIS is not alone in being a product of the October Crisis overreaction. In some important respects, the *Canadian Charter of Rights and Freedoms*[15] itself was an outgrowth of that dark period. The *Charter* embedded rights into Canada's constitutional firmament and gave independent judges the task of preventing rights violations and providing remedies for them.

And just as Bill C-51 rejects the wisdom of the past in relation to CSIS's mandate, it also attempts an end run around fundamental understandings of the *Charter*. It suggests that judges may authorize CSIS to violate not just any Canadian law but also any *Charter* right so long as CSIS does not violate sexual integrity, cause bodily harm, or obstruct justice and so long as the judge determines that CSIS's actions are proportionate to the threat. Put another way, Bill C-51 represents a "back to the future" policy that moves us one step closer to the bad old days of illegalities committed in the name of preventing terrorism.

It is worth examining, therefore, how we overreacted during and after the first October Crisis and why the framers of our traditional national security approach made the decisions they did in an attempt to prevent a repeated overreaction.

Repeated Acts of FLQ Terrorism

Of the 1,405 incidents reported in the TSAS database between 1960 and 2014, 308 are attributed to "separatist" organizations, and 143 include Front de libération du Québec (FLQ) among their keywords. In the period 1963 to 2000, the most common FLQ-related act was the bombing of English-language symbols and federal institutions in Quebec. The terrorist attacks were not simply symbolic destruction of property: they resulted in 5 deaths[16] and 144 injuries.

Most famously, in October 1970, two cells of the FLQ kidnapped, first, British diplomat James Cross and then Quebec Cabinet Minister Pierre Laporte. The terrorists ultimately murdered Laporte. The Cross kidnappers, the so-called Liberation Cell, demanded safe passage to Cuba or Algeria, a

$500,000 ransom, release of "political prisoners," and the name of the informer whose information led to arrests of members of the FLQ and the discovery of dynamite during the summer of 1970. The Quebec government rejected the demands but was prepared to negotiate safe passage out of the country for the kidnappers. Some, including *Le Dévoir* editor Claude Ryan, urged the government to be even more conciliatory toward the terrorists. It did not work out that way, at least not right away.

The Declaration of the *War Measures Act*

At 4:00 am on 16 October 1970, Pierre Trudeau's federal government proclaimed martial law under the *War Measures Act* to respond to an "apprehended insurrection within the Province of Québec."[17] Trudeau did not act alone. He had in hand requests from the Quebec government, the city of Montreal, and the Montreal police. The Montreal police chief wrote, "the slowness of procedures and the restraints imposed by the legal methods and mechanisms now at our disposal do not allow us at this time to cope with the situation."[18] The RCMP, however, had not requested use of the *War Measures Act*.[19] It believed that dogged police work would eventually discover the kidnappers, as it eventually did.

Although in cabinet debates he raised serious doubts about its use, Justice Minister John Turner justified the use of the *War Measures Act* in part because of "an infiltration of FLQ doctrine in certain areas of society in Québec — in the unions, among university students and in the media," as well as the "growing feeling among the people of Québec, particularly citizens of Montreal that they are living under a reign of terror."[20] The suspension of civil liberties was, in other words, partially a response to the perceived spread of dangerous ideology tied to downstream violence. NDP leader Tommy Douglas, who opposed imposition of the *War Measures Act* as "using a sledgehammer to crack a peanut," denounced other attempts to connect the FLQ with a left-wing municipal party in Montreal as "Canadian McCarthyism" that tried to "smear some political opponents by linking them in the public mind with the FLQ."[21]

There are still defenders of the government's actions,[22] but most today accept that the use of the *War Measures Act* was an overreaction that did more harm to Canada than did the underlying acts of terrorism. Indeed, one experienced RCMP member later told the McDonald Commission that the use of the *War Measures Act* delayed efforts to find Cross by as much as a month by diverting police resources to administering the new powers and arresting and interrogating persons unconnected to the kidnapping.[23] Put another way, the heavy-handed response injured not only civil rights — it diverted resources in a manner that undermined security.

Modern Echoes of October 1970

It is useful to juxtapose the substance of the 1970 response with current approaches to security.

National Security Threats and Sedition

The regulations made by the cabinet under the *War Measures Act* declared the FLQ and any other group "that advocates the use of force or the commission of crime as a means of or an aid in accomplishing governmental change within Canada"[24] to be unlawful. This extraordinary declaration created a retroactive crime, by executive decree. Those accused under it subsequently challenged this form of retroactive offence, but the courts refused to question the invocation of emergency powers. One judge of the Quebec Court of Appeal noted, "between commentators on the law and judges charged with applying it, there is often a lack of pragmatism and realism distinguishing theoreticians and practitioners."[25]

The October 1970 regulations were dramatic, but their focus on use of force to achieve governmental change still finds echoes in other parts of Canadian law. It is still a crime in Canada to speak "seditious words," publish a "seditious libel," or participate in a "seditious conspiracy."[26] The seditious intent at the core of these acts is presumed to exist where a person teaches, advocates, publishes, or circulates any writing that advocates "the use, without the authority of law, of force as a means of accomplishing a governmental change within Canada." At the same time, there are a number of defences including good faith efforts to point out errors and defects in government or to remove ill will between different classes of persons.[27]

The sedition concept also finds echo in the "threats to the security of Canada" CSIS is charged with investigating — and, after Bill C-51, disrupting. CSIS's security mandate extends to "activities directed toward undermining by covert unlawful acts, or directed toward or intended ultimately to lead to the destruction or overthrow by violence of, the constitutionally established system of government in Canada," commonly called "subversion."[28] Counter-subversion was the most controversial aspect of CSIS's mandate when created in 1984. Years later, CSIS's review body called for it to be deleted.[29]

Likewise, in 1986, the Law Reform Commission of Canada expressed surprise that our criminal law persisted in criminalizing political speech, given the free expression guarantees of the *Charter*.[30] This inconsistency is resolved, at least in part, by court interpretations that have long narrowed criminal sedition to actual incitements to violence.[31] The crime of sedition, if ever used again, could likely survive *Charter* scrutiny only if limited to threats of violence.

The constraint of drawing the line of free speech at violence is abandoned by Bill C-51. As we discuss below, the constraint is rejected in relation to the bill's new terrorism speech crime of "advocating or promoting terrorism offences in general" (a concept that may be only distantly linked to violence). Unlike sedition or hate propaganda, there is no defence to the commission of this new speech crime.

Bill C-51 also reverts to antiquated concepts of sedition in the powers that it grants government to share information about supposed security concerns. The key passage in the *Security of Canada Information Sharing Act* (*SoCIS Act*), enacted in 2015 under Bill C-51, is "activities that undermine the security of Canada."[32] These activities are defined as those that undermine "the sovereignty, security or territorial integrity or the lives and security of the people in Canada." The new legislation does not stop at this broad definition but includes many examples of activities that could be tied to these risks, such as "changing or unduly influencing a government in Canada by force or unlawful means."

This reference to "unlawful means" casts a much wider net than the *War Measures Act* in 1970, sedition in the *Criminal Code*, or sedition in the *CSIS Act*. All of these instruments required or still require "force" — that is, violence — or at least "covert unlawful means," and not simply any "unlawful means." And "unlawful means" is a broad category reaching such conduct as a wildcat labour strike done in violation of labour law. These older laws were or are directed at actions intended to change governments. In comparison, the new *SoCIS Act* simply speaks of activities "unduly influencing" a government — whatever that means.

The *SoCIS Act* does not stop there: it compiles a long list of supposed security threats that go well beyond those deployed in 1970 under the *War Measures Act*. Indeed, it constitutes a definition broader than any other definition of national security ever codified in Canadian law. These security issues include interfering with critical infrastructure, undermining the security of another state, and interfering with Canada's "economic or financial stability."

As discussed in Chapter 5, we take little comfort in the exemption in the *SoCIS Act* for advocacy, protest, dissent, and artistic expression because this exemption is carelessly drafted to be absurdly overbroad (violent terrorism can be a form of dissent, but one that really should be the subject of information sharing). Because of this unworkable architecture, we doubt that the exemption will be effective as used in practice inside government. Indeed, the exemption will be applied not by judges but internally by government departments, with no serious prospect of sustained, dedicated, independent, arm's-length review.

Our point here is simply that the government's view of security threats has increased significantly since October 1970, including its view of what constitutes sedition or subversion. Bill C-51 announced that security threats now may include, not only actions committed to separatism, but also aspects of environmental, anti-globalization, diaspora, and Indigenous movements. People will not go to jail under the *SoCIS Act*, but the practical reality is that authorities will keep track of more people for what we once called "civil disobedience."

Arrest on Suspicion and False Positives

The *War Measures Act* 1970 regulations authorized the warrantless arrest of those who the police had "reason to suspect" were members of any unlawful association. Police had these same expansive powers to arrest those who advocated the aims of, or gave funds to, unlawful organizations or who advocated force or crime to accomplish governmental change. The *War Measures Act* rules eroded the critical distinction between those who planned to engage in violence and those who were more distant from physical acts of violence but held radical ideas viewed as motivating others to use force.

Law professors at the time argued that the "reason to suspect" language was novel and "peculiar." They also noted that the police saw these new powers as "justifying arrest for any reason, whether or not the police were acting on reasonable and probable grounds"[33] as required by the *Criminal Code*. Once arrested under the 1970 regulations, a person could be detained without charge or judicial review for seven days.[34]

The police used these powers to arrest 497 people during the October Crisis. Most people spent a full week in detention. Only sixty-two were charged by January 1971, and half were released with charges dropped within a month. In the end, only eighteen people were convicted of crimes associated with the October Crisis, including those convicted for the kidnappings and the murder of Pierre Laporte. Courts convicted only two people not otherwise involved in the kidnappings that sparked the crisis.[35]

Measured by this standard, the October Crisis produced a 96 percent "false positive" result. In the medical world, a false positive is a test result that suggests a given condition is present when in fact it is not. In the national security world, a false positive is state action based on a belief that a person is a terrorist or would-be terrorist when in fact that person is not. Among the false positives were union leaders, intellectuals, and writers and poets associated with separatism, including acclaimed singer and actress Pauline Julien. Seven people were even arrested in Vancouver for distributing the FLQ manifesto.[36]

At least two people were arrested and detained simply because they shared the same name as a person on the police list. The police even arrived in the early hours at the Westmount residence of one Gerard Pelletier before being convinced that they were looking for a Gerald Pelletier who was not, in fact, a federal minister in the Trudeau cabinet.[37]

The Quebec ombudsperson subsequently found evidence of police brutality and property damage during the arrests. He ordered that 104 people receive compensation, which the Quebec government agreed to provide.[38]

The October 1970 experience is an important reminder that powers of preventive arrest exercised on grounds of suspicion will result in arrests and detention of people who are not terrorists. And when people are arrested in times of crisis on such a forgiving standard, bad things can happen. For this reason, extreme measures demand extreme checks and balances. And yet we seem to have forgotten this. Bill C-51 extends the period of preventive arrest from a maximum of three to seven days, with judicial extensions made at the twenty-four hour, three day, and five day marks. Unlike equivalent laws in places like Australia, Bill C-51 contains no legislated safeguards on what can be done to people while they are preventively detained. We may come to regret that decision.

A Chill on Fundamental Freedoms

As we have already noted, the *War Measures Act* regulations focused not just on the threat of terrorist violence but also on the advocacy of ideas associated with violence. The offences they created applied to those who communicated statements on behalf of the FLQ and those who advocated or promoted the use of force or crime to accomplish governmental change in Canada.[39] Like the new Bill C-51 terrorism speech crime, the *War Measures Act* crime was an indictable offence subject to five years imprisonment.

Pierre Vallières and others were twice charged during the October Crisis with seditious conspiracy on the basis of speech acts. A judge quashed the first charges as excessively vague. After a six-week politicized trial, a jury acquitted on the second charges.[40] But the fact that no one was convicted of seditious conspiracy or under the *War Measures Act* speech offence is largely of incidental relevance. The impact of these offences is best measured, not by conviction rates, but by expression chill.

Speech was selectively chilled by the broad terms of the October 1970 speech offence. Authorities deterred several university newspapers from printing the FLQ manifesto, even though the mainstream media did so. But even the CBC tempered its journalistic activities out of concern it would run afoul of the speech restrictions.[41] And the warrantless arrests in 1970 included persons detained for distributing copies of the manifesto.[42] That the government did not then prosecute them is no answer to the fact that they were temporally imprisoned and denied their basic civil rights, precisely for exercising free expression.

Speech offences are a special concern to those who make their living through speech. Both the government of British Columbia and the Toronto school board tried to prevent teachers (and in the British Columbia case even university professors) from advocating (and indeed in at least one case even discussing) FLQ positions.[43] University professors represented by Thomas Berger challenged the British Columbia policy, but the court refused to consider their case, reasoning that it was hypothetical because no one had yet been fired for advocating "FLQ policies" in the classroom. An appeal was abandoned when the British Columbia legislature repealed the policy in 1972.[44]

Bill C-51's terrorism speech crime raises similar issues: its breadth is uncertain, but it clearly reaches much further than advocating actual violence. It provides no statutory defences designed to protect free speech. Because its constitutionality in the post-*Charter* era is doubtful and because people engaged in real terrorist propaganda can be pursued under other offences with more serious penalties, prosecutors are not likely to favour this crime. We will probably see few prosecutions and even fewer convictions. But the new speech crime can (and, we think, will) chill speech. And just as in 1970, the new speech crime is an offence that can justify the exercise of other state powers such as peace bonds, arrests, and intrusive searches. In other words, the viability of this sort of offence often matters less than the very fact that it exists.

Were Harsh Measures Effective?

During the Bill C-51 debates, government politicians repeated a mantra: "We reject the argument that every time we talk about security, our freedoms are threatened. Canadians understand that freedoms and security go hand in hand. Canadians expect us to protect both, and there are protections in this legislation that would do exactly that."[45]

It is, of course, true that discussions of security do not threaten freedoms. It is even true that many actions done in the name of security can be calibrated in a manner that does not threaten freedom, or at least mitigates the risks to it. But sometimes state action done in the name of security does unduly jeopardize freedom. The October Crisis is the poster child of that truth in Canada. But did any of these 1970 measures make a difference from a security perspective? It is often impossible to know whether tough anti-terrorism measures are effective. We will never be able to answer the question, what would have happened had Trudeau not used the Act? It is not surprising that there is still some debate about the effectiveness of the *War Measures Act*.

No less a civil libertarian than former McGill University law professor Frank R Scott defended the use of the *War Measures Act*, arguing that a "shock treatment was needed to restore the balance. It was given, and it worked. There was only one death, and it was not caused by the forces of law and order."[46] FLQ-related terrorism did not disappear after October 1970. The TSAS database lists a number of incidents in 1971. But after that, there are almost none. Maybe the use of the *War Measures Act* was successful "shock treatment." Other commentators, however, believe that the explanation for this pattern is more complex and that Québécois were turning away from the violence of the FLQ in favour of the Parti Québécois for a number of reasons, including a distaste for violence.[47]

Laporte's murder — and FLQ violence generally — led many Québécois who might have shared some of the FLQ's grievances to cut ties with the group. The Parti Québécois was in ascendance even before the October Crisis, earning almost a quarter of the vote in the April 1970 provincial election and presenting a democratic alternative for redressing Québécois grievances. No less than Pierre Vallières, a leading FLQ ideologue, renounced support for terrorism and supported the Parti Québécois in the wake of the crisis.[48] He did so at least in part because he feared that further violence might prompt another *War Measures Act* response, crushing the Parti Québécois movement before it could take power.[49] Ultimately, the Parti Québécois was elected to govern Quebec in 1976.

As already noted, RCMP members doubted that the *War Measures Act* was useful from a police investigation perspective. We have already pointed to the high rate of false positive detention under the measures, suggesting that the suspension of liberties scooped very few "bad guys" into the net. And we certainly do know that the use of the *War Measures Act* did not prevent the murder of Pierre Laporte. The FLQ announced that he had been "executed" on 17 October, the day after the *War Measures Act* had been declared. His body was discovered a few hours later.

Were Harsh Measures Popular?

The understandable anger at Pierre Laporte's murder led to high levels of public support, with 88 percent of all Canadians approving of the measures and 86 percent in Quebec.[50] Eminent historian Jack Granatstein spoke in opposition to the use of the *War Measures Act* to a crowd of 5,000 at York University. He recalled being frightened: "The shouts from the students who interrupted my speech were frequent and hostile; the visceral hatred of the FLQ kidnappers and murderers, and as I interpreted it, all Québécois, was palpable."[51]

Robert Stanfield, the Progressive Conservative leader of the official opposition in 1970, had misgivings but voted to uphold the *War Measures Act* rules when they ultimately arrived in Parliament. He later noted, "to many if not most Canadians any questioning of the invocation of the Act was unpatriotic even before the murder of Pierre Laporte." What was so striking to Stanfield was not the government's actions, because "another government might have done that too," but how "the public enthusiastically supported the measure." Stanfield warned that ultimately civil liberties depended on "our willingness to defend them even in times of stress."[52]

Initial reaction to Bill C-51, tabled in Parliament mere months after the October 2014 attacks, was also largely positive. And while the bill's popularity waned appreciably with time, the controversy that surrounded it was heated and coloured by rhetoric from government leaders that, by Canadian standards, was unusually inflammatory. Just like Professor Granatstein in 1970, we are forced to wonder how much of the initial support for Bill C-51 and how much of the fear of what the government repeatedly called "jihadi terrorism" was based on fear of and animus toward today's minority Other — Muslims. As even a cursory examination of historical practice would suggest, national security is very often an exercise in securing a majority at the expense of the liberty of a minority. What the late Ronald Dworkin reminded us about in the wake of 9/11 remains true today: most of us will pay no price in terms of personal freedom because of new and extreme anti-terror laws.[53] Instead, lost freedom is an externality borne by a minority in the interest of protecting or assuaging the fears of the majority.

How Do We Protect Ourselves against Ourselves?

Those who invoked and then supported the *War Measures Act*, including Prime Minister Trudeau, were not authoritarians, oblivious to the importance of rights. They believed that Canada faced a grave threat of terrorism and that they were acting to protect the rights of victims and potential victims. Some of Trudeau's rhetoric in support of the *War Measures Act* found echoes in defences of Bill C-51.

On the night of 16 October 1970, Trudeau warned Canadians "of a new and terrifying type of person" — in this case not a violent "jihadi terrorist" but a "violent revolutionary" whose emergence made it necessary to "root out the cancer of an armed, revolutionary movement."[54] Trudeau described the nature of the terrorist threat by warning that the FLQ presented a danger to "you or me, or perhaps some child" or "innocent members of your family or of your neighbourhood."[55] In 2015, Prime Minister Harper announced Bill C-51 by calling "violent jihadism" "an act of war."[56]

Prime Minister Trudeau overstated the threat. As we discuss in Chapter 3, Prime Minister Harper also overreaches. But it would be wrong to impute malice to their actions. It is hard to imagine a more difficult dilemma than that faced by any leader confronting an adversary prepared to use violence — in today's world, indiscriminate violence — for political purposes. It is highly unlikely that FLQ- or ISIS-inspired terrorists will kill "innocent members of your family." It is, however, something you fear if you have the responsibilities of a prime minister.

Prime Minister Trudeau used a rights-affirming rationale for invoking the *War Measures Act* when he argued that "persons who invoke violence are deliberately raising the level of hate in Canada . . . at a time when the country must eliminate hate . . . . The government is acting, therefore, to protect your life and your liberty."[57] Prime Minister Jean Chrétien's government would use a similar rights-friendly and anti-hate rationale for its post-9/11 terror laws, discussed below.

But good intentions are no guarantee that governments will not over-react to the fear, insecurity, and uncertainty created by terrorism. How do we guard against this risk?

One response is "through good process." One virtue of Bill C-51, as compared to *War Measures Act* regulations, was that it was debated in Parliament and in parliamentary committees before eventually being passed in the House of Commons by a vote of 183 to 96 and in the Senate by a vote of 44 to 28. In contrast, cabinet's unilateral declaration of the *War Measures Act* in the early morning of 16 October 1970 was an executive branch *fait accompli*.

Nevertheless, the benefits of parliamentary debates in fearful times can be overestimated. Democratic institutions can and do overreact. Three days after the *War Measures Act* was invoked, its use was debated in Parliament and approved in a vote of 190 to 16. The *War Measures Act* regulations were then replaced by similar legislation debated in Parliament during November 1970. Parliament enacted this legislation notwithstanding the guarantee of bail and the guarantee against arbitrary detention in Canada's then only codification of rights: the *Canadian Bill of Rights*. Only the NDP voted against the new statute.[58]

In the Bill C-51 context, the parliamentary debate was mired in simplifications and factual and legal misapprehensions, all conducted in a political hothouse environment during the lead up to the October 2015 federal election. This was not a truly deliberative democratic debate, especially in the House of Commons.

We should all be acutely concerned, therefore, that legislation enacted in a fog of uncertainty or crisis, in response to horrific acts of terrorism and with political fates on the line, may often have unintended and undesired consequences.

Sunsets

One common device to deal with this tendency, and to let calmer heads eventually prevail, is the legislative "sunset" — a provision that forces the new measures to expire within a set period unless affirmatively renewed by Parliament, hopefully after thorough reconsideration in light of experience. The 1970 legislation enacted after the *War Measures Act* regulations protected the public and parliamentarians from themselves: it sunsetted the new law as of April 1971 unless Parliament renewed it. With declining public support and no subsequent terrorist incidents, Parliament did not renew the October Crisis law. The sun went down on a bad law.

We followed a similar pattern with at least parts of the original 2001 *Anti-terrorism Act*, as discussed further below. But in contrast to both the October Crisis law and post-9/11 legislation, Bill C-51 contains no sunsets. It is intended to be permanent legislation. The government resisted calls to include sunsets and mandatory parliamentary re-reviews of the law even as support for the bill declined from the time of its introduction in January 2015 to its enactment in June 2015. This is hubris that we may regret in the future.

The Aftermath of Overreaction

Despite the harshness of the *War Measures Act*, the actual treatment of those responsible for its use was relatively lenient. James Cross's kidnappers were allowed to leave for Cuba, and those convicted of murdering Pierre Laporte were granted parole by 1982. Historian Kenneth McNaught supported the use of the *War Measures Act* but also argued that leniency toward the protagonists of the October Crisis was symbolic of a Canadian political tradition that since 1837 has refused to accept political violence but has also been relatively merciful and responsive to political grievances thereafter.[59]

Until the rise of al-Qaida, we have generally not seen terrorists as a sort of permanent enemy to be defeated in a war. As discussed in Chapter 3, ISIS may be no less of a threat than al-Qaida. But in that chapter, we also point to the shortcomings of the warfare analogy. We must recognize that today's al-Qaida- and ISIS-inspired terrorism has a complex sociology, one that is sometimes hard to separate from regional conflicts in places like Syria. And so we support multi-disciplinary measures designed to recognize and respond to the (sometimes maligned) "root causes" of ISIS's attraction to some Muslims.

Diagnosing a cause and devising a response based on that diagnosis is not appeasement. It is logic. More than that, we agree with Professor McNaught that punishing political violence and stemming its underlying causes are both parts of the Canadian political tradition, parts that have contributed to the country's success. In Chapter 13, we will suggest that Canada should invest more in multi-disciplinary measures focused on countering violent extremism and that these measures should take seriously the discrimination and the lack of a sense of belonging in Canada that some Muslims feel.

The October Crisis also demonstrates that harsh measures may be viewed differently by different sectors of the community. For example, Louise Arbour recalled that she "had the sense that English Canada was completely tone-deaf to what was happening in Québec" and "very supportive of the hard line of the federal government." According to Arbour, who would later serve on the Supreme Court of Canada and as United Nations Commissioner of Human Rights, the October Crisis "anchored [her] commitment to fundamental civil rights."[60]

This raises the question of how Canada's new terror laws may provoke varying responses in Canada's diverse society. This is an especially important question because those who may feel unjustly targeted by these laws may not have the same democratic outlets that appealed to many Québécois in the wake of the October Crisis.

For his part, Pierre Trudeau never admitted error in invoking the *War Measures Act*, but he made the enactment of the *Charter* the goal of his political career. He only reluctantly accepted a clause allowing governments to enact legislation notwithstanding fundamental freedoms, legal rights, and equality rights in the *Charter*.

The *Charter* now requires explicit parliamentary legislation to override its rights with such laws being subject to a five-year sunset. In the absence of such an override (which has never been used federally), the *Charter* would have governed state action under the *War Measures Act*. In any event, the Mulroney government replaced the *War Measures Act* with the *Emergencies Act* in 1988.[61] The *War Measures Act* itself had been enacted during a crisis — World War I. It had been used to intern "enemy aliens" during both world wars and was based on a model of emergency legislation that Britain exported throughout its empire.

The new *Emergencies Act* broke this mold of crisis legislation enacted during a calamity. Among other things, it contains pre-commitments against detention done on grounds of race, religion, or ethnic origin. It also provides for compensation, parliamentary debate, and after-the-fact public inquiries if its provisions are invoked. It was based on a desire, absent from the present government's response to the October 2014 terrorist attacks, to learn from past overreactions.

III. RCMP OVERREACTION IN THE 1970S

In important respects, the *Charter* and the *Emergencies Act* were positive after-effects of overreaction in the October Crisis. The 1984 *CSIS Act* had a similar, but more fraught, origin — one that is particularly relevant in light of the changes that Bill C-51 makes to CSIS's original mandate.

Before the creation of CSIS in 1984, the Security Service of the RCMP had responsibility for both security intelligence and national security policing. In the aftermath of the October Crisis, the RCMP was blamed for an alleged "intelligence failure" that failed to prevent the acts of terrorism. In fact, the RCMP had provided rather good intelligence as the dangers from the FLQ escalated in the months before the actual kidnappings. And indeed, as noted above, the RCMP had not sought the imposition of the *War Measures Act* and had even concluded that its use detracted from the police work that eventually discovered the criminals.[62]

Informers Everywhere

But the RCMP's Security Service was stung by criticisms of its failure to prevent the two kidnappings and the subsequent murder of Laporte. It overreacted. It recruited so many informers that by 1972 the police effectively were the FLQ.[63]

Informers, even more than undercover operatives, exist in a secret and shadowy world on the edges of the law. They are important to security work — but using them has consequences. The use of informers can chill the expressive and associational rights of targeted communities that fear informers in their midst. And done improperly, it can complicate criminal trials. We discuss this issue in Chapter 9, in relation to Bill C-44 enacted in 2015.

Institutionalized Illegality

In the 1970s, RCMP tactics went further than recruiting informers. That tale is a cautionary one as we consider CSIS's new powers to break the law under Bill C-51.

In the 1970s, the police and their informers engaged in a pattern of institutionalized wrongdoing and illegal conduct in an attempt to prevent other acts of terrorism in the lead up to the 1976 Montreal Olympics. This police conduct was detected almost by accident: a former RCMP member testified at his own trial for bombing a private residence that he had done much worse things for the RCMP's Security Service. Specifically, he had broken into the press bureau used by left-wing Quebec political groups to steal membership lists.

These revelations culminated in the McDonald Commission, which recommended the creation of CSIS. That inquiry found "noble cause" corruption in the RCMP, which meant that the RCMP believed the noble end of preventing additional acts of terrorism justified illegal means. The Security Service was also freer to break the law because, like its successor, CSIS, it was not frequently involved in prosecutions. This meant that the courts generally were unable to closely scrutinize its conduct.

Instead of prosecutions, the RCMP employed active forms of disruption and dirty tricks in terrorism cases. One example of such disruption was the infamous burning of a barn to either prevent the meeting of the FLQ and the Black Panthers or force them to a location where there was electronic surveillance. Another example involved false communiqués in the name of the FLQ that were, in turn, cited to the government as evidence of the terrorist threat. RCMP illegal conduct also included 400 break-ins targeting, among other things, the office of a separatist newspaper, trade unions, the Parti Québécois, and the premises of left-leaning groups in British Columbia. The Security Service also surveilled MPs, opened mail, made illegal use of income tax information for non-income tax purposes, stole dynamite and a Parti Québécois membership list, and spied on universities, unions, Indigenous groups, and political parties.

The Security Service's dirty tricks did not escalate to intentional or negligent infliction of bodily harm, invasion of sexual integrity, or obstruction of justice — acts that CSIS is barred from committing under Bill C-51. Nor was its illegal conduct pre-authorized by the courts, something that will be true for CSIS under Bill C-51.

But that may be beside the point. As the McDonald Commission stressed, dirty and illegal tricks can erode public trust in security services and imperil democracy.[64] Indeed, the stakes are even higher under the Bill C-51 regime: if CSIS illegalities and breaches of the *Charter* go wrong under

Bill C-51, the reputation of the judiciary as well as CSIS may suffer. As we discuss in Chapter 9, dirty tricks may also make it difficult to prosecute suspects should they turn out to be determined terrorists. This is an even more acute concern today than it was in the 1970s, given the very different threat presented by ISIS-inspired terrorism than by the waning FLQ of the 1970s.

Massive Invasions of Privacy

The RCMP Security Service focused on gathering intelligence, like CSIS today, and not law enforcement. By 1977, the Security Service had 1.3 million entries in its files about 800,000 individuals, including Canadians who visited the Soviet Union and known homosexuals. The McDonald Commission presciently warned about how "access to computer technology greatly facilitates the ease with which information and opinions recorded in these files can be retrieved and correlated."[65]

Although much of the Security Service's illegal behaviour focused on separatists, the McDonald Commission also found illegal conduct outside Quebec with respect to left-leaning organizations, including the Waffle movement of the NDP. It found that the RCMP collected intelligence on grounds that were "so vague and loose . . . as to justify almost any collection program."[66] In addition, tax and unemployment insurance information was used to encourage people to become informers. This led the McDonald Commission to recommend a strict necessity standard for collecting information, and even judicial warrants for some sharing of information.[67] As will be examined in Chapter 5, neither of these features is part of Bill C-51's new law for sharing information.

The McDonald Commission's Vision for a Law-Abiding and Constrained CSIS

The McDonald Commission concluded that security intelligence should be taken away from the RCMP and given to a new civilian intelligence agency that would be subject to a precisely defined legislative mandate, ministerial controls, and review by both a special expert committee and a parliamentary committee.

The commission stressed the importance of ministerial accountability with respect to both the RCMP and a new civilian intelligence agency. It found that the government's directions to the police had been ambiguous. The RCMP was well aware that the Trudeau government's priority was national unity. The political and criminal dimensions of such threats were often conflated. In other words, national security was politicized but in a manner that allowed the government to avoid taking direct responsibility for what was done.

The McDonald Commission saw the compelling need for security, and it argued that any new intelligence agency should be effective: "accurate intelligence about terrorists is needed not only to enable the government and police forces to take effective action against them but also to avoid over-reacting to their threats."[68] Such observations clearly recalled the overreaction of the October Crisis and foreshadowed some post-9/11 security abuses involving inaccurate intelligence.

Finally, the overriding theme and message of the McDonald Commission was that the new intelligence agency and the police should never engage in illegal acts. If an undercover officer or informer needed to break the law, the specific law should be amended to allow such action. The commission did not recommend any general or generic authorization of law breaking by security forces.

That vision has now been abandoned by Bill C-51. In fact, it was a vision contested from the inception of CSIS: in 1983, the government included CSIS law-breaking powers in its first effort to legislate the new CSIS. These and other proposals prompted a storm of controversy, one that ultimately forced a re-think by John Turner's government.

Initial Resistance to the Creation of a CSIS That Could Break the Law

In May 1983, the government tabled a bill to create CSIS. Its most controversial feature would have enabled CSIS to do not only surveillance but "any other act or thing that is reasonably necessary" to address threats. And so "in the face of scandal over illegal and improper acts carried out by the security service, the government was proposing simply to legalize these acts, with only minimal judicial constraint."[69]

In striking contrast with the relative provincial silence on Bill C-51, the 1983 bill prompted fierce opposition by all provincial attorneys general. Civil liberties groups and Peter Russell, the former research director of the McDonald Commission, also resisted the bill. The provincial attorneys general warned that by allowing CSIS to break laws in secret, the bill would undermine the rule of law and the newly enacted *Charter*. They also warned that CSIS conduct "would never be scrutinized by police forces, Crown attorneys, defence counsel, or courts of law . . . . The force is given carte blanche to break any law completely free from any independent publicly accountable scrutiny or review."[70]

The critics of the original CSIS bill were treated seriously and with respect. Parliamentary committees were given time to do important and detailed work — and indeed the Senate committee discussed below advertised nationally for public submissions.[71] And as also discussed below, the original bill was abandoned, and a much improved bill was tabled in Parliament in 1984, an election year. It ultimately became today's *CSIS Act*.

Unfortunately, this process was not replicated for the Bill C-51 debate in 2015, another election year. Here, we simply note one example of how different 2015 was from 1983 to 1984. In 1983, the British Columbia Civil Liberties Association filed a detailed brief identifying shortcomings with the initial CSIS bill. The association raised other, equally pressing, concerns with Bill C-51, decades later. In defending C-51, Public Safety Minister Steven Blaney attempted to discredit the association as one that was myopically opposed to security measures. In an apparent effort to paint the British Columbia Civil Liberties Association as a serial exaggerator, he cited its 1983 warnings without noting (and indeed perhaps without knowing) that they had been directed at a flawed CSIS bill that then never came into existence because of widespread condemnation. Minister Blaney said, "each and every time a government brings forward national security legislation, some groups are fear-mongering."[72]

The contentious 1983 bill also featured a definition of threats to the security of Canada that included "threats against any state allied or associated with Canada" as well as a broad definition of subversion. As will be discussed in Chapter 5, the information sharing provisions of Bill C-51 have an even broader definition of "activities that undermine the security of Canada," which includes activities in Canada that "undermine the security of another state," even a repressive state not allied or associated with Canada.

The 1983 bill's approach was ultimately abandoned in favour of a narrower definition of Canada's legitimate security interests. No such amendments were made to Bill C-51's information sharing law, and the concerns raised by the many critics of the bill were dismissed.

The Pitfield Committee and the Role of Parliament

When the federal government ultimately bowed to widespread criticism of the 1983 bill, it referred the project to a Senate committee chaired by former cabinet secretary Michael Pitfield. The Pitfield Committee worked though the summer of 1983. It held nineteen days of hearings and accepted twenty-five briefs. It proposed a number of amendments that tightened the bill's definition of threats to the security of Canada. It also rejected the law-breaking clause on the basis that it "could give the wrong signal to agency employees"[73] and encourage a culture of law breaking. Instead, CSIS employees would have the same protections as peace officers, which would mean that there would be "no legalization in respect of more serious offences."[74] But the Pitfield Committee, in keeping with the McDonald Commission recommendations, also stressed that CSIS would be a civilian intelligence agency subject to stringent controls and without the coercive powers used by law enforcement.

Bill C-51 abandons the Pitfield and McDonald vision of CSIS as a law-abiding pure intelligence agency. But ironically, Bill C-51 did not fix an oversight in the initial design of CSIS. By prescribing a firm demarcation between "intelligence" and "law enforcement," the initial conception of CSIS complicated anti-terrorism, and specifically prosecution as a tool of anti-terror. It reflected Cold War priorities where terrorism was a threat but far from the prime security threat. As we discuss below, the idea that CSIS should never collect or be concerned with evidence hindered the investigation of the 1985 Air India bombings. It remains a huge flaw to this day.

In one notable departure from the McDonald Commission, the Pitfield Committee rejected the creation of a joint parliamentary committee with access to secret information, including the classified reports prepared by CSIS's expert review committee. In views echoed in the Bill C-51 debate, the Senate committee was concerned that a parliamentary committee would duplicate the work of the expert body and lack the necessary time and expertise to be effective. At the same time, the Pitfield Committee's main concern was "the problem of maintaining the security of information."[75] In other words, the Senate committee did not trust parliamentary colleagues to hold close sensitive information. Implicit in these views were fears that parliamentarians committed to separatism, or those subject to blackmail, might reveal "CSIS operations and information."[76]

These concerns gave short shrift to the integrity of Canadian lawmakers. They ignored the McDonald Commission's counter-view: there was no reason to think that Canadian legislators were less trustworthy than those in other democracies, which did give legislators access to secret information. And yet the government invoked the very same argument about loose-lipped lawmakers thirty years later in the Bill C-51 debate. Justice Minister Peter MacKay implied that security information might be used for partisan reasons and that leaks over controversial Supreme Court appointments demonstrated that parliamentarians could not be trusted with secret information about national security.[77]

The Pitfield Committee was more supportive of the other forms of review that the McDonald Commission had proposed for CSIS. It stressed the importance of an Inspector General to act as "the ministry's 'eyes and ears' on the Service" and as necessary "to maintain an appropriate degree of ministerial responsibility."[78] It also stressed that the Inspector General should not be limited to "after-the-fact review"[79] but should ensure that policies and laws were being respected in real time.

The ultimate *CSIS Act* created an Inspector General. In 2012, however, the government abolished that office, supposedly in an effort to economize on its $1 million a year budget — a justification that former Security Intelligence Review Committee (SIRC) member (and federal opposition parliamentarian) Bob Rae called "frankly just nonsensical. It means less accountability."[80]

The Pitfield Committee also supported the McDonald Commission's recommendation for a specialized review body, eventually named the Security Intelligence Review Committee. It warned that the SIRC would need adequate resources and five members with a quorum of three. It stressed that CSIS's "extraordinary powers . . . must be balanced by a review body with broad powers of its own to enquire and investigate CSIS operations."[81] And it noted the importance of appointing the right people in consultation with other parties to "ensure the credibility of the SIRC would be maintained."[82]

After CSIS and SIRC were created in 1984, SIRC initially met much of this initial promise under its first chair, Ron Atkey. In more recent years, it has been short-handed, underresourced, and dogged with controversy that saw two chairs, Arthur Porter and Chuck Strahl, prematurely resign. In 2015, Porter died while fighting extradition from Panama to face criminal charges in Canada related to his business practices. He had also purported to act as an ambassador for Sierra Leone while serving on SIRC from 2008 to 2011. The next chair, Chuck Strahl, resigned amid controversy in 2014 over ties to pipeline companies that critics complained put him in a conflict of interest with his SIRC duties.

Before he resigned, however, Chuck Strahl, a former Conservative minister, candidly admitted that SIRC no longer had sufficient powers given the increased integration of CSIS's activities with other federal agencies. He told a Senate committee that SIRC, which only has jurisdiction over CSIS and access to information in CSIS's possession, could "tell parliamentarians that, as far as we can tell, everything looks great in CSIS country, but we don't know what happened over that fence; you're on your own."[83] In other words, Strahl recognized that in the modern world, CSIS increasingly worked closely with other federal agencies, but SIRC faced a legislated wall because it had no power to examine those other agencies and chase threads reaching from CSIS to them. Many of the sixteen other federal agencies that can receive information from CSIS are not subject to national security review under the new *SoCIS Act* created by Bill C-51.[84]

The Creation of CSIS

The Turner government accepted most of the work done by the Pitfield Committee and accepted thirty-two changes to the original 1983 bill. That second bill became law in June 1984, containing the features described above. It remained largely untouched from that date until the enactment of bills C-44 and C-51 in 2015.

The government's response to the Pitfield Committee stands in stark contrast to the stubborn recalcitrance of its successor in 2015. To be sure, government MPs introduced and passed five amendments to Bill C-51 during the Commons process. But these changes — best described as incidental, absurd, or confusing — bore only a loose connection to the Commons committee process. There, hearing time was often consumed with wholesale attacks and defences of the bill and a distressing and often embarrassing tendency by government MPs to read speaking notes into the record to stave off responses by those critical of the bill. As we shall discuss throughout this book, too little attention was given to amendments that should have been made, and too little to the few that were. In the Commons (although not the Senate), the actual content of Bill C-51 sometimes took second seat to more generic claims about security. And there was little attempt to learn from the mistakes of past over- and underreactions to terrorism.

IV. UNDERREACTION TO TERRORISM: THE AIR INDIA BOMBINGS

Introduction

If the October Crisis is the hallmark of Canada's overreaction to terrorism, then the 1985 Air India bombings symbolize the epitome of underreaction. For decades, Canadians did not treat seriously enough the twin bombings that resulted in 331 deaths — Canada's largest mass murder. Dr Ramji Khandelwal, who had two daughters on the destroyed Flight 182, told the Air India Commission that the families "started to think that nobody wants to do anything because we are Canadians of Indian origin. We thought at that time, and I think it may be true today too, that it is not taken as a Canadian problem and nobody cares about the lives of Canadians of Indian origin."[85] Air India is a stark reminder of the damage that can be caused by terrorism in Canada, inspired by grievances a world away, and by underreaction to terrorism.

The 1985 Air India bombings were the world's most deadly act of aviation terrorism before 9/11. And yet, in the end, only one person was ever convicted of what was a wide-ranging plot based in British Columbia. Three other related prosecutions of alleged Sikh terrorists collapsed. These failures prompted Prime Minister Harper to create the Air India Commission of Inquiry in 2006. That commission's findings demonstrate clearly what happens when there is no appropriate command-and-control oversight and co-ordination of how our national security agencies, especially CSIS and the RCMP, work together in the difficult process of converting intelligence into evidence.

CSIS Does Not Collect Evidence

The suspected mastermind of the Air India bombings, Talwinder Singh Parmar, was subject to both electronic and physical surveillance by CSIS before the 23 June 1985 bombings. There were considerable delays in obtaining the judicial authorization to wiretap Parmar in part caused by the transition of security intelligence from the RCMP to the new CSIS. Even after a court granted the warrant, there were more delays in translation and analysis of the wiretaps. Once the tapes were translated and subject to analysis, most were destroyed.

CSIS took seriously its new role as a pure intelligence agency that was only supposed to collect intelligence. It interpreted its mandate in section 12 of the new *CSIS Act* to collect intelligence "to the extent that it is strictly necessary" as a restraint on the retention as well as the collection of intelligence. CSIS was influenced by past criticisms of the disbanded RCMP Security Service, which had been custodian of a massive number of files. And so CSIS destroyed most of the wiretaps on Parmar. This destruction continued even after the lead prosecutor asked that the CSIS wiretaps be preserved because of their evidential value.

The tape erasures as well as CSIS's destruction of interview notes with witnesses in Vancouver's Sikh community hindered subsequent criminal investigations and prosecutions. In 2005, CSIS's actions were found by a court to constitute "unacceptable negligence."[86] And then in 2008, the Supreme Court ruled that CSIS had misinterpreted its legislation since 1984 as mandating the destruction of intelligence, even when it might have evidential value.[87] The Court reached the rather sensible conclusion that raw intelligence collected under a proper and focused investigation should be retained because it might constitute the "best evidence."[88]

However, in its 2010 report, the Air India Commission found that CSIS, unlike MI5 in the United Kingdom, had continued to resist its evidential responsibilities. Given this, the police had reluctantly concluded that it was best to minimize their involvement with CSIS.

The Air India tape erasures symbolize CSIS's traditional reluctance to accept that the intelligence it collects in terrorism investigations may also be used as evidence in criminal trials. The Air India Commission regarded the destruction of the tapes and the interview notes as manifesting CSIS's "mantra" that it "does not collect evidence."[89] As the commission explained:

> This accurate statement of fact — that CSIS was not a law enforcement agency and that its mandate was to collect intelligence rather than to support prosecutions — soon lost its original meaning and became a justification for CSIS to withhold information and ignore its potential role as an aid to law enforcement.[90]

This flaw remains uncorrected, even after Bill C-51. Indeed, C-51 makes it worse. As we discuss throughout this book, Bill C-51 now permits CSIS to engage in many of the dirty tricks once performed by the RCMP Security Services, and it does not force CSIS to consider the impact of its actions on the criminal justice system. Indeed, the only response to criticism over CSIS's new illegal conduct powers was a single amendment made by the Commons, confirming that CSIS does not have "law enforcement" powers. This amendment provides new legislative support for what the Air India Commission found had been CSIS's main excuse for doing so much damage to the Air India investigations and prosecutions.

Air India and the Need for Oversight

The Air India investigation underlines the importance of command-and-control oversight ensuring that timely information goes to those in a position to prevent acts of terrorism, including through prosecutions. We will discuss oversight and review at length in Chapters 11 and 12, but at this point note that oversight — as distinct from review — involves the command and control issue of who is in charge.

Just as intelligence that circulated within the federal government a few days before the October 2014 attacks pointed to a possible terrorist attack,[91] there was substantial intelligence in June 1985 pointing to a threat to the single Air India flight departing Canada each week. The intelligence highlighted plots in British Columbia before 1985 to bomb Air India planes, a test blast heard by CSIS in early June 1985 in its surveillance of Parmar (but misinterpreted as a gunshot), and a 1 June 1985 telex from Air India about the threat of a bomb planted in checked baggage. The Air India Commission also heard testimony from James Bartleman, the director general of intelligence analysis in the external affairs department in the mid-1980s. Bartleman had seen intelligence provided by Canada's signals intelligence agency, the Communications Security Establishment (CSE), concerning a specific threat to Flight 182. He had brought this information to the attention of RCMP officials. Even without this specific warning, the Air India Commission concluded that there were enough pieces in the intelligence mosaic to have prevented the bombing.

As in so many intelligence failures, the fault lay not in the pieces but in putting them together. In other words, there was a failure to get intelligence into the hands of the right persons. For this reason, the Air India Commission recommended an enhanced role for the prime minister's national security advisor to co-ordinate intelligence and to resolve inevitable disputes between security agencies — measures the commission regarded as necessary to grease the flow of information between departments.

The post-bombing investigation was also adversely affected by the lack of "a central informed decision-maker"[92] as CSIS and the RCMP essentially competed to solve the case. In other words, the solicitor general (now the minister of public safety) did not ensure that the RCMP and CSIS, which both reported to him, co-operated. CSIS approached its human sources in the Sikh community and promised them confidentiality. As will be seen in Chapter 9, such promises today would give the sources a veto over whether they could provide evidence for the prosecution. And even though it was effectively investigating the largest mass murder in Canada history, CSIS was often reluctant to turn these sources over to the RCMP. And the RCMP, in turn, treated sources and potential witnesses poorly, failing to protect Tara Singh Hayer, who was murdered before he could testify.

Failed Terrorism Prosecutions

The consequences of CSIS's aversion to criminal justice standards arose early, in cases surrounding the Air India massacre. In 1986, prosecutors laid charges against four men for conspiracy to murder an Indian state government minister, based on incriminating information obtained through a CSIS wiretap. While the men were convicted of attempted murder in a separate trial relying on physical (and not wiretap) evidence, the conspiracy charges collapsed after CSIS officials revealed that misleading information had been used to obtain the wiretap warrant.[93] The then director of CSIS resigned, but this was not the only failed prosecution.

Talwinder Singh Parmar, the suspected mastermind of the plot, was prosecuted along with Interjit Singh Reyat in 1986 for explosives offences in relation to the test blast of a bomb in Duncan, British Columbia, shortly before the Air India bombings. The prosecution was hindered by CSIS's reluctance to testify about its surveillance of Parmar. It ended with the Crown calling no evidence against Parmar and dropping the charges. Reyat, for his part, was assessed a $2,000 fine.[94]

A 1987 prosecution of Parmar for conspiracy to commit acts of terrorism in India collapsed when the Crown was unwilling to reveal identifying information about an informer necessary to sustain a wiretap warrant critical to the prosecution. The informer was offered but refused a place in witness protection. The prosecutor admitted, "If I were placed in a similar situation, I would not be prepared to consent to the information identifying me."[95]

A prosecution for an alleged conspiracy to bomb another Air India 747 airplane eventually collapsed because of an unwillingness to disclose the identity of a key police informer, who had lost his privilege against disclosure of his identity because he had played an active role in the investigation.[96]

Canada had an abysmal record of terrorism prosecutions in the aftermath of the Air India bombings. Indeed only one person, Interjet Singh Reyat, was ever convicted (of manslaughter) in relation to the Air India bombings, even though it was clear that others had been involved in a much larger conspiracy centred in British Columbia.

Reyat was first convicted of manslaughter in 1991 for his role in the premature explosion of a bomb that was destined for another Air India plane and that killed two baggage handlers at Narita Airport in Japan. Even that prosecution was fraught because of CSIS's continued reluctance and delays in disclosing intelligence. The prosecutor in this case, James Jardine, concluded that CSIS "failed to come to grips with the thorny issues created by disclosure requirements for full answer and defence in criminal prosecutions." He warned, "there is little value" in only "gathering intelligence for intelligence purposes."[97]

The Air India Acquittals

The trial for the actual bombings of Air India Flight 182 did not start until 2003, almost twenty years after 329 people died when a luggage bomb exploded over the Atlantic. The Crown charged only three persons, including Reyat, who eventually accepted a guilty plea to manslaughter. After a 217-day trial, the remaining two accused, Malik and Bagri, were acquitted in a judge-alone trial.

The trial was a great disappointment for many, especially the families of the victims. The trial judge's finding of a reasonable doubt about Malik's and Bagri's guilt reflected concern about the credibility of key witnesses. The poor performance of witnesses stemmed in no small part from their poor handling as they were transitioned from being confidential CSIS sources to being prosecutorial witnesses and then exposed to public cross-examination in a criminal trial.

One key witness, Ms E, had initially refused to talk to authorities about the bombing, given her concerns for her safety in Vancouver's Sikh community.

She eventually provided valuable information to CSIS after CSIS promised her full confidentiality. Such a promise is not something that the RCMP, with its concern about gathering evidence, would have issued.[98] CSIS then destroyed notes of the interviews with Ms E, something that the trial judge found was unacceptable negligence. Indeed, if Malik and Bagri had not been acquitted in 2005 because of reasonable doubts about their guilt, the trial judge might have stayed or permanently halted the prosecution anyway because of this conclusion about CSIS's destruction of both the Parmar wiretap tapes and the notes of discussions with witnesses.

The trial judge found that Ms E had feigned memory loss concerning key events surrounding the bombing. The trial judge was also influenced by the fact that Ms E had told her initial story to CSIS only after being promised confidentiality. He concluded, "caution is warranted for fear that the person making the statement had no concerns about being called to account for the honesty and accuracy of that statement."[99]

Despite this experience, in 2015 the government institutionalized CSIS promises of confidentiality in Bill C-44. As we will discuss in Chapter 9, the new legislation entitles CSIS to promise future iterations of Ms E confidentiality, regardless of the effect that such promises may have on subsequent prosecutions.

The trial judge's finding of reasonable doubt in the trial was also connected to his concerns about the credibility of Ms D. Like Ms E, Ms D had been a CSIS source originally promised confidentiality. She told CSIS that Malik had confessed to playing a role in the bombings. CSIS passed Ms D to the RCMP but soon regretted it. Ms D was forced into witness protection in 1998 as a result of an RCMP error that had publicly revealed her name. Witness protection ruined Ms D's life by forcing her to have five different residences in five years. By the time she testified in 2003 at the trial, she was a reluctant witness who was not believed by the trial judge.[100]

The Air India Commission concluded that the RCMP had too much control over witness protection. That process should be subject to an independent director and dispute resolution mechanism. In 2013, the government enacted the *Safer Witness Act*,[101] a law that contained neither feature. The government's new legislation allows unsatisfied witnesses to leave the witness protection program. This is, however, not a realistic option for witnesses whose lives may be in jeopardy. The 1998 murder of Tara Singh Hayer, a potential witness in the Air India trial, was a reminder that witnesses face real threats.

The Minor Miracle of an Air India Trial and Verdict

The Air India trial actually could have been even worse — it was a minor miracle that the full trial happened at all. One reason why the Air India trial did happen, without being derailed before a verdict, was that prosecutors and defence counsel were able to agree on many disclosure issues, avoiding the need to litigate CSIS-driven secrecy claims in the Federal Court.

This observation raises another confounding aspect of the way Canada has organized its national security law. In Canada, the Federal Court adjudicates government claims to national security confidentiality made in any proceeding, including a criminal terrorism trial. Under section 38 of the *Canada Evidence Act*,[102] the Federal Court decides whether material should be kept secret and out of the hands of the accused because of the harm that its disclosure would cause to national security. Provincial superior courts trying terrorism cases, meanwhile, retain a residual authority to toss cases (by staying proceedings) if persuaded that secrecy makes a fair trial impossible.

The inevitable result is often protracted satellite litigation in the Federal Court designed to preserve government secrecy. Bill C-51 does not change the *Canada Evidence Act* — but it will likely make these proceedings even more frequent given that accused in future terrorism cases will be certain to seek information about CSIS's new threat reduction activities, possibly done in violation of the law and the *Charter*, and will try to seek access to CSIS confidential sources by arguing either that innocence is at stake or that the source lost the confidentiality privilege by becoming an active agent. If CSIS responds with its usual reluctance to reveal anything that might hint at its sources and methods, these issues will require litigation before the Federal Court and, ultimately, re-litigation before a criminal trial court obliged to decide whether a fair trial is possible.

The Air India trial represented a unique exception that avoided secrecy litigation in the Federal Court: the prosecutor had agreed to allow defence counsel to examine secret material to determine whether it was helpful to the defence on the condition that defence counsel not share the information with their clients. This approach, quite common in American terrorism trials, has not been repeated in other terror trials. Indeed it has been cast in doubt by the Supreme Court, especially where the secret in question is the identity of an informer.[103] As such, this workaround may not recur in future terrorism trials.

Given CSIS's important role in terrorism investigations and its demand for secrecy, the Air India Commission recommended that Canada should abandon the two-step, bifurcated court model: trial judges should be allowed to decide secrecy issues, as is the case in the United States, the United Kingdom, and Australia. And in fact, this approach was used with success in the "Toronto 18" prosecutions, probably Canada's most famous post-9/11 prosecutions to date. But this approach is no longer available today. In the Toronto 18 prosecutions, a trial judge decided that the bifurcated system was unconstitutional because it denied a trial judge access to secret material that may be quite relevant to the trial. The Crown appealed this holding, and the Supreme Court ultimately allowed the appeal and concluded that Canada's two-court system is constitutional. At the same time, it also admonished trial judges not to hesitate to stay or stop a terrorism trial if they believed that the secrecy blessed by the Federal Court order made a fair trial impossible.[104] The result is a complicated two-court choreography that makes Canada's system of terrorism trials slower and more fragile than the systems of other democracies.

All told, the Air India acquittals are a sobering reminder of the difficulties of terrorism prosecutions. Prosecutions are the best way to denounce and punish terrorism. But, as will be examined in detail in Chapter 9, they are exceedingly difficult and demanding. Moreover, Canada still lags behind other democracies in its capacity to conduct such prosecutions.

In particular, terrorism prosecutions are affected by CSIS demands that its sources, its methods, and the information it receives from others be kept secret. Litigation to resolve these secrecy claims is still conducted in Federal Court with the criminal trial judge being left in the difficult position of determining afterward whether a fair trial is possible. And one result of all this complexity and CSIS's fears of disclosure is that the police now make sparing use of CSIS intelligence and sources. Insiders sometimes call this whole regime of attenuated information sharing "less is more." Because of it, the Government of Canada may have information that would put bad guys in jail, but it does not use it. As will become clear in Chapter 9, we think that until we resolve this intelligence-to-evidence conundrum, no Canadian government can truly claim that it is doing everything possible to keep us safe. Bill C-51 makes no effort to cure this problem. In Chapters 8 and 9, we suggest that it probably makes it worse.

"That Was Then, This Is Now"?

Both during the Air India Commission's hearings and during the Bill C-51 debate in early 2015, the government insisted that the problems revealed in the Air India investigation and trial were ancient history. In defending its present RCMP and CSIS arrangements, the government has pointed to a number of successful prosecutions, most notably the Toronto 18 terrorism prosecutions, where two CSIS sources gave important evidence, with one agreeing to enter the witness protection program.

In his 2010 Air India Commission report, however, Justice Major was not persuaded that the problems he discovered were a question of "that was then, this is now."[105] The Air India Commission devoted considerable effort to examining the adequacy of contemporary anti-terror arrangements. It found that the destruction of the tapes and witness interviews had not been an aberration. CSIS had continued to destroy raw intelligence until the Supreme Court concluded in 2008 that CSIS had misinterpreted its law since its inception by destroying raw intelligence. The Supreme Court warned CSIS that it should retain operational notes and other raw intelligence "[w]henever CSIS conducts an investigation that targets a particular individual or group" because "it may have to pass the information on to external authorities or to a court."[106]

Richard Fadden, then director of CSIS, was not enthusiastic about the decision. He argued:

> [it] turned one of our founding principles on its head. Our *Act* instructed us to collect/retain information that was "strictly necessary" in order to determine if a person was a threat. This was seen as *protecting* civil liberties. Now the highest court in the land has told us to do just the opposite. Retaining everything is now seen as the best defence of civil liberties. I am not sure if Canadians or even our national security community can foresee the full effects of this decision.

He went on to predict that "within several years, someone will accuse us of acting like the [East German] Stasi because of the information we are now compelled to keep."[107] Such comments suggest that CSIS remains far from an enthusiastic partner in converting intelligence into evidence. To some extent, this is inevitable in any intelligence agency. The Air India Commission recognized this fact and recommended that CSIS should no longer be able to refuse intelligence sharing about possible terrorism offences. At the same time, it also recognized that conversion of intelligence into evidence for a prosecution will not always be in the public interest. Someone needs to make that call, and that someone should not be captive to the institutional interests of the security agencies.

The commission recommended that a third party, the prime minister's national security advisor, have increased powers to resolve disputes between CSIS and others related to the prioritization of intelligence use and that there be a streamlined process for deciding what CSIS intelligence must be disclosed in criminal trials. The government dismissed this recommendation.

Summary

The Air India bombings and their aftermath are an important reminder of the dangers of underreacting to terrorism. There is an unfinished reform agenda from the Air India tragedy, much more even than from the overreaction of the October Crisis.

One aspect of this unfinished agenda is the need to ensure that intelligence is not only collected but distributed to the right agencies that can use it to take preventive action. Bill C-51 does not do this, no matter what the rhetoric around the new information sharing law. The new *SoCIS Act* allows information to be shared about extremely broad security threats, and not simply about the growing threat of terrorism. But it does not follow the Air India Commission's recommendation that a reluctant CSIS be *required* to share information about possible terrorism offences with someone who can make a decision in the public interest about what should be done with the intelligence.

The Air India prosecutions, as well as related failed prosecutions, are important reminders that a troubled CSIS-RCMP relationship can result in delayed and inadequate disclosure to the accused, reluctant witnesses, and cratered prosecutions. The flawed security architecture that the Air India Commission identified is not a historical artifact: it is still very much with us. Broad disclosure rules, fear that intelligence methods and sources will be disclosed, a cumbersome two-court process for protecting intelligence from disclosure, and problems with witness protection are all still prominent features of our Byzantine system.

And tragically, the government chose to make the system even more unwieldy. Bill C-44 will aggravate problems by giving CSIS human sources a veto over the disclosure of any identifying information unless (in criminal prosecutions) the innocence of the accused is at stake. Put another way, prosecutors may need to take a pass on potentially critical witnesses because they first talked to CSIS.

For its part, Bill C-51 risks miring our already protracted trials in even more uncertainty: defence lawyers will now root around in search of a CSIS agent and threat reduction activities at the heart of a terrorism case. CSIS may be immunized by Bill C-51 against breaking the law, but its conduct will still be fodder for accused's abuse of process claims in subsequent trials, including for entrapment defences. At a time when terrorism prosecutions are likely to increase to deal with the ISIS threat, they will become more difficult.

To be sure, CSIS agents will have more powers to work on their own as "disrupters," like RCMP Security Service agents before them. But interrupting bad guys does not incarcerate them or take them off the street. With Bill C-51, we may have traded criminal incarceration for temporary disruption, followed by endless surveillance as CSIS monitors dangerous people left at large. Moreover, there will be claims of security failures should CSIS eventually abandon surveillance of those it disrupted because of limited resources.

It is especially ironic that a government that stressed prosecutions as the answer for everything from bullying to missing Aboriginal woman has legislated measures that jeopardize the prospect of prosecutions when it comes to terrorism, where they really matter.

V. THE REACTION TO 9/11

Hitting Legislative Targets in a Time of Crisis

If the October Crisis represents overreaction and Air India underreaction, Canada's legislative response to 9/11 shows that we can come close to getting it right. Canada was profoundly affected by the 9/11 attacks on the United States. It immediately felt the effects of America's decisions to close its borders and provided help to over 200 planes destined for the United States.

And within months of 9/11, Canada legislated many new terrorism crimes and special anti-terror powers in the 2001 *Anti-terrorism Act* (*ATA*).[108] The government was legislating not only for a Canadian public shocked by the events of 9/11 but also for the United Nations Security Council. That body had demanded that states criminalize terrorism.

The government was also legislating with an eye to US concerns. Many Americans wrongly believed that the 9/11 hijackers had entered the United States from Canada. The false rumours were not completely implausible given that terrorist Ahmad Ressam — the so-called millennium bomber — had been apprehended by American officials crossing the border in late 1999 and convicted of trying to bomb the Los Angeles airport. And, as during the October Crisis, the Canadian government also argued that strong action against terrorism was necessary to protect rights.

Not every feature of the *ATA* was warranted, and more time and deliberation might have improved the end product. Like Bill C-51, the *ATA* was omnibus legislation covering a host of national security issues. Its strongest components were new anti-terror criminal offences, but the legislation was enacted with an attention to *Charter* constraints and detail that was often lacking in Bill C-51.

The *ATA*'s chief components have weathered the last decade and a half quite well. Critically, the *ATA* created (for the first time) a definition of "terrorist activity," then incorporated into many new *Criminal Code* terrorism offences. The government stressed that new offences were necessary to stop terrorism before it happened — they were, in other words, consciously pre-emptive to a degree unusual in Canadian criminal law.

The omnibus nature of the *ATA* meant that some issues received less debate than they deserved. These issues included the *ATA*'s renovations to Canada's secrecy laws including the two-court system for determining whether classified information had to be disclosed to the accused in terrorism prosecutions and the statutory mandate that the *ATA* gave to the Communications Security Establishment, Canada's signals intelligence service. There was also very little debate about whether new security powers should be matched by enhanced review powers, even though members of SIRC and the RCMP complaints body raised concerns that they might not have adequate powers to review the new security powers.

The *ATA* debate was robust but much less partisan than the Bill C-51 debate.

The parliamentary committees heard from the privacy commissioner and other officers of Parliament and responded to their concerns with amendments, something that did not happen with Bill C-51. Nevertheless, the 2001 debate should not be romanticized. The Liberal government invoked closure, causing former prime minister Joe Clark to complain that the debate made a mockery of Parliament. The government treated the mandate to report to the United Nations Security Council on its anti-terrorism efforts as a mandate to enact new legislation by the end of 2001 even when other countries did not.

The Definition of Terrorism: Debates about Religious and Political Dissent and Unlawful Protest

The definition of terrorist activity was probably the most controversial issue and an important one since that definition remains the operative definition for most terrorism offences and the basis for enhanced powers such as preventive detention.

"Terrorist activity" includes a series of quite specific offences, such as hostage taking, that had been enacted over the years in response to the forms of terrorism most common in the pre-2001 period. But, more notably, it also incorporates a separate more generic and overarching definition that captures mostly serious forms of violence done for political, religious, or ideological motives with the intention of intimidating the public "with regard to its security, including its economic security, or compelling a person, a government, or a domestic or an international organization to do or to refrain from doing any act."[109]

This definition includes not just various acts of violence but also serious disruptions of essential services. In its initial guise, the only exemption where such disruptions were at issue was for "lawful advocacy, protest, dissent or stoppage of work." This use of the qualifier "lawful" unleashed a storm of criticism from unions, Indigenous groups, and others who recognized that protests often violated some law, if only municipal bylaws. In November 2001, the government acknowledged this concern and agreed to remove the "lawful" qualifier while at the same time ensuring that protests that endangered life would still fall within the definition of terrorist activity.

Astonishingly, the Conservative government chose to spark this same debate almost fifteen years later in Bill C-51 when it inserted the same word "lawful" as a qualifier on the exemption for protests, advocacy, and artistic expression grafted onto the sweeping new security information sharing law. As we discuss in Chapter 5, the government's ultimate response was different from the 2001 compromise and created an exemption that will prove very difficult to implement because, on its face, it exempts all protest and dissent, even those that may endanger life.

In the *ATA* debates, the so-called motive clause — the reference in the generic definition to political, religious, or ideological motivations — also prompted controversy, including fears that it would prompt authorities to profile people for their beliefs. The Liberal government responded by adding a "greater certainty" caveat to the definition of "terrorist activity" providing that "the expression of a political, religious or ideological thought, belief or opinion" would not fall within the definition unless tied to the violent acts listed in it.[110]

In 2012, the Supreme Court held that the "terrorist activity" definition and its controversial motive clause did not infringe freedom of expression in part because this provision meant that "[o]nly individuals who go well beyond the legitimate expression of a political, religious or ideological thought, belief or opinion, and instead engage in one of the serious forms of violence — or threaten one of the serious forms of violence" covered by the section "need fear liability under the terrorism provisions of the *Criminal Code*."[111]

Fifteen years later, Bill C-51 was not equally attentive to free expression rights when it enacted yet another new terrorism offence. The new offence applies to advocacy and promotion, not of "terrorist activity" as defined in the *ATA*, but rather of "terrorism offences in general," a vague and undefined phrase. As we suggest in Chapter 10, the new crime could apply to speech potentially distant from actual violence and as such raises *Charter* concerns.

Shiny New Toys: Peace Bonds, Preventive Arrests, and Investigative Hearings

If Bill C-51 was about enhancing CSIS powers leading to disruptions, the *ATA* was about enhancing police tools leading to prosecutions. The *ATA* eased wiretap rules for police terrorism investigations and also created two new and controversial tools: investigative hearings and special recognizance with conditions powers, permitting a novel form of preventive detention.

Investigative Hearings

Investigative hearings allow a judge to order a reluctant person to provide information about a pending, or past, terrorism offence if reasonable attempts have been made to obtain the information through other means. To ensure compliance with the *Charter*, the 2001 law guarantees that nothing a person reveals — and no evidence derived from those revelations — can be used against the compelled witness.

The first and so far only attempt to use an investigative hearing was during the Air India trial. There, the Crown tried to bolster the testimony of one of its reluctant witnesses by trying to compel another witness to provide information in an investigative hearing. The new power was quickly challenged in the Supreme Court, and in 2004 the Court upheld investigative hearings as consistent with the *Charter* but at the price of a presumption that the hearing would be in open court, that the target would have access to counsel, and that judges would observe evidential rules.[112] The *Charter* required all of these restrictions, but they have made investigative hearings an unattractive investigative tool for the police, and the investigative hearing was never resumed in the Air India case.

Peace Bonds and Preventive Detention

The second controversial tool created by the *ATA* was preventive arrests, which are ultimately tied to peace bonds. Since the October 2014 attacks, peace bonds have figured in the RCMP's anti-terror arsenal, but under another provision in the *ATA* that allows judges to impose a peace bond when a person "fears on reasonable grounds that another person will commit a terrorism offence."[113] This stand-alone peace bond provision followed the introduction of similar peace bond provisions for sexual offences in 1993 and gang offences in 1997. A judge ordering a peace bond can impose reasonable conditions to ensure a person's good conduct in the community, and these conditions could last for a year. There is no prescribed outer limit on the nature of these conditions, although constitutional caselaw dealing with other forms of peace bonds prohibits outright detention as a condition.[114] In the *ATA*, a refusal to agree with the conditions could result in a year in jail while breach of one of the conditions could result in two years in jail.

As we discuss in Chapter 7, Bill C-51 maintains this basic architecture but makes it easier to obtain peace bonds. These 2015 changes responded to the fact that the police had sought a peace bond against Martin Couture-Rouleau before he killed Warrant Officer Patrice Vincent in October 2014, but a prosecutor had reportedly refused to seek such a measure. The victim's sister, Louise Vincent, testifying in support of Bill C-51 suggested, "because of the lower evidence threshold [in C-51], . . . most probably Martin Couture-Rouleau would have been in prison, and my brother would not have been killed."[115] The government would repeat Vincent's statements in its support of Bill C-51.

It is difficult to argue with such statements made by those who have lost a loved one. It is also difficult to argue with them because no public report has been released on why the prosecutor declined to seek a peace bond in Couture-Rouleau's case. We are left, therefore, to simply accept the government's unsupported assertion — one that surprises us since even under the original *ATA* language, peace bonds were not difficult to get. Rushed and panicked law making invites mistakes but even more so when parliamentarians and the public do not have basic information about exactly what it is that they are trying to fix. We can contrast this fact-light methodology with Australia's approach: within a month of a similar terrorist attack in Sydney, the Australian government released a seventy-five-page report detailing all government interventions with the terrorist.[116]

Even assuming that the peace bond for Couture-Rouleau would have been granted under Bill C-51's relaxed standard and could not have been granted under the original *ATA* standards, this does not mean that it will prevent terrorism. To be sure, persons subject to a peace bond can be arrested and prosecuted if a breach is discovered. And now they can be incarcerated for as long as four years. Nevertheless, peace bonds, like preventive arrests, are at best a temporary solution. They need to be supplemented at one end with comprehensive programs to counter violent extremism and at the other end by actual terrorism prosecutions.

In 2001, some commentators found the notion of "peace bonds for terrorists" to be "absurd" given that the 9/11 attackers and others had been "prepared to sacrifice their own lives for the cause."[117] This prediction has proven prophetic: despite being subject to a peace bond, Mohamed Ali Dirie left Canada for Syria, presumably to join ISIS.[118] As we discuss in Chapter 7, the emergence of peace bonds as a central plank of police anti-terror tools poses these kinds of Goldilocks-and-the-Three-Bears dilemmas. Peace bonds may be too strong for those who are not terrorists but too weak for determined terrorists.

These standard stand-alone peace bond powers should not be confused with preventive arrests and detention under the *ATA*. The preventive detention provisions included in the 2001 law were comparatively mild. They could be used where police had reasonable grounds to believe that a terrorist activity "will be committed" and reasonable suspicion to believe that the imposition of a peace bond "is necessary to prevent the carrying out of a terrorist activity."[119] Detention required a judicial warrant and the consent of the attorney general except in exigent circumstances. But in exigent circumstances, police could (and still can) detain someone generally for no more than twenty-four hours to bring that person before a judge. Thereafter, a judge could adjudicate the peace bond (ending with the person's release subject to whatever conditions were imposed by the peace bond), order the person released pending that adjudication, or defer the peace bond question and order the person detained for up to another forty-eight hours. This meant that the total amount of detention for a person subject to preventive arrest was limited to three days, a figure below the seven days allowed under the *War Measures Act* during the October Crisis.

Bill C-51 catches up to the *War Measures Act* standard. It increases the maximum possible period of preventive detention to seven days: the initial possible twenty-four hours of detention in exigent circumstances, an initial judicially authorized period of forty-eight hours, and then two possible additional judicially authorized forty-eight-hour renewals. The trigger for the preventive detention and the subsequent peace bond is also relaxed: both will be available if there are reasonable grounds to conclude that a terrorist activity "may," as opposed to "will," be carried out, and now conditions can be imposed if they are "likely," as opposed to "necessary," to prevent the carrying out of a terrorist activity.

The Sun Sets (and Rises) on Special Powers

In 2001, the government responded to concerns about the two new powers of investigative hearings and preventive detentions, and in particular the post-9/11 danger of falsely targeting Muslims, by amending its initial *ATA* bill to include a five-year sunset on both investigative hearings and preventive arrests (but not stand-alone peace bonds). In addition, the government also introduced amendments requiring annual reports on the use of both special powers. There was, however, very little to report as no preventive arrests or investigative hearings were conducted before they were allowed to sunset in 2007, after the opposition parties defeated the minority Conservative government on the sunset question. Thereafter, investigative hearings and preventive detention did not exist in Canadian law again until 2013.

We pause on this point to describe the parliamentary debate in February 2007 on whether investigative hearings and preventive arrests should sunset. That debate was partisan, acrimonious, and not based on merits. In many respects, it foreshadowed the Bill C-51 process in 2015. Indeed, the sunset debate became so personal and disconnected from the underlying issues that now retired Liberal backbencher Irwin Cotler abstained from the final vote, accurately noting that the debate had descended into "bumper sticker slogans and smears."[120]

The parliamentary debate was also marred by a lack of access to classified information about why the police had not used preventive arrests or investigative hearings and by a resistance to any amendment to the provisions. It was also hindered by the fact that Commons and Senate committees had not yet completed delayed five-year reviews of the *ATA*, which would have provided more evidence to guide the debate. Both committees eventually recommended that investigative hearings and preventive detention be retained, albeit subject to some amendments.[121]

On other issues, the approach of the committees differed in interesting ways. The Commons committee took a harder line.[122] It recommended enactment of a new offence against "the glorification and encouraged emulation of terrorism" on the basis that existing laws would not cover "diffuse and untargeted" expression in relation to terrorism.[123] It focused on a 2006 United Kingdom glorification offence and did not place the criminalization of glorification in the broader context of counter-extremism measures. It did, however, recommend that the free speech and fair comment provisions from existing hate propaganda provisions be included, something that was not done when Bill C-51 created a new criminal speech offence of "advocating or promoting terrorism offences in general."

The Commons committee also recommended increased oversight of the CSE and the creation of a parliamentary committee on national security, but without really defining its mandate or whether it would have access to classified information. Two years before the Commons report, the Martin government had tabled a bill to create such a parliamentary review committee, which died with the dissolution of Parliament for the 2006 election. The Commons committee called for its resuscitation. And while the proposal was repeatedly revived in private members bills since that period, the Conservative government had clearly lost interest.

Debate over such a special parliamentary committee re-emerged during the Bill C-51 process but, as will be discussed in Chapter 12, in a polarized, political manner with some in opposition treating the measure as a cure to many of Bill C-51's deficiencies and the governing Conservatives regarding the idea (and, indeed, the concept of enhanced accountability) as "red-tape," foreign to parliamentary traditions or an invitation to dangerous and criminal leaks of information by parliamentarians. Discussion was muddled by a failure to distinguish between the command and control process of oversight and the retrospective process of review, which produces only findings and recommendations.

In its *ATA* review, the Senate committee was more responsive than its Commons counterpart to concerns raised by the Muslim community. It recommended repealing the religious or political motive requirement in the *Criminal Code* definition of terrorist activities and eliminating the *Suresh* exception — so called because it stemmed from a controversial passage in a Supreme Court decision of that name — which would allow immigration deportation of non-citizens to torture in exceptional circumstances.[124] It also recommended enhanced review of national security activities to prevent profiling and appeals for those placed on the no-fly list.[125]

It is difficult to trace much real impact from these reports except insofar as the Commons committee reflected an enthusiasm for an expansive terrorism speech crime — later realized by Bill C-51. The committees' positions on preventive detention and investigative hearings also eventually ruled the day. In subsequent Parliaments, bills to re-enact these two powers were regularly introduced and failed, but this failure stemmed from regular prorogations and dissolutions of Parliament. Finally, in 2013, a bill re-enacting investigative hearings and preventive detention passed Parliament, and the measures returned to Canadian law.[126] But, in a puzzling decision that only means the legislative language cannot be read literally as enacted, the government made no substantive changes to the 2001 provisions despite the 2004 Supreme Court ruling grafting new constitutional expectations onto how investigative hearings must operate.

As with the original 2001 special powers, new sunset and reporting provisions were enacted. That means that preventive detention — now augmented by Bill C-51 — and investigative hearings will sunset "at the end of the 15th sitting day of Parliament after the fifth anniversary of the[ir] coming into force."[127] That fifth anniversary is 19 June 2018. This is the only aspect of Bill C-51 that will face a sunset and only because a prior law enacted in 2013 contained such a best-before date.

Other Legislative Fixes

The *ATA* was not the only security legislation introduced soon after 9/11. Other laws were more of a mixed bag. In amendments planned before the attacks on New York and Washington but only enacted afterwards, the government amended Canada's immigration law, now called the *Immigration and Refugee Protection Act*. In so doing, it created a revamped system of "immigration security certificates," discussed below.

The government also tabled another bill, the *Public Safety Act*, in 2002. This omnibus bill would have given ministers substantial discretionary authority under a variety of acts to take emergency action for security reasons. The government also proposed amendments to the *National Defence Act* permitting the creation of something called, ominously, "Military Security Zones." These zones were to be created at the discretion of the minister of national defence if, in the opinion of the minister, necessary for the protection of international relations, national defence, or security, all terms left undefined by the bill. Among other things, a zone could be declared over material or property under control of the government or, even more ambiguously, over any other place that the Canadian Forces were directed to protect to fulfil a duty required by law. The Canadian Forces would then control entry into this zone, with unauthorized persons subject to forcible removal.

Civil society groups reacted fiercely to the proposal and to similar provisions in later iterations of the bill. The Canadian Bar Association, for instance, worried that the zone provisions would be used to subdue and control democratic dissent. Indeed, media reports suggested that military security zones would be declared around international meeting places in an effort to control regular civil society protests at such events.[128]

When passed in 2004, the *Public Safety Act* no longer included provisions relating to military security zones. It did, however, continue to give ministers discretionary emergency powers. For instance, the new law amended the *Aeronautics Act* to allow the transport minister to direct any person to do anything required to respond to an immediate threat to aviation security.[129] In 2006, the government built on these provisions to create "Passenger Protect," a system that includes a passenger no-fly list. These regulations, in force in June 2007,[130] were used to exclude persons believed to constitute a threat to civil aviation from aircraft. An obvious reaction to the specific nature of the 9/11 attacks, this power ultimately proved too limiting in an era concerned about the movement of foreign fighters to overseas conflicts. More than this, the regime was built awkwardly around the concept of an emergency order, prompting a design in which a boarding was denied only when the person arrived at the airport to embark. Bill C-51 later responded to some of these issues albeit in a manner raising serious procedural concerns discussed in Chapter 6.

Also in 2004, the government amended the *Canadian Passport Order* to allow refusals or revocations of passports "if the Minister [of foreign affairs] is of the opinion that such action is necessary for the national security of Canada or another country."[131] This power remained unamended until 2015, when the government relaxed and broadened the standards for passport revocations and legislated a new process for challenging such rulings, using a budget bill to do so.[132]

In 2005, the government reorganized the solicitor general's department into a Canadian analogue to the United States' homeland security department, cobbling together a new Department of Public Safety and Emergency Preparedness that, among other things, joined the solicitor general's existing ministerial oversight of CSIS and the RCMP but included new responsibilities for the Canadian Border Services Agency and emergency preparedness. The new department also retained responsibilities over the Correctional Service of Canada and crime prevention. In Chapter 11, we suggest that this new department has emerged as a *de facto* lead on national security. Unfortunately, it has not often been treated as a senior ministry and has often been populated with rather junior ministers. Moreover, it may be too overburdened to allow for effective ministerial oversight of the expanding roster of critical and complex national security activities.

And in 2013, while re-enacting preventive detention and investigative hearings powers, Parliament created several new terrorism offences directed at travel to join terrorist groups or engage in terrorism. While offences enacted in 2001 could also be applied to foreign terrorist fighters, these new more precise prohibitions are front and centre in contemporary responses to the ISIS phenomena and represent an exercise of considerable foresight by the government.

Finally, in 2014, Parliament enacted changes to Canada's citizenship laws allowing revocation of citizenship for service "as a member of an armed force of a country or as a member of an organized armed group" where "that country or group was engaged in an armed conflict with Canada," a conviction for treason under the *Criminal Code*, a conviction for a terrorism offence, or a conviction for certain spying offences under the *Security of Information Act*.[133] As we discuss in Chapter 6, citizenship revocation is a troubling tactic certain to raise new constitutional issues.

VI. CANADA'S MIXED POST-9/11 RECORD OF ANTI-TERRORISM

Canadians had a robust and generally civil debate in the wake of 9/11 about whether new anti-terrorism laws were appropriate, and while our legislative record was not perfect, it was respectable. The remainder of this chapter will examine Canada's mixed anti-terrorism record up to the October 2014 terrorist attacks. The highlights include a mostly successful prosecution record, albeit one with few prosecutions. Alas, in many other areas there have been overreactions and abuses including complicity with torture through information sharing, renditions, use of immigration law, and false positives in listing Canadians as terrorists.

The Prosecutorial Record

Prosecutions under the *ATA* have certainly been more successful than those related to Air India. Prosecutors have won most terrorism prosecutions, and the *ATA* terrorism provisions have survived constitutional challenge at the Supreme Court.[134] But these statistics hide a concerning reality: those prosecutions have been surprisingly uncommon. The first one was not even started until 2004, and though the Supreme Court confirmed the conviction in 2012, a parallel British prosecution of co-conspirators had been completed by 2007. At just over twenty, there have been fewer terrorism trials and convictions in Canada than in comparable democracies, even when measured on a per capita basis. Convictions in Canada stand at 0.6 per million population, and in the United Kingdom at 6.4 per million population,[135] even excluding convictions stemming from Northern Ireland.

Part of this tenfold difference stems from a different threat environment. But we suspect that part also stems from Canada's distinct struggles in converting intelligence into evidence. The United Kingdom's domestic intelligence agency, MI5, has accepted its evidentiary role in terrorism investigations in a way that CSIS has not. United Kingdom laws have restricted disclosure obligations, and the United Kingdom uses a streamlined process where trial judges can grant exemptions from remaining disclosure obligations in a way that Canadian trial judges cannot. We return to this issue in Chapter 9.

The Security Certificate Headache

Much more concerning is the practical aftermath of security actions taken outside of the criminal justice system. Our actions under non-criminal laws — and in some cases our extra-legal conduct — have been much less tempered than our criminal trials, bearing all the hallmarks of overreaction. Concerns about unfairness should always be taken seriously in their own right, but they warrant extra attention in a world where al-Qaida and especially ISIS try to recruit people with the message that the West unfairly targets Muslims because of their religious and political views.

Canada embraced immigration security certificates to pursue five non-Canadians who the government feared were associated with al-Qaida. The government's decision to do so proved to be among its most controversial anti-terrorism responses. These proceedings have produced a total of three Supreme Court decisions and well over a hundred lower-court judgments in the Federal Court and Federal Court of Appeal. Some of these decisions were damning, and the net impact was to force a new edifice of checks and balances on a supposedly expeditious process. Most of these checks and balances ran counter to CSIS secrecy preoccupations.

This use of immigration law as anti-terrorism law reflected the reality that most of the *ATA* criminal offences post-dated the conduct at issue in the security certificates. Since the advent of the *Charter*, and unlike during the October Crisis, criminal law cannot be applied retroactively to actions that predate offences. But the use of certificates also sidestepped (at least in theory) the difficulties examined above of conducting terrorism prosecutions.

In security certificates, the government could use secret evidence, often compiled by CSIS and its foreign partners. And it could deny the persons affected by the security certificates — and their lawyers — access to this information. Security certificates are also administrative proceedings, meaning that they are decided by judges on standards much lower than the proof of guilt beyond a reasonable doubt standard applicable in criminal cases (which so clearly contributed to the 2005 acquittals in the Air India trial).

But immigration proceedings have disadvantages. They are intended to result in removals from Canada. In the post-9/11 cases of alleged al-Qaida involvement, Canada sought to remove security certificate detainees to countries with poor human rights records: Egypt, Syria, Algeria, and Morocco. The government relied on the controversial *Suresh* exception, which would allow deportation to torture even while recognizing that such an eventuality would violate one of the firmest rules of international law. Over a decade later, these vexed issues are still being litigated in the three remaining cases. And even if removal is possible without violating rights, it may simply displace and outsource security risks, a matter we discuss in Chapter 7.

In addition, security certificates quickly ran into repeated constitutional objections over procedure. These process disputes have been legion and protracted. For instance, federal courts have had to decide whether the government can rely on evidence procured by foreign governments, possibly through torture. But more generally, courts have grappled with the secrecy question and the extent to which security certificates violate constitutional fair trial expectations by denying the affected individuals — the "named persons" — knowledge of the case against them.

Of Fig Leaves and Adversarial Challenges

In 2002, James Hugessen, a judge of the Federal Court, made a speech in which he explained that "all the national security functions which are laid on the Federal Court have this in common: they involve at one stage or another and sometimes throughout the piece a judge of the Court sitting alone in what are called hearings, but they are held in the absence of one of the parties." He went on to say that he would not make "the customary disavowal" that he is not speaking for the court because "we hate hearing only one party . . . . We greatly miss, in short, our security blanket which is the adversary system that we were all brought up with and that . . . is, for most of us, the real warranty that the outcome of what we do is going to be fair and just . . . . I sometimes feel a bit like a fig leaf."[136]

The idea of secret hearings in which an individual's fate is decided in her absence (and in the absence of her counsel) is generally anathema in Canada. And in 2007, after substantial litigation, the Supreme Court eventually invalidated the original security certificate regime, holding that it violated the *Charter* because of its one-sided process of adjudication and its degree of absolute secrecy.[137]

Parliament responded with an amended system.[138] Given a choice of various alternative regimes for restoring an element of adversarialism to the process, it opted for a system of "special advocates" borrowed from the United Kingdom. These security-cleared lawyers are given access to all the secret information related to the case subject to a firm obligation that they not then disclose any of this information outside of the closed hearing. In that hearing, however, they are charged with defending the interests of the affected person.

This is not a perfect system — named persons are still excluded. Yet those individuals may be in the best position to respond to the case against them, if only to offer up an innocent explanation for seemingly inculpatory evidence. Special advocates are unable to tap into that personal experience because the inculpatory evidence cannot be shared with the named persons. So the lawyers are left to collect as much information as possible from the named persons before seeing the secret information in the hope that something said in those interviews may prove relevant once the actual case is known. This is not a dilemma unknown in Canadian law. In analogous processes used by SIRC in investigating complaints against CSIS, SIRC lawyers are permitted continued contact with the complainant although they must be carefully oblique in their conversations to avoid spilling secret information.

The government rejected this made-in-Canada SIRC approach in the revised security certificate system. As a result, the amended process was more constraining of fair trial rights than it had to be, fuelling renewed controversy.

In the 2014 *Canada v Harkat* decision, the Supreme Court ruled that the amended regime was consistent with the *Charter* because security-cleared special advocates could provide adversarial challenge and because there were minimal disclosure requirements to the named person in the certificate.[139] However, in a pattern that may recur in litigation over Bill C-51, the Court's constitutional ruling also grafted onto the regime additional procedural protections and expectations, including presumptions in favour of continued communication between the special advocate and the named person during the secret proceedings. In so doing, the Court essentially nudged the process toward the more robust system advanced by critics of the legislation in the parliamentary process but resisted by the government.

The Canadian special advocate scheme has had some notable successes. The government has lost cases that it probably would have won (and, indeed, in some cases had won) in the earlier unconstitutional process. This development affirms the importance of hard-nosed adversarialism in defending rights. And the system has not been dogged, as a similar British system has, by complaints from special advocates themselves who feel like "fig leaves" because they cannot access all the information they need.

Legislation Designed to Correct Government Losses?

That may change. It is hard not to view 2015 amendments by bills C-44 and C-51 as an effort by the government to rejig the security certificate process in its favour. The government failed in 2014 to persuade the Supreme Court to recognize that the anonymity of CSIS's informers in security certificates should be protected in the same way as that of police informers.[140] Shortly after the October 2014 terrorist attacks, the government introduced Bill C-44, which provides that any human source or informer who has been promised confidentiality by CSIS can veto any subsequent disclosure unless innocence is at stake.[141] But security certificate and other immigration cases are not about guilt or innocence — meaning that this narrow exception is unavailable in them. As a result, the new law will be challenged under the *Charter*. In the meantime, it will be more difficult to test the reliability of CSIS informers in administrative proceedings, including not only security certificate cases but also those related to no-fly lists and passport revocations.

The Bill C-51 amendments, for their part, attempt to restrict the disclosure that special advocates may receive in a way that may seriously jeopardize their ability to represent the interests of named persons. Such restrictions could have changed the result in the *Re Almrei* security certificate case. There, special advocates discovered that inconsistent statements made by CSIS sources had not been disclosed by the government and that the government had used an earlier favourable statement made by a source at a time when he or she "was highly motivated to curry favour with the Service."[142] Pointing to this case, special advocates supplied a brief during the Bill C-51 hearings that described their personal experiences:

> when the *Almrei* security certificate case began, the government's disclosure obligation was similar to that proposed in Bill C-51, but the government did not disclose *any* of the secret information that the Special Advocates later received in accordance with [subsequent] court orders, which is the information they used to convince the judge that the government's secret case was untenable (the certificate against Mr. Almrei was thrown out by the Court).[143]

Bill C-51 rolls back the system, raising questions about whether special advocates will have sufficient access to information to detect unreliable CSIS evidence and whether the new approach will result in false positives. The special advocates' concerns received virtually no attention in the Bill C-51 debate, drowned out by controversy over less technical and more notorious aspects of the omnibus bill.

The Morphing of Security Certificates and the Peace Bond Process

Practices surrounding security certificates are also relevant to the enhanced ability to obtain year-long peace bonds under Bill C-51. After many years in detention while their endless cases were adjudicated, the named persons in security certificate cases were released into the community but under strict conditions. These conditions provide some sense as to the provisos that may be imposed as peace bonds. The strict house arrest and monitoring conditions imposed on the named persons have been repeatedly challenged[144] and have led some to say that they are worse off than in prison, especially given the constraints imposed on their families.[145]

As more peace bonds are used, one likely by-product will be increased disputes and litigation over the terms and alleged breaches of the peace bonds. Again we have concerns that peace bonds may be too restrictive when applied to those who are not terrorists and too weak if applied to determined terrorists.

The Continued Use of Immigration Law as Anti-terrorism Law

The government has issued no security certificate against a suspected terrorist since 2003. But that does not mean it has abandoned use of immigration law as an anti-terror tool. The security certificate–style process, complete with special advocates, is also available for regular immigration inadmissibility hearings where the government wishes to use secret information. And while it is difficult to track these things, the government has clearly been dealing with at least some suspected terrorists through the standard inadmissibility procedures. One well-publicized case started in February 2015 when a non-citizen alleged to have plans to bomb Toronto buildings was detained and eventually ordered returned to Pakistan.[146]

It is notable that an administrative adjudicator and not a Federal Court judge decides regular inadmissibility matters. Reasonable questions can be asked about whether the government now resorts to inadmissibility processes over security certificates because it prefers its chances in front of adjudicators over those in front of increasingly exacting and national security–experienced Federal Court judges. Such immigration cases combined with frequent extraditions of persons to face terrorist trials in the United States also raise questions about whether Canadian officials recognize that they do not have the capacity that they should have to conduct terrorism prosecutions, the fairest and most transparent means to deal with allegations of terrorism.

Canada's Renditions

If security certificates have been controversial, they have at least had the virtue of being legal processes. Canada's post-9/11 anti-terror tactics have not always been so discriminating. These tactics have included renditions that were, in typically Canadian fashion, less dramatic and much less publicized than their more notorious American counterparts. "Rendition" is the colloquial expression for the extra-legal removal of a person between countries, sometimes to serve trial and (even more controversially) sometimes to be secretly detained, interrogated, and tortured.

Arar, Almalki, El-Maati, and Nureddin

The most famous example of rendition affecting a Canadian is that of Maher Arar. While he was in transit back to Canada, US authorities removed Arar from the United States to Jordan. From there, officials sent him to Syria, where he was detained and tortured before the Syrians released him in 2003. The spark in this chain of events started in Canada. In the wake of 9/11, inexperienced RCMP officers provided American officials with the entire database of their investigations into Arar without vetting the information for relevance, privacy, or reliability and without limiting the use that foreign officials could make of the shared information. The RCMP also asked US officials to place both Arar and his wife, Dr Monia Mazigh, on watchlists, describing them (without foundation) as "Islamic Extremist individuals suspected of being linked to the Al Qaeda terrorist movement."[147]

Canada's conduct during Arar's detention was also disturbing. The Department of Foreign Affairs shared a statement obtained by the Syrians from Arar with the RCMP and CSIS without informing them that the statement was likely obtained through torture. CSIS received information from Syrian Military Intelligence about Arar, again without assessing whether it was the product of torture. And the RCMP sent questions to Syria that created risks that both Arar and fellow Canadian detainee Abdullah Almalki would be tortured.

Arar's case received much attention in Canada, in large part because of the efforts of Dr Mazigh and the human rights community. SIRC and the RCMP complaints body began to investigate the role played by CSIS and the RCMP. As will be seen in Chapter 12, both bodies are limited to examining a single agency whereas multiple Canadian agencies were involved in the Arar case. In 2004, the Martin government appointed a public inquiry headed by Associate Chief Justice Dennis O'Connor of the Ontario Court of Appeal. The inquiry had the whole-of-government jurisdiction to examine the conduct of all Canadian officials, a breadth denied to the permanent review bodies. The commission examined not only the role of CSIS and the RCMP but that of border and foreign affairs officials involved in sharing information about Arar.

The Arar case was followed by a second inquiry, headed by former Supreme Court justice Frank Iacobucci, that examined the related cases of Abdullah Almalki, Ahmad El-Maati, and Muayyed Nureddin, who had all been maltreated in Middle Eastern prisons and fingered by information shared by Canadian authorities. Again, this inquiry was sensibly given the jurisdiction to examine the conduct of all Canadian officials involved in the case. This second inquiry confirmed that information shared by both the RCMP and CSIS with Syrian and Egyptian officials likely played a role in the torture of these three men. CSIS sent questions to Syria for El-Maati to answer, and the RCMP sent information and tried to interview him when he was detained in Egypt. The RCMP sent questions for Almalki to answer when he was detained in Syria in a centre notorious for its use of torture. Information shared by the RCMP and CSIS with foreign authorities about Nureddin probably played a role in his detention and torture in Syria.

These inquiries underlined that effective review of information sharing could not happen unless a reviewing body had a broad, whole-of-government mandate. Even then, there would be black holes: the inquiries could not determine what use American, Syrian, and Egyptian officials had made of the information that the RCMP and CSIS had shared with them.

A Policy on Sharing Information That May Cause Torture

The Arar Commission also made critical policy findings. It recommended that "information should never be provided to a foreign country where there is a credible risk that it will cause or contribute to the use of torture."[148] In addition, information received from countries with questionable human rights records should be carefully assessed for accuracy. The government prepared assorted ministerial directives on this issue, but, as discussed in Chapter 5, versions of directives issued in 2011 stopped well short of an absolute ban on the sharing of information across borders that might induce torture.

A Policy on Enhanced Review

The Arar Commission also advised modernizing independent review of the government's national security activities. In its 600-page second report, the commission found that Canada's review structure enacted in 1984 had not kept pace with the enhanced integration and intensity of national security activities, and in particular increased information sharing.

The government ultimately refashioned the RCMP's review body in 2013 but in a manner that fell well short of the Arar Commission's recommendations. It also failed to address SIRC's limitations and the bigger problem of "stovepiped" and "siloed" review. In Canada's system, review is stovepiped — confined — to a total of three security agencies — CSIS, the RCMP, and CSE, and review bodies are siloed in the sense of not being able to work closely together on joint activities using secret information even while the agencies they review quite sensibly do.

Despite these acute limitations, the government went ahead in Bill C-51 and enhanced information sharing across Canadian agencies, most of which are subject to no independent national security review. It also did precisely nothing to alleviate the limitations on existing review body collaboration, even after four former prime ministers weighed in and recommended that the Arar Commission's recommendations be taken off the shelf.[149] Bill C-51's imbalance was especially notable in relation to CSIS, whose powers were greatly increased, while those of its review body, SIRC, were left unchanged. We return to these issues in our discussion of the unfinished accountability reform agenda in Chapter 12.

In the wake of the commission report, Arar was compensated for his injuries. Almalki, El-Maati, and Nureddin were left to sue in provincial superior court. That lawsuit remains mired in endless disputes over government secrecy, a practice that has let the government stave off financial accountability for its conduct. As will be discussed in Chapter 5, Bill C-51's information sharing provisions even contain a provision that will make it more difficult for other victims of Canada's information sharing to obtain compensation.

Benatta and Jabarah

Not every extra-legal action by Canada culminated in a public inquiry, and so several are less well known. In the days and months after 9/11, Canada provided secret assistance to the United States that it would later regret. One such form of assistance was the extraordinary transfer of at least two suspected terrorists to American custody.

Canada summarily shipped Benamar Benatta over the Rainbow Bridge at Niagara Falls and transferred him into American custody the day after 9/11. The reasons for the transfer remain murky. A contemporary document expresses the panic of the time, indicating that it would be "unimaginable in the present circumstances" for Canada not to act on its "responsibility to protect the security of Canada and the world."[150] Another factor may have been that Benatta, like millennium bomber Ahmed Ressam, was an Algerian who sought refugee status in Canada.

After a six-year ordeal in American custody and long after the FBI had cleared him of terrorism allegations, Benatta returned to Canada. He was granted, first, refugee status and subsequently Canadian citizenship. The Canadian government recently settled Benatta's lawsuit against it.

In May 2002, Mohammed Jabarah was transferred by CSIS from Oman to American custody, where he pled guilty to a number of terrorism charges in the United States. SIRC subsequently found that CSIS had violated five different *Charter* rights during Jabarah's rendition. These included his right as a Canadian citizen to enter and stay in Canada, his right against arbitrary detention, his right to fundamental justice and *habeas corpus*, and his right to counsel. CSIS explained to SIRC that it had relied upon Jabarah's consent without informing him of his right to contact counsel "because CSIS is not a police service."[151] As in the Air India investigation, CSIS used the fact that it is not a law enforcement agency as an all-purpose excuse. SIRC concluded that

> Jabarah [was] a terrorist but also a Canadian citizen, and no matter how despicable his actions, the *Charter* conferred on him certain fundamental rights. SIRC's mission is to protect Canadians' rights by ensuring that CSIS acts within the law. Therefore, the Service must comply with the *Charter* in carrying out its investigations as mandated by the *CSIS Act*, no matter what unexpected circumstances may arise.[152]

The Jabarah case gives especial pause in the aftermath of Bill C-51. C-51 purports to allow the exact *Charter* rights that CSIS violated in that case to again be ignored by CSIS, this time with a Federal Court blessing. The Jabarah case may illustrate the sort of conduct open to CSIS as it undertakes a more kinetic or physical role after Bill C-51.

Omar Khadr and CSIS's Visits to Guantanamo

Better known (and indeed notorious) is the case of Omar Khadr. Khadr was part of a self-described "al-Qaida family." He was only fifteen years of age when he was wounded in battle with the American military during the invasion of Afghanistan and captured. He was subsequently detained at Guantanamo Bay for ten years.

After pleading guilty to a variety of crimes under the controversial US *Military Commissions Act*, including the killing of an American soldier, Khadr was transferred to Canadian custody in 2012. A court granted him bail in May 2015 pending his challenge to the American conviction, but the federal government opposed his release arguing (contrary to public evidence) that it would cause irreparable harm to Canada's relations with the United States. Khadr's saga deserves and has received book-length treatment,[153] but our focus is its relevance to the Bill C-51 debate.

As a result of a 2009 SIRC report, we know that CSIS officials travelled to the Guantanamo military prison camp in February and September 2003 to obtain intelligence from Khadr. SIRC found that CSIS had not taken into account widespread concerns at the time about human rights abuses at Guantanamo as well as Khadr's particular rights as a youth under domestic and international law.[154]

SIRC admitted that there were "no easy answers or solutions" to the dilemmas of "information-sharing with foreign partners, especially in cases where there are human rights concerns, dealing with youth, and interacting with detainees in foreign jurisdictions." Nevertheless, SIRC concluded that it was "disconcerted that there was no apparent meaningful discussion on these issues within CSIS prior to undertaking its travel to Guantanamo Bay to interview Khadr." It concluded strongly that the affair and other post-9/11 developments meant that

> the time may have come for CSIS to undertake a fundamental re-assessment of how it conducts business, and to undergo a cultural shift in order to keep pace with the political, judicial and legal developments of recent years . . . it is incumbent upon CSIS to implement measures to embed the values stemming from recent political, judicial and legal developments in its day-to-day work in order to maintain its own credibility, and to meet

growing and evolving expectations of how an intelligence agency should operate and perform in a contemporary democratic society.[155]

CSIS shared the intelligence it had gathered from Khadr with American officials, the RCMP, and the Department of Foreign Affairs, underlining the reality of information sharing. SIRC held that this information sharing was appropriate but because of its limited powers could not determine what use the other agencies had made of the information that had been shared.

What foreigners do with this shared information is important: as the Arar and related sagas show, international information sharing opens Pandora's box. Foreign partners will often have the upper hand in dealings on their own turf. For example, in the Khadr case, the United States made the recording of CSIS interviews with Khadr a precondition of Canadian access to him. This meant that Canadian courts and officials could not control how that information was used.

CSIS might well have continued its interrogation trips to Guantanamo if not for an injunction issued by the Federal Court.[156] The Canadian court was much more receptive to Khadr's claim of abuse than an American judge who the same year refused to enjoin American officials from mistreating the then seventeen-year-old.[157] Indeed, a subsequent Supreme Court of Canada decision noted that Khadr had been subject to serious and sustained sleep deprivation,[158] euphemistically called the "Frequent Flyer" program, to make him more amenable to interrogation.

The Supreme Court ruled twice that CSIS had violated Khadr's *Charter* rights at Guantanamo. The Court applied the *Charter* to CSIS's activities outside of Canada on the basis that CSIS had participated in a breach of international law by questioning Khadr when he was denied a right to a lawyer or *habeas corpus*, among other things. The Court, however, stopped short of requiring an extremely reluctant Canadian government to ask for his repatriation to Canada as a remedy.

Bills C-44 and C-51 emphatically enhance CSIS's powers to act internationally, including through means that violate foreign and "other" (as in international) law. It remains to be seen how the courts will react as CSIS engages in increased work outside of Canada. They may be more deferential to the demands that CSIS faces acting abroad. At the same time, before these new laws, one Federal Court judge who had authorized CSIS to undertake surveillance of a CSIS target outside of Canada reacted strongly when he learned that some of the surveillance had been subcontracted to foreign agencies. In obvious appreciation of the Arar and Khadr cases, the judge, Justice Mosley, expressed concerns about what might happen as Canada alerts foreign agencies to CSIS targets and loses control over what is done with its intelligence once it is in foreign hands.[159]

In sum, criticism directed at CSIS in the wake of the Mohammed Jabarah and Omar Khadr cases may well explain the government's determination in Bill C-51 to create a Federal Court warrant system authorizing the violation of all *Charter* rights in advance. It still remains to be seen whether the Federal Court would ever become a willing partner in this process or whether such breaches could reasonably meet Bill C-51's admonishment against bodily harm and the requirement that measures be reasonable and proportionate. But until these matters are decided, Bill C-51 raises the real possibility that Canada could repeat its overreactions in the Benatta, Jabarah, and Khadr cases, albeit under the cover and with the blessing of a Federal Court warrant.

The Blacklisted Canadians

Lying somewhere between security certificates and the more extra-legal rendition-related cases are the post-9/11 "listing" cases. One of the many effects of 9/11 was that the international community and most countries doubled down on the blacklisting of suspected terrorists as a means to combat both terrorist travel and the financing of terrorism. The United Nations Security Council had already heavily invested in such a listing mechanism before 9/11 in an attempt to impose asset freezes and travel bans on individual members of first the Taliban and then al-Qaida. The fact that such sanctions did not prevent 9/11 did not deter massive reinvestment in them after 9/11.

United Nations sanctions had traditionally been applied to states and not persons, but this pattern changed in the 1990s in part because of a focus on so-called smart sanctions and disillusionment with the collateral consequences of country-wide, indiscriminate economic sanctions.

But there were problems with the new focus on individuals, at least in the anti-terror area: the basis for listing individuals as terrorists was often secret intelligence produced by member states, and the states were unwilling to share their intelligence with the fifteen countries on the United Nations Security Council responsible for listing and delisting. This meant that the reliability of the intelligence used for listing was not assessed, let alone subject to adversarial challenge. Mistakes were made. And as will be seen, these mistakes affected some Canadians.

Liban Hussein

The first mistake came when in November 2001 Ottawa resident Liban Hussein was listed under the sweeping *Suppression of Terrorism Regulations*, which Canada had enacted in October 2001 under a statute normally used to impose United Nations–mandated sanctions on other states. Hussein had also been listed as a terrorist by the United States and by the United Nations Security Council after he had been indicted in the United States for running an unlicensed money transfer business that had moved $3 million to the United Arab Emirates. He challenged extradition to the United States and the process used in Canada to list him. By June 2002, the Canadian government recognized that somewhere down the line a mistake had been made. The mistake had produced a false positive: a person listed as a terrorist who was not a terrorist. Hussein was paid compensation and soon thereafter delisted by the United Nations.[160]

Abousfian Abdelrazik

Other mistakes took longer to correct. Abousfian Abdelrazik left Sudan and obtained refugee status in Canada in 1992 because of his opposition to the Bashir regime. He came to CSIS's attention in part because he associated in Montreal with both Ahmed Ressam, the attempted millennial bomber, and Adil Charkaoui, then a named person under an immigration security certificate.

Abdelrazik left Canada in 2003 to visit his ailing mother in Sudan but was promptly arrested and held in a Khartoum jail where CSIS agents interviewed him.[161] He was eventually released and cleared by Sudanese authorities of involvement in terrorism. But in July 2006, he was listed by both the United States and the United Nations Security Council as a terrorist associated with al-Qaida: As a result, he was barred from international travel. This and the fact that Canada refused, without giving reasons, to grant an emergency travel document to replace his expired passport meant that he was effectively banished.

The matter ended in Federal Court. In a strongly worded judgment, the Federal Court held that Abdelrazik's *Charter* right as a Canadian citizen to return to Canada had been infringed and ordered the government to facilitate his return. Justice Zinn was not deterred by the fact that Abdelrazik had been placed on the United Nations list as affiliated with al-Qaida or that the United Nations had denied Canada's request that he be delisted. Justice Zinn characterized that listing process as Kafkaesque and stressed that there was no public evidence that Abdelrazik was involved with terrorism. Sensing government reluctance, he retained jurisdiction over the case until Canadian officials could bring the listed and banished applicant to court.[162] Abdelrazik's name was eventually removed from the United Nations list in December 2011, and he is now suing Canadian authorities.

Hard Lessons

Abdelrazik's case is a cautionary tale for the post–Bill C-51 world. It demonstrates the potentially harsh consequences of violating a Canadian citizen's *Charter* right to return to Canada. Given the present focus on foreign fighters, this may be the first *Charter* right that CSIS will seek authorization under Bill C-51 to contravene. Abdelrazik's case demonstrates how Federal Court judges under Bill C-51 might be required to decide whether to limit a terrorist suspect's right to return to Canada. They will have to balance the danger of allowing a suspected terrorist who might have trained with ISIS to return to Canada against the dangers, including mistreatment and death, of forcing such a person to remain in Syria or other countries.

On the other hand, it is also possible to draw positive conclusions from this litany of events since 9/11. The decisions in several security certificate cases and those enjoining CSIS from interrogating Omar Khadr at Guantanamo and ordering the government to allow Abdelrazik to return to Canada demonstrate how Federal Court and appellate judges may make difficult decisions in a principled manner.

At the same time, however, the warrants that CSIS may try to obtain under Bill C-51 to authorize the violation of *Charter* rights constitute a very different type of legal proceeding. They allow judges to pre-authorize *Charter* violations. In other words, the courts will be asked to approve the violation of people's rights under the *Charter* rather than to protect people's rights as they did in the Khadr and Abdelrazik cases. But more than that, the new CSIS warrants will likely be obtained in one-sided hearings, where the persons whose rights will be violated are not represented, and probably will not even know that their rights are at stake. This is different even from the security certificate matters, where named persons at least know that the government is doing something to them and have a modest ability to know the case against them and intervene in it. To an even greater degree, the Khadr and Abdelrazik cases were regular adversarial proceedings. The new CSIS warrant proceedings will not be adversarial, will not be public, will not be appealable, and the warrants will not (generally) be disclosed.

The Abdelrazik case also demonstrates the dangers of false positives in intelligence-driven listing processes. The United Nations Security Council eventually removed Abdelrazik's name from its list of people affiliated with al-Qaida. As is the norm, it gave no reasons to explain the delisting. It thus did not admit a mistake or exonerate Abdelrazik of the stigma of the terrorist label. We can only speculate about the reasons for both the listing and the delisting from the brief intelligence summary that the United Nations provided. It alleged that he was an associate of Abu Zubaydah, a person who was repeatedly waterboarded and subject to other forms of torture while in

American custody. Perhaps Abdelrazik's listing was related to intelligence provided under duress. In truth, we cannot know. Intelligence-based listing processes will always remain opaque and resistant to review and merits-based assessments.

The lessons from false positives run through Bill C-51 and other new laws, and not just in relation to the CSIS warrant proceedings. As will be discussed in Chapter 6, Canada's new 2015 anti-terrorism laws use intelligence-based listing processes with respect to both the *Secure Air Travel Act*[163] no-fly process contained in Bill C-51 and the passport revocation changes made in the order governing passports and the *Prevention of Terrorist Travel Act*[164] contained in the omnibus 2015 budget bill.

These provisions will restrict the movement of individuals where the government believes or even suspects that they will commit a terrorist offence if allowed to fly or use a passport.[165] These standards make it easier to restrict movement by Canadians. The no-fly list once required that a person be an imminent threat to air safety before being listed. The earlier passport revocation process depended on revocation being "necessary"[166] for the security of Canada or another country. Now a passport can be revoked where the minister "has reasonable grounds to believe that the decision is necessary to prevent the commission of a terrorism offence . . . or for the national security of Canada or a foreign country or state."[167]

The new no-fly powers contemplate that such determinations will be made on the basis of information that is shared from a variety of sources, including CSIS, the RCMP, the Canadian Border Services Agency, and the Department of Citizenship and Immigration.[168] Given the very low standard of reasonable suspicion and the use of secret intelligence, the new no-fly list may produce more false positives.

At least the new no-fly and passport revocation lists allow for judicial review. This is an important improvement over the United Nations terrorist listing process, which is still not subject to judicial scrutiny. Nevertheless, the new laws contemplate that Federal Court judges could uphold listing decisions as reasonable even on the basis of information that would not be admissible in a court of law and has not been disclosed or even summarized for those challenging their listing.[169]

In other words, Justice Zinn's criticism of listing processes as Kafkaesque still holds under Canada's new laws. These new laws also say nothing about adversarial challenges by security-cleared lawyers acting as special advocates or friends of the court. They learn nothing, in other words, from Canada's difficult history with secretive security certificate processes.

VII. CONCLUSION

This is a long chapter, and we have expended considerable effort in writing it. We have done so because we firmly believe that history matters and that we may be passing through a period where Canada's history of overreacting and underreacting to terrorism is now only dimly recalled and even less frequently invoked.

The Bill C-51 debate missed many opportunities to learn from the past. The most relevant lesson is the problem of overreaction, illustrated most acutely by the 1970 October Crisis, but also in the more doubtful responses to 9/11.

The widespread illegalities committed by the RCMP in the wake of the October Crisis led to the creation of CSIS, an agency consciously limited to the collection of intelligence. In enacting Bill C-51, the government has now decided that that decision cannot stand the test of time and that our present predicament requires a more muscular covert service.

In its back-to-the-future renovation, Bill C-51 places CSIS on a footing roughly analogous to that of the RCMP Security Service during the era of dirty tricks. In the government's reasoning, those tricks are sanitized by imposing a judicial pre-authorization requirement. But this fix pays short shrift to the role of the courts and especially their job description under the *Charter* to protect rights and not authorize their violation. And so this fix will fuel constitutional disputes and, we hope, a simple resistance by courts asked to embark on this radical constitutional inversion.

Bill C-51 learns little, also, from the sharing of unreliable information about Maher Arar and other Canadians tortured in Syria. While it does not govern international information sharing, it puts in play information of all sorts that will percolate within government and then (we believe) between governments under existing rules without attention paid to the prudential guarantees of good information sharing announced by the Arar Commission. Nor does Bill C-51 fix the serious deficiencies of Canada's antiquated and outmatched independent review system.

Bill C-51 repeats an earlier fondness for secret hearings using secret evidence in its new no-fly process and the related passport revocation system under Bill C-59. The government also did not learn from the hard lessons that have constrained the use of secret evidence in security certificate cases and used both Bill C-44 and Bill C-51 to roll back losses and limit due process.

Meanwhile, Bill C-51 also learns nothing from instances where Canada underreacted to terrorism. It is inattentive to lessons from the government's failure to prevent the 1985 Air India bombings, despite many intelligence warnings, and the subsequent flawed investigations and prosecutions. The Air India Commission in its 2010 report concluded that the pre- and post-bombing failures had stemmed, in large part, from inadequate oversight of the competing agendas of security agencies. The commission also concluded that fundamental problems in the CSIS-RCMP relationship and Canada's systems of terrorism prosecutions remained. It recommended that CSIS should no longer have a discretion not to disclose intelligence about possible terrorism offences. It also recommended fundamental reforms to oversight and terrorism prosecutions.

The October 2014 terrorist attacks gave the government a perfect opportunity to remedy these deficiencies. Unfortunately, nothing in the 2015 laws addresses any of these multiple deficiencies. Moreover, some features of these new laws may have the unintended effect of making the CSIS-RCMP relationship worse both by giving many CSIS sources a veto on whether they can be identified in subsequent terrorism prosecutions and by allowing CSIS to act on its own to disrupt possible terrorist plots.

We rehearse in greater detail all of these issues and more in subsequent chapters, doing our best to suggest alternative approaches for resolving security dilemmas. But before doing so, we believe it is necessary to examine the new threat of ISIS-inspired terrorism that Canada faced in the October 2014 terrorist attacks.

CHAPTER THREE
Threat: An Evolving Terrorist Threat

I. INTRODUCTION

Terrorist Designs

In 2002, an al-Qaida recording singled out Canada — along with France, Italy, Germany, and Australia — for allying itself "with America to attack us in Afghanistan." On the tape, the speaker — likely Osama bin Laden — asserted, "as you kill you will be killed, and as you bomb you will be bombed."[1]

Subsequently, Canadian officials pointed often to this statement — and a follow-up issued in 2005 — in describing the terrorist threat to Canada.[2] Documents seized by US soldiers from his Pakistani compound suggested that bin Laden continued to harbour terrorist designs on Canada (among other countries) up until his death.[3]

Al-Qaida is not the only terrorist group to menace Canada. The Somali terrorist group al-Shabaab has attacked people in Uganda for watching football games and targeted courthouses and other venues in Somalia. Most famously, it killed 63 innocent shoppers in the Westgate Mall in Nairobi, Kenya, and 147 innocent students at Kenya's Garissa University. It also called for terrorist attacks in Canada in February 2015 during the Bill C-51 debate. The video called "upon our Muslim brothers, particularly those in the West, to answer the call of Allah and target disbelievers wherever they are . . . what if such an attack was to occur in the Mall of America in Minnesota? Or the West Edmonton Mall in Canada? Or in London's Oxford Street?"[4]

Al-Shabaab has exercised influence over young Canadians, often of Somali descent.[5] The first Canadian convicted of attempting to leave Canada to join a terrorist group was imprisoned for trying to join al-Shabaab.[6] But not everyone has been caught. Intelligence estimates from several years ago suggest that as many as twenty Canadians have joined the terrorist group. Most notoriously, in 2009, six young Somali-Canadians left Toronto to fight in the organization. At least four of them were killed. Two others reportedly became disillusioned with the terrorist group and left it but remained in Somalia.[7]

Since then, some reports have suggested that Western recruitment into al-Shabaab has declined because "al Shabaab has delegitimized itself" with many correctly concluding that the group does not "understand Islam."[8] The US Department of State is apparently not convinced. In February 2014, it held counter–violent extremism meetings with the Somali community in Toronto and Ottawa.[9] In Chapter 13, we will suggest that such meetings are a good idea, although it would have been a better idea for the Canadian government to assume the lead.

A variety of foreign terrorist groups continue to attract Canadians. This is a dark side of globalization — people may be in Canada one day and transnational terrorists days later. Most recently, ISIS (Islamic State of Iraq and Syria) has been in ascendance. Like its predecessors, that group has issued a threatening call to arms. Weeks before the two terrorist attacks in October 2014, an ISIS audio recording had been shared widely on social media. The propagandist on the recording stated as follows:

> If you can kill a disbelieving American or European — especially the spiteful and filthy French — or an Australian, or a Canadian, or any other disbeliever from the disbelievers waging war, including the citizens of the countries that entered into a coalition against the Islamic State . . . kill him in any manner or way however it may be.[10]

Canadian foreign terrorist fighters associated with ISIS have recorded similar chilling messages.[11]

And in a development that we have probably not seen in the West on this scale since the Spanish Civil War, an apparently swelling number of Canadians and thousands of other citizens of Western countries have joined ISIS in Iraq and Syria, creating a new preoccupation with foreign terrorist fighters.

Terrorist Risk

These terrorist groups have all broadcast sobering messages, and their calls have resonated with at least some people. Stated intent may be an important indicator of threat, especially when associated with groups of great depravity and, indeed, evil. But deciding how and where to respond to evil requires a clear-eyed assessment of the adversary's ability to act on its intent in a manner affecting Canada and Canadians. Put another way, it is important to distinguish between great evil and great risk.

A failure to do so can muddle responses and contribute to the phenomenon of over- and underreaction discussed in the last chapter. On the one hand, we should not ignore an adversary who has promised to harm us, or our interests, and who may have the ability to act on that threat. To do so may lead us to underreact, in the way we did with Air India. But on the other hand, there is serious danger in conflating struggles against evil with an existential crisis. The air campaign over Kosovo in the 1990s, for example, was about confronting evil — crimes against humanity and feared genocide. Canada's participation in World War II was also about facing down evil but was additionally an existential struggle in which there was serious doubt as to whether democracy would persist on the planet.

In an existential crisis, a struggle for survival, many other values in a society may be set aside. Our *Emergencies Act*[12] recognizes this by allowing some suspension of the regular law of the land while also containing valuable pre-commitments not to repeat the mistakes of the past by interning citizens on the basis of race, religion, or ethnic or national origin. It also provides for parliamentary supervision and review (including access to secret information), public inquiries, and compensation to those who have been harmed in responding to existential threats. Too readily asserting an existential struggle in circumstances short of a true emergency — without the safeguards in the *Emergencies Act* — risks creating a permanent emergency, one that sacrifices the rule of law and our other animating values.

There is also danger in conflating depravity with threat and then bundling it with a war metaphor. A failure to distinguish between a true situation of armed conflict and smaller scale criminal conduct can produce an evil greater than the one being confronted. That is because the laws of war accept the use of lethal force as a proper instrument of policy, at least when directed at those labelled combatants; criminal law rules are more demanding, requiring self-defence or other justifications that narrow the circumstances in which lethal force may be used. The laws of war accept that enemies may, and indeed should, be killed without due process; criminal law rules are geared toward due process. The laws of war accept that there will be collateral casualties and that innocents will be injured; criminal law rules do not. The laws of war accept that the object of war is the defeat and submission of an enemy; criminal law is based on an impartial rule of law that does not distinguish between enemies and allies. It is about proportionate and deserved punishment but also rehabilitation of offenders, who in most cases will eventually re-enter the community.

For all of these reasons, we must guard against mixing up terrorism with war, or elevating criminals to warlords.

The ISIS Evil

ISIS is indisputably evil. Speaking of ISIS in September 2014, Prime Minister Stephen Harper said, "We know their ideology is not the result of 'social exclusion' or other so-called root causes. It is evil, vile, and must be unambiguously opposed."[13]

But where does ISIS lie on the threat spectrum? On this question, the statements of our political leaders cast up smoke while providing little clarity on the nature of the fire. Prime Minister Harper told the House of Commons in 2015 that "[t]his group, the so-called Islamic State, represents a direct threat not just to the region. It represents a threat to the world. By word and by deed, it represents a threat to this country."[14] His ministers went further. Foreign Minister John Baird said to a Commons committee in 2015, "In the 21st century the great struggle of our generation is terrorism, and this most recent example with ISIL probably represents the most barbaric, evil form of it we have seen."[15] Speaking to the same committee about ISIS in 2014, Defence Minister Nicholson said, "Let us not mince words. This terrorist organization is not only committing barbaric murders through the systemic killing of religious minorities, but represents a real and growing threat to civilization itself."[16]

Terrorism and defence researchers expressed skepticism at these threat claims.[17] Professor and former Department of Defence analyst Thomas Juneau concluded in a recent report that ISIS "does pose a threat to Canada, but not an existential one that would warrant a massive commitment of resources."[18]

But no doubt influenced by the remarks of political leaders and the media coverage, Canadians see ISIS as a greater threat to world security than foreign states, homegrown terrorism, or al-Qaida.[19] And indeed, in the aftermath of the October 2014 attacks, the political language became even more heated. Referring to Zehaf-Bibeau's lone wolf attack on the Parliament buildings, Prime Minister Harper told visiting German Chancellor Angela Merkel in February 2015, "As you are aware, Madame Chancellor, one of the [ISIS] jihadist monster's tentacles reached as far as our own Parliament."[20] And just days before, the prime minister announced Bill C-51[21] at a campaign-style rally:

Over the last few years, a great evil has been descending upon our world, an evil which has been growing more and more powerful: violent jihadism .... Jihadi terrorism as it is evolving is one of the most dangerous enemies our world has ever faced .... Through their deeds, these jihadists have declared war on Canada and with their words, they urge others to join their campaign of terror against Canadians .... violent jihadism is not a human right. It is an act of war.[22]

The prime minister announced new domestic security laws in a speech that blurred the line between crime and war, a distinction that we suggest a democracy must maintain to avoid perilous overreaction.

The ISIS Risk

How seriously should we take these political statements that Canada is at war with "violent jihadism"? Boiled to their essence, they declare ISIS evil, and they also declare ISIS (and the terrorism it inspires) a serious risk.

There should be no doubt that ISIS's conduct is horrific — its depravities amount to war crimes, crimes against humanity, and a particularly brutal repression of women and girls. And it has done and inspired terrorism. But unfortunately it has no monopoly in these areas. As Professor Steven Pinker, the author of perhaps the most comprehensive recent survey of violence and modern societies,[23] notes:

> In terms of sheer number of victims, they [ISIS] are nowhere near the Nazis (six million Jews alone, to say nothing of the extermination of gypsies, homosexuals, Poles and other Slavs, plus the tens of millions of deaths caused by their invasions and bombings). Mao and Stalin have also been credited with tens of millions of deaths. In the 20th century alone, we also have Pol Pot, Imperial Japan, the Turks in Armenia, the Pakistanis in Bangladesh, and the Indonesians during the Year of Living Dangerously.[24]

Just in our generation, there are many others who would vie with ISIS for first place on the evil roster: those responsible for the Rwanda genocide, the implosion of the former Yugoslavia, the genocide in Bosnia, the crimes against humanity in Kosovo, the war in Darfur, the depredations of the Lord's Resistance Army, and, more generally, the long-standing and devastating conflict in the Congo region and the Bashar Al-Assad regime's conduct in Syria. And we should not forget the Taliban — Canada's long-standing adversary in Afghanistan, responsible for more terrorist attacks, with more fatalities, than ISIS in 2013 according to the most recent Canadian public report on terrorism.[25]

In some of these cases, Canada acted; in others, Canada did not. It is simply not the case, therefore, that we have always treated evil as a serious risk necessitating action as a national security matter as opposed to (as in Kosovo) a reason to act on humanitarian impulses. And so what about that risk? What peril do we face from al-Qaida, ISIS, and the terrorism they inspire?

This chapter tries to answer that question as best it can from publicly available sources of information. The assessment will be, by necessity, imperfect. Canada does not have a government or security services prepared to quantify these matters publicly. The security services speak obliquely about serious, even unprecedented, risks.[26] The politicians speak in the manner cited above.

Canadians are left, therefore, to piece together a portrait of our present security environment from limited public statements by government, thoroughly censored documents obtained through access to information laws, media reports, academic studies, and historical data. This is what we try to do below, and along the way we note the growing array of possible interventions that could be applied to stop would-be terrorists and foreign terrorist fighters. These will all be discussed in detail in subsequent chapters, and range from attempts at dissuasion through various programs to counter violent extremism, to interdiction via no-fly lists and passport denials and revocations, to preventive detention and peace bonds, and ultimately to prosecutions for various terrorism offences.

Our discussion is necessarily provisional: as a society, we need to better understand the various processes of radicalization to violence and the varying risks presented by different terrorist and foreign terrorist fighters to better match specific risks with specific interventions. One size will not fit all. There is a need for ongoing research and evaluation of threats, risks, and the effectiveness of varying responses. It is the purpose of this chapter, and the rest of this book, to contribute to that discussion.

II. UNDERSTANDING THE TERRORIST THREAT

Reporting the Terrorist Threat

This book is consciously about al-Qaida- and ISIS-inspired terrorism. In popular discourse, this form of violent extremism is called "jihadism," or a variant such as "extreme jihadism" or "violent jihadism." Sometimes, Prime Minister Harper has called it "Islamicism."[27] Except where citing others, we use the different and more precise terminology "al-Qaida- and ISIS-inspired terrorism." As will be explored in Chapter 13, we recognize that conflating violence with what for many Muslims is a spiritual process — *jihad*[28] — can be both disrespectful and a barrier to very necessary cross-cultural dialogue. It also rewards those who have appropriated the term to justify violence with a religious stature that they crave, and that co-religionists dispute. We see no virtue in facilitating this appropriation.

What do we mean by al-Qaida- and ISIS-inspired terrorism? We follow Clark McCauley and Sophia Moskalenko in describing the radical al-Qaida-inspired worldview as one comprising a four-part "narrative frame": "(1) Islam is under attack by Western crusaders led by the United States; (2) jihadis, whom the West refers to as terrorists, are defending against this attack; (3) the actions they take in defence of Islam are proportional, just, and religiously sanctified; and, therefore (4) it is the duty of good Muslims to support these actions."[29] The ISIS ideology may differ in some respects but in a manner that is irrelevant to this book.

It is clear, therefore, that our focus is on one particular species of terrorism and one that is associated with Islam. It is fair to ask, why? After all, government documents enumerate threats extending well beyond terrorism including cyber security, the proliferation of weapons of mass destruction, foreign espionage, and foreign interference in Canadian affairs.[30] Indeed, Canada's one and only public national security policy, released in 2004 and never reissued, identified a wide range of threats to Canadians including natural and artificial disasters.[31]

That broad approach seems now to have been supplanted in government's public pronouncements by a closer focus on terrorism, as with the government's 2012 anti-terrorism strategy.[32] We leave aside the question of whether this marked focus on terrorism as a security threat detracts from close consideration of other perils.

But even within this terrorism category, there are many threats. As noted in Chapter 2, historical data suggest that over the last fifteen years, al-Qaida- and ISIS-inspired "lone wolf" terrorism has been less common than other forms of terrorism, especially that perpetrated by white supremacists.[33] For their part, academic studies have looked at right-wing political violence (albeit infrequently).[34] And our own discussion in Chapter 2 focused substantial attention on the FLQ (Front de libération du Québec) terrorism of the 1970s and the Sikh terrorism of the 1980s. More recent CSIS and RCMP documents identify an array of terrorist threats above and beyond Muslim groups and causes.[35] Indeed, there is occasional public controversy over government documents outlining possible threats from extreme fringe elements of environmental and other domestic movements.[36] And in keeping with all this, Quebec police recently told the Senate security committee that

75 percent of their files on extremist threats deal with issues other than "Islamic radicalism."[37]

But the indisputable truth is that al-Qaida- and ISIS-inspired terrorism dominates the government's assessments and public discourse. The government's 2014 public report on the terrorist threat to Canada dealt essentially exclusively with the al-Qaida- and ISIS-inspired threat.[38] The most recent CSIS public report devoted one paragraph to "domestic extremism" and six pages to al-Qaida- and ISIS-inspired terrorism. A 2014 CSIS briefing to the public safety minister listed terrorism — and particularly "Sunni Islamist Extremism" — as the most significant threat to Canada.[39]

Put another way, al-Qaida- and ISIS-inspired terrorism is regarded by policy makers and the security services as today's terrorist preoccupation. It was also the clear political impetus for the laws introduced in 2015, and especially Bill C-51. The "violent jihadism" meme monopolized debate throughout early 2015.

Explaining every facet of why that was the case would require a chapter in its own right, one lying beyond the remit of this book. But we can look to government explanations for the al-Qaida and ISIS focus. The 2014 CSIS briefing described "Sunni Islamist Extremism" as possessing a powerful narrative that inspires others to radicalize to violence. It is also dynamic because "extremists are reliant, adaptive and opportunistic."[40] For its part, CSIS's 2014 public report described the internationally destabilizing impact of al-Qaida- and ISIS-inspired terrorism and its ripple effects in Canada. According to CSIS, there are

> three primary ways in which terrorism continues to threaten the safety and security of Canadians:
> - First, terrorists continue to plot direct attacks against Canada and its allies at home and abroad with the aim of causing death and disruption;
> - Second, terrorists seek to conduct activities on Canadian territory that support terrorism globally, including fundraising to support attacks and militant groups;
> - Third, terrorists and their supporters employ social media to reach individuals in Canada for operational purposes and to radicalize them. Some of these radicalized individuals may conduct attacks before travelling abroad or travel overseas to obtain training or to engage in terrorism in other countries. They endanger themselves and pose a risk to the countries to which they have travelled. Should they return to Canada, they may pose a threat to national security by attempting to

radicalize others, train them in terrorist methods, or conduct terrorist attacks on their own.[41]

This last issue breaks into two components. First, Canadians travelling to join overseas terrorist groups become foreign terrorist fighters. This phenomenon is not new but has "become more pressing" with participation in "conflicts such as Syria, Somalia, Iraq and Afghanistan."[42] Indeed, international concerns are now so acute that in late 2014, the United Nations Security Council recognized foreign terrorist fighters as a threat to international security. In Resolution 2178, it called on all states to take measures to prevent the travel of foreign terrorist fighters as well as to counter radicalization, recruitment, and organization.[43] Second, the last bullet in CSIS's list raises the question of domestic radicalization to violence and so-called lone wolf attacks by al-Qaida- and ISIS-inspired individuals, otherwise unconnected to those organizations. In 2012, Canada's intelligence co-ordinating body — the Integrated Threat Assessment Centre — called "domestic extremists who subscribe to the AQ ideology" "the most serious threat within Canada."[44] These "Western Islamists" (who include converts to "radical Islam") "understand Western culture, speak its language and can move easily within its societies."[45]

Given the clear prominence that the government places on al-Qaida- and ISIS-inspired terrorism, we have consciously chosen to make it our focus as well in this book. The more difficult task we face, however, is measuring the scale of that threat and quantifying the risk it presents.

Measuring the Foreign-Terrorist-Fighter Threat

We begin by examining the concept of "foreign fighting" — a concern that animates the third bullet point in the CSIS assessment cited above.

What Is a Foreign Fighter?

The "foreign fighter" is a sometimes poorly defined concept in part because it amounts to "an intermediate actor category lost between local rebels, on the one hand, and international terrorists, on the other."[46]

Historically, foreign fighters have more in common with insurgents than international terrorists. While foreign fighting and terrorism may overlap in some instances, analysts note that foreign fighters "(1) originally join a localized insurgency, (2) tend to perpetrate . . . attacks within the confines of the insurgency, and (3) do not primarily target non-combatants."[47] As another expert puts it, foreign fighters are "insurgents in every respect but their passports."[48]

In his historical survey of the phenomenon, David Malet defines "foreign fighters" as "noncitizens of conflict states who join insurgencies during civil conflicts."[49] Likewise, Thomas Hegghammer defines a "foreign fighter" as "someone who leaves or tries to leave the West to fight somewhere else."[50] In a more refined delineation, he describes a foreign fighter as one who "(1) has joined, and operates within the confines of, an insurgency, (2) lacks citizenship of the conflict state or kinship links to its warring factions, (3) lacks affiliation to an official military organization, and (4) is unpaid."[51] We rely on these definitions although we follow others who include among foreign fighters those who are paid but who do not have a primarily mercenary motive.[52]

The History of Foreign Fighting

Western citizens who volunteer to fight in foreign insurgencies are not a recent historical phenomenon. Most famously, they include those who left their homes to fight in the Spanish Civil War or the 1947 Arab-Israel war that resulted in the creation of Israel.

In recent times, "foreign fighter" is a concept that has become conflated with conflicts in the Muslim world. In part, this is because arguably all but two of the "large-scale, global and private foreign fighter mobilizations in the twentieth century" were in Muslim-majority countries.[53] It also reflects, however, the fact that issues regarding foreign fighters and their recruitment have become more pointed for many governments in the aftermath of 9/11 because of the (often presumed) association between foreign fighting and international terrorism.

Certainly, the pattern of citizens (Western or otherwise) fighting in civil conflicts in the Muslim world is not unique to the post-9/11 period. In fact, of the seventy armed conflicts in Muslim states since 1945, foreign fighter contingents from any number of countries served in eighteen,[54] including, for example, the war in Bosnia.[55] However, the pace of participation seems to have increased — sixteen of eighteen conflicts in the Muslim world involving foreign fighters arose since 1980, with most occurring during the 1990s and into the first decade of the twenty-first century.[56] Hegghammer attributes this increased tempo to the emergence in the 1970s and 1980s of a new, extreme pan-Islamic social movement in Saudi Arabia, one that acquired substantial wealth from the oil crisis of the period and was fuelled, in part, by global events such as the conflicts in Lebanon and Afghanistan.[57] These same historical events are also associated with the rise of al-Qaida.[58] Perhaps for this reason, post-9/11 analyses often link foreign fighters with either al-Qaida[59] or the related, but distinct, issue of radicalization.[60]

Foreign Fighters and Terrorism

"Foreign fighters" have a "life cycle" divided into two discrete periods, both of which have galvanized state attention and concern: departure to the conflict zone and return to the country of origin. Distinct policy preoccupations arise at each stage.

Departure enhances the supply of recruits to fight or otherwise participate in foreign conflicts, with possibly serious consequences for life, foreign relations, and international stability. Return amounts to the re-entry of a potentially further radicalized individual equipped with new means and methods into a domestic civil society to which he may wish to do harm.[61] When a person returns from fighting with a foreign terrorist group, the risk is that she will continue her terrorist activities in the countries to which she returns.

Much of current concerns about foreign fighters (including those articulated by the recent United Nations Security Council Resolution 2178) stem from this fear of return. Essentially, the "return" preoccupation can be summarized as follows: even though some of the foreign fighters "may not return as terrorists to their respective countries . . . all of them will have been exposed to an environment of sustained radicalization and violence with unknowable, but worrying, consequences."[62] Put another way, fears "center around the threat of a 'bleed out' as jihadi veterans, equipped with new knowledge of fighting, training, recruitment, media and technical skills in building bombs, take their skills elsewhere—potentially facilitating the initiation or escalation of terrorism in their home country or in other arenas, and enhancing the power of insurgencies and terrorist groups."[63]

The "bleed out" theory has anecdotal support, especially in relation to returnees from the Afghan conflicts of the 1970s and 1980s. In addition to forming the core of al-Qaida, these fighters "played important roles in the Algerian civil war, the uprising of jihadi groups in Egypt against the regime of Hosni Mubarak, the Chechen rebellion against Russia, and the Bosnian civil war."[64]

But uncritically pooling foreign fighters together with international terrorists misses substantial nuance in the "life cycle" and risks provoking policy responses based on category errors. First, it is notable that in the past, Muslim foreign fighters, al-Qaida, and now ISIS have often "competed over resources" and "do not have exactly the same political preferences."[65]

Second, as a strict legal matter, becoming a foreign fighter should be distinguished from international travel for the purpose of joining a terrorist group or to engage in terrorist training or activity. The two may overlap — it is possible that the foreign fighter fights for, or in the company of, a terrorist group during a foreign armed conflict. For example, al-Shabaab is both a listed terrorist entity under Canada's *Criminal Code*[66] and an armed military group in Somalia in that country's prolonged internal armed conflict. A Canadian journeying to fight with al-Shabaab is therefore both a foreign fighter and a person joining a terrorist group. A Canadian joining a rebel group in Syria is, meanwhile, a foreign fighter. And unless he joins a group "that has as one of its purposes or activities facilitating or carrying out any terrorist activity"[67] or that is a terrorist entity listed under Canadian law — for example, Jabhat al-Nusrah[68] or ISIS[69] — he is not serving with a terrorist organization. The person is not, in other words, a foreign *terrorist* fighter.

Third, conduct during the "fighting" phase may not necessarily overlap with terrorism. Mere participation in an armed conflict, without something more, is not terrorism. If we want it to be a crime, we would need to follow Australia and update our foreign enlistment law to bar participation in modern conflicts involving insurgencies.[70]

Fourth, as a factual matter, there is reason to question the "bleed out" theory. Statistically, becoming a foreign fighter does not mean that a person will subsequently become a terrorist. Hegghammer examined the association between foreign fighting by those journeying from the West and what he calls "domestic fighting" — that is, attacks mounted in Western countries. Based on data from 1990 to 2010, he identified 945 "foreign fighters" as having left North America, Western Europe, and Australia to fight in conflicts in the Muslim world.[71] These data are, of course, imperfect, and Hegghammer suggested that the figure could be as high as 7,500.[72] Whatever the absolute number, it far outstripped the equivalent figure of "domestic fighters" — that is, terrorists — in the West. Hegghammer placed the "estimated total number of Islamists in the West who, in the period between 1990 and 2010, were prepared to proceed directly to domestic attacks without going abroad first" at 294.[73] In other words, foreign fighting remained much more common than domestic fighting in the sample group studied by Hegghammer. Critically, he also found that no more than (and possibly considerably less than) "one in nine foreign fighters returned to perpetrate attacks in the West."[74]

In short, the correlation between foreign fighting and domestic terrorism is far from automatic. The 1:9 ratio of foreign to domestic fighting suggests that substantial law enforcement and intelligence resources may be devoted to a constituency of which only 11 percent will progress to domestic acts of terror. For this reason, Hegghammer urged that "[p]rosecuting all aspiring foreign fighters as prospective domestic terrorists has limited preventive benefits, because so few of them, statistically speaking, will go on to attack the homeland."[75] He did not address the degree to which those who might wish to leave the West to join foreign terrorist fights but are prevented from doing so then go on to plan and perpetuate violence. But in both cases, Western states have to be careful not to conflate support for foreign fights with support for domestic terrorism.

At the same time, a 1:9 ratio of returning domestic terrorists among foreign fighters is worrying. It is a more powerful statistical predictor than other independent variables associated with forecasting terrorism.[76] Moreover, Hegghammer's data suggest that "the presence of foreign fighter returnees increases the effectiveness of attacks in the West" as measured in terms of both the chance that a plot will be executed and the prospects of fatalities associated with these attacks.[77]

And the threat presented by foreign fighters may be becoming worse. Hegghammer's data set ends in 2010 before the implosion in Syria. By early 2014, an estimated 6,000 to 12,000 foreign fighters had entered Syria, a number far in excess of that associated with conflicts from 1990 to 2009.[78] Of this number, 2,800 were believed to be from Western states.[79] Many were joining "extremist opposition groups, such as those linked to al-Qaeda,"[80] including Jabhat al-Nusrah.[81]

More recently, attention has focused on ISIS and its active (and successful) recruitment of Western fighters. The numbers of that group's foreign fighters have further swollen the preceding figures. And in the result the foreign fighter "bleed out" problem may be more extreme in the future than in the historical data set used by Hegghammer.

III. CANADIAN FOREIGN TERRORIST FIGHTERS

Canada produces some of these foreign terrorist fighters. Two Canadian men died in a 2013 al-Qaida-linked terrorist attack at an Algerian gas plant that killed as many as sixty individuals.[82] That same year, a Canadian fighting with terrorist group (and armed insurgency) al-Shabaab reportedly participated in a deadly attack in Mogadishu.[83] As already noted, a score of Canadians have apparently joined that Somali terrorist group. Others have joined ISIS, and it is the siren call of this group that is the most alarming recent development.

What Is ISIS?

The Islamic State of Iraq and Syria is a transnational Sunni Muslim insurgent and terror group that has declared a Caliphate and has controlled territory in parts of Iraq and Syria since 2013.[84] ISIS was originally affiliated with al-Qaida (specifically its franchise in post–US invasion Iraq). It was "al-Qaida in Iraq" that, under Al Zarqawi in 2004, first beheaded a prisoner wearing a Guantanamo-style orange jumpsuit.[85] But al-Qaida disassociated itself from

ISIS in June 2014 in part because of ISIS's emphatic brutality directed often toward other Muslims. Some of these acts of brutality include videotaped beheadings of captives (again, often dressed in orange jumpsuits), torture (including the burning alive of a captured Jordanian pilot), slavery, and sexual violence.[86]

Canadians cannot ignore the fact that ISIS operates not just in Iraq but also in Syria. Syria is the country where Canadians such as Maher Arar were tortured by the Assad regime. The Assad regime is implicated in war crimes, repression of minorities, and brutal atrocities in Syria's civil war.

The connection between ISIS and the Assad regime is murky. The Assad regime encouraged foreign terrorist fighters to fight against American-led Coalition troops and others in Iraq during the Unites States–led occupation of that country in part to distract them from challenging the regime itself.[87] An outgrowth of that period, ISIS now fights against Assad's forces, but it also fights against other anti-government insurgents, including the Syrian Kurdish militia, the Free Syrian Army, and tribal militias who are each fighting to gain or retain control on multiple fronts.[88]

Reports allege that ISIS's leadership includes a group of prisoners who were freed from Syrian jails by Assad in 2011 in an attempt to subvert the opposition.[89] A former member of the Syrian Security Services told an Abu Dhabi newspaper that "[t]he regime did not just open the door to the prisons and let these extremists out, it facilitated them in their work, in their creation of armed brigades."[90] ISIS has since destroyed not only ancient antiquities but Syrian jails notorious for torturing the regime's political opponents.

ISIS has thrived in the aftermath of the 2003 invasion of Iraq, where, even today, an extreme sectarian environment pits Sunnis against Shias because of American mismanagement of the occupation. The shortsighted blacklisting of Sunni Ba'athists who served under Saddam Hussein drove many trained fighters into the original anti–United States insurgency and now an awkward alliance with ISIS.[91]

Some of ISIS's leadership may also have organized in US detention facilities. Abu Bakr al-Baghdadi, a leader of ISIS, was interned by the Americans after the invasion of Iraq. The US general once in charge of detainees in Iraq commented, "if you look at how Baghdadi has set up the top leadership of ISIS, you can see how skilled he is. The guys at the top are all very skilled managers. Many of them are former Ba'athists." He added that Baghdadi "learned, from being in detention himself, that if you don't manage the prison well, the detainees will just organize themselves against you . . . his strategy has been to recruit his cadres from the prisons where jihadis were detained. He knows where to find the hard-core radicals."[92]

ISIS differs from al-Qaida and other terror groups in its focus on forming an immediate geographic Caliphate. Indeed, it is a rarity among terrorist groups in that it controls territory and the revenues that go with it. Since late 2013, ISIS has operated several oilfields in Eastern Syria and has reportedly drawn revenue from oil sales to the Assad regime. It uses this revenue to maintain its independence from al-Qaida.[93]

ISIS is also differentiated by its glorification of extreme and graphic violence and by having "the most sophisticated propaganda machine of any extremist group."[94] ISIS broadcasts professionally edited videos and utilizes controlled (or inspired) social media campaigns via Twitter and Facebook targeted directly at its mass audience.[95] As already noted, ISIS propaganda has encouraged attacks on the West, including Canada.[96]

ISIS and Canada

Canadians have grown used to the threat posed by al-Qaida since 9/11, including that terrorist group's repeated threats against Canada. ISIS, however, is new and different and (because of its media prominence) more immediate.

Many Canadians learned about ISIS only in early October 2014 when Canada committed itself to assisting the United States in bombing the group's approximately 30,000 fighters — half of whom are probably foreign recruits. Prime Minister Harper argued that ISIS had committed "the most unspeakable atrocities against the most innocent of people" and had "specifically targeted Canada and Canadians, urging supporters to attack 'disbelieving Canadians in any manner,' vowing that we should not feel secure, even in our homes."[97]

In late October 2014, Canada joined the American-led coalition against ISIS in Iraq. Six hundred military personal were deployed as part of Joint Task Force–Iraq, and six CF-18 fighter aircraft support the coalition in the conduct of airstrikes against ISIS forces, infrastructure, and equipment.[98] Another sixty-nine armed forces personnel are also working in an advisory and assistance role providing strategic and tactical advice to Iraqi security forces.[99] In March 2015, the Canadian mission was extended for a year and expanded to include ISIS targets in Syria.

Exactly how this armed conflict will play out — and whether Canada and its partners have a real strategy to guide their tactics — remains unclear. In his report on Canada's anti-ISIS military campaign, Professor Juneau suggests that while Canada may be justified in contributing to forces combatting ISIS, there is a danger that a military defeat of ISIS itself will not address the factors in both Iraq and Syria that led to its rise.[100]

Canadians in ISIS

Whatever its larger impact on geopolitics, the conflict in the Middle East has ripples in Canada.

It is difficult to know how many Canadians have already joined ISIS, and the government has yet to produce a comprehensive and itemized accounting. In early 2014, the government was aware of more than 130 individuals with Canadian connections who were abroad and suspected of engaging in terrorism-related activities.[101] It was also reported in October 2014 that the RCMP was tracking 90 individuals who intended to travel or had returned from overseas.[102]

These numbers have drifted upward. During its 2014–15 hearings into security threats to Canada, the Senate security committee learned that

> 93 Canadians have been identified as seeking to join Islamist extremist groups like the Islamic State of Iraq and Syria (ISIS), al Qaeda, Boko Harem, and al Shabaab. Eighty radicalized Canadians have been identified as participating with terrorists overseas and have returned to Canada and approximately 145 Canadians are believed to be abroad providing support to terrorist groups.[103]

An internal government speaking-note document put the number of Canadians engaged in terrorism-related activities in Syria by early 2014 at thirty.[104] In April 2015, CSIS Director Michel Coulombe told the committee that the number of Canadians travelling to Iraq and Syria had increased by 50 percent in the past few months.[105]

While exact figures remain publicly unreported, the general numbers suggest that Canada has an active network of individuals who are radicalizing people to become violent extremists and to fight for ISIS. Who are these Canadians?

Andre Poulin and His Recruits: "Life in Canada Was Good . . . . But . . . You Cannot Obey Allah Fully as You Can by Living in a Muslim Country, in an Islamic State."[106]

Andre Poulin was a troubled youth in Timmins, Ontario. He converted to Islam in 2009 when he was still a teenager. He moved in with a Muslim man and his female partner because he wanted to live a Muslim life. Poulin had an affair with the man's partner, and he accused the man of "living an un-Islamic lifestyle." Poulin threatened to kill the man, claiming that the man was intending to convert to Christianity. He was charged with threatening the man and breaching peace bond conditions requiring that he have no contact with the man. Poulin pled guilty and was sentenced to twelve months probation in 2010.[107] The prosecutor in the case recalled that Poulin had told him that "he doesn't care if he went to jail. Then he says that nobody is going to help him and that everybody is out to get him. He said something had to be done and he talked about sacrificing himself."[108]

Poulin left Timmins for Toronto and recruited others, including four young Bangladeshi men from Toronto, to go to Syria. Some of these individuals were convinced by their families to return after initial trips, but some subsequently went back to Syria. One of these men later made extremist comments on Twitter praising the Ottawa terrorist attacks. This caused his Twitter account to be suspended.[109]

Poulin was a successful recruiter both in person and on video. In July 2014, ISIS released a video depicting Poulin, which has been described as a "masterpiece of extremist propaganda."[110] In the video, Poulin states, "Life in Canada was good. I had money. I have good family. But at the end of the day, it's still dar al-kufr [a land of disbelief] and at the end of the day you cannot obey Allah fully as you can by living in a Muslim country, in an Islamic state."[111] He adds, "I was like your everyday regular Canadian before Islam. I had money. I had family. I had good friends . . . . I was a very good person, and you know, majahideen are regular people too . . . . We have lives, just like any other solider in any other army."

The Poulin video indicates how ISIS is a different and in some respects a greater threat than al-Qaida. Whereas al-Qaida focuses on recruiting a small vanguard of terrorists, ISIS attempts to appeal to the masses. Poulin explains in the video, "We need engineers, we need doctors, we need professionals. We need volunteers. We need fund-raisers. There is a role for everybody."[112]

The video then shows Poulin in combat with the Syrian Army and seemingly being killed by it. A narrator, in perfect, unaccented English, then urges that Poulin's death was a good thing because "[h]e answered the call of his Lord and surrendered his soul without hesitation, leaving the world behind him. Not out of despair and hopelessness, but rather with certainty of Allah's promise."[113] The narrator also asserts that Poulin "accepted Islam in a land at war with Islam," namely Canada, which he characterizes as a "land with few Muslims, in a land where evil, kufr [disbelief] and sin called him from every direction and corner to succumb to Satan and to his desires."[114] Poulin's story is just one of many, but it underlines how ISIS has appealed, and continues to appeal, to some Canadians.

Another well-known Canadian ISIS fighter was Damian Clairmont. He converted to Islam after dropping out of high school and being diagnosed with mental health issues. In 2012 he left Canada. CSIS informed his mother a few weeks after his departure that he was fighting with a terrorist group in

Syria. Clairmont's death in a battle with the Syrian Free Army was confirmed in January 2014.[115] As will be discussed in Chapter 13, Clairmont's mother, Christianne Boudreau, has been active (although not entirely successful) in calling for Canadian government support of programs to persuade young people like her son not to leave for foreign terrorist fights, and to assist the reintegration of those who return to Canada.

Mohamed Ali Dirie, whose story is recounted also in Chapter 7, pled guilty to smuggling weapons in relation to the Toronto 18 terrorist plot in 2009. He was given credit for five years pre-trial custody, and he served two years in a special handling unit with other convicted terrorists. While in a Canadian prison, he was able to receive a hidden video, *Return of the Crusaders*, that features scenes of injured women and children in Iraq and a call for terrorist attacks by bin Laden.[116] He may have become further radicalized in prison — he certainly was not de-radicalized. He was released in October 2011 and immediately placed on a peace bond to prevent him from leaving Canada because of concerns that he would participate in what he believed were "unjust wars" involving Western aggression.[117] Despite the peace bond, Dirie was able to leave Canada on a false passport in 2012 and was killed in Syria in 2013.[118]

John Maguire, a Muslim convert, left Ottawa for Syria in early 2013. ISIS released a video of Maguire praising the October 2014 terrorist attacks in Canada.[119] As will be discussed below, he was subsequently charged with terrorism offences, but the government believes that he was killed in Syria.

Aisha: "There's No Way I Would Have Let Her Leave If I Knew Now That She Was Going to the Craziest War Zone in the World."[120]

Other stories of youth lured by ISIS messaging have become increasingly common in Canadian media. One such story is that of "Aisha," who at twenty-three became radicalized and travelled to Syria to join ISIS in the summer of 2014. Her sister Rabia recalled noticing Aisha withdrawing from her family and social circle. Aisha began dressing more traditionally and spent a great deal of time on her computer. Rabia believes that a woman in Edmonton offering an online course on the Qur'an recruited Aisha to go to Syria. The woman apparently offered the course online after she had been asked to leave an Edmonton mosque.

Aisha's sister indicated that CSIS had approached her family before Aisha left Canada. Rabia said to journalists, "They told us she had been interacting with people they thought were dangerous and were influencing her in a negative way, but they didn't give us enough information and it was all very vague."[121] Rabia stated that if CSIS had provided more information, the family would have acted differently: "I would have ripped her passport up. There's no way I would have let her leave if I knew now that she was going to the craziest war zone in the world."[122]

As we discuss in Chapter 8, Bill C-51 gives CSIS the power to do more in these situations — and, indeed, the need to speak to families was often cited in support of the new CSIS powers. As we also discuss in Chapter 8, however, the new powers reach much further than this modest objective. Bill C-51 also makes it easier to revoke passports and to place people on a no-fly list, as discussed in Chapter 6.

The October Attackers: Foiled Foreign Fighters?

And there are also the people who the government has been able to stop from joining ISIS. Some of these may go on to live peaceful lives in Canada. Others do not.

Martin Couture-Rouleau converted to Islam in 2013. The twenty-six-year-old man came to the attention of the police because of extreme postings on Facebook that suggested support for ISIS. Authorities seized his passport in the summer of 2014 to stop him from leaving Canada to fight for ISIS in Syria.

In 2013, Canada added four new offences to the *Criminal Code* that were specifically designed to apply to those who, like Couture-Rouleau, attempted to leave Canada to engage in terrorist activity abroad. Even before that, Canada had charged and prosecuted a would-be foreign terrorist fighter for his efforts to join the Somali group al-Shabaab.

We do not know why police did not charge Couture-Rouleau in the summer of 2014. The RCMP explained this fact as follows: "we cannot arrest someone for having radical thoughts. It's not a crime in Canada."[123] But authorities did have enough information about more than radical thoughts to revoke a passport. We can only surmise from the press statements that there was insufficient evidence admissible in an open court of Couture-Rouleau's darker travel designs. As we discuss in Chapter 7, we also do not know exactly why an RCMP request for a peace bond against Couture-Rouleau was turned down that summer. It seems clear that prosecutors concluded there was insufficient evidence, but there was obviously enough information (on a very similar evidentiary standard) to revoke a passport. So, again, we wonder whether this was a question of a government in possession of good intelligence but not intelligence that authorities were prepared to use in court.

It is astonishing that we do not have clear answers to why the government acted as it did in Couture-Rouleau's case. As we note repeatedly in this book, the lack of information about governmental involvement with the October attackers can be contrasted with the seventy-five-page report that Australian governments (both federal and state) produced about their interaction with Man Haron Monis within a month of his terrorist attacks in Sydney in December 2014.[124] The absence of comparable information in Canada makes it difficult to know whether the government's response to the October attacks was appropriate. In particular, are new measures to prevent people like Couture-Rouleau from leaving Canada effectively co-ordinated with measures to deal with them after they have been denied travel? We return to this issue in Chapter 11. We do know that on 20 October 2014, Couture-Rouleau, apparently motivated by anger at the Canadian bombing mission in Iraq and Syria, ran down two Canadian Armed Forces soldiers, killing Warrant Officer Patrice Vincent.[125]

Michael Zehaf-Bibeau — the man who shot and killed Corporal Nathan Cirillo at Ottawa's war memorial and then stormed the Parliament buildings — may also have been an aspiring foreign fighter. He too had applied for a passport. This passport application was delayed for reasons that are not entirely clear, and Zehaf-Bibeau came to Ottawa seeking a Libyan passport as his father was Libyan. That application also was delayed, and the man ultimately resorted to violence in Ottawa "in retaliation for Afghanistan and because Harper wants to send his troops to Iraq."[126]

Zehaf-Bibeau was reportedly "very low on CSIS' radar."[127] But in truth, just as with Couture-Rouleau, we can only speculate on why he slipped through the cracks. This information vacuum did not stop the government from legislating without evidence, or at least explanation, about what had gone wrong. The information deficit relating to what the government knew and did about the two October 2014 attackers also raises issues of oversight and review, which will be discussed in Chapters 11 and 12.

Common Features

For our purposes here, it is notable that while each story we recount above is unique, there are constant themes in recent ISIS recruitment patterns. Many actual or aspiring foreign fighters have had troubled adolescences, often with mental health and addiction problems. Many have converted to Islam and may have only a rudimentary understanding of the religion. Almost all were attracted to strict and intolerant forms of Islam promoted both online and in person by some charismatic leader.

This online environment can exploit feelings of youthful frustration, marginalization, and discrimination. It may also facilitate a search for identity and purpose.[128] The message is that by joining the cause of foreign terrorist fighters, people will help others and find camaraderie and great adventure.[129]

As is suggested by some of the incidents described below, recruits are often found in clusters. This suggests that real-world interpersonal relations may also matter. Some recruits may be guided by internal group dynamics in narrow peer groups and may resist interventions by family, friends, and those in the Islamic community. Many believe they are combatting the oppression of Muslims and joining a noble cause.

IV. CRIME AND PUNISHMENT?

The government reacted to the October attacks. The end of 2014 and the first half of 2015 were filled with a renewed focus on reports of foreign terrorist travel and also arrests, charges, and peace bonds related to such travel. In some cases, no charges were laid. In other cases, peace bonds were used as a less drastic alternative to charges.

While the government repeatedly pointed to each incident as proof of the heightened security risk, we must be wary of drawing firm conclusions about the threat environment from this surge. After the October attacks, the RCMP moved hundreds of members from other policing areas to bolster the ranks of its national security investigations. The scale of this resource move was unprecedented for the force.[130] More police translate into more police activity, and with it more arrests.

Where charges have been laid, we await trials, and so we do not know whether the charges will be sustained. We cannot rule out the possibility of an overreaction somewhat similar to that discussed in the last chapter, after two terrorist attacks in October 1970. Peace bonds are most problematic because they may offer no ultimate adjudication of guilt or innocence. We must also be wary of attributing this upswing to Bill C-51, which was being debated throughout this period. All of the cases were dealt with under existing laws, and not under any of the new powers or crimes in Bill C-51.

These recent charges also underline the need for further investigation of precisely why Couture-Rouleau was neither charged nor made the subject of a peace bond.

The Charges

In December 2014, a fifteen-year-old Montreal youth was charged with committing robbery for the benefit of a terrorist group. Police also alleged that he was planning to leave Canada to engage in terrorist activity abroad.[131] Police said the boy's father had discovered stolen money secreted in the family's backyard and notified authorities. The father suspected his son had become radicalized, and police said they had found "jihadi-related material and videos" on the boy's computer.[132]

Police charged a total of six Ottawa-based men with terrorism offences in the first half of 2015. In January 2015, they arrested Ashton Larmond at the Montreal airport and detained his brother, Carlos, in Ottawa. The twenty-four-year-old twin brothers had previous criminal records and were recent converts to Islam. They have been charged with various terrorism offences. Suliman Mohmed, a twenty-one-year-old Ottawa man, was subsequently charged with conspiracy to participate in a terrorist group.[133]

In February 2015, the police charged twenty-five-year-old Ottawa resident Awso Peshdary along with two others (charged *in absentia*). These others were twenty-three-year-old John Maguire and twenty-seven-year-old Ahmad Waseem, both believed to have joined ISIS and been killed in Syria. The three men were charged with various terrorism offences including participating and counselling others to participate in the activities of a terrorist group.[134]

Maguire fought with ISIS, a crime, and praised the October 2014 terrorist attacks in Canada calling for others to engage in similar attacks. Waseem returned to Canada to recover from wounds sustained fighting in Syria, but despite pleas from family and the Muslim community, he returned to Syria, where he posted on his Twitter account, "Canadian Muslims guess what 'high risk traveller' made it to Sham [historic name for Syria]."[135]

Peshdary had been investigated in a previous terrorism investigation and charged with domestic violence, but he was acquitted when his wife refused to testify against him. Originally a Shia Muslim, he had converted to Sunni Islam but had reportedly been asked to leave two Ottawa mosques because of his extremism. He is also said to have been involved with religious activities in Ottawa high schools and Algonquin College.[136]

A seventeen-year-old male from Edmonton was charged in March 2015 with attempting to leave Canada to commit terrorist acts and participate in the activities of a terrorist group. The arrest followed reports that three others who had left Edmonton in 2013 had been killed while fighting for ISIS.[137] Little is known about this case in part because it involves a young offender, but the judge has ordered a psychiatric assessment of the accused to determine whether he is mentally fit to stand trial or might have a mental-disorder defence.[138]

In April 2015, two eighteen-year-olds from Montreal, Sabrine Djaermane and El Mahdi Jamali, were charged with and pled not guilty to explosives offences and various terrorism offences including attempting to leave Canada to participate in the activities of a terrorist group.[139] Both attended Collège de Maisonneuve in east-end Montreal.

In July 2015, police charged a thirty-three-year-old man in Fort St John, British Columbia, Othman Ayed Hamdan, with three terrorism charges related to online activities for ISIS. The charges included counselling murder and other violence for the benefit of a terrorist group, here ISIS.[140]

And, in a twist, the RCMP also laid charges against a Somali man visiting Canada alleged to be one of the chief protagonists in the 2008 Amanda Lindhout hostage-taking in Somalia. During Lindhout's 460-day ordeal, the accused reportedly "directed much of the torture she endured, watching impassively as a serrated knife was held to her throat, and terrorizing her mother with ransom demands."[141] Ali Omar Ader is charged with hostage-taking, a venerable offence that predates 9/11.

These twelve cases are on top of outstanding charges laid before the October 2014 attacks. In July 2014, the RCMP laid its first terrorist travel charges against Hasibullah Yusufzai, a man police believe left for Syria in January 2014.[142] Police also laid charges *in absentia* in 2011 against two Winnipeg men, twenty-seven-year-old Maiwand Yar and thirty-year-old Ferid Ahmed Iman, for various terrorism offences stemming from their plans to "travel to Pakistan for terrorist training, with plans to later join the insurgency against NATO forces in Afghanistan."[143]

The Peace Bonds

As discussed in detail in Chapter 7, the police also increased the tempo of peace bond restraints on feared aspiring terrorists. Merouane Ghalmi, a twenty-two-year-old former kick-boxing champion, agreed in March 2015 to a peace bond that required him to submit to electronic monitoring and monitoring of his computer usage. He also agreed not to travel outside of Quebec or to possess material that promotes violence or extremist ideologies.[144] In May 2015, he was charged with breaking a condition of the peace bond, namely that he not access or attempt to consult "[t]errorist material using any means, or material which promotes violence or which promotes extremist or radical ideas, in whole or in part, for political, religious or ideological purpose, objective or cause."[145]

A friend of Ghalmi, Daniel Minto Darko, agreed to a peace bond in April 2015 that included the condition that he not communicate on social media with a terrorist group or anyone in Syria, Turkey, or Malaysia.[146]

Twenty-year-old Seyed Amir Hossein Raisolsadat was arrested in Prince Edward Island with police alleging that he had beans that could produce the deadly toxin ricin, but no terrorism charges were laid. Instead, the University of Prince Edward Island chemistry student agreed to a peace bond requiring him to remain in Prince Edward Island, report to the police weekly, and be of good behaviour.[147]

Aaron Driver, a twenty-three-year-old Winnipeg man who had discovered and been converted to Islam online, was arrested in June 2015.[148] He refused to agree to a peace bond but after eight days in custody was released on bail subject to nineteen conditions. These included the wearing of a GPS bracelet, the surrender of his passport, a bar on computer use and possession of any object with ISIS or al-Qaida symbols, no contact with people from these groups, the restricted use of social media, a curfew, and an obligation to participate in "religious counselling."[149] He was re-arrested after a financial surety, his landlord, retracted her support because of comments Driver had made to the media defending the October terrorist attacks and the publicity the case had received, but again released on strict bail conditions. The case may remain in the news as Driver has indicated that he will challenge the peace bond process under the *Charter*.[150]

Stopping Departures and Missing Others

A number of students from the Collège de Maisonneuve in Montreal reportedly left Canada in January 2015. It is unclear whether they left to join ISIS or for other reasons. Another man, Sami Elabi, left Montreal for Syria in 2013 and posted a video in 2014 in which he burned and shot his Canadian passport.[151] Acting on tips from parents, the RCMP arrested ten young people, including four who attended the Collège de Maisonneuve, at the Montreal airport in May 2015. They were subsequently released without charge but with their passports confiscated.[152]

A week later, Prime Minister Harper announced increased funding for RCMP terrorism investigations at the same airport. He responded to these arrests by stating, "obviously we have great sympathy for the families affected," but "there is no legitimate reason of any kind in this country for someone to become a violent jihadist or a terrorist or to join any kind of group that is involved or advocates that kind of activity. It is totally unacceptable to Canada and Canadians and unacceptable to this government."[153]

V. CANADA'S PARTIAL RESPONSE TO THE ISIS THREAT

So given all this recent activity, how well is Canada doing in responding to the terrorist threat — especially that from foreign terrorist fighters? That is ultimately the topic of this entire book. Here, we simply raise recurring issues.

Canada started off well, but not perfectly. Parliament enacted a bill in 2013 adding four new terrorism offences to the *Criminal Code*. The original terrorism crimes enacted in 2001 could reach foreign terrorist fighting or aspiring foreign terrorist fighters, and in fact they did. Mohamed Hassan Hersi was convicted and sentenced to ten years "for attempting to participate in a terrorist activity."[154] The conviction followed Hersi's arrest at Toronto Pearson International Airport in March 2011 as he was about to leave for Cairo, Egypt. The prosecution argued successfully that Cairo would have been a stopover on his journey to Somalia, where Hersi had intended to join al-Shabaab.[155] The full story of this prosecution is told in Chapter 9.

But even if technically redundant, the new 2013 offences at least made the crime of foreign terrorist travel crystal clear, and there is value in such a clear statement of prohibited conduct. These offences criminalized leaving or attempting to leave Canada for the purpose of facilitating terrorism, participating in the activity of a terrorist group, committing an offence for a terrorist group, or committing an offence that is a terrorist activity.[156]

Creating New Hammers: "Other Kinds of Societal Programs, Such as Education and Outreach, Are Not within the Scope of This Bill."[157]

During its enactment, Senator Linda Frum explained that the government's impetus for the 2013 terrorism travel bill was "the recruitment of Canadians by terrorist groups who urge them to travel overseas to fight and engage in terrorist activity. These young people may not have any links or connections to terrorist groups or activities and may, in fact, be acting alone."[158] And she identified the Somali terrorist group al-Shabaab as possessing "one of the most effective Internet recruitment programs developed by extremist groups. It uses the Internet to encourage young people, including young Canadians, to leave their homes to engage in terrorist activities in Somalia and provides training for them in Somalia."[159]

For her part, Senator Mobina Jaffer responded that she was well aware and "not proud" of young men leaving to join al-Shabaab. But she also asked whether the bill responded to concerns expressed by some youths that "they have not felt included in our great country's fabric." Senator Romeo Dallaire amplified this concern: "disenfranchised youth, especially from Canada's Aboriginal and immigrant populations, can grow to present a national security threat." He added that Canadians "among the ranks of Somalia's al-Shabaab" can

threaten our country or simply the international community . . . . This could even influence our diasporas in our country. This is unacceptable.

This is bigger than law. This is the way we actually keep this country as a cohesive entity in order to continue to thrive into the future and not just survive. The question is, are we introducing legislation to survive, or are we bringing about legislation and other programs in which we will be able to thrive and to maximize these youth to their full potential?

Senator Dallaire also asked whether youth would be prosecuted under the new offences, noting, "then we run the risk of creating another situation like Omar Khadr's, which has been embarrassing for Canada and quite troublesome for our legal system."[160]

On behalf of the government, Senator Frum rejoined that the bill was only concerned with "anti-terrorism policies. Other kinds of societal programs, such as education and outreach, are not within the scope of this bill."[161]

And that, in a nutshell, is what is wrong with Canada's response to the threat: it is focused simply on punishment. The 2013 bill simply added four new criminal offences, punishable by a maximum of fourteen or ten years imprisonment, to the *Criminal Code* while also reinstating provisions for preventive arrests and investigative hearings discussed in Chapter 8.

The laws introduced in 2015 — bills C-44, C-51, and C-59 — are also simply tactical instruments, albeit ones that are much vaster in their reach. They provide government with a host of tools, many of them hard-nosed and focused on disruption. But the government has given no clear indication of how these tools will work together and, more generally, what our anti-terror strategy now is. We can deny suspected foreign terrorist fighters exit from Canada, but then what? Do we prosecute them all? And do we also prosecute all returned fighters? Or do we rely on peace bonds or CSIS disruption? Is there any role for education or outreach? Where is our endgame and exit strategy?

The limits of a hard-nosed approach are obvious. In a July 2015 report, the Senate security committee expressed concern and astonishment about Canada's modest record of criminal prosecutions:

[T]here are approximately 93 Canadians — so-called "high-risk travellers" — the authorities believe want to leave Canada to engage in terrorist activities . . . . [And] eighty Canadians have returned to Canada after participating with Islamist fundamentalist groups. Many of these people return with terrorist training, combat experience and may therefore pose a security risk to Canada. There have been relatively few charges, prosecutions or convictions for participating in or providing material support to the jihadist movement.[162]

The Senate committee is right that the rate of charges, described above, seems modest in the face of these numbers. So too is the rate of convictions since 9/11, discussed in Chapter 9. Part of this mismatch stems from resources — as we note repeatedly in this book, terrorism proceedings are expensive and protracted. And terrorism investigations are incredibly resource intensive. One recent British Columbia investigation, Project Souvenir, focused on the al-Qaida- or ISIS-inspired plan of John Nuttall and Amanda Korody to bomb the provincial legislature. The undercover RCMP "sting" culminating in their arrest lasted 128 days. A total of 249 police officers were involved at one time or another, with between 20 and 30 involved daily. Prosecutors submitted 102 hours of video and audio surveillance as evidence in the trial. The primary undercover officer testified in court for 47 days, and the trial lasted 4 months.[163] This sort of effort cannot be sustained over hundreds of cases.

And this was a relatively simple trial — the plot was a purely domestic one. But even then it was not over. As we finish this book, the defence is raising an entrapment complaint, arguing that police manipulated the defendants into their criminal actions. And the defence is seeking information concerning a possible related CSIS investigation into the plotters, arguing that it could shed light on the RCMP's conduct.[164]

As we will repeatedly argue, evidence and secrecy issues like these are the bugbear of Canadian anti-terror law. And they become instantly more complex when the discussion turns to foreign terrorist fighters. Foreign-terrorist-fighter convictions will often depend on prosecutors' proving beyond a reasonable doubt at least something about the accused's intended or past conduct in a war zone. The resulting evidentiary problems are daunting especially if the only available information comes from intelligence sources. Indeed, in the context of war crimes, Canada has struggled with prosecutions involving foreign conduct even in relation to conflicts that have ended and where investigations can now be brought in peacetime circumstances. These investigations have been expensive and protracted, and the outcome of prosecutions uncertain.[165] These experiences do not augur well for prosecutions brought contemporaneously with ongoing conflicts.

We see criminal law as an important — vital — tool in our anti-terror arsenal. It should be used more, and we should be thinking about how its use can be facilitated. But it must not be the only tool, and, indeed, there are times when criminal incarceration will be counterproductive. It is one thing to prosecute and incarcerate people for overseas depravities. But should every person who has left Syria disillusioned with that conflict be locked up regardless of his conduct in it? Perhaps, but if we decide on that course of action, we should do so attentive to Hegghammer's historical survey suggesting that only a small minority of returning foreign fighters have gravitated to domestic terrorism in the past.

And even prosecution and imprisonment requires an exit strategy. In this respect, we should heed observations made in 2012 by Canada's intelligence co-ordinating body, which noted that "Western Islamists" are sometimes "further radicalized in prisons in countries such as Canada, the United States, Britain, France and Spain."[166] Put another way, zealous and unremitting prosecution of foreign fighters, no matter what the circumstances, may be an overreaction, one that produces tomorrow's new terrorist menace.

All this means that criminal law alone is not an exit strategy from our security dilemmas. To be sure, criminal law is a necessary strategy but not a sufficient one. We need a bevy of different instruments in our toolkit, and they should include forms of outreach that will be discussed in Chapter 13. We need a strategy to guide the use of these tactics. And we need to have effective oversight, review, and evaluation of how the strategy is implemented, matters to which we return in Chapters 11 and 12.

Tactics without Strategy Is the Noise before Defeat

The government knows we need to do some serious strategic thinking, and at one point it seemed to be doing that. In 2012, Canada's first (and only) anti-terrorism strategy drew on an earlier United Kingdom equivalent.[167] It comprised four elements labelled "Prevent," "Detect," "Deny," and "Respond." In announcing the policy, the government explained as follows:

> First and foremost is prevention — because preventing terrorist ideologies from taking hold of vulnerable individuals is the best scenario. The Strategy also lays out how Canada works every day to detect individuals and organizations who may pose a terrorist threat; to deny terrorists the means and opportunities to carry out their attacks; and to respond to acts of terrorism in a manner that mitigates their effects.[168]

The announcement emphasized the need for "strong partnerships" with "local governments, communities, leaders, academics and citizens." And it pledged to promote greater engagement with Canadians to "build awareness, not fear." It also acknowledged the need for more learning: "How do we define and measure effectiveness? And, how do we determine if our programs are in fact working when success is measured by the absence of an event?"

We believe that all of these considerations are elemental in a successful anti-terror policy. And part of the promise of the new policy was realized through the Kanishka research project, currently set to expire in 2016. Among other things, this initiative helped create, for the first time, a consortium on anti-terror research, the Canadian Network for Research on Terrorism, Security and Society (TSAS). One of us sits on the executive and has benefitted from the wisdom assembled there and in the joint academic and government workshops that it organizes. And the research projects spearheaded under the umbrella of that organization have begun to change the landscape of our understanding. For instance, in Chapter 2, readers will already have encountered the TSAS-based statistical analysis of terrorism in Canada.

But in other respects, the 2012 policy appears largely to have disappeared in both public and government consciousness. In the flurry of legislative activity in 2015, the government made no real and persuasive effort to tie its new laws to the 2012 anti-terrorism strategy.

Nor did the government pay heed to other thinking applicable to antiterror policy. The Air India Commission of Inquiry proposed solutions for fixing the real impediment to close CSIS-RCMP co-operation, which stemmed from the unwillingness of CSIS to share intelligence that may be dragged into court as evidence. The earlier Arar Commission had laid out detailed ideas to address our outmoded national security review structure. A past Senate committee report proposed useful ideas on some of these same issues.[169] The Privacy Commissioner has named solutions to problems that impair that office's ability to protect privacy in national security matters.[170] CSIS's review body has repeatedly noted how its antiquated legal structure prevents it from "following the thread" when CSIS operations implicate other agencies, as they often do. Private member's bills have proposed viable systems of enhanced parliamentary review. As we discuss in many places in this book, none of this learning mattered in early 2015.

Unlike Australia and the United Kingdom, Canada has no independent reviewer of anti-terrorism law empowered to see secret information, to react to new government bills, to report on performance under existing laws, and generally to keep the big picture in mind while advising the public and parliamentarians on the wisdom or failings of the government's anti-terror laws and policies. Nor do Canada's parliamentarians see secret information, and when government officials speak to them, those officials generally do so in oblique and imprecise terms, preferring speaking lines to hard data. This is a huge strategic disadvantage. It means that there is no real independent counterweight to executive government in assessing the risks we face and assessing our responses to them. Secrecy means that we often do not know if the government has over- or underreacted until it is too late.

In the result, there is a real risk that we are now embarked on a strategy of accumulating new tactics without either a clear sense of what those tactics can and should achieve in the area of anti-terror or a commitment to open discussion and evaluation of how they fit together and work (or not).

Organizing a Re-think

We are in no position to conduct a re-think based on full and secret intelligence about the threat, but in this book we want to raise the core issues. In the chapters that follow, we will examine the range of new tools that were enacted in 2015 to deal with the terrorist threat and situate them in a broader context, including that of known cases of their use and often-rejected reform proposals. We will evaluate the strength and weakness of each of these instruments and also ask questions about how they fit together (or do not). As will be seen, the weaknesses of some of these tools often relate to the danger that they may constitute an overreaction to terrorism producing false positives — treating people as terrorists when they are not and violating their rights. At the same time, a weakness of some anti-terror tools is that they potentially underreact to terrorism. For example, "peace bonds for terrorists" or even increased powers of preventive arrest may constitute an underreaction for the minority of would-be or returned terrorist foreign fighters who may be willing to engage in violence in Canada.

Matching the appropriate instrument to the appropriate threat level in individual cases is, alas, more an imperfect art than an exact science. Therein lies some of the enduring challenges of anti-terrorism and the frequent and perhaps inevitable occurrence of under- and overreaction to a terrorist threat that is both evolving and real.

But we can certainly load the odds in our favour: to the extent that we labour under structural shortcomings that make us more prone to over- and underreaction, we must devote considerable attention to ensuring that anti-terrorism activities are subject to adequate review and oversight so that we can learn from mistakes and make necessary adjustments. In this book, we belabour concerns about how we have (dis)organized our anti-terror responses — most notably, in the way we structure and oversee the relationship between intelligence services and the police. This is a perennial source of underreaction including the difficulties that Canada has experienced in conducting terrorism prosecutions. And we raise preoccupations with our anemic review systems — now inadequate checks on overreaction. We also stress the need for new tools for whole-of-government oversight and responsibilities to ensure effective and rational co-ordination of our growing anti-terrorist toolkit.

Fixing these problems — or at least mitigating them — is within our means as a society, a topic we address in the last few chapters of the book. However, in the chapters immediately following this one, we begin our march through the existing tools in our toolkit.

The Threat Escalator

In approaching the toolkit, we have borrowed and then revised the approach suggested by Canada's 2012 anti-terrorism strategy: a list of objectives tied to escalating terrorist perils. We have, however, bundled these objectives differently to match them to particular types of threats.

To explain our approach, we borrow from Clark McCauley and Sophia Moskalenko's research on radicalization to violence. They propose an action radicalization pyramid, running from the politically inert at the base, through activists, to radicals, and then to terrorists at the much smaller pyramid tip.[171] As we discuss in Chapter 13, considerable caution is warranted in imagining that radicalization leads naturally to violence. A pyramid like this is not "stage theory" — it is not meant to imply that individuals progress along a railway track from one stage to another. Political ideology and grievance is not a conveyor belt to terrorist activity.[172] But the pyramid idea has the benefit of illustrating a hierarchy of risk while also communicating that the greatest risk is attributable to only a small subset of the larger pool of persons harbouring radical ideas.

We have departed from McCauley and Moskalenko's nomenclature by dividing the pyramid into four tranches:

- Neutral: a person who is presently unconnected to radicalization
- Apologist: a person who celebrates or justifies past acts of terrorist violence
- Extremist: a person who engages in a form of radicalized discourse or boasting, endorsing the full al-Qaida or ISIS worldview and political violence but without crossing the line to criminal incitement. Within this broad category, there may be people who authorities suspect are gravitating toward the criminal threshold and who pose a risk necessitating measures short of criminal arrest. This category could, therefore, be further subdivided. For example, the RCMP "High Risk Individual" framework is a form of triage prioritizing security files into one of four priorities: Priority 1 (in-country or inbound and presenting an immediate terrorist threat), Priority 2 (in-country and presenting a possible threat), Priority 3 (in-country and presenting a non-immediate threat), and Priority 4 (out of country).[173]
- Terrorist: a person who commits a terrorism offence

We then match the tranches on the threat escalation triangle with categories of anti-terror response tools (see Figure 3.1, below):

- Dissuade: multi-disciplinary counter–violent extremism programs (Chapter 13)

- Watch: surveillance and monitoring (Chapter 4)
- Share: information sharing (Chapter 5)
- Interdict: constraints on movement (Chapter 6)
- Restrain: constraints on liberty short of criminal incarceration (Chapter 7)
- Interrupt: tools to stop feared terrorist attacks when other measures are unavailable (Chapter 8)
- Prosecute: criminal incarceration (Chapter 9)
- Delete: prosecution and deletion of extremist speech (Chapter 10)

We portray the results graphically in Figure 3.1, below. With the exception of "dissuade" — a topic we address at the end of the book because it is so underdeveloped in Canada and is a critical reform requirement — our book follows the order of the threat escalator tools, travelling toward the apex of the radicalized action triangle. In our next chapter, we begin this process by addressing "watch," the tools of surveillance and monitoring.

Figure 3.1: The Anti-terror Threat Escalator

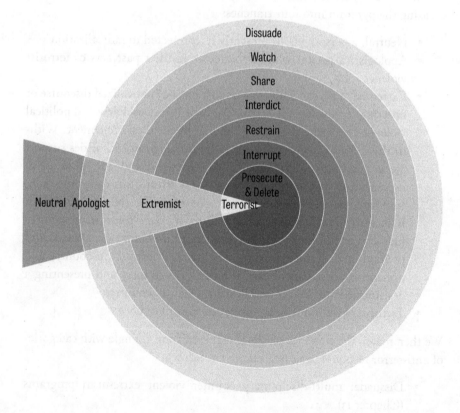

CHAPTER FOUR

Watch: Surveillance of Threats

I. INTRODUCTION

Crime

In March 2015, a jury found Chiheb Esseghaier and Raed Jaser guilty of a terrorist plot to destroy or derail a VIA Rail train between Toronto and New York. A substantial part of the evidence against the men — both non-Canadians living in Canada — stemmed from secretly recorded conversations they had held with an undercover FBI agent, often in person. Crown evidence in the case also relied heavily on evidence from what is known as a "Part VI" *Criminal Code* wiretap, which allows police to intercept "private communications" — often telecommunications. Absent the judicial wiretap authorization, police intercepts would be a crime. They would also infringe section 8 of the *Canadian Charter of Rights and Freedoms*, which guarantees that "[e]veryone has the right to be secure against unreasonable search or seizure."[1] Where this standard is violated, police generally cannot rely on the fruits of their surveillance in court. A duly authorized warrant is usually what makes a search reasonable and ensures that evidence obtained from it can be used in a criminal trial.

Police need evidence — not a lot, but some — to obtain one of these wiretap permissions in the first place. And in the VIA Rail investigation, a superior court judge authorized the police intercepts on the strength of evidence drawn from two surveillance wiretap warrants earlier issued by the Federal Court to CSIS and allowing that agency to eavesdrop. CSIS does its own spying — not to catch criminals but to investigate "threats to the security of Canada," a broadly defined understanding of national security found in the *Canadian Security Intelligence Service Act.*[2] Under that statute, CSIS must seek warrants for surveillance where on "reasonable grounds" it believes that a warrant is required to investigate security threats — in other words, in circumstances where absent the warrant CSIS would violate the reasonable expectation of privacy protected by section 8 of the *Charter.*

CSIS conveyed information from the Federal Court–authorized wiretaps to the RCMP through what are known as "advisory letters." These letters are carefully scribed and formal disclosures of CSIS information that police can then use for criminal investigation purposes. And police used the material from the advisory letter to obtain their Part VI warrant.

The defence counsel knew all of this because police investigative warrants and their supporting information are disclosed in the course of a criminal prosecution. And, indeed, even without a criminal trial, the existence of Part VI surveillance needs to be shared with the target after the end of an investigation and the passage of time.

But CSIS itself needed evidence — not a lot, but some — to persuade the Federal Court to issue its earlier warrants. And some of the supporting material used by CSIS — its core affidavit or sworn statement — to obtain its own warrants was not conveyed to the police as part of the advisory letter. CSIS guards against sharing its sources and methods even to the police for fear that those sources and methods will be disclosed to the accused under the broad disclosure obligations that apply in Canadian criminal trials. And so, as intended, the police were not able to give this affidavit document to the defence.

In the VIA Rail trial, defence lawyers sought the underlying CSIS affidavit. They wanted to see if, in obtaining its own warrants, CSIS had been sufficiently forthcoming with the Federal Court. If the defence lawyers could show that the CSIS warrants had been improperly obtained, then the Part VI police wiretap that depended on the CSIS surveillance information might itself be invalid for constitutional reasons. And this could well knock the police intercepts out of the trial. In other words, CSIS's intelligence warrant played a foundational role in the criminal trial, illustrating that "intelligence" and "evidence" are not watertight compartments.

But CSIS did not want to disclose to the defence the full content of its affidavit presumably because it would betray information on CSIS's sensitive sources or methods. The result was a delicate (and unusual) negotiation between CSIS, the prosecutors, and the criminal trial judge about which portions of this CSIS material could be disclosed to the defence without triggering protracted secrecy litigation in a parallel Federal Court process of the sort discussed in Chapter 9.

Only portions of the CSIS affidavit (or summaries of them) were then provided to the defence, who used them to attack the validity of the CSIS warrant. And in fact the trial court concluded that parts of the CSIS material used to obtain the original Federal Court CSIS warrant included misstatements and omissions, including in relation to the role of a confidential informer. But the trial judge found that the misstatements and omissions in the CSIS affidavit were not so serious as to invalidate the CSIS warrant, or cause a chain reaction that would knock the police intercept information out of the trial.

And so the police wiretap evidence remained available to the prosecutors. It was admitted into the criminal trial, and both men were convicted.[3]

Intelligence

In 2007, CSIS sought a surveillance warrant from the Federal Court to investigate "threat-related activities CSIS believed individuals would engage in while traveling outside of Canada."[4] As noted, CSIS is supposed to investigate "threats to the security of Canada," and since 1984 it has done just that. And when its surveillance has been sufficiently intrusive to trigger section 8 of the *Charter*, it has gone to the Federal Court to seek warrants.

But CSIS has usually directed its gaze inward, to threats on Canadian territory. This case was different and involved covert surveillance in a foreign country. The legal issues were novel. Indeed, there was doubt about whether and when the *Charter*'s section 8 protections reached beyond the territory of Canada — and that issue remains murky to this day. And so CSIS clearly acted with an abundance of caution in applying for a warrant.

The first Federal Court judge turned the warrant application down, concluding that the court had no power to issue a warrant extending outside the country for activities that were quite likely to violate foreign privacy laws and state sovereignty. But sometime after, another judge allowed a second warrant application covering some of the same people. He had been persuaded by CSIS's pledge that the intercepts, while directed overseas, would all be physically done in Canada.

In a remarkable sequence of events described at length in Chapter 11, the judge later learned that CSIS had sought, in association with Canada's own signals intelligence agency, the Communications Security Establishment (CSE), the assistance of so-called Five Eyes allied spy agencies — those of the United Kingdom, the United States, Australia, and New Zealand. Calling CSIS and its government lawyers back before him, the judge concluded that they had breached their duty of candour, the requirement to be perfectly frank with a judge deciding whether to issue a warrant. In an obvious reference to the Maher Arar case, discussed in Chapter 2, the trial judge also warned that once Canada lost control of intelligence, bad things can happen. He held that CSIS did not have the legal authority to seek Five Eyes assistance to spy in other countries and that no judge could authorize them to do so.[5]

Information Is the Currency of Prevention

These two case studies illustrate three important lessons. First, surveillance is closely connected with information sharing: making sure the fruits of the investigation go to the right people. This is a matter we examine closely in Chapter 5. But surveillance law in Canada is complicated and highly "judicialized" — that is, judges perform a form of oversight by pre-authorizing operational use of intrusive surveillance. In this book, we use the term "oversight" to describe precisely this sort of advance authorization or command and control of security agency activity.

Second, these case studies point to the practical importance of surveillance — "watch" — as an anti-terror tool in the toolkit proposed in Chapter 3. Every counter-terrorism investigation starts with information: an initial tip, a formal disclosure, a leak, or some other spark of data that prompts an investigation, which in turn then rifles out more information. Canada's 2012 counter-terrorism strategy brands this branch of activity "detect": "To counter the terrorist threat, knowledge is required on the terrorists themselves, their capabilities and the nature of their plans."[6]

Early detection is vital. Anti-terror investigations are often aimed at anticipating and pre-empting threats. In this environment, surveillance and monitoring of anticipated threats and timely distribution of relevant information between security and intelligence agencies are essential.

But there is a third lesson to be drawn from these case studies: the trade-off between the "watch" tool and privacy. Surveillance trenches on the right to be left alone. Excessive surveillance, and then the sharing of its fruits, raises the spectre of an omniscient state. Canada's Privacy Commissioner warned in 2005 that "the logic of anti-terrorism could permeate all spheres of law enforcement and public safety and this could result in large-scale systems of surveillance that will increasingly erode privacy rights in Canada."[7] Democracies tend, therefore, to be suspicious of the surveillance state, and they have been for a very long time. One further case study illustrates this point.

In the 1760s, British parliamentarian John Wilkes published an anonymous series of pamphlets critical of the King. Much irked, the King's officials issued a "general warrant" responding to this "seditious libel." This warrant authorized a search and arrest of those responsible. And it did so without specifying in any greater detail the identity of the persons against whom this power was to be exercised. Under this warrant, the Crown's henchmen ultimately arrested Wilkes and forty-nine others and seized papers after breaking into homes. Upon securing release from the Tower of London, Wilkes and several others sued the officials responsible for the warrant.

In a celebrated series of decisions,[8] the presiding judge, Lord Camden, invalidated the warrant. In relation to the forcible search of the houses, he observed, "there is no law in this country to justify the defendants in what they have done; if there was, it would destroy all the comforts of society; for papers are often the dearest property a man can have."[9]

This early "national security" case — perhaps one of the most famous decisions of the late eighteenth century — galvanized opinion in colonial America and was a clear impetus to what became the Fourth Amendment of the US Constitution:[10] "The right of the people to be secure in their persons, houses, papers, and effects, against unreasonable searches and seizures, shall not be violated, and no warrants shall issue, but upon probable cause, supported by oath or affirmation, and particularly describing the place to be searched, and the persons or things to be seized."

That amendment in turn was the inspiration for our own section 8 of the *Charter*. Briefer than its American counterpart, section 8 has come to guard the same United States–style requirements: intrusive searches must be authorized by a person able to act judicially, according to demanding expectations. Lord Camden's decision shaped a legal dichotomy that persists to this day between when a state can merely observe and when it can actively search and seize.

In this chapter, we examine how Canada's important "watch" tool works and where it faces serious challenges. Along the way, we highlight the significance of the 2015 anti-terror laws. While Bill C-51[11] did not expressly address watch, it will likely have implications for surveillance related to the bill's creation of a broad new speech crime that can be a predicate for surveillance. The bill also contemplates that CSIS can delegate some of its new threat disruption activities, even when conducted under warrant, to other traditional "watchers" including CSE and even potentially to foreign agencies, companies, or other persons. For its part, Bill C-44[12] was motivated largely by a desire to enhance CSIS's watch arsenal and to ensure that CSIS could be authorized to engage in surveillance outside of Canada. We also discuss the implications of an important 2014 law: Bill C-13, *Protecting Canadians from Online Crime Act*.[13]

In this chapter, we touch on themes that recur throughout book: the tension between rights and security, the difficulties of co-ordinating activities between different security services, the permeable border between the national and the international with respect to transnational terrorism, the occasional incoherence of governing law and the opacity of government decision making under it, the importance of serious command-and-control oversight, and the need for robust back-end independent review that audits security service activity against standards of law and propriety.

II. SURVEILLANCE 101

The state can spy on you. But if its spying interferes with a "reasonable expectation of privacy," it must be authorized by a carefully crafted judicial warrant to be constitutional.

This rule originates in those famous Lord Camden common law cases of the 1760s, as developed through later caselaw under the constitutional rules of the United States and now Canada. It is essential to appreciate, however, how this Camden model was first and foremost a response to physically intrusive state interventions.

Lord Camden's decisions cannot properly be read without an eye to an older common law tradition codified by the expression that an "Englishman's castle is his home." Boiled to its essence, this colourful chestnut is a celebration of a personal sovereignty over physical property. The Camden paradigm protects property because it constrains state access to these zones of personal sovereignty. Put another way, in its inception, the Camden model was about protecting geography and not about limiting access to information. Certainly, in its defence of geography, Camden operated to protect information, but only incidentally and only in an information-poor world. In such a world, tangible information is found in specific locations, for example an office desk where letters are stored, and access to this information requires a physical intrusion of the state into these places. So personal sovereignty over spaces equates to control over the information found in them.

Round Peg, Square Hole

All of this is to say that the Camden model was originally designed to protect privacy in a now bygone era in which information always had a specific geography. It works when what the state wants to spy on is in the confines of your house, with shades drawn.

But as soon as you venture out from your proverbial castle, your rights become more doubtful, and the state's power to spy more sweeping. And more than that, the Camden model works awkwardly when the information that the government wishes to collect becomes more mobile and more vulnerable to intercept beyond the brick and mortar of the castle. Your house may be your castle; the Internet cloud may not be.

In the 1920s, the new frontier for privacy was telephone communications. What relevance did the Camden model of privacy have for this form of distance-spanning conversing? In *Olmstead v United States*,[14] a majority of the US Supreme Court answered, "none." The Court held that "[t]he language of the Amendment cannot be extended and expanded to include telephone wires reaching to the whole world from the defendant's house or office. The intervening wires are not part of his house or office any more than are the highways along which they are stretched."[15]

This position was met by a forceful dissent by Justice Brandeis, one of the first notable purveyors of a self-standing concept of privacy. Brandeis warned of an unduly narrow construction of the Fourth Amendment, hinging on geography and the physical nature of the intrusion. He argued that what mattered was any government interruption of the right to be left alone — that is, of privacy.

Surveillance Privacy and New Technologies

Brandeis's position, if not his precise approach, was adopted decades later by the US Supreme Court in *Katz v United States*,[16] a decision that later heavily influenced the Canadian Supreme Court's approach to section 8 of the *Charter* in the pivotal *Hunter v Southam*[17] decision, which prevails into the current period.

Another wiretap case, *Katz* (and specifically Justice Harlan's concurring decision) is the origin of the "reasonable expectation of privacy" doctrine — that is, the protections of the Fourth Amendment require "first that a person have exhibited an actual (subjective) expectation of privacy and, second, that the expectation be one that society is prepared to recognize as 'reasonable.'"[18]

The concept of reasonable expectations of privacy guides application of constitutional search and seizure protections to this day in the American and Canadian legal traditions. The central idea behind the cases relating to this concept was that privacy protects people and all their reasonable expectations of privacy, and not only their physical places such as their homes.

Yet while *Katz* abandoned an exclusive preoccupation with physical intrusion in a constitutionally protected geographic *place*, it still concerned itself with *zones*, that is, circumstances where a person can be said to enjoy personal sovereignty because of the reasonable expectation of privacy. *Katz* did not convert the Camden paradigm into a self-standing protection of information itself. Refinements ever since have focused on circumscribing the scope of the "zone."

A Jurisprudence as Clear as Mud

So, for instance, in the Canadian caselaw, privacy interests include "informational privacy."[19] Exactly what this category includes is a matter of judgment. The Supreme Court of Canada has said that "s. 8 of the Charter should seek to protect a biographical core of personal information which individuals in a free and democratic society would wish to maintain and control from dissemination to the state. This would include information which tends to reveal intimate details of the lifestyle and personal choices of the individual."[20]

What this means in practice is often in the eye of the beholder. Thus, for most judges in a Supreme Court case about police access to hydro bills in an investigation of a suspected grow-op, "[d]isclosing information about electricity consumption is not invasive nor revelatory of the respondent's private life." A dissenting minority came to the exact inverse position,[21] demonstrating how utterly subjective the Camden model (applied in the new world of footloose information) can be.

Another frontier issue raising similar questions is whether individuals have a reasonable expectation of privacy in relation to digital trails that they may leave on the Internet. Here, the Court has continued to decide the matter on a case-by-case basis and perhaps with imperfect consistency.

And so in the 2014 *R v Spencer* decision the Court updated the Camden paradigm for the Internet age.[22] *Spencer* was about Internet subscriber data in a police investigation of child pornography. The information in question was the name, address, and telephone number of the customer associated with a particular IP (Internet protocol) address. It was, in other words, the most benign form of data attached to an IP address. In a nutshell, the Court nevertheless held that the *Charter*'s section 8 protections against unreasonable searches and seizures extended to this subscriber data. In key passages, the Court wrote:

> [T]he police request to link a given IP address to subscriber information was in effect a request to link a specific person (or a limited number of persons in the case of shared Internet services) to specific online activities. This sort of request engages the anonymity aspect of the informational privacy interest by attempting to link the suspect with anonymously undertaken online activities, activities which have been recognized by the Court in other circumstances as engaging significant privacy interests . . . .[23]

The Court's recognition of the concept of anonymity as part of the interests protected by section 8 is potentially revolutionary — it goes to the heart of one of the key dilemmas in our current information-rich environment, discussed below: is the electronic superstructure of communications — metadata — protected by the *Charter*'s privacy rules?

But still the vital "reasonable expectation of privacy" undergirding any section 8 analysis will always depend on what the Court calls the "totality of circumstances." And this foggy concept translates into something uncomfortably close to a "gut test." More than this, the Court so far seems inclined to extend the reach of conventional *exceptions* to the warrant requirement to new technologies despite the very dramatic implications these exceptions have when applied to the new data machines.

For instance, only months after *Spencer*, the Court concluded that police were constitutionally entitled to search smartphones located on the persons of those lawfully arrested without a warrant subject to several (probably unsustainable in practice) safeguards.[24] Conventional "searches incident to arrest" exceptions to the warrant requirement make sense to, among other things, protect the police and the public from concealed weapons. But they are much more concerning when extended to handheld computers in common use and capable of holding more data than a fair-sized library — and much more intimate and personal data at that.

Big Data and Quaint Law

In sum, the Camden model of traditional geographic-based privacy protection struggles to accommodate the "right to be left alone" in our technological era. Piecemeal judicial determinations like *Spencer* renew this classic protection and prolong its life, but the traditional model may be on life support, and *Spencer*-style decisions may constitute the last battles of an unsustainable war. That is because we now live in an information-rich era. In terms of sheer quantum, the bytes of data flowing through this information-rich period dwarf what has come before. In the computer age, data are accessible, transmissible, and retainable in manners hardly envisaged a decade ago, let alone by Lord Camden.

And so there is a disconnect between the information-rich computer era and the Camden paradigm of privacy protection. It is not that this disconnect is new; rather it is that in an information-rich environment, the disconnect risks swamping the protections offered by the Camden model, giving it an almost quaint quality. This is one reason why firm rules on what can be done with information once collected — information sharing — are as important as rules on when information can be collected by the state in the first place. Judicial protections geared to the acquisition of information will only provide partial protections of privacy if they do not extend to the subsequent sharing and use of the information.

III. NATIONAL SECURITY SURVEILLANCE IN CANADA

The challenges of privacy in the modern age and the limitations of the traditional approach to the protection of privacy are apparent in anti-terror investigations.

In Canada, an alphabet soup of government agencies collects information. But a smaller subset engages in true invasive searches, including intrusive forms of surveillance that would be unlawful and unconstitutional without court authorization. CSIS and the RCMP (and other police forces) have search and seizure powers in the area of national security. The CSE, Canada's signals intelligence service, has a more complicated role when it comes to spying on Canadians and persons in Canada.

Law Enforcement: Police

Wiretapping Private Communications

The police powers of intrusive surveillance are long-standing and stem potentially from a number of sources in the *Criminal Code*. But the key electronic intercept authority is found in Part VI of the *Criminal Code*, a series of provisions first introduced in 1974 as a special protection against electronic eavesdropping in a pre-*Charter* era. It represents a traditional Camden model for the protection of privacy.

Part VI applies to "private communication," basically any "oral communication" or any "telecommunication" made by someone in Canada or intended by that person to be received by another in Canada in the reasonable belief that it will not be intercepted by someone else. Unauthorized intercept of a private communication by anyone (government agencies included) is a crime.[25] But there are exceptions. Peace officers, for instance, may intercept private communications in emergencies to stop serious harm to a person or property.[26]

More typically, though, a judge must first authorize the intercept — a practice that predates section 8 of the *Charter* but that is now demanded by it. Police must have reasonable grounds to believe that intercepts will assist in investigating a crime. And in the usual case, judges issue authorizations where satisfied that the intercept would "be in the best interests of the administration of justice" and where persuaded that the intercept is the last, best investigative tool available to police.[27]

The rules for terrorism investigations are more relaxed: there is no need for the judge to be satisfied that the intercept is the last available option. Intercept authorizations for anti-terror investigations may also last longer — for up to one year.[28] Moreover, under Part VI, the surveillance target is supposed to be notified eventually of the wiretap — but police in anti-terror investigations may more easily obtain extensions delaying this notification.[29] These more forgiving standards in terrorism investigations contribute to what senior government lawyer Stanley Cohen has described as the post-9/11 state's "enlarged capacity to peer into the individual's private life," including its power to "examine the trappings of simple associations and lifestyle, and ambiguous activities that the jurisprudence has often described as 'mere preparation.'"[30]

Following Electronic Trails

The rules governing intercept of computer data are more uncertain and complex. There have, for instance, been debates about whether email communications fall within the special Part VI system for intercept of "private communication," discussed above, or instead whether they are a form of written communication stored in computers and subject to regular search warrants.[31] Likewise, the precise status of direct "text messages" sent between mobile devices, and which warrant regime they fall within, has been disputed all the way to the Supreme Court.[32]

These debates are highly technical, even for lawyers. But they are important. For instance, in the aftermath of the Supreme Court's groundbreaking *Spencer* decision in 2014, it is no longer permissible for police to ask service providers to provide even basic data about Internet subscribers without a warrant. This has greatly complicated the more informal way in which police once investigated computer-based activity, much to their disgust.

Although the government may be trying to confine *Spencer* to its facts,[33] the decision does bring what are known as metadata within the Camden paradigm. These metadata have been compared to "data on data" — that is, they constitute the contextual information that surrounds the content of an Internet transaction or communication. In a 2013 report, the Privacy Commissioner of Ontario compared metadata to "digital crumbs" that reveal "time and duration of a communication, the particular devices, addresses, or numbers contacted, which kinds of communications services we use, and at what geolocations."[34]

But in *Spencer*, the Court never addressed "what sort of warrant" is now required for this electronic spillover information. It just suggested that some sort of judicial pre-authorization is required. The government then finished pushing through Parliament its controversial 2014 bill, C-13, which it billed as a "cyberbullying" law.[35] But this new statute also established special new judicial authorization regimes to search new sorts of data created by technology — including metadata (called "transmission data" in the law). Now, a judge may authorize the use by peace officers of a transmission data recorder where there are "reasonable grounds to suspect" that a criminal offence has been or will be committed and that the data will aid the investigation.[36] Or a judge may order disclosure of this information in the possession of a person — typically an Internet service provider — to the peace officer on a similar standard.[37]

This standard — reasonable suspicion — is an increasing favourite of the government, and it was later littered throughout Bill C-51. But it is a much lower standard than that usually associated with the Camden model — reasonable grounds to believe (sometimes labelled reasonable and probable grounds).[38] For definitions of the "suspect" versus the "belief" standards, readers may wish to refer to the annex to Chapter 1. For our purposes, reasonable suspicion amounts to the lowest evidentiary threshold in Canadian law, one that has been associated with brief stops by the police and the use of sniffer dogs, not with access to one's communication history, as revealed by metadata, or putting someone on the no-fly list (as Bill C-51 allows, and is discussed in Chapter 6). Put another way, Parliament is making it easier for authorities to get hold of "data about data" than it would be to, for instance, intercept actual voice communications. At some level, this more relaxed standard for seemingly banal metadata makes sense — but only if one ignores the real significance of this information.

Metadata are stored by communications providers potentially indefinitely and are amendable to compilation, linking, and tracing. Metadata can be used to paint a quite intimate portrait: work and sleep habits, travel patterns, and relationships with others. From these data, observers may develop detailed inferences about places of employment, patterns and means of travel, frequency of visits to doctors and pharmacies, visits to "social or commercial establishments," religious and political affiliations, and the like.[39]

Reviewing this kind of information may be more invasive of privacy than even intercepting the actual content of communications. Massachusetts Institute of Technology computer scientist Daniel Weitzner considers metadata to be "arguably more revealing [than content] because it's actually much easier to analyze the patterns in a large universe of metadata and correlate them with real-world events than it is to through a semantic analysis of all of someone's email and all of someone's telephone calls . . . ."[40]

Metadata associated with Internet use may also reveal notable amounts of personal information. A study by the Privacy Commissioner of Canada concluded that subscriber information such as IP addresses[41] may "provide a starting point to compile a picture of an individual's online activities, including: online services for which an individual has registered; personal interests, based on websites visited; and organizational affiliations."[42]

Even more concerning than the direct privacy implications of metadata is the amalgamation of these data with other information, a process that some have called "Big Data." One definition of "Big Data," a colloquial expression, is "the storage and analysis of large and/or complex data sets using a series of [computer-based] techniques."[43] Big Data may involve the linking together of discrete and separate pieces of information to create a mosaic portrait of a person's life.

What Bill C-13 does is deploy a (watered-down) Camden model for metadata without taking a step back and considering whether that model manages the duelling preoccupations of privacy versus public safety in a sustainable or sensible manner. It responds to changes in communications technology producing metadata simply by lowering the standard for searches to reasonable suspicion. It will, of course, be challenged on constitutional grounds.

Bill C-51 and Opening the Door to Spying on Speaking

Bill C-51 is not a surveillance law, but it does have surveillance-related implications for police "watch" powers. These implications stem from the knock-on effect of the new speech crime that Bill C-51 enacts. The government may now jail people who by speaking, writing, recording, gesturing, or through other visible representations "knowingly advocate or promote the commission of terrorism offences in general" while at minimum aware of the possibility that the offences may be committed.[44]

As we argue at length in Chapter 10, the outer limit of this new offence is not clear — "terrorism offences" is a sweeping concept in Canadian law, and that sweep is increased to a potentially astonishing degree by the new offence's invocation of "terrorism offences in general." We have serious doubts whether it is consistent with the free speech protections found in section 2 of the *Charter*. The new crime is capable of reaching what we call radicalized boasting — expressions of radical views far distant from actual terrorist violence.

And while it sits on the books, it will have important side-effects. If radicalized boasting is now a crime, even if conducted in a private conversation, the state is authorized to use investigative tools to detect such behaviour. The new Bill C-51 speech crime would justify computer metadata searches on the relaxed reasonable grounds to suspect standard. And it is yet another "terrorism offence" that justifies the special, more easily obtained, Part VI terror-crime wiretap warrants, in this case aimed at detecting the wrong kind of vocalized thoughts. And, of course, to detect the wrong type of speech, police may need to monitor all sorts of other speech during which the bad things might be said.

This means that while Bill C-51 says nothing about wiretaps, it has the effect of increasing the range of circumstances in which police may obtain intercept authorizations.

Security Intelligence Spying: CSIS

Bill C-51 does not affect CSIS's spying authority — it is instead directed at expanding the range of things that CSIS can do on top of spying, as discussed in Chapter 8. Nevertheless, the distinction between threat reduction, especially when assisted by CSE or other watchers, and surveillance may be a thin one.

A Cacophony of Different Standards

Bill C-13, enacted in 2014, also does not affect CSIS directly. But it does create an awkward disjuncture between when CSIS and when the police can collect electronic communication metadata.

Under CSIS's rules in the *CSIS Act*, there is one warrant process for all sorts of searches — everything from wiretaps to rifling through dresser drawers — that applies regardless of what is being searched. As already noted, CSIS seeks a Federal Court warrant where it "believes, on reasonable grounds, that a warrant . . . is required to enable the Service to investigate a threat to the security of Canada." It may also seek a warrant on the same standard to assist (from within Canada) the minister of national defence in "the collection of information or intelligence relating to the capabilities, intentions or activities of . . . any foreign state or group of foreign states."[45]

But after Bill C-13, the police may obtain a warrant to collect metadata for criminal investigation purposes on a lower standard than is available to CSIS in its national security investigations. Specifically, the police now need only show reasonable grounds to "suspect" while CSIS must still meet the reasonable "belief" standard.

This kind of discrepancy may be sufficiently subtle to worry only lawyers, but it raises the usual sort of coherence and interpretation headaches. Police presumably will be able to share metadata they collect, under the regular *Privacy Act* justifications and the information sharing regime in Bill C-51, discussed in Chapter 5. And so depending on how these very uncertain rules are interpreted, CSIS may have indirect access to data that CSIS itself could not legally collect but that might still be shared by police under permissive information sharing laws. Indeed, CSIS often receives more information from the police than it gives to the police for complex reasons that will be explored in Chapter 9. This suggests that the police will use their new powers under Bill C-13 to feed metadata to CSIS.

Exactly who will review this practice of information sharing from the police to CSIS and how carefully are perplexing questions. Independent review of security and intelligence agencies is discussed in Chapter 12. There, we describe the extent to which back-end compliance auditing — review — varies among security agencies and the extent to which review bodies are prohibited from close joint investigations, even while the agencies they scrutinize collaborate. In particular, we note that the RCMP is subject to what may prove a weaker review regime than CSIS, again magnifying our concerns about the police giving CSIS information under Bill C-13 that CSIS might not otherwise be able to obtain directly.

For our purposes here, we note simply that the sort of anomalies created by Bill C-13 reveal the extent to which the state's response to technology, surveillance, and law reform is a series of Band-Aid and ad hoc solutions, not a systematic re-think. This approach creates a danger that the restrictions placed on one security actor, such as CSIS, can be circumvented by relying on another security actor, such as the police, that may have broader legal authorities and may be subject to less onerous forms of independent review.

Spies without Borders

Coherence problems also arise in the area of international spying. We discussed at the beginning of this chapter the conundrum faced by CSIS as it seeks to survey covertly Canadians travelling abroad. When and if a court can authorize spying in violation of a foreign law and when and if CSIS can act without such a warrant were contested legal issues.

The other key 2015 anti-terror law — Bill C-44[46] — tried to resolve this issue, but it did so in a manner creating new legal doubts. That law now makes it abundantly clear that CSIS security intelligence investigations may be conducted "within or outside Canada."[47] The more interesting alteration is in the amendments to the Federal Court warrant provisions. These amendments permit CSIS to seek and obtain a warrant from the Federal Court for overseas investigations. And "[w]ithout regard to any other law, including that of any foreign state, a judge may, in a warrant . . . , authorize activities outside Canada to enable the Service to investigate a threat to the security of Canada."[48]

This new approach could produce a distinctively Canadian version of allied intelligence agencies infamous for their disregard of foreign and international law. It is too much to say that under the combined bills C-44 and C-51, CSIS would mimic, say, the CIA's foreign adventures, and especially its paramilitary roles. But it is now certainly the case that foreign and international law are no obstacle to the exercise of CSIS's powers.

Politically, it will be awkward for the Federal Court to bless violations of foreign law and foreign state sovereignty — each judge must be acutely aware of the reputational consequences, personal and institutional, of a CSIS foreign operation that goes wrong, complete with revelations of an undergirding warrant. But legally the Bill C-44 change likely lies within the competence of Parliament, although the matter is not without doubt.[49] In the Canadian system of parliamentary sovereignty, Parliament generally has the power to legislate a departure from international law so long as it is sufficiently emphatic in doing so.[50]

However, the new warrant-power amendment creates its own uncertainty. Namely, it is not clear when CSIS is actually *obliged* to obtain a foreign surveillance warrant. Even after Bill C-44, the *CSIS Act* simply instructs CSIS to seek a warrant where it believes "on reasonable grounds that a warrant is required." In a domestic surveillance operation, these grounds arise when failure to obtain a warrant would violate section 8 of the *Charter*, or the criminal prohibition on unauthorized intercepts in Part VI of the *Criminal Code*. But the applicability of these two laws — and especially the *Charter* — to matters outside Canada's borders (and thus to foreign surveillance) is uncertain. This is especially so because the *Charter* generally does not reach outside of the country's borders. In *R v Hape*,[51] the RCMP had conducted an overseas criminal investigation with the express consent of the foreign authorities and in partnership with them. The Supreme Court looked to international law and the principle of the comity of nations to construe the reach of the *Charter* and concluded that section 8 of the *Charter* did not reach the RCMP's conduct in that case.

As a consequence, the existing "reasonable grounds" threshold that obliges CSIS to seek a warrant is unhelpfully ambiguous when applied to the new warrant powers in this bill. Given *Hape*, when should CSIS reasonably believe that it needs a warrant, as opposed to its having the power to act on its own?

It may be that the courts will ultimately decide that a warrant is required whenever foreign surveillance involves covert interception of telecommunications. It may also be the case that a court will construe the provision as requiring a warrant any time an operation may violate international or foreign law. These would be sensible standards, ones that extend beyond surveillance and might also affect the approach taken with the other sorts of CSIS powers created by Bill C-51 and discussed in Chapter 8. These two threshold standards would also constitute an approach consistent with the overall structure of the *CSIS Act*. After Bill C-44, CSIS's governing law emphatically specifies that CSIS may perform its security intelligence investigations "within or outside Canada." It does not, however, go on to specify that CSIS may do so in violation of foreign and international law.

The only place where Parliament has currently anticipated actions in violation of foreign or other (e.g., international) law is in relation to the new competency of Federal Court judges to issue warrants for overseas CSIS investigations. In this manner, the Federal Court warrant becomes the gateway to any international law violation — the only gateway. Passing through this gateway is, therefore, the only conceivable manner in which CSIS's mandate can be construed as reaching violations of international law.

It follows that the trigger for the warrant under the new Bill C-44 regime is every circumstance where CSIS believes on reasonable grounds that foreign or international law might be violated. If CSIS acts in one of these circumstances without a warrant, it acts outside of its jurisdiction and therefore unlawfully. Under this view, CSIS would seek to obtain the protective cover of a warrant before it violated foreign or international law.

Superimposing a judge onto these circumstances would at least avoid awkward legal gaps. Unless a Federal Court warrant is triggered by invasive extraterritorial surveillance, neither foreign nor Canadian privacy law is brought to bear on the operation. And, in the result, whatever safeguards exist do so entirely at the discretion of the Canadian executive government. The result would be a legal black hole of the type that may be associated with CIA conduct, such as renditions.

But because the bill is not emphatic, establishing the proper standard triggering CSIS's obligation to seek an extraterritorial warrant may require another round of litigation. As we discuss in Chapter 12, the Federal Court warrant process is a one-sided affair, in which the government is the only party along with at best an *amicus curiae*, or "friend of the court," providing some challenge function. The warrant process is also a deeply secret process, and (unlike Part VI warrants) CSIS warrants are never disclosed outside of comparatively rare circumstances, like those in the VIA Rail trial, where they are material in later criminal proceedings. The Federal Court decisions leading to CSIS warrants are also rarely disclosed — although the court has a policy of releasing redacted versions of cases that raise important legal issues.

In the result, the standards applicable to CSIS's new foreign surveillance warrants will be decided behind closed doors, and the outcome may not be entirely clear to anyone outside of government. This reality affirms the importance of robust independent review of CSIS conduct by its review body, SIRC, another subject of Chapter 12.

A Roving Electronic Eye: The Communications Security Establishment

We turn now to the third member of the key "watcher" triumvirate: CSE. CSE is the Canadian version of the National Security Agency, the US signals intelligence agency made (in)famous by the Edward Snowden revelations. There is nothing in the 2015 legislation that mentions CSE. Nevertheless, CSE will be an important player in implementing the new powers provided to the police and especially CSIS.

Some background is required to understand this assertion. By law, CSE's mandate is to acquire and use "information from the global information infrastructure for the purpose of providing foreign intelligence" (Mandate A); to provide "advice, guidance and services to help ensure the protection of electronic information and of information infrastructures of importance to the Government of Canada" (Mandate B); and to provide "technical and operational assistance to federal law enforcement and security agencies in the performance of their lawful duties" (Mandate C).[52] In other words, CSE is principally an electronic eavesdropping agency that collects what is known as "signals intelligence" or SIGINT.

To perform any spying, CSE must be lawfully authorized to do so, that is, it must be able to lawfully access the electronic data. CSE may spy on foreigners and on Canadians, but the rules that apply to each of these scenarios are radically different. Put bluntly, for foreign spying there are no real legislated rules; this is a legal black hole. For spying that may implicate Canadians there are several legislated provisos.

Spying for Other Agencies

Mandate C, described above, is the most straightforward scenario, especially with respect to domestic spying.

A Helping Hand

Here, CSE may assist other government agencies — such as CSIS or the RCMP — in intercepting information and providing technological wherewithal that these other agencies may not have. Given the mandate of most of these bodies, these intercepts could involve Canadians or communications within Canada (although, for its part, the RCMP has said that it does not call on CSE to "target Canadians").[53]

Such domestic and Canadian-related intercepts would be legal only if the other agency (typically CSIS or the RCMP) itself has lawful authority for the intercept. In other words, CSE can act as a technological appendage of the other two key watchers where those watchers themselves are acting lawfully. Put yet another way, CSE may spy on Canadians on behalf of CSIS or the RCMP where those agencies themselves are lawfully permitted to perform the surveillance.[54] The legal authority exercised by the requesting agency creates a safe harbour for CSE.

The 2015 Laws and Assistance to Partners

That means that to the extent lawful CSIS and police powers expand, so too does the possible scope of CSE's operations in support of these agencies under its Mandate C. In principle, CSE may provide technological assistance to the RCMP in executing its lawful searches for the speech barred by Bill C-51's new speech crime.

CSE will unquestionably be involved in CSIS's extraterritorial spying, now firmly authorized by Bill C-44. And CSE will almost certainly provide assistance to CSIS where CSIS engages in threat reduction activities, that is, physical steps to reduce threats to the security of Canada, discussed in Chapter 8, now authorized by Bill C-51. In one of the few specific statements made about how these new CSIS powers might be used, CSIS director Coulombe focused on "disrupting a financial transaction done through the Internet, disabling mobile device use in support of terrorist activities, and tampering with equipment that would be used in support of terrorist activities."[55] Such an approach to the use of the new powers would combine surveillance with disruption.

The technological wherewithal to perform these and related electronic disruptions may lie in CSE, not CSIS. Indeed, Edward Snowden's 2013 disclosures, discussed further below, point to a sophisticated "offensive" CSE electronic interference ability.[56] This is exactly the sort of aptitude that CSE might now be expected to deploy under its Mandate C, described above, in support of CSIS's Bill C-51 powers.[57]

Scrutinizing an enhanced CSE-CSIS or CSE-RCMP relationship will fall on the review bodies for each of these agencies. Unfortunately, as discussed in Chapter 12, these accountability bodies are restricted in the extent to which they can carefully scrutinize joint security service operations — each review body is "siloed" to its own agency and cannot share confidential information in a manner permitting joint reviews.

Spying under Its Own Steam

The legal situation with CSE's Mandates A and B is much more complex. Under its Mandate A, CSE can collect "foreign intelligence" — that is, "information or intelligence about the capabilities, intentions or activities of a foreign individual, state, organization or terrorist group, as they relate to international affairs, defence or security."[58] Much (probably almost all) of this foreign intelligence is just that: foreign. There is no Canadian or person in Canada implicated in the intercepted communication. Here, the law does not prescribe any specific rules on intercept authorizations. This is a legal black hole that opens the door in principle to a no-holds-barred approach to activities in foreign states.

No Targeting of Canadians

On the other hand, CSE's rules insist that its Mandate A foreign intelligence activities and also its Mandate B computer system security functions shall "not be directed at Canadians or any person in Canada; and . . . shall be subject to measures to protect the privacy of Canadians in the use and retention of intercepted information."[59]

Squaring this expectation with the reality of webbed or networked communication is challenging. In a world whose telecommunications systems are networked together, even "foreign intelligence" may have a Canadian nexus — for instance, it may be that a telephone call sent to or originating in Canada might be intercepted. Similarly, CSE surveillance may capture the communication of a Canadian located overseas. As the government has acknowledged, "the complexity of the global information infrastructure is such that it is not possible for CSE to know ahead of time if a foreign target will communicate with a Canadian or person in Canada, or convey information about a Canadian."[60] Some Canadian material will incidentally be caught in CSE's broad net.

The Metadata Challenge

The issue of incidental capture of Canadian-origin data is particularly acute with CSE's collection of metadata,[61] an issue that came to public attention after Edward Snowden's 2013 disclosures. Snowden — a "leaker" or "whistleblower" depending on one's perspective — ignited a mainstream (and social) media frenzy in mid-2013 by sharing details of classified US National Security Agency surveillance programs with the *Guardian* and *Washington Post* newspapers.[62]

The US National Security Agency, one of those Five Eyes spy services with which Canada's CSE partners, collects and archives metadata on millions of Internet and telecommunication users.[63] The National Security Agency revelations fuelled media, academic, and other speculation about whether similar surveillance programs exist in Canada. That attention focused on CSE. In 2013, journalists unearthed tantalizing clues concerning a Canadian metadata project.[64] In early 2014, a Snowden document pointed to some sort of CSE metadata-analysis project implicating travellers accessing the WiFi (wireless) network at a Canadian airport.[65] More recent disclosures point to a powerful CSE ability to extract massive quantities of data from the international electronic communications infrastructure.[66]

These revelations prompted questions about the legal basis for any collection initiative[67] and the extent to which CSE was governed by robust accountability mechanisms. They also sparked an ongoing constitutional lawsuit brought by the British Columbia Civil Liberties Association.[68] Part of that lawsuit will focus on whether the metadata collected by CSE differ from the personal papers at issue in the Lord Camden decisions. Or, put more concretely, are metadata information of a sort that gives rise to the sort of privacy protections Lord Camden was defending and that is now protected under our constitution?

Mind the (Accountability) Gap

Until the resolution of this *Charter* challenge, metadata collected by CSE now escape Camden-style rules.

CSE's law does recognize that "there may be circumstances in which incidental interception of private communications or information about Canadians will occur."[69] The law permits the minister of national defence to issue a "ministerial authorization" authorizing CSE to collect "private communications" in performing its Mandate A and B functions, described above, where persuaded that satisfactory privacy protections are in place. "Private communications" in CSE's law is defined in the same way as it is in Part VI of the *Criminal Code* — basically, telecommunications originating from or directed at a person in Canada.

In practice, ministerial authorizations have been issued on a just-in-case basis — that is, because one can never be sure that the communications intercepted will lack a Canadian nexus, authorizations are sought regularly to make sure that CSE remains on-side the law. Compared to warrants issued by judges in police investigations (and those in CSIS investigations), ministerial authorizations are general, relating to a class of activities rather than to specific individuals or targets. Still, this looks a little bit like a conventional Camden-style approach.

But looks are deceptive for two reasons. First, this model possesses the trappings of the Camden model of independent pre-authorization but fails to honour its specifics. CSE is conducting searches that, by the government's own acknowledgement, capture (however incidentally) the sort of private communications protected by section 8 of the *Charter*. But these searches are never authorized through a warrant issued by *someone able to act judicially*. Instead, the minister of national defence — currently Jason Kenney — issues the authorization. The minister's exact statutory duty under the *National Defence Act* is to manage and direct "all matters relating to national defence."[70] As such, he is hardly the independent and disinterested reviewer of government search and seizure requests required by the *Charter*. It is difficult to imagine a court honouring the section 8 jurisprudence and viewing an executive actor as a proxy for the impartial judge promised in it.

All of this is to say that CSE's current Mandate A and B regimes are vulnerable to a court challenge — they are very hard to reconcile with section 8 caselaw. There is no evident reason why the CSE approval regime could not draw on CSIS precedent and have a judge rather than a minister issue the authorizations to CSE. Certainly, CSE collection is different than conventional warrants. It is directed at classes of information, not individuals. But even with that proviso, there is no reason why a judge could not step into the shoes currently occupied by the defence minister and offer independent oversight of what exactly CSE is proposing to do. This would have the welcome effect of preserving the promise and integrity of the *Charter*'s section 8 while still meeting the government's pressing objectives in relation to foreign intelligence.

Bill C-622, a private member's bill sponsored by Liberal MP Joyce Murray, would have done just that, but the government defeated this bill in the most recent Parliament without much effort and without much of a debate.[71] We discuss this bill in Chapter 12.

The CSE ministerial authorization model is also underinclusive as measured against the classic Camden model. Section 8 protects all information where there is a reasonable expectation of privacy. And as *Spencer* demonstrates, that may include metadata. But CSE's ministerial authorization regime applies only to "private communications," a statutorily defined term that the government appears to have interpreted narrowly to *exclude* metadata.[72] Metadata collection has not fallen, in other words, within even the ministerial authorization system. This means that it is performed without mandatory, outside, advance oversight of any sort, and in practice is instead done pursuant to general ministerial policy directives.

In these circumstances, we are acutely dependent on robust back-end independent review by CSE's review body, the CSE Commissioner. We return to this issue in Chapter 12 but note at this juncture that the CSE Commissioner has no ability to require CSE to change its practices. In other words, the CSE Commissioner is a review body that can make findings and recommendations but is not an overseer that, like the minister of national defence, has command and control authority.

IV. CONCLUSION

"Watch" tools are an ingredient of any successful anti-terror strategy. In their absence, anti-terror responses would be limited to physically intercepting future Michael Zehaf-Bibeaus dashing from war memorial to Parliament Hill. Put another way, our responses would often be too late.

But watch tools are surreptitious in an open, democratic society that is rightfully suspicious of powers exercised in secrecy. One solution is to superimpose over those actions independent court oversight, judicializing surveillance. Canadian law accomplishes most of that, but imperfectly. CSE remains outside the umbrella of judicial oversight. And in laws such as those created by Bill C-13, the precise standard by which judges determine whether invasions of privacy are permissible is relaxed to a reasonable suspicion standard, which may not adequately prevent unreasonable invasions of privacy. The police may obtain metadata under Bill C-13 and share them with CSIS even though CSIS would have to satisfy a higher standard if it were to obtain the same metadata directly.

Bill C-44, for its part, legalizes CSIS extraterritorial covert spying but does so in a manner that leaves doubt as to the precise circumstance where that activity requires advance judicial blessing. It places Federal Court judges in the awkward position of authorizing violations of international and foreign laws, no doubt to save CSIS from criticisms that it is acting lawlessly as some sort of modest variation of the CIA. And while Bill C-51 contains no emphatic provision on surveillance powers, it grants new roles and responsibilities to both the police and CSIS to which watch tools will now be directed. And in practice some of those activities will be undertaken by CSE, in partnership with the police or CSIS. These partnerships may make security sense and practical sense, but in Chapter 12, we will see that the separate review bodies for the RCMP, CSIS, and CSE cannot be partners in the same way that the agencies they review are.

Watch tools were expanded in 2015, a fact that escaped much commentary in debates over the laws. This will not always be a bad thing. But to the extent that the new powers in Bill C-51 — such as the speech crime — themselves overreach to capture private behaviour that should not properly be penalized by the state, the watch powers exercised in support of them trench deeply into a zone that should be privileged in a free society: the right to be left alone.

Moreover, the expanded reach of watch tools should not be considered without close contemplation of how information once collected can then be deployed by the state. This is because the traditional model of privacy protection no longer fits an information-rich environment where data can be collected, retained, and then combined or aggregated in a way not easily appreciated even when the *Charter* was enacted in 1982, let alone when Lord Camden issued his landmark warrant decisions in the eighteenth century. We turn to information sharing in the next chapter.

CHAPTER FIVE
Share: Information Sharing about Threats

I. INTRODUCTION

The Connect-the-Dots Intelligence Failures

In 1985, James Bartleman was the head of the intelligence division at what was then the Canadian Department of External Affairs. He later testified that he had been given a secret Communications Security Establishment document indicating that Sikh extremists were targeting Air India Flight 182. As discussed in Chapter 2, on 23 June 1985, a bomb exploded while Flight 182 was in mid-flight, killing 329 passengers and crew. Another bomb destined for an Air India flight killed two baggage handlers in Tokyo.

Bartleman's recollection — fiercely resisted by the government at the commission of inquiry that followed decades later — was, in the words of that inquiry's head, "credible." More than that, there were other documents "that should have led the Government to have anticipated the bombing of Flight 182 and to have acted to put in place security precautions to minimize the risk." Justice John Major, the commissioner, concluded that "there was enough information in the hands of various Canadian authorities to make it inexcusable that the system was unable to process that information correctly and ensure that there were adequate security measures in place to deal with the threat." The facts that the government had before it created "a mosaic of information which clearly identified a particularised threat to Air India for the month of June 1985. This constellation of factors should have compelled

139

the Government to tailor and implement security measures to meet this identified threat."[1]

These kinds of botched efforts to "connect the dots" are the most notorious (and arguably most commonplace) form of "intelligence failures." In some notable respects, the Air India experience was replicated years later when in 2001 American authorities also failed to piece together the jigsaw puzzle pointing to the 9/11 attacks.

In the findings of the subsequent US 9/11 Commission, the "FBI did not have the capability to link the collective knowledge of agents in the field to national priorities. The acting director of the FBI did not learn of his Bureau's hunt for two possible al-Qaida operatives in the United States or about his Bureau's arrest of an Islamic extremist taking flight training until September 11." The CIA knew about a key FBI investigation "weeks before word of it made its way even to the FBI's own assistant director for counterterrorism."[2] The National Security Agency, for its part, had information in its possession in 2000 that would have helped identify one of the 9/11 hijackers. No one asked for this information. Other information was distributed but in narrow, compartmentalized, and "siloed" channels. Still other information was available, and agencies asked for it, but sharing was impossible, presumably for some bureaucratic or legal reason.

The 9/11 Commission recommended that "information procedures should provide incentives for sharing, to restore a better balance between security and shared knowledge."[3] Likewise, Canada's own Air India Commission urged that the CSIS Act[4] "should be amended to require CSIS to report information that may be used in an investigation or prosecution of an offence either to the relevant policing or prosecutorial authorities or to the National Security Advisor."[5] As we discuss at length in Chapter 9, this recommendation was ignored — and despite the occasional puzzling government claims to the contrary, Bill C-51 does not honour it.[6] Instead, Bill C-51 responds to legitimate concerns about siloed information, so evident in the Air India and 9/11 cases, by throwing wide open the barn doors on information sharing but in such a complex and unnuanced way that the only certain consequence will be less privacy for Canadians.

While Bill C-51 creates a new permissive regime for information sharing about a vast array of security threats, it does not compel information sharing for the most serious security threats, including terrorism. It takes no steps to cure the problem that the Air India inquiry spent four years studying and that we examine in Chapter 9: the critical questions of how intelligence can be shared so as to prevent terrorism and how it can be converted into evidence for court prosecution purposes.

Nor does Bill C-51 prioritize the sharing of information that could prevent another Air India or 9/11. Instead, it risks drowning terrorism-related information in a data haystack that can include information sharing about peripheral matters of all flavours, not all of them consistent with long-standing understandings of national security.

The Careless-Use-of-Authority Intelligence Inquiries

In its few short pages, therefore, the new *Security of Canada Information Sharing Act (SoCIS Act)*[7] enacted in Bill C-51 fails to grapple with the key complaints arising from past intelligence failures while turning a blind eye to another form of failure: careless use of authority.

And that assertion brings us to another story about information sharing: that of Maher Arar. As discussed in Chapter 2, the RCMP's ill-considered provision to American authorities of raw information along with sensationalist commentary on the false affiliation of Arar and his wife, Dr Monia Mazigh, with al-Qaida was the likely cause of Arar's troubling treatment at the hands of the US authorities, including his ultimate rendition to Syria, where he was tortured. Those events culminated in the Arar Commission of Inquiry, where the commissioner, Justice Dennis O'Connor, noted the shortcomings of RCMP information sharing practices and recommended careful steps to forestall a recurrence of the Arar events.

Poor information sharing practices also were revealed by the subsequent Iacobucci inquiry examining the mistreatment of Adbullah Almalki, Ahmad Abou-Elmaati, and Muayyed Nureddin in Middle Eastern jails. Justice Frank Iacobucci concluded that Canadian officials had likely contributed to the maltreatment of these individuals in foreign custody when they had shared information about the detainees (especially suspected terrorist involvement) or communicated suspicions by making efforts to interrogate the individuals or have them questioned by foreign officials.[8]

Framing the Information Sharing Objectives Clearly

Together, these inquiries point to the importance of information sharing — what we call "share." Their findings need to be read in conjunction with one of the points made in Chapter 4: specifically, that our old model of protecting privacy by superimposing "gatekeeping" rules limiting collection does a poor job in an information-rich environment where the government is able to accumulate rich databases of minable data. In other words, traditional privacy protections focus on the acquisition of information whereas modern technology would suggest the need to supervise how information is shared and aggregated.

A modern, twenty-first-century system of information sharing needs to reconcile a number of objectives: to breakdown bureaucratic silos in a manner that enables key "dots" to be connected and information to be aggregated, to oversee information sharing to ensure that CSIS or other agencies do not sit on information that should be shared with agencies that need it, to control the flow of information so that it does not become the ingredient for abuse, and to review internal management of information so that privacy and reliability are not sacrificed in the rush toward an omniscient government. A final issue in an era when the quantity of data may exceed the capacity to draw meaningful intelligence from them is ensuring that the data haystack does not simply add so much chaff that it makes finding real needles even harder.

In this chapter we examine how our current information sharing rules are structured and the challenges they present as measured against these objectives. We then turn our attention to Bill C-51, looking at both what it does and what it fails to do.

II. INFORMATION SHARING 101

National security information sharing is a vast topic. It is both complex and almost entirely opaque given the extent to which it takes place behind closed doors and is rarely the subject of court proceedings. Commissions of inquiry give an occasional peek into how it works. And details sometimes emerge through documents dredged from government under access to information law. In this section, we spell out what we can reasonably know about information sharing rules and practices, at both the international and the Canadian level.

International Information Sharing

Scope

Intelligence sharing among allied states has been a regular practice in the area of military intelligence for decades, most notably among NATO allies. Likewise, the United States, the United Kingdom, Canada, Australia, and New Zealand have engaged in formalized intelligence sharing for generations, especially in the area of signals intelligence, through what is often called the UKUSA agreement, creating what is popularly known as the "Five Eyes" arrangement. The level of co-operation under the UKUSA agreement is so complete "that national product is often indistinguishable."[9]

Since 9/11, the pressure for more regularized international intelligence sharing on terrorism matters has increased. The director of operations of CSIS described the environment for information sharing this way in 2004: "compromising al-Qaeda operatives requires an unprecedented level . . . of cooperation between police, law enforcement, and immigration officials and the like, not just domestically but internationally as well."[10] International instruments encourage this international exchange. After 9/11, the United Nations Security Council instructed all states to

> Take the necessary steps to prevent the commission of terrorist acts, including by provision of early warning to other States by exchange of information . . . [and to] Afford one another the greatest measure of assistance in connection with criminal investigations or criminal proceedings relating to the financing or support of terrorist acts, including assistance in obtaining evidence in their possession necessary for the proceedings.[11]

More generally, intelligence sharing is a key practice in guarding national security interests. Not least, it permits the "acquisition of intelligence that is valuable to decision makers but otherwise unobtainable at an acceptable cost."[12] As such, it is particularly important for small countries such as Canada to tap into the intelligence capacities of larger states. For instance, the RCMP reported in 2007 that it had received seventy-five times more information from partner agencies than it had provided.[13]

Preoccupations with maintaining these necessary intelligence sharing arrangements go a considerable distance in explaining much Canadian government secrecy — the mere chance that disclosure of an ally's secret would impair intelligence sharing is a considerable source of concern for security officials.

Foreign alliances may also explain some overreach. The RCMP was too accommodating in sharing information with the United States in the post-9/11 investigation of Arar and other Canadians later tortured in Syria. In a move severely criticized by the Arar Commission, the RCMP had given American officials the entire investigative file without reviewing its content or attaching caveats that would limit the use that the American officials could make of it.

Intelligence Sharing Agreements

Some information sharing is almost certainly conducted at an ad hoc level through informal means. But there are also many bilateral intelligence sharing agreements. These are themselves often considered "among the most closely guarded secrets of clandestine agencies."[14] It is difficult, therefore, to piece together the full scope and extent of these arrangements. If the Canadian experience is illustrative, however, there are several observations that may be made about intelligence sharing agreements.

First, such arrangements are numerous and now exist between counterpart agencies (and not just as agreements between states per se). As one commentator has noted, "[i]nside large alliances, these [intelligence] organizations behave remarkably like states, with their own treaties, embassies and emissaries."[15] For example, the *CSIS Act* empowers CSIS to "enter into an arrangement or otherwise cooperate with the government of a foreign state or an institution thereof or an international organization of states or an institution thereof" for the purpose of performing CSIS's functions.[16] CSIS reported in 2006 that by 2004–5 it had "more than 250 relationships with foreign agencies in approximately 140 countries . . . . The agreements give the Service access to intelligence that might not otherwise be available to it, and can lead to cross-training, personnel exchanges and joint operations."[17]

As already suggested, Canada, the United States, the United Kingdom, Australia, and New Zealand, meanwhile, collaborate in signals intelligence pursuant to the confidential UKUSA agreement dating in its original form to 1947.[18] As described by Canada's signals intelligence agency, the Communications Security Establishment, "Canada is a substantial beneficiary of the collaborative effort within [this] partnership to collect and report on foreign communications."[19]

Originally a signals intelligence operation, the Five Eyes relationship now extends to co-operation on other security issues and among other security agencies, such as CSIS.[20]

Principles of Intelligence Sharing

While these intelligence sharing agreements are often themselves secret, it would appear that they generally incorporate some regular elements.

For instance, intelligence is often handled under a "need to know" rule — something that the 9/11 Commission questioned as potentially limiting the "dot connecting" abilities of security services. Under the need-to-know approach, "individuals should have access to classified information only when they need the information for their work, and access should never be authorized 'merely because a person occupies a particular position, however senior.'"[21]

Also common are policies of "originator control," sometimes also called the "third-party rule." This feature is designed to remedy the key impediment to intelligence sharing: distrust between the sharing entities. Sending entities, in particular, seek guarantees that recipients will not "defect," that is, employ the received intelligence in a manner that prejudices the sending entity. Not least, senders fear that "[r]ecipients of their intelligence might deliberately or inadvertently share it with hostile third parties, or reveal valuable sources and methods of intelligence to enemies."[22] Put simply, "originator control" places control over the use and distribution of the information in the hands of the state from which it comes. For instance, a 1996 Canada-Australia agreement on sharing of "defence-related" information provides that "the receiving Party shall not disclose, release or provide access to Transmitted Information . . . to any third party . . . without the prior written consent of the originating Party or unless such disclosure, release or access is otherwise in accordance with the provisions of another agreement or arrangement between the Parties."[23]

Analogous provisions are likely commonplace in other international information sharing agreements. CSIS told a Canadian Federal Court in 1996 that the information it receives is "invariably provided in confidence and on the explicit or implicit understanding that neither the information nor its source will be disclosed without the prior consent of the entity which provided it."[24] This principle is "widely recognized within the policing and security intelligence communities."[25]

Originator control in both international and domestic information sharing may be exercised through the use of "caveats." Caveats are "written restrictions on the use and further dissemination of shared information."[26] Countries such as Canada take these provisos very seriously — as noted, we are a net recipient of information and so cautious about what we do with other people's secrets. CSIS, for example, told the Federal Court in 1996 that "CSIS receives sensitive information, not just because of the third party rule which requires CSIS to treat the information as confidential, but also because there is confidence on the part of information providers that the Canadian government understands the need for confidentiality and has in place practices and procedures to safeguard information."[27] Without this confidence in Canada's ability to restrict disclosure, some allies "may discontinue the alliance or association. Others may continue their alliance, but with a reluctance to be candid."[28]

Originator control limits, in principle, the receiver's downstream ability to use the information without permission of the originator. Permission might be sought for any number of reasons — not least the use of the information in a judicial proceeding. However, intelligence services may be loath to seek this permission. As one commentator put it, the "mere request to a foreign intelligence organization for such permission, and for declassification, could easily foster an atmosphere of concern, not only over protecting sources and documents passed previously, but also whether it should continue to do so."[29]

The Torture Question

Recognizing the Hard Dilemmas

Unquestionably, the most controversial aspect of international intelligence sharing relates to information sharing and torture or other forms of cruel, inhuman, or degrading treatment. The causal link between sharing and maltreatment goes both ways. Most famously, given the Arar and Iacobucci inquiries, information shared by Canada can contribute to the causal chain leading to maltreatment of prisoners at the hands of a foreign government. We call that "outbound" information.

But "inbound" information arriving from a foreign government can itself be the product of torture or other forms of maltreatment. This issue has arisen most notoriously in the infamous security certificate immigration proceedings, where some information deployed by the Canadian government in trying to make out its case has been extremely suspect. We discuss security certificates in Chapter 7. It is illegal to use information procured by torture in Canadian legal proceedings[30] — and this kind of evidence has been rejected where the circumstances of its origin are known.

But using information derived from torture in court proceedings is one thing. Using it for other purposes is another. Imagine the following situation: on 22 June 1985, while working at CSIS, you receive a telex from a liaison with the Indian police that, summarized to its essence, reads, "we have a member of a Sikh militant group in our custody, and we've given him our usual treatment, and he's told us there is a bomb in the baggage of Air India Flight 182, scheduled for departure soon from Toronto." You know, and are right, that torture is practised by the Indian police of the era and that the "usual treatment" in this missive is a euphemism for torture. Question: Do you tip off the RCMP and airport security officials to search the baggage for Air India Flight 182 again? If you do, you have used the tortured intelligence, but in a very different manner than, for example, using it in a judicial proceeding.

Sharing outbound information with less than fastidious allies raises similar dilemmas. Should Canada sit on information directly material to a planned terrorist event in a repressive regime for fear of what might happen to the perpetrators should the information be shared?

At some level, the debate on these issues boils down to a dispute between two camps. On the one hand are those who urge that any use of torture-derived information creates a "market" that may fuel the persistence of this horrific practice. On the other are those who conclude that in exigent circumstances the injury caused by failing to take steps in response to torture-derived intelligence outstrips the evil of torture. Likewise, some analysts will argue that the risk of harm stemming from a feared terror attack can outweigh the dangers that outbound information sharing with an abusive government will lead to the torture of persons in its custody. Confusing this debate (especially on the inbound question) are contested assertions about whether any information elicited through extreme interrogation can ever be accurate — instead, it may just produce a series of wild goose chases that distract from more meaningful security strategies.

These are not easy questions. In 2006, we were part of a group of academics, lawyers, and human rights experts that proposed the "Ottawa Principles on Anti-terrorism and Human Rights." Among other things, that group debated at length about how best to reconcile the absolute ban on torture contained in international law with the sorts of inbound and outbound dilemmas flagged above. The compromise position was a firm reassertion of the ban on use of information procured by torture (and also cruel, inhuman, and degrading treatment) in any "judicial, administrative or other proceeding" (except those necessary to prove the existence of this abuse). But on the bigger question of use outside of this context, the experts proposed this standard:

> Information, data, or intelligence that has been obtained through torture or cruel, inhuman or degrading treatment or punishment may not be used as a basis for:
>
> (a) the deprivation of liberty;
>
> (b) the transfer, through any means, of an individual from the custody of one state to another;
>
> (c) the designation of an individual as a person of interest, a security threat or a terrorist or by any other description purporting to link that individual to terrorist activities; or
>
> (d) the deprivation of any other internationally protected human right.[31]

Put simply, the Ottawa principles do not impose an absolute ban. They would allow the use of torture-derived intelligence from India to be used to prevent the Air India bombings. They would not, however, allow that information to be used to prosecute, extradite, or deport someone or as a basis for limiting anyone's rights. In essence, the Ottawa principles are designed to put a stop to "fruit of a poisoned tree," that is, visiting disadvantage on a person or constraining a person's liberty because of torture-derived intelligence. But this would not stand in the way of using the Air India warning in the manner imagined above.

The Ottawa principles reaching outbound sharing are more opaque: "States must ensure that their receipt, dissemination and use of any information, data, or intelligence to and from other states does not result in the violation of human rights."[32] It is, in fact, very hard to articulate nuanced standards to govern how a democratic information-supplying state should guard against repressive regimes simply violating assurances on how they will use information supplied to them.

At the very least, however, such assurances should be sought. And, as the Arar inquiry concluded, there will be instances where information simply cannot be shared because the risk of resulting maltreatment is too high. The Arar Commission also warned that the high stakes of information sharing will generally be played out in secret without judicial review. It stressed the need for independent, audit-based review and pointed as well at the inadequacy of Canada's siloed and partial system of review (discussed in Chapter 12).

Canada's Response

Canada has struggled to address some of these issues. Controversially, in 2011, then Public Safety Minister Vic Toews issued "ministerial directions" to Canada's key security and intelligence agencies on "information sharing with foreign entities."[33] This innocuous title betrayed little of these administrative instruments' actual content.

These directions focused on information sharing "when doing so may give rise to a substantial risk of mistreatment of an individual." They were, in other words, new policies on the thorny issue of information sharing and torture. The directions are permissive of information sharing that might induce (or be the product of) mistreatment, limiting and controlling how that sharing might take place but not precluding it absolutely.

When reported in the press in 2012, the new directions elicited a hostile reception from opposition politicians and the human rights and legal community.[34] The 2011 directions represent a shift in emphasis from their closest predecessors. An earlier 2009 ministerial direction, for example, seemed to bar use of inbound torture information — CSIS was not to "knowingly rely upon information which is derived from the use of torture" — and there was no emphatic instruction allowing outbound sharing that might contribute to torture.[35]

But at the same time, it is also clear that CSIS operational policies implementing these directions overpromised by asserting unverifiable and implausible guarantees that shared information was not the product, or a contributing cause, of torture. They also, understandably, held the door open to information sharing even in the face of substantial risk of mistreatment, as in the Air India scenario discussed above.

The 2011 directions may be an honest rendition of longstanding government practice in at least some agencies, consolidating tacit practices into a single code of conduct for the three key security and intelligence services within the minister of public safety's portfolio. At core, they provide a high-level system of approval for inbound or outbound information sharing tied to torture, where the stakes are high enough, but do not impose an obligation on the minister to pre-authorize such decisions (a striking omission).

Through a Glass, Darkly

Exactly how these directions are being used is not entirely clear — there has certainly been no public reporting on the issue. Documents released under access to information law provide, however, some hints.[36]

In 2013–14, the RCMP considered sharing information under the ministerial direction in five cases. In every single instance, the information at issue contained an element of outbound sharing. In each case, the RCMP internal approval process denied information sharing permission. The RCMP, of course, is aware of its difficult history in the Arar case. It is also acutely aware that its practices will usually culminate in an open court criminal process, during which its investigative tactics will be exposed and subject to close scrutiny. This prospect exercises a discipline on the RCMP that is not nearly as acute for CSIS.

CSIS reportedly relied on the 2011 information sharing ministerial direction ten times by 2014. In one case, the matter fell outside the supervising CSIS committee's jurisdiction. One case was referred to the CSIS director for his consideration because of the risk of maltreatment, but the need to share information was superseded by events. The committee issued permission to share in six cases. In two of these cases, the information was shared on condition that proper assurances against mistreatment were obtained from the recipient. In the four other cases, the committee authorized the information sharing because it was "unlikely that mistreatment had occurred" or because it concluded that "sending the information would not cause a substantial risk of mistreatment." These six cases comprised four cases of outbound sharing and two of inbound sharing. The committee denied only two of the ten requests, and in both denials the use of inbound information in a Federal Court proceeding was at issue. This pattern is consistent with a particular wariness when there is the prospect that a court will assess doubtful information sharing, illustrated also by the RCMP practice.

We know nothing about the particulars of the circumstances in which CSIS did share information and cannot evaluate the merits of the CSIS decisions. This is unfortunate because how the directions are used is material to the question of their legality — and there is reason to question whether full use of these directions would be compliant with the *Canadian Charter of*

Rights and Freedoms[37] and Canada's international obligations.[38] For instance, use of the directions to justify outbound information sharing with knowledge of the likelihood of torture may give rise to international criminal culpability and impose an obligation on Canada to prosecute those officials who are sharing the information.

There is also an obvious *Charter* issue raised by the directions. For instance, certain use of the directions to authorize outbound information sharing could violate the section 7 guarantee of fundamental justice whenever life, liberty, or security of the person is jeopardized.[39] But this is not a sure thing — much will depend on the facts in individual cases. And those facts will be hard to come by. It is not likely that the government will willingly release the details of its practice in specific cases. In the result, a challenge to the policy may require a frank challenge to the directions themselves without evidence of their use, something that would make the applicant's case more difficult. As a Canadian Bar Association resolution protesting the CSIS direction noted, "decisions to share information pursuant to the Direction tend to elude judicial review and public oversight due to the circumstances in which they are made."[40]

At some level, that is perhaps the most pernicious aspect of a policy articulated, not in legislation with reporting obligations, but in the form of executive fiat. Put simply, the public will not know what the state is doing unless and until a scandal like that which engulfed Maher Arar arises.

Until then, we depend on executive good faith and the operations of accountability bodies with limited resources and capacities, like the Security Intelligence Review Committee. But even that body cannot police the conduct of entities outside its narrow mandate over CSIS. The Security Intelligence Review Committee started to examine the Arar case but was unable to follow the thread that lead from CSIS not only to the RCMP but from the RCMP to customs officials and from Canadian agencies to foreign officials and back to CSIS and the RCMP. A public inquiry was necessary to run all the threads down, but a public inquiry of course depends on a scandal forcing the government to appoint one. All of this means that for organizations like the Canada Border Services Agency (CBSA), which has no review body, use of the directions may be largely immunized from independent scrutiny.

As both of us have argued in the past,[41] if the government wishes to nuance its approach to torture-derived-information sharing, it should also layer on procedural nuance including periodic reporting on the number of times the 2011 directions have been deployed and the mandatory provision of details to independent review bodies each time one of the directions is used to justify sharing. Otherwise, in the hothouse of inside-government thinking, dissenting views may be lost, and the willingness of the 2011 directions to touch torture with a ten-foot pole may produce even shorter poles in time.

The Privacy Question

Privacy issues also loom large in the world of information sharing. As discussed in Chapter 4, much privacy regulation in Canada is focused on the collection issue, that is, rules limiting what government can collect about the private lives of Canadians and people in Canada and how that information can be collected. But collection, monitoring, and surveillance are just the first tranche of privacy issues. As we also discuss in Chapter 4, the real frontier in a world of Big Data is what happens to information while in the possession of government — and especially how it might be shared and aggregated.

In a work like this, we do not outline in full the privacy rules on information sharing.[42] For our purposes, it is important simply to recognize that the starting point in the federal *Privacy Act* is that there is to be "no disclosure" of personal information collected by the government without consent of the individual concerned.[43] But, as is so often the case, this opening premise is so riddled with exceptions that the exceptions in large measure swallow the rule, or at least complicate it to a mind-boggling degree. For example, the *Privacy Act* allows subsequent disclosure of information for "consistent purpose and use"[44] — that is, for the same purpose as it was originally collected for. This is a large exception that government agencies have relied upon for "discretionary latitude to operate effectively within their mandates."[45] The *Privacy Act* also allows disclosure for prosecutorial and lawful investigation purposes,[46] for research purposes,[47] and even for general purposes where the public interest outweighs any harm to privacy,[48] to cite some examples.

There is also another important exception that basically subordinates the *Privacy Act*: information disclosure is permitted "for any purpose in accordance with any Act of Parliament or any regulation made thereunder that authorizes its disclosure."[49] There are many such trumping laws in the national security area, including in the *Aeronautics Act* (for passenger information) and the *Proceeds of Crime (Money Laundering) and Terrorist Financing Act* (for financial information). Some *Privacy Act*–trumping laws were included in little-noticed amendments contained in the omnibus Bill C-51.

All of this would be awkward enough, but on top of this cacophony of various statutory rules on information sharing, there are also constitutional principles. Information sharing should not be employed by state agencies to circumvent constitutional privacy protections. Law enforcement agencies, for example, may not avoid constitutional search and seizure rules under section 8 of the *Charter* by receiving otherwise protected information from administrative or other bodies not subject to the same constitutional strictures.[50] Where law enforcement agencies propose obtaining private information that is protected by a reasonable expectation of privacy from other bodies, warrants must be obtained, even in circumstances where disclosure of personal information is permissible under the *Privacy Act*.[51]

Likewise, after the Supreme Court's recent decision in *Wakeling v United States*, information collected by warrant retains constitutional protections. And if it is then shared without being governed by a clear law, with reasonable safeguards, and in a reasonable fashion, that behaviour too is unconstitutional.[52] *Wakeling* concerned the sharing of intercepted private communications by the RCMP with US authorities in a drug case. The intercepts were authorized under Part VI of the *Criminal Code*, the key wiretap provision in Canadian criminal law (discussed in Chapter 4). But even so, the case was decided with an eye on Canada's largest post-9/11 scandal: Canada's sharing of false and unreliable information about Maher Arar. As one judge noted, "The torture of Maher Arar in Syria provides a particularly chilling example of the danger of unconditional information sharing."[53]

CSIS information sharing, in particular, raises post-*Wakeling* concerns: even as compared with the somewhat sparse language of Part VI of the *Criminal Code*, CSIS information sharing is not governed by a clear law with reasonable safeguards. The *CSIS Act* is permissive without providing the level of safeguards that several of the judges saw as being met by Part VI (which other judges saw as actually insufficient).

The inevitable fallback for the government will be generous sharing permissions in the *Privacy Act*.[54] However, the highly generic, non-intercept or agency-specific nature of these permissions may make the *Privacy Act* "authorization" so ambiguous that a court might disagree that it meets even section 8's basic first requirement of "authorized by law" under the *Charter*. This matter is undecided, and there is always the prospect that the Supreme Court will find something magical in the national security context. But we think that it would be frankly unbelievable for the Court to conclude that the sharing of RCMP intercepts is sensitive and that the sharing of CSIS intercepts is less sensitive.

And so the *CSIS Act* will need to comply with the constitutional standards discussed in *Wakeling*. This is a train heading down the track, but the government seems to have ignored this *Charter* jurisprudence. The result is that much of the 2015 legislation will be challenged under the *Charter*, creating further uncertainty about the new powers.

III. BILL C-51'S NEW *SECURITY OF CANADA INFORMATION SHARING ACT*

What the government did do was unleash a convoluted new domestic information sharing law that will twist the government lawyers asked to construe it into pretzels.

Bill C-51's information sharing regime is motivated by a real problem. During debate over the bill, proponents regularly posed the following scenario: Passport authorities are aware of a Canadian who persistently reports lost passports to the Canadian embassy in a Middle Eastern country. The officials suspect that this person may be feeding passports to foreign fighters. But they can see no way to overcome Canada's privacy laws and send their concerns to CSIS.

This is an untenable situation. As correctly noted in an internal CSIS briefing note that predates Bill C-51:

> Currently, departments and agencies rely on a patchwork of legislative authorities to guide information sharing . . . . Generally, enabling legislation of most departments and agencies does not unambiguously permit the effective sharing of information for national security purposes. When combined with the "consistent use" provision of the Privacy Act as well as Charter considerations, the legislative ambiguity in various enabling pieces of legislation hinders information sharing for national security purposes, and correspondingly, attitudes and overall approaches become reflexively cautious. The absence of a clear authority to share information for national security purposes amplifies this challenge.[55]

The question is, however, what to do about this. The answer is "Not Bill C-51." As the CSIS briefing note goes on to state, "Existing legislative authorities and information sharing arrangements often allow for the sharing of information for national security purposes. With appropriate direction and framework in place, significant improvements are possible to encourage information sharing for national security purposes, *on the basis [of] existing legislative authorities.*"[56]

Bill C-51 departs from this advice by superimposing over the existing legal regime a new security information sharing umbrella law: *SoCIS Act*. In so doing, it adds new uncertainty and complexity to the already muddled information sharing system. That new law articulates a series of generally laudable objectives in its (unenforceable) preamble and "purposes and principles" portions and then presents a series of legal principles that risk creating more problems than they cure.

As urged above, any modern national security information sharing system must have four objectives:

1) breakdown bureaucratic silos in a manner that enables key "dots" to be connected, even when intelligence agencies left to their own devices are reluctant to share

2) control the flow of information so that it does not become the ingredient for abuse

3) oversee internal management of information so that privacy and reliability are not sacrificed in the rush toward an omniscient government

4) ensure that the data haystack does not simply add so much chaff that it makes finding real needles even harder

Measured against these standards, the *SoCIS Act* fares very poorly.

Mind-Numbing Complexity

Canada's Broadest Definition of Security

We need now to get into the details. We begin with an overview of the *SoCIS Act*'s core provisions. The Act would allow those within the government of Canada to share information about the new and vast concept of "activities that undermine the security of Canada."[57] It is difficult to overstate how broad this new definition is, even as contrasted with existing broad national security definitions such as "threats to the security of Canada" in the *CSIS Act*[58] or the national security concept in the *Security of Information Act*,[59] Canada's official secrets law.

The new *SoCIS Act* defines an activity that undermines the security of Canada as *any* activity, including any of the activities then enumerated as examples, "if it undermines the sovereignty, security or territorial integrity of Canada or the lives or the security of the people of Canada." The phrase "people of Canada" means "people in Canada" or *any* citizen or permanent resident who is *outside* Canada.[60] Put another way, the definition reaches any activity that "undermines" (whatever that means) the life or security of any single Canadian anywhere in the world. This is quite staggering, and it risks sweeping virtually everything under the security label. This raises a variety of concerns. An obvious one is privacy. A perhaps less obvious one is the problem of finding needles in a boundless security haystack. If everything is a security matter, then effectively nothing may be.

This concept of undermining the security of Canada is the "headline" or *chapeau* — where it is satisfied, the new information sharing system is triggered. But the *SoCIS Act* also includes a long list of broadly conceived

154

examples of activities that *could* undermine Canadian security. The listed items are mere illustrations — not a fixed and closed menu of activities that undermine security. But each of these examples can trigger the new information sharing system *if* it arises in circumstances where the government thinks that the *chapeau* definition is also met. During the Bill C-51 debates, government politicians urged that the requirement the *chapeau* elements be satisfied was a meaningful constraint on the breadth of the listed examples. But since the *chapeau* definition itself is vast and uncertain, we suspect that whatever constraint it imposes will be largely illusory.

Already, as this discussion probably communicates, the *SoCIS Act* introduces a large measure of subjectivity, complexity, and uncertainty into the system.

Lots to See under the Chapeau

What are the listed examples? "Terrorism" is identified as one.[61] Even there, the choice was made to use the undefined term "terrorism" as opposed to the better understood, codified, and still very broad concept of "terrorist activity" found in the *Criminal Code*. Other activities on the enumerated list are "interference with critical infrastructure" and "an activity that takes place in Canada and undermines the security of another state."[62]

Also included is the incredibly broad concept of "changing or unduly influencing a government in Canada by force *or* unlawful means."[63] This phrase looks a lot like the antiquated concept of subversion. Subversion is not unknown in Canadian law, but the notion of subversion found in the *CSIS Act* definition of "threats to the security of Canada" focuses on violence and "covert unlawful acts" directed at destroying or overthrowing the constitutionally established system of government in Canada.[64] The related concept of "sedition" in the *Criminal Code* also focuses on unlawful use of force to accomplish governmental change in Canada.[65]

This requirement for violent political change is not found in the new *SoCIS Act*. Subject to comments below on the protest exception, the Act potentially extends to trivial unlawful acts such as breaching municipal by-laws in efforts to "unduly influence" (whatever that means) a government (any government) in Canada. The concern about influencing governments is found in United Kingdom terrorism law, but it has been criticized by many there and was not used in Canada's 2001 *Anti-terrorism Act*, which requires more forceful acts of compulsion or intimidation.

An Exception That Was Too Narrow but Now Swallows the Act

The only exemption in the *SoCIS Act*'s definition of "activities that undermine the security of Canada" is for "advocacy, protest, dissent and artistic expression."[66] Initially, this exemption included the qualifier "lawful" before the list of exempted activities. The word "lawful" provoked controversy during the Bill C-51 debate. "Lawful" conduct would, of course, exclude blockades. It would also exclude workplace strikes inconsistent with labour law and street protests lacking the proper regulatory permits. Put another way, "lawful" does not mean "non-criminal." It just means "without lawful authority."

The risk was that once labour, Indigenous, or environmental protesters broke one law — including a municipal bylaw — they would fall outside the limited safeguards in the new *SoCIS Act*. They could be subject to security information sharing involving at present (the number could increase) seventeen different federal institutions including revenue, finance, and health as well as CSIS, CBSA, the RCMP and the Communications Security Establishment.

On this specific issue, the government appeared to be deliberately rejecting the compromise approach found in the original 2001 *Anti-terrorism Act*. That law had codified the then new concept of "terrorist activity" and extended its reach to serious interference or disruption of an essential service. But, after controversy, it then excluded circumstances where the disruption stemmed from (even unlawful) protests and strikes so long as they were not intended to cause death or bodily harm, endanger life, or cause serious risk to health. Predictably, the same controversy reappeared during debate over Bill C-51. Under pressure from civil society groups (and after having regularly rejected their concerns, sometimes obnoxiously), the governing Conservative party amended the bill in the House of Commons to delete the word "lawful."

We were astonished by this change. We had proposed that "lawful" be dropped but then recommended the same 2001 compromise noted above: we recommended excluding both lawful and unlawful protest and advocacy but *only* so long as it was not intended to cause death or bodily harm, endanger life, or cause serious risk to health.

We think that not all protest and advocacy should be exempted from the new information sharing regime. Violent protest or advocacy of a sufficient scale *can* be a national security issue justifying information sharing. After all, anyone dimly aware of the history of terrorism appreciates that terrorism can be a form of "protest" or "advocacy," depending on how you define those concepts. Terrorism is certainly a form of "dissent."

But by simply dropping the word "lawful," the new *SoCIS Act* seems to preclude new information sharing powers in relation to *any* sort of protest or advocacy or dissent, no matter how violent. And so government officials will now need to spend a lot of time wondering if, for example, violent conduct is "protest," "advocacy," or "dissent," an unnecessary headache that just compounds the incoherence of the Act. Government lawyers will find a way to work around this carelessly drafted exception. The problem is that the public, and perhaps even review agencies (because of claims of solicitor-client privilege), will not know whether government lawyers have interpreted an unworkable exemption effectively out of existence.

Powers to Do What Exactly?

That incoherence is then compounded by the operative powers in the *SoCIS Act*. In its key operative provision, the Act contemplates that more than 100 government institutions may, unless other laws prohibit them from doing so, disclose information to any of 17 (and potentially more) federal institutions if "relevant" to the receiving body's "jurisdiction or responsibilities" in relation to "activities that undermine the security of Canada," including "in respect of their detection, identification, analysis, prevention, investigation or disruption."[67]

If the point was to create a tent big enough to accommodate every eventuality, this power does it but at the expense of clarity and predictability. We have already discussed the concept of "undermining the security of Canada," a concept whose contours we have described as complex and confusing. Now we must ponder the meaning of "jurisdiction or responsibilities." These are legalistic terms capable of definition — but that definition may lie in the eyes of the beholder, a point we will return to below. The same is true of the term "relevant." In plain language, "relevant" here means "having a sufficient bearing on" whatever lies within the agency's jurisdiction or responsibilities. As the Privacy Commissioner noted in his critique of Bill C-51, much more falls within the orbit of "relevant" than would be captured by the more modest term "necessary." "Necessary" means "needed."

The long list of specific mandates — and especially "prevention" and "disruption" — then add more uncertainty. If an agency, say CSIS, has the power to "prevent" or "disrupt" anything that falls within the "undermine" security definition, does that mean information can be shared with that agency *pre-emptively*? That is, must the sharing agency be persuaded that the activity in question actually has undermined or does undermine security? Or can a mere fear that it might, in the future, undermine security justify information sharing with an agency that can pre-empt the risk? If so, then the *SoCIS Act*'s already vast concept of national security becomes an even vaster concept of things that may at some unknown point in time undermine security.

There is a safeguard of sorts: the new information sharing power is "[s]ubject to any provision of any other Act of Parliament, or of any regulation made under such an Act, that prohibits or restricts the disclosure of information."[68] This means that it must comply, among other things, with the *Privacy Act*. As already discussed, the *Privacy Act* bars disclosure but then removes that bar under a whole host of broad exceptions. For that reason, the *SoCIS Act*'s subject-to-other-laws proviso is not an impressive one.

The *SoCIS Act*'s entire architecture creates confusion and uncertainty. And in so doing it rejects the lessons from the Arar Commission, Air India inquiry, and US 9/11 Commission. It threatens privacy as the government seems to want to include almost everything under its radical and novel definition of security interests. At the same time, the *SoCIS Act*'s overbreadth threatens security by making it difficult to focus on terrorism. The Act allows the government to share just about everything while it rejects the Air India inquiry's recommendation that CSIS *must* share intelligence about terrorist offences, if not to the police than to someone who is in charge and who can take responsibility for the proper use of the information.

Walking through a Hypothetical

This next section will confuse our readers — which is exactly the point. Right out of the gate, we need to wonder about whether the new *SoCIS Act* matters very much for national security sharing between the mainstream agencies with roles in this area such as the RCMP, CSIS, CBSA, and the Communications Security Establishment. To a large extent, these agencies are already webbed together by customized information sharing rules stemming from information sharing understandings that are based on laws, such as the *Privacy Act* or more specialized information sharing regimes in the statutes applying to each agency.

Does the *SoCIS Act* expand the existing basis for disclosure where it already exists under the law, at least for some agencies? The intuitive answer is "yes, it must fill gaps, or why bother." But the Act is drafted inelegantly: as noted, disclosure is "[s]ubject to any provision of any other Act of Parliament, or of any regulation made under such an Act, that prohibits or restricts the disclosure of information." We do not know how to read this phrase. It must mean that the *Privacy Act*'s limitations on disclosure and also its exceptions to those limitations all apply. But do these existing exceptions then mark the outer limits of how the new *SoCIS Act* can be used? That is, does the Act permit disclosure *only* to the limit of the existing exceptions under the *Privacy Act* or other statutes? The question then becomes again, "why bother?" Nothing new would be added by the introduction of the *SoCIS Act* — information sharing would be neither increased nor decreased relative to the pre-existing situation.

We also quickly reach a conundrum. The *Privacy Act* specifies that personal information may be disclosed for "any purpose in accordance with any Act of Parliament or any regulation made thereunder that authorizes its disclosure."[69] Maybe Bill C-51 is another example of such an Act that authorizes disclosure — and, indeed, in separate amendments to existing laws made by Bill C-51, the grounds for disclosure by different agencies are expanded. Or maybe at its incoherent worst, the *SoCIS Act* permits disclosure subject to existing rules, and the existing rules permit disclosure only in accordance with the *SoCIS Act*. Around in paradoxical circles we go.

We cannot resolve these questions. But we imagine that the inside-government interpretations guiding application of the *SoCIS Act* will struggle to construe it as expanding the information sharing legal status quo, while at the same time being attentive to existing legal disclosure rules. A circle will be squared, painfully. Again, however, the public will not know how this badly drafted law is actually being interpreted. The rule of law will suffer as a result, and we strongly suspect that privacy will also suffer.

A Cautionary Tale of Bad Laws and the Officials Who Are Saddled with Them

We imagine that the result may be quite messy, a point best illustrated with a law professor favourite: the hypothetical. Let us assume that in the course of its regular and legitimate activities and under its existing information collecting rules, CBSA collects travel information on all persons exiting and entering Canada.

Using Big Data techniques, CBSA assembles a portrait of travel to, among other places, Turkey. Turkey is an entry point for many persons joining ISIS (Islamic State of Iraq and Syria). During border searches, CBSA finds that some Turkey-bound voyagers are travelling with large amounts of cash in excess of amounts plausibly correlated with travel needs, raising suspicions about whether they are engaged in illicit financing of some sort of activity in their overseas destination. CBSA has also compelled persons returning from the region to disclose the passcodes on their smartphones and downloaded archived geolocational data from them, giving some sense as to where those phones have been. (In fact, under the *Customs Act*, CBSA has the power to search cellphones at the border without warrants. Recently, it charged a traveller for refusing to disclose the passcode that would have allowed the traveller's smartphone to be subjected to such a search. By the time you read this, that charge will undoubtedly be before the courts, where it faces challenge on constitutional grounds.[70] We discuss CBSA border powers in Chapter 7.)

From its Big Data exercise, CBSA determines that one small region of suburban Toronto is a disproportionate source of Turkey-bound travellers, especially young males. From smartphone geolocational information, CBSA is also able to establish that some have travelled in or near Syria. CBSA concludes, therefore, that its data may reveal some sort of hotbed of foreign fighter financing, possibly involving the transfer of funds to ISIS. This is information that most reasonable people would agree should be shared with the security services.

Throwing Information over the Fence

CBSA's lawyers ponder the question of how to get this information to CSIS. There is, in fact, an existing information sharing agreement between the two agencies. It predates Bill C-51 and provides that the two agencies will "exchange information or intelligence . . . in the possession of one Participant related to the operational requirements of the other Participant or for the purpose of de-conflicting investigations, subject to their respective mandates and authorities." It also specifies that "collection, use, disclosure, retention and disposal of personal information and customs information will conform to all relevant Canadian legislation, regulations and government policies including . . . the *Privacy Act*, the *Customs Act*, the *CSIS Act*, *IRPA*, the *Canadian Charter of Rights and Freedoms*."[71]

Now the lawyers will also need to consider the implications of Bill C-51's new information sharing act. In so doing, they immediately encounter serious headaches of the sort noted above. It may be that they decide the *SoCIS Act* adds nothing to their powers of sharing. Or they may conclude it provides an overarching authority to be considered in making any sharing decision. This latter approach is a reasonable conclusion, and so we will follow that path.

Playing Twister with the New Law

In performing their analysis, CBSA lawyers decide to proceed in the following way: First, they will need to consider whether any of the CBSA information in our hypothetical scenario truly falls within the orbit of the "undermine" security concept in the new *SoCIS Act*. Given the ISIS subject matter, it probably does, either under the Act's undefined reference to "terrorism" or even with respect to activities that undermine the "security of another state," such as the Assad regime in Syria. CBSA concludes that both of these security concerns reach the level of undermining Canadian security as defined in the headline or *chapeau* of the *SoCIS Act*, a reasonable conclusion given the breadth of the concept of "undermining the security of Canada."

Second, CBSA lawyers will need to decide whether the information is "relevant" to CSIS's "jurisdiction or responsibilities." Here, there is utter definitional uncertainty. Since 1984, CSIS has been tasked with collecting "to the extent strictly necessary" intelligence on activities "that may on reasonable grounds be suspected of constituting threats to the security of Canada." Moreover, after Bill C-51, where CSIS has "reasonable grounds to believe a particular activity constitutes a threat to the security of Canada," it may take measures to reduce that threat.[72]

So what is CSIS's "jurisdiction or responsibility"? Can it be *anything* that CBSA's lawyers think CSIS itself might think is relevant — however incidentally — to "threats to the security of Canada"? The *CSIS Act* definition of that concept has four categories: espionage or sabotage, foreign-influenced activities, terrorism, and subversion. Is it enough if the CBSA information falls into one of these categories? CSIS's primary responsibilities relate to investigating (and now reducing) these threats. But its investigations may be triggered only where it has "reasonable grounds to suspect" a threat. Moreover, it can collect information in those investigations only to the extent "strictly necessary."

So does CSIS's "jurisdiction or responsibility" under the new *SoCIS Act* reach only situations where these two supplemental requirements are met? If yes, then CBSA can only share information whose significance is such that it would meet these supplemental requirements, and CSIS would itself be able to collect it through a threats investigation. If no, and "jurisdiction or responsibility" is broader than situations in which CSIS's own investigations would be triggered, then CSIS will now be able to receive (and then potentially further share) information that it is not legally entitled to collect on its own.

In our hypothetical scenario, the information does seem to relate to terrorism and so to a "threat to the security of Canada." The *CSIS Act* definition of terrorism is "activities within or relating to Canada directed toward or in support of the threat or use of acts of serious violence against persons or property for the purpose of achieving a political, religious or ideological objective within Canada or a foreign state."[73] The CBSA information seems to fit that standard. Assume also that CBSA takes the conservative approach to the headache raised above and concludes that its information is information that would provoke CSIS (on "reasonable grounds to suspect") to start an investigation or operation in response. And the CBSA information would be exactly the sort of information that meets the "strictly necessary" threshold. CBSA concludes, therefore, that the information lies within CSIS's "jurisdiction and responsibility."

But Is the Sharing Authorized?

But the analysis is hardly over because the information must be shared only in "accordance" with other laws. Other laws governing disclosure surely include the *Privacy Act*, which says, in essence, "no sharing, but . . . ." And the "but" or justifications for sharing are exceptions that practically gut the rule.

And so we need to review the *Privacy Act*'s rules of disclosure. It could be that CBSA might make out a "consistent use" justification for sharing: the information was originally collected for national security purposes, and so it can be shared for this reason. But let us assume, as seems likely, that at least some of the information was collected for a number of other reasons related to CBSA's vast array of border responsibilities and then combined with assorted other data after collection. In our hypothetical, CBSA only connects the dots about the cluster of travellers by using Big Data techniques. So "consistent use" is not a full blessing for the disclosure.

CBSA could also point to the "lawful investigation" justification for information disclosure under the *Privacy Act*. But that justification requires the investigating authority — in this case CSIS — to make the request in writing. We would then be faced with the Monty Pythonesque situation of CBSA wanting to give CSIS information so that CSIS can start an investigation but requiring first that there be an existing CSIS investigation so that the information may be requested. (Recall, a CSIS intelligence investigation is initiated only on a "reasonable grounds to suspect" standard, requiring at least some existing information already in CSIS's possession.)

Alternatively, as seems most likely, CBSA could rely on other statutory permissions allowing information sharing found in the laws that it itself administers. But here, of course, there are more headaches: these laws all have different rules.

For instance, under the *Excise Tax Act*, as amended by Bill C-51, CBSA may share "confidential information" "if there are reasonable grounds to suspect" that the information is "relevant" to "an investigation of whether the activity of any person may constitute threats to the security of Canada" as defined in the *CSIS Act*.[74] Because this definition and the *CSIS Act* itself line up closely, excise tax information may flow to CSIS fairly readily. But, of course, our possible foreign fighters are not flagged because of their excise taxes but because of their travel patterns and geolocational data.

Since the geolocational data were seized under the *Customs Act*, that statute would govern the data's disclosure. The *Customs Act* allows disclosure where CBSA reasonably regards the information as relating to "national security or defence of Canada."[75] Bizarrely, after Bill C-51 it also allows disclosure "in accordance with the *Security of Canada Information Sharing Act*." But this reference creates an impossible paradox: the *SoCIS Act* allows disclosure in accordance with other statutes, but here the other statute in question, the *Customs Act*, specifies that disclosure is to be done in accordance with the *SoCIS Act*. Rather than remain on that merry-go-round, the (by now exhausted) CBSA lawyers may simply conclude that the geolocational data relate to "national security" and "defence," both named under the *Customs Act*, and so can be disclosed. They go home for a well-deserved weekend, and a stiff drink.

Oops, We've Done It Again . . .

The CBSA lawyers return well rested from the weekend, during which they have read some of the privacy caselaw from the Supreme Court. They realize that they should revisit the information sharing issue because they may have implicated their colleagues at CSIS in a *Charter* violation.

They recognize that CBSA would be providing to CSIS information seized from a smartphone after a traveller was compelled to provide the passcode. If CSIS had wished to obtain the information itself, it would have required a judicial warrant. CBSA used its special powers to seize otherwise constitutionally protected data at the border and would then be providing that data to CSIS in what might reasonably be regarded as an end run around section 8 of the *Charter* under existing caselaw.[76]

Of course, no one would know about the *Charter* violation because no one outside of government would know about this information sharing, and even if this were the rare instance where the Privacy Commissioner or the Security Intelligence Review Committee happened upon this single transaction in a sea of operations, it could only admonish, not really enforce anything. We discuss the difficulties faced by the Privacy Commissioner further below.

CSIS's review body, the Security Intelligence Review Committee, cannot even force CBSA to reveal how information that it provided to CSIS had been obtained — its review jurisdiction begins and ends with CSIS. There is no specialized, independent reviewer of CBSA. No one is ever in a position to get this question in front of a court to adjudicate the constitutionality of CBSA sharing and CSIS receiving this type of information.

More Round Pegs Meeting Square Holes, Requiring a Lawyerly Hammer

Now on to the travel information in our hypothetical scenario. As fate would have it, the *Immigration and Refugee Protection Act* allows the government to make regulations on CBSA information disclosure "for the purposes of national security, the defence of Canada or the conduct of international affairs."[77] Regulations now in place allow CBSA to disclose information about passengers that "relates to terrorism" or "terrorism-related crimes or other serious crimes, including organized crime, that are transnational in nature."[78]

For CBSA, things look good. Except they aren't: under the immigration law, "terrorism" is not a defined term but has been construed by the courts to mean an "act intended to cause death or serious bodily injury to a civilian, or to any other person not taking an active part in the hostilities in a situation of armed conflict, when the purpose of such act, by its nature or context, is to intimidate a population, or to compel a government or an international organization to do or to abstain from doing any act."[79] This is actually *narrower* than the definition of "terrorism" in the *CSIS Act*, and it is also narrower than the concept of "terrorist activity" in the *Criminal Code*. Both of these statutes include serious violence against persons *and* in some instances property, not just "serious bodily injury to a civilian."

And meanwhile, how are we supposed to construe "terrorism-related crimes"? The *Criminal Code* uses (and defines) the different term "terrorism offences," which reaches all sorts of conduct, including terrorism financing. Under the immigration law, the phrase "terrorism-related crimes" is undefined, but to be consistent with court definitions of "terrorism" in the immigration context, it presumably relates to crimes involving bodily harm. So would that concept include terrorism financing, which is a few steps removed from actual violence causing bodily harm? Recall that the real issue with our suspicious travellers is that they may be shuttling cash to ISIS, not fighting for it.

Well, the CBSA lawyers decide to apply common sense and conclude that whatever the angels on this particular legal pinhead, the information should go to CSIS. Perhaps they simply conclude that these conflicting disclosure rules should be "read up" in some manner to allow sharing of information that meets the new "undermine" concept in the *SoCIS Act*.

Meanwhile, in a scene multiplied across many different departments and many different cases, similar decisions are made by other government agencies when confronted by the mass confusion of Canada's security information sharing regime. And so information flows but only because officials perform (perhaps doubtful) mental gymnastics to overcome the inadequacies of Canada's incoherent laws, not because those laws establish a sensible, workable system based on the rule of law.

Wallpapering over a Fissured Wall

Maybe it is obvious to government lawyers how all of this is to work. But as readers may suspect, we think it will work because the government makes its work, in spite of the law, not because of it. In a system built on legality, we sincerely doubt that this is the most elegant approach to dealing with the silo problem identified by the Air India and 9/11 commissions. It may reflect the poor and likely hurried drafting of Bill C-51 and the speed with which it was rushed through Parliament and committees in a highly partisan environment.

Missing the Point

Nor do we think that the *SoCIS Act* cures the problem identified by the Air India Commission. Put simply, this issue revolves around the considerable difficulty that CSIS has sharing information with the police. In Chapter 9, we consider at great length this "intelligence-to-evidence" problem.

This issue is close to notorious in Canadian security circles and was the source of much of the Air India Commission's close inquiry. Joseph Fogarty was until fairly recently the United Kingdom security liaison to Canada, and he is a man intimately familiar with the security services of both the United Kingdom and Canada. Testifying before the Senate committee studying Bill C-51, he offered his views:

> [A] key difference at the time [of Fogarty's assignment to Canada] be- tween the U.K. and Canadian operational systems was that CSIS and the RCMP had not been provided with a framework within which they could both share information extensively and also protect themselves from the disclosure of sensitive capability and relationships when encountering the criminal justice system.[80]

For all the government's fanfare around the *SoCIS Act*, it does nothing to dispel Fogarty's concern, a point we explore in Chapter 9. It does not compel CSIS to share, something that the Air India Commission identified as a key reform.

Information Sharing Run Amok and Drowning in Data

As this discussion suggests, we do not hold the new information sharing regime in high regard, measured against its security objectives.

Here we add another concern related to the extreme breadth of the "undermine" concept at the heart of the new legal regime: there is an acute concern in security discussions that we are now overloaded with too much information. In 2009, the then head of CSIS revealed in a public speech that

CSIS was retaining so much information on targeted investigations that he predicted "within several years someone will accuse us of acting like the Stasi because of the information we are now compelled to keep."[81] CSIS now retains information for important due process reasons, after being told by the Supreme Court to do so, but there are key questions about how well all this data flow can be managed.

We now have the technology to store and mine unprecedented amounts of data. The haystacks are exponentially expanding, but it is also becoming more difficult to find the needles of actionable intelligence that could prevent a future Air India bombing. That is because there appears to be too little analytical capacity and rigour. And even when intelligence of a threat is produced, as occurred before the 22 October 2014 attack on Parliament,[82] sufficient oversight is not there to ensure that the intelligence is distributed and used to best advantage.

The *SoCIS Act* risks more of the disease of agencies drowning in data. It allows scores of government institutions to convey vast amounts of data to the security services. These data may include a vast range of information that is viewed by the sharing agencies as reaching the "undermine" level on diverse matters such as the domestic activities of separatist, Indigenous, and environmental groups, the security of other states, and harm to infrastructure. We have concerns, augmented by what is being learned from the Snowden leaks about the collection of Big Data, that officials applying the new Act may be unable to see the most immediate dangers of terrorism in the tidal wave of newly shared information.

The history of terrorism is littered with intelligence failures, including the failures to appreciate fairly specific intelligence to prevent the 9/11 events, the Air India bombings, and possibly the 22 October 2014 attack on Parliament. Recent events in Europe and Australia suggest that authorities have often known the perpetrators of terrorism but have not predicted their conduct. If we have been unable to process warning signals properly even in relation to terrorism, what are the implications of information sharing that reaches the vast universe of matters labelled a security risk in the *SoCIS Act*?

We fear that if everything is a security matter (as it appears to be under this Act), nothing is. The advent of Big Data, prompting agencies to rely on computer algorithms and not gumshoe detective work, may aggravate this problem, not solve it.[83] In sum, we fear that the new *SoCIS Act* may make it more, not less, difficult to single out information and intelligence that could help stop an act of terrorism. We admit we may be wrong. The security professionals may be able to separate the wheat from the chaff. But we are confident as lawyers in concluding that the *SoCIS Act* will produce a lot of chaff.

From Rumour to Action

More than that, a chaff-heavy new system raises serious civil liberties concerns. Notably, the new system appears to have learned little from Maher Arar's experience. Arar's experience points to the pernicious consequences of sharing unreliable information. The commission of inquiry into the Arar matter made a number of concrete recommendations on information sharing. Because of that inquiry's focus, these recommendations were directed at the RCMP, but they are best practices for all national security information sharing.

Among other things, those conducting national security investigations should be extremely well trained including on how to analyze information with accuracy, precision, and a "sophisticated understanding of context."[84] Information sharing decisions should be centralized and governed by clear policies on screening for reliability, relevance, and accuracy.[85] Caveats limiting who can have access to the information and how it can be further transmitted must be attached to shared information.[86] And most importantly, integrated information sharing must be matched and balanced with integrated review by independent review bodies[87] able to initiate their own investigations to ensure reliability, relevance, and compliance with *Charter* and privacy rights.

In what we have called "Arar amnesia," there is nothing in the *SoCIS Act* about steps to ensure the reliability and accuracy of the information that is shared. This should give everyone serious pause. We raise, here, the injustice-related implications of sweeping information sharing of intelligence with varying levels of reliability. Improperly shared information may result in rumours and innuendo being reconceived as fact and used to justify action, sometimes of a very troubling sort.

There is one place where the government seems to have had the Arar experience in mind: the *SoCIS Act* legislates a very robust qualified immunity should someone seek to obtain compensation for harms done as a result of "good faith" information sharing (e.g., Arar or other Canadians tortured in Syria in part because of Canadian information sharing, or Abousfian Abdelrazik, who was detained in Sudan).[88] Neither the Arar nor the Iacobucci commission found an absence of good faith among government officials, despite the dire consequences of their behaviour. And so the Act could preclude most civil recovery should someone in the future be harmed or even killed as a result of the sharing of information, as long as the subjective purpose behind the sharing was earnest, even if the conduct was negligent or ill-executed.

Meanwhile, the new *SoCIS Act* invokes caveats but only in its non-binding "guiding principles" portion. An initial version of the Act even provided what we called an "anti-caveat" provision authorizing further sharing "to any person, for any purpose."[89] The government thankfully amended this provision after Bill C-51 was introduced. Nevertheless, originator control and caveats continue to be enforced not by law but by the expectation of reciprocity: if violated, future information sharing may be imperiled. The Act does not enhance this (sometimes underwhelming) safeguard.

The issue of independent review is ignored completely, a matter discussed further below and in Chapter 12. This means that, as in the Arar affair, a failure to place caveats or restrictions on subsequent disclosure may not be detected or remedied, except by accident. It also means that oversharing — sharing of information that is not within the jurisdiction and responsibilities of the body receiving the information — may not be detected. It is important to recall here that information sharing does not require judicial warrants or oversight.

Privacy and the Omniscient Government

At some important level, the *SoCIS Act* seems aimed at achieving what Stanley Cohen once identified and criticized as "a unitary view of government information-holding." Writing in 2005, he observed:

> A belief exists . . . that the government should consider legislative change that will allow it to view all data collected by institutions as belonging to one party — the government. Government institutions would merely be custodians of what would essentially amount to a centralized pool of personal information. Needless to say, this unitary view of government information-holding is highly controversial and has never been officially endorsed. By this view, the government would reserve the right to share information horizontally for greater protection and security when it is in the public interest to do so.[90]

Bill C-51 comes close to an official endorsement of this unitary view. And it is important to underscore again that this unitary approach is not tied to terrorism alone but to the broadest definition of national security in Canadian legal history. As the Privacy Commissioner warned in his critique of Bill C-51, "All Canadians — not only terrorism suspects — will be caught in this web. Bill C-51 opens the door to collecting, analysing and potentially keeping forever the personal information of all Canadians in order to find the virtual needle in the haystack."[91] He also reasoned that with the enactment of the bill, "17 government institutions involved in national security would have virtually limitless powers to monitor and, with the assistance of Big Data analytics, to profile ordinary Canadians, with a view to identifying security threats among them."[92]

·   The *SoCIS Act* ignores the chilling impact that information sharing and total government awareness may have on expressions of dissent, even with the Act's (overbroad and therefore unworkable) exception. Nor are we persuaded that mere information sharing is benign. As we have underscored above, the experience with commissions of inquiry in the past decade shows that information sharing can be the causal origin of significant harm. To be sure, information sharing is necessary to prevent terrorism, but it must be disciplined by more carefully and narrowly drafted legislation than Bill C-51, and it must be subject to adequate review structures, which are not in place in Canada.

Moving Past Bill C-51

In sum, many of our concerns would be resolved — or at least muted — by three changes. First, it is past time to fix definitively information flows between CSIS and the police. No government is serious about security until it applies itself to this task. We discuss this issue in Chapter 9.

Standardized Definitions

Second, the government could reduce the complexity (and subjectivity) of its information sharing regime by standardizing national security information sharing rules throughout the statute books, rather than simply papering over an overly messy system with an even messier umbrella "undermine" concept and a sloppy set of operative rules on disclosure.

If the prevention of terrorism is to be the highest priority, then there may be a case for special rules that give priority to sharing terrorism-related information — not rules that are equally permissive of the sharing of information related to lesser security threats. But whatever the case, it would be better to harmonize a common and reasonable definition of national security and then embed it in the law, not overlay it on existing concepts that remain operative and thereby raise the coherency nightmares explored above.

Enhanced Review

Third, even the best statutory language cannot eliminate subjectivity and also the possibility that secretive interpretations of the rules may lead to unwarranted use of information sharing powers. Correcting this prospect requires a real investment in a new accountability mechanism.

The government's backgrounder on Bill C-51 expressed confidence that the review functions of the Privacy Commissioner and the Auditor General "will help maintain the appropriate balance between protecting the privacy of citizens and ensuring national security."[93] But the Arar Commission found that while the Auditor General did valuable work on national security, "it [did] not have the expertise to review RCMP national security activities [there at issue] to ensure their legality and propriety"[94] and that privacy commissioners did not have sufficient resources to adequately provide accountability in this area.[95] Indeed, in 2014, the Privacy Commissioner's office underscored continued difficulties in reviewing national security matters and called for wholesale reform.[96] This reform has not come to pass. When Bill C-51 was being debated in Parliament, the Privacy Commissioner warned that scrutinizing activity under the new *SoCIS Act* would stretch his resources, leaving other areas of his large mandate potentially unguarded.[97] It is also notable that the Privacy Commissioner's remit extends only to "personal information." While that concept is broadly defined in the *Privacy Act* as "information about an identifiable individual,"[98] it may not reach all the information that might be at issue under the new sharing regime.

In this respect, consider the implications of whole-of-government information sharing and the "mosaic effect" of aggregated data: Government agencies may each individually share pieces of information that themselves do not include information about "an identifiable individual." The government might argue that this sharing is ungoverned by the *Privacy Act*, and unreviewable by the Privacy Commissioner. But once assembled through Big Data processing, the information may be combined to present a mosaic that does raise serious privacy concerns. Bits of information that themselves are not attached to people may be assembled so as to say a lot about the behaviour of a now imputable individual. The government might urge that the point of assembly is where the *Privacy Act* attaches and not before. Such an approach would greatly limit the ability of the Privacy Commissioner to investigate and review the whole "life cycle" of information sharing within government.

The government backgrounder on the *SoCIS Act* also noted that there are review bodies for CSIS, the RCMP, and the Communications Security Establishment but again disregarded the Arar Commission's finding that the existing three specialized review bodies could not adequately review information sharing between institutions because they could not share secret information amongst themselves or conduct joint investigations and reviews.[99] In other words, all-of-government total information awareness is not being matched by all-of-government total review and accountability. Such a system does not exist in Canada.

What the new *SoCIS Act* does is break down barriers between government agencies in a clumsy and uncertain manner while keeping specialized national security review bodies carefully corralled to a narrow subset of agencies. And it asks the Privacy Commissioner to expend resources and exercise powers that his office has said are insufficient. This is a recipe for disaster, as we will discuss in Chapter 12. For present purposes, it suffices to say we find inspiration in the expectations outlined by a minority of the Supreme Court in the *Wakeling* cross-border information sharing case described above:

> Canadian law enforcement officers may subjectively intend to serve justice by sharing information. However, improper or hazardous sharing is unlikely to come to light without record-keeping, reporting or notice obligations. Moreover, accountability is not only about fostering compliance with the letter of the law; it is about giving oversight bodies, legislators and the public the information that they need to ensure that statutory powers are necessary and are used appropriately.[100]

The minority proposed new transparency mechanisms — including after-the-fact reporting on the scale of information sharing to Parliament itself.

For his part, the Privacy Commissioner recommended that Bill C-51 "should be amended to include an explicit requirement for written information agreements" covering "what is to be shared and how, when information is to be retained, when it must be disposed of, and include robust accountability measures to assign responsibility for and review of sharing, including direction on how documentation disclosed or received should be handled."[101] We would go one step further: information sharing should be carefully logged, and notice of when the *SoCIS Act* is used should be affirmatively provided to the Privacy Commissioner and other relevant review agencies.

In its present form, the Privacy Commissioner (and other bodies) would be deluged with such notifications. We feel this is so in large part because the *SoCIS Act* is so vast and because an excess of data risks being transferred. Giving the Act a more reasonable scope, of the sort described above, would limit this excessive flow and make a notification system more manageable.

Enhanced Judicial Oversight

We do not think, however, that even meaningful back-end accountability to an auditing review body suffices in the world of Big Data. We discussed at length in Chapter 4 the consequences of the information-rich era for privacy. Back-end auditing does not protect the "right to be left alone" in the manner once promised by the classic Camden approach to warrants, issued in advance of invasive searches.

Other countries may eventually catch up to the modern need to supervise, not simply the collection, but also the processing and aggregation of information. One of the conclusions reached at a recent international conference composed largely of security professionals (that one of us was fortunate to attend in May 2015) was that oversight should focus not simply on the collection but the use of information.[102] In our view, archived data shared and pooled into databases should become the new "Englishman's castle." That is, data may accumulate in databases in a way that triggers reasonable expectations of privacy. We need new rules for when and how those databases can be searched. The new *SoCIS Act* does not address this issue — it makes the issue more urgent if, as the Privacy Commissioner warned, it means that "17 government institutions involved in national security would have virtually limitless powers to monitor and, with the assistance of Big Data analytics, to profile ordinary Canadians, with a view to identifying security threats among them."[103]

We believe that the time has come to adopt the judicial oversight model and to require so-called Firewall Warrants — requiring that approval from a judge be obtained before databases are queried for information that raises reasonable expectations of privacy. Such approval would be granted only where on reasonable and probable grounds the judge is persuaded that the search should be permitted.

Indeed, we believe that Firewall Warrants are probably already a constitutional necessity where law enforcement is inclined to search databases aggregating information originally collected for other purposes. Law enforcement agencies, for example, may not avoid constitutional search and seizure obligations by receiving otherwise protected information from administrative or other bodies not subject to the same constitutional strictures,[104] accumulating it into databases, and then simply searching.

Firewall Warrants would have to limit the sorts of data mining to be conducted pursuant to the warrant. A Firewall Warrant must not be a carte blanche to troll linked databases at will. Instead, the specific searches to be conducted and the algorithms to be used in searching the databases must be approved in advance.

Further, judges (and reviewing bodies) should be concerned with minimization procedures. Even with the most carefully constructed algorithms, any data mining exercise is likely to reveal extraneous information unrelated to the approved search. The state should be obliged to minimize the product of an authorized search: material unrelated to the search's authorized objective should be expunged from the search results. This is especially true in relation to third-party information caught by the search results. Without minimization, the results of approved searches could themselves be archived and constitute a substantial parallel data network to be data mined in subsequent investigations. It will not always be clear at the outset what information is material to the investigation that has prompted the search. Therefore, the obligation to expunge extraneous data should follow the completion of the investigation or, barring that, come after the passage of a modest period of time.

IV. CONCLUSION

The "share" tool, like "watch," is fundamental to an effective anti-terror strategy. But the details matter. Canada has struggled with intelligence sharing for decades. Information does not flow where it should (Air India), or it flows where it should not (Arar). Fixing this problem is not beyond our means. But it requires much more than Bill C-51's papering over of the cracks and its clumsy and confusing drafting. Instead, it requires a sincere and deep re-consideration of all the issues raised in this chapter: breaking down bureaucratic silos in a manner that enables key "dots" to be connected and that actually compels information sharing between recalcitrant agencies (CSIS) and agencies that may need the information (the RCMP); enhanced oversight and enhanced review of information flows to guard against abuses, including invasions of privacy; and careful prioritization of what information should flow to avoid enlarging the haystack to such proportions that it makes finding the needles impossible.

Bill C-51's *SoCIS Act* meets none of these objectives in any real way, but it does erode privacy and create confusion and uncertainty where greater precision is required. We do not think the law's drafters deserve the blame, but the ministers who demanded a rushed job and the broadest definition ever of Canada's security interests probably do. Bill C-51's new information sharing law is an ill-crafted law reacting to a larger systemic problem that requires deep inquiry, not superficial quick fixes.

CHAPTER SIX

Interdict: Restricting the Movement of Threats

I. INTRODUCTION

Algerian Ahmed Ressam came to Canada in 1994 on a crude false passport. Border officials detected the forgery, and Ressam applied for refugee status. He was released pending adjudication of his refugee claim and took up residence in Montreal, living on welfare payments and petty crime. In May 1995, the Immigration and Refugee Board of Canada denied Ressam's refugee claim after he had failed to appear for a critical hearing.[1] In June 1995, he was convicted of shoplifting and ordered to leave Canada. He did not comply, and he was again arrested for theft — in this case pickpocketing — in October 1996 and eventually convicted.[2] Again, he remained in Canada. He was not deported reportedly because of the prospect of his maltreatment in his native Algeria.[3] But he was watched by CSIS.

While in Montreal, Ressam associated with affiliates of al-Qaida, but CSIS did not regard his activities as threatening Canadian security.[4] During this period, however, Ressam did manage to acquire a blank baptismal certificate stolen from the Catholic church. Assuming a new identity, he acquired a real Canadian passport in March 1998. Using this document, Ressam left Canada, and CSIS lost all track of him.

Ressam travelled to Afghanistan, where he attended al-Qaida terrorist camps. There, he acquired explosives training.[5] He also plotted with other Algerians to attack a US airport or consulate. Returning to Canada under his false identity with precursor chemicals for bombs hidden in toiletry bottles, a notebook with bomb-making instructions, and a large quantity of cash, he

175

then sought weapons, chemicals, and phony papers. After his co-conspirators proved unable to obtain travel documents to Canada, Ressam went ahead with his plans alone, selecting Los Angeles International airport as his target.

After a week in Vancouver assembling explosive components with a close friend, he packed the explosives in a rental car and drove onto the ferry between Victoria and Port Angeles, Washington. He and a new United States–based confederate had planned to bomb the airport on 1 January 2000. But, at the border crossing, a US customs agent noticed Ressam's evident nervousness. Subjected to a pat-down search, Ressam panicked and attempted to flee. US authorities inspected the rental car and discovered the bomb material. Ressam was arrested[6] and convicted. He is now known to history as the "millennium bomber."

Ressam's plot was halted. But it was alert border officials that stopped him, not surveillance, intercepts, or intelligence sharing. These officials interdicted what could have been a devastating terrorist attack. Had they not, there is every chance that Ressam would have succeeded. Enhanced tools to physically foil plots and attacks are, therefore, a logical priority in any anti-terror strategy.

Stopping terrorist violence before it occurs is called "deny" in the Canadian government's 2012 counter-terrorism strategy. For the government, "deny" "involves mitigating vulnerabilities and aggressively intervening in terrorist planning, including prosecuting individuals involved in terrorist related criminal activities, and making Canada and Canadian interests a more difficult target for would-be terrorists."[7] Put another way, "deny" includes everything from hardening infrastructure to trials.

We do not find this general and vast concept of "deny" to be a tremendously useful analytical tool. It is too broad and ambiguous to fit into our analytical threat response escalator, explained in Chapter 3. And so in the next five chapters we subdivide "deny" into different categories, each marking a more assertive step on the escalator:

- Interdict: measures that restrict movement
- Restrain: measures that restrict liberty short of criminal incarceration
- Interrupt: measures that are used to stop feared terrorist attacks or threats when other measures are unavailable
- Prosecute: criminal trial and incarceration
- Delete: prosecution and deletion of extremist speech

This chapter covers "interdict," which involves inhibiting the movement of suspected terrorists, either directly or indirectly. Some of these tools reach Canadians while others are available only in relation to foreigners within Canada. In this chapter, we focus first on those tactics that may be directed at Canadians and then on those pertaining to foreigners. Finally, we consider new efforts to turn Canadians into foreigners in the name of anti-terrorism.

II. INTERDICTING CANADIANS

Unlawful Banishment

Under section 6 of the *Charter of Rights and Freedoms*, Canadians have a constitutional right to enter, remain in, and leave Canada.[8] Canadians cannot, therefore, be banished unless the government is able to establish that such a step is a reasonable limitation on the right, justified in a free and democratic society. There are laws that withstand this searching "section 1 analysis." Canadians may be extradited to face criminal proceedings in a foreign court.[9] And if the government weighs competing considerations properly, it may reject petitions by Canadians serving time in foreign jails to transfer to a Canadian prison.[10]

But there is no law like the one enacted in the United Kingdom in 2015 denying citizens re-entry rights on national security grounds.[11] There is also no way other than through a proper extradition that a Canadian can be forced out of the country. This is not to say that renditions — extraordinary and extra-legal removals — have not happened in Canada. In one post-9/11 case, discussed in Chapter 2, CSIS acted precisely in this manner and was criticized by its review body for violating the section 6 (and other) *Charter* rights of a Canadian who had been sent to the United States and later found guilty of terrorism.[12]

In another case, a court found that the government's efforts to banish a Canadian citizen suspected of terrorism had violated his right as a Canadian citizen to return to Canada. In that case, the Federal Court found that CSIS had been complicit in the detention of Canadian citizen Abousfian Abdelrazik in Sudan and that the Canadian government had also impeded his return to Canada, not least by failing to provide a passport, needed for international travel.[13] The court concluded that the government's bare assertion unsupported by evidence that Abdelrazik "posed a danger to national security or to the security of another country" did not amount to a section 1 defence.[14] This case was discussed in Chapter 2 as a post-9/11 overreaction to terrorism, one that violated the rights of a Canadian citizen who was later delisted from the United Nations blacklist as a person associated with al-Qaida.

Crossing Borders

But while Canadians generally cannot be stopped from crossing the Canadian border, they can be closely scrutinized while at it. In some respects, the border is like the neck of a wine bottle: rights narrow there, and the state can do things that it may not do quite so easily within the country.

Here, we are speaking about much more than invasive security screening at airports. At the border, Canada Border Services Agency (CBSA) officers have extensive powers to stop and search persons entering the country, along with their luggage and other property.[15] Crossing the border is one of the few instances outside of actual arrest by the police where state authorities can interrogate someone who is unable to simply walk away (at least not easily). The questioning of people and the examination of people and luggage (including electronic devices) by border authorities is not restrained by the same *Charter* search protections that apply within Canada.[16]

This makes the border a very powerful means of interdiction and allows authorities to question and search people, and their property, on bases that would not justify a police or CSIS search warrant within the country. There is no constitutional error if CBSA subjects a person to a search under the agency's standard procedure on the basis of a "lookout" triggered by police or CSIS information.[17] Indeed, the Arar Commission found that it had been a border lookout from the RCMP to both Canadian and American customs officials that had wrongly identified both Maher Arar and his wife, Dr Monia Mazigh, as persons linked to al-Qaida. As a result, Arar was subjected to secondary inspections by Canadian customs before his eventual detention in and rendition from the United States.[18]

Arar's border search is an example of a false positive: treating a person who is not a terrorist as a terrorist. But Ressam's detection by an alert US border official is an example of a true positive — and one that likely prevented a deadly terrorist attack in the United States.

Extorting Compliance at the Border

Border controls are, in other words, an important tool. But there is a risk that border controls may be used as a pretextual tool for extraneous CSIS or police investigations. In one egregious, recent case, CSIS agents repeatedly questioned Ayad Mejid, believing him to be "an individual who posted extremist literature on the Internet with the intent of inciting violence."[19] Mejid denied these accusations, and after browbeating and pressure he allowed CSIS to review his computer several times. These reviews proved fruitless, and (despite failing a lie detector test) Mejid continued to deny involvement in terrorist propaganda.

Then, several years after this initial CSIS investigation, Mejid accidentally crossed the border. While visiting Niagara Falls, Ontario, he and his family missed a turnoff before the Lewiston bridge to the United States. He turned around on the bridge to re-enter Canada, but because he and his family lacked the papers required at a border crossing, they were detained by the CBSA.

By this point, Mejid was on a CBSA lookout, presumably at CSIS's request, so every time he crossed the border, CBSA would call CSIS. On this occasion, a CSIS officer "'dropped' everything that he was doing and drove as quickly as he could from Hamilton to the border."[20] As a court later found, he did so "to take advantage of Mr. Mejid's detention by a second government agency — the CBSA."[21] The CSIS officer questioned Mejid for one or two hours concerning his alleged online extremist activities, which Mejid again denied. At this point, a CBSA officer searched Mejid's computer, which had journeyed across the Lewiston bridge with him. She looked for child pornography.

The CSIS officer later said that CBSA had conducted this search after "an 'informal request' for advice," to which the CSIS officer had provided "an 'informal suggestion' in a collegial manner between two government agencies."[22] But a court held that the CSIS officer was misrepresenting the facts and had in fact "instructed the CBSA to conduct a search for child pornography."[23] The CSIS officer told the court that he had suspected Mejid might have such predilections because he believed Mejid had had an affair with a teenager and because CSIS had heard other rumours in the community.

The CSIS officer also misled his CBSA colleague: he told her that Mejid had consented to the search. But the CSIS officer later told a court that he did not remember asking Mejid for this permission, and Mejid denied that he had been consulted on the matter.[24]

The CBSA officer was unable to do a thorough search because of limited expertise, and she found no information on the computer related to national security or criminal activity. But before being released from detention, Mejid agreed to meet with the CSIS officer again inside Canada. He did so, concluded the court, as "a condition precedent to leaving the border," not because he wanted to.[25] In the judge's words, "I am persuaded that he was only permitted to leave once he agreed to meet with CSIS a couple of days later."[26] We revisit this case and its aftermath in Chapter 9 and note how the CSIS conduct resulted in the exclusion of child pornography evidence in a subsequent trial and severe criticism by the trial court of CSIS's violation of the *Charter*. But for our purposes here, this case illustrates both the temptation to use and the consequence of using the border to strong-arm Canadians in violation of their constitutional rights. We do not know how often this happens, but Mejid's case shows it clearly does.

It is not clear that such practices would be detected often. A keyword search of the public reports of the Security Intelligence Review Committee (SIRC) suggests that the Mejid case has attracted no scrutiny despite how extreme it is. It may be that SIRC conducted a secret review, but it would not be surprising if SIRC had not. As we discuss in Chapter 12, SIRC can be expected to scrutinize only a small number of CSIS operations annually, and much will be missed. This prospect is enhanced where, as here, the operation involves co-operation with CBSA. CBSA has no review body of its own, and SIRC may review only CSIS conduct. No review agency exists able to put together the pieces in the same way that the court was able to do in the Mejid case.

And the Mejid court was able to play this role only because CSIS not only coerced Mejid in violation of his *Charter* rights but also later decided to enforce criminal law in violation of its mandate. The infrequent nature of judicial review in either criminal or civil courts is one of the main reasons cited by the Arar Commission for expanding independent review to include other security agencies, including CBSA. We know about this particular case only because some prosecutor made the mistake of proceeding with it.

The basic point here is that interdict powers immunized from review by courts run the risk of abuse. As we explore in Chapter 8, CSIS's actions in the Mejid case were also a failed attempt at Al Capone–style collateral enforcement of the criminal law, a strategy that is still not technically available to CSIS under Bill C-51[27] but that may hint at how the agency's new threat reduction powers could be used.

Monitoring Departures

CBSA can search people leaving the country as much as it can people entering the country. But since Canada does not have exit controls and interviews, there is no natural funnel channelling people through a system that would make such searches routine.

That is not to say that people have not proposed such approaches. The Senate national security committee, for instance, concluded as follows in 2015:

> It has become clear that over 145 Canadians have gone abroad to support terrorist groups and approximately 80 have returned. Without entry and exit registration this poses a significant challenge to law enforcement agencies and the CBSA. In this scenario, it is vitally important for Canada's na-

tional security that the government be aware of everybody who is entering or leaving Canada.[28]

The Canada–United States Beyond the Border Action Plan will ultimately implement a bilateral entry and exist information sharing system between Canada and the United States. The Senate committee called for the government to move beyond this development "to implement a system to register the entry and exit of all travellers, Canadians and non-Canadians."[29]

There are obvious logistical challenges to doing so.[30] And privacy also ranks high among concerns. Initially, CBSA proposed retaining entry and exit information under the Canada–United States plan for seventy-five years, which was later reduced to a mere thirty years after protest from the Privacy Commissioner. The planned rollout of the entry and exit recording system anticipates that the information will also be used for law enforcement and intelligence purposes and shared with police and CSIS. In late 2014, the Privacy Commissioner recommended that "each of these expanded uses be demonstrated as necessary and effective, be undertaken in the least privacy-invasive manner possible and be designed so any loss of privacy is in proportion to a substantial societal benefit."[31] Recording and sharing vast numbers of entries and exits reveals how an interdict measure justified as an anti-terrorism tool can morph into a system of sifting through large numbers of false positives — each representing a person who has surrendered an element of privacy as the state seeks to detect uncommon threats. The prospect of the careful modulation advanced by the Privacy Commissioner may now have evaporated in light of the massively expansive information sharing regime established by Bill C-51, discussed in Chapter 5.

The *Charter* would apply to the Canada–United States Beyond the Border Action Plan, but in uncertain ways. A Supreme Court case decided shortly after 9/11 held that the state's interests in preventing unemployment insurance fraud outweighed any residual privacy that people have in the customs declaration cards that they fill out when returning to Canada.[32] That decision suggests, again, that *Charter* protections at the border may not be entirely robust. At the same time, the decision sits uneasily with a more recent Supreme Court case that accepts that anonymity is part of privacy and express more awareness about how otherwise innocuous information can be pieced together to reveal much about a person.[33]

Stopping Departures

Even an extensive entry and exit information sharing regime will not stop international travel except where that system is used to catch people already subject to an arrest warrant under a criminal process or peace bond strictures of the sort discussed in Chapter 7. And yet stopping Canadians from venturing abroad has become a particularly poignant national security concern with the focus on ISIS (Islamic State of Iraq and Syria) and foreign terrorist fighters. Since it is now impossible — legally — to leave Canada without a passport, taking away passports is an obvious means of interdicting Canadian international travel.

Revoking Passports

The government's passport rules are found in the *Canadian Passport Order*.[34] That instrument provides that "any person who is a Canadian citizen under the [Citizenship] Act may be issued a passport"[35] and sets out the requirements to be met before a passport will be issued.

Under rules updated and broadened in 2015, "the Minister of Public Safety and Emergency Preparedness may decide that a passport is not to be issued or is to be revoked if he or she has reasonable grounds to *believe* that the decision is necessary to prevent the commission of a terrorism offence . . . or for the national security of Canada or a foreign country or state."[36] Passport services may thereafter be denied to a Canadian for ten years. Under the 2015 changes, the Minister of Public Safety may also "cancel" a passport,[37] which was described by government officials as a more interim step amounting to a suspension pending a full decision on revocation.[38] The minister may cancel, as opposed to revoke a passport where she has (merely) reasonable grounds to *suspect* that it will prevent a terrorism offence. As discussed in Chapter 4 and set out in the annex to Chapter 1, reasonable grounds to suspect is a lesser threshold than reasonable grounds to believe, and, indeed, amounts to the most undemanding limitation on state action in Canadian law. Passport revocation is an administrative device and not dependent on criminal evidentiary burdens and standards of proof. And while passport revocation raises section 6 mobility rights issues under the *Charter*, its past application in national security matters has been saved by section 1 of the *Charter*.[39]

All this makes passport denial a reasonably pliable tool allowing authorities to bar international travel where persuaded that a person is, for instance, voyaging to become a foreign terrorist fighter.[40] Of course, there must be some proof of the latter objective. Proof of this nature may be collected as a collateral product of a police investigation into crimes, or (probably more likely) it could stem from an investigation by CSIS into a threat to the security of Canada. This secret source of relevant information raises inevitable concerns. The government has acknowledged that passport revocations have been used less frequently than they might have been because of a "concern that the intelligence will not be protected in open proceedings."[41]

Secret Hearings

In direct response to this problem, the government took steps in 2015 to facilitate the use of secret information in any challenge to a passport revocation. Up until that point, a person could challenge a passport revocation through a regular judicial review process in Federal Court, where open, conventional court processes would apply. While the government could shield its secret evidence from disclosure using the *Canada Evidence Act*, discussed in Chapter 2,[42] such an approach allowed courts to balance the competing cases for and against disclosure and sometimes opt for disclosure to preserve other values even in the face of a real security justification. Moreover, even if the government won on secrecy grounds, it might have considerable difficulty relying on the shielded information to support its case, risking a loss on the ultimate issue of passport interdiction.

In Bill C-59, the 2015 federal budget bill, the government resorted to its notorious habit of legislating substantive law in budget bills,[43] and Parliament duly enacted the *Prevention of Terrorist Travel Act*.[44] This statute establishes a brand new appeal system to the Federal Court for passports cancelled on an interim basis on national security grounds. It also establishes new procedures for judicial review of a passport revocation. Both new challenge systems draw on the immigration security certificate process, described in Chapter 7: they allow for secret hearings using secret evidence. As with security certificates, the court must order secrecy, not after a balancing of the competing cases for and against disclosure, but whenever disclosure of the information could harm the government's interests in national security or the safety of any person.[45] Put another way, security secrecy prevails automatically regardless of other interests that might be impaired by this confidentiality.

And, in an example of the recurring due process minimalism in the 2015 laws, the government refused to incorporate a statutory special advocate system, something that is constitutionally required in the security certificate process. In other words, the government did nothing to ensure that intelligence never disclosed to the affected person would still be subject to adversarial challenge by someone whose job it was to test it.

The Federal Court may try to mitigate the risks associated with a closed proceeding by enlisting the assistance of a "friend of the court," or *amicus curiae*, to restore a quasi-adversarial system. But an *amicus curiae* is not a perfect replacement for a special advocate for two key reasons. First, under the security certificate process, "special advocates" are a statutory office with statutory roles and responsibilities. That places them in a significantly more meaningful role than is the case with *amici curiae*. A recent Federal Court decision suggests that the role (and, indeed, the actual presence) of *amici curiae* in *ex parte* proceedings will vary depending on the judge's predispositions and may be more limited than that of special advocates.[46]

Second, although underfunded, special advocates are at least supported by a special support unit, organized at arm's length from the Department of Justice. *Amici curiae* do not automatically benefit from this administrative structure and may end up operating in splendid isolation, with only the resources that they can personally bring (which do not include assistance from their own firms for security reasons, if no other) or that the court provides. Ad hoc alternative arrangements are possible but at the risk of piling more strain on the existing special advocate support unit.

In the Bill C-59 hearings, the government took the view that the special advocate system was unnecessary for passport cancellation or revocation challenges because the consequences are less severe here than with security certificates.[47] To the extent that security certificates may result in the detention and removal discussed in Chapter 7, that is true. But passport revocation also raises a different set of interests and rights. Because a passport is required for any cross-border travel, a revocation makes Canada into a very large prison. The inevitable question, therefore, is whether a passport revocation decision — one that the courts have already said engages *Charter* mobility rights and plausibly also raises *Charter* section 7 liberty interests — must include special advocates for constitutional reasons.

Of course, a special advocate procedural fix would be no silver bullet. Not least, special advocates may have difficulty proving useful if the basis for the passport revocation is information provided by a CSIS informer who has been promised confidentiality and to whom the new CSIS human source privilege in Bill C-44 will apply. We discuss Bill C-44's new secrecy provisions in Chapter 9.

No Security Panacea

Passport revocations will potentially visit considerable hardship on people who are falsely fingered as terrorists on the basis of the undemanding legal standard found in the new rules. There is also an obvious shortcoming to a passport revocation if the person really is a terrorist or prospective foreign fighter: a determined individual may attempt to travel on a false passport.[48] But this action is itself a crime.[49] And so an aspiring foreign terrorist fighter could be prosecuted in another variant of the Al Capone strategy — that is, not for the crime of foreign terrorist fighting per se but for the collateral activity of passport fraud.[50] Since the penalty for knowingly using a forged passport is a possible term of fourteen years, this may be more than a slap on the wrist.[51]

All this means that passport revocation is a potentially helpful tool in dealing with foreign terrorist fighters. But its usefulness should not be exaggerated. Revocation presumably has little or no deterrent effect — there is no public trial. Moreover, revocation is a gatekeeper tool available only at the exit stage of the foreign fighter life cycle. As already noted, it is not a means of forestalling return because of the constitutional right of all Canadians to re-enter the country.[52]

Even more importantly, while passport revocation may make a prison of Canada, that prison may not be sufficiently confining to comfort security officials. If deterred from travelling, a person may be redirected toward domestic terrorism, something that may have occurred with at least one of the October 2014 attackers and probably both.[53] This makes passport revocation a tool to be used strategically in close association with other tools, like the peace bonds to be discussed in Chapter 7 or even the prosecutions discussed in Chapter 9. Interdiction tools should not be used as a replacement for criminal proceedings, and this will require co-ordination, something that we will suggest in Chapter 11 is often lacking in Canada.

The need to use passport revocations strategically appears to be recognized within government. For instance, internal RCMP documents state that it "would *never* knowingly support or recommend a passport action if it would put Canadian lives at risk."[54] To its credit, the RCMP is leading a National Security Joint Operations Centre to "de-conflict" inter-agency decision making over passport revocations: "It is critical that all relevant agencies are consulted to ensure that an action taken by one agency does not impede on another."[55] This centre dates from October 2014 and is described by the RCMP as an "unprecedented interdepartmental collaboration" in the national security area.[56] We discuss it further in Chapter 11, but simply wonder here what was happening before October 2014.

No-Fly Lists

Canadians (along with others) can also be stopped from flying. In 2007, the government deployed powers under the *Aeronautics Act*[57] and that Act's *Identity Screening Regulations*[58] to exclude persons posing a security risk from aircraft. Although the details of Canada's Passenger Protect program are kept secret, there are reasons to conclude that it was a much more modest and restrained affair than the American no-fly list, notorious for both its size and its number of embarrassing false positives.[59]

Procedurally, this Canadian system depended on airlines screening passengers against a list managed by Public Safety Canada. The legal justification for the Passenger Protect program was clear and limited: it responded to "an immediate threat to aviation security or to any aircraft or aerodrome or other aviation facility, or to the safety of the public, passengers or crew members."[60] Except through the most dramatic of contortions, this ground does not include those who intend to travel overseas to fight in a foreign conflict.

In the result, Passenger Protect constituted a round-peg-in-square-hole tool for grappling with travel by Canadians to join foreign terrorist causes: in only rare circumstances will aviation security and foreign-terrorist-fighter concerns overlap. Those circumstances may exist on occasion. Media reports suggest that at least some foreign fighters are on the Passenger Protect no-fly list.[61] However, extreme caution was warranted in trying to extend the reach of the program to deal with the distinct and separate foreign-terrorist-fighter issue. If persons had been placed on the list simply as a means to deter their travel, and not because of plausible concerns about aviation security, the government would have been acting unlawfully.

New System

Bill C-51 changed all that. It enacted the *Secure Air Travel Act*, replacing the old *Aeronautics Act* system. The government can now put someone on the no-fly list where it has reasonable grounds to *suspect* that the person will "engage or attempt to engage in an act that would threaten transportation security" or will travel by air for the purpose of committing a terrorism offence.[62] Recall again that reasonable grounds to suspect is the lowest standard known to law and one that accepts a high rate of false positives — treating people who are not terrorists as terrorists. It seems very likely, for instance, that had Canada possessed a no-fly list in 2001, based on this forgiving threshold, Maher Arar would have been placed on it.

Once a person has been listed, the government may direct an air carrier to stop that person from boarding. The notion that airlines might be asked to stop a person from threatening transportation security or from travelling to commit a terrorism offence occasioned some concern from the airline industry during the Bill C-51 debate. In its original form, Bill C-51 said that the government could direct an air carrier to do anything "that, in the Minister's opinion, is reasonable and necessary to prevent a listed person" from threatening transportation security or travelling for the purpose of committing a terrorism offence.[63] For the airlines, this raised the disturbing prospect of an airline worker being asked to do something reckless[64] like detain or delay a potential terrorist until the police arrived.

In one of the handful of minor amendments the government permitted to the bill, that language was changed to allow the minister to order "specific, reasonable and necessary action."[65] It is difficult to see this change as being more than cosmetic, but it is hard too to imagine that the government really intends to deputize airline workers as a posse.

More Due Process Minimalism

More concerning was the government's now habitual failure to depart from due process minimalism. As with the new passport revocation process, the new *Secure Air Travel Act* establishes a brand new statutory appeal system where the government may use secret evidence in a secret hearing. And, again, the new approach fails to introduce a special advocate check on this closed-door process. This raises a new set of novel constitutional claims, similar to (if less acute than) those noted above for the new passport system.

The government's move followed a challenge in the Federal Court under the old system. Under the original Passenger Protect system, standard judicial review of listing decisions was met with government claims to confidentiality under the *Canada Evidence Act*. In *Canada (AG) v Telbani*,[66] the Federal Court ordered that some information the government wished to keep secret be disclosed to the applicant. As already noted, the *Canada Evidence Act* requires a judge to balance security interests against other concerns, like fair proceedings, in deciding whether to disclose information. But, like the security certificate system and the new passport revocation challenge process, the new Bill C-51 no-fly listing appeal process contains none of this balancing: security secrecy concerns prevail, and evidence will not be disclosed whenever disclosure would harm national security or any person.

An Information River

Bill C-51's *Secure Air Travel Act* also includes expansive new information sharing powers — piling on information sharing powers in a bill that already opens the door wide with its special new information sharing law, discussed in Chapter 5. Under the no-fly powers, the minister of public safety may disclose information to prevent banned travel and, more generally, for aviation security. More than that, the minister may enter into a written arrangement to share the no-fly list with a foreign state. Other agencies such as CBSA and Transport Canada may share information under the Act as well.[67]

None of these bodies is subject to specialized national security review. Any independent review will depend, therefore, on the Privacy Commissioner, an officer whose statutory remit now far exceeds his resources. In her review of Passenger Protect in 2009, the then Privacy Commissioner found that Transport Canada was mostly compliant with privacy rules but did note some shortcomings. Not least, the department had not extended its "oversight activities to verify that airlines are adequately handling and safeguarding Specified Persons List information disclosed by the department."[68]

This concern about sharing the list with airlines is a potentially acute one. Once shared with an airline, the list is presumably accessible to that airline in all of its international destinations. This likely means that it is also accessible to the governments in those international destinations, and some of them may not be benign in the interest that they show in a listed person within their reach.

Surprise Notification

The *Secure Air Travel Act* is also ambiguous on how listed persons will discover their fate. Under the prior Passenger Protect system, the government supplied a list, with names, genders, and dates of birth, to the airlines, who were then obliged to screen passengers by checking listed names against passenger identification when they arrived at check-in. Where passenger data matched those on the list, the airline contacted a special twenty-four-hour Transport Canada office, and a Transport Canada officer then decided whether to issue an emergency order under the *Aeronautics Act* precluding boarding by the passenger, and the RCMP was notified.[69]

As a result, persons were not given advance notice of listing decisions but instead discovered their status only when they arrived at check-in counters (or tried to check in at automated wickets). Transport Canada asserted that advance notification of listed persons not already ticketed would be difficult, if not impossible, because these persons might not be easily located.[70] The *Secure Air Travel Act* is indefinite but structured in a manner that permits the persistence of this "surprise, you're listed" approach. This means that people can never proactively confirm whether they are false positives — not least, because they have identifying information overlapping with that of a person on the list.

The new Act requires a person who has been incorrectly listed to get over the shock fairly quickly and challenge the listing with the minister of public safety within sixty days of being denied boarding. Then there is another sixty-day window for challenging the reasonableness of the minister's decision in Federal Court, with denied passengers perhaps never seeing the critical information that grounded them.

Limits of No Fly

Finally, it is important not to overstate the security benefits of no-fly systems. The no-fly list is just that — a list relating to flying. While denying a person air travel greatly inconveniences departure from Canada, it does not make a journey to places like Syria impossible, especially if the person travels on a false passport.[71] There also remains the risk that grounded flyers will turn their foreign terrorist fighting inward, on Canada.

In sum, interdiction on air travel is an obvious and valid tool, but it is important to recognize that it adversely affects rights, including the rights of Canadian citizens to leave Canada, while offering imperfect protections for security. There is a need for oversight and co-ordination between passport revocation, no-fly listing, and other domestic means of surveillance and restraint, including peace bonds and prosecutions.

We will return to the question of oversight in Chapter 11 and suggest that the minister of public safety has not in the past always been up to the oversight of national security activities, while the number of such activities has expanded in the 2015 laws to include both passport revocations and no-fly listings.

Property Blacklisting

A Buffet of Tools

Seizing potential terrorists' property and freezing their funds might also interdict their designs while avoiding a full trial that generally must establish guilt and terrorist purposes beyond a reasonable doubt. In 2001, Canada introduced new terrorism financing crimes as part of the *Anti-terrorism Act*. But in lesser-known (and rarely used) provisions, the government also has the power to seize property and money outside of a criminal process. And the application of these provisions is not confined to Canadians, covering non-Canadians as much as Canadians.

The first tool is the *Regulations Implementing the United Nations Resolutions on the Suppression of Terrorism*, created after 9/11 in October 2001 and re-crafted in their present form in 2006. Initially, these regulations implemented financial sanctions against al-Qaida (and Taliban) affiliates listed by the United Nations on what is now the Al-Qaida Sanctions List.[72] In Chapter 2, we outline controversies arising from this United Nations listing process, specifically the cases of Liban Hussein and Abousfian Abdelrazik.

In their present form, the regulations allow the government to list someone unilaterally, without the person's name appearing on the United Nations list.[73] Thus, a person may be listed by the government under the regulations where there are reasonable grounds to believe that the person has carried out, participated in, or facilitated a terrorist activity, or is controlled by or acting for someone who has.[74] Thereafter, it is illegal to provide or collect funds with the intention that the funds be used by a listed person or to deal in any property of a listed person, or provide any financial service in respect of that property. It is also an offence for persons to fail to disclose to the security services any property in their possession or control that they believe to be owned by a listed person.[75]

The list of persons subject to these measures is very short. It has thirty-six entries, mostly organizations rather than individuals. The last change to the list appears to have been made in 2006. The regulations appear, therefore, to no longer be an active component of the government's interdiction approach. This is likely a wise decision since a constitutional issue raised during the Hussein controversy, but never resolved because that dispute was settled, exists: whether the government can create comprehensive criminal offences through regulations, without those offences being vetted and enacted by Parliament.

The regulations have largely given way to the system created by the 2001 *Anti-terrorism Act*, which also permits the government to list terrorist entities.[76] Persons then dealing with those listed entities, whether financially or otherwise, are subject to very serious criminal penalties. The *Anti-terrorism Act* list now includes several dozen organizations but no individuals.

Mixed Usefulness

We do not doubt that these tools might be useful in select instances. But, in the past, we have expressed some skepticism concerning the effectiveness of listing and terrorism financing prohibitions given the modest cost of much terrorism.[77] We noted then that the mutation of al-Qaida from a networked terrorist group into an ideology raised doubts about the ability of lists and terrorist financing rules to stop the growth of al-Qaida-inspired terrorism.

We now confront a challenge with ISIS that is both different and similar. Unlike al-Qaida, ISIS controls oil-rich territories from which it extracts considerable revenues. Plausible anti-terror financial responses in this circumstance look a lot more like the traditional economic sanctions associated with state-to-state embargo regimes[78] and less like micro-level criminal law action.

At the same time, ISIS has inspired a radicalized following and lone wolf attacks. Money is probably not a huge ingredient of such attacks, even if the state could predict how and when they might arise. Moreover, any listing of individual members would likely be more than a few steps behind the radicalization to violence and recruitment of new members. The mass appeal of

ISIS makes listing an even more awkward tool to prevent ISIS-inspired travel than it is to prevent al-Qaida recruitment, yet we note with some concern that the United Nations Security Council has doubled down on listing as a means to deal with ISIS.[79] We risk, therefore, serious due process concerns of the sort that has turned the European implementation of listing into knots and finds echoes in Canadian cases like that of Abdelrazik.[80]

Still, there may be innovative means of using existing asset-seizing rules in Canadian law to counter at least some of ISIS's siren song. We note that prosecution and confiscation of assets have been used in several recent cases in Australia to target funds bound for ISIS.[81]

The 2001 *Anti-terrorism Act* created provisions allowing the seizure and forfeiture of property "owned or controlled by or on behalf of a terrorist group" or "that has been or will be used, in whole or in part, to facilitate or carry out a terrorist activity."[82] So property may be seized even before it has been employed in a terrorist activity. Moreover, there need not be an actual conviction — on a beyond a reasonable doubt standard — undergirding the forfeiture. Instead, forfeiture is available by order of a Federal Court judge on a balance of probabilities evidentiary standard.

In the present security environment, property controlled by ISIS can be seized, but an individual's property may also be taken if it has been or will be used to facilitate a terrorist activity. In 2010, Saïd Namouh was convicted of several terrorism offences including facilitating terrorist activity. His acts of facilitation included conducting propaganda activities for a terrorist group.[83] These are described at length in Chapter 10. For our purposes here, however, it is clear that in the right circumstances facilitating terrorist activity can include serving as a terrorist propagandist. There is a realistic prospect, therefore, that those whose Internet activities amount to furthering the activities of ISIS through the dissemination of its message may have their computers and related equipment seized under the property seizure rules.

To be sure, this will not shut down ISIS propaganda permanently, and it is no alternative to the lengthy sentence of imprisonment that Namouh received. But it underlines how interdiction can be used to chip away at terrorist infrastructure one piece at a time without some of the burdens of proof associated with a criminal trial.

III. INTERDICTING FOREIGNERS

Impeding Entry

The mobility right found in section 6 of the *Charter* complicates interdicting Canadians. But the right applies only to citizens; foreigners have no right to enter or stay in Canada. Stopping foreigners with terrorist designs from entering Canada is a complicated undertaking, however, since it depends on accurate intelligence and border control implementation on a massive scale.

In this book, we do not propose a detailed review of the complicated process of visitor and immigrant screening and lookout lists. We confine ourselves to noting that the *Immigration and Refugee Protection Act* specifies a number of circumstances justifying the inadmissibility of a foreign national or permanent resident to Canada.[84] Included among these are several security grounds. To assist border authorities in administering these rules, CSIS conducts security screening of foreign visitors, immigrants, and refugee applicants seeking permanent resident status.[85] Over the last decade, authorities have expended effort to develop systems for pre-screening foreign travellers before arrival in Canada.

This process may implicate CBSA, CSIS, the RCMP, and Citizenship and Immigration Canada. It depends, therefore, on information sharing, and in 2015 the Senate national security committee called for even more such exchanges: "it is reasonable to assume that CIC [Citizenship and Immigration Canada] and the CBSA should be able to request a query of permanent resident and temporary visa applicants against RCMP criminal and CSIS intelligence databases, and a consolidated Canadian intelligence community list of persons of interest, to see if they generate a hit."[86] There is an obvious logic to such a proposal, but, as we discuss in Chapter 5 and repeat further below, the archiving of personal information to larger and larger databases accessible to more and more persons raises acute privacy concerns. There are also pressing concerns about the reliability of the information used to interdict people from entering Canada on security grounds.

Removing Dangerous Foreigners

Detecting Danger

Not every dangerous foreigner will be pre-screened and stopped at the port of entry. And foreigners already lawfully in Canada may only later become dangerous. Removing dangerous foreigners is, therefore, another important form of interdiction: persons inadmissible on security grounds may be deported.[87]

This is a sensible tool, but one that involves some of the same trade-offs and shortcuts discussed above in relation to interdiction tools that apply to Canadians. In immigration matters, the state has a much lower burden of proof than the criminal standard of proof beyond a reasonable doubt, and it can use secret evidence not disclosed to the affected person. This reduces the burden on the state, but it also increases the risk of false positives. And it means that the violence of terrorism is not exposed and denounced as fully as it could be in a public criminal trial. Moreover, to the extent that terrorists are interdicted at the border or removed from Canada, the risk of terrorism may simply be displaced. That said, and as discussed in Chapter 7, Canada has frequently and sometimes controversially relied on immigration interdiction as anti-terrorism law.

There are practical challenges in this approach. Removals are long — currently averaging 851 days — and costly.[88] CBSA currently has warrants for the removal of approximately 44,000 people who have not complied with removal orders. CBSA may not know where inadmissible people are or even whether they are still in Canada. Most of these people, or about 80 percent, are not regarded as security risks, but that still leaves 20 percent. As the Senate national security committee noted, "even if the CBSA places a high priority on removing 'high risk' individuals, the number of people who are in Canada illegally and who have been deemed inadmissible on such serious grounds, is cause for concern."[89] The Senate committee proposed more careful tracking of entries and exits, as discussed above, to ensure better intelligence on how many of these people remain in Canada. But even if agencies are armed with that information, there will still likely be large numbers of people in Canada illegally, and it is not immediately clear how this problem will be solved without the expenditure of substantial resources.

Put another way, there may be future Ahmed Ressams in Canada. We suspect that today a failed refugee claimant with no legal status and with a Canadian criminal record, being watched by CSIS because of feared terrorist affiliations, would be among the high priority removals. But removing people like this to regimes that might maltreat them remains an unresolved conundrum.

Removing Danger

Where there is a risk that someone may be tortured if deported, there are few good solutions. The 2002 *Immigration and Refugee Protection Act* established a procedure for removing people for serious security reasons even where there is a risk of torture. The constitutionality of this procedure is doubtful and depends on how one interprets a 2002 Supreme Court of Canada case called *Suresh v Canada*. There, the Court ruled that deportation to torture would generally violate the *Charter*. Nevertheless, in a controversial departure from international law, the Court left the door open for deportation to torture in undefined "exceptional circumstances."[90]

Canada has since removed people to possible maltreatment, including in instances where the United Nations Committee against Torture has concluded that they face a substantial risk of torture.[91] But we are aware of only one case where it has done so using the "exceptional circumstances" justification.[92] The more usual course has been simply for the court to defer (sometimes in the face of considerable opposing evidence) to an executive determination that there is no serious risk of torture.

The Supreme Court has not yet revisited the issue although it has since emphasized that the *Charter* is to be interpreted consistently with Canada's international human rights obligations.[93] International human rights law bars absolutely removals "where there are substantial grounds for believing that he would be in danger of being subjected to torture,"[94] no matter how grave the security preoccupation. It is only a matter of time before the question reaches the Supreme Court again.

Torture concerns may arise over the government's attempts to remove already-convicted foreign terrorists. For instance, the question of Saïd Namouh's removal to his native Morocco has so far been avoided as premature since he is serving a sentence in Canada for various terrorism offences and will not even be eligible for parole until 2017.[95] What will happen later is another question.

In resolving the dilemma of removal to torture, the government has demonstrated some fondness for "diplomatic assurances" — that is, pledges provided by states that they will not torture an individual. These assurances — intended to guard against an eventuality that is almost always illegal in these states and yet occurs on a sometimes vast scale — have been roundly condemned by human rights organizations as ineffective.[96] The Supreme Court of Canada has also queried their usefulness.[97] It is difficult to imagine that Canada can put much stock in such assurances, except where it exercises considerable influence over the foreign government. But even when it presumably does exercise such influence — as it did over Afghan authorities during the Afghan military campaign — it may not be able to guard the welfare of persons transferred to abusive regimes, including when intrusive inspection regimes are part of the assurances.[98]

Nevertheless, some Federal Court judges have come to view diplomatic assurances as a consideration in assessing the reasonableness of a removal, although bare assurances alone may not be enough without additional evidence suggesting a reduced risk.[99]

Removal as Displaced Risk

In Chapter 7, we outline the dilemmas that Canada confronts when removal is impossible or much delayed because of torture concerns and when the person remains in Canada. Here, we note that removal is, at best, a partial solution.

If the person is in fact dangerous, simply displacing that person to another jurisdiction may not truly eliminate risk, but instead just kick it down the road. The risk may now be borne by foreigners. This is an outcome that many Canadians may regard as acceptable, especially if the possible terrorist is a product of the society to which the person is returned. But as the Ressam case suggests, risky people may just bounce back. Although he had no legal status, Ressam was able to return to Canada — on an illegal Canadian passport.

Making the Canadian border a one-way door for deported security risks — and not a revolving door — raises the border lookout logistical challenges we discuss above. But those challenges are redoubled where people travel on real but fraudulently acquired passports, using assumed identities. In these circumstances, there is considerable appeal to the Senate security committee's recent call for the government to "fully implement a plan to collect biometric information from all foreign nationals arriving in Canada."[100] Biometric data, deployed in an effective screening program, could address the issue of falsified identities.

The government is moving ahead with such a plan, starting with visa applicants. Again legislating substantive changes through its 2015 budget implementation bill, the government introduced changes to the *Immigration and Refugee Protection Act* permitting new regulations on the collection of biometric data from foreigners.[101] It also announced that by 2018–19 it would begin collecting biometric data from 2.9 million non-Canadians annually, in the form of digital photos and fingerprints.[102]

But such data are acutely personal, warehoused in databases, and subject (as is planned) to domestic and international sharing, raising clear privacy issues. In commenting on the *Immigration and Refugee Protection Act* changes, the Privacy Commissioner signalled his support for enhancing the integrity of the immigration system but raised concerns. For one thing, biometrics can produce false positives — and "[e]ven low failure rates can have a significant impact when a system is scaled up to involve thousands or even millions of people." For another thing, centralized storage raises the risk of data breaches, requiring the observance of new privacy-enhancing safeguards. Last, individuals will have no real choice but to relinquish this personal information, "and therefore every effort should be made to inform the individual about the purposes of collection and whether information will or may be shared with another jurisdiction, especially if the information may be used for purposes that it was not originally collected."[103]

Unspoken in these comments is the obvious need for safeguards in the forms of close internal oversight and independent external review. A recurring theme in this chapter, as in so many, is the incomplete review agenda, discussed more fully in Chapter 12.

IV. MAKING CANADIANS INTO FOREIGNERS

The government has more tools of interdiction for foreigners than it does for Canadians. Foreigners have no right to enter Canada, and they can be removed from Canada. And, as discussed in Chapter 7, they can be detained pending removal. Making a Canadian into a foreigner means, therefore, that the government may be able to remove a former citizen from Canada, albeit subject to the deportation to torture concerns discussed above. But stripping citizenship can be disproportionate, arbitrary, and if used only against dual nationals discriminatory. It may also do little to achieve real security objectives.

Security Pre-screening

National security rules have existed in citizenship processes for some time but until recently only as part of the system for becoming a citizen. For instance, a permanent resident may be denied citizenship if subject to an immigration removal order or a declaration from the government that the person constitutes a threat to the security of Canada.[104] A declaration of this sort follows an investigation by SIRC or a retired judge, sparked by a request from the government.[105] CSIS screens citizenship applicants on security grounds presumably to determine whether the government should trigger this process.[106]

Security Denaturalization

But the government has recently concluded that screening as a citizenship gatekeeper is insufficient. In 2014, Canada followed the practice in several other countries — most notably the United Kingdom — in creating a process by which citizenship could be revoked on security grounds.[107] The government may now revoke citizenship for service "as a member of an armed force of a country or as a member of an organized armed group and that country or group was engaged in an armed conflict with Canada," a conviction for treason under the *Criminal Code*, a conviction for a terrorism offence, and a conviction for certain spying offences under the *Security of Information Act*, as well as certain analogous offences under the *National Defence Act*.

But the new provisions do not "authorize any decision, action or declaration that conflicts with any international human rights instrument regarding statelessness to which Canada is signatory."[108] This confusing language responds to the fact that Canada is a party to an international treaty designed to minimize statelessness. When Canada joined that treaty, it did not preserve a right to impose statelessness for national security reasons. That means that, unlike countries that have made this reservation, Canada is barred from producing statelessness on these grounds.

The net result of these 2014 legislative changes is that the reach of the new revocation provisions is confined to those who have a dual nationality or who (under the Act's reversed burden of proof rules) are unable to prove that they have only Canadian nationality. Dual nationals become, in this manner, provisional citizens subject to a revocation process that cannot reach Canadians with only a single citizenship.

The overwhelming majority of those with dual nationality are naturalized Canadians — that is, those who emigrated from other states to Canada. In 2011, 2.9 percent of the total population had dual nationality, and immigrants comprised 79.5 percent of that group. Fully 14.3 percent of all naturalized Canadians were dual nationals, but only 0.7 percent of Canadian-born citizens had other citizenships.[109] Put another way, subjecting everyone with dual nationality to the possibility of citizenship revocation singles out 2.9 percent of the population for a special peril, and more than three quarters of those people are new Canadians.

Constitutional Doubts

As a result of all this, the new revocation rules are vulnerable to a number of constitutional objections.[110] But equality rights should rank chief among them. Section 15 of the *Charter* specifies, "Every individual is equal before and under the law and has the right to the equal protection and equal benefit of the law without discrimination and, in particular, without discrimination based on race, national or ethnic origin, colour, religion, sex, age or mental or physical disability." The new citizenship revocation rules impose differential treatment based on national origin.

Moreover, this differential treatment can be readily equated with discrimination. Since the vast majority of dual nationals are immigrants, a measure singling out dual nationals necessarily visits injury on a class of individuals who have historically suffered prejudice or disadvantage.[111] And even if this were not the case, a measure singling out dual nationals for the peril of citizenship revocation on the basis that they are traitors or terrorists would seem likely to have a prejudicial impact: it risks fuelling the perception that they are inherently more prone to such behaviour than are other citizens.

If the new provisions do violate the *Charter*, it is not clear that they are justifiable as a reasonable limitation on rights under section 1 of the *Charter*. To establish that a limit on a right is reasonable and proportionate, the government must not only invoke an important objective but demonstrate that the limit is rationally connected to the objective, that there is a minimal impairment of the right in question, and, finally, that there is proportionality between the impact on the right and the benefits of the measure in question.[112]

It is not at all clear that a rational connection can be drawn between discriminatory citizenship revocation provisions and the objectives of protecting national security and denouncing disloyalty. A measure singling out naturalized Canadians — or even the broader class of dual nationals — is not rationally connected to those objectives. To show such a connection, the government would have to prove that dual national Canadians in fact present an inherently greater threat to national security or are more prone to disloyalty. The challenge of providing such proof is likely an insurmountable one for the government.

Nor is there a clear claim that the revocation provisions are minimally impairing of rights. If the government's objective is to punish or denounce disloyalty, there are obvious alternative measures that can do that without violating section 15. The *Criminal Code* provisions on treason and terrorism are important examples. If the government's objective is to protect national security, it again has a range of tools available to it, from passport revocation to criminal prosecution. These are all tools that more plausibly comply with the *Charter*.

Finally, the detrimental impact on the rights of dual nationals seems disproportionate to the doubtful contribution that revocation would likely make to protecting national security and punishing disloyalty. The impact of such revocation on the individual might well be severe. In Shai Lavi's words, "the revocation of citizenship is a denial of concrete rights, including the active right of political participation and the passive right of residency, as well as a denial of membership in the community and, with it, the more fundamental right to have rights vis-à-vis the state."[113]

In contrast, citizenship revocation would have, at best, an ambivalent effect in furthering Canadian national security. A dual citizen who lost Canadian citizenship would revert to foreign national status and be subject to immigration removal procedures described above. We would face, therefore, the displacement of risk, not its elimination. It is even less clear that revocation would have any positive effects on the objective of enhancing loyalty.

Indeed, there may be no positive effects on loyalty whatsoever. Selective de-naturalization that would, in most cases, target naturalized Canadians might be expected to have the opposite effect — that is, to fuel a sense of second-class citizenship among the affected communities and erode their feelings of social solidarity with Canada and its government.

Next Steps

An initial and premature constitutional challenge of the new law, raising extraneous objections, was dismissed.[114] More serious constitutional challenges are now underway just as the government has begun using the provisions.

In July 2015, the government began revocation proceedings against Hiva Alizadeh, a Canadian of Iranian decent.[115] Alizadeh became a Canadian in 2007 but was charged with terrorism offences following a 2009 trip to an Afghan terrorist training camp. Upon his return to Canada, he had plotted a terrorist attack. In 2014, he pled guilty to possessing explosive materials for the purpose of endangering life or causing serious property damage in association with a terrorist plot. The judge sentenced him to twenty-four years with a credit of six years for time spent in pre-trial custody in difficult circumstances.[116] Alizadeh will be in his fifties by the time he is released.

If the government is successful in revoking Alizadeh's citizenship, he will then be subject to removal, presumably to Iran, upon completion of his criminal sentence. But, in keeping with the torture concerns discussed above, that removal may itself be a fraught issue. A Sunni Muslim convicted of terror-related crimes and with a reported affiliation with "Kurdish insurgents loosely allied with the Taliban"[117] may not be removable to Shia Iran.

Citizenship revocation followed by protracted immigration removal proceedings mired in claims of torture is a very costly and probably ineffective way of addressing the problem of what to do with a middle-aged former convict. Yet revocation seems now to be the government's preferred course of action in a growing number of cases.

Employed in this manner as a supplemental penalty for a criminal conviction, revocation poses unanswered legal questions. For instance, should criminal trial judges now take revocation into account when deciding what sentences to give offenders, presumably reducing those sentences to reflect the new supplemental penalty?[118]

Revocation's punitive nature also poses assorted procedural constitutional issues. It seems likely that *Charter* section 7 entitlements to procedural fundamental justice will apply to a proceeding with such dire consequences. There are even issues about whether the constitutional rights found in section 11 of the *Charter*, and typically confined to criminal proceedings, might attach to this punitive revocation process, something that would dramatically change the architecture that Parliament legislated in 2014.[119]

As discussed in Chapter 9, the government's preference for displacing risk and deflecting it to overseas locales may reflect its lack of attention to questions of rehabilitation and the prospect that housing those convicted of terrorism offences together may make them more dangerous. We would not be surprised if the government attempts to impose other post-sentence controls on convicted terrorists as more of them come closer to their release dates. Like other forms of interdiction, such measures will be controversial and may well be challenged under the *Charter*.

V. CONCLUSION

The tools and tactics of interdiction that we discuss in this chapter are imperfect. But this is not to say that all of them are unwise or that we oppose their purpose and objectives. Some of that imperfection is inevitable: no measure is a silver bullet guaranteeing our safety. But some of that imperfection is a function of mis-design and the willingness to overlook serious constitutional issues in favour of doing something as forceful as possible in the interests of anti-terror. This propensity is both unnecessary and concerning, and the risk of false positives is high. Some of that risk may be countered by careful amendments, especially changes reversing the government's infatuation with due process minimalism. Risk of overreaction may also be tempered by a robust system of internal oversight and an enhanced system of review, but, as we discuss in Chapters 11 and 12, we are not persuaded our present systems are entirely up to the task.

Still, if Ahmed Ressam tried to come to Canada today, he might not make it in. And if he did, he might not be allowed to stay as long as he did. And he might not be able to acquire fraudulently a Canadian travel document, or leave and return to Canada, or fly on planes within, to, or from Canada. If he were a Canadian, he might not be able to obtain a passport, and, as a convicted terrorist, he might be stripped of his Canadian citizenship.

Of course, he might still slip through the cracks, and even if he did not, we might be stuck with him unless we were truly willing to toss him over to potential torturers in his country of origin. It is important to consider, therefore, what other tools are available to the state to curb the designs of terrorists, foreign or Canadian. In the next chapter, we look at tactics for physically constraining terrorists, short of outright criminal conviction.

CHAPTER SEVEN

Restrain: Limiting Threats

I. INTRODUCTION

Egyptian national Mohammed Zeki Mahjoub came to Canada from Sudan in December 1995. Upon arrival, he immediately applied for asylum. In October 1996, the refugee board declared him a refugee. Thereafter, he married a Canadian citizen and started a family.

In June 2000, he was detained under an immigration "security certificate." That instrument declared Mahjoub inadmissible for security reasons. Documents summarizing the government's position alleged that Mahjoub was a senior member in the militant wing of the Egyptian Islamic Jihad. This group splintered from Egypt's Muslim Brotherhood in order to pursue a more violent path to an Islamic Egyptian state. In 1999, Egyptian courts convicted Mahjoub *in absentia* for his role in the group.

The Canadian security certificate process was (and remains) secretive, and persons in Mahjoub's circumstances were not (and are not) fully apprised of the evidence and the case against them. But the Federal Court affirmed the government's security certificate in October 2001. Thereafter, Mahjoub's actual removal quickly become mired in questions about whether he could be removed to Egypt, where he might be subjected to torture. The resulting delays were protracted. Mahjoub remained in custody, first at the Toronto West Detention Centre and then at the special Kingston Immigration Holding Centre. His imprisonment lasted until February 2007 — a total of six and a half years — at which point a Federal Court judge concluded he would not be removed from Canada in a reasonable time and the risk to security he might pose could be contained by conditions on his release.[1]

At around the same time, the Supreme Court decided a constitutional challenge brought by three other security certificate "named persons" in similar cases.[2] In this first of a series of modern security certificate decisions, the Court invalidated the secretive process and held that the *Charter* required better efforts to square fair trials with secrecy preoccupations. At the same time, the Court also indicated that alternatives to full-time detention, such as release on strict conditions (which was used in two of the cases), were still "less severe than incarceration" even though they also "severely limit[ed] liberty."[3] All five men subjected to security certificates were eventually released on strict conditions.

In 2008, Parliament enacted a new security certificate system incorporating standards responsive to the Supreme Court's holding.[4] And in February 2008, the government issued a second security certificate against Mahjoub under the new process. During this second proceeding, Mahjoub remained free, but under very stringent conditions. His family and friends acted as sureties, posting performance bonds, and he was restrained by a list of conditions on his movement, conduct, use of communications devices, and a willingness to co-operate in surveillance.[5]

But in March 2009, Mahjoub chose to return to prison, telling the court that "he and his family could no longer live with the stringent conditions of his release."[6] He first voiced this intent reportedly "after federal agents' policy of 'eyes-on' surveillance led them to follow Mr. Mahjoub into a closed hospital room, while his wife was having a miscarriage."[7] Reincarcerated for several months, Mahjoub began a hunger strike. In November 2009, he was released under court-imposed conditions less stringent than the original limitations. The revised conditions still ran to several pages and fifty-five paragraphs.

After assorted other legal challenges, in 2013 the Federal Court ruled that the security certificate was reasonable, and concluded that Mahjoub was inadmissible to Canada on grounds of security. He has now appealed this holding and a series of earlier constitutional matters in his case. Throughout these protracted legal disputes (there are over thirty reported decisions in Mahjoub's case), he has remained subject to the November 2009 release conditions, as modified.[8] In total, he has been subjected to either detention or strict conditions on release for over fifteen years. His appeals will consume still more time, as will any subsequent adjudication of whether he can actually be removed to possible abuse in Egypt.

Skipping Town

While Mahjoub fought removal from Canada, Mohamed Ali Dirie, a Canadian citizen, left the country. In the mid-2000s, CSIS was gathering intelligence on Sunni Islamist extremism in an investigation dubbed Operation Claymore.[9] One of the subjects of that investigation rented a vehicle that CSIS could not then subsequently locate. CSIS issued a "lookout" on the computer system accessed by customs officers in the hope the vehicle might be located. In 2005, customs officials identified the vehicle crossing the border, driven by Dirie and a confederate. They searched it and discovered handguns and ammunition. At that time, CSIS had reportedly not formed a settled conclusion on whether Dirie was smuggling weapons for terrorist purposes. CSIS wiretapped Dirie after his arrest and recorded him expressing concerns about the arrest that would have assisted the police in laying conspiracy charges. It did not share this information with the police. But Dirie ultimately pled guilt to six *Criminal Code* offences, including illegal importation of a firearm, and was sentenced to two years.

While serving that sentence in 2006, he was charged with an additional crime — this time, a terrorism offence, as Dirie was now believed to have done the smuggling for the benefit of a terrorist group. More than that, while in prison he viewed himself as still being a member of that group and tried to make connections that would allow him to acquire other firearms and false travel documents. He also tried to recruit other inmates to his extremist worldview and to his group. Indeed, in 2011, authors from the Macdonald-Laurier Institute described him as the "best known example of a terrorist convict actively promoting terrorism behind bars."[10]

The terrorist group in question was not a listed terrorist entity, but rather the now well-known and more ad hoc conspiracy billed the "Toronto 18." After contesting the propriety of the new Toronto 18 charge, Dirie pled guilty in 2009. He was sentenced to an additional seven years, but discounted to reflect time served. As a condition of his subsequent release in 2011, Dirie was subjected to a peace bond with fifteen conditions. Although housed in the *Criminal Code*, peace bonds (more technically, recognizances with conditions) are essentially administrative measures imposing restraints on liberty short of detention, but for reasons that can fall far short of actual proven criminal conduct. Among other things, the peace bond barred Dirie from applying or possessing a passport and obliged him to report to police once every two weeks. Dirie complied for a year, but then stopped doing so. Police obtained arrest warrants, but to no avail. Dirie had left Canada on a false passport for Syria. As of 2013, he is believed to have died fighting in Syria for Jabhat al-Nusrah,[11] a group listed as a terrorist entity in Canada.

Tools of Restraint

Security certificates and peace bonds are a tool on the threat escalator falling within the category of what we call "restrain." While interdict tools inhibit the movement of terrorists, and prosecution results in outright incarceration under criminal sentence, restrain tools permit the state to detain or otherwise impose long-term constraints on liberty for reasons other than criminal conduct. Restraint activities are appealing to the state because they can generally be triggered by less than proof of guilt beyond a reasonable doubt. And as noted, the Supreme Court also approved of restraint as a more proportionate alternative to outright, indeterminate detention under security certificates.[12]

But restraint tools have what we call a Goldilocks problem. They can be too restrictive on liberty when imposed on those who are not really terrorists. A particularly aggressive form of house arrest or other form of liberty constraint can impose real harms on detainees and their families. Conditions such as bans on use of computers and unrealistic curfews may only result in disputes over frequent breaches, on top of the hugely expensive and intrusive process of monitoring the person's behaviour. At the same time, however, there is a bright line between restraint and imprisonment; as a result, restraint may prove too weak for the determined terrorist. Indeed, the idea of "peace bonds for terrorists" was something of an afterthought in the post-9/11 reforms, and they were ridiculed by experienced commentators as manifestly ill-suited for suicide bombers.[13]

Therefore, restraint tools run a dual risk from an anti-terror perspective: they can be an overreaction when imposed on some individuals and may create legitimacy problems not generally experienced in criminal trials, decided in open court on robust evidentiary standards. At the same time, they may be an underreaction when imposed on determined terrorists who require long-term incapacitation of the sort that can generally only be provided by successful criminal prosecutions. And yet, restraint under both *Criminal Code* peace bond amendments and security certificates amendments emerged as one of the prime (and to our mind, curious) features of Bill C-51. The government eagerly repeated claims by the sister of the late warrant officer, Patrice Vincent, that a peace bond restraint would have prevented the 20 October 2014 terrorist attack and kept her brother alive. We, however, do not share this confidence — while restraint may lead to imprisonment if conditions are ignored, it does not in itself produce outright imprisonment.

This chapter first examines immigration restraint measures, an area with the longest existing history as an anti-terror tool. We look then to the now burgeoning and, after Bill C-51, increasingly easy-to-obtain peace bond tool.

II. RESTRAINING FOREIGNERS

Immigration law — most notably in the form of security certificates — permits the detention of non-citizens, pending their removal from Canada.[14] The government can issue certificates against foreigners they regard as inadmissible to Canada "on grounds of security, violating human or international rights, serious criminality or organized criminality."[15] A Federal Court judge then adjudicates whether the certificate is reasonable, and if he or she so concludes, the certificate constitutes a removal order.

We discuss practical issues surrounding use of immigration removal as an anti-terror tool in Chapter 6.

Limiting the Liberty of Named Persons

Here we focus on what happens while the question of removal is being decided. During the process, the named person may be arrested if the government has "reasonable grounds to believe that the person is a danger to national security or to the safety of any person or is unlikely to appear at a proceeding or for removal."[16] The Federal Court reviews this detention soon after and periodically every six months thereafter. The judge can allow the detention to continue, or may order the person released under any "conditions that the judge considers appropriate."[17] A breach of any of the conditions is a criminal offence under both the *Criminal Code* and immigration law,[18] resulting in a possible sentence of two years. Security certificates are, in other words, a potentially potent form of restraint. As with Mahjoub, detentions of the four other individuals named in certificates for anti-terror reasons after 9/11 have been protracted and controversial.

When released on conditions, the conditions themselves have been significant. For example, the conditions under which another named person, Mohammed Harkat, was released in 2006 ran to five pages. Among other things, any computer with Internet connectivity was to be kept in a locked portion of his residence to which he had no access,[19] and he could be incarcerated for two years were he to enter into a room with an Internet-equipped computer. Examples of other conditions included: seven sureties, each committing sometimes substantial amounts of money as a guarantee on Harkat's conduct; wearing an electronic monitoring bracelet at all times; a strict curfew, with solo departures from his house precluded and accompanied departures only on Canadian Border Services Agency approval; strict geographic limits on his ventures outside his house; no visitors other than those listed in the order; no communication with anyone supporting "violent Jihad"; consent to interception by the Canadian Border Services Agency of all communications; consent to Canadian Border Services Agency searches of his house and possessions; surrendering his travel documents; and a bar on possessing weapons.

Endless Disputes, Endless Restrictions

As in the *Mahjoub* case, disputes concerning compliance with conditions have been commonplace, as have disputes concerning their content.[20] And as *Mahjoub* suggests, detention and conditional release risk becoming close to indefinite.

A Record of Failure

Despite almost a decade and a half of trying, the government has yet to remove a single one of the five persons named as alleged terrorist affiliates. Two cases — those of Egyptians Mahmoud Jaballah and Mahjoub — remain in court. The government lost the Hassan Almrei security certificate case in 2009,[21] and its efforts to remove him through alternative means is being contested.[22] His removal to his home country of Syria would be all but impossible given both that country's human rights records and the present conditions in the country, but the government is reportedly still making the effort.

The government withdrew its certificate against Adil Charkaoui,[23] rather than abide by a court order requiring more disclosure to Charkaoui and his lawyers. (Both Almrei and Charkaoui have since sued the Canadian government for their treatment.)

Expensive "Wins"

The government has "won" only two security certificate cases so far, and both are probably best described as pyrrhic victories. We have described the *Mahjoub* case above, and noted its endless trajectory. The Federal Court also ruled Mohammed Harkat's certificate reasonable in 2010.

Harkat's case went up to the Supreme Court, the third security certificate case to reach the high court involving one or more of the five men. In its 2014 decision,[24] the Court dismissed concerns about the different positions reached on a key factual question by different judges, noting that judges were expected to make judgments on the facts before them in their own cases. That issue concerned the implications in both *Harkat* and *Almrei* of the named persons' association with Ibn al-Khattab, a leader of the Arab Afghan mujahidin who was later involved in the Chechen conflict. In *Almrei,* the Federal Court judge concluded al-Khattab could not "be reasonably said to be part of Al Qaeda" and "was not a terrorist in his own right or a terrorist patron" based on the evidence before him.[25] In *Harkat*, a different judge found that the "Khattab groups were not part of the Al-Qaeda core, but were part of the Bin Laden Network" and that they were affiliated with terrorism.[26]

A larger question was the constitutionality of the new special advocate system created in 2008, after the first Supreme Court security certificate ruling. As discussed in Chapter 2, special advocates are security-cleared lawyers who, during the secret hearings, advance the interests of the person named in the security certificate. In other words, they restore an adversarial challenge to the government's secret evidence, something that is a constitutional necessity since the Supreme Court's 2007 ruling in *Charkaoui*.[27] At issue in *Harkat* were a number of related due process concerns outlined more fully in Chapter 2. The Court ruled that the amended regime was consistent with the *Charter*, but also required the process to meet some of the more robust procedural standards critics had sought (unsuccessfully) to incorporate through the original parliamentary process. In other words, the outcome was not a true win on the law for the government, but it was a loss for Harkat. Even then, Harkat continues to remain in Canada. As with all the other named persons, an outstanding issue likely to wend its way through the courts is whether he can be deported to his native country — in his case, Algeria — where he may face torture. (We discuss the problem of removals to torture in Chapter 6.) But in the interim, Harkat is still subject to the security certificate detention and conditional release system, now thirteen years after the government issued the original certificate. The conditions on his release have been relaxed since his initial 2006 release, but they are still substantial.

This is also true for Jaballah and Mahjoub, still contesting (or appealing) their security certificates. In 2010, Jaballah argued that the strict conditions on his release were unhinged from a realistic removal process and risked enduring indefinitely, in violation of the *Charter*. But the government still continues its fifteen-year effort to remove Jaballah. Under these circumstances, the judge concluded that the detention and conditional release system remained proper. He did relax the conditions on release, including barring the Canadian Border Services Agency from opening school letters addressed to Jaballah's children, unless there are reasonable grounds to believe they do not actually come from the schools. The Canadian Border Services Agency is also barred from monitoring the children's calls with children of their own age.[28]

More generally, the conditions on the three individuals still subject to certificates have abated with time. In deciding what standards should govern conditional release, the Supreme Court instructed lower courts to consider a number of variables.[29] One consideration (animating many decisions before and since) has been the impact of long-term detention (and conditional release).

Courts have regularly concluded that protracted constraints on liberty have cut the men off from their extremist associates and diminished the security threat they present. The Supreme Court also observed that long detention means that the government has more time to collect evidence. For this reason, the government's evidentiary onus justifying the limitation on liberty increases with the passage of time.[30]

Horns of Dilemma

If the purpose of security certificates was expeditious removal of feared terrorist risks, it has failed in this regard.

A Three-Walled Prison?

There is some truth in a common government refrain that security certificates create a three-walled prison. The men who have been subjected to these measures "can, and always have been able, to leave the country at any time. They are detained solely by virtue of their refusal to leave Canada."[31] But in relation to the five post-9/11 cases, the missing prison wall requires a leap into the arms of a potentially torturing state. In these circumstances, the prison has three walls, and named persons can choose to walk the plank.

Effectively, the Canadian security certificate labels (or reveals, depending on the truth of the matter) these individuals as members of organizations whose purposes are invariably at variance with the interests of their countries of origin, to which they may be removed. In these circumstances, it should be assumed that foreign authorities have their own agendas to pursue. This gives rise to a prospect of torture that does not exist (or at least is not as acute) with the removal of, for example, spies working for foreign security services, something for which security certificates have been used in the past.[32] The net result is a strong incentive for named persons in terrorism cases to test every boundary of the process — as has happened — producing a protracted, unwieldy system. For this reason, security certificates are poor immigration tools. The bigger question is whether they are effective anti-terrorism tools.

Certainly all immigration law has obvious flaws as a tool of anti-terrorism — we have discussed the issue of displaced risk in Chapter 6. But even in relation to immigration detention, there is a clear shortcoming: it applies only to non-citizens. As the UK House of Lords observed in invalidating a similar detention regime under UK law,[33] there is no reason to assume that foreign nationals (as opposed to UK nationals) present the greatest terrorist threat. This has certainly proved to be the case in the United Kingdom and is increasingly so in Canada.

Security Certificates as Disruption without an Exit Strategy

The government will argue that, whatever the limitations on its reach, security certificates have "worked" by taking dangerous people out of circulation for protracted periods of time and have thereby muted the risk they present. In that respect, the system is a success. But the success comes at significant cost: by the end of the last decade, the government was budgeting $59 million for two-year periods[34] — over $11 million per named person.

In addition, certificates have been extremely controversial. This is true not just because of due process issues, but also because of how it looks when a democratic, human-rights-observing government excludes named persons from parts of their proceedings and seeks to remove them to torture. And the government has been repeatedly caught out for failing to meet its duty of candour when presenting secret evidence to the courts and, in the *Almrei* case, in understanding and interpreting that evidence.[35] For our part, we are extremely skeptical that security certificates are a balanced anti-terrorism strategy. Long-term detention or strict limitations on freedom without a criminal charge in an ultimately fruitless attempt to remove persons may have the effect of "outing" potential threats and limiting their freedom of action; however, it risks being disproportionate to the actual threat posed by these individuals, especially as detention periods lengthen.

Security certificates amount to a system of protracted detention and limited release on conditions (with possible removal from Canada) that allows the state to act on the basis of the perceived "dangerousness" of the individual, without that dangerousness being linked to a specific and imminent threat. In such a system, the focus will inevitably become the person's past behaviour, associations, and beliefs, and not a careful assessment of his capacity to cause serious harm. Our law allows all this in a system with weak evidential controls, where the government need only demonstrate the reasonableness of the certificate and, for detentions, its reasonable belief — close to the lowest standard known to law. This is particularly problematic where, as the *Almrei* decision strongly suggested, the government's case suffered from a flawed understanding of the political environment in Afghanistan, the concept of jihad, and the affiliations and ideologies of persons with whom Almrei associated.

As the different outcome on some of these issues in *Harkat* establishes, high-level geopolitical issues are sometimes contested, and different courts can (and have) come to different conclusions on precisely the same factual questions. But the point here is that any system that depends on perceived dangerousness is prone to misunderstandings and misinterpretations, which feed increasingly untenable suppositions and suspicions. In the meantime, Hassan Almrei was detained for more than seven years, much of it in facilities not designed for long-term detentions. The government spent literally millions of dollars and untold hours of effort to keep him there, while trying fruitlessly to send him to a country inclined to torture people accused of the conduct at issue in his case. This was money and time expended on trying to prove that Almrei was dangerous that was not spent on other matters that might be much more useful to national security.

In some important respects, therefore, security certificates in anti-terror cases have created for Canada the same dilemmas the Americans now face with Guantanamo Bay, albeit for different reasons: protracted limits on the liberty of individuals who can be neither prosecuted or removed. There is no evident way out of this impasse, and so we should be very reluctant to enter it if we can avoid it. And if we do go down this rabbit hole, we need to build in an alternative, de-radicalization exit strategy of the sort we discuss in the section below, on peace bonds, and return to in Chapter 13.

Aftermath

Knowing what it knows now, and with the strictures now imposed after a decade and a half of constitutional litigation, the government has opted not to use security certificates in terrorism matters since the original five cases. There are probably several reasons for this fact.

Criminal Solution

For one thing, Canada's anti-terrorism criminal law is now robust — more so then when the five men engaged in their activities. The 2001 terrorism offences were unavailable for the five men, as crimes cannot apply retroactively under Canada's constitution. Additionally, more recent matters have involved terrorist activity planned in Canada itself, not in the fog of some foreign conflict zone. So the non-Canadian defendants in the VIA Rail case were prosecuted for their rail bomb plot,[36] even when they could have been subjected to security certificates. (Although, at least one of the plotters may have been impossible to remove from Canada anyway.)[37]

As readers may have noted, we often favour efforts to move much anti-terrorism activity into the criminal justice system. It is true that incarceration is expensive, but that is no objection given the costs of security certificates. As we will suggest in Chapter 9, criminal trials are our fairest and most transparent way to expose the violence in terrorism and to denounce and deter it. Criminal trials are a potentially profound counter-narrative in a way that security certificate "secret trials" are not.

Regular Inadmissibility Detention and Removal

Even today, however, the government has not always opted for criminal prosecutions. It has pursued an alternative immigration remedy: the government may detain and deport through regular immigration inadmissibility hearings on a "reasonable grounds to believe" standard a person who is a security risk.[38] And it may use these processes even where the government wishes to use secret information.[39]

As we note in Chapter 2, reasonable questions can be asked about whether the government now resorts to inadmissibility processes because it prefers its chances in front of an adjudicator over those in front of increasingly exacting and national security–experienced Federal Court judges, let alone in front of criminal trial judges who would never allow the state to use secret evidence against the accused. We suggest in Chapter 9 that the overall preference for immigration law over criminal prosecutions may also be related to CSIS's concerns about exposing its secrets, and those of foreign agencies with which it works closely, in Canadian criminal trials. In some large measure, the use of secret evidence in immigration proceedings has helped Canadian officials defer fully grappling with the difficulties of converting intelligence into evidence, a problem that, as we argue in Chapter 9, should no longer be avoided.

We do not know how often regular inadmissibility proceedings are being used as less restrained alternatives to criminal trials or to full-blown immigration security certificate proceedings. But clearly this "substitution effect"[40] is occurring, shifting cases to a less restrained anti-terror instrument. One well-publicized case started in February 2015 when a non-citizen, alleged to have plans to bomb buildings in Toronto as an alternative to joining ISIS, was detained and eventually ordered deported to Pakistan.[41]

Keeping Options for More Constitutional Battles Open

The government still has a soft spot for security certificates. It moved in Bill C-51 to reverse some of its security certificate procedural losses, possibly because the changes will flow over to use of secret evidence in regular inadmissibility proceedings. These amendments restore the government as the gatekeeper of information flows to special advocates, in a way that may seriously jeopardize these lawyers' ability to advance the interests of the named person.

In the *Almrei* case, special advocates discovered that inconsistent statements made by CSIS sources were not disclosed, and the government used an earlier supportive statement made by a source at a time when he or she "was highly motivated to curry favour with the Service."[42] As discussed in Chapter 2, the Bill C-51 changes may make it harder for special advocates to perform this challenge function in the future. And so, just as the rules were becoming more certain and predictable, Bill C-51 has teed up another constitutional challenge. Meanwhile, because Bill C-44 also extends new and absolute statutory identity protections for CSIS informants, it too opens the door to another round of litigation. All of this suggests that immigration law will continue to be an unwieldy anti-terror instrument. Its use threatens rights while offering only partial security in the form of restraint or removals that only displace risks to other countries, with possibility of the bounce back discussed in Chapter 6.

III. RESTRAINING ANYONE
Learning Lessons from Overseas

As noted, security certificates only restrain foreigners. Other countries have laws allowing restraint of their own nationals for national security reasons. These are known as "control orders," or in the current UK law, "terrorism prevention and investigation measures" (TPIM).

The United Kingdom introduced TPIMs in 2011[43] to replace the more restrictive and highly controversial control orders. These earlier devices were created in 2005 after a UK high court decision invalidated indeterminate immigration detention (effectively, still available under Canadian security certificates) as disproportionate and discriminatory in relation to foreign nationals.[44] TPIMs are directed at people that the UK government reasonably believes may engage (or have been involved) in terrorism-related activity, but for whom deportation or prosecution is not feasible. TPIMs last a year and may be renewed once. They are imposed by the government, but are subject to review in court, partly in secret hearings involving special advocates. That means that, like Canadian security certificates, the UK government may impose TPIMs through the use of secret evidence. TPIMs may include a lengthy series of conditions not greatly different from those that have been used in practice for conditional release under Canada's security certificate regime.[45] That said, TPIMs are more moderate; for instance, they do not absolutely bar the use of telephones or the Internet.

The UK government used its original control order regime to impose strictures on a total of fifty-two people. Nine of these, and one additional person, have also had their liberty restricted under the newer TPIMs.[46] But these measures are like "peace bonds for terrorists" — not exactly a silver bullet solution. A number of individuals absconded while on control orders, and under the more recent TPIM system, two of the ten individuals have disappeared.

All of the TPIMs expired by February 2014. This suggests that TPIMs are, in the words of a UK parliamentary committee, "withering on the vine as a counter-terrorism tool of practical utility."[47] The ISIS challenge, however, may revive TPIMs. Under the older control orders, the government could "'relocate' control order subjects, with their families if they so chose, to a town or city some two or three hours' travel from their home."[48] Legislation enacted in 2015 restores the ability to impose "relocation" as a condition under the newer TPIM regime.[49]

The UK Independent Reviewer of Anti-terrorism strongly favoured this change. He recognized that "relocation was in some cases very strongly resented by those who were subject to it and by their families, who spoke of encountering loneliness and racism." But he defended relocation because "it was valued by police and MI5 both as an effective way of disrupting networks that were concentrated in particular areas and as a way of making abscond more difficult."[50]

This development underscores how Bill C-51 is not singular in its focus on disrupting terrorist suspects. At the same time, the United Kingdom has recognized the need for an "exit strategy" from time-limited TPIMs. A UK parliamentary committee urged that all TPIM subjects should be on a "graduated scheme, which commences concurrently with the measures, with the sole purpose of engagement and de-radicalisation."[51] This proposal amounts to the recognition — unfortunately, very rare in Canadian political discourse — that restrain tools are partial responses that must be co-ordinated with, and supplemented by, other interventions.

Peace Bonds

We raise this UK experience to contextualize the situation in Canada. In Canada, the closest equivalent to TPIMs is an anti-terror "recognizance with conditions," better known as a peace bond. As discussed in Chapter 2, there are two types of anti-terror peace bonds: one that may be preceded by preventive detention, and a regular process that does not involve preventive detention (although it can involve arrest under warrant to bring the person to court).[52] We focus here on the regular process, leaving preventive detention to Chapter 8.

Peace bonds are relatively common tools in Canadian law. For instance, a person labouring under a fear (based on reasonable grounds) that an individual may commit certain personal injury offences,[53] sexual offences,[54] certain offences relating to intimidation of the justice system or a journalist, or a criminal organization offence[55] may bring the matter to a provincial court judge (although in some instances only with permission of the attorney general). After 9/11, this list was expanded to include a terrorism offence.[56] A person "who fears on reasonable grounds that another person will commit . . . a terrorism offence may, with the consent of the Attorney General, lay an information before a provincial court judge." If the provincial court judge was persuaded that these reasonable grounds for the fear exist, she could order the defendant to "enter into a recognizance to keep the peace and be of good behaviour" for up to twelve months (and up to twenty-four for a convicted terrorist), and could impose other reasonable conditions. In its original form, refusal by the accused to enter into the court-ordered peace bond was punishable by imprisonment for up to twelve months, and a breach of the bond was a criminal offence, punishable by up to two years imprisonment.[57]

The Use of Peace Bonds Since 9/11

While anti-terror peace bonds have existed for the better part of fifteen years, their use has been infrequent. Unlike in the United Kingdom, where close statistics are kept on the use of anti-terrorism tools, Canada does not report on the use of the regular peace bonds (or much else in this area). Therefore, we are left to piece together statistics from media reports and figures reported, under questioning, by the government to the Senate national security committee. Based on these sources, we estimate the total number of anti-terror peace bonds issued between 2001 and July 2015 at twelve. Six peace bonds were issued as part of the Toronto 18 case. Five of these were imposed as part of a plea bargain. The sixth was applied after the person's sentence[58] — this is almost certainly a reference to Dirie (who, as noted, violated his peace bond by leaving Canada and is believed to have been killed while fighting for at terrorist group in Syria).

Peace bonds were used in the Toronto 18 as a reaction to an uncovered and existing terrorist activity rather than pre-emption in relation to feared conduct. That pattern has since started to shift, as we also discuss in Chapter 3. By the end of 2014, prosecutors obtained an additional two peace bonds, imposed as part of investigations.[59] Then, in the spring 2015, two individuals from Quebec signed peace bonds. Under their recognizances, the men are barred from having communications with each other.[60] Other conditions limit the men's movements and oblige them to wear electronic tracking devices, to cancel Internet service, and to provide police with electronic device passwords. The measures also bar the men from consulting terrorist material online and restrict communications on social media or otherwise with persons linked to a terrorist group.[61] Within a week, police alleged that one of the men had breached the obligation not to consult terrorist material. He was arrested and charged with breaching the bond,[62] an offence that may lead to his imprisonment.

A third man residing in Prince Edward Island and attending the University of PEI as a chemistry student signed a peace bond in March 2015.[63] He was reportedly found with significant quantities of castor beans, the ingredient for the deadly toxin ricin.[64] Police also pointed to documents they discovered, reportedly "with procedures for making calcium phosphide — described as an explosive compound — and a diagram of a small rocket with a section labelled 'warhead.'"[65] The RCMP told the court that it feared the man would commit a terrorism offence using a small rocket and a warhead carrying a chemical or biological agent. This is a public claim that the man described as "sensational" and one that he says has caused great suffering by his family. His lawyer says the rocket diagram was for an item sold at a toy shop: "It's a foot-high piece of cardboard with glue and balsa wood. It's meant to put a little GI Joe up in the air and it parachutes down."[66] The peace bond requires the man to remain in PEI, report to a probation officer and then to the RCMP weekly, and bars him from possessing castor beans, ricin, weapons, explosives, or ammunition.[67]

The twelfth case involves a Manitoba man. Apparently on a CSIS watchlist because of his social media activity in support of ISIS, Aaron Driver was arrested and held in custody in June 2015.[68] Prosecutors claimed that he might participate with a terrorist group, without providing specifics. He spent eight days in jail — an astonishing period, given that peace bonds themselves cannot result in incarceration (and the expanded period for preventive arrest and detention under Bill C-51 is seven days). The man refused to agree to a peace bond, but was released on bail subject to strict conditions. These included a GPS bracelet, surrender of his passport, a bar on computer use, a bar on possessing of any object with ISIS or al-Qaida symbols, no contact with people from these groups, restricted use of social media, a curfew, and an obligation to participate in "religious counselling." The counselling obligation may be first time such a requirement has been imposed by a Canadian court.[69] Driver was rearrested after a financial surety retracted support, but released again on bail. In July 2015, he launched a *Charter* challenge to the peace bond process, making his matter a key case likely to have important implications for the system.[70]

In another case, the police initially arrested two Quebec residents and intended to proceed with peace bonds, but decided instead to file terrorism charges.[71] And in May 2015, the RCMP intercepted ten young people at the Montreal airport, reportedly en route to the Syrian conflict. Subsequently, some "volunteered to be monitored" while others were simply released without their passports.[72] The police do not appear to have sought peace bonds.

Patterns of Use

The twelve peace bonds issued through to mid-2015 reflect a notable pattern. It appears that defendants in some — perhaps most — cases have not resisted the measures in an actual court proceeding. Consent to the peace bond is not truly voluntary — it reflects an obvious desire to avoid a legal process with its attendant bad publicity. The desire to avoid publicity was perhaps most obvious in the case of the PEI chemistry student.

The Trouble with Just Rolling Over

It is understandable that a person might consent to a peace bond in order to avoid a protracted, expensive, and even more stigmatizing open court process. But this consent also means that the state's allegations are not tested in court. This is regrettable. Should we really fear, for instance, that a chemistry student might deliver ricin by rocket? Or is this a case of misunderstanding, in a period of heightened security fears? Either way, the man will bear the terrorist label for the rest of his life.

In other cases, we do not even know the specifics of the allegations because they have never been tested in a full hearing. For instance, in the 2015 Montreal cases, prosecutors refused to divulge details, other than to say that authorities were worried the men will commit a terrorism offence. And because the two men did not contest the peace bonds, police were not obliged to testify at a hearing.[73]

Defendants who consent to peace bonds permit authorities to sidestep a potential difficulty they might otherwise face: the perennial intelligence-to-evidence concern that runs through this book. If the state can bank on consent and avoid the dilemmas of placing intelligence in front of a judge, it may attempt a peace bond even in circumstances where it would be otherwise deterred by a full, open-court adversarial hearing. In this way, a *Criminal Code* proceeding starts to look more like the security certificate proceedings that have been dogged by the "secret trial" label. In other words, too often in peace bonds, there is no trial, just agreements.

A Problem with Evidence?

But even without a full hearing, evidence issues are obviously a key concern: prosecutors cannot legally go forward without evidence, and there is always the prospect of a contested case, as is now occurring in Winnipeg. The reasonable fear that a person "will" — and now under Bill C-51, "may" — commit a terrorism offence is not an overwhelming standard. Like security certificates, it blurs the line between discrete acts and a person's status as a person who, because of past conduct, is thought to be a more or less permanent security or terrorism risk. But this "reasonable fear" is still a standard of evidence, requiring facts. The federal director of public prosecution will approve a peace bond application where "there is sufficient evidence available that a judge could — not that the judge would — find that the statutory requirements or threshold has been met."[74]

We note that the statistical record on peace bond use since 2001 replicates a pattern observed in relation to prosecutions in Canada: they are comparatively uncommon. The fifty-three control order/TPIM measures issued in the United Kingdom, where secret evidence can be used, amount to a rate of one measure per 0.83 million population. With twelve peace bonds, the Canadian anti-terror peace bond rate stands at 0.29 per million, or roughly one-third of the UK rate. Some of this difference is attributable to a dissimilar security environment, but we wonder how much might also be attributed to evidence issues — and especially the intelligence-to-evidence problem.

Certainly, the police will typically know little about what happens overseas in a conflict zone. In discussing the paucity of peace bonds in relation to returning terrorist travellers, justice department lawyers told the Senate committee in 2015, "It's not an easy task to gather evidence as to what someone did in a foreign jurisdiction. [The police] know the people have gone over there. They have strong suspicions about what people have done while over there, but to get evidence as to what they have actually done that would be admissible and convincing in a court of law is, at times, a difficult task."[75]

A Bond to Stop Saying the Wrong Things?

It is notable that the bizarre twelfth peace bond dispute in the Aaron Driver case in Manitoba appears to be the first firmly contested case. It is also the first clear case where the undergirding actions may be related to propaganda, as opposed to more kinetic activities. The peace bond appears to be tied to participation with a terrorist group and not the new Bill C-51 speech crime discussed in Chapter 10. At the same time, the process has focused attention on a man who has given interviews where he voices support for the October 2014 attacks and distinguishes them from attacks on civilians. This in turn led for calls by a member of Parliament that Driver be charged for his speech, potentially under the new terrorism offence of promoting or advocating "terrorism offences in general."[76] All of this raises questions about peace bonds designed to curb speech. The Manitoba case also hints at an anticipated escalation, and an aggressive use of peace bonds for activities removed from actual violence or threats of violence. This escalation may also invite outspoken targets of these peace bonds to breach the peace bonds by speaking out, which may include voicing sympathy for ISIS. Hearings to determine whether someone has breached a speech-related peace bond may be more like trials than the initial, and somewhat mushy, determination of whether there is a reasonable fear that the target may commit some terrorism offences. These mini-breach trials may, however, become political trials that simply amplify the accused's message.[77]

The Couture-Rouleau Mystery

With peace bonds, we also must be conscious of the failure to impose a peace bond on Martin Couture-Rouleau. Couture-Rouleau killed Warrant Officer Patrice Vincent in Saint-Jean-sur-Richelieu on 20 October 2014, using his car to run down the solider and a companion. Couture-Rouleau was well known to authorities before this time. They had revoked his passport because of his apparent ISIS ambitions, but they had not imposed a peace bond.

Just prior to Bill C-51's introduction in Parliament, media reports suggested the police had sought such a peace bond, but prosecutors had turned them down because the evidence was insufficient.[78] Federal prosecutors later told the Senate national security committee, "there was not a request for a peace bond. There was ongoing discussion between the investigators in Montreal and our senior Crowns to see whether or not there would be sufficient evidence to proceed with, among other things, . . . a peace bond . . . . They concluded that, in fact, there was insufficient evidence to meet the statutory threshold."[79] This revelation might explain why police suggested in the lead up to Bill C-51 that they should have the power to seek peace bonds without consent from the Attorney General (in practice, the director of public prosecutions).[80] But the Couture-Rouleau media reporting also fed into the idea that peace bond standards should be relaxed so they could be more easily obtained. Warrant Office Vincent's sister would later tell the Commons security committee that a lower evidence threshold would have saved her brother's life,[81] an opinion obviously welcomed by government politicians.

Since the standards for acquiring peace bonds were already among the lowest known to law — all it required was a reasonable fear that a terrorism offence "will be committed" — and since Couture-Rouleau's passport had already been seized on the basis of evidence meeting another low standard, the true explanation may be more complicated. For instance, was this a question of "no evidence," or rather "no evidence that we want to use in open court because it involves intelligence"? We do not know — the government has never explained the events surrounding Warrant Officer Vincent's death. That silence stands in contrast to the (modest) lessons-learned reporting on the Zehaf-Bibeau attacks in Ottawa and the much fuller report issued soon after a December terrorist attack in Sydney, Australia.[82]

Enter Bill C-51

Whatever the case, the government went ahead and used Bill C-51 to lower thresholds for acquiring peace bonds. They inserted a "may" where the 2001 law used a "will," and also increased the penalties for breaching any peace bond to a maximum of four years imprisonment,[83] while suggesting to judges a new range of conditions. As a result, "[a] person who fears on reasonable grounds that another person *may* commit . . . a terrorism offence may, with the consent of the Attorney General, lay an information before a provincial court judge."[84] If the provincial court judge is persuaded that these reasonable grounds for the fear exist, he may order the defendant to "enter into a recognizance . . . to keep the peace and be of good behaviour" for up to twelve months (and up to five years for a someone with a terrorist conviction), and may impose other conditions to secure good conduct.[85] A refusal by the accused to enter into the recognizance is punishable by imprisonment for up to twelve months.[86] A breach of a recognizance is a criminal offence, punishable by up to four years' imprisonment.[87]

Another Goldilocks Remedy?

Peace bonds are an obvious draw for the police: they do not require the levels of evidence required for an outright prosecution. Instead, authorities must simply prove that they have reasonable grounds for a fear that the target may commit any of a broad range of terrorism offences, one of the lowest standards of proof in Canadian law. And indeed, the past pattern suggests that they may need to prove nothing — the defendant will consent to the peace bond conditions to avoid a court proceeding.

Significant Limitations on Liberty

But no one should discount the impact of peace bonds on liberty interests. The Canadian system differs from the UK TPIM approach: it suggests a number of conditions, but does not set an outer limit. The conditions it does list include wearing an electronic monitoring device, curfew, abstaining from consuming intoxicants, and a bar on possessing weapons and explosives. The judge can also order participation in a "treatment program." One of the issues in the Manitoba case may be whether "religious counselling" is a "treatment program." As discussed below, this condition may allow Canada to address a shortcoming in the UK control order/TPIM approach: the absence of an exit strategy. At the same time, it may also result in claims that forced "religious counselling" violates freedom of religion. The new rules also require the judge to consider ordering the defendant to surrender her passport or other travel documents. At first blush, this measure seems redundant, given the government's passport revocation powers discussed in Chapter 6. But of course, revocation reaches only Canadian passports; a peace bond could reach foreign travel documents.

The new measure tells a judge to "consider whether it is desirable, to secure the good conduct of the defendant, to include in the recognizance a condition that the defendant remain within a specified geographic area unless written permission to leave that area is obtained from the judge or any individual designated by the judge."[88] This is a notable feature, since it means that, in principle, Canada could embark on relocation orders which, in the United Kingdom, are regarded as enhancing the effectiveness of TPIMs (but which are also deeply resented by defendants and their families). Beyond this, the judge may impose other, "reasonable conditions to the recognizance that [she] considers desirable to secure the good conduct of the defendant." This "good conduct" language accommodates many more conditions than the old standard, which allowed conditions tied only to preventing the feared terrorism offence. "Good conduct" has a much broader sweep — and is more ambiguous.

It is not endlessly pliable. In interpreting other peace bond powers containing the "good conduct" language, lower courts have concluded that conditions must have a reasonable nexus to the situation of the defendant and the feared conduct.[89] But in relation to terrorism offences, the feared conduct may be vast, amorphous, and never carefully articulated (at least in public), if the Montreal cases are indicative. The state has, in other words, a substantial discretion to craft conditions. As a result, peace bond conditions may come to look much like some of the conditions imposed on security certificate named persons. It is certainly already clear that peace bonds are being used to restrict communication and Internet use, as were security certificate conditions. For this reason, the potentially formidable reach of the peace bond should not be underestimated. A peace bond is a government-crafted, judicially imposed set of behavioural standards tailored to individual persons. Onerous conditions imposed as a part of the bond may be easily breached, permitting the subsequent incarceration of a feared security risk for behaviour that is benign (even commonplace) in its own right. For instance, a person barred from accessing a room with a computer violates the peace bond by walking into such a room. The person could potentially face a maximum of four years imprisonment for breaching any condition in a peace bond.

The Hair-Trigger

In this manner, peace bonds become a hair-trigger allowing the government to pursue easily proved and potentially banal peace bond violations as a means to incarcerate a person, without troubling itself with a prosecution for terrorism. As such, they are somewhat similar to the Al Capone strategy of charging a suspected terrorist with a different, more easily proven crime, although with the important difference that the breach here will involve behaviour that is not criminal for anyone else. In comments on a related process, David Paciocco called peace bonds "intuitively offensive." It is a way to "extend the reach of criminal consequences where the requirements of full proof cannot be met."[90] Conversely, Gary Trotter was not impressed with the efficacy of "peace bonds for terrorists."[91] We add to these points concerns that the courts have not yet developed a settled jurisprudence in peace bond cases. One can imagine some judges placing the emphasis on the "fear" that the person "may" commit a broad range of terrorism offences, with others perhaps placing more emphasis on the need for the "fear" to be "reasonable." In any event, judges are being asked to make predictive judgments about an accused's risk status. As such, a peace bond hearing is more similar to a bail hearing because both speculate about the accused's level of risks, and both avoid having to determine what the accused did.

Pushed to the extreme, there may be no wrong answers to the speculative questions that the judge must answer. In other words, "guilt" for a peace bond is a matter of awkward prognostication. As the criminal law embraces prevention and risk management, its sharpness as an instrument to determine facts and denounce proven — rather than future — crimes diminishes.

Constitutionality

All this begs inevitable questions about constitutionality. The constitutionality of anti-terrorism peace bonds has never been tested — something that seems likely to change because of the Manitoba case. But the Ontario Court of Appeal upheld a different species of peace bond: that guarding against sex offences directed at minors.[92] There, the defendant urged that the peace bond amounted to a "status offence"; that is, "an offence based on a person's status alone, . . . based on a person's medical diagnosis or even on a person's past criminal record but without any current offending conduct."[93] For this reason, and because of its overbreadth, the defendant argued peace bonds violated the fundamental justice promised by section 7 of the *Charter*.

The court agreed that the peace bond amounted to a restraint on liberty, and thus triggered the application of section 7 of the *Charter*. It concluded, however, that fundamental justice was not offended where the provision was largely geared to bona fide prevention and was not truly penal in nature. It mattered that the peace bond was narrowly tailored, restricting the defendant's liberty in respect to a large, but reasonably discrete group of persons (minors).[94] This allowed "a defendant to lead a reasonably normal life."[95] Some analysts point to this decision in discussing the propriety of anti-terrorism peace bonds.[96] The scope of the peace bond at issue in the Ontario case was, however, much more limited than those likely to be employed for anti-terror purposes. If present patterns are an indication, the anti-terror peace bond will be broader and more intrusive, potentially constraining liberty in *every* dimension of life, including issues of freedom of expression, freedom of association, and mobility rights, among others. It is difficult, in these circumstances, to draw a straight line between the Ontario Court of Appeal holding and a conclusion on the constitutionality of anti-terrorism peace bonds.

IV. CONCLUSION: TOO STRONG FOR FALSE POSITIVES, TOO WEAK FOR VILLAINS

We think peace bonds have an anti-terror role — a potentially important role. But we need to be clear-eyed on the risks. Whenever standards of evidence are this relaxed, the chance of false positives increases. Therefore, peace bonds are vulnerable to overreach. In that respect, they may prove too strong, wrapping the wrong people into their stifling embrace. It is not clear how such false positives will be detected. A defendant intimidated into consent may choose the least awful out of a series of bad options: agreeing to the peace bond conditions. Even if they challenge the measures, a court can remedy only so much when confronted with the modest evidentiary burden the peace bonds process places on the state. When a judge is asked to apply the vague standards of a peace bond, there may be no (or at best, very few) wrong answers. For these reasons, peace bonds — and their merits — are probably a good topic of review by the RCMP's review body, assuming it is able to overcome some of the structural difficulties it will have in reviewing RCMP operational information. Unfortunately, as we discuss in Chapter 12, that body does not have guaranteed access to the intelligence, including CSIS intelligence, that may lie behind some terrorist peace bonds, and has of yet not undertaken a review of the RCMP's national security activities.

At the same time, peace bonds may be too weak for determined terrorists. We opened this chapter with the story of Mohamed Ali Dirie, a convicted terrorist subjected to a peace bond who, nevertheless, absconded and was reportedly killed fighting in Syria. As noted above, absconders have been an issue in the United Kingdom as well, but there may be means of mitigating this risk. The UK experience suggests relocation may be the most effective means of breaking networks and reducing the prospect of flight. But this should not be the first option. Instead, whenever possible, real terrorists should be diverted into the criminal justice system. This is clearly the RCMP's preferred choice — in one Montreal case noted above, authorities started by seeking a peace bond, but switched course to a full prosecution. And RCMP officials told the Senate security committee in 2015, "[i]f we can put a peace bond in place, most of the time we're pretty close to being able to lay a charge."[97] The RCMP sees peace bonds as a stepping stone and not a solution: "With the imposition of conditions on the individual, such as travel restrictions and electronic monitoring, the police can have the ability to monitor and contain an individual's activities while they are under criminal investigation."[98]

This is a welcome approach that goes some way to mitigating our concerns (also articulated in Chapter 9) that Bill C-51 may be moving Canada away from its modest use of prosecutions toward a strategy where disrupt may often be the strongest sanction used against suspected terrorists. But in cases of returned foreign terrorist fighters and perhaps other cases (possibly including that of Couture-Rouleau), the police may be thwarted by problems in converting intelligence into evidence. In such cases, a peace bond may be a second-best remedy that could be too weak in the case of the determined terrorist. In the event that criminal prosecutions do not come to pass and the government remains persuaded that the person continues to pose a threat, we risk a pattern of serial peace bonds: strict limitations on liberty that can be sought and presumably re-sought again and again on the basis that a person is just plain dangerous, and forever dangerous.

As in security certificates, courts should respond to such a pattern by escalating the evidentiary expectation on the state over time, expecting more of it to make its case with the passage of time and the opportunity to collect evidence. But more than that, peace bonds should be twinned with broader, multi-disciplinary counter–violent extremism programs. As UK authorities now believe, intervention should come early in the peace bond term. This may be what the government has in mind in allowing judges to impose treatment program obligations. And it is another aspect of a necessary exit strategy. But as will be discussed in Chapter 13, the government does not appear to have a plan for "treatment programs," and in our federation, they will likely vary from province to province. We are not opposed to treatment and religious counselling, but question whether coercive and publicized peace bonds are the best delivery mechanism.

We also readily acknowledge concerns over whether treatment or de-radicalization programs can be successful. Dirie would not be a likely success story, although we will never know. That said, others may be better candidates. And as we discuss in Chapter 13, getting de-radicalization (or more correctly, disengagement from terrorism) right is perhaps the single biggest challenge we face in dealing with extremism of all stripes. But our key point from this chapter is this: security certificate and peace bond restraint tools are important, but deeply imperfect. They are the Goldilocks remedy. As such, they are best viewed not as solutions, but merely as funnels to the harder process of prosecution and the softer process of dissuading persons from terrorism.

CHAPTER EIGHT
Interrupt: Disruption When All Else Fails

I. INTRODUCTION

Urgency in the Fog of Uncertainty

Imagine the following scenario: Through an exercise of the "share" tool, a reliable foreign intelligence agency warns Canadian security agencies of a potential attack by a terrorist organization at an unspecified time in the near future on an unknown Canadian landmark. The foreign ally fingers an individual in Canada, who is the only known sympathizer in Canada of that terrorist group.

The only connection between the individual and the attack is the person's sympathy with the suspected terrorist group. In other words, the state (1) has reason to believe that an imminent terrorist attack will occur; (2) has reason to believe that a particular group is behind the plot and that a person in Canada may be working with that group; but (3) has no other information connecting that particular individual to the plot.

Under these circumstances, there are no reasonable and probable grounds for a criminal arrest — mere sympathy with a terrorist organization is not itself a crime, even if it could be proved beyond a reasonable doubt in open court.

"Watch" surveillance tools are available — and certainly, the government would be foolish not to monitor the person. Surveillance might produce evidence that leads the authorities to the perpetrator(s) of the planned terrorist attack, or that incriminates the surveillance target with other acts that are offences under Canadian law.

Surveillance is, however, fallible, especially if it must strive to be covert. Faced with an imminent danger from a group with which the individual is associated, the security agencies may reason that neutralization is to be preferred to surveillance, despite the investigative cost of alerting the person to the state's interest.

But the more assertive threat escalator tools are unhelpful. "Interdict," in the form of no-fly rules or passport revocation, is entirely irrelevant in this scenario. "Restraint" in the form of a peace bond might be useful, but as we have suggested in Chapter 7, such a device may be underwhelming when the state is confronted with a real peril. It does not detain the person, although the police may be able to obtain a warrant for arrest pending adjudication of the peace bond.

As a consequence, we are running out of tools: surveillance is imperfect, interdict irrelevant, restraint underwhelming, and prosecution at this point unavailable. What is left?

When the Wheels Fall Off . . .

We have intentionally painted the sort of scenario that drives discussions of what we shall call "interrupt" options — proactive tools designed to forestall a feared terrorist event, available when the wheels fall off more conventional devices.

The fact that our scenario is fictitious should give our readers pause: the other tools described throughout this book are potent, and circumstances where we need to reach beyond them should be very rare, and perhaps more theoretical than real. There is a reason why Canada's chief interrupt tool — "preventive arrest" or "preventive detention" — has never been used, either in its expired, original 2001 to 2007 form or following its revival in 2013.

We should also be very wary of interrupt tools that are used out of convenience rather than true necessity. These are devices that run the highest risk of abusive and counterproductive overreach. They may result in "false positives," resulting in the arrest and detention of people, perhaps with great publicity, who, as it turns out, are not terrorists.

Furthermore, preventive arrests may scuttle ongoing investigations that, if allowed to play out, could provide evidence to support actual terrorism prosecutions — forceful, exacting, and fair instruments examined in Chapter 9.

But with proper safeguards, we believe preventive arrest and detention do have a place in Canada's anti-terror arsenal. In this chapter, we first look at legal tools falling into the interrupt category and explore their structure and scope. We then examine the now infamous Bill C-51[1] developments in this area, and especially the controversial new CSIS "threat reduction measures."

We view these new CSIS powers as poorly situated in our threat escalator model and potentially acting at cross-purposes to it. We also address how, by failing to think through exactly how a CSIS "disruption" role should work, the government legislated provisions that stumble into an unnecessary and deeply damaging constitutional adventure.

II. LAW ENFORCEMENT INTERRUPT

Of all our tool categories, "interrupt" is the most unconventional, and thus most difficult to define. In colloquial usage, the word means "breaking continuity" or "stopping the seamless progress of something." Many tools, used singly or in combination, could serve this purpose in relation to a terrorist plot — stopping someone from boarding a plane or imposing a peace bond may be forms of interrupt. A border stop, of the sort at issue in the Ressam case discussed in Chapter 6, might have the same effect. Convening an investigative hearing under the *Criminal Code*'s anti-terrorism rules could (indirectly) interrupt: it could shake up a plot, place a stick in the spoke of a conspiracy, or jam the gears of a feared lone wolf, at least in theory. It has not yet worked out that way: As discussed in Chapter 2, the only attempt to use an investigative hearing occurred with respect to one of the many reluctant witnesses in the Air India trial. That is, it was a reactive tool, not a pre-emptive one, and even then it did not work. But in principle, investigative hearings may be used pre-emptively in the future.

Here, though, we define "interrupt" more narrowly, to distinguish it from other tools discussed in this book. Interrupt tools are those used where exigency or unavoidable operational impediments make other tools unavailable or ineffective. Interrupt is, moreover, a temporary strategy — it is not a permanent solution, but rather a way for authorities to divert a threat, or at least press the pause bottom in order to get on top of it. As we will argue, one problem with Bill C-51 is the extent to which it departs from these kinds of criteria by giving CSIS broad powers to engage in undefined forms of "threat reduction" — what the government calls "disruption."

Obviously, deciding when to deploy "interrupt" is a matter of close judgment, exercised in the inevitable fog of a real or anticipated emergency. Ensuring its proper application will require clear rules, close oversight, and careful retrospective review, matters discussed in Chapters 11 and 12.

In this section, we focus on three law-enforcement-related "interrupt" powers, which we label investigative interruption, pretextual enforcement, and preventive detention.

Investigative Interruption

Defusing Plots

As a terrorism investigation progresses, peace officers may forestall a terrorist act by removing one of its constituent ingredients. Financing arrangements may be interrupted, key information intercepted, misinformation conveyed, or physical tools associated with the plot denied. Perhaps the best-known (public) example of "investigative interruption" arose in the Toronto 18 investigation.

In 2006, police conducted multiple arrests in southern Ontario. Thirteen adults and four youths were arrested. Combined with charges against another man, these people constituted the Toronto 18. Members of the group discussed bombing prominent locations — "CSIS's office in downtown Toronto, the CBC building in downtown Toronto, Parliament, unspecified military bases and a nuclear power plant."[2] They also developed plans to explode three truck bombs at each of the Toronto Stock Exchange, the Toronto offices of CSIS, and a military base near Highway 401.[3]

The accused were arrested under conventional criminal law rules. Although they knew about the plot soon after its inception, the police did not use special preventive arrest powers, discussed below, that were available when the arrests were made in 2006. This was probably wise: as discussed in Chapter 9, ordinary arrests trigger presumptions of denial of bail in terrorism cases. Moreover, they generally result in pre-trial detention that lasts much longer than the maximum three days allowed under Canada's original preventive arrest provision (or even the seven days now allowed under Bill C-51).

Shooting Blanks

But the police did make sure prior to the arrest that the plotters would not have the means to carry out their crime; that is, they performed an investigative interruption. Undercover CSIS informants, who were ultimately transferred to the police, enmeshed themselves in the group's planning activities. When the group ordered agricultural chemicals to be used in the bomb-making, police ensured that the delivered material was inert, before arresting the accused.[4]

Swapping dangerous material for benign substances is an obvious and prudent practice in an urgent situation. In the Toronto 18 case, the timing suggests that the authorities did so without breaking any criminal laws. The situation would have been more complex, however, if the investigative interruption had implicated police or government agents in illegal activities. In the Toronto 18 case, for example, a key legal issue was at what point a key police informant among the group — Mubinoddin Shaikh — became a "state agent."[5]

A state agent is someone who acts at the direction of the security services and plays an active role in the investigation. A confidential informant, in comparison, is someone who simply supplies information to authorities. The line between the two is a fine one, but a confidential informant's identity is entitled to robust protection from disclosure in court proceedings — the so-called informer's privilege.

In the Toronto 18 case, defence lawyers argued that Shaikh's leadership activities in support of the plot occurred while he was a state agent. They argued that it would be an abuse of legal process to then prosecute co-conspirators acting in response to the state agent's own illegal actions. The challenge failed because the court concluded that, at the time, Shaikh remained a police informant and had not become a state agent. And at any rate, the court also concluded that the accused would have acted in the manner they did even without Shaikh's role.[6] The failure of an entrapment defence in this and other terrorism prosecutions is discussed in Chapter 9.

But what if Shaikh had been a "state agent"? Could he have broken the law? It seems he would have done so by continuing to participate in a terrorist conspiracy — and it is possible the RCMP would have asked him to perform an illegal interruption, such as destroying the property of one of the co-conspirators to foil some part of the plot.

More generally, could the police themselves have broken the law as part of an investigative interruption of a terrorist plot? For example, had the agricultural fertilizer necessary for the bomb-making already been in the possession of the plotters, could the police have broken into the warehouse in which it was stored and destroyed it, or switched it with an inert substance?

Law Enforcement Justification for Illegality

The answer to these questions is "yes" so long as the police had complied with sections 25.1 to 25.4 of the *Criminal Code*.[7]

Called the "law enforcement justification provision," these sections date to 2001 and constitute an extraordinary — and controversial — justification for peace officers, in controlled circumstances, to break the criminal law. The provision was passed in response to the 1999 Supreme Court case of *R v Campbell*.[8]

In that case, the police engineered a "reverse sting" operation by arranging the sale of narcotics to the accused and then charging that person with conspiracy to traffic. A stay of proceedings was sought on the basis that the police had engaged in a serious breach of the law.

In response, the Crown argued that any illegal conduct should be subject to Crown immunity from statutory offences. In the course of considering this argument, the Supreme Court of Canada considered the nature of the relationship between the police and the Crown, noting the existence of "police independence" from the executive branch of government — a concept we discuss further below. On the basis of this independence, the Supreme Court rejected the extension of Crown immunity to the police.

While the significance of this case regarding police immunity has been disputed,[9] Canadian governments and police authorities concluded it placed them on the horns of a policy dilemma, especially in relation to police undercover work in organized crime (and, in today's context, national security).

The Dilemmas

Their concerns are obvious: a criminal organization, in an attempt to identify undercover police agents, would simply require its members to break a law — say, engage in an armed robbery. In that circumstance, an undercover agent would face a dilemma: decline, and be identified as a state agent, or participate, and rely on prosecutorial discretion to ensure that there would not be a prosecution for the crime.

This would be an unwieldy and unfair system, placing the peril of prosecution while providing an important public good — fighting organized crime — on the shoulders of the state agent. It would also force the police into a form of "noble cause" illegality — that is, breaking the law for a higher purpose.

On the other hand, legislating new get-out-of-jail-free immunity provisions for police provoked other concerns. As the Senate committee examining the provisions at the time of their enactment in 2001 noted, "[t]here is something paradoxical about breaking the law in order to better enforce it."[10] This is, as critics observe, "an attack upon the fundamental premise of the rule of law, which is that all persons, including the police, are subject to the law."[11]

The 2001 provisions ran counter to recommendations of the McDonald Commission on RCMP wrongdoing in the 1970s, which rejected the idea of immunity for premeditated criminal offences even by security intelligence undercover operatives.[12] Moreover, the provisions also give immunity to persons acting on the direction of those peace officers who appear (to the agent) to be authorized to give these orders. This could result in somewhat shady actors working undercover for police being instructed by police to break more laws, this time with immunity.

The Safeguards

The provisions do include several safeguards. We underscore these here in some detail, because they become especially material when we examine the new CSIS law-breaking powers under Bill C-51.

First, a substantial portion of the relevant law is made up of rules on approval for law breaking.[13] In this respect, the minister responsible for the police force must personally designate peace officers able to exercise these powers, and may only do so where the peace officers are subject to a system of outside review by non-peace officers. For example, for the RCMP, this would be the Civilian Review and Complaints Commission. In emergency situations, a senior law enforcement official may designate a peace officer as empowered to break the law, but only for a maximum of forty-eight hours. In either case, the authorization may be subjected to conditions, such as limitations on its duration and the nature of the crimes that the officer may commit.

Second, there is an outer limit to law breaking. The provisions cannot justify "(a) the intentional or criminal negligent causing of death or bodily harm to another person; (b) the wilful attempt in any manner to obstruct, pervert or defeat the course of justice; (c) or conduct that would violate the sexual integrity of an individual."[14] Also excluded are certain drug offences (governed by separate immunity provisions in drug enforcement law).

Notably, "bodily harm" means any "hurt or injury to a person that interferes with the health or comfort of the person and that is more than merely transient or trifling in nature."[15] Courts have construed this standard as encompassing both physical and psychological harm — including death threats.[16]

Third, the authorized peace officer can only commit (or direct another to commit) an offence lying within these permissible limits if engaged "in the investigation of an offence under, or the enforcement of, an Act of Parliament or in the investigation of criminal activity" and where the officer also believes on reasonable grounds that committing the offence is reasonable and proportional, given its nature, the nature of the investigation, and the availability of other means to carry out the officer's duties.[17]

Fourth, where the offence is likely to involve loss of, or serious damage to, property, the peace officer must also generally have written authorization from a senior law enforcement official to commit that act (or direct another to do so). And that senior official must believe the act to be reasonable and proportional. This written authorization requirement may be disregarded, but only where it is not feasible to obtain it and at issue is the life and safety of a person, the compromising of the peace officer's identity, or the imminent loss or destruction of evidence.[18]

Fifth, an officer who commits (or directs another to commit) the illegal act must file a report with the proper senior law enforcement official. And every responsible minister must publish annually a public report detailing the number of times a senior official authorized law breaking in exigent circumstances or an illegal act likely to result in loss or serious damage to property, and the nature of the acts then committed in response.[19]

Sixth, the person whose property was lost or seriously damaged must be notified within one year, subject to certain public interest exceptions.[20]

Note that public reporting under the provisions is imperfect — it is confined to exigent use of the justifications or use resulting in loss or serious damage to property. This presumptively covers only a subset of illegal conduct that authorized peace officers (or those they instruct) may commit.

However, at least this much disclosure does exist. And this "tip of the iceberg" peek into policing suggests that, for the RCMP, use of the justification to commit acts involving property damage is comparatively rare — but does involve anti-terror investigations.

For instance, in 2013, five persons were directed to commit a total of thirteen illegal acts of the magnitude triggering reporting, with four acts ultimately carried out. The "nature of the conduct being investigated" was "participating in the activity of a terrorist group and facilitating terrorist activity." And the nature of the acts then committed is described as "providing, making available, etc., property or services for terrorist purposes and using explosives (delivering an explosive substance)."[21] These constituted the only reported uses of the justification by the RCMP for that year.

Anti-terror use appears in earlier reports, although not that frequently and never in relation to a large number of authorizations. In the annual reports from 2003 to 2013, law enforcement justifications for RCMP anti-terror investigations were reported for 2006 (or early 2007), 2010, 2011, and 2013. It is impossible to know about the nature of these activities, unless the matters being investigated result in criminal charges prosecuted in court.

Constitutionality

As suggested, the law enforcement justification provisions provoke substantial unease when examined from a rule of law perspective. Some critics label them a form of "legal lawlessness"[22] and, indeed, the provisions were not enthusiastically embraced by at least some of the parliamentary committees that have examined them.[23]

Their constitutionality has been questioned, although so far, *Charter* challenges appear to have been dismissed in a single reported lower court case. This is not that surprising — to date, the constitutional examination of these provisions has depended on a "rule of law" argument and constitutional "vagueness or overbreadth" objections under section 7 of the *Charter*.[24] Both arguments have been notoriously unsuccessful when used to attack statutes.

Defendants have also proposed that the absence of a prior judicial authorization before police engage in illegal conduct violates the *Charter* section 7 guarantee of "fundamental justice." The single lower court that has considered this argument rejected it, in part because such prior judicial authorization was viewed as impracticable given the circumstances in which the law-breaking justifications were used.[25]

The Catch: The Possibility of Collapsed Prosecutions

In fact, overall, there is surprisingly little judicial treatment of the justification provisions. However, a relatively recent lower court decision places an important gloss on how the provisions are to be interpreted. The Ontario Superior Court concluded that section 25.1 is a defence to criminal charges, but it did not affirmatively *authorize* criminal conduct. The court held that section 25.1 "does not prevent a defendant from relying upon the unlawful conduct of a public officer if it is helpful in the conduct of the defence."[26]

We return to this issue in Chapter 9 while discussing the impact of the new CSIS measures on prosecutions. But for our purposes here, it should be underscored that section 25.1 does not insulate police from defence claims that state agents have entrapped a defendant or otherwise conducted themselves in a manner that might impair a subsequent trial of an accused. And so, police illegality may still be a consideration in applications to stay criminal proceedings or exclude evidence. Put another way, a get-out-of-jail-free card is not permission for the police to circumvent the rules in order to obtain convictions. This means that when police break the law in a terrorism investigation, they know that their conduct will be closely scrutinized if there is a subsequent terrorism prosecution, and that their conduct may jeopardize those cases.

This qualification concerning the effect of section 25.1 is potentially important. It may have the effect of making police wary of acting illegally under the law enforcement justification, for fear of complicating a subsequent prosecution. Police might also reasonably be concerned about novel claims concerning their civil liability exposure for illegal acts, especially now that *Charter* breaches are clearly actionable for damages. And in this regard, it is notable that nothing in the law enforcement justification purports to override the *Charter*. These are all important differences from the new CSIS powers discussed later in this chapter.

Put another way, prudential considerations may push police to use the measure as a last-best alternative, perhaps in true "interrupt" situations. These prudential considerations enhance the more general section 25.1 formalization of "last-best alternative": before breaking the law (or directing another to do so), designated peace officers must take into account "the reasonable availability of other means for carrying out the public officer's law enforcement duties."

Pretextual Al Capone Enforcement

Pretextual enforcement — sometimes also called "preventive charging" or "preventive prosecution" — is a technique on the edge between "prosecute" and "interrupt."

Here, police investigating a terrorism matter may unearth evidence allowing them to enforce assertively other, even minor, criminal or regulatory laws against those believed to pose a terrorist threat. This might involve outright charging and prosecution for these collateral crimes. Much like Al Capone was convicted for tax offences and not for his mobster crimes, this form of collateral enforcement interrupts suspected terrorist threats through expedient use of other laws.

The Bill C-51 speech crime discussed in Chapter 10 may morph into a form of backup, Al Capone–type enforcement, where authorities suspect deeper terrorist involvement but have evidence only of public advocacy with regards to terrorism. Its elements — tied to the wrong speech in the wrong context — are much easier to prove than other terrorism offences. As discussed in Chapter 10, we predict it will be rarely used because of its constitutional infirmities and the limited sentences (maximum five years) it allows. But we can imagine circumstances where those concerns are displaced by a resort to collateral enforcement tactics.

Poking the Bear

Pretextual enforcement of one set of laws may also prompt conduct by suspects that authorities can then act on separately. For example, an Ottawa man attracted police attention in the immediate aftermath of the October 2014 Parliament Hill shootings by allegedly praising the gunman as a hero and martyr and acting in a threatening and provocative manner at a local mosque.

Apparently, as part of an operational choice made in the aftermath of the October shootings, the police monitoring the man decided to conduct a traffic stop on a weekend afternoon — some reports suggested the man had a number of serious driving infractions on his record. The man then allegedly became "combative," began pacing and chanting, and eventually ran. After avoiding a Taser, the man punched a police officer, an assault that drew another officer from a surveillance vehicle into the fray. That second officer (surprisingly) fired a shot at the fleeing man, missing him. A second Taser ultimately subdued the suspect. Police charged him with two counts of obstructing justice and one count of assaulting a peace officer.[27]

Poking Bears Who Would Never Growl?

Pretextual enforcement has obvious attractions — it extends the range of anti-terror tools significantly. But it also raises important issues because it is a potentially dangerous form of anti-terrorism.

Using police powers, not to pursue genuine criminal prosecutions, but as pretextual tools to provoke people who, to that point, were acting lawfully (or at least not violently) is a concerning practice. Used routinely, it may have the effect of creating criminals of people who would otherwise have posed no real threat.

The Ottawa man stopped by police in the October incident described above was, by all accounts, not an upstanding citizen. He had also voiced offensive political opinions and did so in an obnoxious and even aggressive manner. The criminal charges ultimately brought against him following the traffic stop stemmed directly from an apparently pretextual enforcement policy. Put another way, there was a straight line drawn from his expression of offensive political views to a technically legal but seemingly pretextual traffic stop. This straight line should make anyone in a democracy uncomfortable, since there is not necessarily an equally straight line between expressing offensive political views and acting violently on them. Pretextual enforcement, deployed in this manner, looks an awful lot like "provoke" and "create" and not "interrupt."

In the same way, using the new Bill C-51 speech crime as a pretextual enforcement tool could be an overreaction to an extremist speaker who is not actually involved in terrorism. And as we have already suggested, it could be an underreaction if the person is actually involved in recruiting, funding, or planning violence.

Poking Only One Type of Bear?

Singling out people for aggressive pretextual enforcement of real offences is, from one perspective, fully legitimate. But if in the usual course, the minor crimes or regulatory infractions would not attract the same scrutiny from authorities, or galvanize an equivalently harsh response from them, then it can amount to *de facto* unequal treatment under the law.

And since authorities are imposing this unequal treatment on the basis of perceived threats never proven in a court of law, there is the real risk that those suspicions are poorly grounded and reflect untested tunnel vision. In other words, pretextual enforcement can lead to unequal treatment of false positives — people fingered as threats who really are not.

Perhaps the most notorious example of this was the US government's stringent enforcement of conventional immigration laws in the aftermath of 9/11. Infractions include remaining past the expiration of visas, entering the United States without inspection, or entering the country with invalid papers. Almost 800 persons with suspected terrorism connections were detained on these conventional immigration law grounds in the immediate wake of 9/11.

A 2003 US Department of Justice report reviewing this record concluded that administrative practices associated with these detentions produced unduly lengthy periods of incarceration, and in some instances unsatisfactory conditions of detention.[28] The median length of detention between arrest and release or removal from the United States was about 100 days.[29]

This experience suggests that expedient and pretextual use of tools designed for other purposes may become a practice ripe for abuse. It is not a strategy to be undertaken lightly — and calls out for careful policy guidance, possible legislative action, and thorough assessment by robust, independent review bodies.

Violating the Bear's Rights

The most egregious example of a (failed) attempt at Al Capone–style pretextual enforcement in Canada comes not from the police but from a case where CSIS, after years of investigating a terrorism suspect, decided that the best way to proceed was to have the suspect charged with child pornography. This case, R v Mejid,[30] is also discussed in Chapter 6.

In this case, the trial judge found that the CSIS officer took charge of directing a criminal investigation, "clearly outside of his mandate to investigate matters of national security."[31] The suspect, Mejid, complied with CSIS's demand to search his computer "because of a sense of compulsion [in part, stemming from CSIS threats to reveal details of his personal life to family members] rather than making a voluntary choice."[32] The search focused entirely on child pornography — and not terrorism. Such pornography was found and Mejid was reported to the police and prosecuted.

The court then threw out the charges, issuing one of the sternest rebukes of CSIS that we have ever seen, and one that is relevant to the new threat reduction powers that CSIS now has, to be discussed later in this chapter. The CSIS officer, wrote Justice Kelly, cannot simply throw his hands up and say: "I am a CSIS agent and I collect intelligence for national security so I do not have to consider the Charter rights of individuals". Obtaining the computer from Mr. Mejid under the guise of national security concerns is a flagrant abuse of Mr. Mejid's Charter rights. The computer was given to CSIS under false pretences . . . . I am troubled by the atmosphere of coercion and intimidation that the CSIS agents (and in particular Witness "A") seem to have created and been eager to embrace. The very people that are tasked by the federal government to oversee and safeguard Canada's national security are themselves acting in a manner that suggests either a complete lack of comprehension of our Charter rights or else, they demonstrate a total willingness to abrogate and violate these same principles. Neither is acceptable and I find that the Charter breach in this case was serious.[33]

Some readers may see nothing wrong with CSIS's conduct — after all, there were incriminating photos. But CSIS did not find the photos as part of a bona fide security investigation and then transfer that information over to the police. Instead, they decided that since they could not justify their national security preoccupations, they would instead consciously search for child pornography — an Al Capone approach.

As noted above, there may be room for Al Capone–style strategies in national security law for the police. But there is no room for CSIS to exceed its remit and engage in unilateral law enforcement.

As discussed in Chapter 9, CSIS should be sensitive to evidential concerns when it conducts its national security investigations, to better support ultimate prosecutions. But that is not the same thing as CSIS itself conducting law enforcement, well beyond its statutory jurisdiction, especially when (at the same time) it falls back on its regular "we do security intelligence, not law enforcement" mantra to disregard completely the *Charter* rules that govern law enforcement. Whatever the merits of the positions aired during the Bill C-51 debates discussed below, what CSIS did in *Mejid* really was to act as a "secret police."

Mejid has since launched a $10 million lawsuit against the Canadian government for CSIS's conduct in 2011. He claimed that CSIS's "campaign of harassment" destroyed his "reputation, cost him many of his former friends and associations and made him effectively unemployable." He also maintained that he had never associated with any terrorist organization, and suggested that the child pornography–related images found on his computer were planted by CSIS.[34]

We do not know, and may never know, whether the lawsuit has merit. If litigated, we suspect it will encounter many of the challenges of state secrecy claims that have beset other similar claims.

Preventive Detention

The final law enforcement tool in this discussion is designed specifically as an "interrupt" device: preventive arrest or preventive detention.

Like many other expressions in anti-terror law, preventive detention has different meanings to different people. For our purposes, preventive detention is a non-criminal-charge detention designed to prevent future behaviour, rather than to punish or rehabilitate in response to past actions. That is, it is not a criminal law process in which a court trial results in a conviction and a sentence. (We recognize that there is a measure of preventive detention in normal bail practices after a person has been charged. Indeed, in Chapter 9, we examine how those accused of terrorism offences bear the onus of proof when bail questions are adjudicated in court, in part because of an assumption that they might threaten public safety if released pending trial.)

Pre-charge detention is a relatively commonplace feature of anti-terrorism law around the world. Examining foreign analogues is an apple-and-oranges exercise, since legal systems are often quite different, and some countries (such as the United States) have detained people for prolonged periods in extra-legal manners, in offshore detention facilities, and through the manipulation of material witness warrants. One 2010 United Kingdom study ranked seven countries by the duration of their pre-charge detention regimes.[35] The United Kingdom was an extreme outlier, at (then) 28 days. For other states, the numbers (in days) were as follows: Australia (12), Turkey (7.5), France (6), Spain (5), Russia (5), Italy (4), Denmark (3), Norway (3), United States (2), New Zealand (2), and Germany (2).

A Brief History of Canada's Anti-terror Preventive Detention Rules

Canada's anti-terror preventive detention rules are found in the *Criminal Code*. Originally enacted by the 2001 *Anti-terrorism Act*,[36] section 83.3 of the *Criminal Code* is entitled "recognizance with conditions" but called "preventive detention" in the popular discourse.

This provision was clearly designed to foil terrorist plots on the cusp of execution. Stanley Cohen describes its purpose this way:

> The whole scheme is designed to disrupt nascent suspected terrorist activity by bringing a person before a judge who would then evaluate the situation and decide whether it would be useful . . . to impose conditions on the person. The purpose . . . is not to effectuate an arrest but merely to provide a means of bringing a person before a court for the purposes of judicial supervision.[37]

The net effect of the original section 83.3 was (theoretically) to enable a preventive detention on suspicions of terrorist activity for a maximum initial period of twenty-four hours (and perhaps longer if a judge was not available within that period) in emergency situations and then, where the judge agreed to an adjournment but did not release the detainee, detention for another forty-eight hours. Preventive arrest could last, in other words, for a maximum of seventy-two hours.

But to be clear, this was not a self-standing detention regime. The detention was, in principle, linked to a peace bond process not greatly different from that discussed in Chapter 7. That is, when a full hearing was ultimately held after the detention process discussed above, the judge was to consider whether the peace officer had reasonable grounds for his suspicion.

If the officer did, the judge could order the person to enter into a recognizance of up to twelve months' duration, a limitation on the person's freedom equivalent to the other peace bond controls discussed in Chapter 7. As with regular peace bonds, outright detention was not among the conditions that could be imposed. But like the regular peace bond process, a violation of conditions in the recognizance could culminate in incarceration — in some respects, therefore, the peace bond could become a "hair trigger" on outright imprisonment.

By 2007, section 83.3 had never been used. Nevertheless, it remained among the most controversial of the provisions introduced by the 2001 *Anti-terrorism Act*. In particular, the prospect of detention for up to seventy-two hours on suspicion of terrorist activity generated disquiet.

To ease those concerns in 2001, Parliament inserted requirements that the attorney general and the minister of public safety report annually on the use of the section. The preventive detention power also included an automatic sunset provision, terminating the measure in early 2007 unless it was renewed by vote of Parliament. As discussed in Chapter 2, both the House of Commons Standing Committee on Public Safety and National Security and the Senate Special Committee on the *Anti-terrorism Act* recommended in 2006 and 2007 respectively that this provision be extended. However, a motion to renew the provision was defeated in a minority Parliament by the opposition parties in February 2007, after an acrimonious and often unedifying political debate that echoed in some notable respects the toxic politics of Bill C-51.

Thereafter, the Conservative government made several efforts to re-enact the measure. These law projects were foiled, not by the opposition parties, but by repeated prorogations and dissolutions of Parliament that caused the bill to die on the order paper. Finally, in 2013, the measure was re-enacted in essentially identical form to its 2001 version and is again found in section 83.3

of the *Criminal Code*, together with a new sunset expiring in 2018 (or soon after). The new section 83.3 preventive detention provision has still never been used.

Nevertheless, Bill C-51 amended the rules to ratchet down the standards that have to be met for detention and lengthen the duration of that detention to a maximum of seven days.

How Preventive Detention Works after Bill C-51

The mechanics of section 83.3 are now quite complex, and we illustrate their workings in Figure 8.1. Key terms — such as "reasonable suspicion" and "believe" — are defined in the annex to Chapter 1.

Controversies

Section 83.3 was (and remains) controversial. Many civil society groups oppose the concept of pre-charge detention outright. This is a reasonable position: detention without charge prioritizes public safety over "the most fundamental and probably the oldest, most hardly won and the most universally recognized of human rights": freedom from executive detention.[38]

Pre-charge detention should, therefore, be used sparingly, and only in the most limited circumstances. As the hypothetical we began this chapter with suggests, it is an "interrupt" strategy justified only by true emergencies where the risks are grave. We believe that the power to detain in exigent circumstances without judicial warrant should apply only where designed to prevent a terrorist activity that involves a *serious and imminent threat to life, health, public safety, or substantial property damage that threatens life or health.*

Unfortunately, section 83.3 is not so constrained. Its present wording allows preventive detention in more than such serious instances. The provision is tied to the concept of "terrorist activity" in the *Criminal Code*, and that concept in turn is connected mostly to true acts of violence or serious harm. But not always: a terrorist activity may actually be considerably removed from actual acts of violence. For instance, the provision also includes "serious interference with or serious disruption of an essential service, facility or system" (except where caused by advocacy, protest, dissent, or work stoppage, unless these acts themselves are intended to cause bodily harm, endanger life, or cause serious risk to public health). In upholding the constitutionality of the definition of terrorist activity, the Supreme Court recognized that this wording was the broadest and most problematic part of the definition and that it might have to be revisited for *Charter* purposes by the Court if squarely raised on the facts of a case.[39] Further, the section includes not only actual interference with essential services, but "conspiracy, attempt or threat

Figure 8.1: Mechanics of Preventive Detention

Peace officer must believe on reasonable grounds that a terrorist activity may be carried out and suspect on reasonable grounds that a peace bond or an arrest is likely to prevent the carrying out of a terrorist activity

⬇

In exigent circumstances (or if the peace officer has laid an "information" with a provincial court judge) . . .

⬇

Peace officer may arrest and detain the person if officer suspects on reasonable grounds that the detention of the person is likely to prevent a terrorist activity

⬇

Person must be brought before a provincial court judge without unreasonable delay, and within **twenty-four hours**, unless a judge is unavailable

⬇

Judge must order the person released, but he or she may adjourn the matter and continue the person's detention for up to **forty-eight hours** if the peace officer had laid an "information" that demonstrates the need to detain the person in order to ensure they will appear for the peace bond case; for protection or safety of the public; or to maintain confidence in the administration of justice, for example, because of the gravity of the feared terrorist activity

⬇

Judge must order the person released, but may adjourn the matter and continue the person's detention for up to another **forty-eight hours** if peace officer again demonstrates one of the justifications listed above *and* that the investigation in relation to which the person is detained is being conducted diligently and expeditiously

⬇

Judge must order the person released, but may adjourn the matter and continue the person's detention for up to yet another **forty-eight hours** if peace officer again demonstrates one of the justifications listed above *and* that the investigation in relation to which the person is detained is being conducted diligently and expeditiously

⬇

Judge must then adjudicate the matter and may, if satisfied on the evidence that the peace officer has reasonable grounds for suspicion, impose a peace bond for a period of up to twelve months requiring the person to comply with reasonable conditions the judge deems necessary to prevent the carrying out of a terrorist activity. The person must then be released. If the person has been convicted of a terrorism offence, the peace bond may be for two years. If the person refuses to enter into the peace bond, the person may be imprisoned for up to twelve months.

⬇

Person who violates the peace bond may be convicted of an indictable offence and imprisoned for up to four years (or up to eighteen months on summary conviction)

to commit any such act," or being an accessory after the fact or counselling in relation to any such act."

It is thus possible under the post–Bill C-51 section 83.3 to detain someone for up to seven days where a peace officer

- has a credibility-based belief, sometimes described as a bona fide belief, of a serious possibility, based on credible evidence that
- the person *may* counsel another person to interfere seriously with an "essential facility"
- while suspecting on objectively articulable grounds that
- the arrest is *likely* to prevent this counselling or another terrorist activity.

The words "may" and "likely" are highlighted above because these are the standards that were eased by Bill C-51; before Bill C-51, the words were "will" and "necessary" respectively. During the bill's enactment, these relaxed standards attracted condemnation from the bill's opponents.

Turning a Blind Eye to Predictable Issues

For our part, we are not entirely persuaded that the more relaxed standards for obtaining such an instrument are irresponsible — or indeed, that they will make much of a difference in practice.

In part, our indecisiveness reflects the absence of any public record on why section 83.3 has not been used to date. Put another way, we are faced with the same problem running through Bill C-51: does it respond to real legal impediments, or does it simply superimpose a legalistic solution to operational problems resolved only by better resourcing, organization, and better transition of "intelligence to evidence"?

Nevertheless, by reducing the threshold for detention and extending the period of (judicially approved) preventive detention from a maximum of seventy-two hours to seven days, we are concerned that the balance may now have tipped too far toward security and away from liberty.

It would be foolishness to assume that detention based on these now very forgiving standards will mean the right person will always be detained. Again, there will be false positives — innocent people wrongly detained. This is especially so in a case where the outside boundaries of a suspected cell or group are unclear. In the worst case, the current preventive detention system could come close to acting as a dragnet. Under the forgiving evidentiary standards, fairly tenuous connections between individuals may generate the "credibility-based belief" that a given person loosely associated with an investigative target *may* be about to engage in a suspected terrorist activity.

This would be a controversial outcome, with echoes of the October Crisis, and its impact could at least have been mitigated by standards on what can then be done to the person detained. We do not assume the state would visit abuse on the detainee. Nor do we assume that the courts would be inattentive to such abuse. But given somewhat regular revelations of mistreatment of prisoners in various detention settings,[40] combined with the inherently emotive context of terrorism fears, we would be naïve to imagine that the preventive detention system will be immune to mistakes or excess.

Indeed, the extraordinary and potentially high-pressure circumstances of preventive detention make these concerns more acute, as does the fact that we simply have no real history with pre-charge detention (at least not since the October Crisis of 1970).

Matters That Should Have Been Addressed

There is a lengthy list of novel questions. Where will persons subject to preventive arrest be detained? How will they be detained — with the general population, or in solitary confinement? They will retain a right to counsel, but what role will a lawyer play in this unique situation? Will there be limits on detainee interrogation? Furthermore, we will be inventing standards of propriety in terms of, for example, the duration, nature, and circumstances of questioning. Preventive detention is a situation unknown in Canadian practice: a person is being questioned without being charged, but (unlike in every other case in which such questioning is now done) she cannot simply walk away from the interrogator. The person is confined, and nothing in the preventive detention law stands in the way of a campaign to wear down the detainee through seven days of protracted questioning.

Indeed, this possibility is enhanced by the Bill C-51 changes, and not just by the increased duration of the detention. The amended section 83.3 squarely anticipates that detention can be extended in forty-eight-hour cycles to enable police to conduct (sufficiently diligent) investigations. Our preventive detention system has, in other words, become a system of investigative detention. Seven days of detention, brought on by exigent circumstances, but perhaps not always tied to imminent terrorist violence, should not mean seven days of urgent efforts to break down the resistance of a detainee through prolonged interrogation.

As discussed in Chapter 12, judges participate in the process. One would expect this to be a safeguard, but Parliament has attempted to restrict judicial involvement during a preventive arrest to determining simply whether the investigation is being conducted expeditiously. Bill C-51 does not include express provisos guarding against the detainee being abused in a way that may result in false confessions or psychological harm, though we would hope and expect that judges would be concerned with this issue, notwithstanding Bill C-51.

We find particularly striking Bill C-51's failure to address these foreseeable controversies by establishing clear ground rules on the conditions of detention. Close analogues were unavailable. One possibility would be to prohibit questioning, as under Australian preventive detention orders,[41] or to regulate questioning, as is done with respect to Australian Security Intelligence Organisation questioning warrants under the *Australian Security Intelligence Organisation Act 1979* in Australia,[42] including allowing on-site visits by independent reviewers. There would be no harm (and potentially much benefit) in following Australian law and specifying that the questioning of a person subjected to preventive detention under section 83.3 should be conducted only pursuant to conditions imposed by the judge authorizing the detention, and be consistent with the requirement that the detainee be treated humanely and with respect for human dignity, and not be subjected to cruel, inhuman, or degrading treatment as that term is understood in the United Nations *Convention against Torture*.[43]

Given the growing pattern of youth radicalization, the law could also have reasonably included standards applicable to those under eighteen years of age. Bill C-51's changes do assign jurisdiction in section 83.3 matters to youth court judges, not regular provincial court judges, and alter the penalty regime where a young person fails to enter into, or breaches, a peace bond. But there are no youth-specific detention or interrogation rules.

It is not difficult to imagine the controversy prompted by a seven-day detention and interrogation of a fifteen-year-old at, for instance, Ottawa's notorious detention centre. Australian law again provides a useful analogue ignored by Bill C-51's drafters: children under sixteen years cannot be detained, and those between sixteen and eighteen must be detained separately from adults, and may have a parent or guardian visit them.[44]

As in so many other areas, Bill C-51's careless assumption that new powers need not be balanced with new safeguards means that all of these novel issues will need to be worked out piece by piece, by any number of peace officers and prosecutors, in any number of individual cases, in front of any number of different judges. It is difficult to imagine universal standards emerging from this process. It is easier to imagine that many of these issues will be addressed only after avertable mistakes are made and scandals exposed.

III. SECURITY INTELLIGENCE INTERRUPT

We turn now to a novel creature on the Canadian anti-terror scene: "interrupt" by security intelligence services; that is, CSIS. Here, a typology of legal tools is much more difficult, in part because of the secrecy surrounding

CSIS activities, but also because the laws themselves are unnecessarily and dangerously ambiguous.

What Does CSIS Want: The Ambiguous Concept of Disruption

In political and parliamentary debate over the new CSIS powers provided by Bill C-51, the term used by the government and many observers to describe the enhanced CSIS role is "disruption." An official backgrounder on the bill, for example, is entitled "Amending the Canadian Security Intelligence Service Act to give CSIS the mandate to intervene to disrupt terror plots while they are in the planning stages."[45] Throughout the Bill C-51 debates, the new power was repeatedly described as aimed at threat disruption.

"Disruption" is not a legal term, but rather a colloquial expression. In debates over the bill, and in other contexts, it became immediately clear that the term meant different things to different people. For instance, government officials repeatedly asserted that close democratic allies possessed similar powers of disruption, and that Canada was merely catching up with Bill C-51. At no time in the parliamentary debates, however, were the nature of these foreign powers enumerated, or their scope outlined — indeed, CSIS internal documents specify "[d]irect comparisons can be difficult given different systems of government, legal and operational frameworks."[46]

Our own efforts to discover analogues in the countries named by the government gave rise to the suggestion that the government was pointing to a variety of different roles exercised by often very differently situated services in foreign countries and was using these as analogues for much more unbounded CSIS powers. Some interpretations of foreign security law offered by government MPs as talking points on their websites were incorrect, according to lawyers from these foreign countries.[47]

When it came to more specific assertions, Public Safety Minister Steven Blaney repeatedly pointed to the new powers as allowing CSIS to talk to parents of radicalizing children. This is conduct that, measured on our threat escalator, amounts to "dissuade," discussed in Chapter 13, and not "interrupt" as we have defined it.

CSIS Disruption Practices Prior to Bill C-51

Moreover, talking to families is something that CSIS has already done, even under its classic intelligence mandate. Even as parliamentarians debated Bill C-51 — and were told repeatedly that CSIS needed new powers in order to better warn families about radicalizing children — media reported that CSIS was already talking to families of radicalizing children.[48] Documents released under access to information legislation revealed that the CSIS director was advised to explain, if pressed in parliamentary committee hearings, that under Bill C-51, CSIS "could advise a parent or family member of an individual's planned travel and ask them to intervene to dissuade the person from travelling."[49] Asking family members to *intervene* in this manner apparently exceeded CSIS's existing, pre–Bill C-51 mandate, a conclusion difficult to reconcile with 2010 CSIS press statements indicating CSIS "may consider asking a family member or community leader" close to a terrorist suspect to help dissuade extremism.[50] At any rate, not addressed in the internal note was whether the Bill C-51 powers were overkill for addressing this modest objective.

Also lost in much of the debate was the fact that CSIS also engages in "overt" surveillance; that is, making targets aware that it is watching them. A 2010 report issued by CSIS's review body, the Security Intelligence Review Committee, described this practice as a "disruption" technique. In the committee's words, "[w]henever CSIS conducts investigations, an intended or unintended consequence can be to counter — or disrupt — a threat to national security. For instance, making it generally known to targets that their activities are being investigated can reduce the likelihood that the targets will continue with their plans."[51]

"Less Tangible Is Whether Our Actions Push Some People to Radicalize . . . ."

At the time, the Security Intelligence Review Committee expressed some unease with the overt investigation technique: "there are no CSIS guidelines to help with the design and implementation of disruption operations or to prepare for the potential consequences of such investigative activity." Moreover, it noted CSIS's own recognition that "disruption is an activity that departs from typical forms of information collection, and that certain risks must be managed when undertaking this investigative activity." Not least, there is risk that "disruption" could precipitate blowback. As CSIS reported, "Less tangible is whether our actions push some people to radicalize, but our assessment is that it discourages radicalization."[52]

This statement constitutes a less than categorical assurance — and underscores the importance of integrating CSIS conduct into the broader threat escalator we develop in this book. It is certainly asking too much of CSIS to be both a spy agency and act as an effective counter–violent extremism program. There is also a possibility that a visit by CSIS could become something of a status symbol or badge of honour amongst radicalized individuals.

And when and if Canada develops counter–violent extremism programs, CSIS activity must be carefully calibrated to not undermine the viability of these projects. CSIS's new powers under Bill C-51 increase the inevitable risk of "the left hand not knowing what the right hand is doing," a matter to which we return in Chapter 13.

But whatever the case, the legal scope of the new threat reduction measures in Bill C-51 dwarfs what is required for CSIS to speak to families or engage in more overt surveillance. For much of the political debate, Canadians were left in a fog of uncertainty concerning "what CSIS wants." In the next sections, we try to piece together what we do know.

Understanding the New CSIS Powers

With Bill C-51, CSIS is now expressly authorized to "take measures, within or outside Canada, to reduce" very broadly defined "threats to the security of Canada."[53] This is an important addition to CSIS's mandate as an intelligence agency. We must try, as best we can, to unpack what this broad statutory language entails.

Content

"Threats to Canadian security" under the *CSIS Act* are not limited to terrorism but also include espionage and sabotage, clandestine or deceptive foreign influenced activities, or the undermining of the constitutionally established system of government in Canada by covert unlawful acts or by violence. "Advocacy, protest or dissent" are excluded from this remit, but only if "lawful" *and* not carried on in conjunction with any of the threats.[54] In internal documents, CSIS points to this carve-out to assuage fears that it will overreach.[55]

But it is notable that protesters who engage in unlawful activities have less protection under the *CSIS Act* than either under the *Criminal Code*'s anti-terrorism provisions[56] or even Bill C-51's information sharing provisions. (As discussed in Chapter 5, the information sharing law was amended during the parliamentary process to exempt all protests.)

This difference between CSIS's remit and those in other laws is significant, given the uncertain breadth of CSIS's new threat reduction powers. In this last respect, the only categorical restriction is that the new measures must not intentionally or by criminal negligence cause death or bodily harm, violate sexual integrity, or willfully obstruct justice[57] — language clearly modelled on the law enforcement justification in the *Criminal Code*, discussed above. CSIS must also believe that the measures are "reasonable and proportional in the circumstances, having regard to the nature of the threat, the nature of the measures and the reasonable availability of other means to reduce the threat."[58] This language again mimics some of the prudential constraints in the *Criminal Code* law-enforcement justification.

A key difference lies, however, in the introduction of a judicial warrant system. Where authorized by Federal Court warrant, the CSIS "measures" may even "contravene a right or freedom guaranteed by the *Canadian Charter of Rights and Freedoms*" or may be "contrary to other Canadian law."[59] Judges must determine that such violations are reasonable and proportional when issuing the warrant,[60] but Bill C-51 is silent on whether CSIS has to report back to the judge on what was done when executing the threat reduction warrant.

Radicalized CSIS

The CSIS changes are dramatic, even radical, on several different grounds. First, they represent a paradigm shift in Canadian law and policy in terms of the role of a covert security service. Or more correctly, they constitute a reversion to an older paradigm, once exercised by the RCMP Security Service. As discussed in Chapter 2, that agency engaged in widespread illegalities in the 1970s, including theft of Parti Québécois membership lists and the burning of a barn designed to "counter," or what today would be called disrupt, the Front de libération du Québec (FLQ).

CSIS was created in 1984 in response to these illegalities as an agency that would collect intelligence, and only do that when strictly necessary. Parliament accepted CSIS's broad intelligence mandate because it lacked what we can call "kinetic" or physical powers — the powers to do things to people in the physical world (except as necessary to, for example, install a wiretap or listening device). More than this, as already noted, the McDonald Commission that preceded the *CSIS Act* was crystal clear that "noble cause" illegality should not be a feature of Canada's security intelligence. Parliament resisted a 1983 version of the CSIS bill because of widespread concern, including from all provincial attorneys general, that it would allow CSIS to violate the law.

The idea that CSIS should obey the law and only collect intelligence was a particularly important feature for a security service that is much more closely yoked to the political executive than are the police. Unlike the RCMP, CSIS does not have constitutional protections of police independence. The police independence principle is designed to ensure that governments do not order the police to investigate and charge their political enemies while turning away from investigations of their friends. CSIS is (in principle) under much closer control at the ministerial level, a decision made to keep political masters apprised of possible controversial conduct by a covert service.

Secret Police?

Bill C-51 abandons this careful calibration. CSIS's new powers reach efforts to reduce all threats to the security of Canada, including threats associated with subversion and foreign-influenced activity that may be conducted in conjunction with even otherwise lawful protest and advocacy.

Especially when read in tandem with the even broader definition of "security threats" in Bill C-51's proposed information sharing act, this raises precisely the kind of concerns that animated the 1980s debate about CSIS: that today or tomorrow a government may use its legitimate powers of providing political direction to CSIS to encourage the agency to focus on and disrupt its political "enemies" — in today's environment — Indigenous peoples, environmental groups, anti-petroleum protesters, or diaspora groups opposed to allied governments.

Put another way, a number of long-standing expectations changed after Bill C-51. The bill superimposes kinetic powers on the broad mandate CSIS possessed for the last thirty years, when it was a pure intelligence agency. Painted as necessary to forestall terrorism, the new Bill C-51 powers allow CSIS to take physical measures to reduce all threats to Canadian security, including subversive and foreign-influenced threats that may encompass elements of protest and advocacy. And these new CSIS powers may, on the terms of the bill, contravene Canadian law and *Charter* rights, if authorized by a judge.

These changes with their potentially far-reaching effects go a long way to explaining a regular feature of some of the Bill C-51 debate: the soundbite used by some politicians — and especially Green Party leader Elizabeth May — of "secret police."

What Do These Powers Really Entail?

Setting aside fears of a future CSIS unmoored to democratic principles and deployed against mainstream movements, a key question since the introduction of Bill C-51 has been, "what does CSIS really want to do with these new powers?" The mismatch between the vast scope of the new threat reduction powers and the political speaking lines used to justify them — that CSIS needs to speak to families — is stark. Only the most inattentive observer would conclude that the desire to talk to families represents the true motivation behind the changes.

What Would the Law Allow?

In Table 8.1, below, we propose ways in which CSIS *could* use its new powers and comply fully with the new Bill C-51 provisions, but without violating Canadian laws or *Charter* rights.

Table 8.1: Possible CSIS Kinetic Measures Short of Illegality

Threat to the security of Canada	Example of possible measure that does not violate law or the *Charter*, assuming CSIS deems it "reasonable and proportional in the circumstances"
Espionage or sabotage that is against Canada or is detrimental to the interests of Canada, or activities directed toward or in support of such espionage or sabotage	Remotely wiping a data device stolen from a government facility and believed to be in the hands of a foreign intelligence service
Foreign-influenced activities within or relating to Canada that are detrimental to the interests of Canada and are clandestine or deceptive or involve a threat to any person	Providing misinformation to an anonymous foreign environmental funder in an effort to deter them from continuing to clandestinely fund a Canadian environmental group's planned protests in opposition to the Keystone Pipeline Project, a project that the government of Canada sees as a priority and strongly in "the interests of Canada" (This protest is done in conjunction with clandestine "foreign-influenced activities" and so does not benefit from the exception for protests.)
Activities within or relating to Canada directed toward or in support of the threat or use of acts of serious violence against persons or property for the purpose of achieving a political, religious, or ideological objective within Canada or a foreign state	Notifying parents or other persons of influence when CSIS investigations reveal that an individual is radicalizing toward violence, and asking them to intervene
Activities directed toward undermining by covert unlawful acts, or directed toward or intended ultimately to lead to the destruction or overthrow by violence of, the constitutionally established system of government in Canada	Advising a fertilizer dealer not to sell chemicals that may be precursors to a bomb built by a radical secessionist movement

It is also possible to imagine ways in which CSIS *could* act in violation of other laws and *Charter* rights under the new judicial warrant regime. See Table 8.2, below.

Table 8.2: Possible CSIS Kinetic Measures That Would Be Illegal or Violate *Charter* Rights

Threat to the security of Canada	Example of possible measure that violates statute law or the *Charter*, assuming CSIS deems it "reasonable and proportional in the circumstances" and the measure is authorized by Federal Court warrant
Espionage or sabotage that is against Canada or is detrimental to the interests of Canada, or activities directed toward or in support of such espionage or sabotage	• Breaking into a private home in order to destroy equipment CSIS believes may be used to destroy pipelines (absent Federal Court authorization, a violation of the *Criminal Code*) • Calling on the services of the Communications Security Establishment (CSE) under that agency's so-called Mandate C (assistance to CSIS) to infect and destroy the computers of a radical environmental group believed responsible for "tree spiking" but for whom there is insufficient evidence for criminal charges (absent Federal Court authorization, a violation of the *Criminal Code*)

Threat to the security of Canada	Example of possible measure that violates statute law or the *Charter*, assuming CSIS deems it "reasonable and proportional in the circumstances" and the measure is authorized by Federal Court warrant
Foreign-influenced activities within or relating to Canada that are detrimental to the interests of Canada and are clandestine or deceptive or involve a threat to any person	• Draining the bank account of an anonymously foreign-funded environmental group in an effort to impede secret funding of planned protests in opposition to the Keystone Pipeline Project, a project that the government of Canada sees as a priority and strongly in "the interests of Canada" (absent Federal Court authorization, contrary to the *Criminal Code*) • Working with the Canada Border Services Agency to prevent the travel to Canada of foreign anti-globalization protestors believed to be planning a (possibly violent) protest at an international free trade summit hosted in Toronto (absent Federal Court authorization, most likely an irregular use of immigration law) (These protests are conducted in conjunction with clandestine or possibly violent "foreign-influenced activities" and so do not benefit from the exception for protests.)

Threat to the security of Canada	Example of possible measure that violates statute law or the *Charter*, assuming CSIS deems it "reasonable and proportional in the circumstances" and the measure is authorized by Federal Court warrant
Activities within or relating to Canada directed toward or in support of the threat or use of acts of serious violence against persons or property for the purpose of achieving a political, religious, or ideological objective within Canada or a foreign state	• Working with Foreign Affairs and the Canada Border Services Agency to prevent the return to Canada of a citizen who is feared to pose a potential future risk in terms of political violence (absent Federal Court authorization, a violation of the s 6 *Charter* mobility rights) • Calling on the services of CSE under that agency's so-called Mandate C (assistance to CSIS) to bring down a website that CSIS believes may be about to begin recruiting for a group engaged in political violence (absent Federal Court authorization, a violation of the *Criminal Code*) • Calling on the services of CSE under that agency's so-called Mandate C (assistance to CSIS) to bring down a website that CSIS believes may be about to encourage support for a foreign insurgency, one of whose activities includes political violence (absent Federal Court authorization, a violation of the *Criminal Code*; possibly a violation of *Charter* free speech protections) • Starting a cyber-whisper "smear" campaign in order to discredit among his peers an individual regarded as the nucleus of a group that CSIS fears may be radicalizing to political violence (absent Federal Court authorization, probably a violation of the *Criminal Code* and possibly a form of cruel and unusual treatment under the *Charter*)

Threat to the security of Canada	Example of possible measure that violates statute law or the *Charter*, assuming CSIS deems it "reasonable and proportional in the circumstances" and the measure is authorized by Federal Court warrant
Activities directed toward undermining by covert unlawful acts, or directed toward or intended ultimately to lead to the destruction or overthrow by violence of, the constitutionally established system of government in Canada	• Breaking into a private residence to destroy chemicals that CSIS believes may be precursors to a bomb to be used by a radical secessionist movement (absent Federal Court authorization, a violation of the *Criminal Code*)

Given these possible examples, what have we learned about the government's own views on the reach of the new powers? When pressed by senators in committee, CSIS Director Michel Coulombe cited a handful of ways in which the powers could be used, such as "disrupting a financial transaction done through the Internet, disabling mobile device use in support of terrorist activities, and tampering with equipment that would be used in support of terrorist activities."[61] But these examples cited by the director do not exhaust the range of possible CSIS conduct contemplated by the government. Our own access to information requests on this question produced boilerplate speaking notes, but it is possible to examine the entrails of the legislative process and piece together views on how officials think the power might, or at least legally could, be used.

Speech-Suppressing Activities

In the senate proceedings, the minister of justice used examples of past (and quite different) speech-limiting features in Canadian law — such as a judge's *Criminal Code* powers to exclude the public from a courtroom and to remove hate speech from the Internet — in defending the sort of conduct CSIS might undertake.[62]

These examples are, of course, overt activities, done by the state with the full knowledge of the affected person, at least in principle. They are therefore no precedent for secret speech-suppressing activities, such as covert Internet take-downs that bring down a website — an obvious prospect given concerns about radicalization and the Internet. Nevertheless, the government statements do clearly communicate that speech-suppressing tactics are on the government's radar for CSIS, raising clear section 2 *Charter* free expression concerns. We will return to this issue in Chapter 10 and suggest that CSIS threat reduction warrants should not be used as an end run around Bill C-51's new *Criminal Code* provision that allows (open) court orders for the deletion of "terrorist propaganda" from the Internet. That said, we recognize that CSIS threat reduction warrants may apply to the vast amount of such material posted on non-Canadian websites.

Restricting Movement of Canadians

Meanwhile, during the Commons committee process, one government witness used limitations on mobility rights (that is, entering and returning to Canada) as an example of conduct that could be affected by the CSIS measures.[63]

Again, stopping people from coming back to Canada is an obvious (and controversial) addition to the CSIS toolkit. Indeed, in the *Abdelrazik* case discussed in Chapter 6, the government tried (unsuccessfully) to banish a Canadian on security grounds. Moreover, the issue of returning foreign fighters — and whether they should be barred from re-entry — has recently been the subject of heated debate and legislation in the United Kingdom, no doubt a matter watched with interest by Canadian officials.

We suspect that CSIS may well request a warrant that would enable it to take secret measures to prevent a suspected foreign terrorist fighter from either leaving or returning to Canada. This raises obvious section 6 *Charter* mobility rights issues. To the extent that the CSIS measure results in Canadian citizens potentially being stranded in a war zone in, for example, Syria or Iraq, it may even raise questions about section 7 rights to life, liberty, and security of the person and about whether the novel warrant provision for authorizing the violation of *Charter* rights accords with the principles of fundamental justice.

Detention

The new CSIS powers do not preclude even outright detention. The government tabled, and Parliament duly enacted, a "greater certainty" amendment to the original Bill C-51, providing that CSIS has no "law enforcement powers."[64] But this term provides little guidance on whether and how CSIS might detain. Outside of the section 25.1 *Criminal Code* justifications discussed above, the term "law enforcement" is not typically used in Canadian law — the term "peace officer" is generally used in describing the powers possessed by police. As such, the phrase raises new interpretive headaches. We assume it means that CSIS will not have police-like *Criminal Code* powers of arrest. But criminal arrest does not exhaust all the forms of detention exercised by state agencies. And so the amendment does not address the power of detention short of *Criminal Code* arrest.

At any rate, if CSIS wishes to detain or interrogate, it will do so for threat disruption purposes, not "law enforcement" purposes. The government's peculiar language does nothing to dispel concerns about CSIS "security detention" or "detention for security interrogation" activities. Indeed, the fact that CSIS's actions are not to be used for law enforcement leads us to believe that its activities, unlike those of the police, will rarely be reviewed in after-the-fact criminal trials.

Given the disturbing experiences in other jurisdictions after 9/11, the absence of an express, emphatic bar on detention by an intelligence service is alarming. And detention appears to be on the table. In the Commons committee, government MPs defeated a Green Party amendment that would have prohibited detention. In so doing, they complained that "[t]he amendment that is on the floor right now is not consistent with the intent of the bill. *It would unduly narrow the range of possible measures that CSIS could take*, and would so weaken CSIS's capacity to carry out its threat reduction mandate."[65]

In short, CSIS has not possessed detention authority in the past, but it appears it will be able to detain after Bill C-51.

Rendition

More than this, the provision denying CSIS "law enforcement powers" will not bar "rendition." In recent history, rendition is the process by which a person is kidnapped from one jurisdiction and taken to another, sometimes for trial and sometimes for abusive interrogation.

In the words of one government witness, "just the reference to 'rendition' or 'removal to another state' is not necessarily a law enforcement power. So to the extent that the amendment refers to 'law enforcement', it may not be a like thing."[66] Put another way, rendition too remains on the legal table.

Again, our point is that the law permits such activity, not that CSIS will do it. But in reality, CSIS has at least once detained and rendered a Canadian in the post-9/11 period in violation of that person's *Charter* rights and transgressing its then-legal powers. In a 2002 case investigated by the Security Intelligence Review Committee and reported in its 2006–7 annual report,[67] CSIS facilitated the transfer of Mohammed Jabarah, an admitted member of al-Qaeda and a Canadian citizen, from Oman to the United States via Canada. The Security Intelligence Review Committee concluded that Jabarah was "arbitrarily detained" by CSIS in violation of section 9 of the *Charter*. Further, "[b]ecause he was detained, his right to silence as protected by Sections 7 and 11(c) was violated, as was his right to counsel under Section 10. Furthermore, his right to remain in Canada as protected by Section 6 of the Charter (mobility rights) was breached."

In considering the range of actions the government might chose to take with CSIS's new powers, it is also instructive to recall the experiences of Omar Khadr, interrogated by CSIS at Guantanamo Bay in violation of the *Charter*, and Benamar Benatta, removed to the United States in unusual circumstances. All three of these cases are discussed in Chapter 2.

After Bill C-51, with judicial warrant, this treatment of Canadians (as well as non-Canadians) may now be legal (to the extent that Bill C-51 itself is legal). The one solace we take from Bill C-51's strictures is the prohibition against "bodily harm." In the *Criminal Code* context, that term includes psychological harm. We find it difficult to believe that in applying this standard, a careful and conscientious Federal Court judge familiar with the aftermath of past secret detentions and renditions would authorize such forms of extreme conduct.

This assumes, however, that CSIS even needs to seek a warrant. As discussed below, it is not clear in what circumstances CSIS might require a warrant for its overseas (as opposed to Canadian) activities.

Confliction Risks

In sum, this discussion points to the uncertain but staggering range of things that CSIS can do to people under its new powers.

This vast range of potential conduct is precisely why the new CSIS powers are (literally) off the threat escalator chart described in Chapter 3 from an anti-terror policy perspective (and indeed, more than anti-terror, since the new powers extend to the full scope of CSIS's broad national security mandate). These powers are capable of permitting CSIS to act physically against persons and targets in all zones of the threat escalator, except "prosecute."

There is no real guidance provided in the bill as to how CSIS will choose among these many options, and how it will reconcile its activities with those of other agencies exercising their powers. Put another way, Bill C-51 has the legal effect of making CSIS a jack of all trades, able to covertly go where many other agencies also tread. This raises the risk of both operational and legal "confliction" with these other agencies and anti-terror policies.

"More Formal De-confliction Practices Will Need to Be Established"

As we have discussed, police to date have performed "interrupt" functions linked to police investigations. Peace officers in these situations likely remain preoccupied with the effect their conduct might have on any future criminal proceedings and wish to reduce the chances that their activities will lead to acquittals in criminal trials.

CSIS, in comparison, has not traditionally operated in the criminal law space — and has assiduously avoided being swept into it whenever possible. Certainly, over the last fifteen years, CSIS has been increasingly enmeshed in judicial proceedings and has been obliged to evolve — what one former CSIS director called (with considerable disapproval) the "judicialization of intelligence."[68] However, there is no reason to believe that CSIS now has come to culturally approximate the police in viewing viable convictions as the endgame of its operations. Indeed, the amendment to Bill C-51 which provides that CSIS does not have law enforcement powers may re-enforce CSIS's long-standing self-image as an intelligence agency without law enforcement responsibilities.

So, for cultural and institutional reasons and because of the terms of its new powers in Bill C-51, downstream criminal trial preoccupations will not discipline CSIS, at least not to the same extent as the police. This raises important questions.

First, how will CSIS and the RCMP arrange their affairs so that CSIS's kinetic activities do not undermine RCMP criminal investigations, either ongoing or prospective? As discussed in Chapter 9, the two agencies persist in a system of "parallel investigations," managed through an informal de-confliction process with careful controls on the flow of information from CSIS to the RCMP. In that chapter and in Chapter 11, we follow the Air India Commission of inquiry in casting doubt on this process. But whatever shortcomings it had in the past are now aggravated by Bill C-51. The RCMP has, itself, expressed wariness on this front. In internal documents prepared for the parliamentary process, the RCMP indicated:

> More formal de-confliction practices will need to be established to clarify roles and responsibilities so that our activities are transparent and accountable.
>
> The RCMP, with significant relationships with international law enforcement agencies abroad, is concerned that CSIS threat diminishment activities in a foreign country, if detected by the authorities, could inadvertently jeopardize existing relationships on particular investigations.[69]

Second, will someone properly apprise the RCMP, charged with investigating illegality, of unlawful CSIS conduct authorized by the Federal Court, to avoid the "keystone cop" problem of police chasing spies? In internal documents, the RCMP responded to this concern: "The RCMP would need to be made aware of a criminal complaint in the first place. The RCMP, and any other law enforcement agency of relevant jurisdiction, would be responsible for investigating criminal complaints. The RCMP and CSIS will need to formalize robust de-confliction practices to mitigate such potential scenarios."[70]

Third, what protocols will be in place to ensure handover from CSIS to RCMP in the event that CSIS's kinetic activities are still in play when the threat crosses a criminal line? As the RCMP notes, criminal matters lie in its purview,[71] but it would need to know about them before it can act. The idea that CSIS might not inform the RCMP of intelligence that reveals terrorism offences is not fanciful. This is a matter we discuss at length in Chapter 9 in our discussion of the "less is more" intelligence sharing between CSIS and the RCMP and the "intelligence to evidence" conundrum.

Legal Confliction

The poor calibration of the new CSIS powers with other tools on the threat escalator also raises concerns about legal confliction: that is, circumstances where CSIS powers are exercised as a convenient end run around other, more demanding legal rules.

As discussed in Chapter 10, Bill C-51 introduces a new open-court procedure allowing the state to seek judicial authorization to remove terrorist propaganda from the Internet. However, why would the government pursue this approach, when instead CSIS can simply go to Federal Court and, in a secret warrant proceeding, receive authorization to take down a website covertly?

Likewise, if CSIS has the power to detain, why would the government pursue a preventive detention under section 83.3 of the *Criminal Code*, with all its strictures, limits, and open court processes? Instead it may be tempted to obtain a novel CSIS detention warrant through a secret Federal Court process, a venue in which it can use secret intelligence as evidence and circumvent an adversarial process in which that evidence is tested by the detainee. CSIS threat reduction activities could also be a functional equivalent to investigative hearings under section 83.28 of the *Criminal Code*. In either case, the CSIS activities would not be subject to the same reporting requirements or open court presumptions as are the police powers.[72]

Safeguarding against such prospects should guide both operational decision making in CSIS and the Federal Court's exercise of its role. For instance, in deciding whether a measure is reasonable and proportional in the circumstances, both CSIS and the court are to take account of "the reasonable availability of other means to reduce the threat."[73] This phrase should be broadly construed. It is not just the reasonable availability of other means available to CSIS that should matter. Also important is the reasonable availability of other means *anywhere*, by any other agency. In the result, no court should issue a warrant without asking about the impact of CSIS activity on other agencies, and their ability to perform the same functions in a manner less invasive to the rule of law.

Likewise, "reasonable availability" should include any other legal process, no matter that it may be more inconvenient. And especially, an alternative means should never be deemed unavailable because CSIS feels the need to act in secret. Put another way, this reasonable availability phrase should become a form of "rule of law parsimony" — a way of ensuring that state powers are whenever possible used in accordance with conventional constitutional and legal practices. Otherwise, we truly do risk an invisible, parallel justice system where CSIS can do it all under one warrant.

In sum, we see how the idea of a full-service CSIS might be attractive to a government panicked into a policy of throwing anything against the wall and calling it disruption, in the hope that something might work. But there is a real risk of not only creating a messy wall, but of CSIS operations disrupting the work of other agencies — whether on de-radicalization, criminal investigations, preventive detentions, or plain vanilla criminal prosecutions. And there is the peril that CSIS threat reduction will circumvent other legal procedures with their own particular safeguards that do not apply to CSIS's new threat reduction activities, even when conducted under a warrant, creating a parallel, secret justice system.

Checks and Balances

Throughout the Bill C-51 debate, the government responded to criticism over the new CSIS measures by suggesting it was a modest innovation and carefully curbed by checks and balances.

Breaking Laws Like the Police, without the Restraints

At the Senate committee, Minister Blaney cited the RCMP *Criminal Code* law-breaking justification, discussed above, as precedents for the CSIS threat reduction powers.[74]

However, the new CSIS model is shorn of much of section 25.1 of the *Criminal Code*'s transparency features and is broadened considerably in terms of the range of circumstances in which it could be used. Specifically:

- The police justification is limited to criminal law and investigation, a broad scope but not nearly as broad as the scope of "threat to the security of Canada" and one that is much better understood.

- The police justification is limited to violations of the criminal law, and does not justify violations of all law and the *Charter*, as does the CSIS power. It cannot, for example, be used to deprive citizens of their *Charter* rights to leave or return to Canada or to engage in free speech.
- Use of the police justification is more transparent. First, there is a *public* report with at least some data on its use each year and the nature of the police's actual illegal (but exonerated) conduct — something that does not exist for the CSIS power. Second, since the police justification is exercised in the course of criminal law duties, the police conduct is much more likely to come to light in a subsequent criminal proceedings. In comparison, if the CSIS system operates as designed, the precise scope and contours of the CSIS measure will never be revealed publicly. Some reporting is done confidentially to the minister, but public disclosure is merely statistical: all that is required are details on the raw number of new warrants.[75] CSIS's review body, the Security Intelligence Review Committee, is only instructed, meanwhile, to review annually "one aspect of the Service's performance in taking measures to reduce threats to the security of Canada."[76] Third, the person affected by a police activity that causes serious property loss or damage must be notified of the police conduct within one year, subject to exceptions enumerated in the *Criminal Code*. Nothing equivalent exists for the CSIS provisions.

In short, the government has replicated the law enforcement justification to act unlawfully but has omitted many of the key checks on that power employed in relation to law enforcement under the *Criminal Code*.

Judicial Warrant, Sometimes

Understandably, in these new circumstances, the bill's drafters saw need to impose a new accountability feature absent from the law enforcement justification provisions: an advance judicial authorization, by warrant, for CSIS conduct that might violate Canadian law. More than that, they appreciated that the expansive tool being provided to CSIS might implicate CSIS in breaches of the *Canadian Charter of Rights and Freedoms*. We discuss how these warrants work and our concerns about limited powers of judicial oversight in Chapter 11.

But for our purposes here, though, it is important to underscore that there is no automatic judicial authorization requirement: Bill C-51 specifies that the government need only seek a warrant where it has "reasonable grounds" to believe it is required. Section 12.1(3) only requires a warrant where "measures" "will" (not "may") contravene a *Charter* right or other Canadian law. As there is no other indication of where warrants are required (and no established practice in this area, given its novelty), other measures that do not cross the illegality line presumptively do not require a judicial warrant. The only operational oversight in instances where warrants are deemed by CSIS and its legal advisors to be unnecessary will be internal, executive branch controls.

We underscore the extent to which Bill C-51's language raises doubts about whether CSIS will require a warrant for its overseas operations — Bill C-51 allows CSIS to exercise its new powers inside and outside Canada. But Canadian law is almost always confined to the territory of Canada. Likewise, the (confused) jurisprudence on when the *Charter* applies outside Canada suggests that it only applies where government action is in violation of Canada's international law obligations (itself a complex and contestable issue)[77] and (the Federal Court has suggested) where the government conduct is directed at a Canadian citizen.[78] In other words, Canadian law and the *Charter* will be only rarely breached by international operations, and so a warrant only rarely sought by CSIS from the Federal Court.

The one solace we can take from the language in Bill C-51 is that a warrant is required when CSIS violates any "other" Canadian law, an expression that can only be interpreted as including common law. Since the common law automatically incorporates what is known as customary international law,[79] a breach of international customary prohibitions on violating foreign sovereignty should be enough to trigger a warrant requirement. This would then place the Federal Court in the admittedly unenviable position of deciding whether to let CSIS violate the sovereignty of another state.

Contorting the Constitution

But even with all these concerns, the most alarming feature of the new scheme is the prospect that, with a warrant, CSIS can violate the *Charter*.

While legislation authorizing *Charter* breaches is not common, it does exist. We have pointed to examples already in this book. For example, the *Canadian Passport Order* is a legal instrument permitting the government to revoke a Canadian's passport on national security grounds. This decision has the effect of preventing (legal) international travel, and thus obviously violates a Canadian's right to "leave Canada" under section 6 of the *Charter*.

In this instrument, however, the government has "prescribed by law" a limitation, and in an intelligible fashion has alerted the public to a specific *Charter* infringement. A person can, therefore, challenge the measure, and its propriety can be openly adjudicated by a court, which can also decide whether a *Charter* breach should be forgiven by the *Charter*'s section 1 provision (discussed below). This is exactly what has happened with passport revocations in the past, as discussed in Chapter 6.

This pattern of notice and open challenge would also be true of every other legal tool discussed in this book that could raise *Charter* issues: preventive detention, peace bonds, no-fly lists, surveillance powers, criminal offences, and so on. It is not, however, true of the new CSIS powers. Rather, Bill C-51 simply establishes an outer range on permissible CSIS conduct and allows it the power to do whatever it wishes within that range, subject to some prudential considerations that it must take into account. As we have suggested at length, it is not possible to predict the full range of what CSIS might do, nor has the government offered up such a list. Nor is it possible to predict how that conduct might breach the *Charter* or, indeed, which of the *Charter*'s many rights might be infringed.

In the national security area, the closest analogy to this extreme range is found in the *Emergencies Act*,[80] although even that statute (designed for the most dire situations in the life of a nation) offers more constraint. For one thing, conduct under that Act — developed by the Mulroney government — is still governed by the *Charter*, a matter specifically recognized in its preamble. The *Emergencies Act* also triggers various accountability devices, including, in some cases, mandatory public inquiries.

In comparison, the drafters of Bill C-51 wished CSIS to be able to cross the *Charter* barrier where it believed it necessary to do so, but without offering guidance of any sort on precisely when and where and how. Instead, the bill imposes a judicial gatekeeper on CSIS's conduct. The obvious analogy is to the judicial role in authorizing searches and arrests through warrants. However, this is a fundamentally false analogy, as discussed below. And it places the new *CSIS Act* into totally uncharted constitutional territory — not just under the *Charter*, but also in relation to even older concepts of the separation of power between the branches of government.

Why the New CSIS Warrants Are Not like Conventional Search and Arrest Warrants

Search and arrest warrants are part and parcel of *Charter* rights that have qualifying language in the right itself: section 8 of the *Charter* only guards against *unreasonable* searches and seizures. Section 9 only protects against *arbitrary* detention. A search or an arrest warrant satisfies this qualifying language, and therefore a government agency acting under such a warrant *does not breach the Charter*. It is the warrant that preserves the constitutionality of the action. The warrant does not authorize a breach.

Most other *Charter* rights *are not imbued* with built-in qualifying language. There is no concept of *permissible* free speech or *justified* cruel and unusual treatment or *appropriate* mobility rights to enter or leave the country or *limited* habeas corpus. And so there is simply no precedent (and no plausible legal theory) for these *Charter* rights being curbed by a warrant, pre-authorizing constraints.

Why the New Warrants Are a Radical Approach to Section 1 of the Charter

This lack of precedent means the new Bill C-51 provision places judges in a radical new universe. Their task is no longer, as it is with search warrants, to define the limit of *Charter* protections and to prevent their breach, but rather possibly to authorize violations of (any and all) *Charter* rights.

Rights can, of course, be limited under section 1 of the *Charter* (or, in some cases, if the government uses the section 33 notwithstanding clause, which it did not do in Bill C-51). Section 1 reads: "The *Canadian Charter of Rights and Freedoms* guarantees the rights and freedoms set out in it subject only to such reasonable limits prescribed by law as can be demonstrably justified in a free and democratic society." The Supreme Court has developed a sophisticated jurisprudence on section 1.

Under the *Oakes* test, section 1 may save a rights-impairing measure where the government proves that the measure has an important objective, that there is a rational connection between the objective and the means, that there is a minimal impairment of the right in question, and that there is proportionality between the impact on the right and the benefits of the measure in question.[81]

In cases involving discretion exercised by government officials that may violate the *Charter*, the Court has begun deploying a slightly different approach. In the wake of *Doré v Barreau du Québec*,[82] the section 1 analysis in relation to discretionary executive action amounts to consideration of "reasonableness." In deciding that matter, everything would then turn on the facts — was the national security objective motivating the action so pressing as to be proportionate to the right violated?[83]

Probably with this jurisprudence in mind, the government has proposed that a court only issue a warrant for illegal or unconstitutional conduct where reasonable and proportionate. In other words, it is (in principle anyway) the judge's views on these matters that will matter, not CSIS's initial position. Where the judge authorizes the measure, this amounts to an implicit section 1 *Charter* finding.

But this approach ignores the unique legal and procedural context in which the proposed warrant decision would operate. For one thing, in every instance where the *Doré* approach to section 1 has been applied, the power in question is much more closely anchored to a limited and specific range of possible government conduct, and the *Charter* rights potentially at play are not "the entire *Charter*." Put another way, in these other cases, everyone has been given fair notice by the legislation as to what *Charter* rights are imperiled.

Even more critically, we only turn to section 1 in the first place where the rights limitation is "prescribed by law."

"Prescribed by law" is rarely an issue in constitutional disputes, since the government action in question is either expressly authorized in legislation or is sufficiently linked to it to meet the "prescribed by law" standard. In challenges to legislative action, the Supreme Court takes a "flexible approach to the 'prescribed by law' requirement as regards both the form (e.g., statute, regulation, municipal by-law, rule of a regulatory body or collective agreement provision) and articulation of a limit on a Charter right (i.e., a standard intelligible to the public and to those who apply the law)."[84] In Bill C-51, neither this flexible form requirement nor the intelligible standard expectation is met. We cannot predict in advance which *Charter* right is violated, or the specific circumstances or nature of the breach. The standard of what is contemplated is not intelligible to the public. This is precisely why we cannot fit CSIS's new powers neatly into our threat escalator. The full extent of CSIS's new powers to limit *Charter* rights can be decided and revealed only on a case-by-case basis. Assuming warrant decisions will be made public, the public will only know what rights have been limited after the fact.

In addition, all this will be done in the name of reducing "threats to the security of Canada." As examined above, this is an extremely broad concept that is closely intertwined with political freedoms and civil liberties. The *CSIS Act* is not your typical administrative regime; it is one that by design skates very close to the edge of what the state should be doing in a democratic society.

As a consequence, Bill C-51 has more "prescribed by law" shortcomings than those identified by the Supreme Court in "public interest" provisions that once allowed bail to be denied.[85] It offers exactly the sort of vagueness and imprecision that disentitles the measure to a full section 1 inquiry.[86] In the new CSIS powers, the *only* statutory framework translates into: you can do anything to "reduce" broadly defined threats to the security of Canada, including violating every right in the *Charter*, so long as it does not do bodily harm, violate sexual integrity, or obstruct justice.

We are not aware of any circumstances in which the Supreme Court has concluded that such an open-textured invitation to violate the *Charter* is "prescribed by law."[87] That is probably because we have never before seen such an open-textured invitation. This result, when coupled with the extraordinary procedural context in which *Charter* rights will be decided in one-sided and closed-court proceedings (discussed in Chapter 11), takes the new powers out of the category of "novel" and into the realm of "radical."

In sum, Bill C-51's CSIS warrant is an astonishing rupture with foundational expectations about both the rule of law and the role of the judiciary. In our constitutional system, it is for Parliament to prescribe by law the limits on *Charter* rights and for the courts to protect those rights and to determine if limits on those rights are reasonable. Parliament should not avoid democratic responsibility by writing anyone — even judges — a more or less blank cheque to authorize violations of *Charter* rights.

Dragooning Judges

In making judges enablers of executive illegality, and not reviewers of compliance with the *Charter*, the bill also runs roughshod over common expectations about the separation of powers. We appreciate that in Canadian constitutional law, the separation of powers is not a robust limiter. It does, however, exist, and a judge dragooned into an *executive* function of overseeing illegal and *Charter*-violating CSIS conduct is no longer the independent and impartial adjudicator required by the Constitution.

We also believe that the Bill C-51 CSIS warrant system amounts to a drafting of judges into the *legislative* function of limiting *Charter* rights. As we have suggested, it differs significantly from the traditional search warrant process where judges simply decide whether a warrant can be granted to guard against violating the right against unreasonable search and seizure under section 8 of the *Charter*. We do not regard search warrants as a reasonable analogy.

Moreover, the present system is dramatically different from the "investigative hearings" process upheld by the Supreme Court the last time judicial independence was a live issue in a national security context.[88] Most notably, a key ingredient saving the latter process from being unconstitutional was the fact that investigative hearings are held presumptively in open court.[89] That safeguard does not exist in Bill C-51 — CSIS warrant proceedings are conducted in secret.

Moreover, a strong minority of the Court concluded that even the relatively banal investigative hearing system did violence to the role of judges. The dissent concluded that judges were, in effect, being made into police investigators, even though investigative hearings are adversarial hearings held in open court.

Bill C-51 places the legislative power to authorize and limit *Charter* rights on "section 1 reasonableness grounds" into the hands of those few Federal Court judges who have been specially designated to sit in security cases, in secret. This is dramatically different from (and much more concerning than) investigative hearings. It demonstrates a lack of understanding of the role of courts in protecting *Charter* rights and not authorizing *Charter* violations. It gives a handful of judges the *legislative* function of deciding which, among the entire universe of *Charter* rights, may be limited. Those judges are then asked to assume the *executive* function of overseeing how CSIS will engage in conduct that would otherwise violate the *Charter*. All of this is done in a secret and possibly one-sided hearing that will at best produce a heavily redacted judgment released long after CSIS has acted. The result is an absence of the checks and balances inherent in respecting the separate roles that should be played by legislators, the executive, and judges. This problem does not dissolve simply because judges are asked to do the dirty work under the new law.

A Lot of Broken Eggs, but No Omelet

In sum, judges should *adjudicate* whether a *Charter* breach by another branch is prescribed by law and demonstrably reasonable in a free and democratic society. They should not *create* or *pre-authorize* a *Charter* breach because they think it reasonable and necessary. In essence, Bill C-51 invites judges to legislate limitations on rights on an ad hoc basis, in response to a secret government request, and in a manner that simply cannot be predicted in advance or democratically debated in its particulars. Bill C-51 profoundly contorts the judicial role even while it neglects legislative responsibilities for setting out and justifying specific limits on *Charter* rights and the executive responsibility for obeying such precise laws. Our hope is that courts will resist the notion that the legislature can delegate to them powers to limit every *Charter* right and that the executive can violate any *Charter* right, with their connivance.

Our expectation is that the Federal Court will do its best to ensure that CSIS justifies the need for any illegal and *Charter*-violating measures. Ultimately, however, there is considerable risk that we will not really know what is happening in Federal Court. It may be that we will end up with a secret or partially secret *Charter* jurisprudence. Again, in this manner, Bill C-51 sets us up for a secret, parallel justice system.

For this reason, the best chance for addressing these issues may come from a direct challenge to the very existence of this novel warrant provision, and one was predictably commenced in the Ontario Superior Court in July 2015.[90] Such a direct challenge in superior court is far better than waiting for the provision to be used in what would be a likely one-sided and secret warrant proceeding in Federal Court.

IV. CONCLUSION

As this book goes to press, the court challenge to the new and constitutionally suspect CSIS warrant process is just beginning. The government will likely contest it aggressively and any decision on the merits from a trial judge is likely years away. And so it is important to underscore what legislators have done: because parliamentarians turned a blind eye to basic issues of constitutional roles and principles, the burden of defending foundational concepts of our system of democracy and law falls now on the shoulders of underfunded non-profit organizations, through litigation, where the government will challenge their right to do so at every turn. In the final analysis, all that is certain as this legal process unfurls is that there will be more uncertainty, until such time as the Supreme Court decides the matter definitively, perhaps a decade from now.

There Were Alternatives

All of this controversy was predictable, which raises again the question of why the government did not opt for a more intellectually challenging but more constitutionally conventional strategy. Rather than an open-textured "CSIS can do anything and violate any *Charter* right" approach, it could have opted for a legislated, closed-list enumeration of CSIS's new "disruption" powers.

Certainly, some of these listed powers may have invaded constitutional rights (say, the power to interfere with a computer system or the right to leave or return to Canada), but having articulated those new powers clearly and intelligibly, Parliament would actually have exercised its responsibility to prescribe and justify limits on rights under section 1. Parliamentarians would have known exactly what they were allowing CSIS to do, and how it could invade rights. The public would know exactly what rights the government believed should be limited. And any *Charter* challenge could focus on whether any of the discrete, transparent, enumerated powers met the standards of justification under section 1.

Since the provision could be challenged on its face, the question of its legitimacy would be a "clean" and discrete legal issue, not mired in secret CSIS operational preoccupations of the sort that require the Federal Court warrant process to be held in secret when and if it authorizes *Charter* violations on a case-by-case basis. Nor would this more thoughtful and forthright approach have raised collateral questions about the proper role of the courts as defenders of the *Charter*, and not enablers of illegality.

In sum, careful drafting would have restored a system in which Parliament enacts clear rights-limiting provisions that are predictable, intelligible, and challengeable in open court, and the courts are asked to adjudicate their reasonableness. Judges would not have been asked to create new rights-infringing permissions from the ether, on demand, from Canada's covert security service. The government, in other words, might have done the hard work of tabling a bill containing certainty and precision, rather than ambiguity and contingency. The bill's word count would have gone up, but so too its transparency and usefulness.

Giving CSIS Legal Cover or Feet of Clay?

In its attempt to gain legal cover, the government may have inadvertently tied CSIS in knots with its new open-textured "CSIS can do anything and violate any *Charter* right" legal regime. In some respects, the new CSIS warrants are part of what Jack Goldsmith — the American official who withdrew the infamous government memos excusing torture — has described as a heavily legalized approach where intelligence officials demand get-out-jail-free cards and legal cover before they take off the gloves.[91] The new scheme may also constitute defensive lawyering in response to the Security Intelligence Review Committee's criticisms of CSIS for violating *Charter* rights in both the Mohammed Jabarah and Omar Khadr cases, and a trial court's criticism of CSIS's violation of rights in the *Mejid* case. These are the only cases of which we are aware where CSIS has thought it necessary to violate *Charter* rights, and again, we would hope that no Federal Court judge would ever attempt to legalize such illegalities in a threat reduction warrant.

But there is still a real security cost to Bill C-51's open-textured approach, with its rejection of carefully enumerated powers, subjected to thorough, legislated checks and balances. In a regime with certainty and limited powers, the new rules might even have dispensed with a warrant requirement in emergency situations, much like some law enforcement justification powers can be used in emergencies through a "short form" process.

The special irony is that the present, open-textured, sparsely worded Bill C-51 rules require a warrant every time *any* Canadian law is breached:

municipal, provincial, regulatory, criminal, or common law. This means that without a warrant, CSIS cannot technically direct, say, an agent embedded in a terrorist group to run a red light in an emergency, or trespass and destroy chemicals — that is, vandalize property — to be used in a ticking explosive.

If CSIS does not have time or cannot obtain a new threat reduction warrant, it will need to call the police or just fall back on the conventional expectation that prosecutors would never prosecute such wrongs or, if they did, that the defence of necessity would exonerate CSIS's conduct. These may be safe assumptions, but they do make a mockery of the notion (clearly at the front of some legislators' minds) that Bill C-51 presents a coherent new pre-emptive system for urgent security threats.

And so a power with extreme reach that allows a violation of every *Charter* right cannot actually be used in extreme circumstances. That is probably a very good thing, given the extreme reach, but it makes Bill C-51 less than useful in true "when all else fails" "interrupt" situations. In such emergency situations, the best course of conduct may still be to call the police, who can make preventive, or Al Capone, arrests.

Teeing Up a Legacy of Ashes

All of this is to say that a better-tailored Bill C-51 could have avoided placing all *Charter* rights up for grabs. It could have clearly ruled extreme measures, such as rendition and prolonged detention, off the table. It could have better protected rights while giving CSIS clear, but limited, powers to, yes, speak to families, but also if necessary to take specifically enacted actions to interrupt terrorist acts in exigent circumstances.

None of this was done, at least not properly. Parliament did not perform its role of justifying what specific rights must be limited. It simply asked the Federal Court to do the difficult and dirty work it shirked. The result of such radical and reckless law making will be years of *Charter* litigation, producing uncertainty about both the status of all *Charter* rights and the precise ambit of CSIS's additional powers. CSIS's new powers will not improve its image except among those who are thrilled by the prospects of spies taking matters into their own hands, at home and abroad.

And it gets worse. The next chapter will examine how CSIS's new powers may disrupt a traditional and key anti-terror tool: criminal prosecutions.

CHAPTER NINE
Prosecute: The Challenges of Terrorism Prosecutions

I. INTRODUCTION

Mohammed Momin Khawaja was born in Ottawa in 1979. By 2004, the twenty-five-year-old man was a computer contractor at the Department of Foreign Affairs. He was also obsessed with Osama bin Laden and al-Qaida.

The Conspiracy

He entered into correspondence with "the bros" — like-minded others in the United States and the United Kingdom. He joined some of these individuals in Pakistan, where he participated in a "small-arms training camp." He offered his support, including money and technical equipment, to assist "the bros" in their violent designs. In an email to one, Khawaja wrote: "Imagine if there were 10 Sept 11's, wouldn't that accurately bring America down, never to rise again? Yes, I understand that innocent human beings died, but there is absolutely no other way of achieving the same objective with the same effect."[1] He also designed a remote arming device for a bomb that he called the "hifidigimonster," offering to smuggle it to the United Kingdom and to school his confederates in its use.

Canadian authorities learned of Khawaja from their UK counterparts. A UK investigation — Operation Crevice — tracked Khawaja meeting with British associates in London to discuss his remote bomb-triggering device, to be used on British or foreign targets. Canadian police arrested Khawaja in Ottawa on 30 March 2004. The day after, British authorities arrested several confederates in London and charged them with conspiracy to commit several terrorism offences. Khawaja was named by UK prosecutors as an unindicted co-conspirator in a plot to use 600 kilograms of explosive ammonium nitrate-rich fertilizer against a public target in the United Kingdom. The trial of the seven British accused involved a massive amount of evidence. It took fourteen months, including twenty-seven days of jury deliberations. By 30 April 2007, however, five men had been convicted and sentenced to life imprisonment.

The Dispute over Secrecy

Khawaja's prosecution in Canada took much longer. It was delayed by lengthy disputes between the defence and Crown over disclosure of secret information. That process required two rounds of collateral proceedings in the Federal Court under section 38 of the *Canada Evidence Act*,[2] a consequence of Canada's two-court model of adjudicating disclosure of secret information. Many of the secrecy issues revolved around whether material from CSIS and foreign agencies in this transnational investigation had to be disclosed to the accused. The Federal Court ordered that most of it could be kept secret. This meant that the information would not be used by the prosecutor, but also that it would not assist the accused in either undermining the Crown's case or building his own.[3]

Deciding all this took time and substantial judicial energy. This secrecy dispute resulted in at least six reported decisions from the Federal Courts. These decisions included two appeals to the Federal Court of Appeal. In one, the appeal court decided the judge at first instance, Justice Mosley, had put too much secret information into a summary he had prepared for use by Khawaja in the criminal trial.[4] Justice Mosley almost certainly made this error because he knew that the criminal trial judge in the provincial superior court (who was not privy to all this pre-trial litigation) would eventually have to decide whether a fair criminal trial was still possible, even though the Federal Court had ordered so much information to be kept secret. This process also resulted in a failed effort to appeal to the Supreme Court.[5] All of this occurred before the trial even started.

The Constitutional Challenge

Khawaja was the first person charged under terrorism offences enacted after 9/11, and he challenged their constitutionality in pre-trial proceedings before the criminal trial judge. He won that challenge only in part when the trial judge struck out parts of the definition on constitutional grounds,[6] in a manner that actually made proving the case easier for the Crown. The defence unsuccessfully attempted an immediate appeal to the Supreme Court.[7]

The Trial

The criminal trial began in June 2008, more than four years after Khawaja's arrest and more than a year after the UK convictions. The Ottawa trial — before a judge and no jury — took twenty-seven sitting days and ended in September 2008. (The trial of the co-conspirators in the United Kingdom was longer: it took 107 sitting days.) In October 2008, the trial judge concluded that Khawaja did not specifically intend to facilitate the UK fertilizer bomb plot per se, but did possess a more diffuse intent to cause death and endanger life. He was convicted of five terrorism offences,[8] and sentenced to a total of ten-and-a-half years. Khawaja had been denied bail and had been in custody since his 2004 arrest, but the trial judge refused to credit his nearly five years of pre-trial custody at the then general rate of 2:1 because that would have produced a very short sentence, one that would neither denounce or deter terrorism.[9]

The Appeal

Khawaja appealed the conviction, and the Crown appealed the sentence. The Ontario Court of Appeal upheld the conviction (and the constitutionality of the terrorism law) and greatly lengthened Khawaja's sentence to life imprisonment.[10] The defendant further appealed the matter to the Supreme Court of Canada. That Court issued its decision on 14 December 2012, unanimously upholding the constitutionality of Canada's 2001 anti-terrorism law and confirming the life sentence.[11]

All told, almost nine years passed from the arrest to the final appeal decision.

Trial and Tribulation

The *Khawaja* case was Canada's first terrorism trial under the 2001 *ATA*. It is perhaps not surprising it was so protracted, but it was not unusually or exceptionally protracted for a Canadian terrorism trial. And it had the virtue of actually taking place — terrorism trials are rare on the Canadian legal landscape. This infrequency is not just because we live in a generally peaceful society; Canada struggles with terrorism prosecutions for other reasons to be explained in this chapter.

In previous chapters, we discussed a range of anti-terror tools such as watching through surveillance, interdicting through passport denial and no-fly lists, restraining through immigration detention and peace bonds, and interruption through preventive arrests or some other sort of threat reduction tactic. In this chapter, we examine society's most forceful and transparent tool: criminal charges and terrorism prosecutions that, upon conviction, can lead to significant punishment.

The issue in terrorism prosecutions is not generally the absence of criminal offences — conspiracy and attempt to kill or bomb have always been criminal. Instead, terrorism prosecutions present very difficult challenges in terms of producing evidence to prove guilt beyond a reasonable doubt. Why? Because since 9/11, our prosecutions have been directed at preventing violence, rather than simply being reactive to it.

A prosecution indexed to a feared attack depends on evidence very different from that associated with an actual act of violence. To be sure, evidentiary issues can be botched even for post-attack cases. The 2005 Air India acquittals are a stark reminder of that fact. But evidentiary issues become even more complex where plotters are prosecuted for their plotting. We know about this plotting often because of normally secret intelligence, and sometimes intelligence collected by bodies disinclined to see it used in court. For this reason, Canadian authorities have often struggled with converting secret intelligence into public evidence that can prove guilt and in ensuring that the intelligence that they do not use in trials is protected from unnecessary disclosure to the accused or the public. Other countries face similar challenges, but Canada lags behind them. CSIS seems more concerned than some other intelligence agencies about the disclosure of its intelligence in court. There are a number of reasons for this: the accused's broad right to disclosure under the *Charter*; Canada's frequent reliance on foreign intelligence; and Canada's cumbersome two-court approach to protecting state secrets (on display in all its Byzantine complexity in *Khawaja*).

In this chapter, we examine Canada's record of anti-terror prosecutions and enumerate the acute difficulties we have encountered in making them work. We suggest that the two anti-terror laws enacted in 2015 — bills C-44 and C-51 — may make these difficulties more acute, with the result that prosecutions may become more arduous and perhaps more rare.

II. WHAT WE (MOSTLY) DO RIGHT: A ROBUST CRIMINAL LAW

The problem in terrorism prosecutions is not that we have too few crimes. Even before Bill C-51 added the ill-conceived speech offence analyzed in Chapter 10, we had fourteen specific terrorism offences. These included the original 2001, post-9/11 crimes that focused on things like terrorism financing, facilitating terrorist activity, and participating with a terrorist group in a "terrorist activity." Here, we briefly rehearse the content of the most important of these rules. "Terrorist activity" includes most acts of violence done for political, religious, or ideological motives, with the intention of intimidating the public "with regard to its security, including its economic security, or compelling a person, a government, or a domestic or an international organization to do or to refrain from doing any act."[12]

Terrorist groups include ad hoc groups of conspirators — it is possible, in fact, to be a terrorist group of one[13] — who have terrorist activities as one of their purposes. They also include the entities pre-emptively listed by the cabinet as terrorist groups. With two exceptions, all of our completed prosecutions have concerned so-called bunch-of-guys terrorist groups — informal groupings — and not the more formal entities listed in Canada's terror group list.

Facilitation and Participation

"Facilitation" offences prohibit things like: "knowingly" facilitating terrorist activity, whether or not "the facilitator knows that a particular terrorist activity is facilitated; any particular terrorist activity was foreseen or planned at the time it was facilitated; or any terrorist activity was actually carried out."[14]

"Participation" crimes prohibit knowingly "participat[ing] in or contribut[ing] to, directly or indirectly, any activity of a terrorist group for the purpose of enhancing the ability of any terrorist group to facilitate or carry out a terrorist activity." The list of things constituting participation is a lengthy one and includes "recruiting a person for training," providing a skill or expertise to a terrorist group, or entering any country at the direction of or for the benefit of a terrorist group.

Contribution, meanwhile, is gauged by such things as whether the accused associated with persons in a terrorist group or "uses a name, word, symbol or other representation that identifies, or is associated with, the terrorist group."[15]

Our criminal law also includes a host of more traditional terrorist crimes that predate the *ATA*, like taking hostages and aircraft hijacking. And in addition to all these crimes, prosecutors can also charge persons with indictable offences, such as those relating to explosives, or well-established crimes, such as conspiracy to commit murder or attempted murder. And in addition, it is a terrorism offence[16] to commit *any* serious crime for a terrorist group, and it is also a terrorism offence to commit *any* serious crime where the wrongful act also amounts to a terrorist activity. Both of these broadly defined offences are punishable by a maximum of life imprisonment.[17] In short, the criminal law is robust when it comes to terrorism.

Intentional, but Not Endless, Overbreadth

Parliament has defined many terrorism offences in broad and sometimes sweeping terms. Widening the net is exactly what the *ATA* intended. Its proponents urged "the nature of terrorism requires a different approach to disrupt and disable the terrorist network before it can carry out its design."[18] Parliament's objective in 2001 was to disrupt terrorists, not through unlawful acts by CSIS (as in Bill C-51), but by criminal convictions that could be registered long before any act of terrorist violence. This was something that one of us (Roach) did not appreciate enough when the *ATA* was introduced in 2001 but came to appreciate in light of post-9/11 uses of less restrained alternatives to the criminal law both in Canada and abroad.[19]

The post-9/11 terrorist crimes are broad, but there are limits. In *Khawaja*, the Supreme Court restricted the reach of at least some offences so as not to apply to activities presenting a "negligible risk of enhancing the abilities of a terrorist group to facilitate or carry out a terrorist activity." It reasoned that when Parliament enacted the expansively worded and frequently used "participation in a terrorist group" offence it "did not intend for the provision to capture conduct that creates no risk or a negligible risk of harm. Indeed, the offence carries with it a sentence of up to 10 years of imprisonment and significant stigma. This provision is meant to criminalize conduct that presents a real risk for Canadian society."[20]

The Court also rejected the idea that the participation offence was so broad it could apply to doctors or lawyers providing legitimate services to known terrorists. In doing so, the Court stressed the importance that the accused "have the *subjective* purpose of enhancing the ability of a terrorist group to facilitate or carry out a terrorist activity, the accused must *specifically intend* his actions to have this general effect."[21] The Supreme Court's approach mitigates the dangers of a leading American decision holding that people supporting the non-violent and humanitarian activities of a listed terrorist group could nevertheless be guilty of the main American terrorism offence: material support of terrorism.[22]

Still, a few terrorism offences in the *Criminal Code* can be committed without a subjective purpose to engage in terrorism. The most important is the offence of knowingly providing funds to a terrorist group.[23] As in the United States, a person could be guilty under this offence for knowingly sending money to a terrorist group, even if they intend the money to be used to finance non-violent and even humanitarian activities by the group. In the next chapter, we discuss how Bill C-51's speech crime also lacks a link to a terrorist purpose. As such, it constrains speech in a way we believe violates the *Charter*.

Freedom Fighters?

It is easy to agree that the use of violence to express political or religious grievances is wrong in a democracy where people have avenues to dissent. And in assigning criminal blame, our law does not differentiate between the motives of someone who engages in terrorism offences. There is no cause, in other words, that exonerates political violence. But this issue becomes more difficult with respect to those who take up arms as part of a foreign conflict, in rebellion against a tyranny in Assad's Syria or Gadhafi's Libya or, before that, in apartheid South Africa. The so-called Arab Spring was a reminder of an old cliché that has often confounded efforts to define terrorism: one person's terrorist is another person's freedom fighter. The international community is now generally hostile to this view, and Canada follows suit.

The post-9/11 *Criminal Code* definition of "terrorist activity" provides only a limited exemption for freedom fighters; specifically, for acts committed during armed conflicts in accordance with international law. Khawaja argued he was a freedom fighter. But the Supreme Court held that there was no air of reality to the argument that his actions with respect to planned violence in Afghanistan fell within the exemption. The Court stressed that Khawaja's "violent jihadist ideology . . . is fundamentally incompatible with international law" because he was prepared "to take arms against whoever supports non-Islamic regimes," including the idea "that suicide attacks on civilians may sometimes be justified by the ends of jihad."[24] Similar reasoning would likely apply to ISIS and other foreign terrorist groups — by visiting such egregious violence on non-combatants, none of them act in "accordance with" the international law of armed conflict.

But still, "freedom fighter"-like thinking may have informed one Canadian criminal sentencing decision. The *ATA* includes broad laws against terrorism financing, but no one was convicted under them until 2010. In that case, a Sri Lankan Tamil expatriate pled guilty to collecting $3,000 for the Liberation Tigers of Tamil Eelam (LTTE), a protagonist in the long-standing civil conflict in Sri Lanka and also a group engaged in terrorism against civilians. The freedom fighter issue was not litigated, but the court imposed a very lenient six-month sentence. This sentence was upheld on appeal, despite the fact that the accused — who had lost family members at the hands of the Sri Lanka state — was not remorseful.[25] As will be seen, the leniency in this case was exceptional in terrorism cases. More recent trials dealing with the involvement of foreign-based terrorist groups have produced much sterner sentences.

Canada's Laggard Record on Terrorism Prosecutions

So if our law is robust, what about our record of prosecutions?

We set out hard figures in Table 9.1 in the annex to this chapter. On the plus side, prosecutors have won all but one of the anti-terror cases they have brought to trial for conduct since 9/11, under the new laws. This gives them a conviction rate of 95 percent — but this is a misleading number. For one, it does not include the 2005 acquittal — under the older laws — of two men for murder in the Air India bombings after a 217-day judge-alone trial that started in April 2003 and concluded in December 2004.[26] Moreover, it is also misleading because of the surprisingly small number of people actually charged with terrorism offences.

Since 9/11, a government tabulation of Canadian terrorism trials lists twenty-one convictions, in addition to one acquittal and eight instances where charges were stayed or dropped.[27] As a result, the Canadian figure is smaller than the twenty-six convictions in the legally similar, but significantly less populated country of Australia.[28] It is also much smaller than the 411 convictions in Great Britain by 2015,[29] a number that excludes those stemming from Northern Ireland related terrorism. And in the ten years after 9/11, US federal courts tried 1,054 terror-related cases, 578 of which involved "defendants who were formally or informally associated with an Islamist terror group" or the "global jihadist ideology."[30] In this last category, prosecutors secured 376 convictions. Another analysis calculates the number of US convictions for all terror-related offences for roughly the same ten-year period at 494.[31] Translated into convictions per million people, the Canadian conviction figure drawn from the government document is 0.6 per million. The comparable figures for Australia, the United Kingdom, and the United States (now several years out of date) are, respectively: 1.12, 6.4, and 1.54.

Of courses, those numbers are on an upswing since the October 2014 attack and the massive shift of RCMP resources into anti-terrorism. As discussed in Chapter 3, we are aware of fifteen individuals who have been charged with terrorism offences, several *in absentia* and a few who may be dead. Those in custody now await trial. Cumulatively, we calculate that these outstanding matters bring the total number of people charged with terrorism offences since 9/11 to at least forty-five. But between 9/11 and the end of 2014, the United Kingdom charged 721 persons.

Are Only Muslims Prosecuted for Terrorism?

As Table 9.1 suggests, most of our criminal proceedings have involved terrorist group charges. All but one have involved al-Qaida- and ISIS-inspired terrorism. This fact reflects contemporary security preoccupations, but it also raises a question concerning selective use of our anti-terror laws. Anti-terror laws reach all political, religious, and ideological motives, not simply the al-Qaida- and ISIS-inspired brand. The rule of law, unlike a declaration of war against a specific enemy, should apply to all.

Canada is a somewhat notorious terrorism financing hub for a wide variety of foreign terrorist causes.[32] And yet, we have only had a single terrorism financing prosecution — the only conviction for a cause other than one inspired by al-Qaida and ISIS. As others have suggested, there is considerably more work to be done in the area of terrorism financing.[33]

We have also had acts of outright violence that amount to terrorist activity. In 2014, twenty-four-year-old Justin Bourque shot five RCMP members in Moncton, killing three. He later outlined an ideological motive for his conduct, not tremendously different from that of so-called right wing extremists:

> [H]e hated the government and the authorities because of the different rules that were made — gun regulation. He talked about foreign workers coming to work in Canada while some Canadians have no jobs. He was convinced that the police were intimidating and screwing everyone in Moncton by working for the politicians. He repeated a few times how he hated the authorities, the government and the police for working for the politicians . . . . [H]e felt oppressed by the law . . . He was rational and aware of what he was about to do. He consciously decided not to shoot civilians. His battle is with the authority.[34]

In sum, he targeted RCMP officers because he viewed them as "'soldiers' in the employ and propping-up of a corrupt government."[35] Bourque was convicted of murder and attempted murder and will likely spend the rest of his life in jail. But his conduct was not addressed using terrorism provisions, even though his conduct likely satisfied the threshold of terrorist activity and police considered terrorism charges.[36] Bourque is not a one-off. Richard Bain killed one person and injured another in 2012 in an attempt to assassinate Pauline Marois — then Quebec's newly elected premier and leader of the Parti Québécois — on election night. His statement, "the English are waking up" reveals a political motive. He faces fifteen charges including murder, but not terrorism charges.[37]

Data from the Canadian Network for Research on Terrorism, Security and Society (TSAS) suggests 59 percent of lone wolf attacks in Canada in the last fifteen years have been tied to white supremacy, but none have resulted in terrorism convictions.[38] Specific instances of seemingly politically motivated violence reported in the TSAS database between 2010 and 2014 include: arson by the "Anti-Gentrification Front" in Vancouver (2013); and a large number of assault and firearms offences from 2008 to 2013 by members of neo-Nazi group Blood & Honour, including setting one man on fire. There has also been a case involving an actual bombing incident in Ottawa (Royal Bank)[39] that appears to have been motivated by a clear political ideology, tied to anti-globalization. However, all of the matters listed here were treated under non-terror-related criminal offences, even though some might have ticked off the boxes for one or more terrorism offences or have sentences increased on the basis that the crimes also constituted terrorist activity.[40]

There may be good reason for the evident prosecutorial parsimony, faced with these incidents. A prosecutor able to secure a conviction for more conventional offences may see no purpose in also pursing a separate terrorism offence, or seeking an augmented sentence for conventional offences done in association with a terrorist activity. A prosecutor pursuing the terrorism angle would then need to prove the complicated elements of terrorist activity beyond a reasonable doubt, and Justin Bourque could not have been sentenced to a longer term had his prosecutors made that effort. The same is also true for Richard Bain; both men faced (or face) charges with mandatory minimum life sentences — meaning that there is no possibility of an increased penalty for terrorist activity. In other cases, however, terrorism charges might have been viable, if more complex.

"The Attack Does Not Appear to Have Been Culturally Motivated, Therefore Not Linked to Terrorism"

There is a consequence to anti-terror laws that in government rhetoric and practice is directed more or less exclusively at "violent jihadi" crimes. The particularly acute stigma and denunciation associated with terrorism convictions is visited on only one particular brand of terrorist violence — that associated with a minority religion — and not on terrorists from the majority community. The consequence may be pernicious, false impressions of the sort that even Justice Minister Peter MacKay laboured under in 2015.

MacKay commented on a foiled (and possibly ideologically motivated) alleged mass shooting in a Halifax mall: "What we know of these alleged plans for a mass attack against our friends and our neighbours in the province, is that the attack does not appear to have been culturally motivated, therefore not linked to terrorism."[41] This statement — seemingly asserting that terrorism in Canadian criminal law is predicated on a "cultural" motivation — was legally incorrect. But the minister's spokesperson then stated MacKay "was simply relating his understanding of what law authorities have concluded at this point."[42] The minister, in other words, apparently believed that somewhere in Canadian law or jurisprudence, terrorism is predicated on a "cultural" motivation. He may have been using "culture" as shorthand for "religious," but even then, by being underinclusive in his understanding of the true reach of terrorist activity — applicable also to "political" and "ideological" motives — he implied that Canadian law is directed at one (and only one) motive for politicized violence: religion. Some Muslim Canadians took the minister's statement as coded language for "they weren't Muslim so thus, [it's] not terrorism."[43]

MacKay's comments were unhelpful, especially coming from the Attorney General of Canada. But they draw attention to the underlying (and potentially alienating) reality: people who progress to violence inspired by ideologies other than those of al-Qaida and ISIS are almost never being charged for terrorism offences in Canada. Such double standards[44] threaten the essence of the rule of law, one in which criminal justice is supposed to apply even-handedly and not single out particular perceived enemies.

Prosecuting All Foreign Terrorist Fighters?

So we have broad terrorism crimes, but we underuse them and use them selectively. We have special crimes on the books to address foreign terrorist fighters, the principal security concern discussed in Chapter 3. In 2013, four new offences of attempting to leave Canada to participate in a terrorist group, or to facilitate, instruct, or commit terrorist activities were added to the ever-thickening *Criminal Code*. And as we discuss below, even before these specialized terrorism offences, those who left or attempted to leave Canada to engage in terrorism abroad could be prosecuted and punished under Canadian criminal law.

In June 2015, a spokesperson for Prime Minister Harper seemed to suggest all returned foreign terrorist fighters would be prosecuted (and the dual nationals would have their citizenship removed).[45] And the Senate security committee raised concerns in July 2015 that authorities had not already done more to bring such individuals to trial.[46] It reported "eighty Canadians have returned to Canada after participating with Islamist fundamentalist groups. Many of these people return with terrorist training, combat experience and may therefore pose a security risk to Canada."[47] The Senate committee is right to note the mismatch between these numbers and the rate of criminal arrests and prosecutions in Canada. To date, the only clear, would-be foreign terrorist fighter convicted in Canada is Mohamed Hersi. The story of his prosecution is recounted below.

For our part, we doubt that Canada has the capacity to prosecute the eighty returned foreign terrorist fighters reported by the Senate committee. Moreover, throwing people who are not truly dangerous in jail may often be asking for more trouble, especially given documented patterns of prison radicalization in the terrorism area. We raise this issue below and explore it in Chapter 13.

Prosecute If Necessary, but Not Necessarily Prosecute

We are, nevertheless, surprised — and more than a little concerned — that Canada does not have more terror prosecutions, and ideally more prosecutions for politically motivated violence of all sorts. Prosecutions are our principle guard against violent people — they are our primary exit strategy from the threat posed by people who have embarked on the path to outright violence. Prosecutions also have a unique ability to deter and denounce those who might use violence for political ends, either in Canada or abroad. They have a potential to expose the violence in terrorism and to deglorify it. As we have already said, the criminal law has always been based on the firm proposition that no motive — including those derived from political grievances or religious aspirations — can excuse violence. That is an appropriate stance for a liberal state that accepts intellectual and religious pluralism, but draws the line at harm.

Fair criminal trials are a form of counter-narrative. Democracies, unlike terrorists, only punish the guilty. Criminal trials, unlike surveillance and most forms of covert CSIS "threat reduction," will be carried out in public. They do not use secret evidence, as do immigration detention and removal, no-fly listing, and passport revocation. Criminal trials meet the violence and nihilism of terrorism with due process, measured fact-finding, and proportionate punishment. Done properly, criminal trials delegitimize terrorism for all but the most strident observers.

Canada may now be stepping away from its important tradition of using the criminal law to denounce and punish terrorism. We have examined in Chapter 7 the more frequent and problematic use of peace bonds as an alternative to criminal trials. The use of immigration law and removals as anti-terrorism tools has also been rightly controversial. We fear that we may be moving away from our modest use of prosecutions in favour of disruption, peace bonds, and immigration detention and removals at precisely the time when criminal trials can expose the violence of al-Qaida- and ISIS-inspired terrorism and hopefully minimize ISIS's growing appeal.

III. THE EASY CASE WITH JUST THE USUAL LEVEL OF COMPLEXITY

So why do we have so few trials?

Terrorism trials are demanding. The accused goes free if the state cannot prove guilt beyond a reasonable doubt. The accused also walks if the court finds the state has acted improperly through entrapment or other abuses, or if a fair trial is not possible because of the need to protect secrets from disclosure. The 2005 acquittal of Ajaib Malik and Rupidaman Bagri for the Air India bombings,[48] as well as the 2014 acquittal of Khurram Sher,[49] demonstrate that terrorism trials in Canada are not show trials.

To introduce some of the complexities of terrorism prosecutions, we will first examine an "easy" prosecution involving a would-be foreign terrorist fighter, then look at how prosecutions get even more complex and difficult from there.

The Errant Security Guard

Mohamed Hersi should have been a Canadian success story. That is not to say he had it all; he grew up in a single-parent immigrant family in a poor Toronto neighbourhood. He went to high school with six Somali-Canadians who left Canada to join the Somali terrorist group al-Shabaab in 2009 and 2010. As discussed in Chapter 3, al-Shabaab is a brutal terrorist group, best known for killing sixty-two people in its 2013 attack on the Westgate Mall in Nairobi and killing 149 in a 2015 attack on Garrissa University.

But unlike those high school peers, Hersi continued his education and graduated with a health science degree from the University of Toronto. Thereafter, he was underemployed, working as a security guard. One day, a cleaner discovered a USB flash drive in the pocket of Hersi's security guard uniform. The inquisitive cleaner found suspicious materials on the drive, including *The Anarchist Cookbook* and a Canadian Forces operational manual. The alarmed cleaner informed the Toronto police, not CSIS. In many ways, this is what made what followed an "easy" case. For reasons we explore below, calling the police, and not CSIS, simplified the subsequent investigation and prosecution.

But easy is relative: the trial ultimately featured thirteen published judgments on various motions brought by the accused. This legal complexity flowed from how the police responded.

The Sting

The Toronto police took the tip from the cleaner seriously and devoted considerable resources to the investigation. They assigned a young police officer of East African ancestry to go undercover and befriend Hersi. The undercover officer (known throughout the trial as the UC) met with Hersi on about thirty occasions between October 2010 and March 2011. The UC went to Friday prayers with Hersi; the two also went to Toronto Raptors basketball games. Over the course of their relationship, the UC sought Hersi's advice about how he should travel to Somalia to join al-Shabaab. Some of these exchanges were recorded — a wiretap was obtained in late January 2011 and it recorded about eleven of the thirty encounters between Hersi and the UC. The police allowed the elaborate sting to play out. They only arrested Hersi at the Toronto airport when he was to start his journey to Somalia.

The Charges

The police charged Hersi with attempting to participate in the activities of the terrorist group al-Shabaab and of counselling the UC to do the same. These were 2001 *ATA* crimes, combined with old-fashioned inchoate — before the fact — forms of liability thrown in through the use of attempt and counselling (or incitement) charges. These charges demonstrated how our law can capture conduct lying well short of actual acts of violence. They also demonstrate how speech was not exempt from terrorism charges even before Bill C-51's new speech crime, discussed in Chapter 10. The counselling charges hinged on the words that Hersi used in his attempt to recruit the UC to join al-Shabaab.

The Pre-trial Motions

Hersi brought a large number of pre-trial motions. He challenged the Crown's use of a direct indictment that avoided a preliminary inquiry. This procedure is quite common as an attempt to shorten notoriously long terrorism prosecutions, but Hersi argued that it violated the *Charter* because it deprived him of the opportunity to cross-examine the UC before trial. Hersi lost, with the judge noting that Hersi would have a chance to cross-examine the UC at trial, as indeed he did.[50] Hersi also challenged a police wiretap warrant on the basis that the grounds for issuing the warrant were inadequate and based on Islamophobia. The judge upheld the warrant because Hersi had, in fact, told the UC that every good Muslim should consider becoming a *shaheed* or martyr and that he planned to travel to Somalia via Egypt to join al-Shabaab.[51]

This was an important ruling. As discussed in Chapter 4, electronic surveillance plays an important role in many terrorism investigations and prosecutions. And wiretap warrants will invariably be challenged by the accused. The prosecution must be prepared to disclose enough material to show there were sufficient grounds for granting the warrant in the first place. If there was something wrong with the evidence used to obtain the warrant, then that warrant itself risks being flawed, and a flawed warrant would make the invasion of privacy involved in a search or wiretap an "unreasonable" search and seizure. Unreasonable searches and seizures violate section 8 of the *Charter of Rights and Freedoms*. Such a transgression would put in jeopardy any evidence collected through the warrant. Bottom line: a tainted warrant application can have cascading effects that can alter a trial.

Here, the UC could provide the evidence supporting the warrant. This was an easy case because the prosecutors were dealing with an undercover agent employed by the police and not a confidential volunteer or police informant. An informer who wished to keep his or her identity secret would be less useful to prosecutors obliged to show that the warrant was properly granted. And if this had been a CSIS surveillance warrant rather than a police warrant, all bets would have been off in terms of how things would play out, for reasons we explore below.

Hersi also challenged the constitutionality of the offences under which he was charged, alleging that they constituted a thought crime.[52] The trial judge rejected this challenge because of the Supreme Court's decision in *Khawaja*. There, the Court had rejected a similar freedom of expression challenge. The Court had stressed the need for the accused to have a terrorist purpose and to do something that presented some risk of terrorist violence.[53] This sets a fairly high standard, but one that the jury ultimately concluded was satisfied in Hersi's case.

The Evidence the Jury Heard

Each jury member was questioned about whether their ability to try the case impartially on the facts would be affected by the fact that Hersi is black and a Muslim, charged with a terrorism offence. Although the judge ruled that some of Hersi's views on matters such as the Toronto 18 and Omar Khadr were too prejudicial for the jury to hear, the jury heard plenty about Hersi's political and religious views.[54] For example:

- He [Hersi] told the officer that it was every Muslim's duty to consider joining Al-Shabaab and that it should be every Muslim's dream to die as a shaheed (martyr);
- He advised the UC to prepare an alibi to conceal his true motive for travelling to Africa;

- He advised the UC to travel through Kenya, where the UC had connections, and told him how to best get from Kenya into Somalia so that he could link up with Al-Shabaab;
- He warned the UC not to "burn bridges" in Canada as he may be asked to return and "take care" of something, such as people who insult the Prophet;
- He recommended "Inspire" magazine to the UC, an English language online magazine which purports to be published by Al Qaida;
- He and the UC talked about a bomb making article from "Inspire", and the accused told the UC that he did not need to try to make a bomb now because "when you get there they will show you how to make them".[55]

The jury also heard extensive expert evidence to establish that al-Shabaab was a terrorist group, and that one who joined it would be involved in terrorism. Again, this was an easy case. Al-Shabaab has a clear and notorious track record, and in fact in 2010, was listed as a terrorist group by cabinet under the *Criminal Code*.[56]

During the trial, the UC was the star witness. He testified and was cross-examined over forty days of the trial. After two days of deliberation, the jury convicted Hersi of attempting to participate in the activities of the terrorist group al-Shabaab and of counselling the UC to do the same.

Entrapment Issues

Undercover officers and informants have been a staple of many post-9/11 terrorism prosecutions. Police and informers in Canada have also participated in stings, including in the Toronto 18 prosecutions where entrapment was claimed but rejected in two different cases.[57]

In one of them, the Ontario Court of Appeal stressed that the remedy for entrapment, a permanent stay of proceedings that sets the accused free, "is an exceptional remedy to be employed only in rare cases and as a last resort."[58] The most recent test of the entrapment defence will come in the case of John Nuttall and Amanda Korody, now convicted of plotting to explore pressure cooker bombs on Canada Day 2013 at the British Columbia legislature. At the time of this writing, the judge has yet to decide whether the accused were entrapped during an intensive five-month sting.

What is entrapment? In Canadian law, entrapment will occur if the state conducts a sting either without a reasonable suspicion that the accused was already involved in a crime or outside a bona fide investigation. The latter concept was designed to allow undercover police to try to buy drugs or sex in certain parts of town.[59] The concept could, however, be more controversial if applied to everyone who associates with a terror suspect or attends certain religious or political meetings. Even if a suspect has been properly targeted for a sting, the accused will also have an entrapment defence and be allowed to walk if the state induced the commission of the crime with so much pressure that even a reasonable person in the same circumstances would commit a crime.[60]

Prolonged and elaborate stings raise questions about whether those charged and convicted of terrorism offence would ever have engaged in terrorism if left to their own devices. In the United States, a 2014 report by Human Rights Watch lists twenty-seven cases where extensive stings started by the state resulted in terrorism convictions.[61] The report found problematic practices, such as targeting people on the basis of their speech and associations, and preying on those with mental health issues, including mental disabilities. In all of these cases, American juries rejected the entrapment defence.

In Canada, trial judges, not juries, decide the entrapment issue because of a belief that judges are in the best position to ensure the integrity of the justice system. At the same time, however, Canadian judges generally rule on whether the accused has established the entrapment defence only after the accused has been found guilty. A court-ordered entrapment stay after a jury conviction would be quite controversial. And yet, overly aggressive police investigative strategies run the danger of tainting the legitimacy of all terrorism prosecutions and supporting the narrative that the police target Muslims they perceive to be extreme and then manufacture crimes to get them. This was, in fact, a narrative that Hersi and his counsel invoked.

The trial judge had no trouble rejecting Hersi's entrapment defence after the jury convicted him. She found that the undercover officer could properly befriend Hersi, even before there was a reasonable suspicion that Hersi was involved in terrorism. She also found nothing wrong with the UC steering conversations toward terrorism and al-Shabaab. The judge observed that Hersi "needed little if any prodding on any of these subjects . . . Hersi jumped in with both feet. That he now finds them stuck in his mouth is his own doing."[62] She added: "I do not believe that the community would be offended by the length or nature of this investigation. Quite the opposite: given the devastating effects of terrorist acts and the corresponding need to prevent them, I believe the community would be alarmed if the police had done anything less."[63]

All told, this ruling — and others — suggests that informers and undercover officers will have considerable leeway to engage with suspects before a viable entrapment defence reins them in. This will make life easier for the police. But we need to be vigilant. There is a danger that police targeting decisions can be a self-fulfilling prophecy. This could attract allegations that suspects were targeted for elaborate stings largely because of their political or religious views.[64] Again, we underscore the importance of even-handed and measured application of the law to maintaining the integrity of the justice system and the rule of law.

Police who come to depend on investigative strategies just short of entrapment may also steer efforts toward those most vulnerable to stings. Those persons will not always be the most intelligent, most determined, and most dangerous potential terrorists. Put another way, directing scarce resources at low-hanging fruit may mean fewer resources are available for more complicated — and potentially more important — anti-terror investigations.

The Sentence

In the end, Hersi received the maximum sentence possible for the crimes charged: five years imprisonment consecutive on both the attempt and counselling charges, for a total of ten years imprisonment. These maximum sentences reflected the fact that Hersi was not convicted of actual participation in a terrorist group, which itself has a ten year maximum sentence. Rather he was guilty of the incomplete (or "inchoate") offences of attempting to participate in a terrorist group and counselling others to do likewise.

In her strongly worded sentencing ruling, Justice Baltman stressed deterrence and denunciation. She stated that "terrorists are the worst kinds of cowards because they deliberately target innocent members of the public who are not prepared for combat . . . . The message needs to be sent out that anyone who aspires to become part of such evil must pay a heavy price."[65] The judge was understandably disappointed with Hersi, given that Canada had granted his family refuge from Somalia and Hersi had received a university education. Even with these advantages, Hersi "decided to break Canadian laws so he could return to Somalia and perpetuate violence" and "aspired to join a terrorist group that seeks to annihilate those who think differently."[66]

Justice Baltman devoted only two of eighty-eight paragraphs in her sentencing judgment to rehabilitation. She saw no potential for rehabilitation in Hersi, despite the fact that he complied with all bail conditions while free awaiting trial; had no record; was intelligent, educated, and well-read; and had experienced some discrimination in Canada.[67] She concluded "given that the offender has shown a willingness to join cause with a fanatical group that indiscriminately kills innocent civilians, and there is no basis to believe he is likely to reform his views, the need to segregate him from society for society's protection must be the driving factor here."[68]

The judge's evident disgust was understandable. But Hersi's sentence will expire well before his fortieth birthday. Given this, we cannot ignore the danger that Hersi could be further radicalized while in prison and we cannot give up on the undoubtedly difficult task of attempting to rehabilitate Hersi and other convicted terrorists. Although the Supreme Court confirmed a life sentence for Khawaja, it also stated that rehabilitation was still relevant and should be considered on a case-by-case basis when sentencing terrorists.[69] We return to this issue below and in Chapter 13.

Hersi's conviction was not well received by his family. The accused's uncle — who had offered his house so Hersi could obtain bail before trial — told reporters that Hersi's family regarded the affair as "a political trial and nothing to do with the justice system," and went on to state, "We believe this has been orchestrated and fabricated by the police . . . . An innocent person is in custody now." Hersi's lawyer told the press the trial was a "kind of Western show trial" that convicted someone "merely speaking [his] thoughts."[70] But of course, Hersi went well beyond thinking and preparing to join al-Shabaab. He was properly targeted, given the incriminating material that the cleaner found that led to the sting; he was literally caught boarding the plane. Moreover, "merely speaking thoughts" has always been a crime when the speech is designed to incite others to commit crime. In other words, Hersi was not convicted for the mere radicalism that could conceivably be captured by the Bill C-51 speech crime discussed in Chapter 10.

Summary

Hersi's trial was a form of counter-narrative that can expose, denounce, deter, and punish terrorism. But terrorism prosecutions are not easy. Unlike most criminal cases, they often require trials and are not resolved by guilty pleas. The accused have little incentive to plead guilty, given both their ideological motives and the stiff sentences they will likely receive in any event. Hersi's case involved electronic surveillance. It also involved an undercover officer whose conduct was closely scrutinized to determine if there had been entrapment or other abuses. The judge had the power to halt terrorism prosecutions permanently on the grounds of entrapment, abuse of process, or non-disclosure, or to exclude the wiretap material if it had not been properly obtained.

But even with all this complexity, the *Hersi* case was a relatively simple terrorism case. It involved one police force (as best we know) and only one accused. Not every case is *Hersi*. Many others will involve multiple accused and multiple investigators, including CSIS and sometimes foreign agencies. As will be seen, those terrorism trials are much more difficult.

IV. THE NOT-SO-EASY CASES AND HOW THE 2015 LAWS MAKES THEM HARDER

Despite recent convictions like *Hersi*, Canada has struggled with terrorism prosecutions as compared to other democracies. Our terrorism trials are too long, too costly, too complex, and too infrequent. The Air India Commission warned in 2010 that Canada urgently needed to improve its capacity to conduct terrorism prosecutions. It dedicated an entire book of its five-volume report to this topic, and its recommendations were then echoed by a unanimous 2011 Senate committee report.[71] As will be seen, the government then largely ignored these recommendations.

The comparative lack of terrorism prosecutions would not necessarily be a problem if it represented a considered choice to use the less drastic alternatives examined in the previous chapters to deal with modest threats. The problem, however, is that it may reflect Canada's somewhat unique and awkward approach to terrorism investigations and prosecutions. As discussed in Chapter 2, these struggles were first revealed in prosecutions arising out of the Air India bombings and related acts of terrorism in the 1980s.

Terrorism prosecutions in any country will be among the most difficult and complex criminal trials. All countries try cases that involve multiple accused who frequently have little incentive to plead guilty and every incentive to claim that the state has violated their rights or treated them unfairly. Every country struggles with converting secret intelligence collected in terrorism investigations into evidence that can be introduced in a public trial and with shielding unused intelligence from disclosure to the accused.

But Canada faces particular challenges that other states do not. First, Canada has some of the broadest rules in the world requiring material to be disclosed to the accused. This affects how willingly the open court-shy intelligence services work with police, and police with intelligence services. This is an old problem that has precipitated a series of deeply imperfect — and even dangerous — workarounds. Those workarounds will become even more imperfect after 2015's new laws. One of those new laws — Bill C-44 — gives informers or sources who were promised confidentiality by CSIS an effective veto over whether any identifying information about them can be used or disclosed to the accused in a subsequent terrorism prosecutions. The other law — Bill C-51 — creates new incentives for CSIS to sidestep the agony of open court disclosure by taking matters into its own hands with anti-terror threat reduction measures that will not involve arrests or prosecutions.

Second, Canada is afflicted with a cumbersome process where only the Federal Court — and not criminal trial courts — can determine whether material should not be disclosed to the accused because it contains state secrets. This system, which we will call the two-court system, also requires the trial judge in terrorism prosecutions to decide whether a fair trial is still possible in the face of any non-disclosure order made by the Federal Court. The interplay between the two courts has been called "constitutional chicken"[72] because it could result in the collapse of a terrorism trial. These made-in-Canada challenges make terrorism prosecutions more difficult here than elsewhere. They are the features that make the typical terrorism prosecution a "hard case." We address each at length and in turn.

The Burden of Broad Disclosure Rules

Since the landmark, but still controversial, 1991 *Stinchcombe* decision, the Supreme Court has insisted that the accused must have pre-trial disclosure of all relevant and non-privileged information in the prosecutor's possession, regardless of whether it is exculpatory (that is, whether or not it is evidence tending to exonerate the accused).[73] The courts have also decided the accused can gain access to information held by "third parties" to a prosecution, including CSIS, if it is likely relevant.[74]

Canada has some of the broadest disclosure rules in the world. Canada's disclosure rules are broader than the United Kingdom's rules that, since 1996, have been subject to legislative definition and limited to material that would advance the accused's case or undermine the Crown's case. They are broader than American constitutional disclosure requirements, limited to information that would be exculpatory for the accused. Many in the security community hoped that the Air India Commission would recommend legislation curbing Canada's broad disclosure requirements. But the commission declined to do so, concluding that such changes were likely impossible because *Stinchcombe* disclosure requirements are constitutionalized by virtue of section 7 of the *Charter*. And the Supreme Court has never, in the over thirty-year history of the *Charter*, accepted a limit on a section 7 rights — considered the most basic rights to fair treatment in the legal system.

The Air India Commission also concluded legislated restrictions would be blunt, and inevitably over- or underinclusive in particular cases. You cannot predict in advance the relevance of any particular piece of intelligence to a subsequent trial. Instead, it proposed "a more practical and efficient means to address the constitutional obligations to disclose intelligence" in order "to improve the process that can be used to obtain non-disclosure orders on the facts of the particular case."[75] Specifically, it proposed back-end reforms, giving trial judges a new power to make non-disclosure orders tailored to the circumstances of the trial. And it recommended front-end reforms that would require CSIS to adjust to the reality that sometimes intelligence about terrorism would have to be disclosed. The commission was impressed by the

UK experience. There, the domestic intelligence agency, MI5, collects intelligence in terrorism investigations to evidential standards and is prepared, if necessary, to testify in court. This has not been the Canadian experience.

Should CSIS Share Its Intelligence about Terrorism with the Police?

The Air India recommendations would have ended CSIS's power to refuse to disclose to the police intelligence about possible terrorism offences. They would have empowered a person outside the agency — the prime minister's national security advisor — to make the call on whether it was worth running the risk that intelligence might be disclosed. It would be up to the national security advisor — not CSIS — to decide whether the public interest was served, or not, by further disclosure of the intelligence to the police. Once the police received the evidence, the broad *Stinchcombe* constitutional rules for disclosure would apply if there were a prosecution, albeit subject to a new ability of trial judges (as opposed to Federal Court judges) to order non-disclosure on the particulars of their case. Well before the 2014 terrorist attacks, it was clear that the government had ignored and rejected these recommendations. It is easy to understand why the recommendations would not be popular with CSIS. And so, even before bills C-44 and C-51, the government committed us to a dangerous system.

Despite occasional claims to the contrary, Bill C-51 was not a response to the Air India inquiry's call. Although the information sharing act in Bill C-51 facilitates information sharing about a very broad array of security threats, it does not *require* CSIS to share intelligence it collects about terrorism offences. That choice remains with CSIS, undisciplined by any of the reforms proposed by the Air India Commission.

Of "Firewalls" and "Parallel Investigations"

The government suggests that the present system works well. In testimony before the Senate security committee, CSIS director Michel Coulombe disputed the notion

> that we keep files to ourselves and that we decide on our own when it should be passed to the RCMP and that it's normally done too late . . . .
> On the counterterrorism file, we talk with the RCMP every day, we share with them, they are aware of what we do, the targets we have and when it is time for them to engage. It's important to understand when the RCMP does engage, it doesn't necessarily mean we disengage. [RCMP Deputy

Commissioner] Mike [Cabana] talked in his opening remarks about parallel investigations. We are not here to supplement what they do, but we can run parallel investigations.[76]

Officials often point to the Toronto 18 cases at the end of the last decade as a successful example of CSIS and police co-operation, and it was — but only if measured by the undemanding standards by which we in Canada evaluate such things.

A closer look at the success story of the Toronto 18 investigation reveals some uncomfortable realities. Consider this passage from *Ahmad*, a Toronto 18 prosecution:

CSIS was aware of the location of the terrorist training camp . . . . This information was not provided to the RCMP, who had to uncover that information by their own means. Sometimes CSIS was aware that the RCMP were following the wrong person, or that they had surveillance on a house when the target of the surveillance was not inside, but [CSIS] did not intervene.[77]

Reasonable observers might assume that CSIS's failure to inform the police was a one-off mistake, or at worst, a remnant of the cultural divide that bungled the Air India investigation. It was not — it exists by design. The court in *Ahmad* was not condemning CSIS or this practice. Rather, it was explaining a Canadian staple: the parallel police-CSIS investigation. The court described a "firewall" between "parallel" investigations run by CSIS and the RCMP, one that tried to avoid CSIS intelligence "contaminating the police investigation."

The security services defend this system of parallel investigations arduously. CSIS notes, correctly, that its security investigations are triggered on broader grounds — and thus earlier — than are police criminal investigations. They are often the first ones investigating a potential security risk. CSIS's mandate, means, and procedures are different than those of the police and are geared to advising the government of threats, not collecting evidence for prosecutions. And CSIS is determined that its "Crown jewels"[78] — its sources and methods — not be revealed in open court, dragged into a proceeding by virtue of *Stinchcombe* disclosure rules. And so CSIS is extremely cautious in what it tells the police when what it is investigating turns out to be a crime.

You might expect that police and prosecutors would not stand for such a state of affairs, and there have been some glimpses of their unhappiness. One of the frustrated Air India prosecutors argued as early as 1991 that CSIS "must come to grips with the thorny issues"[79] raised by disclosure requirements.

That prosecutor and others had to try to explain to a trial judge why CSIS — applying regular procedures that existed until stopped by the Supreme Court in 2008[80] — destroyed much relevant raw intelligence in the Air India and other cases.

In his 2005 review of the Air India investigation, Bob Rae concluded that CSIS's destruction of most of the wiretaps on the suspected Air India mastermind was not surprising because CSIS believes "its mission does not include law enforcement." He warned however that this "misses the point" because terrorism is a crime and CSIS surveillance "may ultimately be connected to law enforcement."[81] But police and prosecutors today seem to have reluctantly concluded that access to more CSIS intelligence would poison their prosecutions because it would require them to go to Federal Court (potentially in the middle of the terrorism trial in a provincial superior court) to obtain an order that CSIS does not have to disclose its "Crown jewels." And even if they win and the Federal Court makes a non-disclosure order, they may lose. They may lose because the trial judge in provincial superior court may then conclude that a fair trial is no longer possible because of the Federal Court's non-disclosure order.

Put another way, CSIS information may turn into a "poison pill" in subsequent terrorism prosecutions because of CSIS's demands for secrecy.[82] And so the RCMP is happy to receive "hints" from CSIS; this approach is sometimes called "less is more."[83] "Don't ask, don't tell" could be another slogan to describe the distant relationship between CSIS and the police. But the bottom line is, as police officials told the Air India Commission, "sometimes it's better for us not to know things."[84] In saying this, they likely did not have in mind whether it was better that they not know of the existence of a terrorist training camp, or that they were following the wrong suspect.

"One Vision": "Less Is More"

There is some evidence that this less-is-more approach is applied even outside of the terrorism context. Jeffrey Delisle was a Canadian naval officer who spied for the Russians. Canadian Press reported in May 2013 that CSIS knew of the spying but failed to alert the RCMP. The RCMP instead learned of the espionage in 2011, after a tipoff from the FBI, and only then was Delisle arrested.[85] This story is obviously concerning, but applied to terrorism cases, the consequences are even more frightening. The net result of the less-is-more approach is often a quasi-formalized system of nudges and hints that prod police in the right direction. But in the worst cases, the risk is that the police will be left in the dark about what CSIS knows about terrorism. None of this reflects malice, incompetence, or the sometimes destructive relationship between the RCMP and CSIS arising in the early days after CSIS's creation. It reflects official policy. One called— somewhat ironically — "One Vision."

According to a document on One Vision released under an access to information request,[86] CSIS retains discretion about what to disclose to the police and keeps its investigations separate from the police. It is CSIS that decides whether to initiate a consultative process with the RCMP "if deemed appropriate." In other words, CSIS reserves the discretion to keep the police in the dark. Tellingly, the One Vision document relies more on the Arar Commission (which was concerned about not passing on unreliable intelligence) than the Air India Commission (which stressed the need for CSIS to pass on reliable intelligence about terrorism offences to the police). It does mention the Air India Commission, to support the idea of the RCMP sharing information with CSIS. This is acceptable because the RCMP material is presumably already subject to *Stinchcombe* disclosure in any event. What is not mentioned in One Vision is that the Air India Commission wanted a two-way flow of information between CSIS and the RCMP and that it, like the Bob Rae review before it, stressed that CSIS must adjust to a key fact: much intelligence collected in terrorism investigations may have evidential value.

One Vision may be a valiant bureaucratic effort to regularize a difficult situation. The problem, however, is not with good will or personalities at the administrative level. The problem is structural. The problem is the very concept of parallel investigations connected only by "less is more." So what about the claims that CSIS and the RCMP talk every day? To be sure, CSIS agents work with the police in Integrated National Security Enforcement Teams in major Canadian cities. Joint meetings between CSIS and the police, however, are designed to "deconflict," essentially ensuring that the parallel investigations do not collide. And CSIS shares intelligence with the police not in such meetings, but in a "very limited and carefully controlled manner." Step one is a "disclosure letter." This is something of a misnomer because such letters are not for disclosure in subsequent trials. They are essentially "tips" from CSIS to the police.[87]

Step two is a heavily lawyered "advisory letter." A recent RCMP document suggests that such letters provide the police with more information, but in a way that protects human sources and investigative methodologies.[88] At the end of the day, the lines between separate but parallel CSIS and police investigations are maintained. The maintenance of investigations through such tight information control is seen as a victory because it avoids courts holding that CSIS is subject to *Stinchcombe* because its investigation has merged with the police. Indeed, the judge in the Air India trial held that such a merger occurred. He also held that CSIS's destruction of tapes and interview notes with sources was negligent and only avoided determining whether a stay of proceedings was required because he acquitted the accused on other grounds.[89]

In the Toronto 18 case *Ahmad*, the trial judge concluded that because of the police-CSIS firewall, CSIS was not subject to the same disclosure requirements as the police.[90] Similar findings have been made in subsequent terrorism prosecutions including the VIA train plot and the British Columbia Canada Day plot.[91] In all of these cases, CSIS was not subject to the dreaded *Stinchcombe* disclosure standards. But CSIS risks winning the battle and losing the war. Even when not subject to *Stinchcombe*, CSIS is hardly immune from the accused's disclosure demands. Indeed in all of these cases, it had to disclose material to the accused under the slightly less onerous disclosure standard that applies to "third parties." All of this reflects how legalistic national security has become. And it begs the question most pressing for Canadians: does "less is more" keep us safe?

"You Have Been Remarkably Lucky"

Most Canadians would be — and should be — both shocked and scared by revelations that CSIS does not share all of its intelligence about terrorist conduct with the police, even when they know the police are looking in the wrong places. From the outside, "less is more" looks crazy and dangerous. Even with their amped up Bill C-51 powers and with the best intelligence in the world, CSIS cannot arrest a person for criminal law purposes. Nor can it lay charges, leading to a prosecution and incarceration.

The most galvanizing recent statement on the dangers of "less is more" was offered to the Senate security committee studying Bill C-51. Joseph Fogarty, a former UK government security liaison in Canada, condemned Canada's arrangement, noting how poorly it compared to the much more seamlessly coordinated anti-terror endeavours of the UK police and the MI5. Commenting on whether he thought the United Kingdom has anything to learn from Canada's operational arrangement between CSIS and the RCMP, Fogarty observed: "with this particular regime, with the greatest of respect, I wouldn't incorporate a single aspect of it, at the minute, because it's dangerous." And averting to CSIS's failure in the Toronto 18 matter to alert the RCMP to the terrorist training camp and its errant surveillance operation, Fogarty stated:

> if you take that sort of decision on an operation and are running up against
> fast-moving, sophisticated opponents, the consequences could be a tragedy.
> . . . [I]magine a situation in which an MI5 team discovers a Provisional
> IRA camp in the U.K. and decides not to tell anybody about it . . . . It's a

tragedy waiting to happen. You have been remarkably lucky, as a country, that you have not faced fast-moving, sophisticated opponents since 2001 because you could have been living in tragedy here.[92]

We will not always be lucky.

How Bill C-51 Pours Fuel on a Dysfunctional Fire

If you accept, as many security professionals have (but we do not), that "less is more" must stay, then Bill C-51's radical decision to give CSIS more muscular threat reduction powers (discussed in Chapter 8) has a grim logic.

Ray Boisvert, former CSIS director of counter-terrorism, alluded to the possibility that the new threat reduction powers would provide CSIS an attractive alternative to disclosure to the police. He told the Commons committee examining Bill C-51 that:

> While I was with CSIS, I often worried that our tool kit was highly restricted by the Canadian Security Intelligence Service Act. Disclosure rules of the day thwarted the flow of potential intelligence leads. Other impediments hampered the transfer of CSIS intelligence into viable evidence for the RCMP . . . I was involved in it in the Toronto 18 investigation and in subsequent terrorism-related charges. I worked with the RCMP as the director general of counterterrorism. I can tell you it is a very complex choreography. This bill will give CSIS a chance to more directly deal with threats without having to engage in that choreography.[93]

As Boisvert aptly notes, the less is more relationship between CSIS and the police requires a "very complex choreography," where CSIS shares only small parts of its intelligence about terrorist conduct with the police through the exchange of formal, lawyered letters.

If you assume that it is rational and necessary for CSIS to not tell the police that they are following the wrong suspect or do not know the location of a terrorist training camp, it makes sense to give CSIS more powers. That way, CSIS can, if necessary, disrupt the suspect or the training camp that the police may not know about. This is better than letting bombs go off, but it is not a long-term solution. CSIS cannot arrest people (although Bill C-51 does not prohibit CSIS from otherwise detaining them). It can watch and now disrupt people. But that does not put terrorists in jail after a fair and public trial.

Scuttled Prosecutions

We may end up paying a high price for the Bill C-51 fix. The deeper a CSIS operation slides into threat reduction, the more difficult it will be to pull it back in the orbit of the criminal justice system. The more active the CSIS investigation, the more that the evidentiary record will be muddied with CSIS human sources, CSIS methods, and perhaps, controversial CSIS conduct.

Consider the implications of CSIS threat reduction operations for the entrapment issues discussed above. The police have experience in running elaborate stings not only in terrorism cases, but also in murder and drug cases including so-called Mr Big operations. So far, they have avoided stays of proceedings in every terrorism prosecution. Bill C-51 may, however, encourage CSIS to get into the sting business as a form of threat reduction. This is new territory for CSIS, and indeed for other intelligence agencies. The available evidence suggests that mistakes are likely to be made. Prosecutions have fallen apart in the past because CSIS and other intelligence agencies have not paid sufficient attention to the rights of the accused. As discussed in Chapter 8, an Ontario trial judge found that CSIS had violated the *Charter* rights of Ayad Mejid when it coerced him into turning over his computer to CSIS as his "last chance" to prove he was not a terrorist. A subsequent child pornography prosecution against Mejid collapsed when the court excluded files found on the computer. The judge found that over two years, CSIS had engaged in a "systemic course of conduct" that was "abusive and oppressive."[94]

CSIS's Australian counterpart, the Australian Security Intelligence Organisation, engaged in aggressive interviewing of a terrorist suspect and university student that a judge characterized as verging on kidnapping, false imprisonment, and trespassing. In the Australian case, the trial judge ruled that the intelligence agency's "conduct was grossly improper and constituted an unjustified and unlawful interference with the personal liberty of the accused."[95] As in the Mejid case, a prosecution — in that case, for training with a terrorist organization — collapsed after the court excluded evidence improperly obtained by the intelligence agency. A subsequent report by the Australian Security Intelligence Organisation's reviewers recommended that the intelligence agency needed training in evidential standards and that there was a "significant potential" for the work of the intelligence agency and the police "to overlap and clash."[96]

Yet, precisely this sort of conduct could now be authorized by Federal Court judges under Bill C-51's threat reduction mandate, so long as it did not result in intentional or negligent bodily harm or willfully obstruct justice. Such an order might protect CSIS officials from the unlikely chance of being prosecuted themselves, but it will not prevent a person charged with terrorism from arguing that CSIS's new acts of disruptive "threat reduction" justify tossing the terrorism prosecution for abuse of process. This means that if the target of CSIS's new powers is ever prosecuted, defence lawyers will be *duty bound* to try to find out what CSIS did by way of threat reduction before the arrest.

The state will inevitably argue that CSIS's prior threat reduction efforts must remain secret. This will then result in a different type of "very complex choreography" in which the Federal Court will decide whether CSIS disruption should remain secret, and the trial judge in provincial superior court will decide whether a fair trial is still possible after either a Federal Court non-disclosure order or a decision that reveals what CSIS did by way of threat reduction. All this will make our already long and complex terrorism cases even longer and more complex. Or it might mean that our comparatively infrequent terrorism trials become even less frequent. The government may opt not to prosecute because it does not wish to risk too much disclosure of what CSIS was doing in its operations.

The Slide from Modest Prosecutions to Continual Disruptions

One possible knock-on and unintended consequence of CSIS threat reduction powers may be that the problematic RCMP-CSIS "less is more" relationship becomes even more anemic. Put another way, Bill C-51 creates structural incentives for even *more* limited information sharing. For one thing, since CSIS can dance alone, it may not need to trigger police involvement. But more than that: CSIS is reluctant to risk disclosure of its human sources and investigative methods now, as an information-gathering service. It almost certainly will be *even more* reluctant to risk disclosure that reveals potentially controversial threat disruption activities. It will not want these operations ripped into the open by an enterprising defence lawyer. The easiest way to guard against that is: don't tell the police.

If the police are never notified, there is no clear exit strategy. CSIS can never arrest and charge those terror suspects it disrupts. Even under Bill C-51, CSIS still does not have law enforcement powers, something confirmed by one of the rare government amendments made after the bill was tabled. This puzzling amendment — specifying for "greater certainty" that CSIS has no "law enforcement powers" — was a response to those critics who claimed Bill C-51 made CSIS a "secret police." The bill never made CSIS a "secret police," even before the amendment. The statement that CSIS is not a law enforcement agency is more a statement of the problem than a solution. In our nightmare scenario, dangerous people are never locked up: the strongest sanction in Canadian anti-terrorism strategy may often no longer be to prosecute, but instead morphs to interrupt, discussed in Chapter 8. The move from prosecute to interrupt is a concern from both a rights and a security perspective.

From a rights perspective, prosecutions are conducted in a public and fair manner and they attempt to avoid false positives, arising when people who are not terrorists are nevertheless treated as such. CSIS operations are the inverse of transparent and conducted on lower standards than apply in the criminal law. In the foreign fighter context, CSIS operations may also involve the use of foreign agencies and persons in some very dangerous and nasty places.

From a security perspective, prosecutions can incapacitate, deter, expose, and punish terrorism in a way that mere interruption cannot. They can expose the violence in terrorism and deglorify ISIS's attempts to recruit. If CSIS uses its new powers to interrupt a plot, and the plotters then disband, they are still radicalized to violence but never incarcerated. CSIS is left to watch these persons, perhaps indefinitely, for the period during which they remain dangerous. Covert surveillance is incredibly expensive and it is imperfect. And somewhere down the road, some disrupted — but not imprisoned — terrorist will slip surveillance and we will, to use Joe Fogarty's words, "be living in tragedy."

If we are right about this, Canada's lackluster record on terrorism prosecutions may get worse — or at least not improve — even as the terrorism threat increases. If this happens, Canada may buck international trends. In 2009, the then RCMP commissioner observed that "counter-terrorism measures based exclusively on intelligence that falls short of the evidentiary threshold are fraught with danger and difficulty" and predicted that terrorism prosecutions "will be the new paradigm of national security in democratic nations the world over."[97] With Bill C-51, Canada appears to be charting its own novel course.

The Need for Clear-Eyed Oversight

There is only one way out of this impasse: robust, all-of-government oversight co-ordinating a refined and defined anti-terror strategy. Someone needs to be in charge of deciding how new CSIS threat reduction powers interface with other anti-terror tools. As we outline in Chapter 11, we are a long way from achieving the goal of all-of-government co-ordination. It is not that the concept of CSIS threat reduction operations is inherently flawed. As we urge in Chapter 8, a specifically enumerated set of proportionate disruption powers may well be warranted. There may be CSIS actions that can contribute new solutions to our security situation — especially if the targets are amenable to dissuasion. But CSIS threat reduction is no answer if it replaces cases that should be prosecuted.

And so here, as in so many other areas, we need all-of-government co-ordination that deploys disruption powers properly, confining it to where it proves useful and not counterproductive, and ensuring that CSIS co-operates more in those cases where prosecution is necessary.

Does Bill C-51 Help Prosecutions at All?

The government will argue that Bill C-51 is not all bad for prosecutions: Bill C-51 recognizes the value of witness protection by expanding the definition of justice system participants who can be protected by publication bans, closed court rooms, and offences outlawing their intimidation. These newly protected persons can include any persons involved in criminal proceedings because they are providing "security information" and foreign-sourced information that is the subject of secrecy claims.[98]

It is possible that some CSIS sources or perhaps even CSIS agents (who more rarely testify in terrorism trials than do UK MI5 agents) might be comforted by the prospect of publication bans and closed courtrooms. But forms of these protections already existed before Bill C-51 for all informers or prospective witnesses. It is not clear that Bill C-51 adds much that will induce more justice system participation by CSIS or its sources.

How Bill C-44 Makes Prosecutions Harder

Bill C-44[99] received much less attention than Bill C-51, but it presents a more direct threat to criminal prosecutions. It guarantees that any human source or informer who has been promised confidentiality by CSIS can veto any subsequent disclosure that might identify him or her, unless innocence is at stake for an accused in a criminal trial.[100] The new power arose in *R v Nuttall* — the British Columbia Canada Day bombing attempt case where the accused tried to force disclosure of CSIS sources. They abandoned the request when the sources and the CSIS director refused to consent and the trial judge ruled that any application would be within the jurisdiction of the Federal Court.[101] The judge's language suggests that attempts by the accused to penetrate the new CSIS informer privilege, even on the limited "innocence at stake" grounds, will have to be decided by the Federal Court, not the trial judge.[102] This would be an extraordinary development, adding yet another complication to terrorism prosecutions and the "complex choreography" of parallel decisions by the Federal Court and the criminal trial court.

In his Air India Commission report, Justice Major rejected the idea that CSIS sources should enjoy the privilege against disclosure subsequently provided in Bill C-44. He reasoned, "CSIS promises of anonymity to human sources might often be premature and could, if the promises were enforceable, jeopardize subsequent terrorism prosecutions."[103] In the Air India investigation, almost all of the important Crown witnesses were confidential CSIS sources first. Most of them were reluctant witnesses. If Bill C-44 had been law at that time, they simply could have said "no" when police and prosecutors asked them to testify. They could even prevent the prosecutor from disclosing identifying information about them that was necessary to obtain (and sustain from *Charter* challenge) a wiretap or other warrant.

Justice Major was not alone in concluding that a new privilege for confidential CSIS sources was a bad idea. The Supreme Court, in a 2014 immigration security certificate decision, also recognized that "the police have an incentive not to promise confidentiality except where truly necessary, because doing so can make it harder to use an informer as a witness. CSIS, on the other hand, is not so constrained. It is concerned primarily with obtaining security intelligence, rather than finding evidence for use in court."[104] In enacting a new privilege for CSIS sources in Bill C-44, the government recklessly ignored the warnings from the Air India Commission and the Supreme Court. We may live to regret giving CSIS this legislative victory if a terrorism prosecution collapses (or is not even taken) as a result. In sum, allowing CSIS sources and the director of CSIS to veto whether a source can be compelled by police or prosecutors to be a witness in a terrorism prosecution may be a good thing for the sources and for CSIS. But it is not a good thing for terrorism prosecutions.

The best rationale for the new privilege is that CSIS requires human sources to do its work. CSIS sources often risk their reputations, friendships, and even their lives. But it is not like CSIS sources were regularly being outed under the old system. And the new privilege is not absolute anyway, at least in relation to the accused. Now, CSIS sources will certainly be better protected, but in a system that demands fair trials, there will be no ironclad guarantees against disclosure to the person being prosecuted. The accused can defeat the privilege if the source has become an active (rather than a passive) agent in the investigation. One terrorism prosecution of a conspiracy to blow up another Air India plane during the 1980s eventually collapsed because the informer lost his privilege by becoming an active agent.[105]

Accused can also penetrate the privilege if necessary to establish their innocence, albeit potentially now at the cost of fighting the matter via the two-court system of Federal Court adjudication if the trial judge's ruling in *Nuttall* is accepted. It is prosecutors — not defendants — whose hands are tied tightest by Bill C-44 and terrorism prosecutions will suffer as a result.

Witness Protection?

So much will now depend on whether confidential CSIS informers will consent to helping the prosecution. If CSIS sources are reluctant, why not offer them witness protection? Alas, witness protection works better in the movies than in real life. (And even in the movies, it rarely works.) A prosecution of the alleged mastermind of the bombing of Air India Flight 182 collapsed when a police informer refused to consent to having his identity disclosed. He turned down an offer of witness protection and the prosecutor in the case admitted he would do the same in the same circumstances.[106]

Some informers will co-operate, of course. Two CSIS sources were used as witnesses in the Toronto 18 prosecutions. One seemed content with the attention; the other received $4 million.[107] So one solution is to pay CSIS informers to persuade them into the courtroom, and steer them away from exercising their Bill C-44 veto.

Money may, in some cases, buy the state out of the full consequences of premature CSIS promises of confidentiality, but it may also undermine the informer's credibility at trial. In any event, a lot of money may be required. Police are familiar with the danger of being shaken down by sources for money. Indeed, a recent Supreme Court case colourfully described a person seeking police informer privilege as "a disappointed suitor for a potentially lucrative co-operating witness contract and an opportunist, not a police informer."[108] Even without the new power of a veto over disclosure, one Toronto 18 informer received $4 million. With the veto now provided by Bill C-44, he may have received closer to his opening demand for $15 million.[109]

One of the witnesses in the Air India trial was placed into witness protection. The experience ruined her life, ending in divorce, separation from her children, and constant residence changes. Looking to cases like these, the Air India Commission recognized that witness protection was a last resort, but recommended that the program be improved and made independent from the RCMP. The government responded in 2013 with the *Safer Witness Act*.[110] This Act, however, rejects the commission's recommendation that witness protection should be taken away from the RCMP (because of conflicts of interest) and placed in the hands of an independent director. The government also rejected the commission's recommendations about the need for an independent, confidential mechanism to resolve frequent disputes between witnesses in the program and the government over the type of protection provided. Instead, the RCMP remains in control of the program. The main remedy that dissatisfied witnesses have is to take their chances and leave the program.[111]

CSIS can nominate sources for witness protection under the 2013 law. Like Bill C-51's expansion of other witness protection mechanisms to include anyone providing a court with security information, this is a potentially positive development that could assist in the transition of intelligence to evidence. We wonder, however, if either of these devices will be used, given the new ability of a CSIS source or the director of CSIS simply to veto identifying information being disclosed. A veto will be much more appealing to CSIS sources than going into witness protection, even though this decision may harm a terrorism prosecution, and perhaps ultimately, the safety of Canadians.

Making Do

The new CSIS human source privilege was a bad idea, but it is now law. Now security officials and prosecutors will have to find some way to work around this impediment.

The Air India Commission recommended that if CSIS sources were granted the type of privilege they have now received in Bill C-44, it would be irresponsible for individual CSIS officers to continue to make routine promises of confidentiality to almost all of their sources. Such promises should only be granted after legal advice and following a close chain of command.[112] Unfortunately, there is little evidence to suggest that CSIS is becoming more sensitive to the reality that much of the intelligence it collects in terrorism investigations may have possible knock-on effects on terrorism prosecutions. For example, the CSIS director told the Commons committee (which spent just two days studying Bill C-44) that CSIS is not "in the business of collecting evidence," even in today's more complex environment.[113] As we describe in Chapter 2, this is the traditional CSIS excuse for distancing itself from the criminal justice consequences of its conduct. It is precisely the excuse CSIS used for its role in Air India.

And even if CSIS is more careful about promising its sources confidentiality, informer privilege can be triggered by implicit, as well as explicit, promises of confidentiality.[114] Given CSIS's role in collecting secret intelligence, we are concerned that almost all CSIS interviews with human sources could be seen as involving at least an implicit promise of confidentiality. When it enacted Bill C-44, Parliament refused to specify that the new CSIS privilege is only triggered by "an explicit promise of anonymity." And so we are left with language that triggers the privilege whenever a source has received "a promise of confidentiality."[115] Hopefully, CSIS will be responsible and sparing in promising sources confidentiality under the new legislation. At the end of the day, however, CSIS is an intelligence agency without law enforcement responsibilities or experience. It will have strong incentives to promise informants confidentiality when necessary to do its job of collecting intelligence. Under Bill C-44, police and prosecutors, and indeed the Canadian public, will have to live with the promises that CSIS makes at an early stage of investigation, even if those promises render subsequent terrorism prosecutions more difficult or even impossible.

The Burden of Canada's Two-Court Game of "Constitutional Chicken"

Spies will be spies. Intelligence agencies throughout the world are concerned with protecting their sources and methods from disclosure. In most countries, criminal trial judges make decisions about whether intelligence is privileged and need not be disclosed to the accused. This makes sense because trial judges are most familiar with their cases. While they can order that an intelligence operation not be disclosed to the accused, they can also revise this decision later in a trial, should the undisclosed material turn out to help the accused's often-evolving defence or undermine some part of the prosecution's case. Trial judges are in charge of their cases.

Why Two Courts Are Not Better than One

In Canada, however, we have not trusted trial judges with information that the Attorney General of Canada (in truth, often CSIS) claims should be secret. The reasons are speculative but likely revolve around concerns that trial judges, unlike Federal Court judges, do not have facilities designed to store top secret material and perhaps may not have the necessary expertise.

Under section 38 of the *Canada Evidence Act*,[116] specially designated Federal Court judges decide whether material that, if disclosed, would harm national security, national defence, or international relations should be given to the accused, perhaps in redacted or summarized form. These are the same judges who decide whether to grant CSIS warrants and who decide challenges to the use of secret evidence in immigration cases, no-fly cases, and passport revocations.

Federal Court judges have not only secure facilities, but also indisputable national security experience. Yet they have little, and often no, criminal trial expertise and even if they did, they would be asked to make disclosure decisions without being familiar with all of the facts of a trial that, in many cases, has not yet started. The Federal Court judges work hard — the section 38 process is an arduous one for all concerned and they must make decisions with the clock ticking on the *Charter* right to a trial in a reasonable time. But the Federal Court often has to make rulings about what can be shielded from disclosure without the full context.

The disclosure decisions made by the Federal Court are generally made before the terrorism trial starts. As seen in the discussion of the *Khawaja* case at the start of this chapter, pre-trial disclosure decisions can be appealed to the Federal Court of Appeal and potentially to the Supreme Court before the terrorism trial even starts. The Air India Commission noted that this is not the norm in criminal trials and recommended that such pre-trial appeals be abolished.[117] The government refused, likely because of concerns that it should be able to appeal Federal Court decisions that required some of CSIS's "Crown jewels" to be disclosed. After all this litigation in Federal Court, the trial judge then has to accept whatever non-disclosure decision the Federal Court makes. But that is not all. The trial judge must then make the difficult decision whether to halt the prosecution because the Federal Court's non-disclosure order has made the trial unfair.

The trial judge may not even know the specifics of the CSIS and perhaps foreign intelligence that the Federal Court has ordered should not be disclosed. Again, this raises both rights and security concerns. Stopping a terrorism prosecution may threaten public safety. Allowing a trial to run without the accused — and potentially even the trial judge — knowing about CSIS intelligence that might truly assist the defence runs a risk of a miscarriage of justice, as occurred in some infamous IRA cases, such as the Birmingham Six case in the United Kingdom, in part because of lack of full disclosure to the accused.[118]

Rejected Proposals to Reform the Two-Court System

The Air India Commission found that this two-court system was unsustainable, especially if secrecy issues arose in the middle of a jury trial and had to be litigated and potentially appealed in the Federal Court.

A non-terrorist trial collapsed when secrecy issues involving national defence information arose in the middle of a jury trial. A second trial was held and resulted in a conviction, but only after twenty months of pre-trial secrecy litigation in the Federal Court. The experienced trial judge, indeed the same trial judge as in *Khawaja*, observed that the two-court process was "cumbersome, and in this case was destructive of the trial process then in mid-course." Justice Rutherford warned of the dangers of "throwing in the towel and saying that we have no capacity to administer criminal justice in cases where national security issues are at stake . . . ."[119] For this sort of reason, the Air India Commission recommended that Canadian trial judges, like trial judges in Australia, the United Kingdom, and the United States, should be able to make — and if necessary, revise — non-disclosure orders during the course of terrorism trials.[120] In other words, trial judges should be in complete charge of their trials. The federal government rejected these recommendations without any public explanation.

Rejected Charter Challenges to the Two-Court System

The federal government might not have wanted to take powers over secrecy matters away from the Federal Court even in criminal cases, but it could have allowed the two-court system to die a slow and well-deserved *Charter* death. One of the judges in the Toronto 18 prosecutions held that the system was unconstitutional because it denied trial judges the right to control their own trial. This avoided trips to the Federal Court during Canada's most successful large-scale prosecution.

But unfortunately, this approach will not recur. The government appealed the constitutional ruling and won. The Supreme Court recognized that the two-court system could "cause delays and pose serious challenges to the fair and expeditious trial of an accused, especially when the trial is by jury,"[121] but decided that the two-court system was constitutional because the trial judge could always stop a trial, should the Federal Court's non-disclosure order make it impossible for the accused to have a fair trial. The Court stressed that "the trial judge may have no choice but to enter a stay." Some participants in the case argued that this approach "puts the Attorney General and the trial courts in the dilemma of playing *constitutional chicken*."[122] For its part, the Court expressed the hope that a sensible application of section 38 would avoid such a result, perhaps using the intermediary of a security-cleared special advocate as a link between Federal and trial courts.

That the Supreme Court refused to strike down the two-court system illustrated that *Charter* litigation remains an imperfect instrument for law reform. And so now, if the trial judge threatens to stay proceedings because of a Federal Court non-disclosure order, the Attorney General of Canada will have to decide whether to blink and abandon the secrecy claim. The police and prosecutors will urge the Attorney General to abandon the secrecy claim, so that years of investigation and prosecution will not go down the drain. Where its intelligence is at stake and especially when some of the intelligence originated from foreign sources, CSIS will argue that disclosure of its "Crown jewels" will harm its continued ability to produce intelligence.

We cannot know who will win these battles within government. We do not even know who decides who wins, although in Chapter 11 we will see that the Air India Commission recommended that the prime minister's national security advisor should resolve such disputes. We are, however, reasonably certain that such battles between spies and cops in the game of constitutional chicken will not make terrorism prosecutions either more efficient or attractive.

Unworkable Workarounds

The two-court system was avoided in the Air India trial, but only because the parties agreed that defence lawyers could examine CSIS documents to see if they contained useful information. They did so, on the condition that they not discuss or share the CSIS documents with their clients. While this approach has been used in the United States, it may no longer be viable in Canada. There is reason to believe that secret access to documents by lawyers unable to share that material with clients violates ethical duties.[123] The Supreme Court has also cast doubt on this approach where the secret in question is the identity of an informer.[124]

The two-court system was most recently avoided in the VIA Rail plot prosecution because the prosecutor wisely gave the trial judge unprecedented access to secret CSIS material.[125] Hopefully this approach will recur. However, the 2015 laws may make such a sensible approach less likely. A judge in the British Columbia Canada Day plot has even suggested that issues under Bill C-44's new statutory CSIS source privilege must be resolved in Federal Court.[126] Moreover, the two-court system may be impossible to work around in foreign terrorist fighter cases that involve secrecy claims to protect intelligence Canada has received from foreign sources — secrets that Canada will generally protect at all costs and so will want to confine to a handful of Federal Court judges.

At Best, an Inefficient and Risky System

Even if we are lucky and no terrorism prosecution is stayed because of secrecy, all the evidence suggests that our two-court system bogs down terrorism trials. In *Khawaja*, the two-court system obviously occasioned substantial delay and was the principal reason that trial was so much longer than its UK counterpart. Terrorism prosecutions — or at least those that involve secrecy claims generally made on CSIS's behalf — will continue to be longer than those in other democracies. The pre-trial (or even in-trial) litigation of secrecy issues places the Federal Court judge in a difficult position given that the issues at trial may not have crystallized. Similarly, the Canadian system places the trial judge in a difficult position of having to accept the disclosure decisions of the Federal Court and decide whether the drastic remedy of a stay is necessary because a fair trial is impossible.

Summary

Canada has a troubled history of terrorism prosecutions, and there is nothing in the 2015 legislation that will improve this record. At most, Bill C-51 has some modest and duplicative witness protection provisions. Meanwhile, CSIS actions under both bills C-44 and C-51 at early stages of terrorism investigations may inadvertently take terrorism prosecutions off the table and out of the anti-terrorist toolkit.

Our position is not that prosecutions are always warranted, or that the demands of prosecution should always trump those of intelligence. It is simply that the government's desire to give CSIS more powers, coupled with its inaction on the Air India Commission's warnings about the present system, will have the unintended effect of making terrorism prosecutions even more difficult, even when they really are the best solution. And the government has done all this at a time when the foreign terrorist fighter problem may require more prosecutions to expose, incapacitate, denounce, punish, and deter the threat.

V. IMPRISONMENT: AN EXIT STRATEGY FROM OUR EXIT STRATEGY?

In criminal proceedings, people go to jail. That is the point — dangerous people are incapacitated in a real way. That is one of the strengths — on top of transparency — of prosecutions. But what happens next? Even prosecution is not always a permanent solution.

Criminal Charges and Denial of Bail as Longer Forms of Interruption

At some level, even bringing charges is a form of anti-terror disruption. Once charged, most accused in terrorism cases will be denied bail pending trial. This fact alone makes criminal charges more attractive than other mechanisms, such as preventive detention, which is discussed in Chapter 8. Once denied bail, the accused will remain in pre-trial detention for much longer than the seven days of preventive arrest provided in Bill C-51.

Since 2001, an accused charged with a terrorism offence has a reverse onus on bail. This means that the accused must establish that pre-trial detention is not necessary to ensure their attendance at trial, to protect the public, or to maintain public confidence in the administration of justice. Although a few accused of terrorist offences — such as Mohamed Hersi, Misbahuddin Ahmed, and Khurram Sher — have obtained bail pending trial,[127] most of those accused of terrorism offences have been denied bail. The reasons are obvious. Those who have plans to engage in foreign terrorist travel or have already engaged in such travel will generally present a flight risk that can justify denial of bail. And even if accused can convince a judge that they are not a flight or safety risk, they will increasingly be subject to pre-trial detention under the public confidence grounds.

In the Toronto 18 prosecutions, Saad Gaya was kept in custody for this public confidence reason, even though his passport had expired while he served two years of pre-trial detention and he could be subject to electronic monitoring. The judge concluded that the pre-trial release of Gaya who had been "demonstrably immersed in a viable plan capable of wreaking catastrophic consequences within Canadian society . . . . would significantly diminish the public's confidence in the administration of justice."[128] The Supreme Court has recently approved this approach, observing that the public confidence ground is legitimate and should be determined by a reasonable person's reactions to the seriousness of the crime and the apparent strength of the prosecution.[129] But the denial of bail is not costless to the state. Traditionally, time spent in pre-trial detention was credited at a 2:1 rate against any sentence imposed, in part to recognize that the time spent in pre-trial detention is "dead time" not counted for eligibility for parole. (The trial judge in *Khawaja* refused to apply the 2:1 rate and Parliament subsequently capped credit for pre-trial custody at a 1.5:1 rate.)[130]

In another terrorism case, the 2:1 rate was applied and this meant that one of the Toronto 18, Asad Ansari — sentenced to six years and five months — was released on the basis of time served because he had served three years and three months in pre-trial custody before being released on strict conditions.[131] The leading academic authority on sentencing in Canadian terrorism cases has found that even after the new pre-trial custody credit cap, "at the lower end of the Canadian spectrum, marginal members of serious plots may continue to receive relatively short sentences, with release after three or four years of custody"[132] mostly spent in pre-trial custody. It is also important to note that pre-trial detention is spent in overcrowded provincial correctional institutes without programming, including programming that targets violent extremism. The significance of pre-trial incarceration for both the accused and society should not, in other words, be discounted.

Lock Them Up and Throw Away the Key?

Part of the appeal of terrorism prosecutions is the prospect of a conviction removing a potentially dangerous person from the community. The life sentences imposed on Momim Khawaja, on appeal, and Zakaria Amara, the ringleader of the Toronto 18 plot, may mean that some convicted terrorists never get out if they cannot convince a parole board that they have been rehabilitated and are no longer a danger to public safety.

Imprisonment Is Just a Long-Term Temporary Solution

But most convicted terrorists will eventually be freed, if only because many terrorism offences have maximum sentences of imprisonment of ten or fourteen years. Of the seventeen terrorism convictions for which sentences had been imposed by July 2015, only four are for life imprisonment. Some may respond that these sentences are too short, given the harm and danger of terrorism. The Supreme Court upheld Khawaja's sentence of life imprisonment in large part because of the seriousness of his conduct, his lack of remorse, and the need to deter and denounce terrorism. But the Supreme Court also rejected a view that rehabilitation has a diminished role in terrorism cases: "[T]he terrorism provisions catch a very wide variety of conduct, suggesting that the weight to be given to rehabilitation in a given case is best left to the reasoned discretion of trial judges on a case-by-case basis."[133] As noted, all of our convictions for post-9/11 terrorism crimes have involved conduct short of actual violence. We have caught and prosecuted people preparing for — and even just anticipating — such violence, because that is what the terrorism laws are designed to do. It is a fundamental principle of criminal justice that sentences must be proportionate to the actual crime and the actual offender.

There is considerable logic in this approach. In Canada's only terrorism financing case — involving several thousand dollars given to the Tamil Tigers — the accused was sentenced to six months. When the government appealed this sentence, the British Columbia Court of Appeal observed, among other things, that the offender's "activities fell at the low end of the scale."[134] Our fear of terrorism and our desire to deter it cannot justify sentences that are disproportionately harsh given what the accused has done.

"In for a Penny, in for a Pound?"

Other plots were not so "low end" — they risked significant death and injury, and as such deserved significant sentences. But they were just that — plots. There was no actual act of terrorist violence. If courts are prepared to turn the screws almost as far as they can go on those who plot, then as soon as the plotting threshold is crossed, the criminal law has no residual deterrence for those considering whether to pursue the plot to its final end. It may well be that the criminal law has no deterrence value anyway for the suicide bomber, but it is reasonable to assume that for every prospective suicide bomber there is a supporting cast of the less blinkered and more doubting — and this supporting cast is more likely to be deterred. "In for a penny, in for a pound" is not the right way to create a criminal deterrence mechanism peeling these people away from terrorist conspiracies.

There is another practical implication to absolutist sentencing in terrorism cases. If "in for a penny, in for a pound" becomes a sentencing principle, we should expect that every terrorism case will be fought to the limits of effort — there will not be much incentive to plead guilty, only to receive the same lengthy criminal sentence. This will compound the expense and difficulty of already expensive and difficult cases.

Terrorist Training Camps behind Bars

We also need to appreciate the consequences of incarceration. It takes people off the street, but when they return, they may be more dangerous than before. We discuss prison radicalization in Chapter 13, but for our purposes here, we note terrorists convicted in Canada have been housed together in a special handling unit.

The segregation of convicted terrorists together is presumably an attempt to prevent the offenders from radicalizing other inmates, but it is hardly likely to contribute to their own rehabilitation. Ray Boisvert, the former CSIS head of counter-terrorism, has commented that while this isolation approach may mean that convicted terrorists "don't infect others," it runs the danger of further radicalization so that when they are released, "they are ready to roll."[135] Canada's intelligence co-ordinating body noted in 2012 "Western Islamists" are sometimes "further radicalized in prisons in countries such as Canada, the United States, Britain, France and Spain."[136] In any event, the imprisonment of all of Canada's convicted terrorist together may not be sustainable, given reports in 2012 that Khawaja had been severely injured by one of the other convicted terrorists.[137]

The fact that some of those in the January 2015 Paris attacks and February 2015 Copenhagen attacks had spent time in prison flags the danger of ignoring issues of rehabilitation and prison radicalization. These problems are complicated in Canada by the fact that many convicted terrorists have served years of pre-trial custody in provincially run jails — a function of the slow pace of Canadian terrorism prosecutions. These holding facilities are notoriously short on rehabilitation services, a fact that (ironically) officials used in an effort to keep Omar Khadr in federal prison to serve out the sentence from his Guantanamo Bay plea bargain.[138]

And we can point to specific instances of apparent prison radicalization in Canada. Mohamed Ali Dirie was imprisoned as part of the Toronto 18 plot — and indeed was already incarcerated on related charges while much of that plot was underway. While in prison (and before he slipped a peace bond to travel to Syria where he is believed to have been killed), Dirie viewed himself as still being a member of the plot and tried to make connections that would allow him to acquire firearms and false travel documents. He also tried to recruit other inmates to his extremist worldview and to his group. Indeed, in 2011, authors from the Macdonald-Laurier Institute described him as the "best known example of a terrorist convict actively promoting terrorism behind bars."[139]

Diversion?

Conscious of the risk that imprisonment may result in further radicalization, officials may themselves be deterred from reaching first for a criminal law solution. Police and prosecutors seem reluctant to lay terrorist charges in some cases of young and misguided individuals, instead relying on dissuasion, peace bonds, and passport revocations. Part of this relates to evidence, and part to the cost and uncertainty of proceeding by way of trial. We suspect, however, that it may also reflect realization that not every problem is a nail best cured with a hammer.

This exercise of discretion is well intentioned and necessary. It will, however, always be more art than science, and we should be wary about its overuse for both security and liberty reasons. A criminal trial is a horrific, arduous process, but it is also a contest in which there are stern expectations on the state. This is much less so with most of the other anti-terror tools discussed in this book. A person subjected to what we call interrupt or restrain tools may never be in a position to clear their name or truly have their day in court. As discussed in Chapter 7, a number of persons subject to peace bonds have agreed to their terms, without the state being obliged to prove anything. Whatever are the considerable flaws of our criminal justice system, many of them exist to guard against false positives. This is much less so for any of the other tools discussed in this book.

Put another way, we remain convinced that criminal trials will remain the fairest and most transparent way to treat would-be terrorists. But at the same time, prosecutors and trial judges must guard against the terrorist label overwhelming their responsibilities to propose and craft sentences that are appropriate — not only for the offence, but the particular offenders. This is especially true for young first-time offenders who are genuinely remorseful and appear amenable to rehabilitation.

This is sociology of the sort we must deploy in a successful anti-terror response. Locking people up — even locking them up for a long time — may only delay our eventual confrontation with the causes of terrorism. As we discuss in Chapter 13, much of the Harper government's rhetoric around this issue (and its comparative neglect of multi-disciplinary approaches to countering violent extremism) has created public and media expectations that anyone convicted of a terrorism offence should be put away for life. Our law does not actually say or do this, and nor should it: terrorism offences are too broad and capture too many people for too much conduct for a one-sized, prison-key-discarding approach to ever be appropriate.

VI. CONCLUSION

Not every would-be or returned foreign terrorist fighter should be prosecuted. In any event, the question of whether they should be is moot. In many cases, such prosecutions will be impossible because of the lack of admissible evidence. Moreover, prosecuting them all would risk overwhelming the system, especially given the inefficiencies in Canadian terrorism trials and the resources they consume.

Nevertheless terrorism prosecutions are necessary in some cases. They have distinct advantages over less restrained and transparent anti-terrorism measures including interdict, restrain, or interrupt strategies. Terrorism prosecutions allow us to expose, denounce, and punish those who intend to engage in terrorism. Our many broad offences in the *Criminal Code* are entirely capable of addressing the terror threats discussed in Chapter 3. Even before the 2013 enactment of four new terrorism offences designed to be applied to those who attempt to leave Canada to join foreign terrorist fights, the Mohamed Hersi case demonstrated that the criminal law could reach those who attempted or urged others to join foreign terrorist fights.

The problem is not (and frankly never has been) the law on the books, but how it is translated into action. The government failed to respond to many identified deficiencies in terrorism investigations and prosecutions in the relative calm before the October 2014 attacks. Subsequent to those attacks, it took steps that will make terrorism prosecutions even more difficult. Bill C-44's new privilege now allows all CSIS sources who have been promised confidentiality to simply refuse to assist the state in a terrorism prosecution. This would have deprived the prosecutor of most of its witnesses in the Air India trial. Prosecutors will now also have to worry not only about protecting CSIS sources from disclosure in terrorism prosecutions, but also about its new powers to engage in foreign surveillance and interrupt security threats. We believe that, together, bills C-44 and C-51 create structural incentives for even *more* anemic information sharing from CSIS to the police. In other words, the "firewall" between parallel terrorism investigations by CSIS and the police may now get even thicker.

The result may be an anti-terrorism toolkit that increasingly stops short of prosecutions and incarceration. This is concerning from a rights perspective — secretive threat reduction "disruption" or "dirty and illegal tricks" measures are ill-suited to a democracy, especially when they also infringe *Charter* rights such as the rights of citizens to leave or return to Canada. It may also be detrimental to security — bad guys need to be imprisoned, and in a democracy, that requires a prosecution.

CSIS's new threat disruption powers make a certain perverse sense under the "less is more" approach that has resulted in CSIS not giving police intelligence about the location of a terrorist training camp. If CSIS will not tell the police about a terrorist threat, it should at least be able to do something about such threats. But the "something" will be shrouded in secrecy and illegality, perhaps approved by a judge. As CSIS goes down its new road of covert disruptions, it may be harder and harder to pull investigations back into the criminal justice system. Prosecutors will realize that it will be very difficult to keep CSIS operations out of court, to ensure that CSIS's sources and methods remain secret, and possibly to avoid an abuse of process claim that may culminate in a stay of proceedings.

CSIS-driven claims of secrecy remain a concern because they still have to be determined in Federal Court, with the trial judge obliged to live with any non-disclosure order, but admonished by the Supreme Court to stay proceedings if there is any doubt that this secrecy will prevent a fair trial. This can result in games of constitutional chicken that undermine confidence in prosecutions as an anti-terrorism tool. We have avoided this two-court system in the past on an ad hoc basis, but we seem to be running out of workarounds. Moreover, secrecy claims that can only be decided in the Federal Court will likely increase under bills C-44 and C-51, especially in cases with an alleged foreign element.

No government should ever have allowed us to reach this impasse. We should not have a system with two possible outcomes: one in which CSIS's threat reduction activities become part of a criminal trial to be protected from disclosure by a protracted Federal Court process, at the risk of a trial judge tossing the case either because of this secrecy or because CSIS's conduct amounted to entrapment or some other abuse of process. And the other: infrequent terrorism trials becoming even less frequent because CSIS will share even less intelligence with the police, but then acts on its own through increasing dosages of threat reduction and surveillance, in an endless cycle of whack-a-mole whose inevitable imperfections put us all at risk.

Canada does not do terrorism trials well, and we are going backwards. Criminal prosecutions are our strongest, sternest, and fairest way of responding to the terrorist threat. Criminal convictions produce solutions that are more lasting than interdict, restrain, and interrupt. Nevertheless, even a conviction and sentence of years does not make the problem go away. Most convicted terrorists will eventually be released, and Canada has already had terrorists further radicalized in prison. In Chapter 13, we will return to the need to address radicalization and rehabilitation of those who have been attracted to terrorist violence. But next, we look at the new speech crime created by Bill C-51.

ANNEX A

Table 9.1: Completed Terrorism Prosecutions in Canada Involving Incidents Occurring after the Enactment of the 2001 *Anti-terrorism Act*

Guide: ss 83.03 (terrorism financing), 83.18 (participating in a terrorist group), 83.19 (facilitating terrorist activity), 83.2 (offence done for benefit of a terrorist group), 83.21 (instructing others to carry out activities for a terrorist group), 83.231 (terrorism hoax)

Source: Internal document marked Canada, *Terrorism Prosecutions in Canada* (as of 16 March 2015), with the outcome updated by these authors to take into account more recently completed trials and terrorism hoax cases added.

Conviction Count	Name	Outcome	Charges	Sentence
Project Awaken				
1.	Khawaja, Momin	Guilty	s 81 (explosives offences) s 83.2 s 83.18 s 83.19 s 83.21 s 83.03	Life
Project O-Sage ("Toronto 18")				
	Aboud, Ibrahim Alkalel Mohammed	–	Charges stayed	Peace bond (1 year)
2.	Adelhaleem, Shareef	Guilty	s 83.18 s 83.2	Life + 5 years, concurrent (minus time served)
3.	Ahmad, Fahim	Pled guilty	s 103 (importing firearms) s 83.18 s 83.21	16 years

Conviction Count	Name	Outcome	Charges	Sentence
4.	Amara, Zakaria	Pled guilty	s 83.18 s 83.2 s 81 (intending to cause an explosion)	Life
5.	Ansari, Asad	Guilty	s 83.18	6 years, 5 months (less time served), 3 years probation
6.	Chand, Steven Vikash	Guilty	s 83.18	10 years
7.	Dirie, Mohamed Ali	Pled guilty	s 83.18	7 years (less time served); peace bond on release (violated terms to travel to Syria, where believed killed)
8.	Durrani, Amin Mohamed	Pled guilty	s 83.18	7.5 years (less time served), 3 years probation
9.	Gaya, Saad	Pled guilty	s 81 (intending to cause an explosion) s 83.2	18 years
	Ghany, Ahmad Mustafa		Charges stayed	Peace bond (1 year)

Conviction Count	Name	Outcome	Charges	Sentence
	Jamal, Qayyum Abdul		Charges stayed	Peace bond (1 year)
10.	James, Jahmaal	Pled guilty	s 83.18	7 years (less time served), 3 years probation
11.	Khalid, Saad	Pled guilty	s 81 (intending to cause an explosion) s 83.2	20 years
	Mohamed, Yasim Abdi		Charges stayed	
12.	Yogakrishnan, Nishanthan	Guilty	s 83.18	2.5 years, 3 years probation
	Youth		Charges stayed	Peace bond (1 year)
	Youth		Charges stayed	Peace bond (1 year)
	Youth		Charges dropped	
Project Summum				
13.	Namouh, Said	Guilty	s 431.2 (explosives offences) s 83.2 s 83.19 s 83.18	Life (plus 8 + 8 + 4 years)
Project Severe				
14.	Hersi, Mohamed Hassan	Guilty	Attempting, s 83.18 Counselling, s 83.18	10 years

Conviction Count	Name	Outcome	Charges	Sentence
Project Samossa				
15.	Alizadeh, Hiva Mohammad	Pled guilty	s 83.18 s 83.19 s 83.2	24 years (less time served)
16.	Ahmed, Misbahuddin	Guilty	s 83.18 s 83.19	12 years
	Sher, Khurram Syed	Acquitted	Conspiracy, s 83.19	
Project Sagittaire				
	Diab, Mouna		Charges dropped	
Project Smooth ("VIA Rail")				
17.	Esseghaier, Chiheb	Guilty	Conspiracy, s 258 (interference with transportation facility) Conspiracy, s 235 (murder) s 83.2 s 83.18 s 83.21	TBD
18.	Jaser, Raed	Guilty	Conspiracy, s 258 (interference with transportation facility) Conspiracy, s 235 (murder) s 83.2 s 83.18	TBD

Conviction Count	Name	Outcome	Charges	Sentence
Project Souvenir				
19.	Nuttal, John Stuart	Guilty	Conspiracy, s 431.2 (placing explosive in public place) s 81 (intending to cause an explosion) s 83.2 s 83.19	TBD
20.	Korody, Amanda	Guilty	Conspiracy, s 431.2 (placing explosive in public place) s 81 (intending to cause an explosion) s 83.2 s 83.19	TBD
Other terrorism cases				
21.	Thambithurai, Prapaharan	Pled guilty	s 83.03	6 months
Terrorism hoax (not a considered a terrorism offence under the *Criminal Code*)				
	Lapolean, Lorne Matthew	Guilty	s 83.231 s 140 (mischief)	2 years probation

Conviction Count	Name	Outcome	Charges	Sentence
	Charest, Lloyd Allen	Guilty	s 83.231 s 137 (fabricating evidence) s 140 (mischief) s 129 (obstructing police officer)	12 months

CHAPTER TEN

Delete: Criminalizing and Censoring Extremist Speech

I. INTRODUCTION

After they kidnapped British diplomat James Cross, the Front de libération du Québec's (FLQ's) first demand was that the press publish their manifesto. It was read on Radio Canada on 8 October 1970 after Prime Minister Trudeau failed to convince the news organization not to publish it. The FLQ manifesto insulted many business and political leaders, including Trudeau. It called on the workers of Quebec: "Make your own revolution in your neighborhoods, in your workplaces . . . . render harmless all the professional robbers and swindlers: the bankers, the businessmen, the judges and the sold-out politicians."[1]

A week later, it was illegal to publish the FLQ manifesto. A regulation made under the *War Measures Act* made it an offence punishable by up to five years imprisonment to communicate statements on behalf of the FLQ or to advocate or promote its "unlawful acts, aims, principles or policies" or the use of force or crime "as a means of accomplishing governmental change in Canada."[2]

Bill C-51 follows in the footsteps of this *War Measures Act* speech crime.[3] It does so by creating a new crime of knowingly advocating or promoting "terrorism offences in general" while knowing or merely being reckless that someone may commit a terrorism offence as a result of the communication.[4] Like the *War Measures Act* offence, this new speech crime is punishable by up to five years imprisonment. A big difference, however, is that the Bill C-51 offence is designed to be permanent, whereas the *War Measures Act* offence lapsed with the emergency.

Bill C-51 also creates a new concept of "terrorist propaganda" defined as "any writing, sign, visible representation or audio recording that advocates or promotes the commission of terrorism offences in general . . . or counsels the commission of a terrorism offence." The government may now seek judicial orders to seize "terrorist propaganda" and delete it from the Internet,[5] and customs officials can seize it at the border.[6]

YouTube Terrorism

The new provisions can be seen as a direct response to videos made by Canadian terrorists. Michael Zehaf-Bibeau, the shooter who killed Corporal Cirillo and assaulted the Parliament buildings in October 2014, is the most famous video maker. In a video captured on his cellphone just before his rampage, he condemned the Canadian military presence in Afghanistan and Iraq, and claimed to be retaliating on behalf of the "Mujahedin of this world" because "Canada's officially become one of our enemies by fighting and bombing us and creating a lot of terror in our countries and killing us and killing our innocents."[7]

But whatever the notoriety of these statements, another famous recording — this one clearly directed at recruiting ISIS (Islamic State of Iraq and Syria) fighters and fuelling more attacks in Canada — may have been the one that inspired the new speech offence. In a video released in December 2014, John Maguire, an Ottawa area convert to Islam who joined ISIS in Syria, stated:

> Oh people of Canada, you are said to be an educated people.
>
> So what is preventing you from being able to put two and two together and understanding that operations such as that of brother Achmed Rouleau of Montreal and the storming of Parliament Hill in Ottawa are carried out in direct response to your participation in the coalition of nations waging war against the Muslim people . . . .
>
> You have absolutely no right to live in a state of safety and security when your country is carrying out atrocities on our people . . . .
>
> Your people will be indiscriminately targeted as you indiscriminately target our people.
>
> I warn you of punishment in this worldly life at the hands of the mujahideen and I would also like to warn you of a greater punishment, and that is the eternal punishment of hell fire promised for those who die not having submitted as Muslims to the one true god of all that exists.

Maguire then goes on to tell Muslims that they must either engage in terrorist violence or emigrate to the new homeland:

> You either pack your bags, or you prepare your explosive devices.
>
> You either purchase your airline ticket, or you sharpen your knife.
>
> You either come to the Islamic State and live under the laws of Allah, or you follow the example of brother Achmed Rouleau and do not fear the blame of the blamers.[8]

The government seemed to justify its new speech offence in Bill C-51 as necessary to target exactly the type of speech at issue in the Maguire video. Justice Minister Peter MacKay argued that the new speech offence was directed at those who "actively encourage some sort of unspecified action should be taken to do something bad against Canadians or our allies, or to do something to support extreme jihadism. Whether specific or unspecific, these statements are harmful."[9] He equated the new crime with existing crimes against hate speech, advocating genocide, and inciting other crimes.[10]

Terrorist Blather

Would Maguire be guilty under the new offence? The first point to make is that Maguire had long since crossed the line between non-criminal and criminal conduct. His travel to join ISIS, his participation with ISIS (including in making the video), and perhaps his instructions in the video to commit violence were already terrorist offences before Bill C-51.[11] In other words, real terrorist propaganda — done for and with terrorist groups — was a crime even before the new speech offence.

But nuance is required in parsing the actual speech itself. Maguire's first lines may amount to the crime of uttering threats but also seem to be an extremist attempt to interpret and justify the October 2014 terrorist attacks. In Europe this might be a crime of "apologie" or glorification of terrorism. The most notorious of European glorification cases is probably that of Denis Leroy. French authorities prosecuted Leroy for his cartoon portraying the 9/11 attacks accompanied by the caption "We all dreamed of it . . . Hamas did it," published in a Basque daily newspaper in southern France days after 9/11. The French authorities charged the cartoonist with complicity in the expansive French crime of "apologie du terrorisme."[12] The government does not believe that its Bill C-51 speech crime reaches this kind of abstract glorification. And we would be shocked if such a prosecution were successful on this continent, given North America's more robust freedom of expression rules. "Hurray for the terrorists" is not, in other words, criminal speech in Canada, at least not because of its content alone.

But the second Maguire quotation above crosses several criminal lines, including under pre–Bill C-51 criminal law. In it Maguire argues that good Muslims should either come and join ISIS (itself the terrorist offence of leaving Canada to participate in the activities of a terrorist group) or do something bad with a knife or explosives in Canada. If saying all this was a crime already, would it also be a crime under the new speech offence? To convict Maguire for the second set of statements under the Bill C-51 speech crime, the prosecutor would have to prove only that he knowingly promoted "terrorism offences in general" while being aware, at minimum, of a risk that someone (regardless of that someone's mental state) might commit an offence as a result. There would be no defence of commenting on matters of political and religious opinion even though Maguire's video contained much (misguided) political and religious commentary. As we discuss at length below, the outer reach of the concept of "terrorism offences in general" and how the elements of the offence work together are utterly ambiguous. But there is also an inner reach — and it seems very likely that Maguire's statements do fall into a zone barred by the new crime.

But the story does not stop there. Someone who re-posts Maguire's videos, or even publishes his statements, could be charged under the new offence as a person who aided the offence. Here, the Crown would have to prove that such a person intended to assist Maguire in accomplishing his objectives. But more than this, the government could seek a court order obliging those who have posted Maguire's video to remove it from the Internet or allowing the government to seize hard copies or other media containing the statements. Here, the intent of the poster would likely be irrelevant: material that fits the definition of terrorist propaganda can be seized or deleted no matter why a person may be reproducing the message.

New Speech Crime as Political Theatre

Of course, we have no sympathy whatsoever for the content of Maguire's message. There are many messages on the Internet with which we sternly disagree. But the criminal law is a blunt instrument for responding to bad ideas, and it is one guaranteed to attract scrutiny under the *Charter of Rights and Freedoms*.[13] In its present guise, the new speech crime and the aspects of it integrated into the concept of terrorist propaganda likely violate the *Charter*.

The state's fight against terrorism is a battle against violence and not a battle against ideas, even extreme ideas. In the 1970s, it was a tactical mistake for the state to charge the radical intellectual Pierre Vallières, sometimes called Quebec's Malcolm X, with counselling crimes though his incendiary and controversial pro-FLQ tracts, including his book *Nègres Blanc d'America*.

Vallières welcomed the prosecutions and wrote that it was "very important for the FLQ and for the Québec revolution to have driven the Crown and the Court to politicize my trial themselves . . . . by placing my writings, ideas, political activities at the center of the debates . . . ."[14] Moreover, he won twice on appeal with the courts holding that his speech was too attenuated from the bombings he was charged with inciting.[15] We expect that the same thing — political trials and ultimately legal (now *Charter*) victories — will happen under the new speech offence.

The focus of the criminal law should be on violence, not ideas, and Maguire was already a terrorist criminal several times over without the new speech offence. Being an ISIS propagandist is a form of participation with a terrorist group that is already criminalized in Canada. And at least one individual, convicted in 2010, is already serving time for exactly this offence, and for facilitating terrorist activity through propaganda for a terrorist group.[16] A second person is facing charges laid in July 2015, not under the new speech offence, but under the existing terrorism offences against counselling or inciting murder and other forms of violence for the benefit of a terrorist group, namely ISIS.[17]

In committing crimes like "participating" with a terrorist group by, among other things, making a promotional recruitment video, Maguire became subject to a penalty much stricter than the five years' imprisonment available under the new speech crime. If a trial were ever held under existing terrorism offences, the content of the video would be almost incidental. All that would matter is that he made the video "for the purpose of enhancing the ability of [a] terrorist group to facilitate or carry out a terrorist activity."[18] And he surely had that purpose.

Put another way, our traditional terrorist crimes are either content neutral when it comes to speech or tied to content that is much more proximate to actual terrorist violence (such as counselling or inciting murder) than is the new speech crime. And, indeed, the more content neutral approach was followed in January 2015 when Maguire (who many believe was killed in Syria) was charged *in absentia* not for his video per se but for facilitating a terrorist activity for ISIS.[19] Such charges put the emphasis where it should be: on violence, not on the ideas and grievances that may motivate violence. Maguire's charges, the July 2015 counselling murder charges, and the earlier 2010 conviction for terrorist propaganda done for a terrorist group all belie the claim made by government that existing laws were inadequate.

Pernicious Propaganda

The government will argue, with some justification, that analogies to the FLQ and Pierre Vallières are quaint and out of date. Much of ISIS's success in recruiting people from Canada and elsewhere has been attributed to its use of social media and slickly edited videos that ISIS and its supporters make available on Twitter, YouTube, Facebook, and other social media. This has made terrorist propaganda more readily available and censorship more difficult. Private Internet companies have co-operated but have not always enthusiastically embraced a policing role. At any rate, the cancellation of Twitter and other accounts has resulted in other forms of social media being used.

The whack-a-mole effort to limit Internet propaganda may be worth it if it stalls the dissemination of terrorist messages.[20] But the whack-a-mole issue is quite different from the issue of having trials and locking up people who say the wrong thing. In other words, "Should propaganda be censored?" and "Should people be jailed for expressing extreme views?" are distinct questions. They do not require an identical answer.

As we discuss below, we think terrorist propaganda — properly defined — should be displaced from the Internet to the extent possible. But, ironically, the Bill C-51 definition of terrorist propaganda (with its tie to the new speech crime) manages to be both overinclusive and underinclusive in not reaching the full range of terrorist propaganda. As we explore in examples below, its careless sweep is such that it can reach speech (and therefore justify censorship under the new propaganda deletion and seizure rules) that may simply express extreme ideas. But, at the same time, it also falls short and fails to censor speech such as how-to manuals about bomb building.

The government may have intended the new speech offence to be its main instrument in a "hearts and minds" approach designed to counter ISIS's attraction to some. But it is far from clear that the new speech offence (and the related propaganda concept) would apply to all of ISIS's propaganda, some of which is more nuanced than grisly examples of beheadings. Take, for example, an ISIS recruitment video featuring Canadian Andre Poulin, released in mid-2014. In his video, Poulin promised recruits the following: "You'd be very well taken care of here. Your families would live here in safety, just like how it is back home. You know we have expanses of territory here in Syria." Another video by a British recruit stated, "Living in the West — I know how you feel — your heart feels depressed. The cure for depression is Jihad."[21]

Like Maguire, Poulin was already a criminal under the original 2001 anti-terror laws simply because of participating in ISIS activities, including the making of this video. But the video itself does not appear to fit the definition of terrorist propaganda or offend the content rules in the new speech crime, as best as anyone can understand them. This might surprise some people. For our part, we do not regret this rare instance of constraint in Bill C-51's speech rules. Banning speech that is not closely tied with violence is not part of our democratic tradition. A free and democratic society does not allow threats of violence, but it has faith that people will reject ideas that condone or even encourage violence. And both past experience and contemporary technology lead us to doubt that the banning of speech can be done effectively, without knock-on effects more detrimental than the benefits achieved.

As we will suggest in Chapter 13, there is a need for a multi-disciplinary approach to tarnishing the lure of ISIS. Put another way, we need to work on the demand side of terrorist propaganda and not resort exclusively or even primarily to heavy-handed and whack-a-mole responses to the supply side. The quick and coercive fix of censorship of speech distantly connected to actual violence will not work and may be counterproductive especially if it deters less coercive "hearts and minds" strategies.

II. THE NEW SPEECH CRIME

Introduction

The new speech crime in Bill C-51 does not reach quite as far as a United Kingdom–style "glorification" of terrorism offence, first recommended in Canada by a House of Commons committee in 2007 and then recommended again after the enactment of Bill C-51 by the Conservative majority of the Senate security committee.[22] Rather the new speech crime seems to draw more inspiration from an Australian "advocacy" of terrorism offence enacted in 2014.[23] Such borrowing is common when terrorism law is hastily drafted, but it raises the question of whether the new crime is appropriate for Canada or consistent with the specific demands of the Canadian *Charter of Rights and Freedoms*.

A Short Review of Criminalized Speech in Canadian Law

In 2007, the House of Commons committee reviewing the 2001 *Anti-terrorism Act* proposed that Canada follow the United Kingdom's lead and enact a glorification of terrorism offence. Members of the NDP and Bloc Québécois dissented on the basis that a glorification offence would infringe freedom of expression.

The position endorsed by the Conservatives and Liberals went further than that apparently advanced in hearings by the B'nai Brith, calling for a new offence of inciting terrorist activities. The committee majority preferred a broader approach because it feared incitement offences, as well as hate crimes, might not apply to "diffuse and untargeted" incitement to terrorism that did not instruct specific persons.[24] This was a view later shared by the government in the Bill C-51 debates. In justifying its new speech crime, the official government backgrounder asserted that "the current law would not necessarily apply to someone who instructs others to 'carry out attacks on Canada' because no specific terrorism offence is singled out."[25]

These views may reflect a misunderstanding of the Vallières case — there, the courts acquitted Vallières on the basis that the Crown had not proven he had incited a specific bombing. But they also recognized that the result might have been different had the prosecutor used a more widely defined indictment.[26]

Speech and Punishment

The government's demand for a new speech crime ignored the ability of existing criminal laws to cover much threatening speech. It was already an offence in Canadian criminal law to counsel the commission of an offence, any offence. Counselling, in modern Canadian law, is a sweeping concept. It means to "procure, solicit or incite,"[27] "induce or advocate — and . . . not merely describe — the commission of an offence."[28] A person who counsels another becomes a party to an offence if the counselled person then perpetrates the offence, or engages in another offence that was likely to be committed because of the counselling.[29] Moreover, a person who intentionally or knowingly counsels the commission of a crime is guilty of an offence even if the counselled crime never occurs.[30]

Counselling can be a terrorism offence. A person who implores others to commit terrorism crimes, including leaving Canada to join ISIS, can be convicted for it. Mohamed Hersi was jailed in 2014 for counselling an undercover officer to go to Somalia and join the terrorist group al-Shabaab.[31] More recently, Othman Hamdan was charged in July 2015 with counselling murder and various forms of assault to benefit ISIS, apparently in the form of online activities.[32]

And counselling is not the only traditional speech crime. We have already discussed seditious libel in Chapter 2 — a much criticized crime arising where one teaches, advocates, publishes, or circulates any writing that advocates "the use, without the authority of law, of force as a means of accomplishing a governmental change within Canada."[33] Also of note is the much more mainstream crime of "uttering threats," that is, saying things that threaten a person with death or bodily harm, or damage to property.[34]

More recent and famous are Canada's various hate crime offences. It is a crime to communicate statements in any public place and thereby incite "hatred against any identifiable group where such incitement is likely to lead to a breach of the peace."[35] And in an offence that served as a clear template for the Bill C-51 crime, advocating or promoting genocide is also a crime — that is, speech tied to the intent to destroy in whole or in part any identifiable group, killing members of the group or "deliberately inflicting on the group conditions of life calculated to bring about its physical destruction."[36] Likewise, and subject to several defences listed below, it is a crime to communicate statements other than in private conversation that willfully promote, as in "actively support" or "instigate,"[37] hatred against any identifiable group.[38] "Identifiable group" has recently been expanded to mean "any section of the public distinguished by colour, race, religion, national or ethnic origin, age, sex, sexual orientation or mental or physical disability."[39]

Terrorist Speech

And all that applies even before we get to specialized terrorism offences. After 9/11, Parliament enacted a host of crimes that, broadly speaking, doubled down on the counselling concept. The application of these terrorist crimes to speech acts has been underappreciated. One reason why the speech reach of Canada's fourteen separate pre–Bill C-51 terrorism offences[40] is not fully understood is because of the complex way in which these offences have been drafted.

One element incorporated in almost all of the terrorism offences is the definition of "terrorist activity" in the *Criminal Code*. "Terrorist activity" includes a variety of politically, ideologically, or religiously motivated acts of violence designed to intimidate the public with regard to its security or to compel governments, international organizations, or even "persons" to act. More notable in the speech context is a little-noticed subclause of the definition stating that a terrorist activity also includes "a conspiracy, attempt or threat to commit such act or omission . . . or counselling in relation to any such [violent] act or omission."[41]

Speech in the form of threats or counselling can, in other words, be a terrorist activity when tied to certain forms of violence listed in the definition. And in addition the many special terrorism offences relating to funding, facilitating, instructing terrorist activity, and participating in a terrorist group can criminalize activity that is itself based largely on particular forms of expression. The end effect is the piling of speech liability on top of speech liability. For instance, a person is a terrorist for soliciting funds[42] to support the speech acts of counselling or threatening to commit a terrorist activity.

This piling of speech crimes is even more obvious with terrorism offences that are emphatically speech related. These include "instructing to carry out terrorist activity" and also "instructing to carry out activity for a terrorist group." Thus, it is an offence punishable by life imprisonment to knowingly instruct,

> directly or indirectly, any person to carry out a terrorist activity . . . . whether or not
> (*a*) the terrorist activity is actually carried out;
> (*b*) the accused instructs a particular person to carry out the terrorist activity;
> (*c*) the accused knows the identity of the person whom the accused instructs to carry out the terrorist activity; or
> (*d*) the person whom the accused instructs to carry out the terrorist activity knows that it is a terrorist activity.[43]

This is an astonishingly broad crime. It is difficult to see, reading its elements, how the Commons committee believed in 2007 that our existing law could not reach statements made where no particular individual is "encouraged to emulate any specific actions."[44] After all, the offence clearly states that it applies to both direct and indirect instruction and that it does not matter whether the speaker instructs a particular person or whether the speaker knows who will carry out the terrorist activity. All that really matters is that the thing instructed be a terrorist activity. And that is not much of a restraint given the breadth of terrorist activity. As already noted, "terrorist activity" itself may involve speech acts of threatening or counselling. And so it would be a crime to instruct someone to threaten an act of terrorist violence.

The statements made by John Maguire in his ISIS video may well have crossed the line into terrorist instruction: "You either pack your bags, or you prepare your explosive devices. You either purchase your airline ticket, or you sharpen your knife. You either come to the Islamic State and live under the laws of Allah, or you follow the example of brother Achmed Rouleau and do not fear the blame of the blamers." It requires no imagination to know what he is instructing.

Furthermore, even if a person does not instruct an actual terrorist activity, instructing *anything* for a terrorist group is a crime — something Maguire also did. It is an offence punishable by life imprisonment to knowingly instruct a person to carry out "any activity for the benefit of, at the direction of, or in association with a terrorist group, for the purpose of enhancing the ability of any terrorist group to facilitate or carry out a terrorist activity."[45] On its face, this offence could apply to propagandists who post material on the Internet or engage in other speech acts so long as their purpose is to enhance the ability of a terrorist group to facilitate or carry out a terrorist activity.

Extrapolating from Supreme Court cases, we do think that there is an outer limit to these broad offences:[46] speech is probably criminalized only so long as there is more than a *de minimis* risk of harm stemming from that speech. So marching in a protest may not satisfy this *de minimis* standard, but recording a video with the express purpose of recruiting persons to a terrorist group likely does. Likewise, preaching a duty to engage in terrorist activity or join a terrorist group likely amounts to terrorist instruction and participation, at least absent further judicial limitation of the broad offences in the name of freedom of speech.

And, indeed, these post-9/11 offences have been used successfully against terrorist-linked speech in the past. For example, in the 2010 *R v Namouh* case,[47] the accused was charged and successfully prosecuted for, among other things, "enthusiastically participat[ing] in most of [a terrorist group's] propaganda activities." The accused had participated in conveying "a message to Austria and Germany threatening terrorist action if their soldiers are not withdrawn from Afghanistan." He had also participated in most of the group's more clearly propagandistic activities including (as described by the court):

1. analyzing the speeches of Al Qaeda leaders
2. inciting violent jihad
3. calling for support for jihadist groups
4. redistributing Al Qaeda materials
5. acting as a spokesperson for captured jihadists
6. singing the praises of jihadist leaders who died for the cause
7. ensuring the security of online communications between jihadists
8. taking part in psychological warfare
9. providing military training with the purpose of implementing violent jihad
10. producing a series of videos called the "Califate Voice Channel," with the aim of transmitting news from the jihadist front
11. publishing jihadist magazines online
12. acting as an official media outlet for two groups taking part in terrorism.[48]

The accused was deeply invested in his cause and was not an idle apologist of things terroristic. This undoubtedly contributed to his conviction for various terrorism offences. The behaviour cited by the court in support of the participation and facilitation convictions ranged from outright threats to speech more distantly linked to violence, including some speech that may simply have amounted to forms of radicalized boasting. Nevertheless, Namouh's speech acts contributed to his convictions because they were uttered in a manner that involved actual participation with a terrorist group. A conviction such as this demonstrates that even speech removed from actual violence could be penalized before Bill C-51.

Two Steps Too Far: United Kingdom–Style Glorification Offence

The Criminal Offences

The United Kingdom *Terrorism Act 2006* introduced two new offences aimed at speech: "encouragement of terrorism" and "dissemination of terrorist publications."[49] Both impose maximum sentences of seven years imprisonment. In both instances, the crimes reach "indirect encouragement" presumed to include statements or publications that glorify the commission or preparation of terrorism crimes whether in the past, future, or generally so long as members of the public could reasonably infer that the glorified behaviour was conduct that was to be emulated in the existing circumstances. Glorification includes "any form of praise or celebration, and cognate expressions are to be construed accordingly."[50]

The United Kingdom's dissemination of terrorist publications offence focuses "not on the original publisher but on those who pass the publication on."[51] It appears to reach Internet service providers and the owners of websites on which people can post statements.[52] In fact, a third provision in the United Kingdom Act established detailed rules for statements or publications communicated via Internet (or electronically).[53] Once a constable gives notice to a person that — in the opinion of the constable — a statement or article is "unlawfully terrorism-related" and that it should be removed from public circulation, absent compliance within two days that person is presumed to endorse the statement or article. (In practice, police give this notice in consultation with the Crown Prosecution Service.)[54]

The presumed endorsement is not an offence in its own right but does narrow the basis for any defence if the person is then charged with encouragement of terrorism or dissemination of terrorist publications. Most people served with a notice, however, may not appreciate such fine legal distinctions.

"Unlawfully terrorism-related" material includes material that directly or indirectly encourages or induces the commission, preparation, or instigation of a terrorism act or that is likely to be useful in the commission or preparation of such acts. As noted, glorification is listed as a form of indirect encouragement.

The Prosecutions

The United Kingdom *Terrorism Act 2006* came into force in April 2006. Between that time and March 2014, there were four instances where the principal charge brought against a person was for encouragement of terrorism,[55] and three convictions.[56] There were twelve instances where the principal charge was for dissemination of terrorist publications,[57] and eight convictions.[58] In some cases, the charge for possession or dissemination of custom, or self-made, al-Qaida-inspired material was redundant. The behaviour recorded on the various videos probably already amounted to another more kinetic terrorism offence.[59]

Some United Kingdom cases involved videos or other materials that portrayed things being blown up or people being killed, sometimes with laudatory narrative and sometimes in an instructional manner.[60] Examples of the latter would include an "anarchist cookbook" compiling bomb-making instructions culled from the Internet[61] or an al-Qaida-inspired how-to manual.[62] Some cases involved materials mixing what might be called extremist al-Qaida-inspired polemics with suggestions on how to commit terrorist acts.[63] Much, if not all, of this would in Canada be captured under existing criminal offences relating to counselling terrorism crimes or instructing terrorist activity.

Criminalizing Extremist Literature

The more troubling United Kingdom prosecutions involved prosecutions for so-called extremist literature.[64] A notable example is *R v Faraz*, a case in which a bookstore owner who had no role in specific terrorist plots was convicted of dissemination of terrorist publications and sentenced to three years imprisonment. The material in question that Faraz sold included 653 copies of *Milestones*, a book by Sayyid Qutb described further below, and 424 copies of *Malcolm X, Bonus Disc*, a film that includes interviews with fighters from Afghanistan. The prosecution led evidence that several of the publications had been found in the possession of past terrorist plotters, and indeed offered a statistical portrait on this point. In sentencing, the trial judge told the accused the following: "It is grossly irresponsible to publish these books in the way that you have published them . . . . They were published differently to appeal to young people who had recently converted to Islam or became more religiously inclined as they got older . . . . These books did glorify terrorism. They implied approving of such attacks as 9/11 or 7/7."[65]

The conviction was reversed on appeal because the Court of Appeal concluded that the use of past cases in which terrorist plotters had been found in possession of the impugned publications was unduly prejudicial: "it is not known (and probably could not be reliably ascertained) how many young Muslim men, who had no terrorist intentions whatsoever, possessed the relevant material or other reasonably comparable material."[66] On this ground, the convictions were quashed.

Free expression interests attracted surprisingly superficial judicial treatment in this and other United Kingdom cases. Defence counsel urged that the publications were not an encouragement to unlawful terrorist acts but rather the expression of political and religious opinion. In a view upheld by the appeal court, the trial judge instructed the jury to disregard the defence's argument to the extent that it encouraged disregard of the law of England and Wales as free speech was not absolute.[67]

In the end, Faraz was successful in his appeal, but only because of the Crown's use of prejudicial evidence. Put another way, this was a procedural loss for the government, not a substantive indictment of glorification crimes.

One Step Too Far: The New Speech Offence in Bill C-51

In Bill C-51, the government stepped back from apparent early enthusiasm for a United Kingdom–style glorification offence, but not very far. It instead enacted a somewhat more restrained offence, inspired by Australian legislation enacted in 2014[68] and drawing on Canada's "advocating or promoting genocide" crime. In so doing, the government added a fifteenth terrorism offence to the *Criminal Code*.

The Excessive Crime

The new speech crime provides as follows:

> Every person who, by communicating statements, knowingly advocates or promotes the commission of terrorism offences in general — other than an offence under this section — while knowing that any of those offences will be committed or being reckless as to whether any of those offences may be committed, as a result of such communication, is guilty of an indictable offence and is liable to imprisonment for a term of not more than five years.[69]

The expression "terrorism offences in general" is unknown in Canadian law, and its exact meaning is impossible to assert with certainty. Certainly, the phrase "terrorism offences" is defined in the *Criminal Code* — and includes all of the terrorist crimes we mentioned above as well as other serious offences committed for the benefit of, at the direction of, or in association with a terrorist group. And so the new offence piles another speech crime onto terrorist offences that already criminalize speech.

The results are striking especially when you consider that terrorism offences (and the underlying concept of terrorist activity) reach conduct outside of Canada as much as inside. Here is an example of speech that advocates or promotes "terrorism offences": "In this era of catastrophic climate change, I believe that all people of good conscience should call on their compatriots to threaten civil disobedience — including threatening outright violence and vandalism intended to risk public health — to stop the flow of oil in Canada's most important pipelines." Converted to legalese, this speech is advocating an instruction to threaten an act that amounts to terrorist activity. The next two examples amount to advocating terrorism financing of a terrorist activity: "I believe that this country should financially support a new rebel movement in the Ukraine prepared to use force to destroy Russian oil and other strategic Russian infrastructure to create new public safety risks for a Russian population that has embraced Russian aggression in the Ukraine." "People should support the struggles to establish Palestine as a well-functioning state. As such they should send money to Hamas to support its efforts in educating, feeding, and caring for children who are suffering in Palestine." Given the listing of Hamas as a terrorist group under Canada's criminal law, as well as its participation in acts of terrorism, this last statement could amount to advocating the provision of property to benefit a terrorist group, a crime regardless of how that property is then used or why that property was given.

All of these statements are controversial, but we believe it is better that they are said and denounced as stupid rather than turned into prosecuted and martyred ideas. Nor do we think that people who aid and abet these kinds of statements — say, by intentionally providing a venue for their speakers — should go to jail, something that is in theory possible under the new speech offence.

Adding Imprecision to Excess: Of Supporting "Extreme Jihadism," Qutb, Fanon, Boycotts, and Conservative Party Ads

The new offence would be bad enough if it reached only this far. But the government chose also to add "in general" to the "terrorism offences" reference. In so doing, it clearly wanted to reach advocating or promoting conduct that could not be as easily reduced to the specific terrorism offences noted in the examples above. As mentioned previously, Justice Minister MacKay went so far as to state that the new offence will apply to those who "actively encourage some sort of unspecified action . . . to do something bad against Canadians or our allies, or to do something to support extreme jihadism."[70]

Minister MacKay's statement should not be ignored, if only because it emanated from the Office of the Attorney General. But, in fact, we are skeptical that it is enough under the speech crime simply to call for "something bad" to happen to a Canadian ally or endorse "extreme jihadism," whatever that is. The "something bad" would at least need to be moored in something cognizable as terrorism, as would the "extreme jihadism." To allude to a small, and rather silly, controversy that arose around the time of the Bill C-51 debates (albeit in relation to hate crimes):[71] We do not think that it is now a crime to say "Boycott Israel."

Nevertheless, Minister MacKay's statement is both revealing and disconcerting. Like some of Prime Minister Harper's statements about "jihadis" declaring "war" on Canada, it blurs the distinct categories of war and crime and suggests a willingness to use both instruments against those who are defined as enemies. The rule of law is supposed to be an impartial instrument that applies to all, and not one that selectively protects "Canadians or our allies," to use Minister MacKay's term.

More plausible, but very troubling, candidates covered by the new speech offence can be found in established (if radical) political literature. Sayyid Qutb was one of the "'intellectual fathers' of the modern Islamic fundamentalist movement."[72] He was the author of the book *Milestones* (as it is known in English), first published in 1964, and the tract that prompted the prosecution under the United Kingdom speech laws described above. *Milestones* is the subject of academic study, and scholars regard it as establishing Qutb "as the twentieth century's most important Islamist thinker and writer."[73] Among other things, the book propounds a doctrine of jihad as holy war of an offensive (and not purely defensive) nature.[74]

Compared by some to Lenin's *What Is to Be Done*,[75] *Milestones* is a revolutionary tract that has clearly influenced Islamist militants, including the terrorist movement led by Osama bin Laden.[76] It is, however, more an ideological treatise than a how-to guide with terrorism tactics or tools. Moreover, as we can attest, it is readily available — including on Amazon websites.

And yet, in this book, Qutb says things that seem to fit what the government had in mind in outlawing advocacy of "terrorism offences in general," tied to "extreme jihadism":

This movement [to abolish "man made" laws] uses . . . physical power and Jihaad for abolishing the organizations and authorities of the *jahili* [basically, non-Islamic] system which prevents people from reforming their ideas and beliefs but forces them to obey their erroneous ways [that is, what they want to do] and make them serve human lords instead of the Almighty Lord.[77]

There is no compulsion in religion; but when the above mentioned obstacles and practical difficulties ["the political system of the state, the socio-economic system and behind all these, the military power of the government"] are put in [Islam's] way, *it has no recourse but to remove them by force* so that when it is addressed to peoples' hearts and minds they are free to accept or reject it with an open mind.[78]

Of course, not all radical thinkers are associated with Islam. Frantz Fanon was born in colonial Martinique and was a leading intellectual influence in the decolonization struggles of the post–Second World War world. Like many people of our vintage (at least), we read his work as undergraduates. Today's professors assigning such readings may wish to consider the extent to which they express agreement with this passage from Fanon's famous anti-colonial polemic, *The Wretched of the Earth*:

> The naked truth of decolonization evokes for us the searing bullets and bloodstained knives which emanate from it. For if the last shall be first, this will only come to pass after a murderous and decisive struggle between the two protagonists. That affirmed intention to place the last at the head of things, and to make them climb at a pace (too quickly, some say) the well-known steps which characterize an organized society, can only triumph if we use all means to turn the scale, including, of course, that of violence.
>
> You do not turn any society, however primitive it may be, upside down with such a program if you have not decided from the very beginning, that is to say from the actual formulation of that program, to overcome all the obstacles that you will come across in so doing. The native who decides to put the program into practice, and to become its moving force, is ready for violence at all times. From birth it is clear to him that this narrow world, strewn with prohibitions, can only be called in question by absolute violence.[79]

On a purely textual basis, these passages by Qutb and Fanon appear to advocate or promote terrorism offences "in general." What else could Fanon's "murderous" struggle using "absolute violence" be, in an armed decolonization struggle? And while Qutb's meaning has been contested, his call for the removal of a socio-economic system "by force" appears to be exactly the sort of generic call to arms that the government wishes to penalize.

Qutb and Fanon are dead and so not amenable to Canadian criminal prosecution. But we ourselves must wonder about our legal exposure for reproducing these passages. Have we "knowingly" promoted (as in encouraged) "terrorism offences in general"? After all, we know what we have done, and we know what these statements say and call for. We would not desire a terrorist outcome — but unlike the "willfully promoting" concept used in the hate crimes that have survived constitutional challenges,[80] "knowingly promoting" does not require us to desire that outcome or have it as our purpose.

Moreover, a final proviso in the offence requires even less fault. All that is required is that the accused either knows that or is *reckless* about whether any terrorism offence may be committed as a result of the communication. "Recklessness" in Canadian criminal law requires only subjective advertence to the possibility or risk that the prohibited act will occur. In other words, people could be on the hook under the new offence if they knowingly promote "terrorism offences in general" while aware of the possibility that someone — anyone — may commit any terrorism offence as a result.

Of course, we would not be alone in "knowingly" promoting "terrorism offences in general" while not desiring a terrorist outcome. Media outlets reproduce ISIS videos all the time. And, indeed, before Bill C-51's enactment, the Conservative party circulated an al-Shabaab terrorism video in an effort to generate donations from party supporters.[81] Even after Bill C-51, it used photographs issued by ISIS showing prisoner executions in a pre-election campaign effort to discredit Justin Trudeau, leader of the opposition Liberal party.[82]

With the change of a word — "willfully" rather than "knowingly" — the government could have drafted its way out of all these endless (but plausible) hypotheticals about violating the new speech crime. And it could also have grafted onto the offence a "purpose" proviso requiring the speaker to desire the terrorist outcome. Many of the terrorism offences in the *Criminal Code* require a terrorist purpose, and this is a praiseworthy and sensible restraint.[83] But it is absent from the new speech offence.

A Speech Crime with No Defences

Not only did the government create needless legal uncertainty that can chill free expression by not requiring willful promotion or a terrorist purpose, but it also refused to add defences analogous to those found in Canada's willful-promotion-of-hatred crime. Defences were something that even the 2007 Commons committee called for when it endorsed a speech crime.

In our chief hate crime offence, it is a defence to willful promotion of hatred for a person (1) to make true statements, (2) to express "by an argument an opinion on a religious subject or an opinion based on a belief in a religious text," (3) to reasonably believe the statements to be true if the statements also "were relevant to any subject of public interest, the discussion of which was for the public benefit," or (4) to "point out, for the purpose of removal, matters producing or tending to produce feelings of hatred toward an identifiable group in Canada."[84] That the statements were made "in private conversation" is also a defence.[85] None of these defences exists for the new speech crime.

Implications of an Unprosecutable Offence

Ultimately, we do not think that any prosecutor with any real career ambitions would ever prosecute someone for expressing simple enthusiasm for Qutb or Fanon, let alone the Conservative party for its ads or someone calling for a boycott of Israel. And we have no doubt that a court would read the offence as narrowly as it could to preclude a conviction, if a prosecution were brought. But that may not matter.

For one thing, free speech is illusory where its persistence depends on the state's choosing not to prosecute. This is particularly so in a heated atmosphere where the government seems to define some of its citizens as enemies. The rule of law requires precise and clear criminal offences — ones that do not assign prosecutors the power to single out enemies and exonerate friends.

And even if there is no prosecution, the overbroad language of "knowingly promoting or advocating terrorism offences in general" is included in the definition of the terrorist propaganda that can be seized or deleted from the Internet by court order, without any inquiry into the speaker's intent. We discuss the implications of this process below.

Outreach to Muslim Communities and Chilling Muslim Speech

The new speech crime's obvious preoccupation with cracking down on radical Muslim speech — "extreme Jihadism" — will chill the expressive and associational activities of those who do not correspond to social expectations of "moderate Muslims." In other words, the government's explanation of the new offence and Minister MacKay's illustrations have thrown fuel on the fire of concerns that the overbroad new offence could be used in a discriminatory manner.

The offence may also have the effect of driving many in the Muslim community away from efforts to engage on political, religious, and social issues that touch on terrorism. As suggested below and as will be elaborated in Chapter 13, this could harm the development of community-based programs to prevent violent extremism, which we think are the most important missing piece in Canada's expanding toolbox of anti-terrorism tools. The RCMP is presently spearheading counter–violent extremism (CVE) initiatives as part of its community outreach projects. In Chapter 13, we urge a broader and deeper community-based investment in such initiatives.

But for our present purposes, consider this hypothetical: An Imam is concerned that though they show no propensity for violence, some of his community members nevertheless hold radical views outside the mainstream. He contemplates proposing that community members participate in an RCMP-led CVE meeting. But the Imam is aware of Bill C-51 and fears what will happen if the RCMP hears statements such as "the use of violence in defence of Islam is just and religiously sanctified and should be supported" or "Canada should be punished because of its foreign policy and for sending soldiers to Muslim lands." Also, as seems very plausible, some community members are known to be keen to send money to overseas groups whose conduct may include acts of violence.

Imagine now that the Imam wisely approaches a lawyer for advice. The lawyer will be aware that the new speech offence does not contain truth or public interest defences analogous to those available when a person is charged with willfully promoting hatred against an identifiable group. The lawyer will also realize that while the new offence requires that the speaker have subjective knowledge about the promotion and advocacy, it merely requires awareness of a risk that anyone might possibly commit a terrorism offence as a result of the speech. Given all this, the lawyer will likely and reasonably conclude that there is a risk some statements made at the meeting by some of the Imam's community members might run afoul of the new offence. He suggests, therefore, that it would be wise not to have the proposed meeting with the RCMP.

Is this a good thing? We think not. Bill C-51 converts the RCMP's "pre-criminal" CVE forum into a criminal space. The result may be that members of a community are deterred from participating and all the while continue to harbour (secret) radical views, and, more critically, perhaps even radical designs. These are the prime candidates for CVE, but they fall off the radar. Indeed, the smarter ones go silent on social media, making it harder to know what they are thinking and doing.

In this result, we are no safer because of the new speech offence. On the contrary, we are probably now at greater risk since what is potentially the most effective pre-emptive tool available to authorities — CVE — has been undermined. And the speech chill means at least some open-source intelligence from social media dries up.

Use of the Speech Crime as a Predicate for Other Investigative Powers

Even if no one is ever prosecuted under the new speech crime or remains silent because of the fear of being charged under it, the new crime can provide a basis for searches (including electronic surveillance), arrests, and the imposition of peace bonds.

All of these powers are tied in various ways to the commission of terrorism offences, and now the knowing promotion or advocacy of terrorism offences in general is such an offence. Attempts to impose peace bonds because people may, in the future, commit the new speech crime would also raise thorny issues about possible prior restraint of speech, where the speech could then be punished both as a speech offence and as a violation of the peace bond.

More than this, the new offence could provide police with a convenient basis to investigate persons on reasonable grounds that they will commit the new speech offence even if the police could not establish reasonable grounds to investigate them with respect to actual terrorist violence.

In other words, the new speech crime moves us closer to the overreaction of the October Crisis, discussed in Chapter 2: it could be used to authorize investigations, searches, and arrests of those who are most vocal in expressing ideas that sometimes may also be held by others who commit terrorism. Such an approach erodes our democratic freedoms, and it can also be counterproductive if it creates well-publicized speech martyrs.

Does the New Speech Offence Violate Freedom of Expression?

So, with all this, is the new speech crime constitutional? The broad, new "advocacy or promotion of terrorism offences in general" crime will be challenged under the *Charter*, probably before anyone is even charged. Indeed, as this book goes to print, a challenge is already underway.

Free Expression Includes Bad Ideas

A strong case can be made that the new speech offence is an unreasonable limit on freedom of expression, but that does not mean it will be struck down in full. Cases such as the Supreme Court's first post-9/11 terrorist crime case, *R v Khawaja*,[86] raise the prospect that courts might give the law a limiting interpretation, rather than strike it completely from the *Criminal Code*. In so doing, a court would likely sidestep many of the egregious applications of the law that we note above. But, of course, leaving the offence on the books may still chill the expression of those who are not aware of the restraining interpretations that courts have placed on broadly written offences. Such a result may not even change how the state might use the offence to obtain search warrants and peace bonds, powers discussed in Chapters 4 and 7. Glosses placed on laws by appellate courts do not always find their way into the legal trenches especially in situations without a full adversarial hearing (e.g., search warrants).

It is certainly true that violence and threats of violence are not protected forms of expression. For instance, the conduct declared "terrorist activity" in the *Criminal Code* comprises mostly acts of violence or incitement or threats of violence. That conduct would, therefore, generally fall outside the scope of expression that is protected by freedom of expression under the *Charter*. Likewise, counselling, conspiracy, or being an accessory after the fact is "intimately connected to violence — and to the danger to Canadian society that such violence represents."[87] The government will likely argue that the new speech offence does not violate freedom of expression protected by section 2(b) of the *Charter* on the basis that knowingly promoting or advocating the commission of terrorism offences in general is much the same as these other offences and is not protected expression. That is because it constitutes threats of violence or is a "thing directed at violence."[88]

The government could have bolstered its position that the law does not infringe freedom of expression by sticking to established legal concepts such as counselling, threatening, instructing, and terrorist activity. These are generally well understood and constitutional parts of the *Criminal Code*. By apparently borrowing broader concepts from an advocacy offence enacted in Australia — a country that does not have a constitutional bill of rights — and using the broader and unknown phrase "terrorism offences in general" instead of the established and broad phrase "terrorist activity," the government chose the path of provoking a *Charter* challenge.

The outer parameters of the phrase "terrorism offences in general" remain uncertain, but the phrase would include, at minimum, crimes that are not closely tied to immediate violence or threats of violence, such as terrorism financing or committing an indictable offence in association with a terrorist group. As we have suggested above, it also likely reaches well beyond this to political speech distantly related to actual violence.

Given all this, the new speech offence clearly extends well past speech that is already criminal, and it is instead capable of capturing radicalized boasting and ideological speech that is not closely connected with terrorist operations or violence. This is important. Despite concluding that threats of violence are not protected forms of expression, the Supreme Court has never suggested that speech removed from violence or threats of violence, however unpalatable it may be, should be denied *Charter* protection. Our colleague David Schneiderman has likewise concluded that it "would be surprising . . . if the Court were to exempt speech from s.2(b) protections that is far removed from threats of actual violence."[89]

The Supreme Court's rationale for excluding threats of violence from protected expression has been that threats no less than violence "take away free choice and undermine freedom of action. They undermine the very values and social conditions that are necessary for the continued existence of freedom of expression."[90] In contrast, the advocacy or promotion penalized by the new speech crime leaves the listener with a choice. You can advocate and promote "terrorism offences in general" without voicing a threat to do violence. To say "Freedom fighters in the Ukraine should resist the Russian occupation with violence, even if it means bringing the conflict to Russian cities" or "Good Muslims should give money to Hamas" does not directly threaten violence. Even John Maguire's video, discussed at the start of this chapter, leaves people with a choice about whether or not they will fulfill what he sees as their religious duties. His speech advances an extreme argument leaving it to the listener to be persuaded or not of its merits. This is exactly the substance of free speech: the idea may be a disreputable one, but it remains an idea.

Little Effort to Charter-*Proof*

Our conclusion that the new speech crime covers expression protected under the *Charter's* section 2(b) is bolstered by a number of contextual factors. First, the new concepts of "advocating" and "promoting" reach beyond the current concepts of "threatening" and "counselling" found in the definition of terrorist activity and "instructing," which is already a terrorism offence. Indeed, the new speech offence effectively glues the new concepts of advocating and promoting onto the existing concept of "terrorism offences," which already covers speech. It stacks new prohibited speech acts on top of already broad speech prohibitions. As such, the new speech crime ventures into unknown and likely unconstitutional terrain.

Second, it matters that the government has deliberately omitted a range of defences for legitimate expression similar to those found in other speech crimes, such as willful promotion of hatred. The government argued that omitting such defences was appropriate because they also do not apply to counselling offences or to the offence of advocating genocide. But the advocacy of genocide or the counselling of crimes generally refers to a determinate, relatively precise, and reasonably well-understood and well-circumscribed concept. In contrast, the reference to "terrorism offences in general" is novel, uncertain, vague, and (even in the government's explanation of it) broad and sweeping.

There is a world of difference between saying "Tutsis should be massacred" — promoting genocide — and saying "Throwing off the yolk where a people are oppressed deserves every kind of support we can provide" or even "Good Muslims should leave the west to fight for the Caliphate." It is much more likely that a person charged under the new speech offence would be able to establish that some of the statements made were true, for the public benefit, or good faith arguments of "an opinion on a religious subject or an opinion based on a belief in a religious text."[91] And yet none of these defences is available to restrain the new speech crime.

Attempts to Justify the Speech Crime under Section 1 of the Charter

Even if the new speech crime is found to violate freedom of expression, the offence might be saved as a reasonable limit on the *Charter* right, as was the case with hate speech.[92] To establish that a limit on a right is reasonable and proportionate, the government must not only invoke an important objective but demonstrate that the limit is rationally connected to the objective, that there is a minimal impairment of the right in question, and, finally, that there is proportionality between the impact on the right and the benefits of the measure in question.[93]

A Rational Offence?

The government's case would not be easy, even if we accept that the government's objective in this case is, in fact, stopping terrorism. In relation to demonstrating a rational connection to the objective, the available social science evidence suggests that the causal correlation between extreme speech or attitudes and terrorist activity is not at all a strong one. It may even be close to non-existent. Political ideology and grievance is not a conveyor belt to terrorist activity.[94] For instance, while 5 percent of adult United Kingdom Muslims (a number that translates to 50,000 persons) told pollsters in 2005 that suicide attacks were justified, only a few have acted on such thoughts.[95] Even more stark is that a very high number of United Kingdom Muslims (24 percent) did not categorically rule out violence when surveyed on reactions to the Paris terrorist attack against *Charlie Hebdo*, committed after that magazine had published cartoons of the Prophet.[96] But again, these views have not translated into actual violence.

These are objectionable opinions, but they are just that: opinions. Looking at the 2005 United Kingdom data, Clark McCauley and Sophia Moskalenko estimate that only 1 in every 100 persons espousing the most extreme al-Qaida-inspired narrative makes the move to violence.[97] The link between beliefs and the actual manifestation of violence would be even more remote if measured in relation to the level of reported sympathy for the *Charlie Hebdo* attack. These data suggest that it might be very difficult indeed, as an evidentiary matter, to establish a rational connection between the new speech offence and the actual prevention of terrorism offences.

Least Rights-Intrusive Means?

It is not clear that the new speech crime would satisfy the minimal impairment test. The government would need to establish that it could not pursue its objectives as effectively by less rights-invasive means. It matters in constitutional law whether there are less restrictive existing crimes.[98]

If the government's objective is to forestall terrorism, we have already pointed to the many other crimes that do that without violating free expression or do so in a manner that is more clearly connected to actual harm. These include criminal offences under the pre–Bill C-51 law including existing offences against the counselling or instruction of terrorist crimes. As we have argued at length, speech is already prohibited in existing terrorism offences because almost all of them incorporate references to "terrorist activity," which includes both counselling and threatening political violence. And the government has actually charged and convicted three people with the "instructing terrorist activity" offence (see Table 9.1 in the annex to Chapter 9). This instructing crime seems a likely response to calls for political violence, one that is much more precise and certain than the new speech offence. The government had only begun to explore the degree to which speech associated with terrorism could be prosecuted under existing laws, as in the *Hersi* and *Namouth* cases and with the counselling murder charges laid in July 2015 against an alleged ISIS propagandist. In this context, the rush to introduce a new crime looks more like political theatre than serious anti-terror policy.

Cost and Benefit?

And then we arrive at the question of overall balance. In section 1 analyses, the Supreme Court has increasingly been prepared to compare the overall benefits of a rights-infringing measure with its harmful effects.[99] At the same time, the section 1 test has been refined to ask a more nuanced question: are the harmful effects proportionate to not only the objective of the measure but also "the salutary effects that actually result from its implementation . . ."?[100] In answering this admittedly difficult and speculative question, courts should be attentive to failed opportunities to employ existing criminal offences. These existing laws may accomplish the same beneficial counter-terrorism effects with much less violence to the *Charter*.

More than this, we think that the benefits of the new speech offence are speculative whereas its harms to freedom of expression are manifest. The new offence would penalize substantial amounts of expression far removed from and not often causally related to terrorist activity. The chill effect on speech would be potentially enormous, and the scope of intrusive police investigation expanded. The preoccupation with al-Qaida- and ISIS-inspired violence would single out a particular subset of Canadian society disproportionately, that is, the Muslim community. Unlike the ideological, religious, or political motive requirement in the definition of terrorist activities upheld in *Khawaja*,[101] the new speech offence would have a very direct impact on the chilling of speech even without any discriminatory law enforcement action. It basically outlaws radicalized boasting.

And because of the chill, the new speech offence could be counter-productive to programs designed to counter violent extremism that, if properly conceived, will engage those who have deeply felt grievances and may be inclined to use extremist rhetoric. Another possible negative effect of the new offence is that it may help drive extremist speech underground thus making it immune to both CVE programs and the collection of intelligence.

And what happens after the successful prosecution of a radicalized braggart? We echo a comment found in a threat assessment produced by Canada's intelligence co-ordinating body: "Western Islamists" are sometimes "further radicalized in prisons in countries such as Canada, the United States, Britain, France and Spain."[102] It is a mistake to think that once people are convicted, they drop off the face of the earth or will emerge from prison with a renewed faith in the society that incarcerated them.

In sum, the new speech crime could criminalize the expression of radical and unpopular sentiments that are not closely connected with violence, threats, incitement of violence, or operational communications that would facilitate terrorist activities. It could criminalize those who assist others to convey messages that "promote or advocate terrorism offences in general" while subjectively aware of the possibility that some person (regardless of mental state) may commit any of an infinite variety of terrorism offences as a result of the communication. It would not matter if the statements were made in private. It would not matter if the statements were true or expressions of religious or political opinions. The new offence is constitutionally overbroad compared to existing offences, and it presents substantial downside risk with very little upside benefit. In that respect, the measure is grossly disproportionate.

This new speech offence, the new threat reduction powers given to CSIS, and the new information sharing powers are the most radical and problematic parts of Bill C-51. Prosecutions under the new speech offence would give accused a platform for extremist views and a martyrdom status that they do not deserve. Such prosecutions would support ISIS and al-Qaida narratives claiming that the West is hostile to Islam and Muslim grievances and that it is hypocritical in applying the civil liberties it propounds.

III. DELETION OF MATERIAL FROM THE INTERNET

Despite our serious reservations about both the constitutionality and the efficacy of the new speech offence, we are not blind to the dangers that some speech may recruit terrorists and facilitate terrorism. We do not oppose in principle the Bill C-51 provision allowing for court-ordered deletion of "terrorist propaganda."

The problem lies, however, in the definition. The Bill C-51 terrorist propaganda definition overreaches in incorporating "advocacy and promotion of terrorism offences in general."[103] It has, therefore, all the flaws that we enumerate above, constitutional and otherwise. And that means that this book may possibly be subject to seizure for reproducing statements by Maguire and passages from Qutb and Fanon. Furthermore, as we discuss below, border officials could stop this book at the border without needing any kind of court permission.

Building on Past Precedents

One of the reasons why we support the concept of terrorist propaganda deletion procedures is that they build on past precedents and defined terms of art. The deletion procedures added to the *Criminal Code* in Bill C-51 are based on a provision introduced by the 2001 *Anti-terrorism Act* allowing for the deletion of "hate propaganda" from the Internet after a contested hearing before a court.[104] We are not aware of any such court orders, but we are reasonably confident that, if used, they would be upheld as a reasonable limit on freedom of expression. Judicial orders are more respectful of freedom of expression than a regime that allows the executive to delete material unilaterally, without judicial approval. And the definition of hate speech has been upheld by the courts as a reasonable limit on freedom of expression.

For similar reasons, we support that part of the new terrorist propaganda definition that allows the deletion of material counselling terrorism offences. As we lay out above, "counselling" is a well-understood legal concept. The new rules allow for the deletion of speech that is already criminal because it solicits, incites, or procures the commission of a terrorism offence. A video that tries to solicit people to bomb or murder is already criminal. So too is a video that seeks to recruit persons to a terrorist activity or group. As the Supreme Court indicated in *Khawaja*, "Only individuals who go well beyond the legitimate expression of a political, religious or ideological thought, belief or opinion, and instead engage in one of the serious forms of violence — or threaten one of the serious forms of violence — listed in [the definition of "terrorist activity"] need fear liability under the terrorism provisions of the *Criminal Code*."[105]

For much the same reason, we would not have opposed a modest expansion of the terrorist propaganda definition to reach material that instructs terrorist activity or other conduct done for a terrorist group. Given that a person could already be convicted for such activities,[106] we see no reason why material that conveys this message should not be subject to a judicial deletion order.

We recognize that some knowledgeable people doubt whether content such as that posted by ISIS can ever be truly removed from the Internet. But there is no reason why Internet service providers and search engine companies who do operate in Canada should not be enlisted through judicial order to minimize this material's reach in Canada — that is, to hide it from Canadian Internet users in manners analogous to the European "right to be forgotten" approach.

The Rise but Likely Fall of an Adversarial Process

One of the reasons why we support part of the new terrorist propaganda deletion procedures is that it provides for an adversarial process that can test and challenge governmental claims and guard against false positives that could result in the deletion of legitimate material. To this end, the new provision appropriately provides for notice and broad rights of appeal from decisions about deletion orders and guarantees that a deletion order will not take effect until the appeal period has expired.

On the other hand, we recognize the limitations of this approach. We fear that deletion hearings will frequently be one-sided, like those that we discuss in Chapters 8 and 12 for the new CSIS threat disruption warrants and in Chapter 6 in the context of the no-fly list and passport revocations. This is because notice and appeal rights in the new deletion procedures are restricted to the person who has posted the material. Such a person will be at risk of prosecution for committing the new speech offence, given its breadth and absence of defences. Such a person is hardly likely to turn up and contest a deletion order.

And because of this threat of prosecution, even in cases where deletion applications raise novel and important points of law about what may constitute "terrorist propaganda," they may face no adversarial challenge in the trial court, and no appeal from it. This increases the risk of legal error by judges ordering deletion of legitimate material, and thereby curbing freedom of expression. This fact underlines the importance of judges' employing *amici curiae* — friends of the court — to restore adversarial challenges when the government requests deletion orders. As in other parts of the government's new legislation relating to no-fly listing and passport revocation, however, the law remains silent on these sorts of substitutes for an adversarial contest.

Troubling Alternative Forms of Censorship

We do not expect that the new terrorist propaganda deletion procedures added by Bill C-51 will be used often or perhaps at all. As noted, there has been no reported use of the similar hate propaganda deletion provision in the 2001 *Anti-terrorism Act*.

One practical problem may simply be that most objectionable material may be posted outside of Canada in jurisdictions, including the United States, that do not have similar powers. Another problem is that authorities may have an incentive to use less restrained and less transparent powers. One less restrained approach would be to simply approach Internet companies and ask them to voluntarily remove or hide the material from the Internet. Other less restrained alternative measures would include seizure by customs authorities and the use of CSIS threat reduction warrants. Bill C-51 enables all of these alternatives.

Informal Enforcement and Deletion in the Shadow of the Law

That there are no reported decisions on deletion of hate propaganda from the Internet does not mean it has not happened. Bolstered by the existence of this power, authorities may simply make an informal request of Internet providers, seeking voluntary compliance. The United Kingdom terrorist speech legislation allows just such a backdoor, informal approach, and the United Kingdom government has reported that over 95,000 postings relating to terrorism have been removed from the Internet since 2010.[107] Some, perhaps most, of these postings may have satisfied the definition of prohibited speech, but we suspect not all. In other words, informal and executive-dominated processes run a greater risk of false positives than judicial processes. In this case, the false positive would result in the deletion of protected expression.

Informal demands by the police or others that material be removed from the Internet escape judicial supervision. This underlines the importance of adequate independent review of the security officials who may invoke the new terrorist propaganda deletion procedures without judicial review. In Chapter 12, we suggest that the RCMP review body may not be up to the task of auditing national security activities that do not result in complaints.

Some idea of the pressure that security officials may place on Internet companies to delete material from the Internet is illustrated by an op-ed written by Robert Hannigan, the head of GCHQ (Government Communications Headquarters), the United Kingdom's signals intelligence service and its equivalent to the US National Security Agency or Canada's Communications Security Establishment. Hannigan argues that "most ordinary users of the internet" are ahead of the Internet companies and that "they do not want the media platforms they use with their friends and families to facilitate murder or child abuse." He urges, "we need a new deal between democratic governments and the technology companies in the area of protecting our citizens. It should be a deal rooted in the democratic values we share. That means addressing some uncomfortable truths. Better to do it now than in the aftermath of greater violence."[108] This is strong stuff, and it underlines some of the pressures that security officials may apply to social media firms.

Internet companies, however, confront competing demands from some customers for privacy. American-based companies such as Google, Facebook, and Twitter may have difficulty responding to non-American laws, including the new deletion procedures in Canada's Bill C-51. Hannigan also discounts the degree to which those companies self-regulate. For example, Twitter has cancelled ISIS accounts that threaten violence for violating Twitter's terms of use. But it has no proactive system to deny service to ISIS and (in keeping with privacy expectations) will generally provide authorities with information about users only if the authorities obtain a warrant.[109]

In any event, the basic point is that officials may pressure Internet companies to delete or hide materials and that this process will not have the same transparency or freedom of expression safeguards that deletion orders do.

Seizure by Customs Officials

A little-noticed provision in Bill C-51 added the broad, new category of "terrorist propaganda" to a customs tariff that currently allows customs officials to seize and retain obscene material and hate propaganda at the border. This is typically done without a judicial order, in recognition of reduced privacy expectations at the border.[110] The relevant customs directive provides for detention of the material for up to thirty days while determinations are made about whether the material is prohibited to enter Canada.[111] As an executive-based and closed process, customs seizures run the risk of false positives — seizing material that does not fit even the broad definition of terrorist propaganda.

Our concerns about false positives are not hypothetical. Customs officials have had difficulty in the past applying complex legal tests for "obscenity" to gay and lesbian pornography, manifested most notoriously in the *Little Sisters* court cases.[112] The new definition of "terrorist propaganda" is even more complex than obscenity because it extends to fifteen terrorist offences and other indictable offences committed on behalf of or in association with a terrorist group and, moreover, adds the unfathomable modifier "in general." Determining the meaning of this phrase will necessitate sustained litigation. It is certainly not the kind of expression that customs officials should be applying, according to their own discretion, in border inspections. Customs seizures in the obscenity context have discriminated against sexual minorities. In the terrorist propaganda context, Muslims may suffer the brunt of false positives.

Our concerns are increased by the absence of an independent review body for the Canada Border Services Agency, despite the 2006 recommendations to that effect of the Arar Commission.[113] No one will be in a serious position to scrutinize what the Canada Border Services Agency is doing. A *Charter* challenge to the amended customs tariff is possible, but it would be very expensive. Moreover, even if such a challenge were to caution the Canada Border Services Agency, the courts could continue (perhaps wrongly) to assume that customs officials will be capable in the future of applying the law correctly. Courts made this assumption in *Little Sisters Book and Art Emporium v Canada (Commissioner of Customs and Revenue)*,[114] but problems continued even after the Supreme Court ruling. And these problems were never fully litigated after the Supreme Court denied Little Sisters the advance costs that were necessary to engage in another costly round of litigation.

CSIS Threat Reduction Warrants

The hate and now terrorist propaganda deletion procedures in the *Criminal Code* have the virtue of at least potentially being adversarial processes held in open court. But Bill C-51 provides an alternative warrant process that may be more attractive to security officials seeking to disrupt or take down material on the Internet. This is especially so because, unlike the deletion orders, the warrant can be obtained in secret and can potentially reach material that is posted outside of Canada.

This alternative warrant process provides for a warrant granted by the Federal Court that authorizes CSIS to take measures to reduce threats to the security of Canada. As discussed in Chapter 8, this new power expressly anticipates the violation and proportionate limitation of any *Charter* right, including freedom of expression.[115] The only other restrictions on it are that such authorized measures not intentionally or negligently cause death or bodily harm, obstruct justice, or invade sexual integrity.[116]

We fear that the government could resort to CSIS threat disruption warrants as a less demanding and much more secretive alternative to the *Criminal Code* terrorist propaganda deletion process. If issued, these warrants could authorize CSIS, with the assistance of the Communications Security Establishment or perhaps even a foreign agency, to take measures within or outside Canada to interfere with and block both domestic and foreign websites.[117] The state would not need to convince a judge that the material constituted "terrorist propaganda" as defined in the *Criminal Code* but only that disruption was a proportionate response to the even more expansively defined "threats to the security of Canada," as described in the *CSIS Act*.[118] This concept includes not just terrorism but also subversion and foreign-influenced activities.

The case for using CSIS warrants may be plausible when the website is not within Canadian jurisdiction and so is unamenable to the terrorist propaganda deletion process. In such a case, the Federal Court will be asked to sign off on a new type of foreign cyber-warfare conducted by CSIS, presumably with the Communications Security Establishment's assistance. But, in our view, Federal Court judges should decline end runs around the more open, transparent, and (at least in principle) adversarial terrorist propaganda deletion rules if CSIS seeks such end runs in relation to websites hosted in Canada.

Unlike under the *Criminal Code* deletion provisions, there is no requirement under the CSIS warrant process that targets be given notice. And there would be no possibility for targets to participate in the warrant proceedings — such proceedings are secret and never disclosed. Also there is no provision in this warrant process for appeals to a higher court, as there is with respect to the *Criminal Code* terrorist propaganda procedures.

Given the secret nature of CSIS's work and the accompanying warrant, people may never know that they have been disrupted by the state. They may simply know only that their website has crashed or their computer is acting up. And, indeed, it seems likely that CSIS's review body, the Security Intelligence Review Committee, will now hear more complaints about CSIS activities whenever websites crash or computers act up. Even if most of these complaints are unfounded and if CSIS has nothing to do with a person's computer problems, the complaints will take time to resolve and generate suspicion about CSIS's work. As discussed in Chapter 12, the Security Intelligence Review Committee will also encounter limits in examining the role that the Communications Security Establishment will likely play in assisting CSIS in any electronic disruptions.

In sum, the prospect of this covert end run creates an even greater threat and chill to freedom of expression than open criminal prosecutions or deletion proceedings. As worrying as some parts of the terrorist propaganda provisions added to the *Criminal Code* by Bill C-51 may be, the new CSIS threat reduction warrants are even broader and less restrained, and they allow for covert as opposed to public incursions on *Charter* rights.

IV. AN UNBALANCED STRATEGY

The Limits of Supply-Side Strategies

All of the provisions discussed above for punishing speech and deleting it from the Internet are attempts to reduce the supply of speech that the government believes fuels terrorism. Even leaving aside the tenuous connection between extremist speech and actual terrorism, we doubt the feasibility and effectiveness of the coercive supply-side speech reduction measures contemplated in Bill C-51.

Once one extremist speaker is prosecuted, another may be willing to take that speaker's place if only for the publicity and notoriety provided by the prosecution. Once one website or Twitter account is deleted by court order in Canada or disrupted by CSIS warrant outside of Canada, another will emerge. Our point is not that supply-side regulation of speech can never be justified, but simply that it is a partial strategy. Supply-reduction strategies will make, at best, very marginal contributions to anti-terrorism.

The Need to Reduce Demand

What is entirely missing from the government's new anti-terror law are demand-reducing strategies for dealing with violent extremism. We return to this issue in Chapter 13, but here we note that Bill C-51 does not provide any incentive or statutory basis for such approaches. But, worse than that, the new speech offence could have the unintended effect of making CVE programs more difficult. This is particularly true when, as appears to be the case, security officials, and especially the police, are taking the lead in Canada's delayed CVE programs. These are the people who will be asked to enforce the new speech crimes, even while they are asking "extremists" to speak with them in an attempt to dissuade them from violence.

Bill C-51, unlike the United Kingdom's recently enacted *Counter-terrorism and Security Act 2015*,[119] does not require CVE programs at institutions such as schools, health authorities, and prisons. We acknowledge that moving forward with at least some of these institutions would require provincial co-operation, an important topic that will be discussed in Chapter 13. We also acknowledge that CVE programs that impose obligations on civil society can be controversial, poorly designed, and even counterproductive.

But the bottom line is that CVE programs may be an important tool against radicalization to violence. Such initiatives depend on willing participation by community members, especially members of the Muslim communities given present preoccupations with al-Qaida- and ISIS-inspired terrorism. Effective CVE programs require ample "pre-criminal" space, in which those with radical views — but who show no violent tendencies — are able to voice their views. This space must allow radicalized boasting if only to establish the errors and the dangers of such speech. As we have argued above, with Bill C-51's new speech offence, pre-criminal CVE space is turned into criminal space with the result that participation in these key counter-extremism events may be curtailed.

Criminal offences have a place and should not be ignored in broader anti-terror policies. But we already have robust criminal laws including ones that already apply to much speech. Bill C-51's overbroad speech crime is not conducive to a hearts-and-minds counter–violent extremism strategy. In a democracy, much of the best work in national security depends on consent, not coercion. Bill C-51 charts a different course.

V. CONCLUSION

The new Bill C-51 speech offence is not as speech restricting as European-style glorification or apologie offences (or, at least, we do not think it is). The government deserves credit for not acting on its initial inclinations in this matter. We are, however, disturbed by the fact that even after the enactment of Bill C-51, Conservative senators have been calling for another offence targeting glorification of terrorism.

The British prosecution of a bookstore owner not involved in any terrorist plots for selling the controversial works of Qutb or the French prosecution of a cartoonist who in poor taste drew a cartoon about 9/11 does not strike us as the appropriate way for a democracy to combat terrorism. We have little doubt that such offences would not survive *Charter* scrutiny, even though they have survived more deferential forms of judicial review in Europe.

Nevertheless, we still have pragmatic and principled objections to the new speech offence that Parliament enacted. Research on radicalization to violence is a dynamic and changing area. Nevertheless, it suggests that the casual links between extremist material (which given present preoccupations often means material related to Islam) and actual violence are far from robust. Internet material appears to be more a facilitator than an actual cause of radicalization to violence. This suggests that there may not even be a rational connection between the new offence and the important objective of preventing terrorism.

And even if a court concluded that there is a rational connection between the new speech offence and preventing terrorism, it would be difficult for the government to justify the new offence given the amount of speech that is already criminalized by existing offences. We already have many criminal and terrorist offences that can apply to hate speech, inciting or threatening terrorism, or providing operational instructions about terrorism. Finally, the overall benefits of this new offence are speculative while its harms to freedom of expression are quite clear.

But even leaving aside rights-based *Charter* concerns, we have pragmatic policy-based concerns. Offences directed at the wrong type of speech are simply supply-reduction strategies condemned to whack-a-mole difficulties. They risk a vicious spiral of ineffective deletion orders, including informal and poorly reviewed police deletion requests, enforcement by customs officials, and the use of covert CSIS threat reduction warrants, which could be used to disrupt Internet sites both in Canada and abroad. In Chapter 13, we elaborate on the need for a demand-reduction strategy: a holistic and evidence-based multi-disciplinary approach toward CVE. Unfortunately, the new and unnecessary speech offence in Bill C-51 could be a barrier to such a strategy. It is a mistake.

CHAPTER ELEVEN

Oversight: Who Is in Charge of Canadian Anti-terrorism?

I. INTRODUCTION

The terrorist attacks of October 2014 were security failures. Security failures raise the question, who is in charge? In Canadian security, the practical answer is everyone — the responsible ministers and the heads of the security agencies. Too often, this means no one is in charge.

The October Attacks as a Symbol of a Larger Ailment

Many Canadians understandably had difficulty understanding how an armed terrorist could run across Parliament Hill, encounter resistance at the entrance to Parliament's centre block, but then manage to make it to Parliament's Hall of Honour, only metres from where the prime minister and members of Parliament were meeting. A heavily redacted report by the Ontario Provincial Police, released in June 2015, concluded that one reason for this breach was that no one was in charge. Parliament Hill was defended by "three separate agencies [working] with different communication systems, separate training and limited interactions between their members, operating in silos to provide security to Parliament Hill."[1] The report pointed to numerous prior reviews that had recommended a more centralized security approach, but no action had been taken. It also noted that the attack on Parliament could have had "devastating consequences" had it been better organized.

A further report revealed that, while the RCMP was placed in charge of Parliament's security in February 2015, the consolidation of House and Senate security staff was not complete as of June 2015. Moreover, "challenges remain with regards to communications interoperability with the RCMP."[2] In other words, eight months after a murderous attack that could have been much, much worse, we had not managed fully to dismantle the institutional silos of just those agencies defending Parliament.

These reports did not deal with the failure to increase security, despite intelligence issued days before the 22 October 2014 attack, warning of a possible attack.[3] They also did not deal with the chaos after the shooting, in part caused by poor evacuation, communications, and lockdown procedures. They did not deal with the unorganized deployment of Ottawa police — something discussed in an Ottawa Police Services assessment[4] — or the fact that it took eight hours to verify that Zehaf-Bibeau was the only attacker.[5]

The OPP's report confirmed comments made by a retired leader of Canada's elite Joint Task Force 2 special forces counter-terrorism unit: the fragmented approach to defending Parliament is "symptomatic of some of the larger issues that we have in Canada," with an approach to security that is "siloed and stovepiped. So, inside Public Safety, inside DND (Department of National Defence) and inside Foreign Affairs, you've got silos of information that don't necessarily translate down to the folks on the shop floor." He added, "it is a systemic issue about how we bring together those different security forces, actors, so that we've got a coherent approach."[6]

In other words, no one has been in charge.

The Need to Understand Security Failures

There is a huge danger in second-guessing the difficult decisions that security officials must make in allocating scarce surveillance and other resources. There is also a huge danger in promoting the ultimately false view that we can prevent every terrorist attack.

Nevertheless, we have been struck by the absence of sustained questioning about whether the October attacks were preventable and who was responsible for the inadequate measures taken that failed to prevent the attacks. And again, a large part of the inattention may be because of the lack of availability of publicly accessible information close to a year after the attacks, a reaction that can be contrasted with Australia's detailed seventy-five-page report released shortly after a December 2014 terrorist attack in Sydney.[7]

Unfortunately, this lack of information is not unprecedented. Canada has been slow to learn from past security failures. A commission of inquiry into the 1985 Air India bombings was only appointed in 2006. It found that the RCMP and the Communications Security Establishment (CSE) did not share intelligence about specific threats to Air India planes in June 1985. The RCMP allowed all of its bomb-sniffing dogs to attend a training session, thus making them unavailable, on the day the luggage bomb that later exploded over the Atlantic made its way through Canada's three largest airports. The commission catalogued how CSIS and the RCMP worked at cross purposes after the bombings and how the poor treatment and protection of witnesses helped explain why only one person was convicted of manslaughter for the largest mass murder in Canadian history.[8]

Both during the Air India Commission and during the debates about the new 2015 terrorism laws, the government has consistently taken the position that the security failures revealed by the Air India disaster are a thing of the distant past. The commission — and some security professionals who testified about Bill C-51[9] — disagreed. We share these concerns about the effectiveness of our security response.

Poorly Understood Facts Make Bad Law

Instead of asking hard questions about the enforcement of existing laws and whether the October 2014 attacks could have been prevented through better-resourced and organized security, the government concluded that vast new security powers were necessary. Politicians cited the emotionally powerful testimony of Louise Vincent,[10] the sister of the murdered soldier at Saint-Jean-sur-Richelieu, and of Bal Gupta,[11] the able and tireless chair of the Air India 182 Victims Families Association. Both of these individuals testified to committees studying Bill C-51, and asserted that the new laws could have kept their loved ones alive.

In the absence of more information, however, it is not possible to know whether Martin Couture-Rouleau, the terrorist who murdered Warrant Officer Patrice Vincent on 20 October 2014, would have been subject to a peace bond under Bill C-51's lowered evidentiary threshold. The RCMP anticipated the Senate asking whether the new peace bond powers would have stopped Couture-Rouleau. Its prepared response, provided in internal documents, is a non-response. It simply pointed to the lower thresholds, without actually addressing the question whether a peace bond would have been granted or have mattered on the ground.[12] Similarly, Bill C-51 permits increased information sharing about all range of security threats, but it does not prioritize or actually require information sharing about terrorism, a long-standing problem most manifest in CSIS's sharing practices and the one the Air India inquiry urged be fixed.

Understanding the Challenge

And so, in this chapter, we go beyond the Bill C-51 debate on hard-nosed new powers and examine the need for better oversight, to ensure that agencies respond to past failures and make the best possible use of the tools in their anti-terrorist toolkit. In other words, this chapter focuses on the need for responsible ministers, and ultimately the prime minister, to be in charge. Oversight provides a much-needed check when security responses begin tilting toward over- or underreaction.

Democracies may never get that delicate and evolving balance right. Course corrections will always be necessary. But better oversight should ensure that capable and informed hands are on the rudder at all times. It can also help promote confidence that the system is capable of learning and recovering from its mistakes.

II. DEFINING THE TERMS

There has been much talk of the need for accountability for and enhanced "review and oversight" of the new powers provided in the 2015 legislation. Four former prime ministers and a bevy of former judges and security watchdogs weighed in on the "review and oversight" issue in February 2015.[13] As we discuss in Chapter 12, we agree completely with their arguments that Canada needs enhanced and integrated review of national security activities by independent watchdogs and by parliamentarians with access to secret information.

But much of the Bill C-51 debate on this issue was marred by the fact that many conflate the distinct meanings of review and oversight. Loose language and muddled thinking is a real danger. Without conceptual clarity at the start, there will only be confusion and disappointment, even if reforms are implemented.

Review and Oversight Defined

Review refers to the ability of independent bodies retrospectively to evaluate security activities.[14] A reviewer does not have operational responsibility for what is being reviewed. The Security and Intelligence Review Committee, the CSE Commissioner, and the Civilian Review and Complaints Commission for the RCMP are all examples of review bodies. They conduct reviews in after-the-fact audits. They also hear complaints from individuals. At the end of the day, reviewers make findings and recommendations.

Oversight refers to a command and control process — the power to issue directions, influencing conduct before it occurs.[15] Review bodies do not have the power to oversee anti-terrorism activities, though they can make findings about failings and can make recommendations on improvements. In fact, review bodies *should not* have oversight roles. In the Arar Commission, Justice O'Connor expressed concerns that combining review with an oversight role that intruded on the management of the agency could compromise the independence of the review body by implicating it in the decisions being reviewed.[16]

Oversight is an executive branch function. In the Air India Commission reports, Justice Major warned that such "oversight is of critical importance" and should be practised both by responsible ministers and through an enhanced role for the prime minister's national security advisor.

Efficacy Based Co-ordination and Oversight

The Air India Commission focused on "efficacy-based oversight," which it defined as examining "whether the agencies have the competence and capacity to do their jobs" and "whether their activities are sufficiently co-ordinated to accomplish the ultimate job of preventing terrorism."[17]

This reference to co-ordination is vital. Co-ordination involves bringing different parts together into a coherent and effective whole. And effective co-ordination requires command and control powers to ensure that one hand works with the other. Command and control, including sanctions, can be the "bad cop" face of oversight. A "good cop" approach, including rewards, can induce different agencies to work together in a co-ordinated manner.[18]

Co-ordination, buttressed with sufficient command and control, is an important, but too often neglected, oversight requirement in modern anti-terrorism — a discipline that often involves the use of multiple instruments across the whole of government. We have identified some of these multiple instruments in the threat escalator discussed in Chapter 3 and then explored them in subsequent chapters. For example, someone needs to ensure that once a suspected foreign terrorist fighter is denied exit from Canada through a no-fly listing or passport revocation, another agency engages in surveillance and investigation of that person.

Co-ordination is particularly challenging in the anti-terrorism context because it may often require firm management across agencies and even ministries. In other words, effective co-ordination requires someone who can not only see the big picture, but also break down silos and require the individual agencies to work together in the public interest. In keeping with this discussion, the Air India Commission stressed the need for a clear understanding of who is in charge. The "siloed" and uncoordinated nature of the system was the main obstacle to anti-terror effectiveness.

Accountability and Accountability Gaps

Accountability is a term that lies somewhere between review and oversight. It refers to the process by which officials and organizations provide explanations and justifications for their conduct. A body can demand an accounting even if it does not have the power to control or change the behaviour for which it is demanding an explanation.[19] In other words, a review body that is not in the chain of command can still demand accountability. So too can those in the chain of command, such as ministers, who have oversight powers. Accountability, like review and oversight, can relate to either the propriety or efficacy of conduct.

Accountability gaps occur when reviewers or overseers do not have adequate powers, information, or resources to match the conduct that is being reviewed. Since 9/11, all democracies have struggled with accountability gaps in national security matters. These gaps have been created as governments move to more intense and more integrated "whole of government" national security activities, but without always ensuring that reviewers and overseers have correspondingly enhanced whole-of-government powers and adequate resources to keep pace with what is being reviewed.[20] For example, Canada's signal intelligence agency, the CSE, will more frequently work with CSIS in assisting the latter to exercise its new threat reduction powers under Bill C-51. Nevertheless, the two agencies are overseen by different ministers and reviewed by different review agencies.

In other words, accountability gaps occur when reviewers and overseers remain stuck in twentieth-century silos while security agencies break down walls and escape silos in order to work with domestic and foreign partners. Accountability gaps may have been created unwittingly at first, given the rapid response to 9/11, but their persistence many years later raises questions of whether governments are truly interested in fixing them.

Accountability gaps are a matter of concern because they create risks to both rights and security. Whole-of-government activities may violate rights, such as privacy. Inefficient practices and lack of effective co-ordination of multiple anti-terrorism instruments undermine security.

III. OVERSIGHT: WHO IS IN CHARGE?

Ministerial Accountability?

A central question in oversight is, who is in charge? The traditional answer in parliamentary democracies has been the responsible minister, able to issue directions and directives. In his testimony to the Senate security committee,

Richard Fadden, the prime minister's national security advisor, reminded senators,

> that under our system of government, all of the agencies here represented have a minister of the Crown. Under our system, they are accountable to that minister, who is accountable to you. I find it interesting that in this debate about oversight and review, we tend to ignore the responsibility of ministers. I must say, when I was Director of CSIS, I never considered my minister to be a rubber stamp.[21]

Fadden is constitutionally correct that the responsible minister is in charge. For example, the minister of public safety has responsibility for both the RCMP and CSIS. In theory, such a minister, assisted by an expert civil service, should have been able to resolve the long-standing conflicts between the two agencies.

In practice, however, ministerial responsibility for national security matters has never been particularly robust. The McDonald Commission found that ministerial responsibility for RCMP illegalities in the wake of the October Crisis was murky at best, and that elected politicians, including Prime Minister Trudeau, were too willing to disclaim responsibility for the manner in which the RCMP investigated and disrupted national security threats.[22] The commission stressed the importance of ministerial responsibility going forward, while also recognizing that the prime minister and his civil servant staff in the Privy Council Office had an important co-ordinating role.

Much time has passed since the 1981 McDonald Commission report. Canada has experienced a long-term trend, accelerated under the Harper government, of "governing from the centre."[23] The Air India Commission revisited the question of ministerial responsibility in 2010. It was pre-occupied with the question of who is in charge. It tied many of the failures it found in both the pre- and post-bombings phases of the Air India investigation to the fact that no one was in charge. Such an environment helped explain why the agencies could claim that each was doing its job, even in the face of blatant security failures.

Justice Major found that the minister responsible for both CSIS and the RCMP had not resolved the constant conflicts between the two agencies that dogged the botched investigation. He concluded that "[w]ithout a central informed decision-maker to direct the entire Canadian counter-terrorism landscape, CSIS and the RCMP were left to proceed according to their own lights and based on their view of the needs and best interests of their own institution. In the competition and mistrust that ensued there were no winners."[24]

Justice Major also found that the CSE — answerable to the defence minister — had not shared important intelligence. In the result, the Department of Transport did not receive intelligence it needed about threats to the single Air India plane that left Canada weekly. And in one of those weeks, tragically, the flight was laden with a luggage bomb that exploded over the Atlantic.

The Minister of Public Safety as a National Security Lead?

If ministerial responsibility in national security is an inadequate form of oversight, this should be corrected. Doing so would require a clear answer to this question: To which minister are the security services responsible, and for what?

The Public Safety Minister's Increased Responsibilities

One possibility is the attorney general of Canada, that is, the minister of justice. The McDonald Commission recognized in 1981 that one benefit of having CSIS report to the minister of justice would be the "virtue of the prestige of the Minister and the Department of Justice both within and outside of government."[25] But the commission ultimately concluded that the then–solicitor general's department was a more logical venue for CSIS, in part because of the heavy workload in Justice and the possibility of conflict between CSIS oversight responsibilities and the attorney general's law officer role.

At the same time, the McDonald Commission warned of the danger that the solicitor general's department might be preoccupied with many other areas, including its responsibility for prisons and corrections. The possibility of distraction has increased with time. The rebranded Department of Public Safety and Emergency Preparedness (Public Safety Canada) includes not just the RCMP, CSIS, and Corrections within its portfolio agencies, but also now the Canada Border Services Agency (itself a massive amalgamation of border control bodies).

The 2015 laws give the minister of public safety considerably more powers and responsibility over anti-terrorism matters. Now, the minister of public safety is confirmed in the lead role with respect to the no-fly list formalized by Bill C-51. Under the 2015 budget bill and changes to the order governing passports, the minister of public safety will also take the lead role in revoking passports to prevent terrorist travel.[26] And the minister of public safety also has responsibilities in relation to new citizenship revocation powers, enacted in 2014 and now in force.

The minister of public safety has had longstanding responsibility under the *CSIS Act*[27] to approve CSIS warrant applications to the Federal Court.

Now, the minister — and in practice the minister's delegate — will be asked to approve of requests by CSIS for new warrants to conduct extraterritorial investigations under Bill C-44 and to engage in threat reduction activities that violate Canadian laws (including possibly the *Charter*) under Bill C-51.

As Richard Fadden suggests, the minister of public safety should not be a "rubber stamp" when signing off on these warrants. The minister, as advised by the senior civil service, should play a challenge function. Warrants are, however, only a small part of CSIS's work, and CSIS is a small part of the minister's portfolio. The minister of public safety is an increasingly busy person and even with assistance, the minister's office may have difficulty establishing priorities for a sprawling department and keeping track of security agencies with increased and broad powers.

Multiple Ministerial Responsibilities for Legal Proceedings

Even with enhanced responsibilities, the minister of public safety is far from a centralized anti-terrorism overseer.

The architects of the 2001 *Anti-terrorism Act*[28] gave the attorney general — and, in practice, the attorney general's delegate — an oversight role of sorts in anti-terrorism: attorney general consent is required for terrorism offence criminal proceedings, terrorism peace bonds, and all but the exigent use of preventive detention. Legally, provincial attorneys general may employ this power (although the attorney general of Canada would still play a special role with respect to secrecy matters). In practice, though, terrorism criminal law is principally a federal preoccupation, and the federal attorney general law officer powers are exercised in practice by the federal director of public prosecutions, acting as the federal attorney general's lawful delegate. Indeed, the Air India Commission thought these functions should be further centralized into an office of the Director of Terrorism Prosecutions, subject to the attorney general of Canada's direction.[29]

The attorney general consent requirement can help ensure that a criminal proceeding or peace bond process does not disrupt an ongoing intelligence operation and is consistent with a broader anti-terror strategy. That objective depends, however, on adequate co-ordination between the attorney general (and now, in practice, the director of public prosecutions) and the minister of public safety (and the intelligence agencies under the Public Safety portfolio). Here, as elsewhere, there is a danger that separate agencies operating in silos may work at cross-purposes.

To give one possible example: As discussed in Chapter 10, we are concerned that Bill C-51's new speech crime, penalizing the "advocacy or promotion of terrorism offences in general offences," and its related Internet deletion procedures may chill freedom of expression and also inhibit attempts to counter violent extremism. We do not believe that the reasonable exercise of prosecutorial restraint and consent by the director of public prosecutions is a cure to this problem. But it is certainly better than no restraint whatsoever. Will prosecutorial discretion be exercised with an eye to the possible knock-on effects on other tools in the anti-terror toolkit?

There are also issues of federal and provincial co-ordination. Quebec has recently proposed its own anti-radicalization bill to deal with hate speech and speech inciting violence.[30] It is not at all clear how these laws will operate with the new *Criminal Code* speech offences and deletion procedures, or interact with counter–violent extremism outreach programs at both the federal and provincial levels.

There is also an overlap between the Internet terrorist propaganda deletion procedures that the attorney general must approve and CSIS threat reduction warrants that the minister of public safety must approve. As discussed in Chapter 8, Internet take-downs effected by CSIS threat reduction measures may be attractive to the government because they can apply outside of Canada and do not require notice or adversarial challenge in an open court. How will ministerial oversight systems choose between deletion hearings started by the justice department and Internet disruption started by the public safety department? All this is to say, again: someone had best be in charge.

Multiple Ministerial Responsibilities for Terrorism Financing

Ministerial co-ordination issues also arise in the area of terrorism financing. Canada has a poor record in enforcing laws in this area. The minister of finance has overall responsibility in this area, but other departments are involved in a complicated horizontal co-ordination, including the departments of Foreign Affairs, Public Safety and Emergency Preparedness, Justice, and Revenue. Canada's financial intelligence agency, the Financial Transactions and Reports Analysis Centre, has an arm's length relationship with all departments but works with the Canada Revenue Agency, the Canadian Border Services Agency, CSIS, CSE, the RCMP, and the Public Prosecution Service of Canada within the Department of Justice.

If terrorism financing regulation is to be effective, there is a need to ensure the appropriate flow of financial intelligence in and out of all these multiple agencies.[31] Bill C-51's convoluted information sharing law may ultimately *allow* intelligence to flow, but it does not *require* that the intelligence flow from sometimes close-lipped agencies. It also does not establish terrorism or terrorism financing as a priority among the almost infinite range of security threats that the new information sharing law identifies.

Multiple Ministerial Responsibilities for Activities Outside of Canada

After Bill C-44, CSIS may now obtain warrants to conduct foreign spying, in violation of foreign law. The minister of public safety or the minister's delegate must approve applications for such a judicial warrant. But in authorizing a warrant application (assuming a warrant is even required), the minister or delegate will need to consider whether the proposed activity will result in political embarrassment and harm foreign relations.

It is very easy to imagine CSIS stepping on the toes of the Department of Foreign Affairs and the military while engaged in foreign adventures. Indeed, it may even adversely affect relationships with foreign police. RCMP documents reflect this concern: "The RCMP, with significant relationships with international law enforcement agencies abroad, is concerned that CSIS threat diminishment activities in a foreign country, if detected by the authorities, could inadvertently jeopardize existing relationships on particular investigations."[32]

Retired diplomats Paul Heinbecker and Daniel Livermore have raised concerns that CSIS's increased foreign footprint could make it a *de facto* foreign policy maker, one that may act in a manner contrary to the foreign policy interests as defined ultimately by the minister of foreign affairs. They point to how whistle-blower Edward Snowden's revelations about CSE spying on Brazil meant that "years of diplomatic time, effort and commitment went up in smoke." They raise the question about oversight: "[W]ho decides what to do when CSIS, or CSE, or another Canadian agency, has an operational objective that conflicts with the broader mandate of the ambassador for all of Canadian operations in a given country?" Based on years of senior experience in government, they conclude that "*de facto* responsibility for making a flawed system work falls to the Canadian public service, especially senior executives of the Privy Council Office (the PM's department), Foreign Affairs, CSIS, CSEC, the RCMP, Immigration and National Defence." Why? "Because ministers have effectively punted on this issue . . . ."[33]

In other words, ministerial accountability does not work well in the multi-departmental national security context. Someone needs to be in charge to resolve disputes between different agencies and ministries.

The government has argued that CSIS's new foreign powers will be controlled by the need for warrants from the Federal Court. But as we discuss below, CSIS will not always need a warrant from the Federal Court for foreign operations. And at any rate, a Federal Court judge who decides whether to issue a warrant to CSIS will not be well positioned to consider the possible foreign relations blowback if a CSIS threat reduction operation that violates foreign and Canadian laws falls apart. That is not the judge's job.

Only the minister of public safety — presumptively in close consultation with his Departments of Foreign Affairs and National Defence counterparts or someone at the centre of government — will be able to determine the perhaps harmful effects on foreign relations or national defence of CSIS activities outside of Canada. This is a tall order that will require a strong cabinet minister and a robust bureaucratic apparatus.

The Public Safety Minister's Stature

And so the question is whether the minister of public safety is up to this essential co-ordinating role.

Alas, the minister of public safety, and its predecessor the solicitor general, has not been a particularly plum cabinet position. Turnover in the public safety portfolio has been fairly commonplace. And in the cabinet that introduced the 2015 bills, Minister of Public Safety Steven Blaney was the eighteenth cabinet member in order of precedence. This is not unique. Wayne Easter ranked twenty-eighth in precedence when he served as solicitor general in Jean Chrétien's cabinet. Ranking in the order of precedence is not legally significant, but it may reflect the reality that few senior politicians willingly choose the Public Safety portfolio. The most able and ambitious cabinet ministers may try to avoid Public Safety. It has not generally been a launching pad for the prime minister's position. Policing, prisons, border control, emergencies, or indeed national security tend to generate bad news.

One exception to this pattern was Anne McLellan. She had previously served as minister of justice and then minister of health, and was the fifth in order of precedence and also deputy prime minister while serving as the very first public safety minister under Prime Minister Paul Martin from late 2003 to early 2006. If national security is to be a priority and if there is to be a chance for effective co-ordination of increased security powers such as supervision of the troubled CSIS-RCMP relationship, it will be important in new governments that the Department of Public Safety is viewed as a senior ministerial appointment that attracts the most experienced and capable ministers and civil servants, on a par with Justice and Foreign Affairs.

It may also be time to consider whether the bundle of broadly defined public safety matters under the Public Safety Canada umbrella makes sense, or simply dilutes Canada's ability to respond effectively to security threats.

Whether any of this re-think happens or not, the minister of public safety will — for better or worse — be a key person in determining how the new security powers are exercised.

The Minister of Public Safety's Many Responsibilities

But the minister of public safety cannot be in charge if he does not know what is happening. This is a constant challenge in a department whose core and portfolio agencies have 52,000 employees, a $6 billion budget, and a role that spans federal corrections, intelligence, federal policing, border security, emergency management, and crime prevention.

CSIS's Abolished Inspector General

Until recently, the minister was kept informed on CSIS conduct, in part, through reports submitted by the CSIS Inspector General. Described as the minister's "eyes and ears" in CSIS,[34] and as "an early warning system,"[35] the Inspector General examined CSIS's operational activities for compliance with law, ministerial directives, and CSIS's own policies.

The Harper government abolished the Inspector General office in 2012. This change will be discussed in the next chapter because the duties of the Inspector General have been transferred to the Security Intelligence Review Committee (SIRC), the agency that reviews CSIS's work. Nevertheless, the abolition of the Inspector General also affects the minister's command and control oversight of CSIS. The Inspector General directly reported to the minister on matters such as the accuracy and retention of CSIS's intelligence, CSIS's foreign operations, and how it executed its warrants. They did so in a manner that was independent of both the deputy minister of public safety and the director of CSIS. The minister of public safety could also task Inspectors General to conduct investigations to help the minister discharge an oversight role.[36]

Out of the Loop? Failures to Keep the Minister of Public Safety Informed

In its most recent annual report, SIRC warned that the new system without an Inspector General is not working well. Specifically, it found that the minister was "not always systemically advised" or "informed" of CSIS activities that "may have significant adverse impact on Canadian interests, such as discrediting the Service [CSIS] or the Government of Canada, giving rise to public controversy."[37] If the minister is to exercise an oversight role, the minister must be informed before the activities are a *fait accompli*.

And if the minister was not adequately informed of what CSIS was doing before the 2015 expansion of CSIS powers, there is a severe danger that the minister will not be adequately informed of CSIS's new activities — which include enhanced extraterritorial investigations, enhanced powers to bestow privileges to protect CSIS human sources from identification (including in-court proceedings), enhanced discretionary information sharing, and novel new powers to take physical measures to reduce threats to the security of Canada, possibly in violation of the law and *Charter* rights. To be sure, the minister will have to sign off on CSIS warrants, and there are new CSIS reporting obligations regarding threat reduction powers, but many of CSIS's new powers will not require warrants and many others are outside the scope of the enhanced reporting provisions.

In addition, the minister has newly codified responsibilities under the no-fly list and with respect to passport revocation. The Canada Border Services Agency — which also reports to the minister of public safety — will have new powers to seize terrorist propaganda at the border.

In short, the minister of public safety and his officials now have even more on their crowded agenda, even as the existing co-ordination issues involving agencies reporting to different ministers persist. Matters will inevitably slip through the cracks. We think oversight with effective co-ordination will require more than an effective public safety minister. It will also require investment at the centre of government.

The Prime Minister's National Security Advisor

After studying both the numerous failures in the Air India bombings investigation and the current relationship between the RCMP and CSIS, the Air India Commission did not have faith that ministerial responsibility, and in particular the Department of Public Safety, would provide central co-ordination and resolve inevitable disputes between security agencies. Instead, it proposed an enhanced role for a position that is virtually invisible to Canadians: the national security advisor to the prime minister.

Who is this person? The first thing to note is that this is a senior civil service appointment, first created in the Privy Council Office in 2003. The Privy Council Office (PCO) serves as the prime minister's civil service, and it provides civil service support to the cabinet. The national security advisor is not a member of the political staff in the Prime Minister's Office.

PCO performs a national security function. Its Security and Intelligence Secretariat "[a]dvises on national security and intelligence issues" and "[c]oordinates federal activities within the security and intelligence community," among other things.[38] But security issues are a small subset of PCO activities.

National security co-ordination does not feature in Canada's Privy Council Office's four strategic priorities, as revealed in PCO's most recent performance report.[39] Instead, national security appears as one of a very long list of matters on which PCO provides advice to the prime minister. Indeed, it is bundled with international affairs as a "subgroup." Reporting on its activities in 2013–14, PCO "worked to build strong relationships within the Canadian and allied intelligence communities to increase information sharing and enhance collaborative efforts" and "[p]rovided advice and support to the Government on the development of national security policy, legislation and programs with a view to enhancing the Government's ability to counter current and emerging threats." These two vast responsibilities come toward the end of a list of thirteen activities in the area of national security and international affairs, almost all of which involved international affairs rather than security. The entire national security and international affairs subgroup staff had ninety-seven "full time equivalents," a significant number but nevertheless one of the smallest subgroups in PCO.

Within the PCO, the national security advisor has a low profile and no organizational website. CSIS describes the national security advisor's role as follows:

> Advises the Prime Minister on security matters and strengthens the capacity of the Privy Council Office to develop and implement an integrated policy on national security and emergencies. The Advisor supports the Security, Public Health, and Emergency Committee to Cabinet, and coordinates integrated threat assessments and inter-agency cooperation among security organizations through the Integrated Terrorism Assessment Centre.[40]

The Air India Commission recommended a national security advisor with a "bit more oomph."[41] Justice Major's very first recommendation in the Air India Commission report was to enhance the role of the national security advisor, giving that office new operational and decision-making responsibilities. These new duties would include:

> To supervise and, where necessary, to co-ordinate national security activities, including all aspects of the distribution of intelligence to the RCMP and to other government agencies . . . ;
>
> To resolve, with finality, disputes among the agencies responsible for national security;

To provide oversight for the effectiveness of national security activities; and

To carry out the government's national security policy in the public interest.[42]

A Special Senate Committee on Anti-terrorism chaired by Senator Hugh Segal endorsed Justice Major's recommendation in a unanimous 2011 report. The report reasoned that "national security issues are too important to be entrusted to a single department or agency, and it should not be the role of a minister to be involved in the management of any national security investigation."[43] Like the Air India Commission, the Senate committee recommended that the national security advisor should co-ordinate and ensure the effectiveness of national security activities and resolve disputes among agencies. It also recommended that CSIS should be required to share relevant intelligence with the national security advisor that it was not willing to share with the police. In addition, it affirmed the Air India Commission's recommendation that the national security advisor should play a role in ensuring better co-ordination and effectiveness of the way multiple agencies in multiple departments dealt with terrorism financing.[44]

The government rejected the key, enhanced national security advisor recommendation of the Air India Commission. This response likely reflected testimony heard by the commission about the continued importance of ministerial responsibility,[45] as well as assertions that Canada (unlike the United States) did not need a "national security Czar."

The government's Air India action plan did contemplate introducing "legislation to clarify authorities for information sharing for the purposes of national security."[46] This came eventually in Bill C-51's *Security of Canada Information Sharing Act*.[47] What was missing, however, was the idea that CSIS should be *obliged* to share information about terrorism offences with either the police or the national security advisor. This central recommendation made by the Air India Commission and then reaffirmed in 2011 by the Senate committee simply fell off the radar.

"I Have Virtually No Power; I Have a Fair Bit of Influence . . . ."

The rejection of all these recommendations became crystal clear when the current national security advisor testified before the Senate security committee reviewing Bill C-51. Richard Fadden commented:

I think it's fair to say I have virtually no power; I have a fair bit of influence on the national security front. The other thing I do have is if I think there's a real problem, I have access to the Prime Minister and ministers.

So I think Mr. Major [the Air India inquiry commissioner] was thinking of something with a bit more oomph in it in the sense that he wanted it to be based in statute and be given specific powers. Again, that's a matter for government and Parliament to decide, but I think both my predecessors and I have sort of evolved to something fairly close to what Mr. Major was suggesting. I certainly never found, when acting on behalf of the community, reluctance when problems are brought to people's attention for people to correct them. On the rare occasions where it happened or it happened to my predecessor, it has been brought to the attention of our political masters, which it seems to me is not a bad way of resolving the issue.[48]

Fadden urged that even without "operational powers" or displacing ministerial lines of accountability, he was not powerless: "to be candid, as an agent of the Prime Minister in these matters, I think it's possible for the NSA to have some influence."[49]

We do not doubt the informal but significant "influence" of the prime minister's national security advisor. The prime minister has ultimate responsibility for national security and we expect that when his national security advisor talks, the agencies listen, carefully. That said, influence is not the same as responsibility. Influence is a discretionary matter: sometimes those who have it exercise it; sometimes they do not. Responsibility, however, involves more transparency and more formal command and control oversight powers to ensure that agencies co-ordinate their activities. Effective co-ordination may require intervention even at the operational level where necessary to resolve disputes between competing security agencies and between security agencies and other parts of government.

The Need for Enhanced Central Co-ordination and Oversight: Making Strategy Out of Tactics

With the 2015 laws, the need for central oversight identified by Justice Major's Air India Commission and Senator Segal's Senate committee has increased. As this book recounts, those laws create a plethora of new anti-terrorism tools, many of which may lead us down the path toward both over- and underreaction. Legislated tactics will not translate automatically into an anti-terror strategy. Strategy will require careful thought, but then also substantial co-ordination.

Take, for example, the co-ordination of no-fly listing and/or passport denials with surveillance in Canada. It may be appropriate to prevent a person from leaving Canada to join the Islamic State of Iraq and Syria (ISIS) or another foreign terrorist group, but there is a need to ensure that appropriate actions — including surveillance, peace bonds, arrests, or prosecutions — are used when that person remains in Canada.

The RCMP has recognized this need, establishing in October 2014 a National Security Joint Operations Centre. Partner agencies, including CSIS, the Canada Border Services Agency, Citizenship and Immigration Canada (and, where necessary, the Department of National Defence, CSE, and the Department of Foreign Affairs), are "co-located at the RCMP's National Operations Centre in Ottawa to facilitate the real-time exchange of information, and support the coordination of operational responses on a daily basis." This is a laudable initiative, albeit one that dates only to October 2014 and so remains nascent. But there are key questions. This body appears aimed at "individuals under criminal investigation for terrorism offences." What about the people who are not yet subject to such investigations? And who decides the matter when differences of opinion arise between the different agencies? As the RCMP notes, this "coordinated approach to operational decision making . . . neither replaces nor impedes the member agencies' prerogative to make independent operational decisions consistent with their respective mandates and applicable laws."[30] It appears, therefore, that the RCMP centre attempts to co-ordinate activity in a system in which everyone is in charge.

Meanwhile, after the 2015 changes, there may well be more friction and disputes between CSIS and the RCMP over how CSIS handles its new ability under Bill C-44 to grant its human sources a confidentiality privilege, immunizing them in most instances from being identified or called as witnesses. The Air India Commission opposed a CSIS source privilege because of concerns that CSIS had incentives to extend this privilege routinely to its sources and would do so unilaterally without consulting police and prosecutors. CSIS does not labour under the same sort of concerns as do police about the difficulties that this privilege can cause to subsequent prosecutions.

Senator Segal's Senate committee recommended that in appropriate cases a CSIS source could be protected by police informer privilege, but only if the source was shared with the police and the police invoked the privilege. In other words, CSIS should not unilaterally be able to extend a privilege that would prevent police and prosecutors from identifying CSIS sources during the course of prosecutions. It also contemplated that the national security advisor would resolve disputes between CSIS and the RCMP about accesses to human sources,[51] something ignored in the 2015 legislation.

Another issue will be whether CSIS's new threat reduction powers under Bill C-51 will encourage CSIS to embark on its own trajectory and share even less information with the police or otherwise conduct itself in a manner that results in fewer prosecutions.

This is not a theoretical concern: RCMP documents assert that after Bill C-51, "there will be additional pressure on the RCMP to de-conflict with CSIS in a timely manner to ensure that criminal investigations are not negatively affected — for instance through inadvertent interference with the chain of evidence or preventing the ability to lay criminal charges." And "[m]ore formal de-confliction practices will need to be established to clarify roles and responsibilities so that our activities are transparent and accountable."[52]

It is, of course, open to the minister of public safety to issue directives to CSIS on these issues, but it will also be important for someone at the centre of government to monitor the effects of CSIS's new powers on criminal investigations and prosecutions. Again, who will oversee this process and make sure it works?

As we argue in Chapter 3, there may be policy reasons for preferring not to prosecute young would-be terrorist fighters. Nevertheless, it should not be up to CSIS to determine unilaterally the government's policy on this matter by making decisions that prejudice downstream prosecutions. Someone, whether it be the minister of public safety or the prime minister's national security advisor, had best be in charge.

The Need for Enhanced Central Co-ordination and Oversight: Foreign Adventures

We have already noted that the new 2015 laws accord CSIS a new ability to conduct investigations and threat reduction activities abroad and even to violate Canadian and foreign laws when doing so. And we have suggested that without co-ordination, this could be a recipe for disaster and international embarrassment.

We advance the argument above that the minister of public safety needs to consider these matters. But we also think that ministerial oversight alone will not work when CSIS bumps into other ministries and other national security interests. There needs to be co-ordination at the centre. The ultimate co-ordinator is of course cabinet and the prime minister, but close cabinet involvement runs the risk of politicizing these issues.

This is one reason why independent civil servants within the Privy Council Office, such as the national security advisor, have an important role to play. Under a whole-of-government approach, the inter-departmental buck should stop somewhere.

The Need for Enhanced Whole-of-Government Co-ordination and Oversight: A Voice of Reason in a Sea of Information

Co-ordination at the centre is also required to establish priorities and discipline for whole-of-government information sharing. As explained in Chapter 5, Bill C-51's information sharing law allows seventeen different agencies to receive security information from over 100 different federal agencies. Bill C-51 is, however, silent on what information must be shared. This raises a danger that each agency will be influenced by its own bureaucratic interests in deciding how much information to disclose.

The new information sharing law defines almost everything as a security matter. There is a pressing need for someone to establish priorities for information sharing and to co-ordinate all the moving parts. If the agencies do not work well together, however, some of the sterner "bad cop" techniques of oversight may also be necessary. Without effective central co-ordination and direction, the government may not be able to keep its promise to the families of the Air India victims and other victims of terrorism that information will be shared and so will aid in preventing terrorism. Again, central direction and co-ordination is necessary to ensure that the appropriate amount of information flows through the system and gets to the right people.

The basic point is that someone in government should establish and assume responsibility for what information is collected and shared. This issue is too important to be left to the discretion of each agency, operating in its own silos. Again, our mantra: someone needs to have clear responsibility and be in charge. If every minister and agency head is effectively in charge, there is a danger that no one will take responsibility for the ultimate result. An obvious person to play this role would be the national security advisor. And the outcome should not depend on whether the prime minister's national security advisor chooses to exercise his influence; it should be a responsibility.

Falling Behind Our Close Allies

In Chapter 12, we discuss how Canada has failed to keep pace with reforms in other democracies designed to provide more effective whole-of-government review of whole-of-government security activities. The idea frequently promoted by Minister of Public Safety Blaney during the Bill C-51 debates that Canada's approach is the "envy of the world" demonstrates a disturbing degree of ignorance of what other democracies are doing, and not just with review. If we also think we are doing fine with oversight and co-ordination, we risk being complacent, an attitude that wears thin in the face of the security failures of October 2014.

The United Kingdom Experience

The United Kingdom has a Joint Intelligence Committee and a National Security Council, both run from the United Kingdom Cabinet Office. Through these bodies, the United Kingdom has developed a more detailed mechanism of co-ordination for multi-agency and multi-ministerial national security activities than has Canada.

In the United Kingdom, the National Security Council meets weekly and involves relevant ministries and, when required, the heads of the agencies. It is chaired by the United Kingdom prime minister, with the prime minister's national security advisor serving as the secretary of the council. The United Kingdom national security advisor also chairs a permanent secretaries group in the national security area.[53]

In crises, the United Kingdom prime minister chairs COBRA meetings, named after the Cabinet Office Briefing Rooms in which they are held. That process is not without critics. A former police officer, present during COBRA meetings relating to the 2005 London bombings and the 2007 Glasgow airport terrorist incident, has criticized the meetings as focusing too much on politics and too little on operations.[54] This is a danger in asking politicians to play an increased oversight role. Giving senior civil servants the lead function, and ensuring that a minister or prime minister assume responsibility for any direction they provide to the civil service, may mitigate this danger.

For its part, the Joint Intelligence Committee includes the heads of all three intelligence agencies as well as military intelligence. It directs intelligence collection and analysis and advises the prime minister. David Omand, who served as its head, has stressed how the Joint Intelligence Committee's practice of formulating collective decisions led all the members to better appreciate the others' perspectives and "may be one reason why the UK has been able to work across domestic/overseas and policy/intelligence organizational boundaries on counter-terrorism . . . in ways that other nations with their more compartmentalized intelligence and police structures have not yet achieved."[55]

Something like a Canadian version of the Joint Intelligence Committee may be developing, but may not yet be formalized. Fadden told the Senate committee examining Bill C-51 that

> . . . once a week, I call a meeting of the chiefs of all the agencies that regularly deal with questions of national security. That way, we can coordinate our activities and bring each other up to date with regard to the major events of the week or the day. Every morning, I receive a communication on what is going on in the area of national security. If necessary, I communicate with the agency directors . . . . We encourage information

sharing and ensure that the centre where I work is aware of what people are doing. If we believe that an issue is particularly sensitive, we ensure that the minister responsible for the agency is informed, or we inform the Prime Minister.[56]

Such developments will be even more necessary given the need to co-ordinate the exercise of new security powers under the 2015 legislation. Such weekly meetings should be formalized and adequately resourced and staffed.

Australian Developments

In the wake of a Sydney terrorist attack in December 2014 causing the death of two people, the Australian government proposed the creation of a new executive counter-terrorism committee, to be chaired by a national counter-terrorism co-ordinator, who was appointed in May 2015.[57] The new counter-terrorism committee is designed "to ensure that all agencies are working in the closest possible harmony" and that that counter-terrorism "needs to be more consistently whole-of-government in outlook. We must ensure all relevant government departments and agencies bring their expertise to bear."[58]

The Australian government augmented this plan by designating the attorney general as the lead minister in charge of counter-terrorism, with responsibilities for prosecutions, intelligence, terrorism financing, and counter-violent extremism programs. A case can be made that the Canadian minister of public safety has become the *de facto* lead on anti-terrorism, especially given the new enhanced terrorism powers assigned to that minister in 2015. Nevertheless, the Canadian development does not appear to be a conscious and considered redesign, at least as compared to the more robust Australian approach.

Summary

Parliament has now given security agencies — and particularly CSIS — many more powers. In doing so, the government has continued to ignore the 2010 advice of the Air India Commission about the need for enhanced oversight to ensure that agencies, notably CSIS and the RCMP, work together in the public interest. Retired Supreme Court Justice John Major — the Air India Commissioner — felt strongly enough about this issue that he testified in both the Commons and Senate committees that reviewed Bill C-51 about the need to give the prime minister's national security advisor enhanced powers.

Richard Fadden, the prime minister's current national security advisor, testified that he has a "coordinating and not an operational role," but that ministerial accountability remains the prime method of oversight. As indicated above, he conceded "Mr. Major was thinking of something with a bit more oomph in it in the sense that he wanted it to be based in statute and be given specific powers. Again, that's a matter for government and Parliament to decide . . . ."[59] The government has decided. It decided that enhanced oversight, like enhanced review, was not necessary. This may be an error that we will come to regret.

Given that the government seems content to rely on ministerial accountability, it is important to recognize that the minister of public safety has evolved into a *de facto* lead department on terrorism. Given this evolution, this ministry should be reserved for some of the most experienced and capable ministers and civil servants. Consideration should also be given to shedding some of the ministry's sprawling portfolio so it can better focus on its national security responsibilities.

A priority for the minister of public safety must be making sure that CSIS's new powers and privileges are not exercised in a manner that will unwittingly compromise subsequent criminal investigations and terrorism prosecutions. The minister will also need to ensure that terrorism-related no-fly and passport interdiction are co-ordinated, when necessary, with measures to minimize the risk that would-be foreign terrorist fighters present in Canada. And the minister will also have to ensure that CSIS and the RCMP co-ordinate the use of their new and overlapping disruption powers.

Alas, we are not optimistic this will happen, because ministers of public safety have been unable to resolve RCMP and CSIS conflict in the past. They have allowed a less-than-optimal distant "less is more" relationship to emerge between the two agencies, a matter we examined in Chapter 9.

Even if an energetic minister of public safety steps to the plate, supported by the department's capable officials, there is still a need for central co-ordination. Who will ensure that CSIS's new powers to investigate and reduce security threats outside of Canada do not step on the toes of the Department of Foreign Affairs and the Department of National Defence?

Who will ensure that the attorney general's consents to preventive arrests, peace bonds, and terrorism prosecutions are exercised in co-ordination with the intelligence and now threat reduction operations that are subject to oversight by the minister of public safety?

Who will ensure that sufficient intelligence flows in and out of the various ministries and agencies that must work together if Canada is to enforce its seldom-enforced laws against terrorism financing?

Who will ensure that counter–violent extremism programs are not dominated by the police and intelligence agencies, but will work with federal and provincial departments with responsibilities and powers over health, education, social services, and citizenship?

Who will ensure that new CSIS and police powers to engage in temporary forms of disruption are not exercised in a way that causes long-term damage to both prosecutions and community relations?

We think that the prime minister's national security advisor will need to co-ordinate Canada's expanding anti-terrorist toolkit, establish priorities for information sharing, and, when necessary, resolve disputes between agencies.

IV. PARLIAMENTARY OVERSIGHT?

What about "parliamentary oversight"? As will be discussed in Chapter 12, Canadian parliamentarians should have access to secret information so they can perform a *review* function. But we do not think they should perform *oversight* — a role in making operational decisions. They are in no position by expertise, training, or disposition to do so. And even if they could, the American experience with Congressional oversight suggests that it might not be a good idea. Congress does not engage in true oversight in the command and control sense; instead, US law requires congressional intelligence committees to be kept "fully and currently informed of the intelligence activities of the United States, including any significant anticipated intelligence activity."[60]

Members of Congress from both parties were apprised of various activities of the US national security agency that were of dubious legality and that invaded privacy. They essentially did nothing, until *The New York Times* in 2005 and Edward Snowden in 2013 drew attention to them. There is considerable reason to believe that legislators who are brought into the operational tent are tainted in their subsequent ability to exercise effective review of executive government action.

Parliamentary committees could, as is done in Australia, be given some role in reviewing the listing of terrorists and terrorist groups. This would of necessity require that they have access to secret information. This might be a positive development, but it is doubtful that busy parliamentarians could do as good a job in reviewing listings as the courts. They would be able to bring political common sense to such exercises, but this should already be achieved through requirements for ministerial approvals and reviews. And at any rate, political common sense may not always be sensible, especially where serious liberty and reputational interests are at stake.

The single place where Parliament does have a command and control power of sorts is in enacting legislation and, to a lesser degree, in approving budgets. Unfortunately, the Bill C-51 debate underlined real limits in the parliamentary process. The five amendments that the government accepted after Bill C-51 was introduced appear not to have originated in the Commons committee's hearings. As discussed in Chapter 5, one of the amendments is particularly awkward because, if taken literally, it could prevent the sharing of information about even violent forms of protest and dissent, including terrorism.

The Senate committee that reviewed Bill C-51 did not propose any amendments, but it held much more informative hearings than in the Commons. Other Senate committees have made important contributions to increasing understanding of complex national security issues. Nevertheless, on Bill C-51, Conservative senators acted so as to ensure passage of the law in time for the 2015 federal election. The Senate committee made an unenforceable commitment to review the bill in five years.[61] But even assuming that review comes to pass, it will not be grounded in the full facts without access to secret information.

V. JUDICIAL OVERSIGHT

The government has stressed that new CSIS and police powers in Bill C-51 will be subject to judicial oversight. Indeed, Minister of Defence Jason Kenney even suggested that Bill C-51 "doesn't give new powers to police or intelligence agencies but rather to judges, to courts, who, for example, can order the detention of a suspected terrorist for up to seven days."[62] This position is ironic for a government that has complained of judicial activism. It also happens to be misleading. The security services did receive new powers. And it is an overstatement to suggest that judges will oversee all of these activities, or that they can truly be effective in relation to those areas where they are involved.

No Serious Prospect of Judicial Scrutiny of Information Sharing

Judicial warrants are a form of command and control oversight — pre-authorization for state conduct. But judicial warrants are only required for a subset of activity authorized in Bill C-51. There is *no* judicial oversight contemplated with respect to the sweeping Bill C-51's information sharing law, the *Security of Canada Information Sharing Act.*

The Arar Commission stressed the limits of courts in reviewing information sharing. In this area, judges are not proactive overseers — they can only respond to misconduct when it becomes the subject of litigation. Because of secrecy, "affected individuals may never know that they have been subject to a national security investigation. This reduced level of judicial oversight is a further reason for independent review."[63] Even if individuals do know of state wrongdoing, they may not have the resources to bring a court challenge. And even if they were well-financed, they would confront serious barriers to their action, in the form of government secrecy claims.[64]

It is well known that Maher Arar received a $10.5 million settlement of his claim against the government for the consequences flowing from the information sharing in his case. But other Canadians who were tortured in Syria, in part because of Canadian information sharing, have faced delays and roadblocks when suing the government.

Future civil suits stemming from the sharing of unreliable and perhaps false information may be more difficult because of section 9 of the new information sharing Act: "no civil proceedings lie against any person for their disclosure in good faith of information under this Act." Neither Justice O'Connor nor Justice Iacobucci — the commissioners who conducted the inquiries into foreign maltreatment and Canada's role in it — found that Canadian officials had acted in bad faith. Section 9 may only protect specific individuals from liability, but it is possible that the government will also attempt to shelter behind its broadly defined form of qualified immunity.

Judicial Review as Opposed to Oversight

Sometimes matters will come before courts. But the same confusion between review and oversight also affects assessment of the judicial role under the new legislation.

The new laws governing the no-fly list and terrorist-related passport revocations provide for challenges by affected persons through judicial review. But this can only happen after a person has been listed and denied the ability to leave Canada. Executive decisions will be overturned only when they are unreasonable. This is not command and control oversight. It is review, likely with a healthy dose of deference.

As has been the case for some time, officials, and not judges, will decide who will be placed on no-fly lists and denied passports. Indeed it would be strange (but alas not unprecedented given the new CSIS powers in Bill C-51) to think that judges would pre-authorize a violation of a citizen's right to leave Canada. Judges are supposed to protect rights and ensure that the government can justify their violations, not authorize their violation.

The Judicial Role in Preventive Arrests and Peace Bonds

Judges will play a more proactive role in supervising preventive arrests and formulating peace bonds. Except in cases of exigent circumstances, judges must pre-approve preventive arrests. And as discussed in Chapter 10, judges will decide whether a person arrested preventively may remain in detention.[65]

In addition, peace bonds may now be ordered on the basis of reasonable fears that a person "may" as opposed to "will" commit a terrorism offence. If the person does not enter in the peace bond willingly, a judge may adjudicate the matter, and impose the conditions on that person's liberty.[66]

But note that while judges will decide these matters, they do so on standards constrained by the legislative framework enacted by Bill C-51. Absent a successful *Charter* challenge, it is Parliament that decides the criteria for these judicial assessments, not the judges. And the judges' only role is to determine whether the police have satisfied the standards that Parliament has set.

Because Parliament has lowered the threshold for using these new powers, it has increased the risks of false positives. There will be instances where someone who is not a terrorist is nevertheless subject to preventive detention or a peace bond. Because of the (false) association with terrorism, such persons may experience adverse publicity, stigma, and ruined reputations. Authorizing a judge to bless government conduct justified on low standards will not avert this problem.

The limits that Parliament has placed on the judicial role are most clearly seen in the provisions in Bill C-51 that govern whether a person subject to preventive arrest can be detained for the maximum period, expanded from three to seven days. On the one hand, there will be judicial hearings within the first twenty-four hours, and then within three and then five days of detention. This is a praiseworthy restraint on state power. On the other hand, Bill C-51 tells the judge to approve extensions of preventive arrest to the maximum of seven days where "the investigation in relation to which the person is detained is being conducted diligently and expeditiously."[67] The result is a form of judicial oversight, but a very constrained one that greatly facilitates preventive detention for investigative reasons.

The Judicial Role with respect to CSIS Warrants

Bill C-44 and Bill C-51 give specially designated Federal Court judges new roles in authorizing CSIS to conduct surveillance and engage in threat reduction in violation of Canadian and foreign laws, including the *Charter*. Many readers might be comforted that a judge will bless (or not) this conduct, and the government's defence of both bills stressed this judicial role. Nevertheless, it is extremely important to understand the nature of the warrant process in order to understand the limits of judicial oversight.

For one thing, a warrant is not always required. It is extremely unclear under what circumstances a warrant is required under Bill C-44 for foreign operations, a matter discussed in Chapter 4. And a warrant is required for threat disruption only where it will (in CSIS's eyes) violate the *Charter* or any Canadian law. Judges will never be asked to consider measures that fall short of this threshold. Moreover, since Canadian law generally only applies in Canada, it should not be assumed that this threshold will frequently be met in international operations or that CSIS will rush to court seeking a warrant for foreign threat reduction activities.

Role of the Federal Court

When CSIS does come to court, what happens? Under both Bill C-44 and Bill C-51, Federal Court judges may grant warrants "without regard to any other law, including that of a foreign state."[68] Under Bill C-51, judges will even be able to grant CSIS a warrant to contravene the *Charter* provided that they are persuaded the proposed measure is proportionate to the threat and the availability of alternative solutions.[69] The measures must also not intentionally or negligently inflict death or bodily harm, invade sexual integrity, or obstruct justice.[70]

Only specially designated Federal Court judges are able to grant CSIS warrants. At present, fourteen Federal Court judges have been "designated" by the Chief Justice of the Federal Court to hear CSIS warrant cases.[71] These judges typically hear CSIS applications alone.

The specially designated judges on the Federal Court are in a difficult position. They need to be aware of and educated about common issues that confront CSIS. This may be particularly true with respect to the technology that CSIS may use when executing warrants and also with respect to the conditions that CSIS may face when executing warrants outside of Canada. Judges must also make efforts to co-ordinate rulings to ensure consistency.

Presumably, to address these issues, the court has held closed-door special sittings — that is, a sitting of a panel of judges — in exceptional circumstances. These have occurred, for example, when the chief justice considered it necessary to hear from the director of CSIS, the general counsel of CSIS, and/or CSIS personnel on procedural questions that implicated more than a single case — that is, crossover issues. When the special sittings addressed procedural or evidentiary matters relevant to future cases, the "designated judge seized of the case proceeded to adjudicate the specific matter alone, but the other designated judges were able to obtain the benefit of the information or evidence provided during the sitting."[72]

These special meetings make obvious sense. They raise, however, another issue: the appearance of bias. In a different context, a leading Supreme Court case held that the appearance of judicial independence suffered and there was a reasonable apprehension of bias as a result of a meeting between a governmental minister and the chief justice of the Federal Court about the scheduling of matters before the court in a contested case.[73] The analogy is not precise because the target of a CSIS warrant is never involved and indeed typically never informed about the CSIS warrant. But the concern is obviously acute for members of the court.

For these reasons, during special sittings, the court has included a "neutral third party, such as a retired Justice of the Supreme Court." Should the issue arise, the latter would then be able to confirm that "the subject matter discussed was entirely appropriate."[74] The court also has the inherent authority to invite security-cleared lawyers, most plausibly drawn from the special advocate roster. It seems advisable to have someone raise questions from the perspective of potential warrant targets to ensure an element of adversarialism and to further maintain the appearance of impartiality.

We also question whether special sittings on issues of public law — such as the constitutionality of the power Bill C-51 gives Federal Court judges — should be held in private at all. These are important questions of public interest, and wherever possible, judges should ensure they are also decided in the public eye.

The One-Sided Nature of the Warrant Process

But in the end, actual CSIS warrant proceedings are *ex parte* and *in camera*. This means that they are held in closed court (*in camera*) with only the government side represented (*ex parte*). This is typical for all warrant applications — there would be no logic to a system in which the target of a covert surveillance operation is apprised of that operation so that the person could appear to make representations on whether it should be authorized.

Nevertheless, it is important to underscore the consequence of this one-sided process. Our system of justice typically depends on an adversarial process in which judges weigh the views of two sides, each with an incentive to set out thoroughly its position. Commenting on another type of *ex parte* proceeding, Justice James Hugessen stated in 2002 that judges "greatly miss . . . our security blanket which is the adversary system that we were all brought up with and that . . . is for most of us, the real warranty that the outcome of what we do is going to be fair and just."[75]

One safeguard in an *ex parte* proceeding is a firm requirement that the government be perfectly candid with judges. It must bring all relevant information to the judge's attention. We believe that the government is generally observant of this firm obligation. However, there are instances where it has breached this duty. There are now several Federal Court decisions complaining that CSIS has failed to meet its duty of candour in closed door proceedings.[76] It is very difficult to know whether these reports represent the sum total of CSIS shortcomings; a failure to be candid is something that is, by definition, very difficult to detect.

The Potential Role of Amicus Curiae in the Warrant Process

As we suggest with special sittings, the Federal Court may try to mitigate the risks associated with *ex parte* proceedings by enlisting the assistance of security-cleared lawyers as a "friend of the court," or *amicus curiae*, to restore a quasi-adversarial system.

Such an approach in the warrant context is an approximation of the special advocate role in the immigration security certificate proceeding. As discussed in Chapter 7, special advocates are responsive to constitutional requirements set down by the Supreme Court for immigration security certificates.[77] Although Bill C-51 does not provide for their appointment, the Chief Justice of the Federal Court indicated just after Bill C-51 became law that security-cleared friends of the court would likely play a role as the Federal Court considered the government's first application for threat reduction warrants.[78] This is a safeguard that supplements the silence of Bill C-51 on this important issue.

And so, the discretionary appointment of such friends of the court for the new CSIS threat reduction warrant proceedings is welcome. Nevertheless, it should not be conflated with the different and constitutionally guaranteed role that the same security-cleared lawyers play as special advocates under immigration law security certificates. In other words, it is important to recognize the extent to which a CSIS warrant process differs from even the imperfect situation under a security certificate.

First, under the immigration security certificate process, special advocates are a statutory office with statutory roles and responsibilities. This places them in a significantly more meaningful role than is the case with friends of the court, appointed at the discretion of the judge. Indeed, a recent Federal Court decision suggests that the role of friends of the court in *ex parte* proceedings will vary depending on the judge's predispositions and may be more limited than that of a special advocate.[79]

Second, although underfunded, special advocates are at least supported by a special support unit, organized at arm's length from the Department of Justice. Absent special arrangements, friends of the court do not automatically benefit from this administrative structure. They may operate in splendid isolation, with only the resources they can personally bring (and which do not include assistance from their own firms or, typically, outside experts for security reasons) or that the court itself provides.

Third, friends of the court have no independent standing to bring appeals. As a result, warrant decisions are unappealable by any party other than (in practice) the government.

Fourth, whatever the imperfections of the immigration security certificate process, at least there are "named persons" aware that their interests are being adjudicated and able to provide information to the special advocate. Indeed, after the *Harkat* decision of the Supreme Court,[80] there is a presumption in favour of ongoing communication between the special advocates and the named persons, subject to care that the special advocates disclose no secret information, as well as minimal disclosure standards allowing the named persons to know the case against them.

The presence of a named person able to feed information to the special advocate is critical to the lawyer's effectiveness — there is a source of information other than the government, and inconsistencies and contradictions in the government's position may be made obvious and then adjudicated by the court.

None of these qualities exist in the CSIS warrant context. No named person will be able to point out factual flaws in CSIS's justification for the warrant. No named person will be able to submit that there are less drastic alternatives to what CSIS proposes. A friend of the court who has access only to the government's version of events may have difficulty determining whether statements by CSIS informers that may lie at the heart of the warrant application are indeed reliable, especially if facts are obscured by the new Bill C-44 privilege that protects the informer's identity. It would be wrong, therefore, to imagine that an *amicus* can correct all the shortcomings of the closed and otherwise one-sided CSIS warrant process.

American Developments in Improving the Warrant Process

It is worth contrasting the Bill C-51 approach with developments in the United States. The United States Privacy and Civil Liberties Oversight Board condemned secretive authorizations, absence of appeals, and no robust special advocate system in a 2014 review of warrants granted to the National Security Agency.[81] The 2015 *USA Freedom Act* responded to these recommendations and provides for both friends of the court and declassified warrant decisions when "a novel or significant"[82] legal point is raised in a warrant application. The law also enables individuals and organizations to act as friends of the court when they can provide "technical expertise" to counter that provided by the government.[83] These friends of the court will have "expertise in privacy and civil liberties, intelligence collection, communications technology, or any other area that may lend legal or technical expertise"[84] to the court. In other words, the new US law pushes against secrecy in warrant cases in a way that Bill C-51 does not.

Absence of Retrospective Judicial Review of Warrants

Once a CSIS warrant walks out the courtroom door, judicial oversight usually comes to an end. CSIS warrants, unlike *Criminal Code* warrants, are not designed to produce evidence that can be tested in criminal trials and appeals. This too limits the usefulness of a judicial role.

CSIS investigations only become the subject matter of trials in rare circumstances, and even then these are usually procedural disputes as to whether CSIS must reveal information about its conduct, and to what extent. As discussed in Chapter 4, a CSIS warrant became relevant in the recent VIA Rail plot trial in Toronto because it provided the basis for a *Criminal Code* wiretap that was used in the prosecution. The trial judge found that some of the information used to obtain the CSIS warrant was misleading, but that even with this material excised, there were still sufficient legal grounds for the warrant. Therefore, the police *Criminal Code* wiretap derived from the CSIS warrant could be used as evidence.[85] But cases like these — where CSIS warrants are reviewed in criminal trials — are uncommon. Especially when CSIS operations are directed toward threat reduction, as opposed to collecting information, the CSIS warrant will rarely be subject to indirect review by a criminal trial judge.

For these sorts of reasons, the Arar Commission noted that the comparative lack of prosecutions in the national security area means that the courts provide less accountability in national security investigations "than they do for other criminal investigations."[86]

Nor are there other means by which a target is informed of the CSIS warrant. While police wiretap surveillance authorizations under Part VI of the *Criminal Code* must be disclosed to the target after a passage of time, CSIS warrants are never disclosed. CSIS warrants remain secret and mistakes in them or in their execution are rarely discovered, and if they are discovered, even more rarely publicly reported.

Accidental Oversight? The Case of Re X

Finally, there is no true "feedback" loop to the judge issuing a CSIS warrant allowing the judge to scrutinize what CSIS purports to do pursuant to the warrant against the actual terms of that warrant.

What is authorized and what is done by CSIS may not always correspond, as a recent Federal Court decision suggests.[87] In *Re X*, the court only learned of the gap between a security intelligence warrant authorization and CSIS conduct by accident. A judge with a wealth of experience in national security, Justice Mosley, noted inconsistency between the actual content of the warrant and practice attributed to his warrant, as hinted at in public reports of SIRC and the CSE Commissioners. His subsequent actions demonstrate the potential of continuing judicial oversight of how CSIS warrants are executed, although they also reveal governmental resistance to such oversight.

The Initial Warrant

In 2009, Justice Mosley issued warrants to allow CSIS to intercept foreign communications of Canadian citizens outside of Canada. These warrants authorized the communications intercepts on the basis that, while they might involve overseas communications, the intercept would be done *within* the territory of Canada. It was this fact — and this fact alone — that appeared to satisfy him that he had jurisdiction to issue the warrants and that the CSIS conduct would comply with international law, and specifically, the prohibition against violations of foreign territorial sovereignty.[88]

It was never entirely clear from the limited public record in this case how an intrusive intercept of a foreign communication could be done within Canada, without reaching out (electronically) and hacking communications overseas, in presumptive violation of some foreign law. But more significantly, subsequent controversy stemmed from CSIS's non-observance of this Canadian territorial expectation. CSIS, in co-ordination with the CSE, outsourced the intercept function to the Five Eyes foreign intelligence alliance. Intrusive surveillance was not, therefore, confined to the territory of Canada, and was instead conducted by one or more Five Eyes allies — that is, the signals intelligence agencies of the United States, United Kingdom, Australia, or New Zealand (Canada is the fifth member).[89] Moreover, this Five Eyes alliance surveillance was not confined to their own territories, but involved intrusive surveillance in third party states.[90]

"A Deliberate Decision to Keep the Court in the Dark . . . ."[91]

Some of these facts were publicized in the annual public reports of the CSE commissioner and SIRC. Upon learning of them, Justice Mosley convened a new hearing on his own initiative. It is reasonable to infer that he was not happy.

Justice Mosley was assisted in this new 2013 hearing by a security-cleared friend of the court. He also had access to the CSE commissioner's secret report to the minister, which reveals the potential for judges and executive watchdogs to assist each other. At the same time, as Professor Reg Whitaker has observed, it is noteworthy that it was Justice Mosley — a "vigilant and skeptical judge" — who raised the alarm bells and followed the trail, and not the executive watchdogs.[92] Indeed, it seems apparent that those watchdogs had misunderstood the content of the warrants under which CSIS was operating.

In declassified reasons released in December 2013, Justice Mosley concluded that CSIS had misled him by not revealing its plans to draw on the assistance of CSE's Five Eyes signals intelligence foreign partners in carrying out the surveillance. He called this a "deliberate decision to keep the Court in the dark about the scope and extent of the foreign collection efforts that would flow from the Court's issuance of a warrant."[93]

Justice Mosley concluded that the tasking of foreign agencies by Canadian officials to conduct the surveillance was unlawful. He was rightly not happy that CSIS had tried to use his warrant as "protective cover,"[94] and he stressed that his warrant did not and could not authorize the use of foreign agencies to conduct surveillance.

Notably, this would no longer be necessarily true under Bill C-51, which authorizes CSIS to enlist "another person"[95] to assist in the execution of threat reduction warrants, without even requiring that the judge who authorized the warrant be informed of this critical fact. It is possible, therefore, to see the new warrant procedures enacted in 2015 as an attempt to ensure that CSIS has the "protective cover" of warrants when it violates Canadian or foreign law and the *Charter* and when it enlists third parties to help execute the warrant.

A Failure to Connect Dots

What happened in the Justice Mosley case was not an isolated occurrence. Drawing on a SIRC report, Justice Mosley noted that foreign assistance had been used in as many as thirty-five warrants issued since 2009. The legality of all this activity had escaped scrutiny until it drew Justice Mosley's attention, although the review bodies had acute concerns about the wisdom of enlisting foreign partners.

This was consequential. Justice Mosley stated emphatically that he shared the concerns of these review bodies that Canada could lose control of intelligence that it asked its foreign partners to collect. He stressed the grave risks that may arise when Canada relinquishes control over its intelligence,[96] as demonstrated by the torture of Maher Arar and other Canadians, in part because of Canadian information sharing with the United States and other foreign partners.

Justice Mosley's decision should not be taken as good evidence that the accountability system "works." It is, at best, a form of "accidental accountability." The system "worked," but by happenstance and not design. As will be discussed in Chapter 12, his decision depended on the happenstance that CSIS had enlisted CSE to execute its warrant, and the happy coincidence that CSE is scrutinized by an independent review body. If CSIS has instead enlisted other partners in, for example, the Department of Defence, the Department of Foreign Affairs, or the Canadian Border Service Agency, no review body would have reported on the activities of those departments or agency. There is no review body to do so.

And in fact, as we have said, the new 2015 laws allow CSIS to do exactly this: recruit assistance from other agencies in executing its functions. In some cases the judge may be aware of third-party assistance because it is specifically authorized in the warrant,[97] but in other cases the judge will not know: CSIS is independently authorized under Bill C-51 to seek the assistance of "another person" in executing a threat reduction warrant without prior judicial approval and is not even required to inform the judge about who has assisted in the execution of the warrant.[98]

The Mosley decision also suggests that no one had contrasted the actual content of the warrant that was issued in 2009 with how CSIS executed the warrant, in this case with the assistance of CSE and still-unnamed foreign partners. The judge who knew the content of the warrant only learned of how it was executed because it happened to be reported (and incorrectly described as actually authorizing the activity in question) in the review body reports.

The absence of formalized, standing, "feedback" loops between authorizing judges and review bodies is one of the many striking omissions in the Canadian national security accountability system. Even a perfect feedback loop would have disadvantages, because it would slowly move judges in our adversarial system toward a model of investigating magistrates, as found on the European Continent. We acknowledge that some may prefer such a system, but it has not been our system, and our judges are not trained or equipped for this task.

We believe, nevertheless, that Federal Court judges should contemplate structuring feedback loops by creating more formal links with SIRC. Under the amended *CSIS Act*, judges may impose "any terms and conditions that the judge considers advisable in the public interest."[99] It is our hope that judges would consider correcting deficiencies in the area of formalized feedback loops by imposing a requirement that the minister request a special review by SIRC[100] of CSIS's performance under the warrant at issue and then report the outcome to the court. Such an approach would ensure some follow-through on the back-end execution of the warrant that we fear might otherwise not take place.

This is not a perfect solution. We are not terribly optimistic that this strategy will mitigate overreach in the use of the new security powers. As we discuss in Chapter 12, SIRC does not have the power to review the work of other agencies that will assist CSIS in executing its warrants. These others include CSE, an agency we expect will routinely assist CSIS in engaging in foreign surveillance and electronic disruptions. We also recognize that placing such judicial mandates on SIRC will increase the formidable challenges that SIRC already faces and could impede its ability to audit other parts of CSIS's work, including those done without warrant. We develop the theme in Chapter 12 that review cannot cure overly broad security powers.

A Secret Jurisprudence on Warrants without Appeals

The Justice Mosley case demonstrates that unexpected things can happen when CSIS executes its warrants. It is easy to image unexpected and even bad things happening as CSIS executes new warrants that allow it to investigate outside of Canada and to physically reduce security threats both outside and inside Canada. But will we ever know if anything bad does happen? Will there be any remedy if it does?

The warrant target is not informed or notified of the content of the warrant, or even of its existence. Even if a judge appoints a friend of the court to play an adversarial role, such an *amicus* will generally not be able to bring an appeal.

Appeals are creatures of statutes, and there are no provisions in Bill C-44 and Bill C-51 providing for appeals of decisions on whether to grant the new CSIS warrants. Even if appeals were possible, only the government is in a real position to bring them — and it did appeal (unsuccessfully) the Justice Mosley decision.

Nor will the decisions by Federal Courts to issue warrants be published, or at least published in full form. In the VIA Rail plot case, for example, the initial CSIS warrant decision has not been released and the name of the issuing Federal Court judge is not even mentioned in the trial judge's decision. We only know about the CSIS warrant because the trial judge in this case was granted extraordinary access to the affidavit used in the CSIS warrant, with the RCMP keeping all the secret material under lock and key at a location outside the courtroom.[101]

In these circumstances, there is a danger that the Federal Court caselaw on CSIS warrants will be a secret jurisprudence, or one that will be released only well after the fact and in such heavily redacted form that it will be difficult to evaluate the decisions that the judges have made.

Bill C-44 and Bill C-51 are silent on the issue of whether warrant decisions can be made public, effectively leaving this critical decision to the judges. This compares unfavourably with developments in the United States. Responding to the fact that many US *Foreign Intelligence Surveillance Act of 1978*[102] court decisions authorizing the collection of mass information remained secret until revealed by the Snowden leaks, the 2015 *USA Freedom Act* places a duty on the US director of national intelligence to make public "to the greatest extent possible" any *Foreign Intelligence Surveillance Act* court decision "that includes a significant construction or interpretation of any provision of law . . . ."[103]

There was no comparable attempt to promote greater transparency under the laws enacted in Canada during the same year. Even if Canadian judges do their best to disclose as much as possible, most of the material in CSIS warrant decisions will continue to remain secret and rarely be subject to appeal or indirect review by another judge.

Summary

So how do we evaluate the government assertion that Bill C-51 will be adequately checked by accountability to judges? It does not persuade.

As seen above, many of these new powers, including those involving information sharing, will not be subject to any judicial oversight. Others, such as the no-fly list, will only be subject to judicial review of the reasonableness of the executive's decision after the fact. Judges will make important decisions about preventive arrests and peace bonds, but absent successful *Charter* challenges, the standards that judges will apply will be the low standards that Parliament established in Bill C-51. These standards create a greater risk of false positives than the prior standards for preventive detention and peace bonds.

The most potent form of judicial oversight in the new laws is the ability of specially designated Federal Court judges to decide whether to grant CSIS new warrants that allow them to take physical measures both inside and outside of Canada to reduce threats to the security of Canada. The government seems happy to enlist judges in this enterprise, but it is one that may strain the capacities of even the most able and dedicated judges. And it will not be a process producing transparent and appealable decisions, made after adversarial argument from both sides.

A particular challenge, as dramatically revealed by Justice Mosley's decision in *Re X*, is that judges will have difficulty supervising how CSIS executes threat reduction warrants. Judges trained in an adversarial system may not have the information and resources they need to ensure CSIS, and the other agencies and persons it enlists, do not go beyond the terms of the warrant. We may have to continue to rely on accidental accountability as in *Re X* because Bill C-51 does not even require CSIS to inform the judge who issues the warrant about the assistance it receives from others when it then conducts its operation inside or outside of Canada.

Federal Court judges will have to fashion their own accountability structures and feedback loops. They should require close reporting back by CSIS including of any third-party assistance in executing a warrant. They may try to rely on SIRC and other independent reviewers, but, as discussed in Chapter 12, these reviewers may not have adequate powers and resources to assist the judges, especially when CSIS enlists other domestic and foreign agencies in its new threat reduction activities.

VI. CONCLUSION

Much of the debate about the need for enhanced "review and oversight" of Canada's new security powers in 2015 has been based on muddled thinking. And this thinking has blurred the critical distinction between review as an after-the-fact process that results in findings and recommendations, and oversight as a process involving real-time command, control, and co-ordination strategies.

Confused thinking is never a good thing, but it was particularly unhelpful in the Bill C-51 debate to the extent that it oversold the virtues of special parliamentary committees having access to secret information, or the expansion of SIRC's jurisdiction. Such reforms would result in much-needed enhanced *review*, but they will not improve the real-time *oversight* of national security activities.

The most important form of oversight is practised, not by Parliament, but by the executive. The government has argued that existing oversight, as practised by ministers, is adequate, but it is not, as determined by the Air India Commission's findings and as evidenced by the security failures of October 2014.

The minister of public safety has emerged as the big winner in the 2015 laws. He will have to approve new CSIS warrants to conduct surveillance outside of Canada and to engage in threat reduction within and outside of Canada. He also has newly codified responsibilities with respect to the no-fly list and security-related passport revocations.

It is hoped that the minister will exercise all of these new responsibilities with vigilance and wisdom, but the fact remains that Public Safety Canada is a very busy and very diffuse department. It has a $6 billion budget and over

52,000 employees. Its employees are involved not only in national security matters but policing, corrections, border security, and crime prevention.

If the Department of Public Safety is now the *de facto* lead on national security matters, it should at the very least be recognized as one of the most important ministries. It should not be treated as a junior post, reserved for ministers who do not have the experience for Justice, Finance, Health, Defence, or Foreign Affairs.

We share the concerns of the Air India Commission and Senator Segal's Special Committee on Anti-terrorism, that the minister of public safety has traditionally been unable to resolve conflicts between CSIS and the RCMP. Unfortunately, the government has rejected the Air India Commission's recommendation that the prime minister's national security advisor be given enhanced powers and responsibility to oversee all-of-government national security matters. And now we fear that disputes between the RCMP and CSIS may increase, given the new powers and privileges that CSIS received in 2015.

Even if such disputes do not arise, there is a need for someone to be in charge and provide strategic whole-of-government direction about how the expanded anti-terrorist toolbox is deployed. This is especially important given that the new *Security of Canada Information Sharing Act* contemplates that 17 different institutions can receive security information from over 100 federal agencies and departments. There is a need for someone to make sure that the right information flows and the wrong information does not. Unfortunately, no one seems to be in charge — just as was the case when a terrorist entered our Parliament.

Oversight of information sharing is especially important because the government has rejected the Air India Commission's call for CSIS to be required to share intelligence about possible terrorism offences. The Air India security failures — and quite possibly the failures of parliamentary security on 22 October 2014 — can fairly be attributed to the absence of someone being in charge of a Canadian security apparatus that, left to its own devices, is most comfortable remaining in traditional silos.

The government stressed the virtues of judicial oversight in defending Bill C-51. Leaving aside the fact that much activity, including enhanced information sharing and CSIS threat reduction activities that do not violate laws, will not be subject to any judicial oversight, the government's arguments overstate the virtues of judicial oversight. CSIS will be able to seek judicial warrants in secret hearings that will be one-sided. To counter this reality, Federal Court judges should insist on the appointment of security-cleared friends of the court to restore adversarial challenge. Bill C-51, unlike the *USA Freedom Act*, does not try to avoid the damage that a secret warrant jurisprudence may cause to confidence in the judiciary as a transparent institution that protects our rights.

Federal Court judges who issue new threat reduction and foreign surveillance warrants should place as much information as possible in the public domain. They should also attempt to develop back-end accountability structures to ensure that the warrants have been properly executed. This will be no easy task given the novelty of these powers, the fact that they will now be exercised beyond Canada's shores, and the fact that CSIS can enlist other persons who may not be subject to independent review to help them execute their warrants. CSIS's main partner in disruption — especially foreign or electronic disruption — is CSE. CSE is subject to independent review, but as will be seen in the next chapter, its reviewer cannot share secret information with SIRC. All of this suggests that the Federal Court judges will have trouble controlling how their warrants are executed, and that the help they will need may not be available.

Finally, all of our criticisms of the limits of judicial oversight bracket the important arguments we make in Chapter 8: namely, that the new CSIS threat reduction warrant scheme threatens the rule of law and the constitutional role of the judiciary by asking judges who are supposed to uphold the law and the *Charter* to authorize and take responsibility for their violation by an intelligence agency — all so that CSIS has the "protective cover"[104] of a warrant for activities that we will likely never know about.

CHAPTER TWELVE
Review: Accountability Gaps

I. INTRODUCTION

Debate on Bill C-51[1] often focused on whether its new powers would be subject to adequate review. As we argue in Chapter 11, that discussion was often muddled, confusing "review" with "oversight." But the focus on review — after-the-fact assessment or auditing of performance against prescribed standards — was a vital one.

The government's position was clear. Public Safety Minister Steven Blaney repeatedly defended the existing review structure, and especially the Security Intelligence Review Committee (SIRC) that reviews CSIS, as "the envy of the world."[2] Defence Minister Jason Kenney stressed the importance of judicial review, going so far as to argue that Bill C-51 "doesn't give new powers to police or intelligence agencies but rather to judges, to courts, who, for example, can order the detention of a suspected terrorist for up to seven days."[3]

Others in the government characterized enhanced review as "needless red tape"[4] and suggested that parliamentary review — a topic of considerable discussion — handed "oversight" over to politicians.[5] Justice Minister Peter MacKay argued that parliamentarians could not be trusted with access to secret information because they had leaked information about judicial appointments in the past.[6]

But many others disagreed that Canada's existing review structure was adequate, let alone "the envy of the world." Four former prime ministers — Jean Chrétien, Joe Clark, Paul Martin, and John Turner — published open letters in *La Presse* and the *Globe and Mail* in February 2015. They argued that "the lack of a robust and integrated accountability regime for Canada's national security agencies makes it difficult to meaningfully assess the efficacy and legality of Canada's national security activities. This poses serious problems for public safety and for human rights." The former prime ministers, joined by former judges, privacy commissioners, and members of SIRC, noted that the government had not implemented either the 2006 recommendations of the Arar Commission for expanded independent review or earlier Martin government proposals that would have given a statutory committee of parliamentarians access to secret information. They concluded that the new powers in Bill C-51 meant "Canada needs independent oversight and effective review mechanisms more than ever . . . ."[7]

The extraordinary letter prompted precisely no amendments to Bill C-51. The government did, however, double SIRC's budget in an April 2015 budget. The new funding was welcome. It was needed to meet even SIRC's regular obligation to review CSIS's intelligence activities, and needed even more urgently given CSIS's new powers at home and abroad under the 2015 laws.

Nevertheless the increased funding did not deal with *the* fundamental problem: SIRC still lacks statutory authority to examine the large number of other federal agencies with which CSIS increasingly and sensibly works. In the result, SIRC and counterparts reviewing the Communications Security Establishment (CSE) and RCMP are able to review only part of the Canadian government's national security apparatus. And when they do review that narrow subset of bodies, they cannot collaborate in sharing secret information or conducting joint review investigations.

In this book, we call the review bodies' inability to work collaboratively with each other the "silo" issue. We call Canada's unfortunate pattern of limiting specialized review to only three security agencies the problem of review "stovepiping."

"The Trail Is Not Going to Stop Nicely and Neatly at CSIS's Door . . . . You Come up to an Imaginary Wall . . . ."

The former prime ministers are not the only ones who have complained about the inadequacy of review. SIRC has made no secret about the consequences of siloed review when CSIS interacts with other agencies. In 2013 Chuck Strahl, then the chair of SIRC, warned:

> once in a while, the trail is not going to stop nicely and neatly at CSIS's door. It blends not just into CSE . . . but also others. Other agencies, by necessity nowadays, are working closely with CSIS, and increasingly we're

going to need some way of chasing those threads. Otherwise, we'll have to tell parliamentarians that, as far as we can tell, everything looks great in CSIS country, but we don't know what happened over that fence; you're on your own.

Strahl elaborated:

we are increasingly nervous or wary of the fact that you come up to an imaginary wall, if you will, where we examine everything that CSIS does, but now it involves other departments. It might involve a no-fly list. It might involve CBSA or CSE . . . , and so on, but our authority extends only to CSIS in our review process. So I think . . . the government would be, wise to look at . . . how we can make sure that we don't, when we're chasing a thread and trying to make sure that Canadians' rights are being protected, run up into the legislative wall of saying, "Well, yes, but you can only look at CSIS, even if the new thread continues on into CSE . . . ," as an example. That is one thing I would encourage you to think about.[8]

SIRC observations — repeated in several different ways in 2015 — went unacknowledged by the government. During the Bill C-51 debate, the government dismissed criticism of its inaction on review by pointing to the all-of-government responsibilities of the Privacy Commissioner and the Auditor General. It never addressed concerns that these bodies could not reasonably be expected to review what is effectively national security writ large — their subject matter responsibilities are very narrow and do not reach reviewing for compliance with all law and policy.

The government's confidence in these agencies exceeded that of the review bodies themselves. In a report released in early 2014, the Office of the Privacy Commissioner commented on the inadequacy of its power to review national security information sharing powers, despite their significant impact on privacy. And like SIRC and other reviewers, the Privacy Commissioner's office lacks the power to conduct joint investigations with other review agencies[9] even while the agencies that it is reviewing are increasingly conducting joint operations. In other words, it too is kept to its silo.

"Canadian Legislators Are . . . Essentially out of the Loop . . . ."

Meanwhile, Canadian parliamentarians have complained that they are essentially alone among Western democracies in being unable to access security information classified as secret. Senator Hugh Segal argued that this situation is unacceptable because it "means that elected Canadian legislators, unless ministers, are essentially out of the loop, lacking and having no way to acquire the expertise and facility necessary to conduct competent, diligent and discrete legislative oversight on behalf of Canadian taxpayers."[10]

It's Not Like No One Has Been Thinking about It

None of this inadequacy is a surprise. The Arar Commission, in its second and mostly ignored report in 2006, concluded that Canada's expert review structure was inadequate. To break down silos, it recommended that the independent review bodies be connected by "statutory gateways" permitting them to share secret information and conduct joint investigations.

The government did not act on this recommendation. Its 2013 *Enhancing RCMP Accountability Act*[11] fell well short of the Arar Commission's recommendations. Among other flaws, it did not allow the newly revamped Civilian Review and Complaints Commission for the RCMP to share information or conduct joint reviews with SIRC or the CSE Commissioner, even while it was empowered to conduct joint investigations with provincial law enforcement reviewers.

The Arar Commission also recommended that the mandates of both the reformed RCMP review body and the existing SIRC be expanded to encompass more of the government agencies that have so far escaped review. The government failed to pursue this cure for stovepiping. And it stubbornly persisted on this course even when in Bill C-51 it massively expanded the scope of (supposedly security) information sharing to and between seventeen government agencies, only three of which are subject to specialized review.

The government turned a blind eye to review even as the new powers accorded to CSIS explicitly allowed that service to enlist assistance from other agencies — including those subject to no review — to perform its new threat reduction activities.

A Strategy of Muddling Through with Crossed Fingers

Accountability gaps may have spontaneously emerged after 9/11, but they are no accident today. A lawyer might call the government's attitude "willful blindness." The government's defence of Canada's review structure is not only unconvincing: it can threaten the credibility of the entire review structure. The aftermath of the Edward Snowden revelations in 2013 is a case in point. Edward Snowden leaked details of classified US National Security Agency surveillance programs to leading newspapers.[12] Thereafter, Snowden's chief journalistic partner, Glenn Greenwald, adopted a strategy of "serial" releases of Snowden documents, including a regular trickle of Canada-specific materials on various surveillance issues.[13] This dribble of material has kept the matter in the public eye and focused attention on Canada's National Security Agency equivalent (and partner): CSE.

In response to the Snowden revelations, the reviewer of the CSE — the CSE Commissioner — stressed that CSE was not directing its intercepts at Canadians or persons in Canada when collecting information on entities outside Canada for the purpose of foreign intelligence.[14] These phrases mirror those found in provisions enacted shortly after 9/11 to define CSE's mandate, but it is not at all clear how the government interprets CSE's mandate and governing rules[15] or how those fit some of the Snowden disclosures. This is not to say that the Commissioner is wrong or captive to the agency it reviews. The Commissioner's office operates under serious constraints and is also subject to Canada's particularly excessive culture of secrecy in security matters. But by standing in front of criticism and queries directed at CSE, it has prompted serious people to ask serious questions about the adequacy of review as a concept.

Critics accurately point out that reviewers do not review all of an agency's activities but only audit a subset of the agency's activities, a subset that must shrink in relative terms as the budget and powers of the agency increase.[16] Critics also note how the United States' much-vaunted system of congressional accountability failed to prevent successive rounds of National Security Agency activities that were revealed by leakers, most recently Snowden.[17] Such critiques suggest that much of the faith that has been placed in increased review as a means to temper the new powers in our security laws may be overly optimistic. And they are right: review alone is not sufficient. Review is a partial and after-the-fact audit function. Reviewers make findings and recommendations. They do not have the powers to implement reforms or to prevent abuses or security failures. Such actions are beyond their scope and above their pay grade. Such actions can be achieved only by effective oversight of the sort described in Chapter 11.

But to say that review alone is insufficient is not to say that it is not important.

Our Impasse

Canada, like much of the world, is struggling with accountability gaps created by the disjuncture between accelerated whole-of-government and transnational security activities, and aging siloed and stovepiped review structures. At the same time, other democracies are attempting to close such accountability gaps. New privacy and civil liberties boards with a whole-of-government mandate have been created in the United States and United Kingdom. France created a parliamentary committee for security intelligence in 2007. Australia created a joint parliamentary committee on intelligence in 2002 and subsequently expanded the jurisdiction of its Inspector General. That review agency plays a role similar to SIRC but is not stovepiped to a narrow subset of the Australian intelligence community.

Canada in contrast has been inert. It has done nothing to close the accountability gaps. Indeed, it moved in the wrong direction in 2012 by abolishing CSIS's Inspector General apparently to save its $1 million annual budget. And still, in 2015, government politicians insisted, against all evidence, that Canada's review structure remained state of the art, even the envy of the world. It is time to move beyond such smugness. Review is no cure for overbroad powers. It can, however, be a canary in the coal mine, warning about overreactions that result in rights violations and underreactions and inefficiencies that can result in security failures. Our accountability gaps are becoming canyons, and ultimately our rights and our security may suffer as a result.

In this chapter, we propose steps to remove ourselves from this impasse, focusing on parliamentary and expert review and adding some words on judicial review.

II. PARLIAMENTARY REVIEW: KEEPING POLITICAL EYES ON THE FOREST

Canada is alone among its "Five Eyes" partners (the United States, the United Kingdom, Australia, and New Zealand) in not giving any parliamentarians (other than ministers) routine access to secret information. Indeed, it is close to alone among Western democracies in this respect.[18]

To be sure, regular standing or ad hoc committees in the House of Commons and in Canada's unelected Senate examine policies and proposed laws related to terrorism and national security. Nevertheless, they do so without the benefit of classified information, including basic information such as the number of people listed on Canada's no-fly list. As discussed in Chapter 2, regular parliamentary committees in both houses conducted separate, extensive, and much-delayed five-year reviews of post-9/11 terrorism legislation. A similar five-year review was conducted of the *Canadian Security Intelligence Service Act*[19] in the 1980s but was hindered by the lack of access to secret information.

Overall, Canada's parliamentary performance in national security has been unimpressive. With some notable exceptions, regular parliamentary committees — and Parliament as a whole — have not played a systematic or concentrated role in reviewing the activities of Canada's security agencies. Indeed, some critics describe their performance in this area as utterly inadequate.[20]

The Rejected Vision of the McDonald Commission

In 1981, the McDonald Commission examining wrongdoing by the RCMP Security Service — CSIS's predecessor — recommended the creation of a joint parliamentary committee on intelligence, able to hear classified information in private. The commission recognized the risks of leaks but concluded that Canadian legislators were no less trustworthy than those in other democracies.[21] It contemplated a small committee of experienced members of Parliament and senators including leaders of the opposition parties or those appointed by them.

The McDonald Commission suggested that its proposed parliamentary committee "should be as much concerned with the effectiveness of the security intelligence organization as with the legality or propriety of its operations."[22] The committee would have jurisdiction over all intelligence matters except criminal intelligence matters involving the RCMP. It would hear *in camera* (private) briefings from the minister responsible for CSIS as well as from SIRC. If it had come to pass, this proposal would have responded to a present problem: although SIRC produces public annual reports with general discussions of its activities, it also writes many more (presumably) detailed classified reports for the minister of public safety that Parliament never sees.

Although the government accepted many of the McDonald Commission's recommendations in devising the new CSIS, it rejected the idea of a parliamentary committee. In 1983, a Senate committee concluded that a parliamentary committee might duplicate the review work of SIRC. It pointed to "vagaries of time, changes in membership and overwork" that beset all legislative committees. Its main objection, however, was "the problem of maintaining the security of information." One concern was that Canada's reliance on intelligence from foreign partners meant that leaks of other people's secrets could spark problems in intelligence sharing arrangements. The Senate committee also cited the "partisan motivations"[23] of legislators as a concern. And there was an unstated apprehension that some members of the parliamentary committee might then (or in the future) be committed to the separation of Quebec.

This was a delicate subject as some of the RCMP illegalities that led to the creation of SIRC were aimed at the Parti Québécois, elected as the provincial government of Quebec in 1976. Based on our own inquiries, the sovereignist issue remained a concern for the Harper Conservatives, who were initially supportive of a parliamentary committee. The presence of an avowed separatist party — the Bloc Québécois — with official party status in the federal Parliament until 2011 raised the prospect of sovereignist members sitting on a national security committee.

As a result, nothing much has changed in the area of national security legislative accountability since the rejection of the McDonald Commission's recommendations. To be sure, some regular parliamentary committees — especially in the unelected Senate — have issued some valuable reports revealing deficiencies in Canada's security operations. And in 2010, parliamentarians in a minority Parliament asserted their ancient parliamentary privileges in an attempt to hold government to account by compelling access to secret documents in the Afghan detainee controversy.[24]

But that protracted effort to examine whether the Canadian military was complicit with torture when it transferred Taliban detainees in Afghanistan to Afghan officials resulted in no lasting reforms. Instead, it produced an ad hoc compromise with government that allowed a few members of Parliament, assisted by retired judges, to have limited access to at least some secret documents. This protracted $12-million process culminated in the disclosure in redacted form of a minority of the requested documents. But the matter eventually lost political momentum, and the work of the ad hoc committee did not continue after the majority Conservative government was elected in 2011.

In short, parliamentarians on Senate and Commons standing committees have been denied the full and wide-ranging access to secret information that is needed to ask the right questions of security officials in any expectation of meaningful answers. They have been unable (and in many cases unwilling) to resist the notorious reluctance of security officials to volunteer information. In the most recent example, the Senate security committee wrote, with understated exasperation, about the challenges associated with its study on Canadian security risks: "the committee was concerned by its inability to extract a direct answer from officials about the number of Canadians that have left to join terrorist groups abroad."[25]

Modest but Unimplemented Reform Proposals

Looking to the Five Eyes experience, most people have concluded that creating a more robust parliamentary role requires legislation: using a statute to set up not a regular parliamentary committee that is a creature of Parliament but an administrative body with special statutory powers, populated by parliamentarians. The legislation would entitle parliamentarians to participate in a more robust national security review function but subject to the same strict statutory rules that govern civil servants' access to and use of secret information.

In 2004, the Martin government tabled a discussion paper looking to the foreign experience and identifying means of enhancing the parliamentary role in national security matters. It proposed the legislative creation of a "National Security Committee of Parliamentarians" in its 2004 security policy.[26] An interim committee of parliamentarians that included Peter MacKay — a subsequent minister of defence, foreign affairs, and justice in the Harper government — recommended a committee with access to secret information modelled on that possessed by SIRC and with members who were sworn to secrecy but otherwise clothed in parliamentary privilege.[27]

Momentum was gathering. In 2005, the Martin government tabled Bill C-81 to establish such a "National Security Committee of Parliamentarians."[28] The bill went no further than first reading in the Commons before it died on the order paper with the dissolution of Parliament for the 2006 election.

The proposed Martin-era national security committee of parliamentarians was significantly less robust than the model proposed by the interim committee of parliamentarians. The Martin committee would have had a broad mandate but fairly weak powers to demand information and no powers to make secret information public. The mandate of the committee was to review the following:

(*a*) the legislative, regulatory, policy and administrative framework for national security in Canada, and activities of federal departments and agencies in relation to national security; and

(*b*) any matter relating to national security that the Minister refers to the Committee.[29]

Reports prepared by the committee would be filed annually with the prime minister, who would then table a version in Parliament, redacted for information that would be injurious to national security, defence, or international relations.

The provisions for access to secret information in the bill were modest, if not weak. The committee could request information from ministers, but the responsible minister could refuse to provide information or provide redacted information or only a summary of the information. The minister's decision to withhold information was final and not subject to review. The bill even provided the minister with a checklist of reasons *not to* provide information, including claims of solicitor-client privilege, the extent to which the information concerned an actual investigation or operation, the provenance of the information being from a foreign source, and the need to protect confidential sources and methods.

The Bill C-81 proposal was, in large part, modelled on the Intelligence and Security Committee in the United Kingdom, itself a creature of statute with members appointed by the government as opposed to a parliamentary body. This United Kingdom body has been criticized in Britain for its inadequacies.

The United Kingdom committee received increased powers in 2013, and these reforms allow the committee access to a greater breadth of secret information albeit still subject to the government's veto.[30]

Had it been enacted, Bill C-81 would have established something unusual in the Canadian context: a legislatively created committee comprising members from both the Senate and the Commons. Such joint membership would take advantage of the considerable ability of senators to gain expertise on national security matters — and also to often be considerably less partisan than their colleagues in the House of Commons. The committee's members were to be appointed by the Governor in Council — in reality the government. They would hold tenure at the government's pleasure until the dissolution of Parliament.

Given these terms, the committee would be a *de facto* executive body staffed by parliamentarians. Indeed, the bill explicitly specified that the committee was not a committee of Parliament and carved out exceptions to the general rule that the executive branch could not employ parliamentarians. These provisions meant that the committee would enjoy none of Parliament's constitutionalized powers and privileges, including its inherent power to compel evidence and summon persons. Also it could not hold non-compliant persons in contempt, a power that Parliament threatened to employ with mixed success to gain access to documents relating to the Afghan detainees.[31]

Under the bill, individual members' parliamentary privileges concerning immunity for the communication of information were emphatically abrogated.[32] Committee members would be sworn to secrecy and named "persons permanently bound by secrecy" under the *Security of Information Act*, Canada's official secrecy law. In other words, if they leaked secrets, they would be vulnerable to prosecution and imprisonment, just like any employee of CSIS and SIRC.

The Harper government did not support the bill or its successors even though the Commons committee reviewing anti-terrorism law recommended in 2007 that it be reintroduced.[33]

Current and Defeated Reform Proposals

Bill C-81 has been resuscitated five times in subsequent Parliaments, generally as a Liberal private member's bill. It has never passed. The most recent version — sponsored by former solicitor-general Wayne Easter — replicated the details of Bill C-81 but failed to reflect the 2013 upgrade to the powers of the United Kingdom committee that had inspired the original Martin-era proposal.[34]

Conservative Senator Hugh Segal proposed a stronger bill in the most recent Parliament, based on 2011 recommendations by a Senate special committee reviewing anti-terrorism law. The Segal bill followed the SIRC model of giving members access to everything except cabinet confidences.[35] It also proposed giving the committee the traditional powers of parliamentary committees to compel the attendance of persons and the production of papers.[36]

Both of these proposals were on the parliamentary order paper before the government introduced the 2015 security laws, but neither proposal attracted government interest or support.

Liberal MP Joyce Murray sponsored a third private members bill, which was also on the parliamentary roster in the last Parliament.[37] It provided a more comprehensive and systematic approach to accountability, attempting to improve the executive and judicial oversight of CSE and then grafting on a revised parliamentary review system for the national security community writ large. In terms of oversight, it required that the head of CSE inform the minister of defence and the prime minister's national security advisor of significant issues. It also would have required CSE to inform the minister and the CSE Commissioner (the expert review body for the CSE) of operations that would affect the privacy of Canadians. And it would have required record keeping with respect to the information sharing requests that CSE received from law enforcement and other intelligence agencies. Last, it would have replaced the current system of ministerial authorization of CSE privacy-endangering activities with judicial authorization, at least with respect to information involving Canadians.

In relation to review, the Murray bill proposed an innovative "Intelligence and Security Committee of Parliament" with six members of Parliament and three senators. It attempted to counter majority-party domination by providing that no more than four members could be from one political party. The committee could also retain its own staff — an important feature of any committee wishing to become an independent source of expertise. Following the SIRC model and like its counterpart in the Segal bill, the committee would have access to all information except cabinet confidences, and its members would be permanently bound to secrecy under the strict terms of the *Security of Information Act*.

This impressive and wide-ranging bill was supported by both the Liberals and the NDP, but it was defeated by the government on 5 November 2014 in a 142 to 120 vote. Roxanne James, the parliamentary secretary for the minister of public safety, was the only member to speak for the government, and she argued that the measures in the bill were "needless and duplicative in nature" and would "increase the cost to taxpayers."[38]

And a committee will cost money. Any proposals for increased parliamentary review must also confront the fact that Canadian committees do not have the same research capacities as American or British committees. A national security committee's effectiveness will depend on having security experts able and willing to advise the committee members. Moreover, Canadian parliamentarians, unlike American and British ones, are disadvantaged in not retaining their own independent specialist lawyers to assist in understanding the growing complexity of national security law and in proposing thorough questions for witnesses. Above all else, however, a committee's effectiveness will depend on a clear-eyed assessment of what it can and should do, a matter we address below.

Red Herrings in the Bill C-51 Debate about Parliamentary Review

After the Afghan detainee matter, no serious discussion about parliamentary review occurred until the Bill C-51 debate in early 2015. As noted, four former prime ministers joined by former officials wrote an open letter calling for enhanced review, including parliamentary review.[39]

We have no doubt that the government's opposition to the former prime ministers' call was driven, in part, by raw partisanship. But it was also animated by a repeat of the Liberal government's 1984 resistance: the fear that Canadian parliamentarians would leak secret information.[40] The leaky politician argument is not persuasive. We doubt that Canadian parliamentarians are more treacherous than their counterparts in other democracies. In any event, they would know that they would likely go to jail under the strict terms of Canada's official secrets law if they leaked information.

A second, more subtle, government rationale for rejecting enhanced parliamentary review was communicated by repeated assertions that parliamentary "oversight" of national security was foreign to our parliamentary traditions. This argument often pointed to the "oversight" role of the US Congress and its inapplicability in Canada. But this debate often misrepresented exactly what oversight means in the United States, imagining that Congress commands security operations. As we note in Chapter 11, it does not. The argument muddled after-the-fact review (the real issue in play in every major reform proposal discussed above) with invasive operational command and control. This managerial form of oversight is not evidently on anyone's legislative agenda, but the opposition parties abetted this confusion with confused descriptions of what they intended in calling for parliamentary "oversight."

For our part, we agree that parliamentary committees should not engage in command and control oversight. Such activities are basically unknown for a legislative body, with a few minor exceptions. As suggested in Chapter 11, oversight is a function that should be undertaken (and improved) by ministers or the prime minister's national security advisor. In the absence of any actual proposals for command and control and real-time oversight by parliamentarians, finger pointing over parliamentary "oversight" is a red herring and simply reflects sloppy thinking that allows "review" and "oversight" to be used as interchangeable terms.

The government's third argument for rejecting enhanced parliamentary review was that it would be duplicative. As noted above, Roxanne James stressed this argument in justifying the government's defeat of the Murray bill. James's views were not a new objection. The concern that a parliamentary committee would duplicate the work of SIRC was also part of the Turner government's reasons for rejecting the McDonald Commission's call for a new special parliamentary committee.

We are not, however, persuaded that parliamentary review would be duplicative of the important work of SIRC and other executive watchdogs, especially given the role that we describe below for such a parliamentary body. We note that the Australian parliamentary committee possesses more powers than any existing Canadian committee, and yet it co-exists in a system with the Inspector General, which in turn has a much broader review jurisdiction than SIRC. If Australia has managed both expert and parliamentary review, it is unclear why Canada cannot do the same.

We also note that a parliamentary committee with access to secret reports by SIRC and other review bodies could help ensure that the agencies and the responsible ministers are questioned about the deficiencies revealed in those reports. This would not be duplication; it would be parliamentary follow-up that could help prevent both security over- and underreactions.

Nor would the committee be necessarily preoccupied with the same issues as the expert bodies. The McDonald Commission predicted that a parliamentary committee would be concerned with the efficacy of the government's security efforts and not just their propriety whereas SIRC, the CSE Commissioner, and the RCMP review body, as well as the courts, are focused on the propriety and legality of security activities. In our proposal, outlined below, we go even further in differentiating the role of parliamentary and expert review. In short, the government's three arguments against enhanced parliamentary review — leaks, the "oversight" red herring, and duplication — are not persuasive.

A Role for a Parliamentary Committee with Access to Secret Information

So, given all this, what contribution could a Canadian parliamentary committee with access to secret information make to accountability in the security sector? Here are some ideas.

Pinnacle Review

Parliamentary committees may be better suited than expert bodies to reviewing the big picture and addressing questions of overall efficacy and strategy.

A parliamentary committee with access to secret information would be in an excellent position to see and evaluate the full national security "forest" while expert review bodies focus on the particular "tree" contained in their silo. In Canada, there simply is no independent body that sees the "forest." The absence of such pinnacle review leaves our system vulnerable to both overreaction and underreaction to security threats.

The Air India Commission stressed the dangers of the broader public interest's becoming lost in inevitable battles between security agencies with different and sometimes conflicting mandates. This is exactly the forest-like consideration that should concern a specialized parliamentary review committee with access to secret information. In this respect, a parliamentary committee is a supplement to expert committee review, not a replacement and not a competitor.

The Martin government's Bill C-81 recognized this objective. It would have created a committee with a broad remit, allowing it to review "the legislative, regulatory, policy and administrative framework for national security in Canada, and activities of federal departments and agencies in relation to national security."[41]

Review for Efficacy and Propriety

Parliamentarians should be concerned with the propriety of security conduct but also its efficacy and wisdom. Among other things, they should question the effects on both rights and security of CSIS's conducting surveillance and "kinetic" activities. They should inquire about information sharing between different agencies of government, bound to increase under Bill C-51 with troubling implications for both privacy (within the Privacy Commissioner's remit) and security prioritization and strategy (within no review body's remit).

The government has stressed that (and exaggerated the extent to which) CSIS's new powers will be subject to judicial oversight, but judges are not in a position to make judgments about how CSIS's actions have affected Canada's foreign and economic relations with other countries.

As discussed in Chapter 11, the responsible minister and ultimately the prime minister must make these difficult calls. Nevertheless, there is a need for retrospective review that focuses on whether the executive has made the right decision or should make the same choice in the future. A parliamentary committee with a whole-of-government mandate to examine how the entire security system operates and that has access to secret information would be in a good position to force us to learn from past mistakes and recommend adjustments to avoid either overreacting or underreacting to terrorism.

Monitoring Trouble Spots

Parliamentarians with access to secret information could monitor trouble spots that emerge among security agencies.

As we argue in Chapter 9, one traditional trouble spot that may get worse is the relationship between CSIS and law enforcement. Without access to secret information, parliamentarians will simply not know whether CSIS is exercising its new powers in a manner that harms prosecutions or makes them impossible. A parliamentary committee with access to secret information could also ask whether there has been appropriate follow-up where a person has been forced to remain in Canada by reason of the no-fly list or a passport revocation. Did someone then guard against the prospect that the foiled foreign terrorist fighter would turn inwards, against Canada? Answering this question requires scrutiny of the work of multiple agencies from multiple departments.

In our present system, no review body is positioned to comment on whether there is satisfactory whole-of-government co-ordination and information sharing. Indeed, a parliamentary committee with access to secret information might have been able to conduct a lessons-learned exercise on the October 2014 terrorist attacks, something that has yet to be done and might otherwise be difficult in Canada without the appointment of a commission of inquiry.

Ministerial References

We also think it is important that ministers with national security responsibilities or the prime minister be able to task any new committee with specific investigations. Although commissions of inquiry have made important contributions to the development of Canadian national security policy, they cost a fortune, take much time, and can themselves be delayed by legal challenges.

In some cases, a well-researched parliamentary committee inquiry and report could be more timely and certainly less expensive. Moreover, recommendations made by parliamentary committees may have a better chance of being implemented than those made by commissions of inquiry, which dissolve at the end of their activities and can conduct no follow-up.

Following Up on Classified Review Reports

A parliamentary committee with access to secret information would be competent to review the many confidential reports that SIRC and the CSE Commissioner routinely provide to ministers. At present, there exist over 200 classified reports that have been prepared by SIRC and the CSE Commissioner on some very important matters. Declassified or short redacted public versions of a few of these reports are available — such as SIRC special reports on CSIS's activities in relation to the post-9/11 rendition of Mohamad Jabarrah and its questioning of Omar Khadr at Guantanamo. And these studies have placed very important and distressing information in the public domain. But most reports remain closely guarded, and their content is sometimes difficult to infer from public summaries. Two recent top-secret SIRC reports have the following question-begging titles: "CSIS's Use of an Emerging Area of Expertise" and "A Sensitive CSIS Activity."[42]

A parliamentary committee with full access to those reports could question ministers on how they responded to the classified findings and recommendations in them. And a parliamentary committee could, in appropriate circumstances, question a minister in public about a failure to address expert body recommendations, without revealing any of the secret details. Such questioning could improve the critical process of ministerial oversight of agencies. It could also attempt to break down silos by questioning multiple ministers about how different agencies work together (or not) on important crosscutting security matters.

Conducting Periodic Reviews of the Effects of Legislation

Major pieces of security legislation such as the *CSIS Act*, enacted in 1984, and the first *Anti-terrorism Act*, enacted after 9/11, have traditionally contained provisions that mandate five-year reviews by parliamentary committees. Neither Bill C-44 nor Bill C-51 requires such review, but the Senate security committee that reviewed Bill C-51 stated that it will conduct one.[43]

Five-year reviews are no excuse for enacting bad laws, but they could provide warnings and help Parliament adjust laws should they produce pernicious and unanticipated effects. At the same time, however, parliamentary committees may have difficulties gauging the precise effects of laws unless they have access to the increasing amount of information that the government classifies as secret.

Without statutory change, a committee reviewing Bill C-51 will be dependent on whatever information the government, expert watchdogs, and courts have made public about how the new security powers have been exercised. Information sharing under Bill C-51 does not require judicial approval and is in many cases subject to no dedicated or adequate review. The new CSIS powers and the no-fly listing in Bill C-51 will be shrouded in secrecy. In all these areas, any future parliamentary legislative review will be flying blind and dependent on the usual imprecise and indefinite answers that seem now to be regularly received from officials and ministers.

This does not need to be the case. A parliamentary committee with access to secret information could review whether the predictions that we and others have made about the adverse effects of the new laws have come to pass.

Elevating the National Security Debate

Some claim that a parliamentary committee might make security issues less partisan, but there are no guarantees. The House of Commons committee that examined Bill C-51 did so in a highly partisan manner. The Senate committee that examined Bill C-51 was more credible in the witnesses it called and more rigorous in its questioning of them. But that committee ultimately divided on partisan lines and proposed no amendments in an obvious effort to ensure that the legislation would be enacted before the 2015 election.

Joyce Murray's private member's bill proposed an interesting attempt to prevent partisan and government domination of a new committee by providing that no political party should have a majority of committee members. This is a worthy idea.

In the final analysis, we hope that partisanship might be muted as it has been on the United Kingdom committee. If serious parliamentarians undertaking a serious task outside of the limelight prove unable to set aside their often petty differences, that is condemnation of our system of government, and not just a national security committee of parliamentarians.

Much of the legitimacy of a parliamentary committee might be earned from its engagement with civil society and the media, rather than its relying strictly on its membership. Any parliamentary committee will have to win public confidence through its work.

Increased parliamentary review could increase both parliamentary and public knowledge of security matters. At the same time, the challenges for parliamentarians — especially those in the Commons — of mastering security matters should not be underestimated. For example, Bill C-51 lists seventeen different departments and agencies that could receive security information under its very broad parameters. It creates two new security statutes on information sharing and the no-fly list, and it amends fifteen other statutes including the *CSIS Act*, *Criminal Code*, and *Immigration and Refugee Protection Act*. It raises complicated constitutional issues. Many of the deficiencies in these laws cannot be understood unless you are familiar with a very large pile of review and commission of inquiry reports.

Even the most diligent parliamentarians, with their many other responsibilities, would struggle to stay on top of the complex and growing security file. The Canadian House of Commons has one of the highest turnover rates among democracies.[44] Our members of Parliament — and often, by extension, our ministers — are less experienced in their chosen political profession than their counterparts in close allies.[45] There are virtues to having such high turnover — having fresh ideas is among them. But there are also consequences to having a Parliament of rookies. Institutional knowledge takes time to acquire, and in Canada it frequently walks out of the building (or at least the responsible committees). This truth frustrated the protracted five-year review of the original 2001 *Anti-terrorism Act*.[46] And having appeared before the Commons and Senate security committees and having been observers of their conduct throughout our professional careers, we believe that this truth continues to afflict our parliamentary committee processes.

More Helping Hands

These are not arguments against a new parliamentary committee with access to secret information, but they do suggest that we should not regard parliamentary review as a panacea.

These arguments also suggest that we must mitigate foreseeable difficulties. In this respect, we think that an enhanced committee would be assisted in its task by another British and Australian innovation: a special reviewer of anti-terrorism law. Independent reviewers have a statutory mandate to issue reports on government performance under anti-terror law and are entitled to see secret information. But even more notably, they have also reacted to legislative ideas and government policy proposals, creating a considerable volume of independent, thorough, and public expert policy analysis. This material has then figured prominently in subsequent parliamentary deliberations on anti-terror law.

In principle, one would think that Canada's existing review bodies would assist in policy deliberations by offering their views on the merits of bills and policy proposals. SIRC once did this in the 1980s, during the mandatory five-year review of CSIS. That tradition now seems to have waned. With the exception of the Privacy Commissioner, review bodies are extremely circumspect, even ambiguous, in opining on bills. This may reflect the fact that because they hear complaints, they view themselves as quasi-judicial and are therefore reluctant to participate in policy making. It may also reflect the effect of operating in a security intelligence community whose culture is not conducive to the open expression of views.

Indeed, it is not even clear that these bodies are able to express views on policy in private. Whatever the government claims in the Bill C-51 debate to the contrary, it appears that the government did not hold advance consultations with review bodies, unless you consider notification (in general terms) consultation.

The net result is that a lot of expertise on policy matters is never communicated to executive government, let alone parliamentarians. Even if review bodies were able to discuss secret issues with a parliamentary committee empowered to hear such information, this would not necessarily translate into a more forthright discussion with review bodies on the legislative policy implications of these issues. Rather, the conversation might focus instead on the more micro-operational matters scrutinized by the reviewers.

We think, therefore, that there is a real need for a Canadian independent reviewer of terrorism laws able to fill this gap. This reviewer function need not involve a new bureaucracy but instead, as in the United Kingdom and Australia, could be done by an adequately resourced, motivated individual with access to relevant secret information.

One of us has comprehensively reviewed Canada's experience with periodic review of anti-terrorism law and contrasted it to the experience in the United Kingdom and Australia.[47] That assessment concluded that independent reviewers when coupled with an adequately resourced and stable parliamentary committee might help overcome some of the difficulties experienced in Canada's traditional legislative process, especially at the Commons level.

First, this independent expert policy reviewer may overcome problems of complexity and scope in anti-terrorism law. With a wide-ranging mandate, an independent evaluator would identify lacunae and difficulties that might otherwise escape the attention of parliamentary committees and place them on the official agenda. In so acting, the independent evaluator would function in a manner analogous to existing officers of Parliament, like the privacy commissioner, who are able to bring matters within their subject-matter roles to the attention of appropriate parliamentary committees.

Repeated annual or special reports by an independent reviewer also militate against the gradual normalization of anti-terrorism laws and powers.

In other words, they guard against the prospect that these laws will fade from the media and public consciousness and lurk below the radar screen in Canada's statute books. Anti-terrorism provisions — especially those in Bill C-51 — are radical enough that they should not be left unscrutinized. This reporting may also galvanize more regular (and transparent) policy thinking within executive government as it appears to have done in the United Kingdom. United Kingdom government responses to independent review have produced a corpus of documents and discussion papers, many of which are much more informative than the cagey government reaction in Canadian legislative proceedings.

And independent expert policy review might take some of the high (and low) politics out of parliamentary deliberations on anti-terrorism issues. A credible, independent evaluator should be difficult to ignore or paint in a partisan light. One wonders how the carefully considered views of such an evaluator might have affected the disappointing and superficial parliamentary debates on preventive detention and investigative hearings in February 2007, discussed in Chapter 2, or the even more disappointing Bill C-51 parliamentary process.

Moreover, a stable system of independent expert policy review, coupled with executive response and parliamentary examination, might generate a more generalized expertise in the area of national security law. Ideas would be tested and debated in public venues potentially allowing rapid, but reasonably carefully vetted, responses to crises that might emerge in the future. Policy actors, well apprised of the legal and policy terrain by the expert policy review, might have the capacity to focus not simply on hot-button issues that arise in legislated responses to crises but also on the more detailed and complex issues that may otherwise escape scrutiny. The result may be parliamentarians — with their democratic legitimacy — possessed of the expertise that is required to question executive-driven security policies.

Summary

Canada lags well behind other democracies in parliamentary review of national security. Given how much information is classified (including overclassified) as secret, it is difficult for parliamentarians to engage in credible review without access to secret information. They often do not know the right questions to ask. When they do ask the right questions, they often do not receive a full answer. Even basic data such as the number of those on no-fly lists and most of the review reports prepared by SIRC and the CSE Commissioner are classified as secret. At present, no Canadian legislator has access to such information. This severely diminishes the ability of Parliament to hold security officials accountable for either overreactions that result in security abuses or underreactions that result in security failures.

Properly equipped, educated, with adequate goodwill, and assisted by independent expert policy review, parliamentary review bodies could function much better than they do presently. We are regularly impressed with how other Westminster democracies debate national security law reform. We do not think that they always arrive at good outcomes, but the truth is that the United Kingdom Parliament is much more intelligently engaged in national security law issues than is our own. This may reflect the fact that other Parliaments are given real responsibilities in the security area, and often then try to live up to them. The contrast with our own disappointing parliamentary tradition is stark.

That said, legislative access to secret material is no panacea that will eliminate accountability gaps or cure the effects of bad laws. Moreover access to secret information with no mechanism for parliamentarians to then advise the public causes its own dilemmas. Although increased legislative review may help increase parliamentary and public knowledge of national security matters, it is a mistake to place too much faith in legislative review of national security activities or to ignore the possibility that such review may give the government some legislative cover for questionable activities.

That means we also need robust, credible, expert, and amply resourced executive watchdog review.

III. EXECUTIVE WATCHDOG REVIEW

Overview

There are only three specialized national security review bodies in Canada: SIRC (for CSIS), the Commissioner of the CSE, and (to a lesser degree) the RCMP Civilian Review and Complaints Commission. There are a few agencies with very narrow and specific mandates that perform all-of-government review, such as the Privacy Commissioner (for privacy) and the Auditor General (for financial management). But these last two bodies have neither the mandate nor the expertise to assess national security operations per se. As noted, the Privacy Commissioner has indicated that its powers are not up to the task of reviewing information sharing in the security context.[48]

There are no national security review bodies for the many other Canadian government agencies implicated in Bill C-51. The whole-of-government approach to security is epitomized in the new *Security of Canada Information Sharing Act*,[49] which allows any federal institution to share security information with seventeen different departments. Again, only three of these bodies (CSIS, CSE, and the RCMP) are subject to national security review.

The Canada Border Services Agency (CBSA) presents an obvious omission. CBSA performs both law enforcement and intelligence functions. It also shares information with other agencies, including CSIS. It is subject to no independent review. Indeed, as best we know, it is the only law enforcement body in Canada not scrutinized by a review body or a police services board of some sort. In the result, outside scrutiny of CBSA occurs sporadically, for instance during occasional coroner's inquires when persons in its custody have died.[50] In the most recent Parliament, a private member's bill, S-222[51] sponsored by Senator Moore, proposed an Inspector General for CBSA. It received second reading in the Senate but died when Parliament was dissolved for the October 2015 election.

As we have suggested, review in Canada is both stovepiped and siloed. Review bodies are empowered to review only their specific agency, and then they are legally limited in their ability to co-ordinate investigations and reviews. Indeed, press reports indicate that the government has even suggested co-ordination would violate Canada's official secrecy laws, with their stiff criminal penalties.[52]

"It Is Essential That There Be Institutional Co-operation among Review Bodies . . . ."

For exactly these reasons, the Arar Commission found in 2006 that the existing review structure was inadequate. Commissioner O'Connor reached this conclusion after looking at the increased security information sharing in government that had both contributed to Arar's torture in Syria and uncritically conveyed information from the torture cells of Damascus back to multiple agencies in Ottawa.

Justice O'Connor based his recommendations on the simple and sound principle that review must match what is being reviewed. As he explained:

> It is essential that there be institutional co-operation among review bodies where there is institutional co-operation among the bodies being reviewed for four specific reasons: to avoid gaps in accountability, to attempt to avoid reaching inconsistent or differing conclusions about the co-operative activities; to provide a unified intake system for national security complaints, and to avoid the burden on agencies of duplicative review.[53]

He recommended that SIRC be given new powers to break out of its silo, share secret information, and conduct joint investigations with other reviewers such as the CSE Commissioner. He also recommended a response to stovepiping: SIRC's jurisdiction should be expanded to reach the national security activities of Citizenship and Immigration Canada, Transport Canada, Foreign Affairs, and Financial Transactions and Reports Analysis Centre of Canada. He also called for an enhanced RCMP review body able to review CBSA. And he proposed that the review bodies form a co-ordinating committee to oversee co-ordination of their respective review functions.

None of these changes has come about despite the passage of almost ten years, an acceleration of security agency integration, and repeated reports — including by SIRC itself — on the inadequacy of the review structure.

Before Bill C-51, the Arar Commission's 600-page policy report had been left to gather proverbial dust. Interest in the report was revived during the Bill C-51 debate when four former prime ministers favourably cited the report and called for enhanced review.[54] And even the Senate committee that later blessed Bill C-51 called for reform in the review area.[55] With the passage of Bill C-51, we should not let the dust settle again.

Why National Security Agencies Should Be Subject to Independent Review

Even long before security powers swelled in 2015, the Arar Commission warned that national security activities

> involve the most intrusive powers of the state: electronic surveillance; search, seizure and forfeiture of property; information collection and exchange with domestic and foreign security intelligence and law enforcement agencies; and, potentially, the detention and prosecution of individuals. The use of such powers may adversely affect individual rights and freedoms.[56]

Unlike regular criminal investigations, national security matters are deeply secret. The writ of Canada's information access laws usually stops short of national security matters. Those who have been investigated may be forever oblivious to this fact and in no position to complain about misconduct. Indeed, if no legal proceeding is commenced, no charge is laid, and if no decision is made to commence a prosecution, none of the investigation undertaken by the authorities will ever be tested before an impartial decision maker.

Even where courts are implicated, that review may be attenuated and curtailed by special secrecy or other rules that constrain the full expression of the adversarial system on which Canadian justice is predicated.[57] As explored above, Parliament, meanwhile, traditionally has a modest role in security and intelligence review because of limits on its time and lack of access to secret information.

For all these reasons, national security lacks many of the checks and balances deemed essential in other aspects of Canadian political and legal life. Absent these checks and balances, the proper functioning of national security agencies depends heavily on the integrity of those who populate them.

There is no reason to doubt that integrity on an individual level. Every bureaucracy suffers, however, from its own shortcomings, some of which are serious. A bureaucracy immune to external scrutiny may find it difficult to resist the temptation to stretch uncertain boundaries. It may also stray into patterns, policies, or groupthink impairing its effectiveness. Such practices may result in either overreactions causing human rights abuses or risk averse behaviour that may result in underreactions causing security failures.

Elements of Effective Review

These considerations all counsel the need for effective executive watchdog review mechanisms — audits and complaint systems able to measure agency compliance with legal or other standards and query problematic behaviour. National security law expert and government lawyer Stanley Cohen aptly captures the standard to be applied in national security review: trust, but verify.[58]

Effective review requires certain design elements. An expert group that developed and agreed to the "Ottawa Principles on Anti-terrorism and Human Rights" set out the following elements:

1) Review must be conducted by a body that is independent of the government and the agencies that it reviews. The body is not, in other words, both the watcher and the watched.

2) This body must be mandated to audit, review, and assess the legitimacy of security intelligence actions.

3) It must have real powers to review and investigate at its discretion, compel and examine even secret information, respond (and propose resolutions) to public complaints, make public reports of its findings and conclusions, and have in place a means to protect and secure confidential information.[59]

The Arar Commission proposed its own similar list of design criteria:

1) Review should ensure compliance with national and international law and "standards of propriety that are expected in Canadian society."[60]

2) It should enhance accountability of security and intelligence agencies to the government and ultimately Parliament and the public.

3) By enhancing accountability, a review system should encourage the public credibility of and public trust in the agency. To achieve this goal, it should be independent and staffed in a transparent manner by qualified individuals. It should also disclose, as much as possible, details of its actions and findings.[61]

The Arar Commission stressed that any credible review mechanism for propriety should have unrestricted access to secret information and the ability to initiate its own audits or investigations. Put another way, it should be able to self-initiate review. The commission was not opposed to review bodies also adjudicating public complaints but recognized that in many cases those affected by national security will not know or be in a position to complain.

SIRC and Review of CSIS

As discussed in Chapter 2, CSIS was created in 1984 with a number of external and independent controls. SIRC is the best known of these controls.

The Security Intelligence Review Committee

During the Bill C-51 debate, the government repeatedly called SIRC the "envy of the world" and pointed to it as the best evidence for its argument that Canada's existing review structure was adequate.

And when SIRC was created, it was ahead of its time. It lived up to its promise in its early years, under its first chair, Ron Atkey. British academic Peter Gill reviewed the impact of SIRC during the period 1984–88 and reached largely favourable conclusions.[62] But Gill's assessment of SIRC may constitute the high-water mark. Academic assessments thereafter have been more critical, if less systematically comprehensive. In 1992, Professor Reg Whitaker acknowledged the "very significant public presence" of SIRC during its first five years.[63] Whitaker observed that SIRC had not yet been co-opted by the agency it was charged to review, a perennial threat for SIRC-like institutions. At the same time, he warned that Canada was entering an era of policy drift and institutional inertia and that only public scandals would be likely to shake this inertia.[64] By 1996, Whitaker was raising concerns about SIRC's performance.[65] Professor Wesley Wark subsequently commented in 2002, "SIRC has been invisible and silent since Sept. 11. It failed to undertake an immediate review of Canadian security intelligence knowledge surrounding the attacks, one more sign that SIRC has lost its early edge."[66]

A Barely Visible Presence?

But while a handful of academics have written about it, in truth SIRC is not a closely studied operation. Indeed, its work attracts surprisingly little public attention. Between 1984 and 2010, SIRC was mentioned in the major Canadian daily newspapers a mere 853 times,[67] and 157 of these mentions were in 1994, the year of the controversy generated by the so-called Bristow Affair.[68] More typical years have between ten and fifty mentions in major Canadian dailies.

These results pale when compared to those for other Canadian federal watchdog agencies. For instance, there were more than 5,500 articles featuring the activities of the Access to Information Commissioner during the period 1984 to 2010.[69] Meanwhile, the Privacy Commissioner's work in the first ten years of the millennium featured in over 1,600 newspaper stories.[70]

Much of the coverage of SIRC that does exist was sparked by its public reports, some of which have been critical of CSIS. That said, the 1994 coverage of SIRC was particularly critical of SIRC itself — the term "lapdog" appeared in association with SIRC in eight published items that year.[71] The agency has also attracted at least one regular media critic. Long-time CSIS critic and journalist Andrew Mitrovica wrote:

> It's time that SIRC stopped being a dumping ground for former politicians, and well-connected (and, no doubt, well meaning) business people, doctors and ex-bureaucrats with little or no experience in intelligence matters. It's time that SIRC be given the money, powers and experienced investigators it so desperately needs to do what on paper, at least, is an important job.[72]

Grading SIRC

For our part, we do not know how well SIRC functions, and not for lack of trying. A comparison of SIRC's activities against the CSIS budget from its creation through to the beginning of this decade appears to indicate that SIRC activity — measured in reports — has been more or less static even while CSIS's budget and scale of operations has increased. In the result, the proportion of reports per unit of CSIS budget has fallen.[73]

What this means is unclear. It could be that fewer reports are necessary because CSIS's own internal governance is more robust. Or it could mean that SIRC was less productive. Or it could mean that SIRC was in stasis and unable to increase the scale of its operations even as CSIS increased its own tempo. Based on what we know about SIRC's resource constraints, we are inclined to the last view. But the bottom line is this: caution is in order when evaluating the work of SIRC (or the CSE Commissioner). While we can try to extrapolate from trends in the *quantity* of its activities, we simply cannot evaluate the *quality* of that work because most of it remains secret.

Although SIRC publishes a declassified annual report, it lists over 200 secret reports submitted to the minister starting in 1986.[74] (And the CSE Commissioner lists over 80 classified reports since 1997.[75]) The process in which decisions are made about publication is less than transparent. Given the government's sustained practice of overclaiming secrecy, it is difficult to think that only two of these reports could be declassified, as is the case at the time of this writing.

SIRC and other review bodies should be encouraged to put more of their work in the public domain and, if necessary, to challenge any extravagant governmental claims of secrecy in court. We should be able to review the reviewers. But until then and until we have a parliamentary committee truly able to press the issue, we must simply presume that they do the best work possible.

Staffing

"Best work possible" is a relative concept. SIRC has up to five part-time "members" supported by a small staff. The members of SIRC are appointed by the Governor in Council (effectively, cabinet) for five-year terms and sworn into the Queen's Privy Council for Canada. This appointment is made, at least in principle, after consultation with the leaders of official parties in the Commons. The posting is a part-time one, with SIRC members meeting periodically (which we understand to be about five or six times) during the year.

SIRC has often been understaffed during recent years. Until recently, it stood at three members. When Bill C-51 was tabled in Parliament, the prime minister announced the appointment of a fourth member, Dean Ian Holloway of the University of Calgary's Faculty of Law. The government subsequently filled the remaining vacancy with Justice Pierre Blais, a former chief justice of the Federal Court who had previously served as solicitor general and minister of justice. Appointed to replace a retiring member was a third person: Marie-Lucie Morin, who was a retired civil servant and had previously served as the prime minister's national security advisor. They joined former senior RCMP member Gene McLean and noted lawyer Yves Fortier. Together, these five constitute a particularly impressive SIRC roster.

Budget

In 2014, SIRC employed an executive director and seventeen staff members and had expenditures totalling $2,901,300,[76] a tiny fraction of CSIS's operational budget, and proportionally smaller than through much of its history.

In 2012, one of us attempted to paint a statistical portrait of SIRC's financing that included data from SIRC's beginnings through fiscal year 2010.[77] SIRC's funding has always been modest relative to that of CSIS. Between 1985 and 2009, its funding averaged 0.77 percent of CSIS's funding. At certain periods — especially in the early 1990s — its funding fell well below this level, before moving back to average or above-average levels in the early 2000s. In 2004, SIRC's funding rose to its highest level ever — 0.97 percent of CSIS's funding — after a 2002 request from SIRC that its funding be increased to reflect the increased size of CSIS post-9/11.[78]

More recently, SIRC spending relative to that of CSIS fell to the lowest levels in its history. In 2008–9 and 2009–10, SIRC spending was 0.56 percent and 0.51 percent of CSIS spending.[79] CSIS's budget for 2011–12 was $540 million.[80] SIRC's budget during the same period was $2.57 million, or 0.5 percent of the CSIS budget. This would appear to be the worst funding level relative to CSIS ever witnessed during SIRC's history. The 2014–15 estimates place CSIS's budget at $516 million and SIRC's at $2.8 million, or 0.54 percent of the CSIS budget.[81] While not as abysmal as earlier in this decade, this figure remained below historical levels.

In the April 2015 budget, however, the government announced its intention to provide SIRC an additional $2.5 million a year, effectively doubling SIRC's budget. SIRC's executive director, Michael Doucet, told the Senate committee examining Bill C-51, "with the increase in funding, SIRC's future looks more promising."[82] He noted that the new funding would help SIRC fulfill its statutory mandate to review at least some aspects of CSIS's new threat reduction mandate and that SIRC would review such CSIS activities conducted both under warrants and in cases where CSIS did not seek a warrant. He also noted that the new funding was required to meet SIRC's expectations that its reviews of CSIS work would increasingly involve foreign operations, which were very expensive to review.

Access to Secret Information

Under the *CSIS Act*, SIRC has broad rights to CSIS information.[83] It may not see cabinet confidences, but it does regularly see data supplied to CSIS by foreign governments and agencies.[84] Members of SIRC and its employees must comply with all security requirements under the *CSIS Act* and take an oath of secrecy.[85] They are also "persons permanently bound to secrecy" under the

Security of Information Act[86] and are therefore subject to that statute's penalties for wrongful disclosure of sensitive information.

Despite these legal powers, there have been occasions where SIRC has felt that it has not been given full access to information and even has been misled by CSIS. In its 2013–14 annual report, SIRC noted that it "had been seriously misled by CSIS" during the investigation of a complaint. SIRC found that CSIS had violated its duty of candour during some *ex parte* (closed) proceedings by not proactively disclosing material information.[87] In the same report, SIRC noted that it had encountered significant delays when conducting two reviews and investigating two complaints.[88] SIRC's executive director reported that he had had to personally intervene "to ensure that staff received complete information."[89] These comments are troubling as CSIS gears up to exercise its new powers.

Review Functions and Difficulties

SIRC's review of CSIS activities has always been partial — it does not and cannot review every activity. For instance, SIRC has explicitly stated that it does "not have the resources to examine all warrants granted to the Service." Instead it looks "at a certain number of warrants as part of its annual review activity."[90] It has commented that its "snapshot" approach "allows SIRC to manage the risk inherent in being able to review only a small number of CSIS activities in any given year."[91]

SIRC reviews seven or eight review topics per year, with its annual report containing summaries of these reviews.[92] It can also be tasked by the minister or by legislation to conduct specific reviews. Since the abolition of the Inspector General, discussed below, one of SIRC's existing reviews must involve certifying that the CSIS director's report to the minister is sound. Under Bill C-51, at least one of the reviews will have to involve CSIS's new threat reduction powers. We have also suggested in Chapter 11 that Federal Court judges may wish to call on SIRC to review how CSIS executes its new threat disruption warrants. But there are consequences to more and more "must review" topics: statutory and any judicial mandates for reviews reduce the time and resources that can be spent on discretionary risk management reviews.

Under the *CSIS Act*, the outcome of a SIRC investigation is conveyed to the minister and the CSIS director, along with SIRC's recommendations. As discussed in Chapter 11, SIRC is a review — and not an oversight — agency. Its recommendations are not binding on CSIS and the government.[93]

Abolition of the Office of the Inspector General

From 1984 to 2012, an Inspector General also reviewed CSIS's activities. The Inspector General was appointed by the Governor in Council and was responsible to the deputy minister of public safety. Described as the minister's "eyes and ears" in CSIS,[94] the Inspector General monitored compliance by the service with its operational policies and examined its operational activities.[95] To this end, the Inspector General was given full access to CSIS's information except cabinet confidences.[96]

The Inspector General also certified whether the reports provided by the CSIS director were adequate and whether they revealed any action of the service that the Inspector General viewed as an unauthorized, unreasonable, or unnecessary exercise of its powers.[97]

As mentioned in Chapter 11, the government eliminated the position of inspector general in 2012. This unanticipated move, buried in a budget bill, was characterized as a cost-cutting measure, saving the government a very modest $1 million annually. The government asserted that there would be no net degradation in review because the Inspector General's functions would be assumed by SIRC. SIRC added two additional staff members when it took on this new role. Eight persons had staffed the abolished Inspector General's office.

"It Takes You at Least a Year . . . to Learn the Right Questions to Even Ask the Service."

The former inspector general of CSIS, Eva Plunkett, was critical of the surprising abolition. She called it "ridiculous" to think that SIRC could do the same job of probing CSIS that her office had done.[98] She further asserted "they don't do the same kind of work at all," and "they don't go into the same depth, the same detail."[99]

Plunkett acknowledged that while SIRC had a small full-time staff, its appointed members worked part-time and met in Ottawa "only periodically." "She suggested that's no substitute for taking on the task full-time, as she did, meeting with CSIS officials regularly at the agency's headquarters."[100] She also warned, "It takes you at least a year in the job to learn the right questions to even ask the service."[101]

Plunkett was not alone in thinking that her office was important. In his assessment of SIRC's early years, Professor Gill attributed at least part of SIRC's success as arising "because SIRC has been able to make use of the Inspector General's resources by tasking him . . . to carry out reviews."[102]

Growing Concerns about SIRC's Siloed Jurisdiction: "Bill C-51 Has Not Been Matched on the Accountability Front."

The Arar Commission in its 2006 report stressed that SIRC had difficulties monitoring CSIS activities such as information sharing involving work with other agencies. The commission recognized the importance of increased integration of security activities in the post-9/11 environment but recommended that SIRC's powers be expanded to allow it to keep pace.

In its 2012–13 annual report, SIRC similarly warned that it "must be flexible enough to follow up and effectively review CSIS activities and investigations, even when they cross over with other agencies and departments." In light of increased "technological interconnectivity," SIRC needed "legislative tools and matching government resource commitments to ensure that the checks and balances enshrined in the Committee remain relevant and effective."[103]

SIRC's concerns about the inadequacies of its legislative tools have persisted even after the government doubled its budget. SIRC's executive director told a Senate committee in May 2015 that while "Canada's rather limited national security activities were carried out in silos" when SIRC was created thirty years ago, "CSIS now liaises and works closely with numerous federal partners on a daily basis. This increased integration and information sharing amongst national security entities, which is further fuelled by Bill C-51, has not been matched on the accountability front." He re-iterated SIRC's call "for amendments to its enabling legislation to give it the ability to conduct joint reviews with other review bodies and to follow the thread . . . . Under our current legislation, SIRC cannot conduct joint reviews or share operational information with other review bodies."[104]

This truth has concrete consequences.

"Neither of Us Has Clearance to Delve into the Details of the Other's Operation."

One of CSIS's most frequent partners is CSE, Canada's signal intelligence agency. Although CSE directs most of its activities abroad, it can help CSIS execute any domestic (or now, after Bill C-44, international) warrant. In 2013, Chuck Strahl, then chair of SIRC, was asked about co-operation between his review agency and that for CSE. He noted, "neither of us has clearance to delve into the details of the other's operation. Both committees have issued reports saying, in essence, that we need to work together more . . . ." He warned that he could tell parliamentarians only that "everything looks great in CSIS country, but we don't know what happened over that fence; you're on your own."[105]

Nothing in the new 2015 laws allows the two review agencies to conduct joint reviews or to work together by sharing secret information.

"This Study Does Not Constitute . . . the Complete Picture on This Subject."

Another example of the limitation on SIRC's ability to review Canada's increasingly integrated national security activities concerned SIRC's inquiry into the Abdelrazik matter. Abousfian Abdelrazik is a Canadian whose efforts to return to Canada after being maltreated in Sudan were repeatedly foiled by the Canadian government.[106] In its annual report, SIRC noted that while Abdelrazik remained in Sudan up until 2010, it had focused on CSIS activity in 2003 and 2004 because thereafter the case "became much more complex, and began to draw a number of other Canadian agencies into significant roles." SIRC observed that

> a raft of other Canadian government departments — notably DFAIT, the RCMP, CBSA and Transport Canada — (as well as foreign government agencies) commenced wrestling over his fate. SIRC is unable to ascertain the extent to which any of these entities may or may not have acted on CSIS's advice, or to what extent CSIS information factored into the decision-making of others. Indeed, SIRC has no review jurisdiction beyond CSIS and, therefore, had to limit its commentary to what the Committee knows solely as it pertained to the Service's involvement.[107]

SIRC found fault with some of CSIS's involvement in the case but effectively placed a warning label on its findings:

> This study does not constitute the definitive or complete picture on this subject. Other information is likely to emerge from the broad range of documents or reports held by other Government of Canada departments and agencies that were equally involved, as well as from ongoing legal processes. As it stands, Abousfian Abdelrazik's story has yet to be fully written.[108]

This was not the only time that SIRC affixed a disconcerting disclaimer on its reports. Its assessment of CSIS's involvement with Afghan detainees noted that it could amount to "only one piece" given the involvement of many more actors in the Afghan theatre.[109] As we discuss next, SIRC's confessions about the limits of its own powers are especially noteworthy given the nature of CSIS's new powers, including the power to enlist third parties to assist its increased threat reduction, foreign surveillance, and information sharing activities.

The Effects of the New Laws on SIRC's Work

Information Sharing

Many of the new powers accorded CSIS in 2015 allow it to work with other agencies. This makes security sense. It is, however, an accountability nightmare.

A prime example is increased information sharing. As SIRC's executive director has explained, "[w]ith Bill C-51 comes increased information sharing for the purposes of national security. As a result, over 100 Government of Canada institutions can share information in respect of activities that undermine the security of Canada without any clear standards for disclosure." He explained that "legislative constraints on SIRC will make it increasingly difficult for [SIRC] to provide robust assurances on CSIS's activities to Parliament and Canadians." He told the Senate committee examining Bill C-51 that giving SIRC the "ability to follow the thread and conduct joint reviews is absolutely vital to accountability,"[110] but the committee made no amendments before the bill became law.

CSIS can now receive information from other departments that may not fit into CSIS's mandate, tied to a definition of threats to the security of Canada in the *CSIS Act*. Some of that shared information might not be reliable. CSIS will also be assisted by CSE and an open-ended list of other agencies in executing its new threat disruption powers. Hopefully, SIRC will use its existing powers and enhanced budget to examine the information that CSIS receives, but it will remain powerless to examine what happens on the other side of the CSIS fence.

De Facto *Creation of a Foreign Intelligence Service*

Both Bill C-44 and Bill C-51 now clearly permit CSIS overseas operations, and these are expected to increase. The implications of creating a "foreign intelligence service" in this haphazard manner are considerable and deserving of their own close scrutiny.

Buried in these two bills, this creep toward a foreign intelligence service has attracted virtually no serious discussion, except by Professor Wesley Wark during testimony on Bill C-44.[111] SIRC director Michael Doucet, in his testimony before the Senate security committee, indicated that SIRC's foreign-based reviews had increased from 20 to 40 percent and that he expected this tempo to further increase under the new laws adopted in 2015. He also indicated that SIRC's current practice of visiting one of CSIS's foreign postings each year was not adequate and would increase. Nevertheless, there are concerns that just as CSIS's increased foreign adventures require new expertise and skills

— including languages other than English and French — so too will SIRC's skill set need to expand.

Assistance from Other Persons in Threat Reduction

Bill C-51 will increase dramatically the sorts of activities that CSIS may undertake, including new and unspecified measures to reduce threats to the security of Canada. These new powers are discussed in detail in Chapter 8, and here we focus on their implications for review where CSIS works with other agencies outside of SIRC's stovepiped jurisdiction.

The amended *CSIS Act* contemplates that a judge may "order any person to provide assistance" that "may reasonably be required to give effect to a warrant" authorizing surveillance or threat reduction.[112] The judge may also order that the "person" offering assistance be kept confidential in the public interest.

More than this, the Bill C-51 changes contemplate further assistance or subcontracting to "another person" provided that certain proportionality-based criteria are met, presumably as decided by CSIS itself.[113] Such additional assistance would not be authorized by the judge who grants the warrant but by a CSIS official (or potentially someone else included in the initial warrant).

One serious problem is that SIRC cannot examine the activities of such other persons, including those within government departments such as CSE, Foreign Affairs, and the Department of National Defence. Officials within these departments are the most likely to be enlisted to help CSIS engaged in "kinetic" activities to reduce threats to the security of Canada. We would stress, however, that the list is open ended. It could include private individuals or corporations or even foreign officials, agencies, or governments.

To do a proper job of discharging its review functions, including the provision in Bill C-51 that it "review at least one aspect of the Service's performance to reduce threats to the security of Canada,"[114] SIRC needs powers to compel relevant information from anyone who has provided CSIS with assistance in executing its warrants. SIRC lacks these powers. The result is that CSIS could subcontract the execution of its new threat reduction warrant to others who are not subject to SIRC review.

Even a much-overdue expansion of SIRC's jurisdiction to encompass other Canadian federal agencies that work with CSIS would leave an accountability gap. One of the lessons of the Maher Arar saga is that even the most robust of review bodies — in that case, a public inquiry with whole-of-government powers to compel the production of secret information — is powerless to review the actions of foreign governments.

Summary

To all but the most ill-informed, the claim that SIRC is the "envy of the world" is absurd. Both the Arar Commission and SIRC itself have raised concerns that SIRC's powers are inadequate given that CSIS, quite appropriately, increasingly works with other agencies. To its credit, the government has significantly increased SIRC's budget and ensured that it now has a full (and impressive) membership. Nevertheless, budget increases are no substitute for a much-needed increase in legal powers if SIRC is to have any chance of keeping pace with CSIS's increased powers.

CSE Commissioner

The CSE Commissioner is a sitting supernumerary or retired judge who, under the *National Defence Act*,[115] has access to secret information in order to examine the legal propriety of CSE activities. The Commissioner also hears complaints about CSE.

Under most of its mandate, the CSE is restricted from directing its powerful intercept capabilities at persons in Canada or Canadians. The Commissioner has an obligation to alert the minister of national defence if he concludes that CSE has acted in violation of the law.

The CSE Commissioner is a part-time appointment, like the members of SIRC, and has a modest staff of eleven, with eight dedicated to review, and a budget of $1.9 million.[116] Unlike for SIRC, there has been no reported budget increase for the CSE Commissioner even though CSE's work will likely increase as it helps CSIS exercise its new powers. Like SIRC, the CSE Commissioner is also a siloed and stovepiped review body unable to review agencies other than CSE, share secret information, or conduct joint investigations with other review bodies, including SIRC.

This is a particularly egregious deficiency given the frequent co-operation between CSIS and CSE. The inter-agency collaboration will increase under the 2015 laws, which give CSIS increased powers to act outside of Canada and to engage in threat reduction — including electronic forms of disruption, which may require CSE's assistance. Indeed, part of CSE's mandate is to assist CSIS or the police in the execution of warrants, and it is likely that CSIS will trigger this authority and be assisted by CSE, especially outside Canada but also potentially within Canada.

CSE may also be an important player under the new *Security of Canada Information Sharing Act* since it is capable of both receiving and sending information under the new law. One concern is that CSE could receive information that is not within its mandate, which is designed to minimize the impact of its activities on the privacy of Canadians. The title of a recent classified CSE report to the minister of defence is intriguing in this respect: "A Review of the CSE Office of Counter-terrorism." The foreign-terrorist-fighter phenomenon blurs much of the divide between foreign and domestic matters that CSE's jurisdiction is premised upon.

In his testimony to the Senate committee examining Bill C-51, Justice Jean-Pierre Plouffe, the current CSE Commissioner, stated his support for statutory gateways, of the type recommended by the Arar Commission, allowing operational information to be shared between his office and SIRC. He stated that such reforms were "much more important in the evolving context of ever greater cooperation between law enforcement, intelligence and security agencies . . . ."[117] In a letter to the chair of the Commons committee examining Bill C-51, he stressed that review agencies, like the agencies they review, needed to share information:

> Sharing of information among the existing review bodies would allow one
> to alert another as to what information was being shared, to follow the trail
> of that information and to ensure that the sharing of information complied
> with the law and that the privacy of Canadians was protected.[118]

In his Senate testimony, he also specifically raised concerns about the review of technical and operational assistance that CSE could provide to CSIS under its new warrant powers and stated that he might require new resources to this end. But, again, under the existing siloed jurisdiction, the Commissioner could review only the CSE side of such assistance and would have no access to secret and operational information about how CSIS executed the warrant.

Civilian Review and Complaints Body for the RCMP

The Civilian Review and Complaints Commission for the RCMP hears complaints arising from all of the RCMP's activities throughout Canada. It has a budget of about $9 million and presently has only a single chair, without a national security background, acting without other members. Much of the body's work is dominated by the handling of about 3,500 complaints a year, which cover matters ranging from allegations of police officer rudeness to allegations of the use of unnecessary force or having contributed to a death in custody. The RCMP commission generally reviews only the RCMP's resolution of about 200 of those complaints each year. Although the RCMP has received new powers in Bill C-51 and has dramatically increased the resources that it devotes to national security policing, there has been no reported increase in the budget of its review body or apparent attempt to devote more resources to the review of the RCMP's national security activities.

The RCMP commission is the creation of the, perhaps misnamed, *Enhancing RCMP Accountability Act*, enacted in 2013.[119] Much of the parliamentary debate at the time focused on the RCMP's notorious personnel problems and issues relating to independent investigations of the use of force. Lost in the shuffle was the government's implicit rejection of many of the Arar Commission's recommendations.

The Arar Commission noted that "many of the RCMP's national security activities will remain secret and thus will not be subject to complaints."[120] And the commission was concerned that even when people knew they should complain, complainants from the Muslim community would be reluctant to come forward.[121] It also recommended that the handling of complaints related to the RCMP's national security functions might require the assistance of security-cleared advocates to provide adversarial challenges to secret evidence not disclosed to complainants.[122]

For these reasons, Commissioner O'Connor proposed an RCMP accountability body with SIRC-like powers to conduct self-initiated reviews or audits and to have access to all secret information except cabinet confidences. He also recommended that the new body be able to share secret information and conduct joint reviews with SIRC and the CSE Commissioner. And it should have members appointed with expertise in national security matters who are able to prepare public reports on review of the RCMP's national security activities.[123]

The 2013 legislation failed to implement most of these recommendations. To be sure, the renamed RCMP commission was given the power to conduct audit-like reviews into "specified activities of the force."[124] But the new Act prioritized complaints over review by providing that reviews could be conducted only after the RCMP commission certified with the public safety minister that it had sufficient resources to ensure the handling of complaints. A lean agency may never have the time or resources to conduct self-initiated reviews of national security activities. This approach ran directly counter to the Arar Commission's warning that only self-initiated review, and not complaints, could get to the bottom of the RCMP's national security activities, including information sharing.

The new legislation also compromised on the Arar Commission's key recommendation: any effective review body must, like SIRC and the CSE Commissioner, have access to secret information. Under the 2013 law, the RCMP review body can ask for secret information if it is relevant and necessary, but the RCMP can refuse to provide it, citing the need to protect operational information and intelligence from foreign sources. The RCMP has this power of rejection even though the review body is bound by strict secrecy legislation.

In the case of disputes over RCMP refusals, the 2013 legislation mimics the unwieldy process used to resolve the Afghan detainee affair: it anticipates that a retired judge will be appointed to make recommendations. The judge's confidential recommendations will not be binding, and the legislation is unclear about what happens if there are continued disagreements between the review commission and the RCMP brass. The whole thing could end up in court with taxpayers footing the bill for prolonged *Canada v Canada* proceedings. Such an approach hardly inspires confidence that the new review commission will be able to get to the bottom of RCMP national security activities, including what is done with information that it can now receive under the new information sharing provision.

The 2013 legislation also rejects other aspects of the Arar Commission's recommendations. It authorized the new RCMP review body to conduct joint investigations with provincial review bodies but stubbornly refused to allow it to conduct such joint investigations and share secret information with SIRC or the CSE Commissioner.

The new body has so far made no visible progress in reviewing the RCMP's national security activities. The RCMP commission's strategic plan for 2015–16 focuses on complaints and proposes initiating the body's review work, but it does not expressly mention review of the RCMP's increased national security work, and there has yet to be a specific report on any such reviews.[125] We have been told that there is appetite for such reviews in the commission. But we wonder whether a body with a dominant complaints mandate and a broad subject-matter remit will ever have the resources to exercise an important but highly complicated and potentially resource intensive security review mandate.

Back to the Future: Will the RCMP Repeat Arar-Era Mistakes?

In its 2013 legislation, the government managed to give the appearance of responding to the Arar Commission's major recommendations for improved review of the RCMP's national security activities without actually doing so.

But this is no time for half-hearted national security review of the RCMP. Part of a review body's role is to ask whether the RCMP is repeating the mistakes of the past. For example: Is it blurring the distinction between extremism and terrorism as it did after the 1970 October Crisis? Is it sharing inaccurate intelligence about suspected foreign terrorist fighters as it shared such intelligence about Maher Arar and others tortured in Syria?

Unlike the CSE Commissioner, representatives of SIRC, or the Privacy Commissioner, the chair of the RCMP complaints body, Ian McPhail, QC, did not ask for new powers or more resources to better work with other reviewers is his testimony on Bill C-51. He alluded to "certain limits" on the body's access to information but concluded, "I am confident that the RCMP recognizes the value of independent civilian review and will cooperate with the commission in fulfilling its mandate." He asserted that with respect to the information sharing provisions in Bill C-51, "the commission is well positioned to review that type of activity, including the policies, procedures and internal oversight mechanisms that would undoubtedly accompany the implementation of such legislative changes within the RCMP."[126] McPhail did not address, however, the review body's inability to review what other agencies did with RCMP information or the fact that the RCMP may refuse its request for secret information.

These are especially important challenges in the current climate. Under the CSIS and RCMP "less is more" approach to information sharing discussed in Chapter 9, the RCMP shares far more intelligence with CSIS than CSIS — the intelligence specialist — shares with the RCMP.[127] This should be an area for close attention since the RCMP has struggled with creating and sharing accurate intelligence about terrorism. As discussed in Chapter 2, this was true in the aftermath of the 1970 October Crisis, and it was certainly true in the Arar affair. The RCMP's production and improper sharing of unreliable intelligence that falsely labelled Maher Arar an al-Qaida associate was in part a function of police officers without adequate national security training being moved into the complex and intelligence-driven world of national security policing in the immediate aftermath of 9/11.

Could something similar to the Arar debacle be happening in the wake of the October 2014 terrorist attacks? By the start of January 2015, the RCMP had reassigned an astounding 600 members from other duties into national security policing.[128] National security policing is highly specialized work that requires very different skills than most other forms of policing. Yet over 600 new people are dealing with the geopolitical and ideological complexities of the foreign-terrorist-fighter phenomenon. Put another way, this is the time for specialists, and police officers are not interchangeable widgets.

The RCMP knows this, of course, and even before the October attacks, it appreciated the virtue of careful staffing and training in its federal policing area. But only the civilian review and complaints body for the RCMP can really tell us whether the mistakes of the post-9/11 Arar era are being repeated. Perhaps they are not. But perhaps new mistakes are being made. The sad truth is that we do not know and we may never know. The only review body that could answer these pressing questions may not have the necessary resources, powers, or expertise to review the RCMP's increased national security activities, including information sharing.

Of the three existing review mechanisms, the RCMP's review mechanism is much weaker than either SIRC or the CSE Commissioner. This is a cause for grave concern especially because the RCMP has dramatically ramped up its anti-terrorism activities in the wake of the October 2014 attacks and in response to the foreign-terrorist-fighter threat. Only a small number of the RCMP's national security cases will end up in the courts. There is a danger that the rest will not be reviewed by any outside eyes.

Privacy Commissioner

The government has argued that the Privacy Commissioner provides whole-of-government review for information sharing under Bill C-51. The Office of the Privacy Commissioner does indeed have a broad organizational mandate that includes all of the federal public sector. But it has a very narrow subject-matter jurisdiction: it is limited to personal information handling and issues related to privacy.

Its role in protecting privacy is muted by the many permissions in the *Privacy Act*,[129] allowing the sharing of personal information for a wide range of law enforcement, "consistent use," and public interest justifications, on top of a lengthy list of other cases where disclosure is specifically authorized by a federal law or regulation. Bill C-51 builds on these permissions. As Professor Lisa Austin has observed, Bill C-51's compounding of these existing authorizations for disclosure amounts to a kind of "sleight of hand" that pretends there are protections for privacy when they are largely absent.[130] We discuss this issue in Chapter 5. As the Privacy Commissioner correctly warned parliamentarians studying Bill C-51, "[n]o level of review can address inadequate standards" for the protection of privacy or other rights.[131]

The Selective Removal of Silos

But good review is still important. In a 2014 report, the Privacy Commissioner raised concerns about out-of-date legislation limiting the office's ability to share information and conduct joint reviews with other reviewers.[132] This concern was echoed in the current Privacy Commissioner's submission to the Commons committee examining Bill C-51: "a system which proposes removal of silos between government departments for information-sharing purposes must provide for the same removal of silos for the bodies which ensure their activities are compliant with the law."[133] In other words, the government has been selectively removing the silos for its own information sharing while retaining silos for review agencies.

The Privacy Commissioner noted that while his office had a $24 million budget, it had a massive responsibility in relation to privacy concerns of all sorts in both the public and the private sector. He undertook to review earnestly the privacy aspects of Bill C-51 but warned, "our review may not be fully effective without some additional resources, as the Act will greatly increase information sharing both in volume and in terms of the complexity of the legal issues involved."[134]

There has been no announcement of new resources for the Privacy Commissioner to review the security information sharing that is bound to increase under Bill C-51. Even if more resources were forthcoming, the Privacy Commissioner would "not have jurisdiction to examine in general the lawfulness of the activities of national security agencies."[135] The Privacy Commissioner has, quite reasonably, contrasted his limited jurisdiction with that of the US Privacy and Civil Liberties Oversight Board, which "extends to constitutional matters, legal matters and matters of effectiveness."[136]

How Review in Canada Lags behind Review in Other Democracies

Despite claims that Canada's review system is the envy of the world, Canada has no review body with specialized security expertise that examines all-of-government security activities. In Canada, we trust but often do not verify. In comparison, other democracies have made efforts to close accountability gaps created by whole-of-government approaches to security.

United States

Following recommendations from the 9/11 Commission, the United States created the Privacy and Civil Liberties Oversight Board in 2004 intelligence reform legislation. This body has a whole-of-government remit and can offer advice on privacy and civil liberties tied to all terrorism policy issues, including information sharing. It considers reports from the privacy and civil liberties officers of eight agencies, including from the Attorney General, Defence, State, Treasury, Health and Human Services, Homeland Security, CIA, and from the Director of National Intelligence.[137]

After one of its members resigned in 2007 claiming interference from the White House, the board was reconstituted as an independent agency with five members serving staggered six-year terms. The chair of the board is a full-time position. The Senate must ratify appointments to the board. It has a bi-partisan composition of retired public servants, judges, and academics.

One of the board's recent reports examined both the National Security Agency and *Foreign Intelligence Surveillance Act of 1978* (*FISA*) court performance in the collection of metadata. The National Security Agency is the American signals intelligence agency, much in the news after the Edward Snowden disclosures of 2013. The *FISA* court is the secretive judicial body that authorizes at least some of the National Security Agency's activities. The 200-page report was based on two public forums and classified briefings with officials from the Office of the Director for National Intelligence, National Security Agency, Department of Justice, FBI, and CIA. Board members also met with White House staff, a former presiding judge of the *FISA* court, academics, privacy and civil liberties advocates, technology and communications companies, and trade associations.

The board had access to classified opinions by the *FISA* court, various Inspector General reports, and additional classified documents relating to the operation and effectiveness of the programs. Board staff conducted a detailed analysis of applicable statutory authorities, the First and Fourth Amendments to the US Constitution, and privacy and civil liberties policy issues.[138] Congress adopted some of the board's recommendations on the need for adversarial challenge and greater transparency in the operation of the *FISA* court in the 2015 *USA Freedom Act*.[139] From review to reform, this was an impressive performance, one that has not been matched in Canada.

United Kingdom

The United Kingdom too has begun developing whole-of-government security review. The Interception of Communications Commissioner reviews all intercepted communications, regardless of what agency conducts the interception. Thus, the Canadian stovepiping and silo problems would not afflict it, at least insofar as intercepts are concerned. Similarly the Office of Surveillance Commissioners reviews surveillance across multiple agencies.

The United Kingdom has also created its own Privacy and Civil Liberties Board in 2015 legislation. It remains to be seen how this new board will work.[140] We assume it will co-operate with the independent reviewer of terrorism legislation, who also has government-wide jurisdiction and access to classified information. So far, the two experienced independent reviewers since 9/11 have made many valuable and detailed studies.[141] The United Kingdom's new Privacy and Civil Liberties Board will also work with the United Kingdom's special security committee of parliamentarians, further formalized in 2013 legislation.[142]

The contrast with Canada is stark: the United Kingdom government has increased both parliamentary and independent expert review at the very same time that the Canadian government has eliminated CSIS's Inspector General and dismissed calls for increased review as duplicative red tape.

Australia and New Zealand

SIRC's closest equivalent in Australia is the Inspector-General of Intelligence and Security.[143] The Australian Inspector-General has jurisdiction not simply in relation to the Australian equivalent of CSIS but also with respect to other members of the Australian intelligence community, although the Inspector-General's precise role varies from agency to agency. The Australian Inspector-General examined all Australian agencies that had been involved in the arrest of an Australian citizen in Pakistan and his subsequent detention in Egypt and Guantanamo.[144] The contrast with SIRC's disclaimer that it could not get to the bottom of the Afghan-detainee or Abdelrazik affairs is stark.

The Australian Inspector-General has complaints and review jurisdiction over six different agencies spanning both civilian domestic and foreign intelligence agencies and military intelligence, including signals intelligence.[145] As a result of 2010 legislation, the Australian prime minister can task the Inspector-General to inquire into any intelligence or security matter relating to any federal department or agency.[146]

In its examination of the Australian Inspector-General, the Arar Commission noted several advantages of its "multi-agency jurisdiction" including "a comprehensive view of the activities of various intelligence agencies" and the "ability to scrutinize integrated and information sharing activities."[147]

New Zealand also has an Inspector-General with a wider remit to examine system-wide issues than exists for Canada's stovepiped bodies. The New Zealand Inspector-General can review the activities of the New Zealand Security Intelligence Service, New Zealand's CSIS analogue. But the Inspector-General may also examine issues with respect to signals intelligence and telecommunications, including hearing complaints from telecommunications companies. Recently, New Zealand eliminated the requirement that the Inspector-General be a retired judge and provided for an advisory committee to assist with that officer's work.[148]

In short, comparable democracies have invested in enhanced review of national security activities. Canada has not.

IV. CHANGING COURSE

So if we are falling behind, how do we catch up? The obvious starting point is to dust off the Arar Commission's recommendations. As noted, the Arar

Commission recommended in 2006 that SIRC's mandate be expanded to include the national security activities of Citizenship and Immigration Canada, Transport Canada, Financial Transactions and Reports Analysis Centre of Canada, and the Department of Foreign Affairs. A revitalized RCMP review and complaints agency was to have jurisdiction to review the national security work of the Canada Border Services Agency. The Arar Commission also recommended that statutory gateways be created between SIRC, CSE, and the RCMP review body to allow them to share secret information and conduct joint reviews. Finally, the three chairs of the review committees joined by an independent chair would co-ordinate reviews and ensure that there was no duplicative or excessive review.

All of these recommendations recognized the need for whole-of-government review to match whole-of-government security responses. At the same time, the Arar Commission ultimately opted for maintaining institutional knowledge and expertise by recommending that an expanded SIRC, the CSE Commissioner, and the RCMP complaints and review body all remain in place. It did not propose one great big, fused über–review committee, or "super-SIRC" that could review all national security activities.

The Changing Review Environment Since the Arar Commission

Time has passed since the Arar Commission made its recommendations in 2006. The government reformed the RCMP accountability body but stopped short of giving that entity full access to secret information or creating gateways to allow it to conduct joint reviews with SIRC or the CSE commissioner. The new legislation prioritizes complaints against almost 20,000 RCMP officers over review even though the Arar Commission had stressed that the latter was critical in the national security context. The body has so far underperformed, with no apparent review of the RCMP's national security activities.

Nor have we made any progress on the parliamentary committee front. In 2006, it was realistic to expect that a new Conservative government with its commitment to strengthening parliamentary committees might adopt some version of Prime Minister Martin's 2005 proposals for a national security committee of parliamentarians. The Afghan detainee affair strengthened the case for a parliamentary committee with access to secret information, but the government was content to rely in that case on a special ad hoc process. The most recent indication that parliamentary review is distant from the Harper government's agenda was the attempt during the Bill C-51 debate to paint it as unsuitable to our system,[149] despite its presence in the United Kingdom, Australia, and New Zealand.

For its part, SIRC's brand has been tarnished by the exploits of Arthur Porter, the former chair of SIRC who resigned in late 2011 after revelations concerning his doubtful business dealings. Meanwhile, media reports in 2014 suggested that three of the then members of SIRC had ties to pipeline companies, an area of acute sensitivity since CSIS was charged with investigating threats to the security of these facilities.[150] SIRC Chair Chuck Strahl eventually resigned as a result.

This was an unfortunate, almost artificial, controversy. There is no reason to assume that SIRC members' lawful and transparent private activities impair their SIRC responsibilities — nor can they be expected to abandon those activities. SIRC members serve part-time and are paid at rates well below what they would receive in the private sector. Nevertheless, the episode reveals the level of public sensitivity over review in the national security area. Reviewers in a secretive sector who conduct their affairs in secret should expect that public apprehensions of bias will be acute.

SIRC now has a second wind. Its most recent annual report was particularly hard hitting.[151] Its funding has effectively doubled, assuming the pledges in the 2015 budget are met. And most of its membership has recently turned over. More than that, it now includes (effectively for the first time) people with existing and substantial national security experience.

But still, we confront the structural problems of silos and stovepipes. We believe it is time to expand the remit of SIRC.

One Reviewer for All: The Case for Whole-of-Government National Security Review

A strong case can be made that with the intensification of whole-of-government approaches to security — manifested more notoriously in Bill C-51's expansive information sharing law and by CSIS's amplified powers to enlist other bodies in its activities — the time has now come for a "super-SIRC" that can review all of the government's national security activities.

A super-SIRC review body would have many advantages. It could follow the trail of intelligence, information sharing, and other national security activities throughout government without the need for statutory gateways between review bodies. It would provide a focal point for complaints about the government's national security activities. It would also avoid what the Arar Commission recognized are legitimate concerns about overlapping and potentially duplicative review.

Of course, there will be start-up costs. We do not underestimate the demands or transition costs of creating a super-SIRC, or indeed even implementing the more limited expansion recommended by the Arar Commission.

SIRC's existing core expertise in reviewing CSIS and the CSE Commissioner's CSE-related competence would need to be retained and integrated into any new body. Moreover, the new body would have to develop expertise working with a broad and diverse range of federal agencies including the RCMP, the Department of National Defence, Foreign Affairs, Trade and Development, CBSA, and so on. And we need to be attentive to police independence issues in relation to the RCMP. But none of these considerations are insurmountable.

A one-committee approach might also enable economies of scale in terms of resources, permit full-time members and therefore greater expertise, and open the door to broader representation of expertise and interests. One of the successful features of Canada's existing review mechanisms is that, while situated in the executive, they are hybrid institutions. The CSE Commissioner and public inquiries benefit from the presence of retired or sitting judges. When it is staffed attentively, SIRC has the advantage of incorporating other leading figures including former senior parliamentarians from all the major political parties. A new revamped committee might include these elements (something that the present SIRC is doing) but also follow the practices of the US Privacy and Civil Liberties Oversight Board by engaging more with the public than do Canada's current review bodies. A larger more diverse and better resourced super-SIRC should be concerned about not only questions of legality but broader questions of propriety and even efficacy.

For example, the US Privacy and Civil Liberties Oversight Board has concerned itself with the efficacy of mass data collection programs.[152] The contrast between review for propriety and review for efficacy can be overstated because it is difficult to determine the proportionality of security measures (a key feature under the *Canadian Charter of Rights and Freedoms*) without making some cautious judgments about their effectiveness.

A super-SIRC should continue to have access to all relevant material (other than cabinet confidences) regardless of its classification. And any review body — including those that exist now — should challenge governmental claims of secrecy in court if necessary. Indeed, review bodies are already competent to refer reference questions to the Federal Court,[153] something that the Information Commissioner has done[154] but that the security review bodies have not. Such challenges should be rare, but they would provide more transparency and perhaps leverage than the current process of closed-door negotiations about what can be made public.

Another move that would be better than the status quo would be to allow a super-SIRC to submit its classified reports to a parliamentary committee that could then question the responsible minister(s) and agency head(s) on their responses to the super-SIRC's findings and recommendations.

It is, of course, highly unlikely that a super-SIRC will be created. The security establishment in Ottawa has too much leverage. In Canada, its power is increased by concerns and preoccupations that enhanced accountability may result in disclosures threatening intelligence sharing relationships with the foreign agencies upon which Canada relies.

The government has prioritized giving security agencies and especially CSIS more powers. Now that CSIS has more powers, there may be little incentive or energy to revisit the neglected question of matching the enhanced powers with enhanced and adequate review. And we caution again that even if review reform comes onto the agenda, better review of overbroad security powers will not be an antidote to the need for reform of those powers. Our reviewers are more than a few steps behind our integrated security activities, but even whole-of-government reviewers will be, by design, at least some distance behind the agencies that they review.

V. JUDICIAL REVIEW AND THE LIMITS OF JUDGES

One of the government's main defences of its new laws was that the new security powers in them are subject to judicial oversight and review. In Chapter 11, we discussed how this is an exaggerated claim and examined generally the process of judicial oversight involving warrants. In this chapter, we focus on judicial review — a process that occurs after, sometimes long after, a security activity has taken place.

Judicial review is valuable. Like independent executive watchdog review, it allows a fresh and independent set of eyes to evaluate what the executive has done in the name of security. Judges should be concerned about the human rights that can be violated during national security activities. Since 9/11, there have been some notable examples in Canada and elsewhere where courts have abandoned their traditional deference to government's national security activities. Without judicial intervention, for example, security-cleared special advocates would never have been created to challenge the secret evidence that the government continues to rely upon to justify detention and strict controls in the immigration security certificate cases.

Unfortunately, the government's 2015 security laws make judicial review a muted check. The new no-fly provisions in Bill C-51 and the new passport revocation provisions in the budget bill both provide for judicial review in Federal Court after internal appeals have been exhausted. As discussed in Chapter 6, this is a positive development that provides for the possibility of a judicial delisting remedy. That said, such a remedy depends on the details of the law. In the case of the no-fly list, judicial delisting would require the judge to declare the government's suspicions that a person would travel for terrorist purposes unreasonable.[155] Absent a successful *Charter* challenge to the process or its substance, judges will reverse the government in only the rarest of circumstances since the review standard is so accommodating of the executive branch.

When determining whether a no-fly listing or passport revocation is reasonable, a judge is specifically empowered by the new laws to consider secret evidence that will not be disclosed to the listed person because of security concerns. But the 2015 changes ignore the important role that security-cleared special advocates can play when a judge is placed in the difficult position of evaluating secret evidence.

As we discuss in Chapter 11, we believe that judges should respond by exercising their inherent discretion to allow security-cleared lawyers to challenge (aggressively if necessary) both the determination that the evidence must remain secret and its merits and reliability. This is particularly important since the new laws allow judges to depart from conventional rules of evidence. Legal rules of evidence are designed to help ensure the reliability of the information that is ordinarily used in court. As such, the rules of evidence systemically inquire into the sources and methods used to produce the evidence. This is, of course, anathema to intelligence agencies. The new no-fly list and passport revocation provisions contemplate that a judge could affirm the state's decision to penalize someone on the basis of hearsay — what a person thinks she has heard from another — or on the basis of intelligence that may turn out to be unreliable.

The Supreme Court decided in 2007 that it was unconstitutional to allow the government to use secret evidence in the security certificate cases without any adversarial challenge. The Court stressed that the state had to respect basic principles of fairness not just in criminal trials but whenever it restricted a person's liberty or security of the person.[156] The subsequent special advocate scheme that Parliament created was a minor but rare Canadian success story, with the Supreme Court holding that the result was constitutional.[157] The scheme should have been specifically incorporated into those parts of the 2015 laws that ask a judge to evaluate secret evidence not disclosed to those whose rights to leave (and potentially return to) Canada are effectively denied.

VI. CONCLUSION

As we stressed in Chapter 11, clear thinking about the differences between oversight and review is necessary if we are to have realistic expectations about the value of review. Whether practised by a new parliamentary committee with access to secret information, by a super-SIRC, or by existing review bodies, review is a retrospective exercise that results in findings and recommendations. Reviewers cannot prevent overreactions that result in human rights abuses. They also cannot prevent underreactions that result in security failures. But they can assess decisions that the agencies have made with fresh and untainted eyes, propose "lessons learned," and flag looming difficulties.

There are accountability gaps in all democracies, but Canada's accountability gaps were particularly pronounced before 2015, and in 2015 they became larger still. Alone out of our Five Eyes partners (and most Western democracies), Canada still does not give any parliamentarians access to secret information. This means that Parliament essentially flies blind on the details.

Like the public, parliamentarians remain uninformed about security failures, including the October 2014 attacks. They do not know the classified details about the foreign-terrorist-fighter threat or our response to it. This must stop.

Unless Parliament asserts itself in the manner last witnessed in the Afghan detainee dispute, the price for parliamentary access to secrets is likely to be a statutory committee whose members are bound by secrecy laws and who cannot rely on parliamentary privileges. This will increase parliamentary knowledge about what is being done and what is not being done in the name of security, but it will also burden parliamentarians with secrets that they cannot, on pain of prosecution and punishment, make public.

We believe that greater parliamentary involvement in security policy is overdue. Boiled to their essence, many of the arguments against such a committee are arguments against Parliament, not its enhanced role in this area.

Still, even the best parliamentary body will not displace the need for expert review. We have proposed that Canada learn from the experience of the United Kingdom and appoint an independent reviewer of anti-terrorism law to smooth some of the structural difficulties with parliamentary competence in national security law and policy. An independent reviewer would help parliamentarians who are able to devote themselves only part-time to national security ask the right questions of the professional and circumspect security mandarins.

Even more critically, we urge a reinvestment in our expert watchdog agencies. SIRC was state of the art when it was created in 1984, but comparable Australian, American, and British reviewers are now much closer to having a whole-of-government mandate that is fit to review whole-of-government security. In stark contrast, SIRC, the CSE Commissioner, and the RCMP complaints body remain deliberately stovepiped and siloed, and the rest of government escapes review even while its security activities become both more intense and more integrated.

Canada's accountability gaps may have occurred accidentally after 9/11, but since then they have been deliberately maintained by a government ignoring or debasing the 2006 recommendations of the Arar Commission and labelling reformed review "needless red tape."

The time has come for Canada to renovate its review structure. It is no longer acceptable that Canada alone of the Five Eyes security powers does not trust its parliamentarians with secret information. It is time to replace the siloed and stovepiped SIRC, CSE Commissioner, and RCMP accountability body with a super-SIRC possessing jurisdiction to review all of the government's national security activities. Such reforms are necessary to ensure that Canada keep pace with other democracies, let alone become a credible "envy of the world."

Even if all of this happens, closing accountability gaps will remain an uphill battle. Effective after-the-fact review is no cure for overbroad and unconstitutional security laws. Nevertheless, effective review that feeds into effective oversight and informs an evidence-based anti-terrorism strategy is our best guard against overreactions of the sort that contributed to Maher Arar's torture. It is also our best early warning system for underreactions and dysfunctional practices like the ones that contributed to the failed Air India investigation and those that may have been present with respect to the October 2014 attacks.

CHAPTER THIRTEEN

Dissuade: An Ounce of Prevention and the Sociology of Anti-terrorism

I. INTRODUCTION

The Foreign Terrorist Fighter

Damian Clairmont went through many different phases in his short life. Friends said that at one point he had "looked like a rapper in a ball cap and baggy basketball clothes."[1] Then he outfitted himself like a fashion model. As a Roman Catholic, he wore a crucifix. He had ambitions to join the military. But he fought depression, dropped out of high school when he was fourteen years old, and tried to kill himself by drinking antifreeze when he was seventeen. After that, he stayed in a group home, took medication, and was treated by a psychiatrist. At one point, police arrested him for attempting to buy ecstasy.

Friends said, "It seemed like he was trying to find himself." He turned to Islam, renaming himself Mustafa. Initially, this seemed to bring him peace. But Clairmont was soon "preachy and judgmental," calling on friends to convert. He urged one to avoid a military career, claiming that "the Canadian military was killing Muslims like him." He became secretive and argumentative, propounded 9/11 conspiracy theories, and made claims about anti-Muslim media bias. Unemployed and on disability benefits, he began hiking with his prayer group and spending time in the gym. He also talked about moving to a Muslim country to study Arabic, naming Egypt as a possible destination.

And despite predictions that Clairmont — a "big talker" — would never follow through, he did leave Canada and his Calgary home. Christianne

Boudreau, Clairmont's mother, only found out that her son was in Syria when CSIS officers arrived at her door in December 2012. CSIS had been watching Clairmont as part of a two-year investigation into an extremist group.

Clairmont may first have joined the al-Nusra Front, an al-Qaida affiliate listed as a terrorist group in Canada. He seems to have joined ISIS (Islamic State of Iraq and Syria) sometime in 2013, adopting the *nom de guerre* Abu Talha al-Kanadi ("The Canadian"). While with ISIS, his infrequent communications with the outside world suggest an increasingly radicalized religious worldview, a hostility to Muslims with views differing from his, and a general contentment with his lot.

In January 2014, the twenty-two-year-old Clairmont was reported killed, defending his base in Syria.

The Foreign Terrorist Fighter's Mother

Since that time, his mother, Boudreau, has campaigned tirelessly for various community-based counter–violent extremism (CVE) programs, but with little apparent assistance from the federal government.

She has spearheaded an effort to bring Germany's Hayat (Arabic for "life") model to Canada.[2] Hayat is a German-based CVE program initiated by the Centre for Democratic Culture and aimed at families and friends of those at risk. It has enjoyed some success and participates in a twenty-four-hour helpline financed by the German Office for Immigration and Refugee Affairs.[3] Hayat's fledgling Canadian version focuses on family counselling. It has no government support and relies entirely on charitable donations.[4] It has not yet been able to implement a twenty-four-hour helpline.[5]

Boudreau is also part of a multinational group named Mothers for Life, which issues pleas through social media for sons and daughters to return from foreign terrorist fights and hopes to assist them in their subsequent reintegration into civil society. Its appeals should not be dismissed: the group relies on both the ability of mothers to prevail on their children and religious reasoning — "remember that even the Prophet Muhammad (peace and blessings be upon him) said: 'Paradise lies at the feet of your mother.'"[6]

When asked to comment on Mothers for Life, a spokesperson for Prime Minister Harper asserted that returning foreign fighters would be prosecuted and that if they were dual nationals, their citizenship would be revoked. Boudreau rejoined, "That's not an answer. There are other ways — better ways, we believe — to make us safe. And Europe is seriously exploring them. I hope Canada will be part of that."[7]

Are we? And if not, should we be? In this chapter, we address these questions, focusing on the anti-terror tool left unaddressed in earlier chapters: dissuade. In Chapter 3, on our "threat escalator" tool, we portrayed dissuade as the broadest and least coercive response to the threat of terrorism — and, more specifically, radicalization to violence. As we discuss below, CVE objectives are also consistent with the "prevent" prong of the government's 2012 anti-terrorism policy.

II. THE HIGH AND LOW POLITICS OF CVE PROGRAMS

Given its significance as a first-level response, it may seem puzzling that we have left this topic to the penultimate chapter. We have done so for two reasons. First, CVE initiatives may be the best "exit strategy" from many of the shortcomings of other tools that we have discussed in this book. Watch, share, interdict, restrain, interrupt, and even prosecute get you only so far. They are temporary solutions even when they involve criminal convictions that may endure for years. We need an endgame, one best discussed at the end of a book.

The Fog of CVE Strategies

The second reason is that while CVE strategies may be the last, best hope for many of our security dilemmas, they are both embryonic and opaque, especially in Canada. They depend on sociological research that is underdeveloped and on practical experience that is slender. The government grey literature in the area is filled with models, best practices, diagrams (often triangles like the one we use in Chapter 3), and checklists. The research literature is filled with caveats and calls for more close inquiry to flesh out the theories or limited empirical samples (often focusing on terrorists without control groups). Indeed, empirical literature on the topic is comparatively sparse, creating the risk of an echo chamber in which policy conclusions are extrapolated from a slender experiential foundation.

This means that the discussion in this chapter is the most provisional of any in this book. It is the new frontier. This is especially true in Canada, which, as will be seen, has yet to implement a full-fledged CVE program — let alone evaluate it and then adjust it in response to slowly evolving knowledge about what works, what does not, and what may even be counterproductive.

As present, there is much talk of the need for "community engagement," but this underestimates the diversity of Canada's Muslim communities.[8] There is also a focus on security that asks much of these communities but offers little in return, especially in terms of needed social and mental health services, matters within provincial jurisdiction.

The High Politics of CVE Programs

CVE programs are highly political — potentially more political and controversial than even the other tools that we have discussed in this book. There are two reasons for this, one good and one not so flattering. The obvious reason for political sensitivities is the scope of CVE initiatives. CVE initiatives are about reacting to behaviour that is perfectly legal, even innocent, to stop a feared slide to more antisocial and illegal conduct. CVE initiatives embrace false positives — sweeping people into programs and potentially bringing them to the state's attention because of what they think and feel and how they act in a society that generally makes thinking, feeling, and acting guarded liberties.

CVE programs must fight, therefore, not to be overinclusive in applying risk prediction models that, in truth, have all the inevitable flaws of the social sciences: they try to predict the conduct, not of physical phenomena responsive to Newton's laws, but of research subjects with free will. Done poorly, a CVE program is the gateway to a Big Brother state lurking at the shoulder of every disgruntled teenager with a bad Internet habit.

More than this, in their struggle not to be overinclusive, CVE programs must also be attentive to other divides in society. They can focus on generic extremism, and government discussion papers can dilute case studies of al-Qaida- and ISIS-inspired radicalization to violence with those of skinheads and anarchists. But if your primary feared security risk is al-Qaida- and ISIS-inspired terrorism, your CVE model will include a close focus on Islam. This means that CVE strategies will subject a religious minority — one that may already be the focus of animus from majority communities — to potentially searing state scrutiny and many demands. It also means that, as discussed in Chapter 9, you will be underinclusive in failing to target extremists who may commit politically or religiously motivated violence that has nothing to do with Islam. In a perverse feedback loop, this in turn may adversely affect co-operation with Muslim communities to the extent that they themselves may fear far-right terrorist violence and perceive discriminatory double standards.

Canada's Low Politics: "This Is Not a Time to Commit Sociology"?

These problems of effectiveness, sweep, and discrimination (perceived or real) afflict contemporary CVE programs everywhere. But, in Canada, there is a second political problem. How it arose, we are not quite sure. But for some incomprehensible reason the political leadership of the Harper government frowns on social science–driven measures as tools of terrorism deterrence. It seems to equate efforts to understand — and ultimately prevent — terrorism with an inquiry into "root causes." It then treats that phrase as tantamount to appeasement and making excuses for violence.

In response to the foiled 2013 VIA Rail terrorist attacks, Prime Minister Harper asserted, "This is not a time to commit sociology, if I can use an expression . . . . these things are serious threats, global terrorist attacks, people who have agendas of violence that are deep and abiding threats to all the values that our society stands for."[9] This "commit sociology" line — twinning a social science with a verb commonly used in relation to crimes — first appeared in the prime minister's condemnation of Liberal leader Justin Trudeau's comments about understanding root causes and the 2013 Boston Marathon bombing.

Government politicians have also seemed inclined to terminology that fosters unease in the Muslim community, and, indeed, is insulting to at least some of its members. In 2007, Prime Minister Harper argued, "the major threat is still Islamism."[10] This neologism is relatively common, used even in some of the literature that we cite below, but its precise meaning and virtue have occasioned at least one book-length debate.[11] In most instances, it seems to denote a conservative Muslim religious ideology more than outright violence.[12] Whatever the case, the prime minister's use of the term drew objections from the Canadian Muslim community and caused some diplomatic fallout, and the government recanted the term's uncertain breadth by affirming that the prime minister intended a focus on outright violence.[13]

Then, the prime minister responded to the January 2015 terrorist attacks in Paris by stating that "the international jihadist movement has declared war. They have declared war on anybody who does not think and act exactly as they wish they would think and act."[14] In introducing Bill C-51 at a campaign-style rally in the same month, he declared, "Our Government has never hesitated to call jihadi terrorism what it is," again claiming that "jihadists" had "declared war" on Canada.[15] As we note below, the political executive seems to take a studied interest in using the common but ultimately counterproductive term "jihadi" now coupled with a war metaphor typically deployed in an armed conflict against states, not a contest with an inchoate ideology.

In June 2015, Prime Minister Harper announced new anti-terror funding, urging as follows: "All civilizations, all civilized nations are today faced with an enemy who hates everything about our existence: freedom, democracy, tolerance, openness. Our Government does not hesitate in calling this enemy by its name, violent jihadism, and as we do not hesitate to condemn it, we do not hesitate to confront it either at home or abroad."[16] And in discussing radicalization to violence, the prime minister asserted in January 2015 that it is a crime and that it "doesn't matter what the age of the person is, or whether they're in a basement, or whether they're in a mosque or somewhere else."[17] Muslim groups responded with alarm at the suggestion that mosques were the font of violent extremists. They called these comments "extremely divisive" especially in light of "anti-Muslim violence and vandalism at places of worship . . .": "[I]t was very disturbing to see the prime minister create this kind of impression in the minds of Canadians, that there's something wrong going on when there isn't anything of that sort."[18]

The prime minister's statements were followed by Minister Peter MacKay's suggestion, discussed in Chapter 9, that terrorist crimes occurred only where there was a "cultural" component, regarded by many as coded language for "Muslim." The justice minister made this comment at around the same time that the prime minister exhibited a heated and disproportionate focus on a woman who wished to wear a niqab while swearing her citizenship oath.

And, in the first question directed at a Muslim witness at the Commons committee examining Bill C-51, Conservative MP Diane Ablonczy placed "on the record" allegations that the witness's group had ties to terrorist organizations, allegations that the group's executive director categorically and cogently denied on behalf of the group, stating that they were based on "innuendo and misinformation" and were "precisely the types of slanderous statements that have resulted in litigation that is currently ongoing."[19] The incident precipitated considerable commentary in the media including subsequent denunciations by prominent members of the Muslim communities, who compared attacks on Muslim witnesses to US Senator Joseph McCarthy's famous anti-communist slurs.[20]

Meanwhile, as discussed in Chapter 10, the governing Conservatives recycled terrorist propaganda from al-Shabaab and ISIS to elicit campaign donations. And in July 2015, the Conservative members of the Senate national security committee issued a report on the Canadian security situation that contained several laudable ideas but also several surprisingly ill-conceived ideas.[21] One of them — proposing that the "federal government work with the provinces and the Muslim communities to investigate the options that are available for the training and certification of imams in Canada"[22] — was likely a response to concerns that Imams were trained in foreign institutions, some of which favoured values inconsistent with those in Canada. The government dismissed this particular recommendation. But in the present political climate, the proposal was still perceived by critics as singling out Muslim religious leaders and by the National Council of Canadian Muslims as "feeding into this 'us versus them' narrative that could also give legitimacy and credibility to the ideology of violent extremists."[23]

In February 2015, columnists were expressing concern on this same theme. Stephen Maher wrote, "Harper will add fuel to the fire, linking terrorism to mosques — as he did when he introduced C-51 — inveighing against niqabs in fundraising emails and scaring everyone by warning about 'jihadist monsters' at every opportunity."[24] Professor Charles Taylor, a renowned political philosopher and co-chair of Quebec's 2007 commission on reasonable accommodation of cultural and religious minorities, accused the government of fuelling anti-Muslim sentiment and making recruitment to al-Qaida- and ISIS-inspired violence easier: "Ask yourself what are the recruiters for Islamic State saying? They're saying (to Muslims), 'Look, they despise you, they think that you're foreign, you're dangerous, you're not accepted here, so why don't you come with us?' . . . The more you make it sound like that (is true), the more you're helping them. And it's strange that people don't see this."[25]

The government rhetoric came mere months before a Statistics Canada study showing that hate crimes against Muslims were increasing even while those against other religions were dropping. The report also observed that Muslim women were more often targeted than women in other groups: "This may be related to the fact that the practice of wearing head coverings may make religious identity more visible for Muslim women than for men."[26]

All of this creates a risky, even toxic, environment for Canada to start the already difficult task of pursuing CVE strategies.

Low Politics and Bad Security

The precise content of CVE programs is, of course, disputed. But one essential ingredient is a counter-narrative that disputes the ideological claim of al-Qaida, ISIS, and like-minded entities that the West is at war with Islam. That ingredient has so far been missing in Canada. A government that responds with a "clash of civilizations" discourse and associates jihad with terrorist violence at every apparent opportunity risks, however unintentionally, affirming the al-Qaida- and ISIS-inspired political narrative, not countering it.

Such a government also undermines the much more sophisticated CVE programs undertaken by government officials, including those in the security services. Whatever politicians may say, Canadian government agencies do, in fact, view the government's anti-terrorism strategy as aiming "to get at the root causes and factors that contribute to terrorism by actively engaging with individuals, communities and international partners."[27] And these agencies must live with the consequences of the government's overheated rhetoric.

Canada as Outlier: "What's Easy Is to Pass Tough New Laws. Harder Is . . . . Returning to Everyday Life . . . ."

Other countries are charting a different course. The White House hosted a Countering Violent Extremism Summit the week of 17 February 2015 while Canada was starting to debate Bill C-51. In addressing the summit, President Obama urged the international community to remember that "[v]iolent extremists and terrorists thrive when people of different religions or sects pull away from each other and are able to isolate each other and label them as 'they' as opposed to 'us'; something separate and apart. So we need to build and bolster bridges of communication and trust."[28] At the summit's conclusion, President Obama was clear that he did not consider the United States to be at war with Islam, or even radical Islam, but rather with terrorists:

> Al Qaeda and ISIL and groups like it are desperate for legitimacy. They try to portray themselves as religious leaders — holy warriors in defense of Islam. That's why ISIL presumes to declare itself the "Islamic State." And they propagate the notion that America — and the West, generally — is at war with Islam. That's how they recruit. That's how they try to radicalize young people. We must never accept the premise that they put forward, because it is a lie. Nor should we grant these terrorists the religious legitimacy that they seek. They are not religious leaders — they're terrorists. And we are not at war with Islam. We are at war with people who have perverted Islam.[29]

This discourse is the mirror image of that used by political leaders in Canada at exactly the same time.

Even Australia's famously pugnacious prime minister has been more open to nuance than his Canadian counterpart. In a fierce June 2015 speech with its own fair share of alarming language, Prime Minister Tony Abbott outlined many of Australia's heavy measures against foreign terrorist fighting, including proposals inspired by Canadian legislation to strip citizenship. But (at least in this speech) he never used the word "jihad" or other religiously pointed terms. And he underscored the following:

> In the end, though, the only really effective defence against terrorism is persuading people that it's pointless. We have to convince people that God

does not demand death to the infidel . . . . We need everyone to understand that it is never right to kill people just because their beliefs are different from ours. Above all, we need idealistic young people to appreciate that joining this death cult is an utterly misguided and wrong-headed way to express their desire to sacrifice.[30]

Implicit in Abbott's comments is a recognition — one largely absent from the Canadian public debate but probably recognized within government agencies — of the limits of the justice system as a means to prevent violent extremism. Indeed, rising concerns about prison radicalization underline that the justice system's most forceful tool — successful prosecution — may in some cases add to the problem.

A uniformly hard-nosed approach can be shortsighted. Looking at his country's experience with CVE programs, Danish Police Superintendent Allan Aarslev concluded, "What's easy is to pass tough new laws. Harder is to go through a real process with individuals: a panel of experts, counselling, healthcare, assistance getting back into education, with employment, maybe accommodation. With returning to everyday life and society. We don't do this out of political conviction; we do it because we think it works."[31]

Securing Canada?

To be sure, there are those who regard the Canadian political executive's recent speaking lines as flinty-eyed truth telling about a troubled religion, objectionable only to apologists, professors, and the thin-skinned.

We find these views on religion objectionable, but in a book on security law and policy, what matters is whether this political discourse translates into good security. We think that it does not: it offers no appreciable security gain but does risk undermining the very ingredients necessary to counter violent extremism. Ultimately, security in a democracy depends on consent and willing collaboration by all communities in a collective effort.

In some respects, it may be beneficial that we have not implemented a full-fledged CVE program in our present politicized environment. We must ensure that the rhetoric of the government does not presage a drift to a form of CVE program that conflates ideology with risk or risk with crime.

III. WHAT DO WE KNOW ABOUT RADICALIZATION TO VIOLENCE?

Countering violent extremism requires an understanding of its causes. And that means we need to "commit sociology" in this chapter.

While there is a vast literature on radicalization to violence, empirical studies are comparatively uncommon,[32] and the conclusions of this research must be regarded as partial and provisional. Nevertheless, a growing corpus of empirical research focuses on radicalization to violence (or "terrorist radicalization"). Many of these studies are relatively recent and focus on post-9/11 preoccupations with religious terrorist radicalization.[33]

Radicalization in Context

A first point to emphasize is the distinction between radicalization and radicalization to violence (or violent extremism). Radicalization may be defined as "changes in beliefs, feelings, and actions in the direction of increased support for one side of a political conflict."[34]

Extremist al-Qaida-Inspired Ideology

As we note in Chapter 3, Clark McCauley and Sophia Moskalenko describe al-Qaida-inspired political discourse as comprising a four-part "narrative frame": "(1) Islam is under attack by Western crusaders led by the United States; (2) jihadis, whom the West refers to as terrorists, are defending against this attack; (3) the actions they take in defence of Islam are proportional, just, and religiously sanctified; and, therefore (4) it is the duty of good Muslims to support these actions."[35]

McCauley and Moskalenko also propose a "pyramid of opinion radicalization." At the base of this structure are Muslims who do not subscribe to any of the four parts of the al-Qaida-inspired discourse. In the tier above these is a smaller tranche of those who agree that the West besieges Islam. Next are those who also believe that al-Qaida-inspired terrorists act in defence of Islam and with moral and religious justification. Finally, the peak of the pyramid encompasses the even smaller group of persons who subscribe not only to these views but also to the view that it is a Muslim's duty to participate in Islam's defence.[36] McCauley and Moskalenko point to polling data supporting their view that the number of people ascribing to the views associated with each tier of the pyramid generally declines the further up the pyramid one climbs.[37]

"The Greatest Myth Alive Today in Terrorism Research": Ideology Equals Violence

To supplement their opinion radicalization pyramid, McCauley and Moskalenko propose an action radicalization pyramid running from the politically inert at the base through activists to radicals and, then, to terrorists at the much smaller pyramid tip.[38] They dispute, however, that individuals progress linearly from one stage to another. Political ideology and grievance is not a conveyor belt to terrorist activity.[39] Violent extremism is not, in other words, the inevitable, or even likely, product of ideological radicalization.

This fact needs to be underscored and double underscored because it is so often misunderstood and the source of considerable mischief. It may be reasonable to use a pyramid to portray gradients as McCauley and Moskalenko do, and as we also attempt in Chapter 3. But it is not, as the New York police once proposed, useful to "think of the radicalization process in terms of a funnel."[40] As John Horgan, director of the International Center for the Study of Terrorism at Pennsylvania State University, puts it, "[t]he idea that radicalization causes terrorism is perhaps the greatest myth alive today in terrorism research."[41] Or in the words of an internal United Kingdom government report, "We do not believe that it is accurate to regard radicalisation in this country as a linear 'conveyor belt' moving from grievance, through radicalisation, to violence . . . . This thesis seems to both misread the radicalisation process and to give undue weight to ideological factors."[42]

This is true even for extremist al-Qaida-inspired ideologues. As we describe in Chapter 3, McCauley and Moskalenko calculate that only 1 in every 100 persons espousing the most extreme al-Qaida-inspired narrative makes the move to violence.[43] The process of radicalization to violence is, therefore, more complex than simply harbouring radical opinion. Non-violent radical groups may in some cases be in competition with violent radical entities,[44] rather than being their "farm teams." Moreover, there are instances where people are drawn to politicized violence without first having developed radical ideas.[45]

In short, the connection between radical and extremist ideas and an actual willingness to engage in terrorist violence is tenuous, even non-existent. Indeed, Canada should be acutely conscious of its own recent experience with seeming insta-converts to Islam, moving in a short time from being socially disgruntled to being religiously obsessed and, ultimately, to being politically violent. One recent academic study estimated that in North America, "coverts to Islam comprised nearly 35 percent of the foreign fighters and almost 50 percent of potential fighters."[46] But other studies have warned that religious conversion per se is probably a poor indicator of the risk of further conversion to a belief in inter-group violence.[47] Taken together, these patterns suggest that it is plain dangerous to imagine some sort of linear and staged progression from religion to radical ideology to terrorism. Our recent Canadian experience also counsels against placing the entire burden of countering extremist violence on the minority religious community with which people suddenly decide to affiliate in their quickstep to violence.

Indeed, it may be that even for those raised in Muslim families, the move to al-Qaida- or ISIS-inspired violence amounts to a different form of "conversion" experience more akin to that associated with cults. As such, the move to religiously inspired violence may be best understood through the lens of a sociology that studies religious conversions and fanaticism[48] and not a more myopic inquiry trying to identify some inherent flaw in Islamic belief.

Radicalization to Violence

If harbouring nasty (religion-related or other) ideas is a poor indicator of *violent* extremism, then establishing exactly in which circumstances a person may become violent is an important research and policy question. The social science data are sparse. As Professor Lorne Dawson notes in his study of radicalization to violence among the Toronto 18, researchers "have yet to explain why only a few individuals, from among the many subject to the same conditions become terrorists."[49]

Empirical studies to date suggest no single socioeconomic profile for a person radicalized to violence in Europe. Individuals radicalized to violence "vary widely in terms of age, socioeconomic background, education, occupation, family status, previous criminal record, and so on."[50] These individuals are, in fact, "strikingly normal in terms of the socioeconomic variables analyzed."[51] Still, Europe-wide case study research points to a finite number of "personality types or roles" within radicalized terrorist groups.[52] The "leader" is "a charismatic and idealist[ic] individual with a strong interest in politics and an activist mindset." The "protégé" is a "young, intelligent, at times vocationally or educationally accomplished individual who admires the entrepreneur and shares his activist mindset." The "misfit" often comes from "a troubled background, maybe with a record of involvement with petty crime or with drug abuse." Finally, the "drifter" is a "person who appears to join the group through social connections to individuals already in the group or in the group's periphery."[53]

Each of these "types" may radicalize to violence for different reasons, suggesting that there is no single profile useful for understanding terrorist radicalization. Leaders and protégés "join through a deliberate and conscious process driven by political grievances." Misfits see membership as a means to start afresh and deal "with personal problems or a troublesome past." Drifters are motivated by such things as "loyalty to friends, peer pressure, coincidental encounters with a charismatic recruiter, or . . . search of 'adventure.'"[54] These misfits and drifters may be bereft of radical ideas and motivated by interpersonal preoccupations. They are, in other words, members of al-Qaida-inspired groups by happenstance, and not by ideological predisposition, at least initially.

Other studies support these findings. An examination of radical recruitment in Holland suggested three central influences behind terrorist radicalization. First, some individuals radicalize in a quest for "meaning, stability, and respect."[55] Often living on the margins, these are frequently individuals with a history of petty crime and educational difficulties. Second, some individuals radicalize to violence in "search for community." Former "outsiders" distinguished by a "pious lifestyle" with "quiet and intense" religious beliefs fall into this class.[56] Last, some individuals radicalize to violence as "a reaction to perceived injustices committed against Muslims in conflict areas such as Afghanistan or the Palestinian territories or Europe itself" and appear to "provide intellectual and social leadership to the rest of the group."[57] They are "typically more resourceful, better educated, slightly older, more knowledgeable about religious texts, better Arab-speakers, and in general more self-assured."[58] Their views may alienate more moderate co-religionists. In the result, these ideological radicals "tend to expend much energy on criticizing competing and nonviolent interpretations of Islam, in which their followers might potentially find alternative sources of community and meaning."[59]

Other researchers have emphasized the particular importance of these leaders in cementing a move to radicalization to violence by others. As one recent study on radicalization to violence and the Bali bombings observed, "[t]he credibility of individuals taking on leadership roles is one of the main factors that leads individuals to join terrorist groups."[60] Specifically, a charismatic leader can "help promote a potent 'us versus them' psychology, setting in motion powerful group dynamics centred on ideology."[61] These findings suggest that "charismatic leaders" may be catalysts that can mobilize others, including protégés, misfits, and drifters.

The Role of the Internet

Both terrorist organizations and radicalized individuals make use of the Internet, including as an "'information weapon' to increase their visibility and to publicize their activities."[62] Francesca Bosco divides Internet activities related to terrorism into three classes: Internet use as an organizational tool, for waging psychological terror, and for publicity and propaganda.

Some persons radicalized to violence create Internet content that is then consumed by others. This active Internet use is most often invoked in discussions of the link between the Internet and radicalization. But the precise nature of the relationship between terrorist use of the Internet and radicalization and violence is debated. Some analysts doubt a causal relationship.[63] An internal Public Safety Canada analysis reports:

> there is little actual evidence that [the Internet] plays a dominant role in radicalization. More likely it has a facilitating and enabling role, such as in maintaining network contacts and reinforcing ideological messages that have already been internalised by their audiences. Face-to-face human contact appears to remain crucial to recruitment and the group dynamics that can drive radicalization, at least radicalization to violence.[64]

Past studies support these assertions. Dutch empirical research suggests:

> The youngsters in the [research] sample did not radicalize due to Imams, parents, surfing on the Internet, or individually seeking out extremist texts and propaganda. They radicalized due to interaction with a significant other — a charismatic leader, a family member, or a trusted peer — and frequently within smaller groups increasingly isolated from the rest of society.[65]

The significance of this charismatic group leader far outstrips that of other potential sources of radicalization: "Online propaganda or fiery Internet preachers might prime an individual toward a certain way of thinking, but seem secondary to real-life relationships when it comes to violent radicalization."[66]

Other researchers see the Internet as influential, though to varying degrees.[67] For instance, Marc Sageman's influential "leaderless jihad" thesis posits that the Internet facilitates a loose, leaderless network of independent, leaderless terrorist organizations.[68] Moreover, Internet propaganda may fuel moral outrage that may trigger violent action.[69] The Internet's interactive aspect may compound this effect. Internet "forums and websites act as an echo chamber where only the same opinions and ideas are discussed," creating a new normal for participants constantly exposed to the same ideas.[70] Some ISIS recruits go to Syria after interacting online with ISIS members there.

In sum, while the Internet alone may not be a cause of radicalization to violence, it may serve as a "driver and enabler for the process of radicalization," a forum for radicalizing propaganda, a venue for social networking with the like-minded, and, then, a means of data mining during the turn toward violence.[71]

These findings lead us to support the limited Internet deletion procedures advanced in Chapter 10, but with considerable caution. Leaving aside *Charter of Rights and Freedoms* concerns about freedom of expression,[72] there are real limits to the ability to control the supply of extremist literature. It is very easy to set up new websites or repost content on a different forum. Even more importantly, one report suggests that negative or repressive measures may have little impact on the "conversational" aspect of the Internet. Thus, "while it may be possible to remove, filter or hide content that is available from relatively static websites, large parts of the internet — chat rooms, instant messaging, virtual worlds and networking sites — are going to remain largely unaffected. Negative measures, therefore, are unlikely to be fully effective, and . . . their deployment generates wider costs."[73]

Turning People Around: De-radicalizing or Disengaging?

If we know something — although not a lot — about radicalization to violence, how much do we know about reversing the process? It turns out we know very little. As Professor Paul Bramadat notes, "the study of de-radicalization is so new that it is also difficult to anticipate what kinds of efforts might delegitimize violent radicalism."[74]

Different Strokes for Different Folks

But this does not mean that researchers and practitioners are inactive in this area. A clear preoccupation in some de-radicalization discussions is persuading people to abandon the radical beliefs said to motivate and justify their violence. This is probably futile if it becomes our ultimate focus. For one thing, it may be difficult to persuade people to think differently. For another, it is unnecessary.

De-radicalization and de-radicalization from violence are distinct objectives.

The reasonable objective is to change the methods through which people pursue their beliefs, not the beliefs themselves. On balance this is a much more plausible objective, and one that is best suited for liberal democracies. As John Horgan has discovered in his empirical work, "the disengaged terrorist may not necessarily be . . . 'deradicalized' at all . . . . In fact, in the sample of former terrorists I interviewed from 2006 to 2008, while almost all of the interviewees could be described as disengaged, the vast majority of them could not be said to be 'deradicalized.'"[75]

How do we achieve a disengagement form of de-radicalization? The literature on de-radicalization suggests that no one model suits all radicalized personality types. While measures that establish alternative social communities or economic opportunities may draw some away from radicalism, leaders, who are more strongly ideological, are likely to be unresponsive to such measures. For these ideological diehards, Anja Dalgaard-Nielsen suggests that "preventive and disengagement efforts should probably be based on the attempt to impact on the thinking of these individuals through credible anti-violence voices in their own community coupled with various attempts at democratic inclusion, to combat the notion that constitutional politics is an ineffective way of seeking to address grievances."[76] Put in more concrete terms, it may be worth disputing contorted religious logic — a process that would depend on a credible religious figure — but we should avoid a program that depends on arguing with ideologues over whether, for example, Islam is under attack by Western crusaders led by the United States. Al-Qaida-inspired ideologues are not the only people with strong objections to Western foreign policy in the Middle East, and to paint that history as purely benign risks discrediting the program.

A more viable alternative may instead be the following: "Well, if you believe that, then the evident course of action is to become politically engaged and change our policies." Indeed, a useful CVE program would provide the tools to do just that: advance democratically acceptable solutions to grievances. In this manner, a belief — entirely acceptable in a free society however unpopular it may be — is steered toward conduct that is also entirely acceptable — even essential — in a democratic society. There is evidence that those who disengage from violence may often engage in other more benign activities motivated by the same radical ideologies.[77] Government institutions may not be in the best position to offer alternative strategies for acting on perhaps radical ideologies, pointing to the importance of robust civil society institutions.

Canada's history is proof of concept. In Chapter 2, we point out how similar strongly held ideological commitments can produce radically different outcomes: the terrorist Front de libération du Québec (FLQ) versus the democratic Parti Québécois. The ideology is not the enemy — the violent conduct is. This fundamental point was lost in some of the excesses of the 1970 October Crisis, but Canada fortunately reclaimed this important distinction and sustained it through two heart-stopping referendums on Quebec sovereignty.

What is the delivery system for this disengagement approach? Dalgaard-Nielsen notes in a meta-study focusing on de-radicalization programs in Europe, Southeast Asia, and the Middle East that "all place emphasis on trust building, on a constructive and benevolent rather than accusatory approach, and on demonstrating a fair and professional approach on the part of the authorities."[78] In her view, these strategies are "well-placed" given "what social psychology tells us about cognitive consistency, dissonance, and reactance."[79] Dalgaard-Nielsen recommends *against* "fixed curriculum, mandatory ideological re-education, and a strong reliance on the power of rhetoric and arguments" given the risk of reinforcing rather than discouraging radical views.[80] In short, we must be flexible, subtle, and smart.

Counter-narratives

Viable disengagement-from-violence strategies obviously extend beyond the propagation of counter-narratives. But credible counter-narratives are an important tool in any such approach, one that may usefully be represented on the Internet. Counter-narrative strategies do not curb speech but rather try to refute radicalized speech in favour of "pluralism, democracy, and the (peaceful) means through which good ideas can be advanced."[81] Strategies for doing so vary but include obvious efforts to rebut "cult personalities," to challenge extremist ideology,[82] and especially to address "legends of injustice and oppression."[83] In some sense, counter-narratives seek to outcompete more pernicious speech in the famous "marketplace of ideas" associated with an open society. They rely on reason, not repression.

But the counter-narrative in this context cannot be ham-handed government propaganda. Community groups may be better positioned to create and deliver anti-violence messages,[84] while government actors are better suited to deal with the political counter-narrative. Government's primary role may, therefore, be to help "create awareness, convene relevant nongovernmental actors, build capacity, and foster media literacy."[85] A June 2015 international ministerial meeting in Australia "acknowledged that effective strategies to counter the threat of online radicalisation require governments to act beyond legislative and law enforcement measures to engage with the community in partnership with industry to promote positive messaging and counter misleading and harmful terrorist narratives."[86] One of the meeting's outcomes was to establish a "network of civil society groups to foster peer-to-peer learning and partnerships, including with the private sector, and assist with identifying and better utilising leaders and influencers across the region to reach target audiences." There was also a recognition of the need "to invest in enhancing the role of communities to challenge terrorist propaganda, including by building the technical capability of grassroots organisations to elevate non-extremist voices that resonate with target audiences."[87]

The Internet will always contain a lot of dangerous content, and it is not realistic to expect people, even children, to abstain from online surfing. A better approach is to focus on Internet safety and awareness programs, sensitizing young people and their parents to extremist messaging, in addition to online bullying, predators, and pornography. Other approaches include co-operation with technology companies that are willing to provide technical assistance, grants, free advertising, or other support facilitating the online presence of, among other things, Muslim thought leaders with messages contrary to those of al-Qaida-inspired extremists.[88]

Likewise, government may enable connections between community groups and media and public relations professionals able to assist in crafting more compelling messages.[89] Still other initiatives may include such things as government support for terrorist victims' documentation on the Internet of their own suffering, in answer to the glorification imagery of terrorist ideologues.[90] This could be more effective and would surely be cheaper than relying on terrorism prosecutions to unmask the brutal violence in terrorism. Former violent extremists, including returned foreign terrorist fighters, are well positioned to convey the needed message that there is nothing heroic or Islamic about violent extremism.[91]

Counter-Violent Extremism versus Counter-Ideological Extremism

If we know a little bit (but not enough) about radicalization to violence and if we know a little bit (but not enough) about de-radicalization from violence, then the next tempting frontier is intercepting people before they radicalize at all, that is, before they become extremist ideologues.

This, however, is a fraught and perilous ambition. Again, it is important to be conscious of the "greatest myth" in terrorism studies: ideas equal violence. Radical ideas are not the problem. Acting violently on them is. Rolling back interventions to target those with concerning ideas on the theory that such interventions stall a progress to violence is just that — a theory. And, given the data discussed above showing loose correlations between radical worldviews and violent extremism, it is not a very good theory.

Commenting on the United Kingdom experience, Anthony Richards correctly warns against "suggesting that there is some kind of intrinsic link between certain non-violent dogmas and terrorism." And he cautions against excluding "large sections of the population who exercise their democratic right to hold . . . unpalatable views" but who "have no truck with the use of violence."[92] There is real danger that European societies will be especially amenable to implementing laws based on the ideas-equal-violence myth because they often accept the doctrine of militant democracy[93] — that is, that democracies can and should ban speech and associations of those who do not accept democracy.

A CVE Program of False Positives: The United Kingdom's Prevent

In fact, to some appreciable degree, the United Kingdom has travelled down a path from a counter–violent extremism strategy to a counter–ideological extremism strategy. Channel is one aspect of the United Kingdom's Prevent strategy first started in 2006. Introduced in its present form in 2012, Channel uses existing collaboration between local authorities, the education and health sectors, social services, children's and youth services, offender management services, the police, and local communities. In 2015, the Channel program was entrenched in law by the *Counter-terrorism and Security Act 2015*.[94] This statute allows the secretary of state to issue both general guidance and more specific directions to "specified authorities" including local governments, correctional officials, educators (including universities), health care providers, and the police.

The United Kingdom government has published statutory guidance for those who implement the Channel program.[95] Once an individual is referred to the program, police will make an initial assessment as to the nature and extent of the individual's vulnerability.[96] This information is then presented to a panel chaired by the statutorily responsible local authority. Depending on the nature of the referral, the panel may also include social workers, teachers, correctional officials, and officials involved with immigration, housing, and child services.[97] United Kingdom guidance pamphlets emphasize that "Channel is not about reporting or informing on individuals in order to prosecute them. It is about communities working together to support vulnerable people at an early stage, preventing them from being drawn into terrorism."[98] A study obtained from Public Safety Canada through an access to information request indicates that over 1000 individuals have been referred under this program since its inception, with 88 percent of these individuals referred "due to concerns about jihadi terrorism."[99]

On one level, an all-of-society CVE program is attractive, and the United Kingdom approach has the virtue of not treating CVE initiatives as a stalking horse for police. But the initiative is controversial, not least because of what triggers its interventions. The Prevent strategy defines extremism to include "vocal or active opposition to fundamental British values, including democracy, the rule of law, individual liberty and mutual respect and tolerance of different faiths and beliefs."[100] Local authorities, schools, health care workers, universities, and others have a duty to assess the risk of persons' being drawn into both violent and *non-violent* extremism.

Setting aside how this will be administered, the focus is staggering. A lengthy list of academics in the United Kingdom have argued that Prevent's approach to extremism is based "on the unsubstantiated view that religious ideology is the primary driving factor for terrorism" and that "this serves to reinforce a prejudicial worldview that perceives Islam to be a retrograde and oppressive religion that threatens the West. PREVENT reinforces an 'us' and 'them' view of the world, divides communities, and sows mistrust of Muslims."[101] In a scathing critique of the Prevent strategy, leading anti-terror and radicalization scholar Andrew Silke has similarly concluded, "everything is pitched in terms of counter ideology, even though ideology is not the prime mover in terms of bringing people into terrorism. That is a mistake. It is not going to be effective in terms of preventing people becoming radicalised. And it diverts attention from other causes which play a role in why people become involved in terrorism."[102]

Current efforts in the United States to create a new CVE office have sparked similar resistance from civil liberties groups who argue that the United Kingdom effort "has been widely criticized for alienating the very communities it was seeking to influence and for lacking any means of measuring effectiveness." They warn as follows:

> Despite years of federally-funded efforts, researchers have not developed reliable criteria that can be used to predict who will commit a terrorist act. CVE training that conveys vague and unsupportable "indicators" of violent extremism will only result in further civil rights and privacy violations, unreliable reporting to law enforcement, and will waste investigative resources.[103]

These critiques are not necessarily fatal for a CVE program, but they do suggest a need for caution and careful evaluation, not least because some forms of CVE strategy may not be effective in preventing violence and because some approaches may even be counterproductive, especially if they stigmatize and stereotype target groups.

Keeping the Eye on the Prize: All-of-Society Counter-violence

An all-of-society CVE program should aim only for disengagement from — or non-engagement with — violence, not for an ideological purging of disfavoured views. It should not do what the social sciences cannot and try to predict which wrong-headed ideas will culminate in violence, intervening through state mechanisms on their detection. A proper CVE program must avoid this trap. It can and should include the counter-narrative strategies described above and engagement and trust building with otherwise isolated and potentially alienated communities. It is about partnerships and collaboration — a resilient society in which values are internalized, not imposed.

Uncomfortable Bedfellows

A CVE program that is not ideologically motivated may have to enlist those who have or at least once had the wrong ideas. A United Kingdom–style counter–ideological extremism approach disqualifies ideological extremists from being CVE agents. Again, the research is imperfect, but it seems short-sighted to exclude those who share the ideology but not the methods of a person turning toward violence. We should be wary of CVE systems that depend on proselytizing state actors or even non-state actors with views completely inimical to those of the radicalized individual. As noted, the state has a vital role in facilitating CVE programs and their counter-narratives. But the agents of persuasion are almost certainly not right-thinking Mounties or even teachers from backgrounds dramatically different than those of their charges.

We obviously do not want to legitimize those with unpalatable ideas. But it may be possible to engage without endorsing. Under a Dutch CVE initiative (with a narrower focus on violent extremism than exists in the United Kingdom), authorities worked with "moderate mainstream Mosques" to challenge the "radical narrative." But the government was not committed to ideological orthodoxy:

> Regarding the most conservative segments in the Muslim community, the authorities, while adopting a zero tolerance policy towards Salafists, recognized the need to maintain an informal, behind the scenes contact with them. There were also instances when Salafists were used as mentors in individual interventions, as some radicalizing individuals refused to be mentored by anybody else.

This "engagement without empowerment of Salafists" was described as a key lesson in a study released under access to information law by Public Safety Canada,[104] but one that may now be at odds with other parts of government policy, including the new Bill C-51 speech offence, discussed in Chapter 10.

Co-ordinating CVE Programs in a Federation

As in every other area we discuss in this book, there needs to be co-ordination. The European Commission identified acts of violent extremism that could, in many cases, have been prevented if practitioners had worked together and shared information.[105] State and non-state partners need to have the ability, knowledge, and capacity to share concerns and information and to develop a unified approach to supporting individuals at risk. A real challenge for Canada will be the federal division of powers and the fact that key areas — education, health, and social services — are in provincial jurisdiction. But the federalism challenge is not insurmountable. Nothing stops the federal government from providing leadership and spending in areas of provincial jurisdiction.

Some federations are managing to start multi-disciplinary CVE programs. Australia announced a new CVE program in August 2014, led by the Attorney-General's Department but including federal departments of education, employment, human services, social services, immigration, and health.[106] One interesting and community-based feature of this program is Australia's efforts to compile a directory of community-based CVE initiatives providing "religious and multi-cultural mentoring, specialized mental health services, education and employment counselling, youth and community work, including sports programs, case management and telephone and/or online counselling." The directory is supported by a grants program that will enable a wide range of community groups, including religious groups, to implement a wide range of multi-disciplinary services for those at risk of being radicalized to violent extremism.[107]

The fact that the United States is a federation has not stopped it from funding pilot CVE programs in three American cities. These programs often involve a range of local partners from the education, health, and social service sectors,[108] sectors that are only now being included in Canada's nascent and delayed federal CVE program, of which, as will be seen, the RCMP has taken the *de facto* lead.

IV. WHAT IS CANADA DOING?

Converting this sociology and comparative experience into operational policy in Canada is not easy especially when the sociology is provisional and when the political leadership has signalled a distaste for it.

In introducing Bill C-51 for third reading, Senator Bob Runciman argued that given terrorists were prepared to die for their cause, anti-terrorism success should be measured in terms of "prevention rather than prosecution."[109] By prevention, he must have been referring to disruption and interruption powers because nothing in Bill C-51 (or any federal law) addresses CVE strategies: the federal government's report on implementation of its anti-terrorism plan admitted that Canada lagged behind in CVE programs.[110] Indeed, documents obtained under access to information law suggest that the United States has taken the lead on some CVE issues *within Canada*.

In February 2014, the US Department of State planned and conducted CVE meetings with Somali-Canadian communities in Toronto and Ottawa in conjunction with a United States–funded Somali organization from Minnesota. This program had apparently been commenced without informing the Canadian government. Canada's Department of Public Safety was eventually consulted and played some role.[111] Nevertheless, it is telling and embarrassing that American officials appear to be more invested in conducting at least some CVE programs in Canada than is the Canadian government.

In fairness, federalism complicates matters in Canada. With our federal division of powers, the path to CVE programs involves a march through provincial capitals. But with provinces facing apparent federal inertia, there is a danger of ill-calibrated responses. Quebec's June 2015 rollout of its own CVE approach was unhelpfully twinned with a revival of the Quebec Charter of Values project including a controversial bill to prohibit persons — in reality Muslim women — from receiving or providing public services with their face covered.[112] Federal politicians are not, in other words, the only officials to conflate ideology with violence and alienate at least some parts of the diverse Muslim communities.

At the federal level, Public Safety Canada is charged with leading "a coordinated, whole of government approach to" countering violent extremism.[113] It has, for example, launched a new community outreach program geared to "storytelling" or walking through concrete accounts of radicalization to violence at community meetings,[114] and it has invested in a new, fairly sparse, website.[115] It is also deeply involved in international forums and dialogues, both multilaterally and with Five Eyes partners, on best practices in CVE programs. And it participates in the training of frontline police officers.[116]

In practice, though, the government appears to have invested the RCMP with the core on-the-ground CVE lead in a program that has been delayed — and renamed the "Terrorist Prevention Program." That initiative seems to have been mired in bureaucratic limbo although we hope that true progress is being made. We worry also that it may in practice have been compromised by the RCMP's last-minute decision in September 2014 to withdraw from a joint initiative with Muslim groups to produce the *United against Terrorism* pamphlet, which was specifically designed to counter violent extremism among young Muslims and to demonstrate that groups like ISIS pervert Islam. We discuss that sad saga below.

Public Safety Canada also regularly points to its support of the Cross-cultural Roundtable on Security in describing its CVE work. Unfortunately, the longstanding roundtable has generally been seen to be ineffective. A former member has cautioned that the government in its international meetings overstates the significance of the roundtable as a "major initiative."[117] Most recently, the roundtable has been mired in controversy over the government's decision, discussed further below, to suspend one of its Muslim members over alleged extremism as a student.[118]

In sum, Canada honed its coercive anti-terrorism toolkit in 2015 to include a new speech crime and powers of interdiction and disruption, but attempts to dissuade people from being drawn into terrorism have suffered from comparative neglect. Indeed, we have argued in Chapter 10 that the enactment of a new and overbroad offence against "advocating or promoting terrorism offences in general" could chill, rather than facilitate, outreach to those most at risk of being attracted to terrorism. Likewise, suspicions generated by aggressive use — or even perceived use — of peace bonds, no-fly listing, passport cancellations, or CSIS's new threat reduction powers might make affected communities more apprehensive about dealing with the state when and if a more robust CVE program knocks on their door.

The Weak "Prevent" Link in Canada's Counter-terrorism Strategy

As noted in Chapter 3, Canada's 2012 counter-terrorism strategy is structured around four mutually reinforcing elements: prevent, detect, deny, and respond. These categories are sometimes difficult to disentangle, and we have used a more functional approach in this book.

Nevertheless, the government strategy's definition of "prevent" is a helpful starting point, focusing "on the motivations of individuals who engage in, or have the potential to engage in, terrorist activities at home and abroad. Canada aims to target and diminish the factors contributing to terrorism by actively engaging with individuals, communities and international partners."[119] Counter-radicalization efforts like government engagement with communities and the introduction of alternative narratives are classified as preventive measures.

The Wrong Definition: ". . . Extreme Views Which, in Turn, Lead to Violence."

Things get off to a bumpy start. In its *2014 Public Report on the Terrorist Threat to Canada*, the government defines "radicalization to violence" as the "process by which individuals are introduced to an ideology that encourages movement towards extreme views which, in turn, lead to violence."[120] The report warns that this process can take place "in religious institutions, schools, prisons, online and any other place where like-minded people come together" and that persons of influence play a major role in determining whether radicalization occurs.[121]

Right away, officials embark on the wrong path: they announce a focus on ideology and seem to imagine a linear process that simply cannot be justified by the empirical literature. In a 2014 backgrounder, officials again come close to propounding an ideological "railway track" theory of radicalization to violence: "Radicalization to violence is the process by which individuals *adopt an ideology that encourages movement from moderate, mainstream beliefs towards extreme views.*"[122]

Fortunately, more nuance is contained in internal government briefing notes. For instance, in a briefing note to the Moroccan government, the department of public safety noted, "While radical thinking is not a problem in itself, it becomes a threat to national security when Canadian citizens, residents or groups promote or engage in violence."[123] But this disparity in pronouncements raises issues about why the messaging has been different to the Canadian public than to a country where Islam is the established state religion.

The *2014 Public Report on the Terrorist Threat to Canada* improves when assessing challenges and articulating objectives. It candidly acknowledges that while Canada has enjoyed some success with respect to detecting, denying, and responding to terrorism, its weakest performance has been with respect to prevention: "a distinct challenge remains for the Government under the 'Prevent' element of Canada's Strategy."[124] The official report announces, correctly in our view, that "the means to help prevent violent extremism ultimately lie within communities."[125] It affirms a commitment to building partnerships with Canadian communities and asserts that "the focus of these partnerships is to develop resilience and foster critical thinking about extremist messaging, and to help devise effective means to intervene during the radicalization-to-violence process."[126]

Unfortunately, the need to build trust seems to have fallen by the wayside in the politicized and fearful environment in the months following the October 2014 attacks. As we argue further below, some of the government's politicized actions have made it very difficult for the government to engage in partnerships with Muslim communities. A new culture of distrust would compound the shortcomings of Canada's weak preventive efforts. This is no small thing. It could fatally undermine future efforts.

The Cross-cultural Roundtable on Security

The Cross-cultural Roundtable on Security was established in 2005 to "engage Canadians and the Government of Canada in an ongoing dialogue on national security in a diverse and pluralistic society" and to facilitate "a broad exchange of information between the government and communities on policy initiatives and programs relating to national security and the impact of such programs on Canada's diverse communities."[127]

A good idea at the time, the roundtable has not been a force in the area. Indeed, it has emerged as a top-down institution. A 2011 Senate report concluded that it was perceived "less as a roundtable discussion and more as a one-way briefing from the Department" of Public Safety.[128] The roundtable holds only a few meetings each year, and recently it has held none — the full roundtable appears not to have met since November 2013, assuming its website is current.[129]

Rejected Advice from the Roundtable

In some cases, the government appears to have rejected advice received from its roundtable. For example, a 2011 roundtable meeting on radicalization to violence recommended the use of the term "Al-Qaeda inspired terrorism" "as a way of describing the threat accurately to Canadians, while being sensitive to communities' concerns over labeling."[130] We have adopted this advice in this book, but the political executive has aggressively rejected it.

In January 2014, an eight-person subgroup of the roundtable prepared a report on CVE strategies for the Department of Public Safety. It cautions that CVE strategies must distinguish between "radical thoughts versus radicalization to violence, as radical thinking has historically supported progressive social change."[131] In other words, the roundtable followed the emerging consensus that violence and not radical ideology should be the target of CVE programs. The roundtable recommended increased community outreach, the creation of counter-narratives, and the creation of a central website for CVE initiatives through public-private partnerships with password-protected access for practitioners.[132] To our knowledge, these recommendations have not all been acted upon, although Public Safety Canada has joined the roundtable in "discussions with groups of young people on the subject of the paths to violent extremism and potential intervention points."[133]

A Controversial Suspension

In April 2015, the government suspended one member, Hussein Hamdani, from the roundtable while it investigated statements that the forty-two-year-old corporate and estates lawyer had allegedly made as a student in 1996, and his past associations. Hamdani responded by claiming that he, like all other members of the roundtable, had been "vetted by CSIS and the RCMP" and by speculating that his suspension was related either to his opposition to Bill C-51 or to his support of the Liberal party.[134] Hamdani was one of three Muslim lawyers who during the Bill C-51 debates warned about anti-Muslim innuendo and "a new spate of fear mongering reminiscent of McCarthyism being promoted through parliamentary institutions."[135]

The chair of the roundtable and the mayor of Hamilton expressed support for Hamdani — previously reported as having saved at least ten local youth from extremism by giving them "legitimate avenues to voice their grievances."[136] Minister of Public Safety Blaney had earlier praised Hamdani for his anti-extremist activities in Hamilton.[137] The minister denied that Hamdani was suspended for political activities,[138] but the whole affair has probably weakened an already weak Cross-cultural Roundtable on Security.

Kanishka Project

One of the (few) recommendations of the Air India Commission that the government did accept was the creation of a fund for research about terrorism named after the Boeing 747 that exploded over the Atlantic. At present scheduled to expire, Kanishka has funded considerable academic work in anti-terrorism research. It has also contributed to CVE initiatives, with Public Safety Canada documents pointing to a "recent focus" on "fostering government-civil society" partnerships.[139]

A new website called "Extreme Dialogue" funded by the Kanishka project was launched in February 2015. It includes a series of short films about two people affected by violent extremism. One is a former right-wing extremist, and the other is Christianne Boudreau, the mother of Damian Clairmont. But other than these short films, the website's content seemed quite thin when last viewed.[140] In any event, it is unclear how this project is currently being employed (if at all) in Canadian schools or in other educational settings.

CSIS Interventions

Members of Damian Clairmont's family criticized CSIS both for not informing them of its concerns about Clairmont until after he had departed Canada in November 2012 and for not taking steps to prevent his departure.[141] These criticisms may be a partial explanation for the new CSIS threat disruption powers, discussed in Chapter 8.

Still, as early as 2010, CSIS engaged in some interventions with respect to potential foreign terrorist fighters. A CSIS spokesperson explained that CSIS "may consider asking a family member or community leader" close to a terrorist suspect to assist[142] even though CSIS would later produce documents for its Bill C-51 appearance suggesting that it needed new legal powers to intervene in such manners.[143]

In truth, little is known about the extent or nature of CSIS's engagement with would-be or returned foreign terrorist fighters. As discussed in Chapter 8, CSIS has engaged in "overt" surveillance, that is, making targets aware of the fact that it is watching them, described as a "disruption" technique. In the Security Intelligence Review Committee's words, "Whenever CSIS conducts investigations, an intended or unintended consequence can be to counter — or disrupt — a threat to national security. For instance, making it generally known to targets that their activities are being investigated can reduce the likelihood that the targets will continue with their plans."[144] At the time, in 2009, the Security Intelligence Review Committee expressed some unease with the technique: "there are no CSIS guidelines to help with the design and implementation of disruption operations or to prepare for the potential consequences of such investigative activity." Moreover, it noted CSIS's own recognition that "disruption is an activity that departs from typical forms of information collection, and that certain risks must be managed when undertaking this investigative activity."[145] There is risk that "disruption" could precipitate blowback. To its credit, CSIS seemed aware of this possibility and reported as follows: "Less tangible is whether our actions push some people to radicalize, but our assessment is that it discourages radicalization."[146]

In its assessment, the Security Intelligence Review Committee noted that such activities went beyond CSIS's then mandate to simply collect intelligence and recommended that they be dealt with by ministerial guidelines.[147] It is not known whether ministerial guidelines or other restraints have been placed on the program. Bill C-51 now provides a statutory mandate for CSIS to engage in a broad range of steps, including those that break the law, to reduce threats to the security of Canada. As we argued in Chapter 8, blowback to CSIS intervention becomes a more acute concern as CSIS deploys these more muscular powers.

Community Policing

The major component of the government's prevention efforts so far appears to be community policing. The RCMP has a National Security Awareness and Community Outreach program, which is described as a "comprehensive effort to engage all of Canada's ethnic, cultural and religious communities in the protection of Canada's national security."[148] The goal of the program is to build mutual trust between the RCMP and communities affected by national security investigations by opening and maintaining regular lines of communication through meetings and community-based events.

The 2014 *Public Report on the Terrorist Threat to Canada* announced that the RCMP was developing a larger CVE program. This program is to be focused on intervention and will mobilize "community resources and local law enforcement to recognize and address individuals at risk of becoming radicalized to violence."[149] An internal RCMP document describes the "Terrorism Prevention Program" (TPP), which at present involves "TPP officers" working "with investigators within the INSETs [Integrated National Security Enforcement Teams, which conduct criminal investigations] to identify those individuals showing signs of being radicalized to violence that have been brought to the RCMP's attention."[150] Those individuals that the TPP officers contact "are not yet actively engaged in criminal terrorist activity," allowing TPP officers to work "in consultation" with those "in the mental health field, [and] education and community leaders."[151]

The apparent emphasis on people drifting toward violence, as opposed to simply voicing ideological complaints, is a good one. But a Terrorism Prevention Program twinned with Integrated National Security Enforcement Teams raises concerns that its interventions, in some cases at least, may be too tardy. These will be people already on criminal investigators' radar. That said, the RCMP is in a difficult position trying to find the sweet spot between a Terrorism Prevention Program intervention that comes too early and one that comes too late, especially given the Arar Commission's warnings that the RCMP should not stray too far from its law enforcement role when conducting terrorism investigations.[152] And there is no reason to think that RCMP interventions are immune from the possibility of counterproductive blowback, again raising acute sensitivities about when and with whom the RCMP intervenes.

Although it was slated to begin in December 2014, Minister Blaney informed the House of Commons that the RCMP's new program would not be fully operational until late 2015.[153] In any event, it has only eight full-time employees and an original budget of $1.1 million, which will be raised (by the 2015 budget) to $3.1 million.[154] Internal RCMP notes from April 2015 warn that the Terrorism Prevention Program is underfunded: "Resource pressures are negatively impacting our ability to deliver the TPP as fully as possible since the RCMP's Program hinges on the ability to take a national approach to training police officers on intervening with at-risk individuals radicalized to violence. This is a resource intensive undertaking."[155] In other words, this program is both delayed and modest.

Rehabilitation and Prison Radicalization

Canada has done little to address prison radicalization to violence, an issue that has become pressing given that some of the attackers in both the Paris and the Copenhagen terrorist attacks in 2015 had served time in prison. As we discussed in Chapter 9, there is also evidence of similar trends in Canada.

To be fair, Canada is no different than most western democracies in neglecting the rehabilitation of terrorists. We may have to look elsewhere for inspiration. Singapore has a Muslim minority of about 15 percent of the population. More than sixty members of that minority have been imprisoned under that country's *Internal Security Act* on suspicion of terrorism. Given Singapore's reputation for stern punishment, it may be expected that such suspected terrorists would never be granted freedom. Indeed, you might expect that they would be executed under Singapore's death penalty.

Such expectations would be wrong. Between 67 and 80 percent of imprisoned terrorists in Singapore have been released after graduating from an intensive program in which members of the Muslim community engage with both prisoners and their families to show that their attraction to violence is based on a distorted view of Islam.[156]

The Singapore approach to rehabilitation could not simply be exported to Canada. But, in any event, it is difficult to imagine the present federal government working closely enough with Muslim communities to allow a Canadian version of such a program. Indeed, the federal government seems much more intent on trying to strip convicted terrorists of Canadian citizenship so that they can be deported from Canada than on rehabilitating them in prison. The government has defended this approach on the basis that "the NDP and the Liberals opposed this, but the majority of Canadians agree with us that those who commit the most serious crimes of state forfeit their right to Canadian citizenship."[157]

"Some Very Dysfunctional Voices Will Fill That Vacuum"

In 2012, the government announced a controversial plan to cut the part-time jobs of fifty non-Christian chaplains in Canada's prisons.[158] This came at a time when about 6 percent of the federal inmate population was Muslim.[159] And the government plan ignored a call in a 2010 Macdonald-Laurier Institute report that the Correctional Service of Canada should employ enough Imams to ensure that their place was not taken by radical prisoners or volunteers.[160]

The government's plan seemed to have been motivated by a concern about a Wiccan priest, but a spokesperson argued that it would save $1.3 million and avoid picking among religions. The spokesperson also suggested that the remaining Christian chaplains would respect the freedom of religion of "convicted criminals" by providing services to the general population. Not surprisingly, Muslim, Jewish, and Aboriginal groups denounced the plan as discriminatory.[161]

Even before the announcement of the plan, Muslim religious advisors had complained about lack of training from Corrections Canada.[162] Yasin Dwyer, a Muslim chaplain who had worked with members of the Toronto 18, resigned in protest of the government plan. He warned, "We need to make spirituality relevant and real. Why? Because a vacuum will be left and perhaps some very dysfunctional voices will fill that vacuum if someone is not offered the ABC's of what Islam is all about."[163] Dwyer's successor was reportedly an Imam who had never worked in a prison and was not qualified in the religious community.[164] The shortage of Muslim advisors in one prison resulted in a man convicted of murdering his wife and three daughters leading Muslim prayers in a bullying manner.[165]

The Canadian approach can be contrasted with that of the United Kingdom. That country has not segregated those convicted of terrorism together, has integrated Imams into prison management, and has created a Prison Service Extremist Unit.[166]

While the United Kingdom has ramped up its efforts, Canada has privatized them. The government has hired a private company called Kairos Pneuma Chaplaincy Inc, established by former Christian chaplains, with its name taken from the New Testament. It would appear to have no listed Muslim officers or directors.[167]

Although recent documents indicate that Corrections Canada lacks "specific correctional programs targeted at radicalized offenders,"[168] it has recently shown some interest in prison radicalization. This is a positive development, but there are many challenges. The government's ill-considered 2012 plan, like other incidents, has disgruntled Muslims and other non-Christians who understandably feel targeted. Lack of resources also seems to be an issue with Corrections Canada hinting in annual reports that it does not have adequate resources for such programs.[169] Effective programs will require correctional authorities to work more closely with Muslim communities than they have in the past. Another complication is that accused terrorists serving long periods of pre-trial custody may be confined within provincial institutions.

Community-Based Re-entry and De-radicalization

As discussed in Chapter 9, the government's official position on returned foreign terrorist fighters appears to be that they will be prosecuted and, if possible, stripped of citizenship.[170] None of the reported eighty foreign terrorist fighters who have returned have so far been prosecuted in Canada. Some returnees have been prosecuted in the United Kingdom. The mother of one of them complained, "The police say 'mothers come forward', you can trust us, we will help. But now they will see what happened to my son. What kind of person would go to the police if they think their son will get 12 years in prison? Nobody wants to do that. I did not want that."[171]

In Chapter 3, we examined the available evidence on returned foreign fighters and suggested that there was little support for the notion that every returned foreign fighter — or even more than a tiny minority — would resort to terrorism in Canada. Some will, and some truly should be prosecuted if they have committed war crimes, crimes against humanity, or terrorism in foreign fights. But the fact is that we will only be able to secure a handful of convictions. We have expressed doubts in Chapter 9 whether Canada has the requisite capacity for a large number of such complicated prosecutions. Also citizenship stripping, which can be done only to those foreign fighters who hold dual citizenship, will be arbitrary and discriminatory and will be challenged under the *Charter* on that basis.

And there is another danger of discriminatory impact if only returned ISIS foreign fighters are prosecuted and not others such as those who have fought with the other factions, assuming their conduct has been problematic. That does not, however, mean that nothing should be done when foreign fighters return to Canada. Close consideration of reintegration will soon become a serious issue in Canada if present trends continue. Some foreign fighters who return home may be disillusioned with fighting or the extremist narrative, and these people may actually be a huge resource for CVE efforts. Others may be physically and emotionally traumatized by what they have witnessed.

One European report has warned that prosecuting all returned foreign fighters is not advisable and to the extent that it may result in short prison terms could even make the problem worse.[172] It advocated a long-term multi-agency approach to reintegration that would be individualized for every participant.[173] Research published in Australia found that the most successful reintegration programs were not organized by security agencies but nevertheless had some central co-ordination.[174] Canada has no federally supported multi-agency "exit program."[175] Instead, Canada has spent much of 2015 expanding and hardening its anti-terrorism toolkit.

Summary

Even before Bill C-51, it was security officials in the RCMP, CSIS, and the government (in its Cross-cultural Roundtable on Security top-down briefings) who took the lead in responding to the danger of Canadians attracted to ISIS. With the possible exception of Quebec, Canada has fallen behind other democracies that are involving health care workers, social workers, and teachers — not just security officials — in CVE work.

In the United Kingdom context, terrorism experts Clive Walker and Javaid Rehman have praised the focus on the causes of terrorism and the broader hearts-and-minds approach but have warned of the danger that controversial laws and anti-terrorism practices may work at cross-purposes with the former. They have also warned of the dangers of CVE initiatives being dominated by police and intelligence officials.[176] In Canada, such officials not only dominate CVE initiatives, but they often seem to be the only engaged players.

Most of us are scared when a police or CSIS officer knocks on our door. We may be suspicious even if the officer invites us for coffee and is, this being Canada, very polite. Especially after Bill C-51's enhancement of security powers, and given the pattern of enforcement of terrorism laws, Muslim communities have more reason to be apprehensive than most. RCMP and CSIS officers may be well-intentioned in their CVE efforts, but given the nature of their jobs, there are few positive benefits that they can offer to those with whom they engage in CVE work. International standard-setting bodies have also cautioned that a security-focused relationship can be counterproductive and increase distrust among targeted communities, which often want social, educational, and health assistance.[177]

One advantage of a multi-disciplinary approach is that health care workers, social workers, and teachers can offer more actual assistance than security officials to the targeted community. Most parents want their children treated and educated, and they will see more coercive responses such as no-fly listing, arrest, and peace bonds as a last resort. Moreover, teachers, social workers, and health care providers can take a more holistic approach. They can be concerned with the well-being of those whom they assist, and not just with whether they are security threats.

That said, we are not opposed to either the police or CSIS trying to dissuade Canadians from joining foreign terrorist fights. The minister of public safety reported that 647 police officers had participated in counter-terrorism "information officer" workshops in 2014–15, which had included training "in how to detect signs of radicalization" — a considerable investment.[178] But, like most CVE activities, the verdict is out, and the results should be carefully evaluated. There also needs to be some central co-ordination so that the RCMP and CSIS do not conflict in their CVE efforts. The dysfunction of the "less is more" CSIS-RCMP relationship, discussed in Chapter 9, should not be repeated in the implementation of CVE initiatives, although this is a distinct possibility if a failed CVE encounter leads to a more focused intelligence or criminal investigation.

We have no doubt that security and Public Safety Canada officials will do their best — the government documents in our possession are testimony to that and their considerable dedication and diligence. And in Canada the RCMP has an important crime prevention mandate. But it remains a law enforcement agency. As discussed in Chapter 7, it has arrested, detained for days, and sought and obtained peace bonds for a number of suspected foreign terrorist travellers in the aftermath of the October 2014 terrorist attacks. Under Bill C-51, it will have responsibility for enforcing the new speech offence, as well as other terrorism crimes. This means that it may need to arrest people who speak the wrong words in the wrong context.

Members of the public — especially in Muslim communities — may be reluctant to share information if they fear that it will result in the arrest and perhaps prosecution of their loved ones. This will not always be the case, of course. Parents do alert authorities. The families of ten youths in Montreal told authorities about their concerns, and the result was the arrest of the youths on 15 May 2015, although not their prosecution. In some cases, such arrests or other forms of disruption by security officials may be the only way to help desperate parents and prevent youths from leaving to engage in foreign terrorist fights. Nevertheless, such youths remain vulnerable to prosecution under Canada's terrorism law, and community and family members have to rely on the restraint and discretion of security officials. This only underlines the need for trust.

There is also a danger that radicalization to violence may be too far along by the time the RCMP or CSIS can intervene under their mandates. Teachers, doctors, and social workers, regulated under provincial legislation, may be better situated to detect violent extremism at an earlier stage where it will hopefully be more easily countered. But there is no evidence we can find that these front-line non-security workers or even correctional officials have received serious CVE training. The federal division of powers may bear part of the blame, but, as discussed above, Canada seems to lag behind its fellow federations of Australia and the United States in even experimenting with multi-disciplinary CVE programs.

Even if the federal and provincial governments can co-operate in implementing a multi-disciplinary CVE program (and that is a big if), the emerging consensus seems to be that community groups should also play an important role. This raises a second thorny issue: the strained relationships between the federal government and at least some parts of Canada's diverse Muslim communities. We now turn to the strengths and weaknesses of CVE initiatives headed by state and community groups respectively.

Content Analysis: Canada's CVE Literature

As in other areas affecting CVE strategy, the available data, especially in Canada, for comparing community- and state-based CVE initiatives are not robust. For this reason, we now attempt to add to it by scrutiny and content analysis of two recent Canadian CVE publications, *United against Terrorism* and *Youth Online and at Risk* — both documents responding to the risk of ISIS-inspired terrorism. The first was a rare grassroots initiative prepared by Muslim organizations, with assistance from the RCMP. The second was prepared by the RCMP itself, without apparent input from Muslim communities.

(Dis)United against Terrorism

United against Terrorism is a thirty-eight-page pamphlet that challenges the extremist messages of violence inspired by al-Qaida and ISIS through extensive quotes from the Qur'an.[179] It attempts to persuade those who may be attracted to extremism to contact others in the community, as opposed to security officials, about their views, and it attempts to channel views and grievances into peaceful and democratic outlets. It was prepared in a collaborative manner by the Islamic Social Services Association, the National Council of Canadian Muslims, and the RCMP. It should have been a rare and notable "prevent" success story. It was not.

The RCMP pulled its support for this project at the last minute before the official launch of the publication in September 2014. The official RCMP explanation for its withdrawal was that the publication had an "adversarial tone."[180] The booklet does advise people to exercise their *Charter* right to counsel when being interviewed by the RCMP or CSIS.

But documents disclosed under access to information law paint a more complex and political picture. They cite concerns about ongoing libel litigation brought by the National Council of Canadian Muslims against spokespersons for Prime Minister Harper, who had alleged that the council had links with a terrorist group. The government also reacted negatively to the pamphlet's call to abandon the term "jihadi" in describing terrorism — a call consciously rejected when the government later branded its counter-terrorism strategy in the wake of the October 2014 terrorist attacks.[181]

The federal government's withdrawal from the project did not mean that all governments ran away from the project. The Manitoba justice minister affirmed his government's satisfaction. And the US State Department later tweeted a link to a news story about the publication, although this caused a stir in the right-wing American press (a stir that was carefully monitored by the RCMP and Public Safety Canada.)[182]

Words Matter

United against Terrorism signals that words matter and that the state should be careful in choosing the words used to interact with Muslim communities. Some may be tempted to dismiss these concerns as semantics and political correctness, but they feature prominently in the pamphlet. And they reflect a social reality that anyone interested in a real CVE program must acknowledge. The use of inappropriate or offensive words can be a real barrier to respectful and constructive relations with a community. It is simple common sense and politeness to be careful with your choice of words if you truly want to communicate with and hopefully persuade others.

United against Terrorism expresses concerns with a number of words that feature prominently in discourses about Muslims and terrorism. For example, it carefully distinguishes "radicalization" from violence:

> All of us have views and opinions that others would define as radical, if not extreme. Radical thought and action does not necessarily translate into terrorism. In fact, radicals can play a highly positive role, both in their communities and in the larger political context (although admittedly this role is often only acknowledged after the fact). Again, radical views only become a problem when they are used to promote or condone violence or other forms of extremist behavior, including terrorism.[183]

We have suggested earlier in this chapter that social science supports this distinction and that CVE programs start on the wrong foot when they focus on radical ideologies.

United against Terrorism also questions the use of the term "moderate Muslim" and asks why the same term is not applied to others, including Christians, Jews, and atheists.[184] Again, this underlines the importance of being sensitive to equality values in all anti-terrorism efforts. It also makes sense given that much of the ISIS narrative is based on ISIS presenting itself as an alternative to perceived discrimination and double standards toward Muslims in Western democracies. By making this point and cautioning about "anti-radicalization," the booklet alerts readers to the peril of counter–violent extremism becoming counter–ideological extremism.

The J-word

One of the most striking warnings in *United against Terrorism* — one that the government, security services, courts, academics (including us), the media, and the general public have repeatedly ignored — is against the danger of using the term "jihad" or "jihadi" as a pejorative word equated with terrorism.

The publication explains, "Jihad is an Arabic term meaning striving, struggling and exertion in the path of good. Every day a Muslim struggles with his/her desires and does good and strives to be a better human being he/she is performing jihad."[185] The document goes on to argue that "the media, law enforcement, intelligence agencies and politicians" have been "counterproductive" and have "emboldened the terrorist" by "applying the noble concept of Jihad to terrorism."[186]

In Chapter 3, we pointed to this sort of explanation for our own choice of terminology in this book. On reading *United against Terrorism*, we are left with the impression that many Muslims may have the same negative reaction to careless use of "jihadi" as many Christians would have to calling the considerable violence done by Christian religious extremists[187] "evangelical terrorism."

The concerns expressed in *United against Terrorism* about "jihadi" are not idiosyncratic. As noted above, the Cross-cultural Roundtable on Security recommended in November 2011 that the government avoid terms associating terrorism with religion and be sensitive to labelling communities.[188] And this view echoed that voiced in a 2009 RCMP analysis, which had also pointed to the religious connotations of the term and warned that "by referring to extremists as *jihadis* we effectively recognize their actions as being in the path of God and, therefore, legitimate."[189] In all cases, the government rejected the advice it received.

Engaging with Islam

United against Terrorism squarely engages with Islam. The preface suggests that both violent extremists and Islamophobes use "the same cut and paste approach to the Quran to argue that Islam condones terrorism":

> The Quran is very clear in advocating for Muslims to be just in all situations. All human life is sacred and the Quran equates the murdering of one person to murdering of all of humanity.
>
> *"If any one slew a person — it would be as if he slew entire humanity: and if any one saved a life, it would be as if he saved the life of entire humanity."* *(Quran 5:32)*
>
> Clearly, in Islam, responsible citizenship is advocated and violence is condemned.[190]

As will be seen, below, an equivalent RCMP document understandably hesitates to engage with Islamic religious doctrine. Although some may again dismiss this as political correctness, the lack of state engagement on issues of religious doctrine reflects principled equality concerns about not singling out religions.

Drawing on Community Resources

United against Terrorism is not state centred. It urges its readers to "seek out a counselor, or an Imam or elder to vent your feelings and find constructive ways to deal and address your concerns,"[191] *not* security officials. Other proposed forms of engagement include "political lobbying for action, raising awareness of issues through media and civic engagement and fundraising for humanitarian relief through registered charities."[192]

In some ways, this approach attempts to persuade people to follow a path to political action rather than the path of attraction to violence that many Québécois followed after the October Crisis, described in Chapter 2. It is an approach consistent with the available disengagement-from-violence research examined earlier in this chapter.

The Dangers of a Police-Centred Approach

Despite its last-minute withdrawal from the project, the RCMP still has a section in *United against Terrorism*. This section illustrates tensions that may emerge between community- and state-based approaches to CVE initiatives. The RCMP section of *United against Terrorism* states that the "the earlier the police can be informed of suspicious behaviours, the better."[193] As noted, other parts of the booklet urge people to consult an Imam or religious advisor first.

The booklet predates Bill C-51. The RCMP's advice for early police involvement does not address concerns about Bill C-51's new speech crime reaching radicalized discourse or that the RCMP might open an investigation potentially leading to preventive arrest, peace bonds, or criminal charges. Nor does the RCMP section mention advice found in other parts of the booklet suggesting that it is best to have a lawyer present when talking with the RCMP or CSIS.[194] This reflects the different perspectives that Muslim communities and the RCMP bring to CVE issues.

The Government's Last-Minute Disavowal of United against Terrorism

The RCMP disassociated itself from *United against Terrorism* the day before its official launch, on 29 September 2014. As noted, the official line was that the publication was "too adversarial," presumably because of its reference to the right to counsel under the *Charter*.[195]

Over 700 pages of internal RCMP and Public Safety Canada documents obtained through access to information law paint a more complex, but murky, picture. These documents suggest that the RCMP's collaboration started with its involvement in a well-received 2013 community meeting, hosted in a mosque by the Winnipeg-based Islamic Social Services Association. This meeting challenged both extremism and Islamophobia. The RCMP then worked enthusiastically on the handbook, exchanging and refining many drafts and with plans for a senior officer to participate in its official launch.

The day before the launch, RCMP emails indicated that there was "very good rapport between" the RCMP and the National Council of Canadian

Muslims, the other sponsoring group. The RCMP officers working on the ground did "not foresee any issues, only that any revisions be shared as soon as" possible.[196] Officials were just waiting "for a green light" from the public safety minister's office and the Privy Council Office.[197]

The green light never came. An email chain from the morning of the launch that includes the signature line of a member of the prime minister's office noted that one of the contributors was the National Council of Canadian Muslims and that the council had "filed a notice of libel in the Ontario Superior Court of Justice that accuses an official in the PMO of acting 'maliciously' in comments allegedly made in respect of that organization."[198] These are presumably the same sorts of comments that Conservative MP Diane Ablonczy placed "on the record" at the Commons security committee when the National Council of Canadian Muslims appeared as a witness on Bill C-51, sparking the considerable controversy described above. The council has repeatedly and categorically denied these allegations.[199]

Another apparent sticking point for the higher-ups was the handbook's criticism of terms such as "Islamic terrorism" and "jihad," on the basis that they associated Islam with violence. Speaking lines were prepared for the RCMP stating that it was not responsible for the handbook's content and that it had not agreed to abandon the use of such expressions.[200] All told, the documents suggest that the RCMP had no trouble working with national and local Muslim organizations before issues went to higher and political levels.

The RCMP's Youth Online and at Risk

The RCMP publication entitled *Youth Online and at Risk* is quite different in tone and scope from *United against Terrorism*. In a well-intentioned effort to balance al-Qaida- and ISIS-inspired terror with other forms of violence, the RCMP publication points to not only the Air India bombings but also "pipeline bombing in western Canada."[201] State agencies may, for good reason, try to be neutral in their CVE efforts lest Muslims accuse them of an exclusive and discriminatory focus on religious terrorism. This is generally a virtue, but the twenty-six-page pamphlet probably overreaches in its attempt to link all terrorism together. For example, it suggests that the Unibomber and Timothy McVeigh were motivated by "similar reasoning" to "militant Muslims in the West" who have a "sense of moral outrage at conflicts in Chechnya, Kashmir, Iraq and Afghanistan."[202]

And, again, in a likely well-intentioned effort to avoid an exclusive focus on Muslims, the RCMP pamphlet looks at anarchist movements, albeit in a manner that demonstrates how government narratives can be self-serving.

The pamphlet cites online discussions by "anti-globalization and anarchist groups" at the Toronto G20 protests as an example of material that "distorted police action" and may have motivated protesters to engage in violence.[203] The booklet is rather tone-deaf to the significant ill will toward police caused by the largest mass arrests in Canadian history at the Toronto G20 protests. In any event, such matters are peripheral to the very different threats presented by ISIS recruitment videos.

The dominant picture painted by the RCMP booklet is that the Internet is a very dangerous place. The booklet notes that "videos showing attacks using improvised explosives and be-headings can be found" as well as other forms of terrorist propaganda. It features general and perhaps unrealistic warnings that call on parents and teachers to monitor teenagers' Internet use and call the RCMP and Internet providers if extremist material is found.[204] There is no sustained emphasis on encouraging youths to be critical consumers of what is on the Internet. The message seems to be "stay away."

The RCMP publication, unlike *United against Terrorism*, does not attempt to persuade young persons to channel their grievances in a more constructive manner. Given its Internet focus, and despite some modest warnings on this point, the publication risks affirming impressions — rejected by a Public Safety Canada analysis obtained by an access to information request — that the Internet plays a dominant role in radicalization, as opposed to informal networks and face-to-face contact.[205]

Summary

We believe that the RCMP's anticipated CVE program will be more comprehensive and concrete than its *Youth Online and at Risk*. But that publication does underline perhaps inevitable differences between community- and state-based CVE programs. Community-based approaches will be able to engage in discussion of religious doctrine in a manner that state institutions in a liberal democracy will not. Community-based initiatives will also be closer to the lived experiences and grievances of the particular community, including grievances that the community may have against the state and the police in particular.

This may well result in more of an "adversarial" approach, but the reasons for the RCMP's last-minute withdrawal from the *United against Terrorism* project were more complex than such concerns. They reveal some of the frictions between the Harper government and the National Council of Canadian Muslims (at least), and the government's determination to brand al-Qaida- and ISIS-inspired terrorism as "jihadi terrorism."

United against Terrorism should have been the productive start of relationship building with Muslim communities. Unfortunately, the experience became yet another obstacle to community-based prevention programs.

New CVE Program in Quebec

Although people have left from all parts of Canada to join ISIS, Quebec has been the province most often in the news recently. By June 2015, at least twenty-one people from Quebec had left Canada to join ISIS, had their passports confiscated, been subject to peace bonds, or, in two cases, been charged with attempting to leave Canada to participate in a terrorist group as well as explosives offences. The Quebec cases also include Martin Couture-Rouleau, who perpetrated the 20 October 2014 terrorist attack in Saint-Jean-sur-Richelieu, and Sami Elabi, a suburban teenager who left Canada in 2013 to join a terrorist group in Syria and was later shown in a video burning and shooting his Canadian passport.

In June 2015, Quebec introduced a plan and two proposed laws to combat radicalization that respond to the particular local circumstances in that province but also to the lack of federal leadership. A CVE plan that engages key areas of provincial jurisdiction such as education, health, social services, and corrections is a needed addition to the anti-terrorism toolkit. Unfortunately, however, Quebec's approach has not started well.

Top-Down Surprise CVE Program with an Uncertain Federal Overlap

Representatives from the Quebec Muslim community complained about a lack of consultation and the inclusion in the anti-radicalization initiatives of a controversial "religious neutrality" bill prohibiting people (essentially Muslim women) from providing or receiving public services with their face covered.[206]

Even leaving aside this controversial twinning of separate issues, the second related bill prohibits hate speech and speech inciting violence even though both forms of speech have long been prohibited under the federal *Criminal Code*.[207] And it would provide for court-ordered emergency measures if hate speech presented a danger to the group targeted,[208] covering some of the same terrain as peace bonds under the *Criminal Code*. The bill also provides that those who engage in such speech can be deprived of public subsidies or other licences relating to education and working with youth. This approach, like federal citizenship revocation, seems to be based on a desire to exclude rather than to reform and reintegrate.

These Quebec bills, as introduced in the National Assembly, do little to build on areas of provincial advantage with respect to CVE strategies. They do not follow 2015 United Kingdom legislation requiring local authorities, social services, schools, universities, and prisons to produce and implement plans.[209] As we argue above, we regard the United Kingdom's Prevent strategy as ungrounded in hard fact because of its excessive scope and, in particular, its overbroad definition of extremism, which seems to focus on ideology. That said, we do not object to the idea that institutions should have plans focusing on the real issue of violence, not ideology. And we recognize that the provinces regulate most of the most important state institutions relevant to an all-of-society CVE program.

More Promising Initiatives?

The introduction of the two bills was supported by other, more promising, interventions and buttressed by $10 million in funding — considerably more than that allocated by the federal government for the RCMP's entire CVE program. There were promising proposals for training for teachers and social workers. And the plan includes a twenty-four-hour hotline that friends and families can call. Lise Theriault, the minister of public security, explained:

> [P]arents can call in to one place, they can ask questions. We must be able to refer parents, friends. We must be able to put the right intervenors in place, not just the police . . . . It works in France, in Belgium. This confidential line reassures people and encourages them to learn but also to report.[210]

The system is not without critics, and its success will likely depend on trust. Pointing to Bill C-51, Haroun Bouazzi, co-president of the Muslim and Arab Association for Secularism in Quebec, expressed concern that police would answer the line: "we have trouble seeing how people thinking that their son is in danger of radicalization will call the police."[211] Moreover, it is also true that the effectiveness of such hotlines in Europe has not yet been subjected to thorough empirical evaluation.[212] But we see no reason not to try it, assuming that it is properly constructed to build (and not diminish) public trust among those who use it. There should also be transparency so that parents will know whether the police will be informed should they use the hotline. CVE programs can be harmed if those who engage with them feel that they have been betrayed when police or other security officials take coercive action. This may be necessary in some cases, but there should be fair warnings.

The German hotline — the gold standard for European hotlines — serves as an anonymous and "general point of contact for any individual who is concerned about the (possible) radicalisation of a family member or acquaintance and has questions regarding this topic. The hotline is closely linked with the four family support facilities across the country."[213] People phoning the line are offered targeted assistance, including referrals to specialists and the several non-government agencies with anti-radicalization-to-violence programs, such as Hayat. The system is a partnership between government and non-government entities, but these community partners "do not work as the extended arm of the government, police or security services. They all have a strong history in supporting families either from right-wing extremists or migrant communities."[214] This is an example of a more holistic and community-based approach offering something to the community and not based simply on the state's security needs. The equivalent hotline in France is not anonymous, and calls go to the police. As the reaction to the Quebec plan suggests, this is not likely to be a winning formula, reaffirming the need for careful planning, transparency, and evaluation of CVE programs.

V. CONCLUSION

Why has the federal government been so slow to invest in community-based and multi-disciplinary programs to prevent terrorism given the government's evident concern about foreign terrorist fighters?

One challenge is the federal division of powers. The provinces have jurisdiction over the critical education, health, and social services sectors. This is a real challenge that helps explain why Bill C-51, unlike the United Kingdom's *Counter-terrorism and Security Act 2015*, does not provide a statutory framework for those sectors to establish and implement programs designed to prevent terrorism. That said, the federal government has not followed the example of the Australian and American central governments in providing leadership and funding for local CVE initiatives. The Canadian federal government can always spend money, even in areas of provincial jurisdiction. But it has relied on the RCMP to take the CVE lead despite a growing consensus that security agencies are not best positioned to implement such programs.

Quebec has recently entered the field in response to a significant number of young Muslims in the Montreal area who appear to be attracted to ISIS. Unfortunately, the Quebec program has started poorly as a result of having been twinned with a controversial bill about face coverings. Even Quebec's proposed anti-radicalization legislation focuses on issues of hate speech and speech inciting violence that are already prohibited under the federal *Criminal Code.*

"As Harshly as Possible"

Another challenge that explains the federal government's lack of interest and lack of program development is its enthusiasm for using the more forceful and aggressive tools at hand to express disapproval.

A hint of the radicalization of Canadian anti-terrorism law was reflected in the way that Prime Minister Harper responded to the 2013 Boston Marathon bombing. Immediately after the bombing, Liberal leader Justin Trudeau suggested that it could only have been committed by those who felt "completely at war with innocence, with society" and that there was a need to respond to those who felt they were "enemies of society rather than people who have hope for the future."[215]

These were clumsy words in the immediate aftermath of a bombing that killed 3 and injured over 250 people. At the same time, Trudeau's comments do point to the need to deter people from concluding that suicidal or violent extremism is their only alternative. In any event, Prime Minister Harper reacted strongly to Trudeau's remarks and criticized any attempt "to rationalize or make excuses" for terrorists. Moreover, he promised that his government if faced with similar actions "would condemn it categorically, and to the extent that you can deal with the perpetrators, you deal with them as harshly as possible."[216]

The surviving twenty-one-year-old bomber eventually received the harshest possible response, the death penalty. Canada has not reintroduced the death penalty, but it has neglected issues of prison radicalization and the need to try to rehabilitate convicted terrorists, who will in many cases eventually be released. Ignoring the causes of terrorism and questions of rehabilitation may allow our anger at terrorism to be vented, but in the end it provides only temporary security.

The October 2014 terrorist attacks gave Prime Minister Harper an opportunity to create as harsh and as radical a law as possible. He introduced Bill C-51 in an election-style rally by using the language of war. And he repeatedly used religiously themed language that a 2009 RCMP study, the government's Cross-cultural Roundtable on Security, and the *United against Terrorism* handbook had asked the government to eschew. The prime minister argued, "violent jihadism is not a human right. It is an act of war and our government's new legislation fully understands that difference." He added, "extreme jihadists have declared war on us, on all free peoples and on Canada specifically."[217]

As we discuss throughout this book, we readily accept that the terrorist threat is real, and even evil. But that does not justify an unbalanced anti-terrorism policy that seeks the rhetorical moral high ground at the expense of actual security effectiveness. A policy environment where it becomes politically advantageous to use polarizing polemics and illegitimate — or at least politically dangerous — to explore and respond to the causes of terrorism is a very dangerous place to be.

Canada has expanded and hardened its anti-terrorism toolkit in 2015. As readers will have noticed, we object to much of the toolkit's new content. But, as attentive readers will also have noticed, we are even more animated in relation to its omissions. Among other things, the government has not cured the pernicious "less is more" relationship between the RCMP and CSIS, discussed in Chapter 9. As we argue in Chapter 11, the government has been largely inert at solving long-standing co-ordination and command-and-control oversight problems. And, as outlined in Chapter 12, it has ignored reforms to our independent review system, something more essential now than ever before.

And last but not least: Although the government admitted in 2014 that it was lagging in its implementation of the "prevent" part of its anti-terrorism strategy, it appears to have taken few visible steps to improve "prevent" in the wake of the October 2014 terrorist attacks. Indeed, the government has probably made things worse by straining its relationship with Muslim communities and by enacting a speech offence that may chill both free expression and government outreach to those most at risk of being radicalized to terrorism. This is concerning given the novelty of the ISIS threat and the need to dissuade people from joining it or to reintegrate them if they return to Canada. The government has offered hard rhetoric and hard laws in the wake of the October 2014 terrorist attacks but, ultimately, false security.

CHAPTER FOURTEEN

Conclusion: The Need for a Re-think

I. A WASTED OPPORTUNITY FOR CONSTRUCTIVE REFORM

The terrorist attacks of October 2014 motivated a radical reform of Canada's anti-terrorism law and policy. Unfortunately, the government squandered an opportunity for constructive and sustainable change. Instead, it quickly enacted politicized legislation unanchored to any publicly available account of what went wrong, either with respect to the 2014 terrorist attacks, or to more horrific experiences of the past — most notably, the Air India bombings.

We still have no clear explanation for why one measure — passport revocation — was deployed against Couture-Rouleau, while others, such as peace bonds or prosecutions, were not. Officials told parliamentarians it had something to do with evidence, but we do not know if the October attacks were yet another example of a failure to convert intelligence to evidence, identified as Canada's Achilles heel by the Air India Commission in 2010.

We also do not have a clear accounting of what the government knew about Zehaf-Bibeau, the Ottawa attacker. Nor do we know why the siloed and fragmented security apparatus on Parliament Hill was not consolidated or augmented in light of prior attacks and threats. We know that some intelligence about a possible attack was circulated in the days before the Ottawa incident, but we do not know whether there was an adequate response. Perhaps there are mundane explanations for all these questions, but at present Canadians do not even have those. And yet, the government told Canadians in the winter of 2015 that its new laws would make them safer. Canadians were asked to believe that the government's new laws would do this, even while the government dismissed and discarded recommendations from former prime ministers, ministers, reviewers, and commissions of inquiry.

The government seemed indifferent to evidence of past failures, measured either in terms of underreactions, such as the Air India incident, or post-9/11 overreactions, such as the treatment of Maher Arar. These incidents produced inquiries that made many recommendations about how to restructure our security strategies so that they actually worked and were subject to adequate whole-of-government oversight and review. These commissions also proposed means to make sure that, in making us safer, security services were not making us less free.

And yet, even as it loudly banged the drum on security, the only government ever in a position to act on these suggestions continued to disregard evidence and lessons tabulated from a close study of mistakes made in the recent past. The government also had no time for the more distant McDonald Commission on RCMP wrongdoing in the 1970s, whose recommendations gave rise to our long-standing security arrangements limiting CSIS to the collection of intelligence. Now under the radical reforms of 2015, CSIS will be able to engage in physical action, even including illegal acts that violate *Charter* rights. These dangerous new powers are not matched with increased oversight or review.

II. IGNORING THE AIR INDIA COMMISSION

The Harper government deserves credit for appointing an inquiry in 2006 to get to the bottom of the Air India debacle. Unfortunately, however, the government has only paid lip service to the commission's 2010 report and recommendations. In particular the government has done the following:

1) In Bill C-44, given CSIS sources and the director of CSIS a veto over whether confidential CSIS human sources can be compelled to testify or to provide any identifying information in subsequent proceedings, including terrorism and immigration proceedings. Justice Major in his 2010 Air India report specifically rejected such an approach on the basis that CSIS would make premature promises of confidentiality that would make terrorism prosecutions more difficult.

2) Preserved CSIS's discretion not to disclose its information about possible terrorist activity to the police or others in government. The government did this, even though it had the logical opportunity to include such reforms in Bill C-51 while enacting a very expansive permissive regime for information sharing.

3) In Bill C-51, provided a puzzling legislative reaffirmation that CSIS does not have law enforcement powers in the face of the commission's findings that CSIS had used its traditional lack of law enforcement responsibilities as justification for ignoring the implications of its conduct on future criminal trials. Still able to sit on intelligence with evidential implications, CSIS's new "not law enforcement" disruption powers may now simply throw more wrenches into the spokes of criminal investigations and trials.

4) Consistently maintained that the flaws revealed by the Air India investigation are in the past. This disregards the commission's findings that many of the problems — including a "less is more" information sharing relationship between CSIS and the RCMP — continue to the present day and compromise the ability to conduct terrorism prosecutions.

5) Refused to enhance oversight of the government's whole-of-government national security activities by giving the prime minister's national security advisor new powers to compel the use of intelligence for evidential purposes and to resolve disputes between CSIS and the RCMP and other agencies.

6) In the *Safer Witness Act, 2013*, implemented reforms in the witness protection program that fall short of the commission's recommendations for a program independent of the RCMP with an independent dispute resolution mechanism.

7) Refused to create a director of terrorism prosecutions to ensure expertise and continuity in terrorism prosecutions and to discipline the overuse of claims of national security confidentiality or state secrets that could compromise terrorism trials.

8) In litigation in the Supreme Court,[1] fought for and maintained the unique and cumbersome two-court approach to determining whether information can be protected from disclosure in terrorism prosecutions because of state secrets.

These failings perhaps explain why retired Supreme Court justice John Major condemned the government for not implementing (and even for not reading or understanding) his commission's report and recommendations.[2] He echoed at least some of these concerns about inaction when he appeared as a witness as the Commons and Senate security committees studying Bill C-51.

III. MAKING THE "LESS IS MORE" RELATION BETWEEN CSIS AND THE RCMP WORSE

Not only has the government failed to implement the Air India recommendations, but its 2015 legislation effectively doubles down on the ills that inquiry diagnosed. The new laws will likely make the distant CSIS-police relationship even more distant. The reasons for the peculiar "less is more" relation between CSIS and the police are complex and not widely understood. They have been described in detail in Chapter 9 in this book and in volume 3 of the Air India report. To summarize: they reflect concerns with keeping CSIS secrets out of court at the expense of making our prosecutions more difficult, and our security situation more perilous, than they need to be.

The Air India commission noted that because CSIS is often the first agency at the scene of an emerging security threat — it has the broadest mandate — its decisions on what to do with its information drive the entire federal government response. We are now concerned that Bill C-51 makes CSIS not only the tip of the spear, but potentially the whole spear, as it embarks on its own "threat reduction measures" without mandated consideration of knock-on effects on other tools, such as criminal prosecutions.

What should be done to make matters better? The criminal law tool is our primary defence — only it results in long-term incarceration of bad guys. CSIS needs a culture shift. Specifically, it needs to follow the United Kingdom's MI5 in becoming more accepting of evidentiary standards, at least in its terrorism investigations.

The post-9/11 expansion of terrorism law has dramatically shrunk the pre-criminal zone within which CSIS activities do not matter to prosecutions. The Cold War mantras that "we do not collect evidence" and "our sources and methods must at all costs be protected" are no longer acceptable. Unfortunately, the 2015 legislation makes this culture shift unlikely. We fear that CSIS will continue to promise almost all of its human sources confidentiality, thus giving them a veto over whether any identifying information can be used in legal proceedings. We also fear that Bill C-51 may make CSIS more confident about not sharing intelligence now that it is able, if necessary, to take robust — even illegal and *Charter*-violating — steps to disrupt or reduce security threats.

Very different laws than the ones enacted in 2015 are required. CSIS must be statutorily required to share its intelligence about terrorism activities with persons able to decide whether to act on it, in ways more meaningful, transparent, and lasting than endless disruption. This may also require repeal of the new CSIS human source privilege in Bill C-44, restoring us to the situation the Air India commission preferred: case-by-case consideration in courts as to whether that privilege should be extended. CSIS will firmly resist any such change because of fears its sources and methods will be disclosed under Canada's broad disclosure rules. These fears are not unreasonable. But as the Air India Commission urged, the risk of disclosure can be better managed: it can be mitigated by requiring CSIS to disclose the information, not directly to the police who are bound by criminal law disclosure rules, but to the prime minister's national security advisor or the minister of public safety. These persons would then be able to exercise independent judgment as to whether the public interest requires that intelligence be disclosed to the police, thereby risking its ultimate disclosure by the prosecutor to the accused.

If and when the police receive the intelligence, we can do a better job of protecting it from disclosure than our unwieldy two-court system. Clearly, any legislative restrictions must respect the accused's right to a fair trial. But as in the courts of our closest allies, we should adopt a streamlined process where criminal trial judges (not specially designated judges of the Federal Court) are empowered to make (and revise where necessary) non-disclosure orders issued where the security reason for secrecy is valid and fair trials can still be had because the non-disclosure does not hurt the accused's case.

Unfortunately, the use of Canada's awkward two-court system is bound to increase in the coming years, given the need to protect foreign intelligence from disclosure in the prosecution of alleged foreign terrorist fighters. Attempts to keep secret CSIS informer identities and CSIS methods of threat disruption will also likely generate more satellite secrecy litigation in the Federal Court. All of this will slow down terrorism prosecutions and potentially disrupt terrorist trials.

IV. DISRUPTION AS A TEMPORARY SOLUTION THAT CREATES NEW PROBLEMS

Disruption above All Else

The official name of Bill C-51 is the *Anti-terrorism Act, 2015*. A more accurate title would the *Temporary Disruption of Terrorism Act, 2015*.

Under Bill C-51, CSIS has a new mandate to go beyond intelligence collection and take physical actions to reduce security threats — commonly labelled "disruption" in the political debate. And so, under Bill C-51, CSIS is able to do much of what the RCMP did in the aftermath of the 1970 October Crisis, right down to the barn burning (albeit, only if a Federal Court judge issues a secret warrant). Moreover, CSIS will now, in principle, be able to apply for the cover of a warrant to authorize some of its post-9/11 abuses. These include violations of multiple *Charter* rights when it rendered

Mohammed Jabarah to the United States or when it interviewed Omar Khadr at Guantanamo.

The government will point to the fact that Federal Court judges must authorize any illegalities and violations of rights. It remains to be seen how or even if the courts will accept this novel and problematic new role of authorizing *Charter* violations. We hope that the courts reject this radical innovation and instead continue to see their job as protecting, not contravening, *Charter* rights. Such an approach would follow in the proud tradition of Federal Court judges who, in 2005, stopped CSIS from continuing to travel to Guantanamo Bay to interrogate Omar Khadr and who, in 2009, retained jurisdiction to ensure that Abousfian Abdelrazik returned home after the government essentially banished him, and who, in 2013, called CSIS to account when they discovered the agency had subcontracted the task of spying on Canadians overseas to foreign agencies. In all these cases, the judges did their job of protecting rights. They did not pre-authorize *Charter* violations in order to give CSIS protective cover.

The Disruption of Disruption

Bill C-51's newly enhanced and broad tactics of disruption are certainly preferable to a successful terrorist attack, but they push at the edges of the rule of law. We have been down this road before. In the wake of the October Crisis, the RCMP engaged in disruption (then called countering), much of it illegal and much of it involving false positives — that is, sweeping the wrong people into the net (e.g., the theft of the Parti Québécois's membership list).

But more than simply raising rights issues, disruption is a tactic clamouring for strategy: it is only a short-term — and frequently dangerous — solution. This is true even in the best-case scenario: imagine that CSIS successfully hires and trains agents skilled and talented at disruption. Potential terrorists are disrupted; a critical meeting is stopped; a computer is hacked; a plot is disrupted; a potential foreign fighter is prevented from leaving. Then what? What is the exit strategy? What do you do with disrupted terrorists, especially if they become more inclined to violence as a result of the disruption or other factors? The disrupted, like those tortured in Guantanamo Bay, may become impossible to prosecute, as prosecution would require the outing of too many secrets.

And so CSIS continues to watch, and when necessary, physically disrupt, until one of the disrupted slips from CSIS's radar because of a decision about the allocation of limited resources or simply because of a mistake. And if the previously disrupted, and now disappeared, terrorist does something really horrific in Canada — or almost worse, to one of our allies — we will have a security scandal, one possibly serious enough to spark yet another commission of inquiry. We predict that such a future commission would start its report by recounting the tale of the unimplemented recommendations from the Air India inquiry.

Peace Bonds: A Goldilocks Remedy and the New Security Certificate

Bill C-51 allows the police to interrupt and restrain possible terrorist activities through preventive arrests and detention (now lengthened to a maximum of seven days), along with year-long renewable peace bonds to control the lives of terrorist suspects in the community without subjecting them to criminal charges. These forms of police disruption will be more public than CSIS disruption, but perhaps no less problematic. Peace bonds may become the new legal battleground and create some of the same problems that immigration law security certificates have caused. Here again, we voice concerns about both security and rights.

A peace bond for a determined terrorist may not be enough to keep us safe. It does not actually imprison anyone. Certainly, individuals who breach a peace bond can be punished. But they will be sentenced for breaching curfews, associating with the wrong people, looking at the wrong websites and perhaps (in one current case) not attending religious counselling. They will not be prosecuted or punished for terrorism. Moreover, the peace bond's criminal hair-trigger for otherwise perfectly legal conduct may become a rallying point for those who point to the terrorist narrative about Western overreaction and hypocrisy.

Peace bonds raise legitimate rights concerns. Imposing restraints on the basis of risk and status should be uncomfortable for a democracy. Several people in the first half of 2015 have agreed to terror-related peace bonds, possibly simply to get the matter over and avoid further bad publicity. One peace bond case has provided a Manitoba man with a platform for his pro-ISIS views, but without the certainty of a trial where guilt or innocence can be determined.

Those subject to peace bonds, like those immigration security certificate detainees now released into the community, may be restrained in a form of perpetual limbo. Controversies will arise if peace bonds become the new security certificates. As time goes on those subject to either instrument can plausibly claim that the state has not produced evidence that they are terrorists and that they are being controlled, not for what they have done, but because of, at best, risk and fear, and at worst, because of their religious and political views. In short, this style of disruption risks being a Goldilocks remedy: too strong for those who simply have extreme religious and political views and a poor choice of friends; but too weak for the determined terrorists. Bill C-51's emphasis on disruption offers a false sense of security.

V. IGNORING THE ARAR COMMISSION AND THE UNFINISHED REVIEW AGENDA

Even as the 2015 laws overpromise on security while delivering problematic forms of disruption, they ignore accountability. The government has correctly been moving toward a whole-of-government approach to security, but has been content to leave a siloed and partial review structure in place. Here are the government's sins of omission:

1) Justice O'Connor in his Arar Commission report on review found that Canada's existing review structure had not kept pace with whole-of-government approaches to security, and in particular, the sharing of security information. Arar's case reveals that security information may not always be reliable and can have severe effects on individuals. In Bill C-51, the government accelerated and broadened information sharing, but without enhancing meaningful review of that information sharing in any way.

2) The government doubled the Security Intelligence Review Committee's (SIRC's) financial resources in its May 2015 budget. Nevertheless, it continued to ignore both the Arar Commission and SIRC's own warning that the review body needed new powers to follow the thread in and out of CSIS and that SIRC's jurisdiction should be expanded to cover other security agencies.

3) Justice O'Connor recommended that SIRC, the commissioner who reviews the Communications Security Establishment (CSE), and the RCMP civilian review and complaints body should be able to share secret information and conduct joint investigations. Two of the three bodies asked for these powers when testifying in the Senate about Bill C-51. The government did not respond. It also did not give the RCMP Civilian Review and Complaints Commission statutory gateways to SIRC and the CSE Commissioner in the *Enhancing RCMP Accountability Act* in 2013, even while creating similar gateways to provincial police complaints bodies.

4) The Arar Commission recommended that the existing review bodies be expanded so that they review eight (as opposed to three) agencies with important security functions. This has not been done. The *Security of Canada Information Sharing Act* (*SoCIS Act*) in Bill C-51 designates seventeen agencies as recipients of security information and allows them

to receive security information from over 100 federal agencies and departments. Only three agencies have dedicated national security review.

5) The Arar Commission found that review of national security information sharing by the Privacy Commissioner and the Auditor General was not sufficient. Both the Privacy Commissioner and the Auditor General had limited powers and mandates in the national security field. The government ignored the Privacy Commissioner's criticism of Bill C-51 and his conclusions that he did not have sufficient powers or resources to conduct even the limited privacy-based review of increased information sharing.

6) The Arar Commission found that review of national security activities by the courts, especially information sharing, was not adequate because such secret matters were rarely subject to judicial review. Nevertheless, the government stressed "judicial oversight" as the main restraint on Bill C-51 even though it is not actually required for information sharing and some of CSIS's new threat reduction activities.

7) During the same Parliament in which Bill C-51 was enacted, government parliamentarians defeated three separate private member's bills that all would have created a statutory committee of parliamentarians with access to secret security information, and in one instance, would have enhanced judicial and ministerial oversight over the activities of CSE.

The government's neglect of the Arar Commission's recommendations is particularly shocking given Bill C-51's broad approach to information sharing, the ability of CSIS to delegate its new threat reduction authority to other bodies, and the extraordinary intervention of four former prime ministers during the Bill C-51 debate. These former political leaders, along with other leading figures, endorsed many of the Arar Commission's recommendations. They called for the creation of a committee of parliamentarians to be given access to secret security information, as is the norm in democracies. They persuasively argued that enhanced review could prevent abuses and rights violations and improve security by identifying problem spots.[3] The government ignored them.

Enhanced Review as a Necessary but Not Sufficient Reform

Although we are strongly supportive of enhanced review, we confess that we are more than a little leery about how the review file might be handled in the future. Review is valuable and necessary, but it should not be oversold as a panacea. Review produces findings and recommendations, and the history of Canadian anti-terrorism is littered with forgotten findings and rejected recommendations. We are frankly concerned that even a reform-minded government might attempt to shut the Bill C-51 barn door simply through review reforms. Such improvements would be relatively cheap and easy, but they cannot cure overbroad security powers.

Reviewers, by design, will always be a few steps behind the agencies. Better review is no substitute for effective leadership and command and control oversight of the agencies, together with proportionate security powers that respect the rule of law and our democratic values. That said, it *is* time to move on expanded review. A Martin-era government bill and several private members' bills have proposed a statutory committee of parliamentarians who could have access to secret information but be bound by Canada's official secrets law. A revitalization of these bills would be welcome.

In addition, we would support a move to a "super-SIRC" that would eventually have a whole-of-government responsibility for all national security activities. As a matter of first priority, SIRC should be expanded to include review of the national security functions of the Canadian Border Services Agency, the RCMP, the CSE, the department of foreign affairs, the Financial Transactions and Reports Analysis Centre of Canada, Transport Canada, and Citizenship and Immigration Canada, among others.

If review of the CSE and the RCMP is not brought into SIRC, there should be a statutory gateway that allows SIRC, the CSE Commissioner, and the RCMP review body to share information and conduct joint review of the joint CSIS and CSE operations that are bound to increase with CSIS's new powers, including powers to conduct investigations outside of Canada.

But again we underscore: enhanced review is no excuse for not engaging in targeted reform of overbroad and potentially counterproductive security laws. It also should not be confused, as it frequently was in the debate about Bill C-51, with the need for better oversight involving command, control, and co-ordination, a topic to which we will return to below.

VI. COURTING UNNECESSARY *CHARTER* CHALLENGES

In the discussion above, we have complained that the 2015 laws were poor policy. But there are a number of features of the 2015 legislation that are also of doubtful validity under the *Charter*.

We are skeptical that the constitutionality of legislation is the sole test of its wisdom, but we do not think that the enactment of unconstitutional legislation is a good idea either. It harms the rule of law. It also creates delay, uncertainty, and costs for all concerned. But we are also not rights absolutists. Like our courts, we acknowledge the concept of balance. At its core, a democratic state must perform "a balancing of what is required for an effective response to terrorism in a way that appropriately recognizes the fundamental values of the rule of law."[4] Our *Charter* allows balance, most notably in section 1. But flexibility is not an invitation for short cuts or blank cheques. The government must justify each and every limit that it places on *Charter* rights and it should respect both the rule of law and the legislative role in the separation of powers by being specific about what rights are being limited and why they are being limited. Bill C-51 is notable not so much because it limits rights, but because it violates rights unnecessarily. Moreover, it places potential limits on each and every *Charter* right and does so in a manner that is alien to our legal tradition by dragooning judges into doing the dirty work of deciding what rights should be limited. This is why we believe Bill C-51 is objectionable on *Charter* and separation of powers grounds, in addition to our concerns about its wisdom.

Anticipating the outcome of *Charter* litigation is a perilous endeavour, but here are our predictions of where *Charter* challenges to the new security laws have the best chance for success:

1) The innocence-at-stake exception to the new CSIS informer privilege provided by Bill C-44 is constitutionally underinclusive given the Supreme Court's repeated recognition that section 7 rights are engaged in immigration and other administrative proceedings that affect section 7 rights to life, liberty, and security of the person, and not simply criminal trials. People affected by immigration detention and removal proceedings, passport revocation, and the no-fly list may all have good *Charter* claims in the right circumstances to knowledge about a CSIS informer who has provided important information that the state relies upon in imposing legal consequences.

2) The complex provisions in Bill C-51 amending Canada's immigration law to restrict special advocates' access to secret information not specifically relied upon in the government's case may contravene section 7 of the *Charter*. The provisions may fall below the minimum standards that led the Supreme Court to conclude in 2014 that the security certificate scheme was constitutional. The impact of these new measures should also be judged in combination with the effect of the new CSIS informer privilege, a privilege that the Supreme Court refused to recognize as a matter of common law while upholding security certificates from *Charter* challenges.[5]

3) Bill C-51's *SoCIS Act* may violate sections 7 and 8 of the *Charter* to the extent that it enables information sharing that may be grossly disproportionate, given the government's broadly defined security interests. The sharing and Big Data aggregation of information — especially that

obtained under warrant — may be an unreasonable invasion of residual privacy issues. The lack of effective review compounds this possible constitutional infirmity, while also raising questions about whether the exemption for protest and dissent may be illusory. Since an illusory exception might chill democratic conduct, the new Act may also violate section 2 freedoms of expression and association.

4) The new no-fly list in the new *Secure Travel Act* and passport revocation procedures in the *Prevention of Terrorist Travel Act* may violate section 7 to the extent that they do not provide for any special advocate adversarial challenge of secret information that is relevant to the government's decision. Courts may avoid invalidating these new laws by appointing friends of the court to provide adversarial challenge, thus raising issues as to whether such friends of the court are able to exercise the full special advocate–like powers that may be constitutionally required to the extent that no-fly listing and passport denial implicate *Charter* rights.

5) The new Bill C-51 terrorist offence of "knowingly promoting or advocating terrorism offences in general" may constitute a disproportionate restriction of freedom of expression under section 2, especially because it allows no truth or opinion defences. Additionally, it may be challenged on vagueness grounds. These flaws would also infect the new terrorist propaganda seizure and deletion procedures, to the extent that they incorporate the new speech crime.

6) The new CSIS threat reduction warrants may be challenged as infringing section 7 of the *Charter* and the ancient concepts of judicial independence and the separation of powers to the extent that they permit judges to authorize violations of any *Charter* right in a manner that is unpredictable, invisible to the target, not prescribed by law, and resistant to appeal.

These constitutional doubts should be read in light also of 2014's amendments to the citizenship law, allowing the citizenship of dual nationals to be revoked on security grounds. As discussed in Chapter 6, these changes raise serious issues under sections 15 (equality rights), 7 (fundamental justice procedural rights), and even, potentially, 11 (criminal procedural rights). Moreover, the government's Bill C-13, also enacted in 2014, allows police to collect potentially highly invasive and privacy-corroding metadata on the lowest evidentiary standard known to law, raising the inevitable section 8 issues described in Chapter 4. We list these *Charter* challenges not because we think that *Charter* litigation is the best way to craft national security policy — it is not — but to underline how all this new legislation may be consumed with (and in) *Charter* litigation.

Much of the inevitable litigation over the new security laws could have been avoided had the government been more attentive to *Charter* concerns and less radical when structuring its new laws. In particular, the government could have attempted to articulate and justify what particular *Charter* rights should be limited in CSIS's new powers rather than relying on the radical and novel idea that judges can authorize the violation of any *Charter* right. It could also have been more attentive to careful word choice in its new speech crime, and more mindful of (and less minimalist in construing) the jurisprudence under section 7 of the *Charter*, especially as it relates to adversarial challenge in secret proceedings.

VII. UNDOING THE DAMAGE OF THE NEW LEGISLATION

As we complete this book, both Bill C-51 and the citizenship stripping laws are being challenged under the *Charter*, but we think it would be a mistake for a new government to wait upon the outcome of *Charter* litigation to change the worst features of the laws. At the same time, we do not think that it is particularly realistic to expect a new government to repeal all of the new legislation. Anti-terrorism laws are much easier to enact — especially after a terrorist attack — than they are to repeal. This is especially so in the absence of any sunset or mandatory parliamentary review requirements. No government wishes to repeal, only to be faced with accusations that the law it abandoned may have made a difference in a future terrorist incident (a claim that requires no proof to be politically damaging).

We are also preoccupied with process. One of the flaws of the Bill C-51 debate was the extent to which it arrived in Parliament as a done deal, without any advance consultation and no real prospect of amendment. A government that persists in perceiving itself as the font of all wisdom suffers from hubris, an unedifying phenomenon given our history, outlined in Chapter 2, of overreacting and underreacting to terrorism. Other democracies are better at developing national security laws with wide input, including from informed reviewers of past practices. More than this though, the government needs to contemplate its strategy, and not simply focus on its tactics. Legislating a slew of new tools and then developing, on the fly, expectations of how they will be deployed coherently is a recipe for disaster. Puzzles are easier to solve when you know what picture you are trying to piece together. The 2012 anti-terror strategy was a start, but it needs to be used as a roadmap, not an afterthought as it was during the 2015 reforms.

Only after we have thought strategically is it worth discussing tactical steps. Still, in an effort to spark deliberation, we recommend targeted (if not necessarily surgical) repeals and amendments of many aspects of the recent security laws. We outline those in an annex to this chapter, recognizing that the detailed work of re-crafting our laws should be a collective project with input from many. Indeed, we would recommend that any new government revisit these questions by issuing a detailed lessons-learned document from the October 2014 attacks and other recent developments, and a white paper that provides a range of options that can then be the subject for genuine and open-minded consultation.

VIII. BEYOND LEGISLATIVE REFORMS

Part of the message of this book is that the 2015 legislation has to be evaluated in the context of Canada's existing security laws and architecture. In some respects, this architecture is sound. There has been a score of successful prosecutions since 9/11. Although the actual numbers of prosecutions lags behind other democracies, the conviction rate has been high.

In other respects, however, our security structure requires renovation and re-thinking. Some of this re-crafting may require legislative changes to the legal structure of our anti-terror policy. Other administrative and organizational reforms need not await law-making. Some needed reforms will require the federal government to work co-operatively with the provinces. Below, we list two priorities for consideration.

Enhanced Oversight

In Chapter 11, we distinguished review from oversight and emphasized the need for better co-ordination and oversight of our growing anti-terrorist toolkit. This has to be done not by independent reviewers or parliamentary committees, but by ministers and the prime minister, assisted by an expert and non-partisan civil service. Like the Air India Commission, we stressed the need for someone at the centre of government to have the responsibility for resolving inevitable disputes when agencies disagree on what is now an expanded array of tactics.

We see two main choices for better command and control oversight. One is to recognize that the minister of public safety has become the *de facto* lead on these matters and treat the department accordingly. Alternatively, we could revisit the Air India Commission's recommendation for giving the prime minister's national security advisor responsibilities and powers for co-ordination and oversight. We accept that the national security advisor has considerable influence and meets regularly with the agencies, but influence that can be exercised in a discretionary manner is not the same as ultimate responsibility.

There is a need to ensure co-ordination of our growing anti-terrorist toolkit. Who co-ordinates what is done after a suspected foreign terrorist traveller is denied exit from Canada through a no-fly listing and passport cancellation? Who co-ordinates how to deal with the various circumstances of returned foreign terrorist travellers? Who decides whether the RCMP or CSIS takes the lead in a terrorism case? Who decides whether it is more important to protect the secrets of CSIS and our allies rather than risk disclosure through prosecution? We fear the answer to some of these question is "no one," and to others, "everyone."

Multi-disciplinary and Community-Based Counter–Violent Extremism

The 2015 reforms have increased and sharpened the anti-terrorist toolkit, but we believe there is one tool still missing that many other democracies (including Australia, the United Kingdom, and the United States) are pursuing: a comprehensive multi-disciplinary and community-based program designed to counter violent extremism. The government admitted in 2014 that Canada's counter–violent extremism (CVE) program was far from robust, and it has done little in the interim to improve it. Indeed, it has created new obstacles. To the extent that there is a federal program, the RCMP appears to have the lead. The RCMP is in a difficult position, given its responsibilities to enforce the law, including the new speech offence of advocating or promoting terrorism offences in general. This obligation may deter outreach to those at risk of violent extremism.

If Canadian CVE programs are to catch up with those of other democracies, the federal government will have to work more closely and co-operatively with provincial governments. Provincial governments have jurisdiction over the teachers, social workers, health care workers, and many of the correctional professionals who may be able to assist those at risk of violent extremism, and view their problems through a more holistic lens that is not simply focused on security. Alas, Quebec seems to be the only province moving on these issues, and it is stressing issues of hate speech already covered by federal law.

In addition, the government must attempt to regain trust among at least some segments of Canada's diverse Muslim communities — trust that has been eroded by repeated irritants, including the government's last-minute withdrawal from a rare Canadian CVE success story, the *United Against Terrorism* pamphlet, and its rejection of the advice it has received from its own Cross-cultural Roundtable on Security. Harsh rhetoric about "jihadism" may be a vehicle to express understandable anger and disgust at horrific acts of violence; it may also result in short-term political gain. But it harms respectful inter-societal relations in ways we may later regret.

Caution about CVE programs is required. We need the humility to understand that little is understood about the process of radicalization to violence, which is why a leading academic expert in the area has proposed a "Manhattan project" for "understanding terrorist behavior."[6] Counter-violent extremism programs need to be evaluated and the hypotheses that they may be ineffective or even counterproductive should be explored. We need, in other words, to commit serious and sustained sociology (and psychology). Canada already has the sinews of research projects and support that could contribute to such an undertaking. No CVE program will be perfect, and its failures will become politically contentious. But more effort and evaluation is required. Even our toughest anti-terrorist tool — prosecution and imprisonment — requires an exit strategy. Most convicted terrorists in Canada will eventually — and in some cases, shortly — be released.

IX. APPRECIATING THE LIMITS OF GOVERNMENT

Finally, we need as a society to be resilient. Terrorism is a strategy, not an ideology. And while today's terrorists might brandish one or another particular variant of political, religious, or ideological belief, tomorrow's terrorist will likely favour a different cause. A liberal democracy should accept even radical ideologies, but insist that no ideology justifies violence.

Tragically, we will not always be successful in stopping violence. Even if we had the absolutist system of North Korea, we would not always have a perfect record of success (and indeed, would probably have one that was much worse). In a democracy, we must, by necessity, be prepared to run risks — that is the price of freedom. As the Israeli Supreme Court famously warned, "a democracy must often fight with one hand tied behind its back," but in doing so "it nonetheless has the upper hand. Preserving the rule of law and recognition of an individual's liberty constitutes an important component in its understanding of security. At the end of the day, they strengthen its spirit and its strength and allow it to overcome its difficulties."[7] Jim Judd, the former director of CSIS, has made a similar observation: "Democracies have taken a long period to develop and their values, laws and institutions continue to provide inspiration to those without the luxury of living in one. It is thus essential that in responding to threats such as terrorism we do so in a fashion that best reflects what democracies stand for."[8]

In the final analysis, terrorists will murder innocent people. Certainly, we can do things to reduce risks. We think that Canada has done too little to improve terrorism investigations and prosecutions. We also think it has gone down the wrong paths of disruption that will challenge the rule of law, including the role of courts, speech offences that will challenge freedom, and massive information sharing for massively defined security threats that will threaten privacy.

But no one who bears the mantle of responsibility in our government should ever promise perfect security. That would be a false claim, one that would propel us on a course so deeply constraining of liberties that few of us would want to live in the world that resulted. Laws that overpromise will never deliver, and when they fail, they will ignite a call for still more laws. We confront an endless cycle of counterproductive legal ratcheting, the legal equivalent of squeezing water in a fist. The final result is a clenched fist, but no water.

However, if we cannot aspire to perfect security, we should surely expect rational security that learns from past mistakes. The laws enacted in 2015 in response to the October 2014 attacks were not wrong in trying to prevent terrorism. But read collectively, they bring us no closer to this key objective. Indeed, they constitute a step away from it. It is time for a re-think.

ANNEX

Table 14.1: Legislative Re-considerations

Statute	Amendments
Canada Evidence Act	The security confidentiality provision in s 38 should be amended to allow provincial superior court judges presiding over terrorism criminal prosecutions to conduct their own s 38 analyses and issue their own non-disclosure orders.
Citizenship Act	The security-based revocation powers introduced in 2014 should be repealed. We do not believe they are justified on security grounds and could even be counterproductive to the extent that their intended use against convicted terrorists might provide another excuse for not engaging in issues of rehabilitation and prison radicalization. In any event, they single out dual nationals for an extra peril without a rational basis to conclude that dual nationals present an extra security risk. They also promote the false view that the security threats faced by Canada come from non-citizens or soon to be non-citizens.
Canadian Security Intelligence Service Act (*CSIS Act*)	1) **Human Source Privilege:** The CSIS human source privilege in s 18.1 should be repealed before it takes root and creates even more distance in the CSIS-police relationship and harms the ability of prosecutors to use identifying information from CSIS informers in terrorism prosecutions. This repeal will be fiercely and probably successfully resisted by CSIS.
	If retained, the adverse consequences of the new privilege should be mitigated in a number of ways. First, the language of s 18.1 of the *CSIS Act* could be tightened to minimize the real risk that the privilege will be triggered in virtually all CSIS interviews with its human sources. To prevent this, the new privilege should only be triggered by explicit promises of "anonymity" — as opposed to "confidentiality" — made by someone high in the chain of command at CSIS, or only if there is a formal quid pro quo. This is a second-best solution to repealing the privilege, but one that avoids extending the privilege to almost everyone that CSIS interviews, with harmful consequences for both terrorism prosecutors and everyone adversely affected by CSIS's human intelligence (for example, because perhaps unreliable intelligence is used to place a person on a no-fly list, revoke a passport, deny a person security clearance, and so on). The innocence-at-stake exception should be extended to all proceedings in which life, liberty, security of the person, or other constitutional rights are at stake.

Statute	Amendments
CSIS Act (continued)	2) **Curing "Less is More":** The CSIS discretion to disclose information in s 19 should be amended to compel disclosure to the national security advisor or the minister of public safety of information that CSIS has reasonable grounds to believe might be evidence of a terrorism offence if CSIS does not disclose the information directly to the police. 3) **Threat Reduction Powers:** We are not convinced that Bill C-51's massive change to CSIS's mandate to include physical or kinetic measures to reduce threats to the security of Canada is warranted. If there is room for CSIS disruption, the better course is to enumerate specific actions that CSIS can take, rather than create an open possibility, limited only at its outer range. This would require careful and thorough study and policy premeditation of the sort we do not believe has been done. If the government resists this approach, at the very least it should: • amend s 12.1(3) to remove any reference to the *Charter* being contravened by a measure, thereby rejecting any interpretation of the amendments that suggests CSIS could violate constitutional obligations. The revised provision would read: "The Service shall not take measures to reduce a threat to the security of Canada if these measures may be contrary to Canadian law, unless the Service is authorized to take them by a warrant issued under section 21.1, and the measures will not contravene a right or freedom guaranteed by the *Canadian Charter of Rights and Freedoms.*" • re-craft the outer limits of illegal conduct to include, in addition to bars on bodily harm, obstruction of justice, and violation of sexual integrity, these additional prohibitions: ▪ loss of or serious damage to property that endangers the health or safety of any person; and ▪ detention of a person. • re-craft s 12.2(2) to specify, "In subsection (1), 'bodily harm' has the same meaning as in section 2 of the *Criminal Code* and for greater certainty, includes torture within the meaning of s 269.1 of the *Criminal Code* or cruel, inhuman, or degrading treatment or punishment within the meaning of the UN Convention Against Torture."

Statute	Amendments
CSIS Act (continued)	• limit the new CSIS measures in s 12.1 to counter-terror operations under s 2(c) of the *CSIS Act* relating to "threats to the security of Canada" and terrorism or (if we must have "measures" for other sorts of security risks) limit them to s 2(a) and (c) matters to exclude sedition and foreign-influenced activities. Alternatively, at least amend the foreign-influenced activities mandate in s 2(b) of the *CSIS Act* to follow the 1989 recommendations of SIRC's 1988–89 annual report assessment of the *CSIS Act*, at pages 56–57. This would limit the prospect that CSIS activities might reach many non-violent democratic protest movements, in some way done in conjunction with secret foreign influence (e.g., a foreign funder). • incorporate the statutory special advocate provisions from the *Immigration Refugee Protection Act* into the warrant proceedings and expressly provide these special advocates with standing to appeal warrant decisions. This extra level of scrutiny is appropriate since, by definition, at issue in these warrants is CSIS conduct in violation of the law, and perhaps the Charter, if the amendment above is rejected. Such special advocates would have more powers, especially in relation to appeals, than *amici curiae* who may be appointed at the discretion of the presiding Federal Court judge. • follow *Criminal Code* s 25.3 (for the police) and require a public report with data on the use of CSIS illegal measures each year and general information on the nature of the CSIS's illegal (but judicially exonerated) conduct. • follow *Criminal Code* s 25.4 (for the police) and require that a person affected by CSIS's illegal conduct under a warrant must be notified of the conduct within one year, subject to reasonable exceptions analogous to those enumerated in s 25.4 of the *Criminal Code*. We recognize that these disclosure requirements place the "measures" warrants on a different footing than CSIS surveillance warrants, which are not disclosed. We believe this fitting. First, the very purpose of a CSIS intelligence-gathering surveillance warrant may be defeated if disclosed — that is, the target will change behaviour in a manner

Statute	Amendments
CSIS Act (continued)	that makes the intelligence irrelevant. The new "measures" warrants are said to be about disruption — here, the justifications for permanent secrecy are less persuasive. Operational concerns can be mitigated by provisos, analogous to those for police in the *Criminal Code*, which delay disclosure for legitimate security concerns, like ongoing investigations. Such concerns should be subject to periodic review in the courts to ensure they remain persuasive. Second, even if there is a justification for secrecy, that justifications pales against the public interest in notice of CSIS conduct, that (by definition, given the very existence of the warrant) has violated the law, and under the existing law, perhaps the *Charter* rights of the target. There must be some manner in which a person subjected to this radical conduct can challenge it, since the prospects of any other form of accountability are remote. All of this is to say that if CSIS has *de facto* police powers of the sort found in *Criminal Code* s 25.1, it also needs police-like levels of transparency. 4) **CSIS Extraterritorial Operations:** Amend ss 21 and 21.1 to specify that warrants are required prior to any CSIS foreign operation that might violate foreign or international law.

Criminal Code	1) **Preventive detention**
	   • At the very least, s 83.3(4), allowing detention in exigent circumstances without judicial warrant, should specifically provide that it applies only where the peace officer suspects on reasonable grounds that the detention of the person in custody is likely to prevent a terrorist activity that involves a serious and imminent threat to life, health, public safety, or substantial property damage that threatens life or health.
	   • The law should specify that the questioning of a person subjected to preventive detention in s 83.3 should be conducted only pursuant to conditions imposed by the judge authorizing the detention, and must be consistent with the requirement that the detainee be treated humanely and with respect for human dignity. The person must not be subjected to cruel, inhuman, or degrading treatment

Statute	Amendments
Criminal Code (continued)	as that term is understood in the United Nations Convention on Torture. These standards exist in the equivalent Australian laws. • An alternative approach would be to prohibit questioning, as under Australian preventive detention orders, or to regulate questioning, as is done with respect to the Australian Security Intelligence Organisation (ASIO) questioning warrants under the *ASIO Act* in Australia, including allowing on-site visits by independent reviewers. • Consequential amendments to the *Youth Criminal Justice Act* should make clear that all relevant parts of the *Youth Criminal Justice Act* relating to the taking and admissibility of statements, custody, and recognizances apply to those under 18 years of age who are subject to preventive arrest and/or recognizances. 2) **Peace Bonds** • Anti-terror peace bonds under s 810.011 should include a mandatory reporting requirement, obliging the government to disclose publicly the number and circumstances in which they are used. • Consideration should be given under both regular peace bonds and those stemming from the preventive detention process to legislating a closed list of conditions that judges may impose, making the potential reach of these instruments transparent. • Either sort of peace bond should be subject to only a single renewal, ensuring that these are temporary measures and do not drift into a standing means of subjecting people to control orders. • Research should be conducted on the effects of peace bonds on those subject to them and their families and their effectiveness should be assessed both in relation to less coercive alternatives and in relation to prosecutions. 3) **Speech Crime** • Repeal s 83.221 as unnecessary. If a reluctant government insists on preserving this offense, then: 　■ incorporate defences found in s 319(3) (on hate crimes)

Statute	Amendments
Criminal Code (continued)	<ul><li>expressly incorporate and affirm the defence-like concepts in s 83.01(1.1) to protect expression of political and religious thought, and make it a defence</li><li>raise fault requirement from "knowingly" to "wilfully" advocating or promoting terrorism. This would eliminate unnecessary debate about whether, for example, a political party's fundraising letter containing terrorist propaganda is itself in violation of the new offence.</li><li>raise fault requirements from "recklessness" or awareness of the possibility that someone will commit an offence as a result of the communication, to "knowledge" of the probability that someone will commit an offence as a result of the communication.</li><li>replace "terrorism offence in general" with "terrorist activity" as defined in s 83.01 of the *Criminal Code*, thereby discarding an unprecedented, vague, and *Charter*-vulnerable concept in favour of one with a clear and *Charter*-consistent legislative definition.</li></ul> 4) **Terrorist propaganda** <ul><li>Amend the definition of "terrorist propaganda" in ss 83.222 and 83.223 to remove reference to written and visual material that "advocates or promotes the commission of terrorism offences in general" and limit terrorist propaganda to such material that "counsels" or "instructs" a terrorist activity. This would focus the provision to speech that is indisputably criminal and more closely moored to actual violence.</li><li>Expressly incorporate the special advocate system into the judicial deletion system, thereby restoring an element of the adversarial system where a judicial deletion order is sought and the person who posted the material does not appear to oppose it, perhaps because of concerns of being prosecuted under the new advocacy and promotion offence.</li><li>Repeal provisions allowing enforcement by customs officials because such officials act without judicial authorization and are not subject to independent review.</li></ul>

Statute	Amendments
Prevention of Terrorist Travel Act and the *Canadian Passport Order*	• Sections 4 and 6 should be amended to allow security-cleared special advocates to see any evidence that is not disclosed to the affected person, but is relevant in determining whether the cancellation or revocation of a passport is reasonable. • Cancellations done under the "reasonable grounds to suspect" standard should be clearly time-limited in the statute, after which the passport must either be restored or revoked by the government on the "reasonable grounds to believe" standard.
Secure Travel Act	• The words "reasonable grounds to suspect" in s 8(1) should be changed to the higher standard of "reasonable grounds to believe." • The words "for transportation purposes" could be added after the words "disclosure of information" to make clear the limited and legitimate purposes of sharing of no-fly lists. • Copies of the "written arrangements" in s 12 should be shared with an independent review agency. The involvement of the minister of transport and Canadian Border Services Agency in the administration of this Act is sensible, but should be tied to independent whole-of-government review. • Section 16 should be amended to allow security-cleared special advocates to see any evidence that is not disclosed to the affected person, but is relevant in determining whether the listing is reasonable. Special advocates should also be able to participate in appeals contemplated under s 17 of the Act.
Security of Canada Information Sharing Act (*SoCIS Act*)	This Act is awkward and creates more problems than solutions. It should be repealed and replaced with legislation that standardizes the understanding of national security-justified information sharing in each of the existing laws that allow such sharing, and extends it (reasonably) to those agencies that lack such authorization. The common definition of security interests should be much more modest in scope than the present *SoCIS Act* concept, and be motivated by reasonable security concerns with thought given to prioritizing information related to terrorist threats. It should also meet the Privacy Commissioner's expectations concerning, for example, necessity-based

Statute	Amendments
SoCIS Act (continued)	standards for sharing. It should incorporate (in legally operative provisions) the policy recommendations of the Arar Commission on how to ensure adequate independent review of such information sharing, especially given the absence of judicial review. Put another way, reform in this area should attempt to iron out the inconsistent and often incoherent patchwork of laws, rather than simply papering over them in the manner chosen by the *SoCIS Act*. Doing this properly is a delicate and complex undertaking that will require a meaningful consultation with stakeholders in the very active privacy community, and must not be another government *fait accompli*.
Surveillance and Information Sharing Issues	• Canada's surveillance laws are so riddled with differing standards that they need a thorough overhaul — one that is guided by addressing emerging technological issues (such as metadata). Moreover, it is now essential to recognize that surveillance law that relies on judges acting as gatekeepers is insufficient in a world of Big Data analytics and pervasive information sharing. Considerable thought should be given to an independent authorization system for internal sharing and aggregation through the use of Big Data analytics of previously collected information. One option would be the Firewall Warrants discussed in Chapter 4 • Departures from conventional search-and-seizure judicial authorization systems, as with the CSE, should be corrected. • At the very least, information sharing that, on reasonable grounds to believe, could implicate torture issues should automatically be reported to review bodies for careful review.
Review Issues	• Reform of review should include implementing and creating a committee of parliamentarians with access to secret information — a concept for which there are many precedents in defeated private member bills.

Statute	Amendments
Review Issues (continued)	• Reform should match all-of-government security activity with all-of-government expert review, on the model potentially of the Australian Inspector General for Security and Intelligence and whole-of-government Civil Liberties and Privacy boards in the United States, and most recently, in the United Kingdom. Serious consideration should now be given to harmonizing review of CSIS, CSE, and the national security functions of the RCMP in a renewed SIRC and then giving that super-SIRC remit also over other agencies listed below. • Barring that, statutory gateways permitting existing review bodies to collaborate in sharing secret information necessary for joint investigations should be created. This is especially urgent given the increased likelihood of joint CSIS and CSE operations under the 2015 laws. • The remit of SIRC should be extended to fill obvious review gaps for agencies that are currently not being reviewed by anyone such as the Canadian Border Services Agency, Transport Canada, and Citizenship and Immigration Canada.

Endnotes

PREFACE

1 Craig Forcese & Kent Roach, "When Facing Terror, There Are Limits to What Law Can Achieve" *Globe and Mail* (27 October 2014), online: www.theglobeandmail. com/globe-debate/when-facing-terror-there-are-limits-to-what-law-can-achieve/ article21312060/.

2 Part I of the Constitution Act, 1982, being Schedule B to the Canada Act 1982 (UK), 1982, c 11 [Charter].

3 Listings of many of these articles can be found at www.antiterrorlaw.ca under "op-eds and commentary" and at www.law.utoronto.ca/news/prof-kent-roach-co-creates-antiterrorlawca-experiment-in-legal-scholarship-done-in-real-time.

CHAPTER ONE: INTRODUCTION

1 Ontario Provincial Police, "Independent Investigation into the Death of Michael Zehaf-Bibeau" (June 2015), online: www.rcmp-grc.gc.ca/pubs/parl/opp-zb-eng.htm.

2 Janyce McGregor & Kady O'Malley, "Stephen Harper Makes His Case for New Powers to Combat Terror" *CBC News* (30 January 2015), online: www.cbc.ca/news/ politics/stephen-harper-makes-his-case-for-new-powers-to-combat-terror-1.2937602.

3 Mohammad Fadel, "A Tale of Two Massacres: *Charlie Hebdo* and Utoya Island" in Edward Iacobucci & Stephen Toope, eds, *After the Paris Attacks: Responses in Canada, Europe and Around the Globe* (Toronto: University of Toronto Press, 2015).

4 "West Edmonton Mall Threats Not a Concern for Cheerleading Competition" *CBC News* (7 March 2015), online: www.cbc.ca/news/canada/edmonton/west-edmonton-mall-threats-not-a-concern-for-cheerleading-competition-1.2986085.

5 Kady O'Malley & Kristen Everson, "Conservative Facebook Post on West Edmonton Mall Threat 'Troubling,' Alberta MLA Says" *CBC News* (4 March 2015), online: www.cbc.ca/news/politics/conservative-facebook-post-on-west-edmonton-mall-threat-troubling-alberta-mla-says-1.2981167.

6 Stewart Bell, "Pakistani Man Accused in Toronto Bomb Plot Ordered Deported after Being Ruled a Danger to Canada" *National Post* (5 June 2015), online: news.nationalpost.com/news/canada/pakistani-accused-of-toronto-bomb-plot-ordered-deported-after-being-ruled-a-danger-to-canada.

7 In February 2015, 82% of respondents reportedly supported Bill C-51 but this declined to 72% in May 2015. Among Canadians who reported following the debate about the law, 55% were opposed with 45% supporting it. See "Bill C-51: Support Declines after Months of Protest, but Strong Majority Still Backs Anti-terror Legislation" (25 May 2015), online: Angus Reid Institute angusreid.org/wp-content/uploads/2015/05/2015.05.25-Bill-C-51.pdf. A June 2015 poll suggested that almost equal proportions (39%) supported and opposed (41%) the bill, with one-fifth of voters expressing no opinion. See "Canadians split on Bill C-51" (23 June 2015), online: Forum Poll poll.forumresearch.com/post/306/liberal-support-for-bill-moves-some-votes-to-ndp/.

8 Kristy Kirkup, "Bill C-51 hearings: Diane Ablonczy's Questions to Muslim Group 'McCarthyesque" *CBC News* (13 March 2015), online: www.cbc.ca/news/politics/bill-c-51-hearings-diane-ablonczy-s-questions-to-muslim-group-mccarthyesque-1.2993531.

9 Ontario Provincial Police, above note 1; House of Commons, "House of Commons Incident Response Summary" (3 June 2015) at 9, online: www.parl.gc.ca/about/house/newsroom/articles/2015-06-03-Summary-e.pdf; Royal Canadian Mounted Police, "External Engagement and Coordination: Parliament Hill Incident on Oct 22, 2014 After Action Review" (29 April 2015), online: www.rcmp-grc.gc.ca/pubs/parl/aar-er-eng.htm.

10 Australian and New South Wales Governments, "Martin Place Siege: Joint Commonwealth and New South Wales Review" (January 2015), online: www.dpmc.gov.au/sites/default/files/publications/170215_Martin_Place_Siege_Review_1.pdf.

11 Jean Chrétien et al, "A Close Eye on Security Makes Canadians Safer" *Globe and Mail* (19 February 2015), online: www.theglobeandmail.com/globe-debate/a-close-eye-on-security-makes-canadians-safer/article23069152/.

12 Oxford Dictionaries, online: www.oxforddictionaries.com/definition/english/radical

13 RSC 1985, c C-23.

14 SC 2015, c 20, s 2.

15 SC 2015, c 20, s 11.

16 SC 2015, c 36, s 42.

17 SC 2015, c 9.

18 SC 2014, c 22.

19 SC 2015, c 20.

20 SC 2015, c 36.

21 United Nations Security Council, S/RES/2178. For an examination of this resolution and some early responses to it, see Kent Roach, ed, *Comparative Counter-terrorism Law* (New York: Cambridge University Press, 2015).

22 "CSIS and RCMP One Vision: An Operational Approach to Intelligence and Evidence" undated powerpoint presentation. Access to Information Request A-2014-224.

23 *R v Khawaja*, 2012 SCC 69.

24 *Re Section 83.28 of the Criminal Code*, 2004 SCC 42 at para 39.

CHAPTER TWO: HISTORY

1 Ontario Provincial Police, "Independent Investigation into the Death of Michael Zehaf-Bibeau October 22, 2014, Centre Block, Parliament Hill, Ottawa, Canada" (2015), online: www.rcmp-grc.gc.ca/pubs/parl/opp-zb-eng.pdf.

2 Canadian Network for Research on Terrorism, Security and Society, "TSAS Canadian Incident Database (CIDB) Initial Analysis of Downtown Ottawa and Canadian Military Attacks," online: www.tsas.ca/files/2014/10/TSAS-CIDB-Ottawa-and-Military-Incidents-October-22-2014.pdf.

3 Canadian Network for Research on Terrorism, Security and Society, Incident Database, Incident Details: 1980520090210001, citing A Kellett et al, *Terrorism in Canada 1960–1989*, User Report No 1990-16, (Ottawa: Solicitor General Canada, National Security Coordination Centre, Police and Security Branch, 1991) at 416.

4 *Criminal Code*, RSC 1985, c C-46, s 83.01.

5 See *R v Khawaja*, 2012 SCC 69 [*Khawaja*].

6 See Michelle Shephard, "Right-Wing Extremism a Greater Threat in North America" *Toronto Star* (28 June 2015).

7 "MPs Rap MacKay's Terrorism References," *Halifax Chronicle Herald* (17 February 2015).

8 See Mohammad Fadel, "A Tale of Two Massacres: Charlie Hebdo and Utoya Island" in Edward Iacobucci & Stephen Toope, eds, *After the Paris Attacks: Responses in Canada, Europe and around the Globe* (Toronto: University of Toronto Press, 2015) at 31; Tristin Hopper, "Suspects in Halifax Mass Shooting Plot Had Obsession with Nazi Symbols, Columbine Massacre" *National Post* (17 February 2015), online: http://news.nationalpost.com/news/canada/accused-in-halifax-mass-shooting-plot-had-obsession-with-nazi-symbols-columbine-massacre.

9 Bill C-51, *An Act to enact the Security of Canada Information Sharing Act and the Secure Air Travel Act, to amend the Criminal Code, the Canadian Security Intelligence Service Act and the Immigration and Refugee Protection Act and to make related and consequential amendments to other Acts*, 2d Sess, 41st Parl, 2015 (assented to 18 June 2015), SC 2015, c 20.

10 See Traffic Injury Research Foundation, *Wildlife-Vehicle Collisions in Canada* (August 2012), online: http://tirf.ca/publications/PDF_publications/WildlifeVehicle_Collision_Deliverable1_Eng_6.pdf.

11 See United States Department of Transportation, *Traffic Safety Facts 2001* (December 2002), online: www-nrd.nhtsa.dot.gov/Pubs/TSF2001.pdf.

12 See Thomson Reuters, "New Security Bill Aimed at Combating 'Lone Wolf' Terrorist Attacks Coming This Week" *CBC News* (25 January 2015), online: www.cbc.ca/news/politics/new-security-bill-aimed-at-combating-lone-wolf-attacks-coming-this-week-1.2931216.

13 William Faulkner, *Requiem for a Nun* (New York: Vintage Books, 2011) at 73.

14   Bill C-44, *An Act to amend the Canadian Security Intelligence Service Act and other Acts*, 2d Sess, 41st Parl, 2015 (assented to 23 April 2015), SC 2015, c 9; Bill C-51, above note 9; Bill C-59, *An Act to implement certain provisions of the budget tabled in Parliament on April 21, 2015 and other measures*, 2d Sess, 41st Parl, 2015 (assented to 23 June 2015), SC 2015, c 36.

15   Part I of the *Constitution Act, 1982*, being Schedule B to the *Canada Act 1982* (UK), 1982, c 11 [*Charter*].

16   Walter Tarnopolsky, *The Canadian Bill of Rights*, 2d ed (Toronto: McClelland and Stewart, 1975) at 332.

17   *Ibid* at 330. *War Measures Act*, RSC 1970, c W-2.

18   Quoted in John Saywell, ed, *Quebec 70: A Documentary Narrative* (Toronto: University of Toronto Press, 1971) at 86.

19   See Reginald Whitaker, Gregory Kealey, & Andrew Parnaby, *Secret Service: Political Policing in Canada from the Fenians to Fortress America* (Toronto: University of Toronto Press, 2012) at 287–90.

20   Tarnopolsky, above note 16 at 341, citing statements made in the House of Commons, 16 October 1970.

21   The first quotation is in Saywell, above note 18 at 91. The second quotation is in Guy Bouthillier & Edouard Cloutier, *Trudeau's Darkest Hour: War Measures in Time of Peace, October 1970* (Montreal: Baraka Books, 2010) at 144.

22   See, for example, William Tetley, *The October Crisis, 1970: An Insider's View* (Montreal: McGill-Queen's University Press, 2007).

23   See Whitaker, Kealey, & Parnaby, above note 19 at 288.

24   *Public Order Regulations*, SOR/70-444, s 3 [*POR*].

25   *Gagnon v Vallieres* (1971), 14 CRNS 321 at 350. For contemporary criticism, see Herbert Marx, "The 'Apprehended Insurrection of 1970' and the Judicial Function" (1972) 7 *University of British Columbia Law Review* 55.

26   *Criminal Code*, above note 4, s 61.

27   *Ibid*, s 59. The defences are contained in *ibid*, s 60.

28   *Canadian Security Intelligence Service Act*, RSC 1985, c C-23, s 2 [*CSIS Act*].

29   See Canada, Security Intelligence Review Committee, *Annual Report 1988–89* (Ottawa: SIRC, 1989) (Chair: Ronald G Atkey) at 55ff, online: www.sirc-csars.gc.ca/pdfs/ar_1988-1989-eng.pdf.

30   Law Reform Commission of Canada, *Crimes against the State* (Ottawa: The Commission, 1986) at 35–36.

31   See *Boucher v the King*, [1951] SCR 265. See also ML Friedland, *Legal Dimensions of National Security* (Ottawa: Supply and Services, 1981) at 25.

32   *Security of Canada Information Sharing Act*, SC 2015, c 20, s 2 at s 2 [*SoCIS Act*].

33   Douglas Schmeiser, "Control of Apprehended Insurrection: Emergency Measures vs. the Criminal Code" (1971) 4 *Manitoba Law Journal* 359 at 363.

34   *POR*, above note 24, ss 3 and 9(2).

35   See Dominique Clement, "The October Crisis of 1970: Human Rights Abuses under the War Measures Act" (2008) 42:2 *Journal of Canadian Studies* 160 at 167.

36   *Ibid* at 169.

37   See Tetley, above note 22 at 98.

38   See Tarnopolsky, above note 16 at 347.

39   *POR*, above note 24, ss 4(c) and (g).

40 On the two seditious conspiracy trials, which were unreported in the law reports, see Peter Mackinnon, "Conspiracy and Sedition as Canadian Political Crimes" (1977) 23 *McGill Law Journal* 622 at 635–36. Vallières did plead guilty to one counselling offence in 1972 after he had renounced the FLQ, and he received a suspended sentence: see *ibid* at 636. See also *R v Vallières*, [1970] 4 CCC 69 at 75–76 (Que CA), for use of Vallières's book as part of the prosecution's case.

41 See Clement, above note 35 at 168–69.

42 *Ibid.*

43 See Thomas R Berger, *Fragile Freedoms* (Toronto: Clarke, Irwin and Company, 1981) at 204; Marian Botsford Fraser, *Acting for Freedom: Fifty Years of Civil Liberties in Canada* (Toronto: Second Story Press, 2015) at 55.

44 See *Jamieson v British Columbia*, [1971] 5 WWR 600 (BCSC).

45 "Tories Cut and Paste 'We Reject the Argument That Every Time We Talk about Security Our Freedoms Are Threatened'" *ThinkPol* (25 March 2015), online: http://thinkpol.ca/2015/03/25/tories-cut-and-paste-we-reject-the-argument-that-every-time-we-talk-about-security-our-freedoms-are-threatened/.

46 Quoted in Tetley, above note 22 at 86. See also Michael Freeman, *Freedom of Security: The Consequences for Democracies Using Emergency Powers to Fight Terrorism* (Westport, CT: Praegar Publishing, 2003) at 125–26.

47 See Cameron Crouch, *Managing Terrorism and Insurgency: Regeneration, Recruitment and Attrition* (New York: Routledge, 2010) at 52.

48 See Clement, above note 35 at 175–6.

49 See Judy Torrence, *Public Violence in Canada 1867–1982* (Montreal: McGill-Queen's University Press, 1986) at 39.

50 See Fraser, above note 43 at 54.

51 Quoted in Clement, above note 35 at 171.

52 Quoted in Berger, above note 43 at 210 and 217.

53 Ronald Dworkin, "The Threat to Patriotism" *New York Times Book Review* (28 February 2002).

54 Quoted in Dennis Smith, *Bleeding Hearts . . . Bleeding Country* (Edmonton: Hurtig Publishing, 1971) at 45 and 57.

55 *Ibid* at 54.

56 Prime Minister of Canada, "PM Announces Measures to Protect Canadians" (30 January 2015), online: http://pm.gc.ca/eng/news/2015/01/30/pm-announces-anti-terrorism-measures-protect-canadians-0.

57 Quoted in Dan Loomis, *Not Much Glory: Quelling the FLQ* (Toronto: Deneau, 1984) at 140.

58 *Public Order (Temporary Measures) Act*, SC 1970–71–72, c 2.

59 Kenneth McNaught, "Political Trials and the Canadian Political Tradition" in ML Friedland, ed, *Courts and Trials: A Multidisciplinary Approach* (Toronto: University of Toronto Press, 1975).

60 Quoted in Fraser, above note 43 at 44.

61 *Emergencies Act*, RSC 1985, c 22 (4th Supp).

62 See Whitaker, Kealey, & Parnaby, above note 19 at 283–88.

63 See Jean Paul Brodeur, "Legitimizing Police Deviance" in Clifford Shearing, ed, *Organized Police Deviance* (Toronto: Butterworths, 1982) at 157.

64 Commission of Inquiry Concerning Certain Activities of the RCMP, *Freedom and Security under the Law* (Ottawa: Supply and Services, 1981) at 268–75.
65 *Ibid* at 518.
66 *Ibid*.
67 *Ibid* at 592 (Recommendation 26).
68 *Ibid* at 436.
69 Whitaker, Kealey, & Parnaby, above note 19 at 360.
70 *Ibid* at 359.
71 See RS Ratner, "Lobbying the Senate" (1984) 7:1 *Parliamentary Review* 8.
72 Standing Senate Committee on National Security and Defence, "Issue 15 — Evidence" (30 March 2015) (Chair: Daniel Lang), online: www.parl.gc.ca/content/sen/committee/412/SECD/15EV-52013-E.HTM [Senate Committee on National Security and Defence].
73 Special Senate Committee on the Canadian Intelligence Service, *Delicate Balance: A Security Intelligence Service in a Democratic Society* (November 1983) at 24 (Chair: Michael Pitfield) [Pitfield Report].
74 *Ibid* at 25.
75 *Ibid* at 32.
76 *Ibid*.
77 Senate Committee on National Security and Defence, above note 72.
78 Pitfield Report, above note 73 at 29.
79 *Ibid* at 29.
80 Quoted in "Ottawa Abolishes Spy Overseer Role" *National Post* (26 April 2012).
81 Pitfield Report, above note 73 at 31.
82 *Ibid* at 31.
83 Senate, Standing Committee on National Security and Defence, *Minutes of Proceedings and Evidence*, 41st Parl, 2d Sess (9 December 2013), testimony of Hon Chuck Strahl, Chair of the Security Intelligence Review Committee.
84 *SoCIS Act*, above note 32.
85 Commission of Inquiry into the Investigation of the Bombing of Air India Flight 182, *The Families Remember* (Ottawa: Public Works, 2007) at 102.
86 *R v Malik and Bagri*, [2005] BCSC 350 [*Malik and Bagri*].
87 See *Charkaoui v Canada*, 2008 SCC 38 [*Charkaoui*].
88 *Ibid* at para 49.
89 Commission of Inquiry into the Investigation of the Bombing of Air India Flight 182, *Air India Flight 182: A Canadian Tragedy — The Overview*, vol 1 (Ottawa: Public Works, 2010) at 28 [Air India Inquiry I].
90 *Ibid*.
91 Terry Millewski, "Ottawa Shooting: Federal Security Chiefs Warned Days before an Attack" *CBC News* (24 November 2014), online: www.cbc.ca/news/politics/ottawa-shooting-federal-security-chiefs-warned-days-before-attack-1.2847552; Stewart Bell, "Three Days before Ottawa Terror Attack, Alarm Bells Were Sounding, Intelligence Reports Show" *National Post* (1 March 2015), online: http://news.nationalpost.com/news/canada/security-forces-braced-for-terror-attacks-over-canadas-enhanced-profile-before-ottawa-shooting.
92 Air India Inquiry I, above note 89 at 116.

93 The four men involved in the shooting of Malkiad Singh Sidhu were convicted of attempted murder and sentenced to twenty years: Kent Roach, *The Unique Challenges of Terrorism Prosecutions* (Ottawa: Public Works, 2010) at 98.

94 Commission of Inquiry into the Investigation of the Bombing of Air India Flight 182, *Air India Flight 182: A Canadian Tragedy — Post Bombing*, vol 2 (Ottawa: Public Works, 2010) at 477 [Air India Inquiry II].

95 Quoted in Roach, above note 93 at 112.

96 See *R v Khela* (1998), 126 CCC (3d) 341 (Que CA).

97 Air India Inquiry II, above note 94 at 514–15.

98 See *ibid* at 196.

99 *Malik and Bagri*, above note 86 at para 1232. He elaborated, *ibid* at para 1236: "These statements were provided on a confidential basis and not under oath by a person who falsely claimed loss of memory when testifying."

100 Air India Inquiry II, above note 94 at 222–4.

101 SC 2013, c 29.

102 RSC 1985, c C-5.

103 See *R v Basi*, 2009 SCC 52.

104 *R v Ahmad*, 2011 SCC 6.

105 Commission of Inquiry into the Investigation of the Bombing of Air India Flight 182, *Air India Flight 182: A Canadian Tragedy — The Relationship between Intelligence and Evidence and the Challenges of Terrorism Prosecutions*, vol 3 (Ottawa: Public Works, 2010) at 142.

106 *Charkaoui*, above note 87 at para 43.

107 Richard Fadden, "Remarks" (29 November 2009), online: www.casis-acers.ca/wp-content/uploads/2014/06/Dick-Fadden-CSIS-Speech-To-CASIS-OCT-09.pdf.

108 SC 2001, c 41 [*ATA*].

109 *Criminal Code*, above note 4, s 83.01.

110 *Ibid*, s 83.01(1.1).

111 *Khawaja*, above note 5 at para 82.

112 *Re Section 83.28 of the Criminal Code*, 2004 SCC 42.

113 *Criminal Code*, above note 4, s 810.01(1).

114 See *R v Budreo* (2000), 46 OR (3d) 481 (CA).

115 "Sister of Slain Soldier Delivers Emotional Appeal for Bill C-51" *Toronto Star* (23 March 2015).

116 Commonwealth of Australia and State of New South Wales, *Martin Place Siege: Joint Commonwealth–New South Wales Review* (Canberra: January 2015), online: www.dpmc.gov.au/sites/default/files/publications/170215_Martin_Place_Siege_Review_1.pdf.

117 See, for example, Gary Trotter "The Anti-terrorism Bill and Preventive Restrains on Liberty" in Ronald Daniels, Patrick Macklem, & Kent Roach, eds, *The Security of Freedom: Essays on Canada's Anti-terrorism Bill* (Toronto: University of Toronto Press, 2001) at 241 and 244.

118 See Kent Roach & Craig Forcese, "Legislating in Fearful and Politicized Times: The Limits of Bill C-51's Disruption Powers in Making Us Safer" in Iacobucci & Toope, above note 8 at 154.

119 *Criminal Code*, above note 4, s 83.3(2), as amended by SC 2001, c 41, s 4.

120 House of Commons, *Hansard* (26 February 2007) at 7333.

121 House of Commons Subcommittee on the Review of the *Anti-terrorism Act*, "Investigative Hearings and Recognizance with Conditions" (October 2006) (Chairs: Garry Breitkreuz & Gord Brown); Special Senate Committee on the *Anti-terrorism Act*, "Fundamental Justice in Extraordinary Times" (February 2007) (Chair: David P Smith).

122 House of Commons Subcommittee on the Review of the *Anti-terrorism Act*, "Review of the *Anti-terrorism Act*: Rights, Limits, Security: A Comprehensive Review of the Anti-terrorism Act and Related Issues" (March 2007).

123 *Ibid* at 12.

124 *Suresh v Canada*, 2002 SCC 1 at para 78.

125 Special Senate Committee on the *Anti-terrorism Act*, *Fundamental Justice in Extraordinary Times* (February 2007).

126 *Combatting Terrorism Act*, SC 2013, c 9.

127 *Criminal Code*, above note 4, s 83.32(1).

128 See Canadian Bar Association, *Submissions on Bill C-42* (February 2002) at 11.

129 *Aeronautics Act*, RSC 1985, c A-2, ss 4.76 & 4.77.

130 *Identity Screening Regulations*, SOR/2007-82.

131 SI/81-86, s 10.1 [*Passport Order*].

132 *Economic Action Plan 2015 Act, No. 1*, SC 2015, c 36.

133 *Strengthening Canadian Citizenship Act*, SC 2014, c 22, s 8, amending *Citizenship Act*, RSC 1985, c C-29, ss 10 & 10.1.

134 See *Khawaja*, above note 5.

135 For United Kingdom statistics, see United Kingdom Home Office, *Operation of Police Powers under the Terrorism Act 2000 and Subsequent Legislation: Arrests, Outcomes and Stops and Searches, Quarterly Update to 31 December 2014* (25 June 2015), Table A-13, showing total convictions of 452, with 41 being "Northern Ireland related."

136 James Hugessen, "Watching the Watchers: Democratic Oversight" in David Daubney et al, eds, *Terrorism, Law and Democracy: How Is Canada Changing Following September 11* (Montreal: Edition Themis, 2002) at 384–6.

137 *Charkaoui v Canada*, 2007 SCC 9.

138 *An Act to Amend the Immigration and Refugee Protection Act (Certificate and Special Advocate) and to Make a Consequential Amendment to Another Act*, SC 2008, c 3.

139 2014 SCC 37.

140 *Ibid*.

141 *CSIS Act*, above note 28, s 18.1(4)(b), as amended by SC 2015, c 9, s 7.

142 2009 FC 1263 at paras 163 and 438.

143 "Submission of the Special Advocates to the Standing Committee on Public Safety and National Security Re: Bill C-51" (on file with the authors).

144 See, for example, *Re Mahjoub*, 2011 FC 506.

145 See Colin Freeze, "Under Constant Watch, Terror Suspect Seeks Return to Prison" *Globe and Mail* (18 March 2009).

146 See, for example, Colin Perkel, "Jahanzeb Malik Ordered Out of Canada" *CBC News* (5 June 2015), online: www.cbc.ca/news/canada/toronto/jahanzeb-malik-ordered-out-of-canada-1.3102070.

147 Commission of Inquiry into the Actions of Canadian Officials in relation to Maher Arar, *Analysis and Recommendations* (Ottawa: Public Works, 2006) at 13.

148 *Ibid* at 345.

149 Jean Chrétien et al, "A Close Eye on Security Makes Us All Safer" *Globe and Mail* (18 February 2015), online: www.theglobeandmail.com/globe-debate/a-close-eye-on-security-makes-canadians-safer/article23069152/.

150 Undated government document, online: www.champlaw.ca/images/uploads/casedocuments/benatta/CdnDocuments.pdf.

151 SIRC, *Annual Report 2006–7* at 20.

152 *Ibid* at 22.

153 See Michelle Shephard, *Guantanamo's Child: The Untold Story of Omar Khadr* (Mississauga, ON: John Wiley & Sons Canada, 2008).

154 SIRC, *CSIS's Role in the Matter of Omar Khadr* (July 8, 2009), online: www.sirc-csars.gc.ca/opbapb/2008-05/index-eng.html.

155 *Ibid.*

156 *Khadr v Canada*, 2005 FC 1076.

157 *OK v Bush*, 377 F Supp 2d 102 at 111 (DDC 2005).

158 *Canada v Khadr*, 2010 SCC 3 at para 5.

159 *Re X*, 2013 FC 1275, aff'd 2014 FCA 249.

160 See Craig Forcese, *National Security Law* (Toronto: Irwin Law, 2008) at 260–1; E Dosman, "For the Record" (2004) 62 *University of Toronto Faculty Law Review* 1.

161 See *Abdelrazik v Canada (Minister of Foreign Affairs)*, 2009 FC 580 at para 91.

162 *Ibid.*

163 SC 2015, c 20, s 11.

164 SC 2015, c 36, s 42.

165 See *Secure Air Travel Act*, above note 163, s 8; *Passport Order*, above note 131, s 10.1; *Prevention of Terrorist Travel Act*, above note 164, ss 4 & 5.

166 *Passport Order*, above note 131, s 10.1, as amended by SI/2004-113, s 5.

167 *Order Amending the Canadian Passport Order*, SI/2015-33, s 4.

168 See *Secure Air Travel Act*, above note 163, s 10.

169 See *ibid*, ss 16(6) (e) & (f); *Prevention of Terrorist Travel Act*, above note 164, ss 4(4) (e) & (f).

CHAPTER THREE: THREAT

1 "Osama's List" *National Post* (14 November 2002) A15.

2 See, for example, Commons Subcommittee on National Security of the Standing Committee on Justice and Human Rights, "Evidence" (1 April 2003), (Chair: Derek Lee), online: www.parl.gc.ca/HousePublications/Publication.aspx?DocId=808452&Mode=1&Language=E; Special Senate Committee on the Anti-terrorism Act, "Issue 18 — Evidence" (31 October 2005), (Chair: Joyce Fairbairn), online: www.parl.gc.ca/Content/SEN/Committee/381/anti/18eva-e.htm?comm_id=597&Language=E&Parl=38&Ses=1.

3 See Integrated Terrorist Assessment Centre, *Threat Assessment: Canada — Biannual Update on Terrorist and Extremist Threats* (19 April 2012) (12-35-E) at para 8.

4 Quoted in Keith Gerein, "RCMP Investigating Al-Shabab Video Calling for Terrorist Attack on West Edmonton Mall" *National Post* (22 February 2015), online: news.nationalpost.com/news/canada/al-shababs-call-for-attack-on-west-edmonton-mall-does-not-pose-imminent-threat-to-canadians-rcmp.

5 See CSIS, "Somalia and al Shabaab," online: www.csis.gc.ca/ththrtnvrnmnt/trrrsm/smlnl-shbb-en.php.

6   See RCMP, News Release, "First Individual Convicted in Canada for Attempting to Participate in International Terrorist Activity" (30 May 2014), online: www.rcmp-grc.gc.ca/en/news/2014/30/first-individual-convicted-canada-attempting-participate-international-terrorist.

7   See Stewart Bell, "They Realized What They Were Doing Was Wrong: Two Canadians Quit Extremist Group, al Shabab" *National Post* (12 September 2013), online: news.nationalpost.com/news/canada/al-shabab.

8   Colin Freeze & Joe Friesen, "Why the Canadian Pipeline to al Shabab Dried Up" *Globe and Mail* (30 September 2013).

9   See "Memo for Assistant Deputy Minister United States Department of State Countering Violent Extremism Project in Canada" (undated), Access to Information Request A-2014-00202.

10 "Stephen Harper Condemns ISIS Audio Urging Attacks on Canadians" *CBC News* (21 September 2014), online: www.cbc.ca/m/touch/news/story/1.2773636.

11 See "Message of the Mujhaid 5" (8 December 2014), online: ringoffirenews.files.wordpress.com/2014/12/transcript.pdf. See also Stewart Bell, "ISIS Fighter from Ottawa Appears in Video Threatening Canada with Attacks 'Where It Hurts Most'" *National Post* (7 December 2014).

12 RSC 1985, c 22 (4th Supp).

13 Quoted in Associated Press, "ISIS must be fought 'by any means necessary,' diplomats say" *CBC News* (15 September 2014), online: www.cbc.ca/news/world/isis-must-be-fought-by-any-means-necessary-diplomats-say-1.2766247.

14 Commons, *House of Commons Debates (Hansard)*, 41st Parl, 2d Sess, (24 March 2015) (Hon Andrew Scheer), online: www.parl.gc.ca/HousePublications/Publication.aspx?Doc=188&Language=E&Mode=1&Parl=41&Pub=Hansard&Ses=2.

15 Standing Committee on Foreign Affairs and International Development, "Evidence" (29 January 2015), (Chairs: Peter Kent & Dean Allison), online: www.parl.gc.ca/HousePublications/Publication.aspx?DocId=6846230&Language=E&Mode=1.

16 Standing Committee on Foreign Affairs and International Development, "Evidence" (9 September 2014) (Chair: Dean Allison), online: www.parl.gc.ca/HousePublications/Publication.aspx?DocId=6690807&Language=E&Mode=1.

17 See Nick Logan, "Analysis: Breaking down the ISIS threat to Canada" *Global News* (25 September 2014), online: globalnews.ca/news/1581616/analysis-breaking-down-the-isis-threat-to-canada/.

18 Thomas Juneau, *Canada's Policy to Confront the Islamic State* (Ottawa: Canadian Defence and Foreign Affairs Institute, May 2015) at 4, online: d3n8a8pro7vhmx.cloudfront.net/cdfai/pages/536/attachments/original/1431041975/Canadas_Policy_to_Confront_the_Islamic_State.pdf?1431041975.

19 See Ipsos-Reid, "Three Quarters (73%) of Canadians Support Use of Canadian Ground Troops in the War against ISIS to Stop It from Gaining Own State" (31 December 2014), online: www.ipsos-na.com/news-polls/pressrelease.aspx?id=6719.

20 Prime Minister Harper, *PM Welcomes Chancellor Angela Merkel to Ottawa* (Ottawa: Government of Canada, 9 February 2015), online: http://pm.gc.ca/eng/news/2015/02/09/pm-welcomes-german-chancellor-angela-merkel-ottawa.

21   Bill C-51, *An Act to enact the Security of Canada Information Sharing Act and the Secure Air Travel Act, to amend the Criminal Code, the Canadian Security Intelligence Service Act and the Immigration and Refugee Protection Act and to make related and consequential amendments to other Acts*, 2d Sess, 41st Parl, 2015 (assented to 18 June 2015), SC 2015, c 20.

22   Prime Minister Harper, *PM Announces Anti-terrorism Measures to Protect Canadians* (30 January 2015), online: http://pm.gc.ca/eng/news/2015/01/30/pm-announces-anti-terrorism-measures-protect-canadians-0.

23   Steven Pinker, *The Better Angels of Our Nature: Why Violence Has Declined* (New York: Viking, 2011).

24   Quoted in Jessica Stern & JM Berger, *ISIS: The State of Terror* (New York: Harper Collins, 2015) at 236 (pinpoint to Ecco e-book version).

25   Public Safety Canada, "2014 Public Report on the Terrorist Threat to Canada" (2014) at 9, online: www.publicsafety.gc.ca/cnt/rsrcs/pblctns/2014-pblc-rpr-trrrst-thrt/2014-pblc-rpr-trrrst-thrt-eng.pdf.

26   See Standing Senate Committee on National Security and Defence, "Evidence" (20 April 2015) (Chair: Daniel Lang), online: www.parl.gc.ca/content/sen/committee/412/SECD/52040-E.HTM, Michel Coulombe, director, CSIS: "the terrorist threat to Canada's national security interests has never been as direct or immediate."

27   "Harper says 'Islamicism' biggest threat to Canada" *CBC News* (6 September 2011), online: www.cbc.ca/news/politics/harper-says-islamicism-biggest-threat-to-canada-1.1048280.

28   See David Cook, *Understanding Jihad* (Berkeley, CA: University of California Press, 2005) ch 1 in particular; Abdullah Saeed, "Jihad and Violence: Changing Understandings of Jihad among Muslims" in Tony Coady & Michael P O'Keefe, eds, *Terrorism and Justice: Moral Argument in a Threatened World* (Mebourne: Melbourne University Press, 2002).

29   Clark McCauley & Sophia Moskalenko, "Toward a Profile of Lone Wolf Terrorists: What Moves an Individual from Radical Opinion to Radical Action" (2014) 26 *Terrorism and Political Violence* 69 at 70.

30   See, for example, CSIS, "Threat Overview: Presentation to the Office of the Minister of Public Safety" (18 September 2014); CSIS, *Public Report 2013–2014* (Ottawa: CSIS, 2015) at 23, online: www.csis-scrs.gc.ca/pblctns/nnlrprt/2013-2014/2013-2014_Public_Report_Inside_ENG.pdf.

31   Canada, *Securing an Open Society: Canada's National Security Policy* (Ottawa: Privy Council Office, 2004). For a defence of this "all risk" approach to security threats, see Kent Roach, *September 11: Consequences for Canada* (Montreal: McGill-Queen's University Press, 2003) ch 7.

32   Canada, "Building Resilience against Terrorism: Canada's Counter-terrorism Strategy" (2012), online: www.publicsafety.gc.ca/cnt/rsrcs/pblctns/rslnc-gnst-trrrsm/index-eng.aspx.

33   See Michelle Shephard, "Right-Wing Extremism a Greater Threat in North America", *Toronto Star* (28 June 2015), online: www.thestar.com/news/world/2015/06/28/right-wing-extremism-a-greater-threat-in-north-america.html.

34 See, for example, James Ellis & Richard Parent, *Right-Wing Extremism in Canada* (2014) TSAS WP 13-03, online: library.tsas.ca/entries/right-wing-extremism-in-canada-2/; Yi-Yuan Su & Sue-Ming Yang, *Eco-terrorism and the Corresponding Legislative Efforts to Intervene and Prevent Future Attacks* (2014) TSAS WP 14-04, online: library.tsas.ca/entries/eco-terrorism-and-the-corresponding-legislative-efforts-to-intervene-and-prevent-future-attacks/; Aurelie Campana & Samuel Tanner, *The Process of Radicalization: Right-Wing Skinheads in Quebec* (2014) TSAS WP 14-07, online: library.tsas.ca/entries/tsas-wp-14-07-the-process-of-radicalization-right-wing-skinheads-in-quebec/.

35 See CSIS, *Public Report 2013–2014*, above note 30 at 23; CSIS, *Intelligence Assessment: 2012 Domestic Threat Environment in Canada (Part I) — Left-Wing/Right-Wing Extremism* (CSIS IA 2011-12/115) (23 March 2012).

36 See, for example, RCMP, *Critical Infrastructure Intelligence Assessment: Criminal Threats to the Canadian Petroleum Industry* (21 January 2013).

37 Standing Senate Committee on National Security and Defence, *Countering the Terrorist Threat in Canada* (July 2015) at 1–2, online: www.parl.gc.ca/Content/SEN/Committee/412/secd/rep/rep18jul15-e.pdf.

38 Public Safety Canada, above note 25.

39 CSIS, "Threat Overview," above note 30.

40 *Ibid.*

41 CSIS, *Public Report 2013–2014*, above note 30 at 16.

42 See Public Safety Canada, above note 25 at 3.

43 S/Res/2178 (2014).

44 Integrated Terrorist Assessment Centre, above note 3 at para 10.

45 *Ibid.*

46 Thomas Hegghammer, "The Rise of Muslim Foreign Fighters: Islam and the Globalization of Jihad" (2010/11) 35 *International Security* 53 at 55. For an elaboration on foreign fighter issues discussed in this section, see Craig Forcese & Ani Mamikon, "Neutrality Law, Anti-terrorism and Foreign Fighters: Legal Solutions to the Recruitment of Canadians to Foreign Insurgencies" 48:2 *UBC Law Review* 305 [forthcoming in 2015].

47 J Skidmore, "Foreign Fighter Involvement in Syria" *International Institute for Counter-terrorism* (January 2014) at 11, online: www.ict.org.il/Article/26/Foreign%20Fighter%20Involvement%20in%20Syria.

48 Hegghammer, above note 46 at 55.

49 David Malet, *Foreign Fighters: Transnational Identity in Civil Conflicts* (Oxford, UK: Oxford University Press, 2013) at 9.

50 Thomas Hegghammer, "Should I Stay or Should I Go? Explaining Variation in Western Jihadists' Choice between Domestic and Foreign Fighting" (2013) 107 *American Political Science Review* 1 at 1.

51 Hegghammer, above note 46 at 55.

52 See Joseph A Carter, Shiraz Maher, & Peter R Neumann, *#Greenbirds: Measuring Importance and Influence in Syrian Foreign Fighter Networks* (London: International Centre for the Study of Radicalisation and Political Violence, 2014) at 9–10, online: icsr.info/wp-content/uploads/2014/04/ICSR-Report-Greenbirds-Measuring-Importance-and-Infleunce-in-Syrian-Foreign-Fighter-Networks.pdf. See also Skidmore, above note 47 at 10.

53 Hegghammer, above note 46 at 90. The two exceptions were the Spanish Civil War in the 1930s (International Brigades) and the 1948 Arab-Israeli War (Jewish volunteers): *ibid*.

54 See *ibid* at 60.

55 See Jennifer Mustapha, "The *Mujahideen* in Bosnia: The Foreign Fighter as Cosmopolitan Citizen and/or Terrorist" (2013) 17 *Citizenship Studies* 742.

56 See Hegghammer, above note 46 at 60.

57 See *ibid* at 79ff.

58 See *ibid* at 89.

59 See *ibid* at 55.

60 See *ibid* at 2.

61 See CSIS, *2011–2013 Public Report*, Catalogue No PS71 (Ottawa: CSIS, 2014) at 27, online: www.csis-scrs.gc.ca/pblctns/nnlrprt/2011-2013/index-en.php.

62 Richard Barrett, *Foreign Fighters in Syria* (The Soufan Group, June 2014) at 7, online: soufangroup.com/wp-content/uploads/2014/06/TSG-Foreign-Fighters-in-Syria.pdf.

63 Barak Mendelsohn, "Foreign Fighters — Recent Trends" (2011) 55:2 *Orbis* 189 at 191.

64 *Ibid*.

65 Hegghammer, above note 46 at 89.

66 See Public Safety Canada, "Currently Listed Entities," online: www.publicsafety.gc.ca/cnt/ntnl-scrt/cntr-trrrsm/lstd-ntts/crrnt-lstd-ntts-eng.aspx#2009.

67 RSC 1985, c C-46, s 83.01(1), definition of "terrorist group."

68 See Public Safety Canada, above note 66.

69 See *ibid*.

70 See Forcese & Mamikon, above note 46.

71 Hegghammer, above note 50 at 4.

72 *Ibid* at 5.

73 *Ibid* at 3.

74 *Ibid* at 7.

75 *Ibid* at 13.

76 See *ibid* at 10.

77 *Ibid* at 11.

78 See Skidmore, above note 47 at 5.

79 See Carter, Maher, & Neumann, above note 52 at 7.

80 Skidmore, above note 47 at 5.

81 See Carter, Maher, & Neumann, above note 52 at 7.

82 See CSIS, above note 61 at 13.

83 See *ibid* at 14.

84 See Christopher M Blanchard, *Armed Conflict in Syria: Overview and U.S. Response* RL33487 (Congressional Research Service, Washington DC: 17 September 2014) at 9.

85 See Michael Weiss & Hassan Hassan, *ISIS: Inside the Army of Terror* (New York: Regan Arts, 2015) at 30.

86 See "Foreign Fighters under International Law" *Geneva Academy of International Humanitarian Law and Human Rights* (October 2014) at 11.

87 See Weiss & Hassan, above note 85 at 102–3.

88 See Blanchard, above note 84 at 1 and 10; Robin Yassin-Kassab, "The rise and fall of ISIL in Syria" *Al Jazeera* (19 January 2014), online: www.aljazeera.com/indepth/opinion/2014/01/rise-fall-isil-syria-2014115729257997332.html.

89 See Mario Abou Zeid, "Assad's Last Battle" *Al Jazeera* (11 May 2015), online: www.aljazeera.com/indepth/opinion/2015/05/assad-hezbollah-qalamoun-150509053528098.html; David Blair, "How Assad Helped the Rise of His 'Foe' ISIL" *Telegraph* (22 August 2014), online: www.telegraph.co.uk/news/worldnews/middleeast/syria/11051566/How-Assad-helped-the-rise-of-his-foe-Isil.html.

90 Quoted in Simon Cordall, "How Syria's Assad Helped Forge ISIS" *Newsweek* (21 June 2014), online: www.newsweek.com/how-syrias-assad-helped-forge-isis-255631.

91 See Shane Harris, "The Re-Baathification of Iraq" *Foreign Policy* (21 August 2014), online: foreignpolicy.com/2014/08/21/the-re-baathification-of-iraq/.

92 Quoted in Stern & Berger, above note 24 at 37.

93 See Kenneth Katzman et al, *The "Islamic State" Crisis and U.S. Policy*, R43612, (Congressional Research Service, Washington, DC: 12 November 2014) at 5.

94 Remarks at the Brookings Institution by NCTC Director Matthew G Olsen (3 September 2014).

95 See Raffaello Pantucci & Clare Ellis, Briefing Paper, "The Threat of ISIS to the UK: RUSI Threat Assessment" (London: Royal United Services Institute, October 2014) at 3, online: www.rusi.org/downloads/assets/102014_ISIS_Threat_Assessment.pdf.

96 See Stewart Bell, "ISIS Urges Jihadists to Attack Canadians" *National Post* (21 September 2014), online: news.nationalpost.com/2014/09/21/isis-urges-jihadists-to-attack-canadians-you-will-not-feel-secure-in-your-bedrooms; "Stephen Harper Condemns ISIS Audio Urging Attacks on Canadians" *CBC News* (21 September 2014), online: www.cbc.ca/news/world/stephen-harper-condemns-isis-audio-urging-attacks-on-canadians-1.2773636; "Ottawa Man Urges Attacks on Canadians in Purported ISIS Video" *CTV News* (7 December 2014), online: www.ctvnews.ca/world/ottawa-man-urges-attacks-on-canadians-in-purported-isis-video-1.2136780; Stewart Bell, "ISIS Spokesman Calls for More Ottawa-Style Attacks in Canada, Warning 'What Lies Ahead Will Be Worse'" *National Post* (26 January 2015), online: news.nationalpost.com/news/world/isis-spokesman-calls-for-more-ottawa-style-attacks-in-canada-warning-what-lies-ahead-will-be-worse.

97 Office of the Prime Minister of Canada, "Statement by the Prime Minister in the House of Commons" (3 October 2014), online: http://pm.gc.ca/eng/news/2014/10/03/statement-prime-minister-canada-house-commons.

98 See National Defence and the Canadian Armed Forces, "Operation IMPACT," online: www.forces.gc.ca/en/operations-abroad-current/op-impact.page.

99 *Ibid.*

100 Juneau, above note 18 at 3ff.

101 See Public Safety, *2014 Public Report on the Terrorist Threat to Canada* (Ottawa: Public Safety, 2014) at 3, online: www.publicsafety.gc.ca/cnt/rsrcs/pblctns/2014-pblc-rpr-trrrst-thrt/2014-pblc-rpr-trrrst-thrt-eng.pdf.

102 See Daniel Leblanc & Colin Freeze, "RCMP Investigating Dozens of Suspected Extremists Who Returned to Canada" *Globe and Mail* (8 October 2014), online: www.theglobeandmail.com/news/politics/rcmp-investigating-dozens-of-suspected-extremists-who-returned-to-canada/article20991206/.

103 Standing Senate Committee on National Security and Defence, *Countering the Terrorist Threat in Canada* (July 2015) at iii, online: www.parl.gc.ca/Content/SEN/ Committee/412/secd/rep/rep18jul15-e.pdf.

104 Canada, "Question Period Note: Interventions to Deal with Terrorist Travellers" (Undated), Public Safety ATIP A-2014-00202(2) at 89 (of PDF File).

105 See Ian Macleod, "Spymaster Warns Foreign Fighter Phenomenon Getting Worse" *Ottawa Citizen* (20 April 2015), online: ottawacitizen.com/news/politics/ number-of-canadian-extremist-fighters-abroad-up-50-per-cent-spymaster-says.

106 Quoted in Stewart Bell, "'Regular Canadian' Killed in Syria Conflict Featured in Slick, New ISIS Propaganda Video" *National Post* (11 July 2014), online: news. nationalpost.com/news/canada/regular-canadian-killed-in-syria-conflict-featured- in-slick-new-isis-propaganda-video.

107 See Benjamin Aubé, "Crown recalls curious case of Andre Poulin" *Timmins Press* (17 January 2014), online: www.timminspress.com/2014/01/17/crown-recalls- curious-case-of-andre-poulin.

108 Michael Schmidt, "Canadian killed in Syria Lives On as a Pitchman for Jihadis" *New York Times* (15 July 2014).

109 See "Timmins-Born Ontario Jihadist Recruited 5" *CBC News* (2 March 2015), online: www.cbc.ca/news/world/timmins-ont-born-jihadist-recruited-5-others- for-isis-1.2978988.

110 Stern & Berger, above note 24 at 86.

111 Quoted in Bell, above note 106.

112 Quoted in Stern & Berger, above note 24 at 87.

113 Ibid.

114 Bell, above note 106.

115 "Damian Clairmont Killed While Fighting with al-Qaeda linked rebels in Syria" *CBC News* (15 January 2014), online: www.cbc.ca/news/world/ damian-clairmont-killed-fighting-with-al-qaeda-linked-rebels-in-syria-1.2497513.

116 See Michelle Shephard, "Toronto 18: Ali Dirie Convicted in Plot Dies in Syria" *Toronto Star* (25 September 2013).

117 See "Toronto 18 Member Ali Dirie Was under Strict Court Order" *CBC News* (26 September 2013), online: www.cbc.ca/news/toronto-18-member-ali-mohamed- dirie-was-under-strict-court-order-1.1870190.

118 See "Toronto 18 Member Ali Mohamed Dirie Reportedly Dead in Syria" *CBC News* (25 September 2013), online: www.cbc.ca/news/world/toronto-18-member- ali-mohamed-dirie-reportedly-died-in-syria-1.1868119.

119 See "John Maguire, Ottawa Man Fighting for ISIS, Urges Attacks on Canadian Targets in Video" *CBC News* (7 December 2014), online: www.cbc.ca/news/ world/john-maguire-ottawa-man-fighting-for-isis-urges-attacks-on-canadian- targets-in-video-1.2863655.

120 Natalie Clancy, "ISIS Recruited Canadian Woman to Join Fight in Syria" *CBC News* (25 February 2015), online: www.cbc.ca/news/world/isis-recruiter-in- edmonton-enlists-canadian-woman-to-join-fight-in-syria-1.2970535.

121 *Ibid.*

122 *Ibid.*

123 "Martin Couture-Rouleau, Hit-and-Run Driver, Arrested by RCMP in July" *CBC News* (21 October 2014), online: www.cbc.ca/news/canada/montreal/ martin-couture-rouleau-hit-and-run-driver-arrested-by-rcmp-in-july-1.2807078.

124 Commonwealth of Australia and State of New South Wales, *Martin Place Siege: Joint Commonwealth–New South Wales Review* (Canberra: January 2015), online: www.dpmc.gov.au/sites/default/files/publications/170215_Martin_Place_Siege_Review_1.pdf.

125 See Mark Gollom & Tracey Lindeman, "Who Is Martin Couture-Rouleau?" *CBC News* (21 October 2014), online: www.cbc.ca/news/canada/who-is-martin-couture-rouleau-1.2807285.

126 Tonda MacCharles, "Parliament Hill Shooter Calm in Video Shot Minutes before Attack" *Toronto Star* (6 March 2015), online: www.thestar.com/news/canada/2015/03/06/parliament-hill-shooter-calm-in-video-shot-minutes-before-attack.html; RCMP, "Commissioner Paulson's Appearance at SECU on the Zehaf-Bibeau Video" (5 March 2015), online: www.rcmp-grc.gc.ca/en/news/2015/6/commissioner-paulsons-appearance-secu-zehaf-bibeau-video.

127 MacCharles, above note 126.

128 See Bibi T van Ginkel, *Responding to Cyber Jihad: Towards an Effective Counter Narrative* (The Hague: The International Centre for Counter-terrorism, 2015) at 2–3.

129 See *ibid.*

130 See Ian MacLeod, "Boost in Anti-terror Staffing 'Unprecedented,' Says RCMP Chief" *Ottawa Citizen* (7 March 2015), online: ottawacitizen.com/news/politics/rcmp-hunting-for-terror-accomplices-of-zehaf-bibeau-paulson.

131 RCMP, "15-Year-Old Montréal Resident Charged with Terrorism" (3 December 2014), online: www.rcmp-grc.gc.ca/qc/nouv-news/com-rel/2014/12/141203-eng.htm.

132 Josh Elliot, "Montreal Teen Pleads Not Guilty to Terror Charges" *CTV News* (undated), online: www.ctvnews.ca/canada/montreal-teen-pleads-not-guilty-to-terror-charges-1.2132705.

133 "Suliman Mohamed Accused by RCMP of Participating in Terrorist Group" *CBC News* (12 January 2015), online: www.cbc.ca/news/canada/ottawa/suliman-mohamed-accused-by-rcmp-of-participating-in-terrorist-group-1.2898135.

134 See Nazim Baksh & Adrienne Arsenault, "Terrorism Related Charges Laid against Ottawa Men with Alleged ISIS Ties" *CBC News* (3 February 2015), online: www.cbc.ca/news/canada/terrorism-related-charges-laid-against-ottawa-men-with-alleged-isis-ties-1.2943313.

135 Michelle Shephard, "Islamic State Canadian Fighter Reported Dead" *Toronto Star* (20 March 2015), online: www.thestar.com/news/world/2015/03/20/islamic-state-canadian-fighter-reported-dead.html.

136 See Evan Dyer, "Awso Peshdary, Terrorism Suspect: Who Is He?" *CBC News* (3 February 2015), online: www.cbc.ca/news/canada/ottawa/awso-peshdary-terrorism-suspect-who-is-he-1.2943955.

137 See "Terror-Related Charges Laid against Edmonton Teen" *CBC News* (21 March 2015), online: www.cbc.ca/news/canada/edmonton/terror-related-charges-laid-against-edmonton-area-teen-1.3003232.

138 See Stewart Bell, "Terrorist Threat Has 'Never Been as Direct or as Immediate': CSIS Boss" *National Post* (20 April 2015), online: news.nationalpost.com/news/canada/terrorist-threat-to-canada-has-never-been-as-direct-or-immediate-csis-boss.

139 See "Montreal Teens Charged with Terror-Related Offences" *CBC News* (20 April 2015), online: www.cbc.ca/news/canada/montreal/montreal-teens-charged-with-terror-related-offences-1.3040534.

140 See "Othman Ayed Hamdan Arrested, Facing Terror Charges" *CBC News* (10 July 2015), online: www.cbc.ca/news/canada/british-columbia/ othman-ayed-hamdan-arrested-facing-terrorism-charges-1.3147663.

141 Michelle Shephard, "Amanda Lindhout Speaks Out on Arrest of Somali Man Accused in Kidnapping" *Toronto Star* (14 June 2015), online: www.thestar. com/news/canada/2015/06/14/amanda-lindhout-speaks-out-after-man-accused-in-kidnapping-arrested.html; RCMP, "RCMP Makes an Arrest as Part of Project SLYPE" (12 June 2015), online: www.rcmp-grc.gc.ca/en/news/2015/12/ rcmp-makes-arrest-part-project-slype.

142 See "Hasibullah Yusufzai, of Burnaby, B.C., Faces Terror-Related Charge" *CBC News* (23 July 2014), online: www.cbc.ca/news/canada/british-columbia/ hasibullah-yusufzai-of-burnaby-b-c-faces-terror-related-charge-1.2715769.

143 RCMP, "RCMP Lay Terrorism-Related Charges" (2011), online: www.rcmp-grc.gc.ca/mb/publications/making-difference-faire-difference-vol1/terrorism-terrorisme-eng.htm.

144 See Allan Woods, "Montreal Man Ordered to Cut Ties with Extremists under Rare Peace Bond" *Toronto Star* (27 March 2015), online: www.thestar.com/news/ canada/2015/03/27/montreal-man-ordered-to-cut-contacts-with-terrorists-under-rare-peace-bond.html.

145 Steve Rilavoma, "Merouane Ghalmi Charged with Breaking Conditions of Terror Related Peace Bond" *CBC News* (8 May 2015), online: www.cbc.ca/news/canada/ montreal/merouane-ghalmi-charged-with-breaking-conditions-of-terror-related-peace-bond-1.3067151.

146 See "Daniel Minto Darko Second Quebecer to Sign Terrorism Linked Peace Bond" *CBC News* (10 April 2015), online: www.cbc.ca/news/canada/montreal/ daniel-minta-darko-2nd-quebecer-to-sign-terrorism-linked-peace-bond-1.3028013.

147 See "Terrorism Related Peace Bond for Seyed Amir Hossein Raisolsadat Extended" *CBC News* (22 May 2015), online: www.cbc.ca/news/canada/prince-edward-island/terrorism-related-peace-bond-for-seyed-amir-hossein-raisolsadat-extended-1.3083226.

148 See Allan Woods, "RCMP Seek Peace Bond over Terrorism Fears" *Toronto Star* (9 June 2015).

149 Mike McIntyre & Kevin Rollason, "GPS Tracker Part of Strict Bail" *Winnipeg Free Press* (16 June 2015).

150 See Steve Lambert, "Winnipeg Man Suspected of Planning Terrorism Says *Charter* Rights Violated" *Canadian Press* (30 June 2015), online: www.chrisd. ca/2015/06/30/winnipeg-man-suspected-of-planning-terrorism-says-charter-rights-violated/; "Aaron Driver, Winnipeg ISIS Supporter, Released on Bail for a Second Time" *CBC News* (29 June 2015), online: www.cbc.ca/news/canada/manitoba/ aaron-driver-winnipeg-isis-supporter-released-on-bail-for-2nd-time-1.3131686.

151 Allan Woods, "Quebec and the Lure of Jihad" *Toronto Star* (30 May 2013).

152 See Graeme Hamilton, "Spotlight on Montreal College after Students Accused of Trying to Join Foreign Jihadists" *National Post* (20 May 2015), online: news. nationalpost.com/news/canada/spotlight-on-montreal-college-after-students-accused-of-trying-to-join-foreign-jihadists.

153 "Stephen Harper Puts Focus on Anti-terrorism at Montreal's Trudeau Airport" *CBC News* (21 May 2015), online: www.cbc.ca/news/canada/montreal/stephen-harper-puts-focus-on-anti-terrorism-at-montreal-s-trudeau-airport-1.3082036.

154 RCMP, News Release, "First Individual Convicted in Canada for Attempting to Participate in International Terrorist Activity" (30 May 2014), online: www.rcmp-grc.gc.ca/news-nouvelles/2014/05-30-severe-eng.htm.

155 See Laurent Bastien Corbeil, "Brampton Man Convicted of Terrorism Charges" *Toronto Star* (30 May 2014), online: www.thestar.com/news/gta/2014/05/30/brampton_man_convicted_of_terrorism_charges.html; "Mohamed Hersi Sentenced to 10 Years for Attempting to Join al-Shabab" *CBC News* (24 July 2014), online: www.cbc.ca/news/canada/toronto/mohamed-hersi-sentenced-to-10-years-for-attempting-to-join-al-shabab-1.2716856.

156 *Criminal Code*, above note 67, ss 83.181, 83.191, and 83.201–83.202.

157 *Debates of the Senate*, 41st Parl, 1st Sess, vol 148 (29 February 2012), online: www.parl.gc.ca/content/sen/chamber/411/debates/055db_2012-02-29-e.htm.

158 *Ibid.*

159 *Ibid.*

160 *Ibid.*

161 *Ibid.*

162 Standing Senate Committee on National Security and Defence, above note 37 at 14 & 15.

163 See Aleksandra Sagan, "BC Legislature Bomb Plotters' Entrapment Hard to Prove" *CBC News* (4 June 2015), with embedded Canadian Press story "BC Terror Trial by the Numbers," online: www.cbc.ca/news/canada/british-columbia/b-c-legislature-bomb-plotters-entrapment-claims-hard-to-prove-1.3098654.

164 See Geordon Omand, "CSIS Documents May Point to Entrapment in Case of Alleged BC Terrorists: Lawyer" *Canadian Press* (22 June 2015), online: www.ctvnews.ca/canada/csis-documents-may-point-to-entrapment-in-case-of-alleged-b-c-terrorists-lawyer-1.2435415.

165 For a media summary of Canada's track record in relation to war crimes prosecutions and the reasons for its moderate rate of success, see Wendy Gillis, "Rwandan Genocide: The Long Road to Justice" *Toronto Star* (5 April 2014), online: www.thestar.com/news/world/2014/04/05/rwandan_genocide_the_long_road_to_justice.html.

166 Integrated Terrorist Assessment Centre, above note 3 at para 14.

167 Public Safety Canada, above note 25.

168 Public Safety Canada, "Launch of Building Resilience against Terrorism: Canada's Counter-terrorism Strategy" (9 February 2012), online: www.publicsafety.gc.ca/cnt/nws/spchs/2012/20120209-eng.aspx.

169 Senate Standing Committee on National Security and Defence, *Security, Freedom and the Complex Terrorist Threat: Positive Steps Ahead* (March 2011), online: www.parl.gc.ca/content/sen/committee/403/anti/rep/repo3mar11-e.pdf

170 Privacy Commissioner, "Special Report to Parliament — Checks and Controls: Reinforcing Privacy Protection and Oversight for the Canadian Intelligence Community in an Era of Cyber-surveillance" (January 2014), online: www.priv.gc.ca/information/sr-rs/201314/sr_cic_e.asp.

171 Clark McCauley & Sophia Moskalenko, "Toward a Profile of Lone Wolf Terrorists: What Moves an Individual from Radical Opinion to Radical Action" (2014) 26 *Terrorism and Political Violence* 69 at 73.

172　See discussion in Sophia Moskalenko & Clark McCauley, "Measuring Political Mobilization: The Distinction between Activism and Radicalism" (2009) 21 *Terrorism and Political Violence* 239 at 240.

173　See RCMP, "Questions and Answers: Bill C-51, Q39" (marked "Draft April 17 2015"), released via ATIP request A-2015-04006.

CHAPTER FOUR: WATCH

1　Part I of the *Constitution Act, 1982*, being Schedule B to the *Canada Act 1982* (UK), 1982, c 11 [*Charter*].

2　RSC 1985, c C-23, s 2 [*CSIS Act*].

3　*R v Jaser*, 2014 ONSC 6052.

4　*X (Re)*, 2014 FCA 249 at para 1.

5　This sequence of cases is reported as *X (Re)*, 2009 FC 1058 and *X (Re)*, 2013 FC 1275, aff'd 2014 FCA 249.

6　Government of Canada, "Building Resilience against Terrorism: Canada's Counter-terrorism Strategy" (2013) at 17, online: www.publicsafety.gc.ca/cnt/rsrcs/pblctns/rslnc-gnst-trrrsm/rslnc-gnst-trrrsm-eng.pdf.

7　Opening Statement by Privacy Commissioner of Canada Jennifer Stoddart, *Independent Review Mechanism for the National Security Activities of the RCMP*, Commission of Inquiry into the Actions of Canadian Officials in relation to Maher Arar (16 November 2005).

8　*Wilkes v Wood*, 19 Howell's State Trials 1153 (CP 1763); *Entick v Carrington*, [1765] EWHC KB J98, online: www.bailii.org/ew/cases/EWHC/KB/1765/J98.html [*Entick*].

9　*Entick*, above note 8.

10　See Akhil Reed Amar, "Fourth Amendment First Principles" (1994) 107:4 *Harvard Law Review* 757 at 772.

11　*An Act to enact the Security of Canada Information Sharing Act and the Secure Air Travel Act, to amend the Criminal Code, the Canadian Security Intelligence Service Act and the Immigration and Refugee Protection Act and to make related and consequential amendments to other Acts*, 2d Sess, 41st Parl, 2015 (assented to 18 June 2015), SC 2015, c 20.

12　*An Act to amend the Canadian Security Intelligence Service Act and other Acts*, 2d Sess, 41st Parl, 2015 (assented to 23 April 2015), SC 2015, c 9.

13　*An Act to amend the Criminal Code, the Canada Evidence Act, the Competition Act and the Mutual Legal Assistance in Criminal Matters Act*, 2d Sess, 41st Parl, 2014 (assented to 9 December 2014), SC 2014, c 31.

14　277 US 438 (1928).

15　*Ibid* at 464–65.

16　389 US 347 (1967) [*Katz*].

17　[1984] 2 SCR 145.

18　*Katz*, above note 16 at 361.

19　See *R v Gomboc*, 2010 SCC 55 at para 19 [*Gomboc*].

20　*Ibid* at para 28, citing *R v Plant*, [1993] 3 SCR 281 at 293.

21　*Gomboc*, above note 19 at paras 43 and 142.

22　*R v Spencer*, 2014 SCC 43 [*Spencer*].

23 *Ibid* at paras 47 and 50.

24 *R v Fearon*, 2014 SCC 77.

25 *Criminal Code*, RSC 1985, c C-46, s 184.

26 *Ibid*, s 184.4.

27 *Ibid*, ss 185 & 186.

28 *Ibid*, s 186.1

29 *Ibid*, s 196.

30 Stanley Cohen, *Privacy, Crime and Terror* (Markham, ON: LexisNexis Butterworths, 2005) at 203.

31 See *ibid* at 490ff.

32 See *R v Telus*, 2013 SCC 16.

33 See Alex Boutilier, "Supreme Court Ruling Hasn't Stopped Police from Warrantless Requests for Data" *Toronto Star* (17 September 2014), online: www.thestar.com/news/canada/2014/09/17/supreme_court_ruling_hasnt_stopped_police_from_warrantless_requests_for_data.html.

34 Ann Cavoukian, *A Primer on Metadata: Separating Fact from Fiction* (Toronto: Information and Privacy Commissioner Ontario, 2013) at 3.

35 Above note 13.

36 *Criminal Code*, above note 25, s 492.2.

37 *Ibid*, s 487.015, 487.016, & 487.017.

38 See *Baron v Canada*, [1993] 1 SCR 416 at para 42.

39 Cavoukian, above note 34 at 4.

40 E Nakashima, "Metadata Reveals the Secrets of Social Position, Company Hierarchy, Terrorist Cells" *Washington Post* (15 June 2013), cited in Cavoukian, above note 34 at 3.

41 An IP address "is a numerical identification and logical address that is assigned to devices participating in a computer network utilizing the Internet Protocol": Office of the Privacy Commissioner of Canada, "What an IP Address Can Reveal about You" (May 2013), online: www.priv.gc.ca/information/research-recherche/2013/ip_201305_e.asp.

42 *Ibid*.

43 "The Big Data Conundrum: How to Define It?" *MIT Technology Review* (3 October 2013), online: www.technologyreview.com/view/519851/the-big-data-conundrum-how-to-define-it/.

44 *Criminal Code*, above note 25, s 83.221.

45 *CSIS Act*, above note 2, s 21, cross-referenced to s 16.

46 Above note 12.

47 *CSIS Act*, above note 2, s 12(2).

48 *Ibid*, s 21(3.1).

49 See Craig Forcese, "One Warrant to Rule Them All: Re-conceiving the Judicialization of Extraterritorial Intelligence Collection" (24 June 2015), online: ssrn.com/abstract=2622606.

50 See, for example, *R v Hape*, 2007 SCC 26 at paras 53 and 68 [*Hape*].

51 *Ibid*.

52 *National Defence Act*, RSC 1985, c N-5, s 273.64 [*NDA*].

53 RCMP, "Questions and Answers: Bill C-51, Q32" (marked "Draft April 17 2015"), released via ATIP request A-2015-04006.

54 See *NDA*, above note 52, s 273.64(3).

55 Standing Senate Committee on National Security and Defence, "Evidence" (20 April 2015) (Chair: Daniel Lang), online: www.parl.gc.ca/content/sen/committee/412/SECD/52040-E.HTM.

56 See Amber Hildebrandt, Dave Seglins, & Michael Pereira, "Communication Security Establishment's Cyberwarfare Toolbox Revealed" *CBC News* (23 March 2015), online: www.cbc.ca/news/canada/communication-security-establishment-s-cyberwarfare-toolbox-revealed-1.3002978.

57 See Ronald Diebert, "Who Knows What Evils Lurk in the Shadows?" in Edward Iacobucci & Stephen Toope, eds, *After the Paris Attacks: Responses in Canada, Europe and Around the Globe* (Toronto: University of Toronto Press, 2015).

58 *NDA*, above note 52, s 273.61.

59 *Ibid*, s 273.64.

60 *British Columbia Civil Liberties Association v AG of Canada* (20 January 2014), S137827 (AG's Response to Civil Claim) at para 5 (BCSC) [on file with authors] [AG's Response].

61 See Craig Forcese, "Law, Logarithms and Liberties: Legal Issues Arising from CSE's Metadata Program" in Michael Geist, ed, *Law, Privacy and Surveillance in Canada in the Post-Snowden Era* (Ottawa: University of Ottawa Press, 2015).

62 Barton Gellman & Laura Poitras, "US, British Intelligence Mining Data from Nine U.S. Internet Companies in Broad Secret Programs" *Washington Post* (6 June 2013), online: www.washingtonpost.com/investigations/us-intelligence-mining-data-from-nine-us-internet-companies-in-broad-secret-program/2013/06/06/3a0coda8-cebf-11e2-8845-d970ccb04497_story.html; Glenn Greenwald, "NSA Collecting Phone Records of Millions of Verizon Customers Daily" *Guardian* (6 June 2013), online: www.theguardian.com/world/2013/jun/06/nsa-phone-records-verizon-court-order.

63 See James Bell, "NSA Stores Metadata of Millions of Web Users for Up to a Year, Secret Files Show" *Guardian* (30 September 2013), online: www.theguardian.com/world/2013/sep/30/nsa-americans-metadata-year-documents.

64 See, for example, Colin Freeze, "How Canada's Shadowy Metadata-Gathering Program Went Awry" *Globe and Mail* (15 June 2013), online: www.theglobeandmail.com/news/national/how-canadas-shadowy-metadata-gathering-program-went-awry/article12580225/?page=all#dashboard/follows/.

65 See Greg Weston, Glenn Greenwald, & Ryan Gallagher, "CSEC Used Airport Wi-Fi to Track Canadian Travellers: Edward Snowden Documents" *CBC News* (30 January 2014), online: www.cbc.ca/news/politics/csec-used-airport-wi-fi-to-track-canadian-travellers-edward-snowden-documents-1.2517881. The actual CSE document is posted online: www.cbc.ca/news2/pdf/airports_redacted.pdf.

66 See Amber Hildebrandt, Michael Pereira, & Dave Seglins, "CSE Tracks Millions of Downloads Daily: Snowden Documents" *CBC News* (27 January 2015), online: www.cbc.ca/news/canada/cse-tracks-millions-of-downloads-daily-snowden-documents-1.2930120.

67 See Amber Hildebrandt, "CSE Worried about How Its Use of Canadian Metadata Might Be Viewed" *CBC News* (22 April 2015), online: www.cbc.ca/news/canada/cse-worried-about-how-its-use-of-canadian-metadata-might-be-viewed-1.3040816.

68   See *British Columbia Civil Liberties Association v AG of Canada* (27 October 2014), Vancouver, T-2210-14 (Statement of Claim) (FC), online: bccla.org/wp-content/uploads/2014/12/20141027-CSEC-Statement-of-Claim.pdf.

69   See AG's Response, above note 60 at para 5.

70   *NDA*, above note 52, s 4.

71   Bill C-622, *An Act to amend the National Defence Act (transparency and accountability), to enact the Intelligence and Security Committee of Parliament Act and to make consequential amendments to other Acts*, 41st Parl, 2d Sess, 2014 (defeated at second reading 5 November 2014). In the interest of transparency, one of us (Forcese) was consulted on the drafting of this bill but takes no credit for its content.

72   See Forcese, above note 61 (relying on access to information disclosures).

CHAPTER FIVE: SHARE

1   Commission of Inquiry into the Investigation of the Bombing of Air India Flight 182, *Air India Flight 182: A Canadian Tragedy — The Overview*, vol 1 (Ottawa: Public Works, 2010) at 26 [Air India Inquiry I].

2   National Commission on Terrorist Attacks upon the United States, *The 9/11 Commission Report* (New York: Norton, 2004) at 352.

3   *Ibid* at 417.

4   *Canadian Security Intelligence Service Act*, RSC 1985, c C-23, s 2 [*CSIS Act*].

5   Air India Inquiry I, above note 1 at 195 (Recommendation 10).

6   Bill C-51, *An Act to enact the Security of Canada Information Sharing Act and the Secure Air Travel Act, to amend the Criminal Code, the Canadian Security Intelligence Service Act and the Immigration and Refugee Protection Act and to make related and consequential amendments to other Acts*, 2d Sess, 41st Parl, 2015 (assented to 18 June 2015), SC 2015, c 20.

7   SC 2015, c 20, s 2 [*SoCIS Act*].

8   Government of Canada, Honourable Frank Iacobucci, *Internal Inquiry into the Actions of Canadian Officials in relation to Abdullah Almalki, Ahmad Abou-Elmaati and Muayyed Nureddin* (Ottawa: Public Works and Government Services, 2008).

9   Richard Aldrich, "Transatlantic Intelligence and Security Cooperation" (2004) 80:4 *International Affairs* 731 at 737. The discussion in this part also draws on Craig Forcese, "The Collateral Casualties of Collaboration: The Consequences for Civil and Human Rights of Transnational Intelligence Sharing" in Hans Born, Ian Leigh, & Aidan Wills, eds, *International Intelligence Cooperation and Accountability* (London: Routledge, 2010).

10   Testimony of William John Hooper, Assistant Director of Operations, CSIS, Commission of Inquiry into the Actions of Canadian Officials in relation to Maher Arar (22 June 2005) at 485, online: epe.lac-bac.gc.ca/100/206/301/pco-bcp/commissions/maher_arar/07-09-13/www.stenotran.com/commission/maherarar/2004-06-22%20volume%202.pdf.

11   S/RES/1373(2001) at 2(b) and (f).

12   James Walsh, "Defection and Hierarchy in International Intelligence Sharing" (2007) 27:2 *Journal of Public Policy* 151 at 157.

13   See *Canada v Khawaja*, 2007 FC 490 at para 127 (FC) [*Khawaja*].

14   Richard Aldrich, "Dangerous Liaisons: Post-September 11 Intelligence Alliances" (2002) 24:3 *Harvard International Review* 50 at 50.

15   *Ibid.*

16   Above note 4, s 17.

17   CSIS, "2004–2005 Annual Public Report" at 14, online: http://publications. gc.ca/collections/Collection/PS71-2004E.pdf. This number appeared not to increase by 2010–11: see Security Intelligence Review Committee, "Annual Report 2010–11," online: www.sirc-csars.gc.ca/anrran/2010-2011/sco2a-eng.html.

18   See Philip Rosen, "The Communications Security Establishment — Canada's Most Secret Intelligence Agency" BP-343E, (September 1993), online: Library of Parliament dsp-psd.tpsgc.gc.ca/Collection-R/LoPBdP/BP/bp343-e.htm.

19   Government of Canada, "CSE: Information Kit," online: www.cse-cst.gc.ca/en/ media/information.

20   See Security Intelligence Review Committee, above note 17.

21   Alasdair Roberts, "Entangling Alliances: NATO's Security Policy and the Entrenchment of State Secrecy" (2003) 36 *Cornell International Law Journal* 329 at 337, citing NATO Security Committee, *A Short Guide to the Handling of Classified Information*, Brussels, NATO Archives, AC/35-WP/14: 4.

22   Walsh, above note 12 at 160.

23   *Agreement between the Government of Australia and the Government of Canada Concerning the Protection of Defence Related Information Exchanged between Them* (October 1996), ATS1996 No 16.

24   *Ruby v Canada*, [1996] 3 FCR 134 at para 25 (FCTD) [*Ruby*], citing the Affidavit of Ms Margaret Ann Purdy (then Director General of the Counter Terrorism Branch) (31 October 1994).

25   *Ibid* (court summary of affidavit).

26   Commission of Inquiry into the Actions of Canadian Officials in relation to Maher Arar, *Analysis and Recommendations* (Ottawa: Public Works, 2006) at 13 [*Analysis and Recommendations*] at 49, n2.

27   *Ruby*, above note 24 at para 26.

28   *Ibid* at para 27. Similar views were expressed in this and other cases by the RCMP, Department of National Defence, and Department of Foreign Affairs. See, for example, *Ribic v Canada*, 2003 FCT 10 at para 10 (FC); *Khawaja*, above note 13 at para 122ff.

29   Fred Schreier, "The Need for Efficient and Legitimate Intelligence" in Hans Born & Marina Caparini, eds, *Democratic Control of Intelligence Services: Containing Rogue Elephants* (Aldershot, UK: Ashgate Publishing, 2007) at 37.

30   *Criminal Code*, RSC 1985, c C-46, s 269.1(4). See also *Information and Refugee Protection Act*, SC 2001, c 27, ss 83(1)(h) and 83(1.1); *Mahjoub (Re)*, 2010 FC 787.

31   The principles are contained in Nicole LaViolette & Craig Forcese, eds, *The Human Rights of Anti-terrorism* (Toronto: Irwin Law, 2008), and also online: aix1. uottawa.ca/~cforcese/hrat/principles.pdf.

32   *Ibid.*

33 Then Public Safety Minister Toews issued the CSIS direction to CSIS on 28 July 2011 and directions to the RCMP and the Canada Border Services Agency on 9 September 2011. The directions are found in Public Safety ATIP Request A-2013-00122. For detailed referencing and discussion of this issue, see also Craig Forcese, "Touching Torture with a Ten-Foot Pole: The Legality of Canada's Approach to National Security Information Sharing with Human Rights–Abusing States" (2014) 52;1 *Osgoode Hall Law Journal* 263, online: digitalcommons.osgoode.yorku.ca/ohlj/vol52/iss1/7/.

34 See, for example, Jim Bronskill, "CSIS Can Share Info Despite 'Substantial' Torture Risk" *Toronto Star* (02 March 2012), online: www.thestar.com/news/canada/2012/03/02/csis_can_share_info_despite_substantial_torture_risk.html; Jordan Press, "Torture Risk 'Must Be Real,' Directive Says; Government on Defensive over Information-Sharing Edict" *Ottawa Citizen* (3 March 2013) A3; Kent Roach, "Canada Plays a Dangerous Game" *Ottawa Citizen* (7 March 2012) A13; Kent Roach, "The Dangerous Game of Complicity in Torture" (2012) 58:3 & 4 *Criminal Law Quarterly* 303 ["Complicity in Torture"]. More recently, the direction to CSIS was condemned by a resolution adopted by council at the 2013 Canadian Bar Association meeting: Canadian Bar Association, Resolution 13-08-A, online: www.cba.org/CBA/resolutions/pdf/13-08-A-ct.pdf.

35 "Ministerial Direction to the Director Canadian Security Intelligence Service: Information Sharing with Foreign Agencies" (undated but may date from or around November 2008). See discussion in CSIS, "Public Report 2008–9" at 28, http://publications.gc.ca/collections/collection_2010/sp-ps/PS71-2009-eng.pdf.

36 CSIS ATIP Request 117-2014-386.

37 Part I of the *Constitution Act, 1982*, being Schedule B to the *Canada Act 1982* (UK), 1982, c 11 [*Charter*].

38 For a full discussion of these issues, see Forcese, above note 33.

39 See discussion of all of these issues in *ibid*.

40 Canadian Bar Association, above note 34.

41 Forcese, above note 33; "Complicity in Torture," above note 34 at 306.

42 Readers may wish to refer to other more detailed sources on national security exceptions that allow information sharing: Stanley A Cohen, *Privacy, Crime and Terror: Legal Rights and Security in a Time of Peril* (Toronto: LexisNexis, 2005); Craig Forcese, *National Security Law* (Toronto: Irwin Law, 2008) at 441–3.

43 *Privacy Act*, RSC 1985, c P-21, s 8.

44 *Ibid*, s 8(2)(a).

45 Cohen, above note 42 at 391.

46 *Privacy Act*, above note 43, s 8(2)(e) & (f).

47 *Ibid*, s 8(2)(j).

48 *Ibid*, s 8(2)(m).

49 *Ibid*, s 8(2)(b).

50 See, for example, *R v Colarusso*, [1994] 1 SCR 20 at para 93; *R v Cole*, 2012 SCC 53 at para 69. See also Cohen, above note 42 at 98, 120, and 137.

51 See Cohen, above note 42 at 120.

52 2014 SCC 72 [*Wakeling*].

53 *Ibid* at para 104.

54 See above note 42 and accompanying discussion in the text.

55 CSIS, "Memorandum to the Director, Deputy Minister Meeting on National Security Information Sharing" (5 February 2014), CSIS ATIP request 117-2014-393 at 2.

56 *Ibid* at 5 [emphasis added].

57 *SoCIS Act*, above note 7, s 2.

58 *CSIS Act*, above note 4, s 2.

59 RSC 1985, c O-5, s 3.

60 *SoCIS Act*, above note 7, s 2.

61 *Ibid*, s 2(d).

62 *Ibid*, ss 2(f) and (i).

63 *Ibid*, s 2(b) [emphasis added].

64 *CSIS Act*, above note 4, s 2.

65 *Criminal Code*, above note 30, s 59.

66 *SoCIS Act*, above note 7, s 2.

67 *Ibid*, s 5.

68 *Ibid*.

69 *Privacy Act*, above note 43, s 8(2)(b).

70 See Adam Kovac, "Cellphone Search at Border Raises Legal, Civil Liberties Questions" *Toronto Sun* (6 March 2015), online: www.torontosun.com/2015/03/06/cellphone-search-at-border-raises-legal-civil-liberties-questions.

71 CSIS/CBSA Memorandum of Understanding (2014), paras 3.2 and 5.5, released through access to information.

72 *CSIS Act*, above note 4, ss 12 & 12.1.

73 *Ibid*, s 2.

74 *Excise Tax Act*, RSC 1985, c E-15, s 295(5.04).

75 *Customs Act*, RSC 1985, c 1 (2d Supp), s 107(4).

76 *R v Colarusso*, [1994] 1 SCR 20 at para 93. See also above note 50 and associated text.

77 SC 2001, c 27, s 150.1.

78 *Protection of Passenger Information Regulations*, SOR/2005-346, ss 9 and 3.

79 *Suresh v Canada*, 2002 SCC 1 at para 98.

80 Standing Committee on National Security and Defence, "Evidence" (2 April 2015) (Chair: Daniel Lang), online: www.parl.gc.ca/content/sen/committee/412/SECD/52037-E.HTM.

81 Richard Fadden, "Remarks" (29 November 2009), online: www.casis-acers.ca/wp-content/uploads/2014/06/Dick-Fadden-CSIS-Speech-To-CASIS-OCT-091.pdf.

82 See Terry Millewski, "Ottawa Shooting: Federal Security Chiefs Warned Days before an Attack" *CBC News* (24 November 2014), online: www.cbc.ca/news/politics/ottawa-shooting-federal-security-chiefs-warned-days-before-attack-1.2847552; Stewart Bell, "Three Days before Ottawa Terror Attack, Alarm Bells Were Sounding, Intelligence Reports Show" *National Post* (1 March 2015), online: news.nationalpost.com/news/canada/security-forces-braced-for-terror-attacks-over-canadas-enhanced-profile-before-ottawa-shooting.

83 See Mattathias Schwartz, "The Whole Haystack" *The New Yorker* (26 January 2015), online: www.newyorker.com/magazine/2015/01/26/whole-haystack.

84 *Analysis and Recommendations*, above note 26 at 365.

85 *Ibid* at 366.

86 *Ibid.*

87 See the many recommendations in Commission of Inquiry into the Actions of Canadian Officials in relation to Maher Arar, *A New Review Mechanism for the RCMP's National Security Activities* (Ottawa: Public Works, 2006) [*A New Review Mechanism*].

88 *SoCIS Act*, above note 7, s 9.

89 Bill C-51, above note 6 (First reading 30 January 2015), s 2 at s 6.

90 Cohen, above note 42 at 104.

91 Privacy Commissioner of Canada, "Privacy Commissioner Raises Concerns about C-51" (6 March 2015), online: www.priv.gc.ca/media/nr-c/2015/oped_150306_e.asp.

92 Privacy Commissioner of Canada, "Bill C-51, the *Anti-terrorism Act, 2015*: Submission to the Standing Committee on Public Safety and National Security of the House of Commons" (5 March 2015), online: www.priv.gc.ca/parl/2015/parl_sub_150305_e.asp.

93 Government of Canada, "Backgrounder Security of Information Sharing Act" (30 January 2015), online: http://news.gc.ca/web/article-en.do?nid=926879.

94 *A New Review Mechanism*, above note 87 at 495.

95 *Ibid* at 286, noting that while the Privacy Commissioner reviews some national security activities, it "does not have the resources to thoroughly audit, review or investigate all national security actors."

96 Office of the Privacy Commissioner of Canada, "Checks and Controls: Reinforcing Privacy Protection and Oversight for the Canadian Intelligence Community in an Era of Cyber-surveillance" (28 January 2014), online: www.priv.gc.ca/information/sr-rs/201314/sr_cic_e.asp.

97 See Daniel Therrien, Privacy Commissioner, Office of the Privacy Commissioner of Canada in Standing Senate Committee on National Security and Defence, "Evidence" (23 April 2015) (Chair: Daniel Lang), online: www.parl.gc.ca/content/sen/committee/412/SECD/52067-e.HTM.

98 *Privacy Act*, above note 43, s 3.

99 *A New Review Mechanism*, above note 87 at 483–96.

100 *Wakeling*, above note 52 at para 138.

101 Privacy Commissioner of Canada, above note 92.

102 Director's Report on Ditchley Conference, "Intelligence, Security and Privacy" (14–16 May 2015), online: ditchley.co.uk/conferences/past-programme/2010-2019/2015/intelligence.

103 Privacy Comissioner of Canada, above note 91.

104 See above note 50 and accompanying text.

CHAPTER SIX: INTERDICT

1   See *Ressam v Canada* (1996), 110 FTR 50.

2   See *United States of America v Ahmed Ressam* (20 April 2005), Seattle, CR99-666C (Dist Ct WD Wash) (Government's Sentencing Memorandum) at 2, online: www.investigativeproject.org/documents/case_docs/150.pdf.

3   See Standing Senate Committee on Social Affairs, Science and Technology, "Issue 26 — Evidence" (1 October 2001), Ward Elcock, CSIS Director.

4   See SIRC, *SIRC Report 2002–2003: An Operational Review of the Canadian Security Intelligence Service* (Ottawa: Public Works and Government Services Canada, 2003) at 5, online: www.sirc-csars.gc.ca/pdfs/ar_2002-2003-eng.pdf.

5   See *ibid* at 3.

6   See National Commission on Terrorist Attacks upon the United States, *The 9/11 Commission Report* (New York: Norton, 2004) at 176ff.

7   Government of Canada, *Building Resilience against Terrorism: Canada's Counter-terrorism Strategy*, 2d ed (2013) at 3, online: www.publicsafety.gc.ca/cnt/rsrcs/pblctns/rslnc-gnst-trrrsm/rslnc-gnst-trrrsm-eng.pdf.

8   Part I of the *Constitution Act, 1982*, being Schedule B to the *Canada Act 1982* (UK), 1982, c 11 [*Charter*].

9   See *United States of America v Cotroni*, [1989] 1 SCR 1469.

10 See *Divito v Canada*, 2013 SCC 47.

11 *Counter-terrorism and Security Act 2015* (UK), c 6, ss 2–4.

12 See SIRC, *SIRC Annual Report 2006–2007: An Operational Review of the Canadian Security Intelligence Service* (Ottawa: Public Works and Government Services Canada, 2007) at 20ff, online: www.sirc-csars.gc.ca/pdfs/ar_2006-2007-eng.pdf.

13 *Abdelrazik v Canada*, 2009 FC 580 at para 156.

14 *Ibid* at para 154.

15 See, for example, *Customs Act*, RSC 1985, c 1 (2d Supp), ss 98 & 99.

16 See *R v Monney*, [1999] 1 SCR 652 at paras 42–43.

17 See, for example, *R v Moroz*, 2012 ONSC 5642.

18 Commission of Inquiry into the Actions of Canadian Officials in relation to Maher Arar, *Report of the Events relating to Maher Arar — Factual Background*, vol 1 (Ottawa: Public Works, 2006) at 57–63.

19 *R v Mejid*, 2010 ONSC 5532 at para 10.

20 *Ibid* at para 32.

21 *Ibid* at para 98.

22 *Ibid* at para 37.

23 *Ibid* at para 100.

24 *Ibid* at para 102.

25 *Ibid* at para 104.

26 *Ibid* at para 79.

27 Bill C-51, *An Act to enact the Security of Canada Information Sharing Act and the Secure Air Travel Act, to amend the Criminal Code, the Canadian Security Intelligence Service Act and the Immigration and Refugee Protection Act and to make related and consequential amendments to other Acts*, 2d Sess, 41st Parl, 2015 (assented to 18 June 2015), SC 2015, c 20.

28 Standing Senate Committee on National Security and Defence, *Vigilance, Accountability and Security at Canada's Borders* (Ottawa: Senate, June 2015) (Chair: Daniel Lang) at 9, online: www.parl.gc.ca/Content/SEN/Committee/412/secd/rep/rep16jun15-e.pdf.

29 *Ibid*.

30 See Office of the Auditor General of Canada, Reports of the Auditor General of Canada, Report 5, *Information Technology Investments — Canada Border Services Agency* (Ottawa: Office of the AG, Spring 2015) at 11–13, online: www.oag-bvg.gc.ca/internet/docs/parl_oag_201504_05_e.pdf.

31 Privacy Commissioner of Canada, *Annual Report to Parliament 2013–14: Transparency and Privacy in the Digital Age — Report on the* Privacy Act (Gatineau, QC: Office of the Privacy of Canada, October 2014) at 25–26, online: www.priv.gc.ca/information/ar/201314/201314_pa_e.pdf.

32 *Smith v Canada (AG)*, 2001 SCC 88.

33 See *R v Spencer*, 2014 SCC 43.

34 SI/81-86.

35 *Ibid*, s 4.

36 *Ibid*, s 10.1, as amended by SI/2015-33, s 4 [emphasis added].

37 *Ibid*, s 11.1.

38 Standing Senate Committee on National Security and Defence, "Evidence" (28 May 2015) (Chair: Daniel Lang), John Davies, Director General, National Security Policy, National and Cyber Security Branch, Public Safety Canada, online: www.parl.gc.ca/content/sen/committee/412/SECD/52178-E.HTM.

39 See *Kamel v Canada (AG)*, 2009 FCA 21 at para 68.

40 The government has suggested that it has not used national security justifications for revocations: Standing Senate Committee on National Security and Defence, above note 38, Lu Fernandes, Director General, Passport Program Integrity. But this statement seems at odds with others made in the past and media reporting: Stewart Bell, "Canadian Government Begins Invalidating Passports of Citizens Who Have Left to Join Extremist Groups" *National Post* (20 September 2014), online: http://news.nationalpost.com/news/canada/canadian-government-revoking-passports-of-citizens-trying-to-join-extremist-groups.

41 Standing Senate Committee on National Security and Defence, above note 38, John Davies.

42 RSC 1985, c C-5, s 38.

43 Bill C-59, *An Act to implement certain provisions of the budget tabled in Parliament on April 21, 2015 and other measures*, 2d Sess, 41st Parl, 2015 (assented to 23 June 2015), SC 2015, c 36.

44 SC 2015, c 36, s 42.

45 *Ibid*, s 4(4)(a).

46 *Canada (AG) v Telbani*, 2014 FC 1050 [*Telbani*].

47 Standing Senate Committee on National Security and Defence, above note 38, Sophie Beecher, Counsel, Public Safety Canada, Department of Justice.

48 See Stewart Bell, "Stopping 'Terror Tourism': The Behind-the-Scenes Struggle to Keep Would-Be Jihadists at Home" *National Post* (25 July 2014), online: news.nationalpost.com/news/canada/stopping-terror-tourism-the-behind-the-scenes-struggle-to-keep-would-be-jihadists-at-home.

49 *Criminal Code*, RSC 1985, c C-46, s 57.

50 See Bell, above note 48. See also Michelle Shephard, "Spectre of Terrorism Looms over Passport Case; Man on 'High-Risk Traveller' List Faces Charge of Document Fraud" *Toronto Star* (10 November 2014) A1.

51 See *Criminal Code*, above note 49, s 57.

52 See *Abdelrazik v Canada (Minister of Foreign Affairs)*, 2009 FC 580.

53 See Shephard, above note 50.

54 RCMP, "Questions and Answers: Bill C-51, Q13" (marked "Draft April 17 2015"), released via ATIP request A-2015-04006 [emphasis in original].

55 RCMP, "Questions and Answers: Bill C-51, Q14" (marked "Draft April 17 2015"), released via ATIP request A-2015-04006.

56 RCMP, "Questions and Answers: Bill C-51" (marked "Draft April 17 2015") at 24 (Opening Statement), released via ATIP request A-2015-04006.

57 RSC 1985, c A-2.

58 SOR/2007-82.

59 See Jeffrey Kahn, *Mrs. Shipley's Ghost: The Right to Travel and Terrorist Watchlists* (Ann Arbor: University of Michigan Press, 2013).

60 *Aeronautics Act*, above note 57, s 4.76.

61 See, for example, Douglas Quan, "Canada Urged to Beef Up Security at Border in Wake of Hasibullah Yusufzai Case" *Postmedia News* (24 July 2014).

62 *Secure Air Travel Act*, SC 2015, c 20, s 11 at s 8.

63 *Ibid* at s 9.

64 Standing Committee on Public Safety and National Security, "Evidence" (12 March 2015) (Chair: Daryl Kramp), Marc-André O'Rourke, Executive Director, National Airlines Council of Canada, online: www.parl.gc.ca/HousePublications/ Publication.aspx?DocId=7881995&Language=E&Mode=1.

65 *Secure Air Travel Act*, above note 62, s 9.

66 *Telbani*, above note 46. *Telbani* also supported the use of *amici curiae* in secret hearings, but, as noted, this role may be less robust than that created by statute for special advocates under immigration law.

67 *Secure Air Travel Act*, above note 62, ss 10–14.

68 Office of the Privacy Commissioner of Canada, *Passenger Protect Program: Transport Canada* (Ottawa: Office of the Privacy Commissioner of Canada, 2009) at 14, online: www.priv.gc.ca/information/pub/ar-vr/ar-vr_ppp_200910_e.pdf.

69 Transport Canada, "Passenger Protect — Program Information Package" (October 2006); "*Identity Screening Regulations*: Regulatory Impact Analysis Statement" (2006) C Gaz I, 3463 ["Impact Analysis"].

70 "Impact Analysis," above note 69 at 3474.

71 See Quan, above note 61, for an example of someone on the no-fly list who reportedly circumvented the no-fly strictures by using a false passport.

72 See United Nations, "The List Established and Maintained by the Committee Pursuant to Resolutions 1267 (1999) and 1989 (2011) with respect to Individuals, Groups, Undertakings and Other Entities Associated with Al-Qaida," online: www.un.org/sc/committees/1267/aq_sanctions_list.shtml.

73 *Regulations Implementing the United Nations Resolutions on the Suppression of Terrorism*, SOR/2001-360, s 2.

74 *Ibid*.

75 *Ibid*, ss 3–8.

76 See Public Safety Canada, "Currently Listed Entities," online: www.publicsafety. gc.ca/cnt/ntnl-scrt/cntr-trrrsm/lstd-ntts/crrnt-lstd-ntts-eng.aspx.

77 Craig Forcese & Kent Roach, "Limping into the Future: The UN 1267 Terrorism Listing Process at the Crossroads" (2010) 42 *George Washington University Law Review* 218.

78 See Patrick Johnston, RAND Institute, "Countering ISIL's Financing" (Testimony presented before the US House of Representatives Financial Services Committee, 13 November 2014), online: www.rand.org/content/dam/rand/pubs/ testimonies/CT400/CT419/RAND_CT419.pdf.

79 See S/Council/Res 2178 (2014).

80 See discussion in Forcese & Roach, above note 77.

81 See Andrew Lynch, Nicola McGarrity, & George Williams, *Inside Australia's Anti-terrorism Laws and Trials* (Sydney: NewSouth Publishing, 2015) ch 4.

82 *Criminal Code*, above note 49, ss 83.13 & 83.14.

83 *R v Namouh*, 2010 QCCQ 943.

84 SC 2001, c 27, s 33ff [*IRPA*].

85 See CSIS, "The Security Screening Program" (13 March 2015), online: www.csis.gc.ca/scrtscrnng/index-en.php.

86 Standing Senate Committee on National Security and Defence, above note 28 at 13.

87 See *IRPA*, above note 84, s 33.

88 See Standing Senate Committee on National Security and Defence, above note 28 at 8.

89 *Ibid* at 8.

90 *Suresh v Canada*, [2002] 1 SCR 3 at para 78 [*Suresh*].

91 See *Dadar v Canada (Minister of Citizenship and Immigration)*, 2006 FC 382. See also *Sogi v Canada (Minister of Citizenship and Immigration)*, 2006 FC 799 (removal ordered before the United Nations committee had a chance to consider the matter); Andrew Sniderman, "Jama Warsame Is a Citizen of Nowhere" *Maclean's* (10 December 2013); Jon Woodward, "Canada Deported Man to Torture in Sri Lanka: Affidavit" *CTV News* (8 October 2013); Graham Hudson, "Secret Trials, Torture, and Deporting People under the Radar" *The Inside Agenda Blog* (27 November 2014), online: tvo.org/blog/current-affairs/inside-agenda/secret-trials-torture-and-deporting-people-under-the-radar.

92 See *Nlandu-Nsoki v Canada (Minister of Citizenship and Immigration)*, 2005 FC 17 at paras 21–22.

93 See *R v Hape*, 2007 SCC 26 at para 56. See also *Health Services and Support — Facilities Subsector Bargaining Association v British Columbia*, 2007 SCC 27 at para 79.

94 *Convention against Torture and Other Cruel, Inhuman or Degrading Treatment or Punishment*, 10 December 1984, 1465 UNTS 85, art 3 (entered into force 26 June 1987).

95 See *Namouh v Canada (Public Safety and Emergency Preparedness)*, 2012 FC 1545.

96 See, for example, Human Rights Watch, "Still at Risk: Diplomatic Assurances No Safeguard against Torture" (April 2005), online: www.hrw.org/sites/default/files/reports/eca0405.pdf; Human Rights Watch, "Empty Promises: Diplomatic Assurances No Safeguard against Torture" (April 2004), online: www.hrw.org/sites/default/files/reports/diplomatic0404.pdf.

97 See *Suresh*, above note 90 at para 124.

98 The issue of what happened in Afghanistan was never resolved after the 2011 election, and a Conservative majority government put a stop to a parliamentary investigation. But some sense as to the nature of the concerns is documented in Military Police Complaints Commission, "Commission's Final Report — MPCC 2008-042 — Concerning a complaint by Amnesty International Canada and British Columbia Civil Liberties Association in June 2008" (Ottawa, 27 June 2012).

99 See *Mugesera v Canada (Minister of Citizenship and Immigration)*, 2012 FC 32; *Lai v Canada (Minister of Citizenship and Immigration)*, 2011 FC 915.

100 Standing Senate Committee on National Security and Defence, above note 28 at 23.

101 Bill C-59, above note 43, s 168, amending *IRPA*, above note 84, ss 10.01 & 10.02 (provisions not in force at the time of this writing).

102 See Susana Mas, "Biometric Data Collection Change in Budget Bill Raises Privacy Concerns" *CBC News* (3 June 2015), online: www.cbc.ca/news/politics/biometric-data-collection-change-in-budget-bill-raises-privacy-concerns-1.3095488.

103 Privacy Commissioner of Canada, "Divisions 13, 14 and 15 of Bill C-59, *Economic Action Plan 2015, No. 1:* Submission to the Standing Senate Committee on National Finance" (1 June 2015), online: www.priv.gc.ca/parl/2015/parl_sub_150601_e.asp.

104 See *Citizenship Act*, RSC 1985, c C-29, ss 5 and 20.

105 See *ibid*, ss 19 & 19.1.

106 See CSIS, above note 85.

107 *Strengthening Canadian Citizenship Act*, SC 2014, c 22, ss 10 & 10.1.

108 *Ibid*, s 10.4(1).

109 Statistics Canada, "Obtaining Canadian Citizenship" (2011), online: www12.statcan.gc.ca/nhs-enm/2011/as-sa/99-010-x/99-010-x2011003_1-eng.cfm. In absolute numbers, in 2011, there were 760,285 dual-national Canadians who were born outside Canada and 172,385 dual-national Canadians born in Canada: see Statistics Canada, "Data Table, cat 99-010-X2011026" (2011).

110 See Craig Forcese, "A Tale of Two Citizenships: Citizenship Revocation for 'Traitors and Terrorists'" (2014) 39:2 *Queens Law Journal* 551. See also Audrey Macklin, "Citizenship Revocation, the Privilege to Have Rights and the Production of the Alien" (2014) 40:1 *Queens Law Journal* 1.

111 See, for example, Alan Simmons, *Immigration and Canada: Global and Transnational Perspectives* (Toronto: Canadian Scholars' Press, 2010) at 142.

112 See *R v Oakes*, [1986] 1 SCR 103.

113 Shai Lavi, "Citizenship Revocation as Punishment: On the Modern Duties of Citizens and Their Criminal Breach" (2011) 61:4 *University of Toronto Law Journal* 783 at 805.

114 *Galati v Canada (Governor General)*, 2015 FC 91.

115 See Stewart Bell, "Ottawa Moves to Revoke Citizenship of Convicted Terrorist for First Time Since Controversial Law Took Effect" *National Post* (1 July 2015), online: news.nationalpost.com/news/ottawa-moves-to-revoke-citizenship-of-convicted-terrorist-for-first-time-since-controversial-law-took-effect.

116 See *R v Alizadeh*, 2014 ONSC 5421.

117 "Hiva Alizadeh Pleads Guilty in Ottawa Terrorism Trial" *CBC News* (17 September 2014), online: www.cbc.ca/news/canada/ottawa/hiva-alizadeh-pleads-guilty-in-ottawa-terrorism-trial-1.2768944.

118 For a case where the Supreme Court approved of taking immigration measures into account in sentencing, see *R v Pham*, 2013 SCC 15.

119 See Forcese, above note 110.

CHAPTER SEVEN: RESTRAIN

1 *Mahjoub v Canada*, 2007 FC 171.

2 *Charkaoui v Canada (Citizenship and Immigration)*, 2007 SCC 9 [*Charkaoui*].

3 *Ibid* at para 116.

4   *An Act to amend the Immigration and Refugee Protection Act (certificate and special advocate) and to make a consequential amendment to another Act*, SC 2008, c 3.

5   See, for example, *Canada (Citizenship and Immigration) v Mahjoub*, 2009 FC 248.

6   *Mahjoub (Re)*, 2009 FC 1220 at para 11. The conditions were further revised in *Mahjoub (Re)*, 2013 FC 10.

7   Colin Freeze, "Under Constant Watch, Terror Suspect Seeks Return to Prison," *Globe and Mail* (18 March 2009), online: www.theglobeandmail.com/news/national/under-constant-watch-terror-suspect-seeks-return-to-prison/article20445712/.

8   Above note 6.

9   Except as otherwise noted, the facts concerning Dirie are summarized from *R v Ahmad*, 2009 CanLII 84779 (ON SC); *R v Dirie*, 2009 CanLII 58598 (ON SC).

10 Alex Wilner & Brian Lee Crowley, "Preventing Prison Radicalization in Canada: More Needs to Be Done," online: The Macdonald-Laurier Institute. www.macdonaldlaurier.ca/files/pdf/Wilner_Crowley_Prison_Radicalisation.pdf. See also Alex Wilner, "From Rehabilitation to Recruitment" *True North* (October 2010), online: www.macdonaldlaurier.ca/files/pdf/FromRehabilitationToRecruitment.pdf.

11 "'Toronto 18' Member Ali Mohamed Dirie Was under Strict Court Order" *CBC News* (26 September 2013), online: www.cbc.ca/news/toronto-18-member-ali-mohamed-dirie-was-under-strict-court-order-1.1870190.

12 *Charkaoui*, above note 2.

13 Gary Trotter, "The Anti-terrorism Bill and Preventive Restraints on Liberty" in Ronald J Daniels, Patrick Macklem, & Kent Roach, eds, *The Security of Freedom: Essays on Canada's Anti-terrorism Bill* (Toronto: University of Toronto Press, 2001) at 241.

14 *Immigration and Refugee Protection Act*, SC 2001, c-27, Division 9 [*IRPA*].

15 *Ibid*, s 77.

16 *Ibid*, s 81.

17 *Ibid*, s 82.

18 *Criminal Code*, RSC 1985, c C-46, s 127; *IRPA*, above note 14, s 124.

19 The release order is reproduced in *Harkat v Canada (Minister of Immigration and Citizenship)*, 2006 FCA 215.

20 See, for example, *Re Mahjoub*, 2011 FC 506.

21 *Almrei (Re)*, 2009 FC 1263.

22 Colin Freeze, "'Secret Trial' Defendant Back in Court" *Globe and Mail* (15 May 2014), online: www.theglobeandmail.com/news/national/secret-trial-defendant-back-in-court/article18673894/; *Almrei v Canada (Minister of Citizenship and Immigration)*, 2014 FC 1002.

23 *Charkaoui (Re)*, [2009] ACF No 1208.

24 *Canada v Harkat*, 2014 SCC 37.

25 2009 FC 1263 at paras 441 and 457.

26 *Harkat (Re)*, 2010 FC 1241 at para 3.

27 Above note 2.

28 *Jaballah (Re)*, 2010 FC 507.

29 *Charkaoui*, above note 2 at para. 109.

30 *Ibid* at paras 112 & 113.

31 "Joint Statement by the Hon. Anne McLellan, Deputy Prime Minister and Minister of Public Safety and Emergency Preparedness & the Hon. Irwin Cotler, Minister of Justice and Attorney General of Canada" (14 November 2005), online: nouvelles.gc.ca/web/article-en.do?crtr.sj1D=&mthd=advSrch&crtr.mnthndVl=&nid=183399&crtr.dpt1D=&crtr.tp1D=&crtr.lc1D=&crtr.yrStrtVl=&crtr.kw=royal%2Bassent&crtr.dyStrtVl=&crtr.aud1D=&crtr.mnthStrtVl=&crtr.yrndVl=&crtr.dyndVl=.

32 "Canada Kicks Out Alleged Russian Spy" *CBC News* (26 December 2006), online: www.cbc.ca/news/canada/canada-kicks-out-alleged-russian-spy-1.575294.

33 *A and Others v Secretary of State for the Home Department*, [2004] UKHL 56 [*A and Others*].

34 Public Safety Canada, "Final 2009-2010 Evaluation of the Security Certificate Initiative" at section 2.2, online: www.publicsafety.gc.ca/cnt/rsrcs/pblctns/vltn-scrt-crtfct-2009-10/index-eng.aspx#b08.

35 *Almrei (Re)*, 2009 FC 1263.

36 Alyshah Hasham, "Via Rail Terror Trial: Jury Finds Esseghaier Guilty on 5 Counts, Jaser on 3" *Toronto Star* (20 March 2015), online: www.thestar.com/news/crime/2015/03/20/via-rail-terror-trial-jury-finds-esseghaier-guilty-on-5-counts-jaser-on-3.html.

37 Sam Pazzano, "Raed Jaser Arrested and Released on 2004 Deportation Order" *Toronto Sun* (20 March 2015), online: www.torontosun.com/2015/03/20/raed-jaser-arrested-and-released-on-2004-deportation-order.

38 *IRPA*, above note 14, ss 33, 34, 55ff.

39 *Ibid*, ss 86ff.

40 For an argument that substitutions effects are pervasive in counter-terrorism practices and pose a distinct challenge, see Kent Roach, "Thematic Conclusions and Future Challenges" in Kent Roach, ed, *Comparative Counter-terrorism Law* (New York: Cambridge University Press, 2015) c 24.

41 See, for example, Colin Perkel, "Jahanzeb Malik Ordered out of Canada" *CBC News* (5 June 2015), online: www.cbc.ca/news/canada/toronto/jahanzeb-malik-ordered-out-of-canada-1.3102070; IRB, Reasons and Decision, ID File No 0003-B5-00397 (5 June 2015).

42 *Almrei (Re)*, above note 35 at paras 163 and 438.

43 *Terrorism Prevention and Investigation Measures Act*, 2011, c 23.

44 *A and Others*, above note 33.

45 See *Terrorism Prevention and Investigation Measures Act*, 2011, c 23, Schedule 1; David Anderson, "First Report of the Independent Reviewer on the Operation of the Terrorism Prevention and Investigation Act 2011" (March 2013) at 103, online: terrorismlegislationreviewer.independent.gov.uk/wp-content/uploads/2013/04/first-report-tpims.pdf.

46 David Anderson, "Third Report of the Independent Reviewer on the Operation of the Terrorism Prevention and Investigation Act 2011" (March 2015) at para 2.3, online: www.gov.uk/government/uploads/system/uploads/attachment_data/file/411824/IRTL_TPIMs_2014_final_report__web_.pdf.

47 UK Parliament, Joint Committee on Human Rights, Post-Legislative Scrutiny: Terrorism Prevention and Investigation Measures Act 2011, 10th report of 2013-2014, HL Paper 113 HC 1014 (23 January 2014) at 28, online: www.publications.parliament.uk/pa/jt201314/jtselect/jtrights/113/113.pdf.

48 Anderson, above note 46, at para 3.16.

49 *Counter-terrorism and Security Act 2015*, c 6, ss 16 & 17.

50 *Ibid.*

51 UK Parliament, Home Affairs Committee, "Conclusions of the Home Affairs Committee's 2014 Report on Counter-terrorism" (2014) at para 13, online: www. publications.parliament.uk/pa/cm201415/cmselect/cmhaff/933/93306.htm.

52 *Criminal Code*, above note 18, ss 83.3 and 810.011.

53 *Ibid*, ss 810 and 810.2.

54 *Ibid*, s 810.1.

55 *Ibid*, s 810.01.

56 *Ibid.*

57 *Ibid*, s 811.

58 Proceedings of the Standing Senate Committee on National Security and Defence, "Issue 10- Evidence" (3 November 2014) (Chair: Daniel Lang), Brian Saunders, Director of Public Prostitutions, online: www.parl.gc.ca/content/sen/ committee/412/SECD/10EV-51696-E.HTM.

59 *Ibid.*

60 Allan Woods, "Police Seeking Terror-Linked Peace Bonds against Two Montreal Teenagers" *Toronto Star* (15 April 2015), online: www.thestar.com/news/canada/ 2015/04/15/police-seeking-terror-linked-peace-bonds-against-two-montreal-teenagers.html.

61 *Ibid*; "Mounties Make Terror Arrests in Quebec: At Least Six Suspected of Planning to Join Foreign Extremist Groups" *Toronto Star* (20 May 2015); Monique Beaudin, "Pierrefonds Man Out on Bail under New Bond Limits" *Montreal Gazette* (12 May 2015).

62 Beaudin, *ibid.*

63 Kevin Bissett, "RCMP Allege P.E.I. Man Had Beans Needed to Produce Deadly Toxin Ricin" *Globe and Mail* (20 April 2015), online: www.theglobeandmail.com/ news/national/rcmp-allege-pei-man-had-beans-needed-to-produce-deadly-toxin-ricin-docs/article24039003/.

64 *Ibid.*

65 Michael MacDonald, "PEI Man Signs Peace Bond over Ricin Allegations Made by the RCMP" *CTV News* (22 May 2015), online: www.ctvnews.ca/canada/p-e-i-man-signs-peace-bond-over-ricin-allegations-made-by-the-rcmp-1.2385534.

66 *Ibid.*

67 Michael MacDonald, "RCMP Fears Spur Man to Sign a Peace Bond: Wanted to Make Ricin, Build Rockets, Mounties Say" *Globe and Mail* (23 May 2015).

68 Allan Woods, "RCMP Seek Peace Bond over Terrorism Fears" *Toronto Star* (9 June 2015).

69 Mike McIntyre & Kevin Rollason, "GPS Tracker Part of Strict Bail" *Winnipeg Free Press* (16 June 2015).

70 Steve Lambert, "Winnipeg Man Suspected of Planning Terrorism Says Charter Rights Violated" *Canadian Press* (30 June 2015).

71 Paul Cherry, "Teens Remain Detained during Terror Investigation" *Montreal Gazette* (17 June 2015).

72 Le Perreaux, Colin Freeze, & Tu Thanh Ha, "Integrated Anti-radicalization Effort Key to Defusing Threat, Experts Say" *Globe and Mail* (21 May 2015).

73 Allan Woods, "Montreal Man Ordered to Cut Contacts with Terrorists under Rare Peace Bond" *Montreal Gazette* (27 March 2015), online: www.thestar.com/news/canada/2015/03/27/montreal-man-ordered-to-cut-contacts-with-terrorists-under-rare-peace-bond.html; Graeme Hamilton, "Second Montreal Terror Suspect Signs Peace Bond" *Edmonton Journal* (11 April 2015).

74 Standing Committee on National Security and Defence, "Evidence" (20 April 2015) (Chair: Daniel Lang), George Dolhai, Deputy Director of Public Prosecutions, Public Prosecution Service of Canada, online: www.parl.gc.ca/content/sen/committee/412/SECD/52040-E.HTM.

75 Proceedings of the Standing Senate Committee on National Security and Defence, above note 58.

76 Caroline Barghout, "Aaron Driver Defends ISIS, Parliament Hill Attack, Denies He Is a Threat" *CBC News* (24 June 2015), online: www.cbc.ca/news/canada/manitoba/aaron-driver-defends-isis-attack-on-parliament-but-denies-he-s-a-threat-1.3124815; "MP James Bezan Wants Aaron Driver Charged with Inciting Terrorism" *CBC News* (25 Jun 2015), online: www.cbc.ca/news/canada/manitoba/mp-james-bezan-wants-aaron-driver-charged-for-inciting-terrorism-1.3127204.

77 *Criminal Code*, above note 18, s 811.

78 Leslie Ferenc, "RCMP Tried to Get Peace Bond on Quebec Man Who Killed Soldier," *Toronto Star* (15 Jan 2015), online: www.thestar.com/news/canada/2015/01/15/police-tried-to-get-peace-bond-on-quebec-man-who-killed-soldier.html.

79 Senate, above note 74.

80 Standing Senate Committee on National Security and Defence, "Evidence" (27 October 2014) (Chair: Daniel Lang), RCMP Commissioner Bob Paulson, online: www.parl.gc.ca/content/sen/committee/412/SECD/51670-E.HTM.

81 Alex Boutlier, "Slain Soldier's Sister Fights for C-51" *Toronto Star* (24 March 2015).

82 Ontario Provincial Police, "Independent Investigation into the Death of Michael Zehaf-Bibeau," online: www.rcmp-grc.gc.ca/pubs/parl/opp-zb-eng.pdf; *Martin Place Siege — Joint Commonwealth–New South Wales Review* (January 2015).

83 *Criminal Code*, above note 18, s 811.

84 *Ibid*, s 810.011(1) [emphasis added].

85 *Ibid*, s 810.011(3).

86 *Ibid*, s 810.011(5).

87 *Ibid*, s 811.

88 *Ibid*, s 810.011(10).

89 *R v Louis*, 2014 BCSC 1029.

90 David Paciocco, "Constitutional Casualties of September 11: Limiting the Legacy of the *Anti-terrorism Act*" (2002) 16 *Supreme Court Law Review* (2d) 185 at 200.

91 Trotter, above note 13.

92 *R v Budreo* (2000), 46 OR (3d) 481 (CA).

93 *Ibid* at para 24.

94 *Ibid* at para 32.

95 *Ibid* at para 39.

96 See, for example, Stanley A Cohen, *Privacy, Crime and Terror Legal Rights and Security in a Time of Peril* (Toronto: LexisNexis Butterworths, 2005) at 221.

97 Standing Senate Committee on National Security and Defence, "Evidence" (20 April 2015) (Chair: Daniel Lang), Mike Cabana, Deputy Commissioner, Federal Policing, Royal Canadian Mounted Police, online: www.parl.gc.ca/content/sen/committee/412/SECD/52040-E.HTM.

98 RCMP, Questions and Answers, Bill C-51, Q5 (Marked "Draft April 17 2015"), released via RCMP ATIP request A-2015-04006.

CHAPTER EIGHT: INTERRUPT

1   Bill C-51, *An Act to enact the Security of Canada Information Sharing Act and the Secure Air Travel Act, to amend the Criminal Code, the Canadian Security Intelligence Service Act and the Immigration and Refugee Protection Act and to make related and consequential amendments to other Acts*, 2d Sess, 41st Parl, 2015 (assented to 18 June 2015), SC 2015, c 20.

2   *R v Ahmad*, 2010 ONSC 5874.

3   *R v Abdelhaleem*, [2010] OJ No 5693 at para 2.

4   *Ibid* at para 47; *R v Gaya*, 2008 CanLII 24539 at para 51.

5   *R v NY*, 2012 ONCA 745 at para 109ff.

6   *Ibid* at para 112ff.

7   *Criminal Code*, RSC 1985, c C-46.

8   [1999] 1 SCR 565.

9   See, for example, Marc Gorbet, "Bill C-24's Police Immunity Provisions: Parliament's Unnecessary Legislative Response to Police Illegality in Undercover Operations," (2004) 9 *Canadian Criminal Law Review* 35.

10 Standing Senate Committee on Legal and Constitutional Affairs, "Twelfth Report" (4 December 2001) (Chair: Lorna Milne), online: www.parl.gc.ca/Content/SEN/Committee/371/lega/rep/rep12deco1-e.htm.

11 Standing Committee on Justice and Human Rights, "First Report - Interim Report" (Adopted by the Committee on 21 June 2006; Presented to the House on 22 June 2006), online: www.parl.gc.ca/HousePublications/Publication.aspx?DocId=2315361&Language=E&Mode=1&Parl=39&Ses=1.

12 Commission of Inquiry Concerning Certain Activities of the Royal Canadian Mounted Police, *Freedom and Security under the Law: Second Report, Volume 1* (Ottawa; Supply and Services Canada, 1981) at 542.

13 *Criminal Code*, RSC 1985, c C-46, ss 25.1ff.

14 *Ibid*, s 25.1(11).

15 *Ibid*, s 2.

16 *R v JJ*, 2010 ONSC 735 at para 336, leave to appeal refused, [2010] SCCA No 161 [*JJ*].

17 *Criminal Code*, above note 13, s 25.1(8).

18 *Ibid*, s 25.1(9).

19 *Ibid*, ss 25.2 & 25.3.

20 *Ibid*, s 25.4.

21 Public Safety Canada, "2013 Annual Report on the RCMP's Use of the Law Enforcement Justification Provisions," online: www.publicsafety.gc.ca/cnt/rsrcs/pblctns/nnl-rprt-lw-nfrcmnt-2013/index-eng.aspx.

22 See, for example, Gregoire Charles N Webber, "Legal Lawlessness and the Rule of Law: A Critique of Section 25.1 of the Criminal Code" (2005) 31 *Queen's Law Journal* 121.

23 See Standing Senate Committee on Legal and Constitutional Affairs, above note 10.

24 *Canadian Charter of Rights and Freedoms*, Part I of the *Constitution Act, 1982*, being Schedule B to the *Canada Act 1982* (UK), 1982, c 11 [*Charter*].

25 *R v Lising*, 2007 BCSC 906.

26 *JJ*, above note 16 at para 282.

27 Shaamini Yogaretnam, "Chanting, Tasers and Gunfire" *National Post* (30 October 2014); Shaamini Yogaretnam & Andrew Seymour, "Ottawa Man under Investigation Had Called Parliament Hill Shooter a 'Martyr'" *Ottawa Citizen* (31 October 2014).

28 Office of the Inspector General, United States Department of Justice, *The September 11 Detainees: A Review of the Treatment of Aliens Held on Immigration Charges in Connection with the Investigation of The September 11 Attacks* (Washington, DC: Department of Justice, 2003) at 195.

29 *Ibid*, estimated from figure 9 at 105.

30 *R v Mejid*, 2010 ONSC 5532 [*Mejid*].

31 *Ibid* at para 100.

32 *Ibid*.

33 *Ibid* at paras 111 & 112.

34 Isabel Teotonio, "Brampton Man Sues Government Alleging CSIS Harassed Him" *Toronto Star* (27 May 2011).

35 Liberty, "Terrorism Pre-Charge Detention: Comparative Law Study" (July 2010), online: www.liberty-human-rights.org.uk/sites/default/files/comparative-law-study-2010-pre-charge-detention.pdf.

36 SC 2001, c 41 [*ATA*].

37 Stanley A Cohen, *Privacy, Crime and Terror: Legal Rights and Security in a Time of Peril* (Toronto: LexisNexis Butterworths, 2005) at 218.

38 *A and Others v Secretary of State*, [2004] EWCA CIV 1123 at paras 154–55.

39 *R v Khawaja*, 2012 SCC 69 at paras 72–74.

40 See, for example, André Martin, Ombudsman Ontario, "The Code" (June 2013), online: www.ombudsman.on.ca/Ombudsman/files/45/450c6aa8-3481-43d6-bce1-8141fa6bbbda.pdf.

41 *Criminal Code* (Cth), Act No 12 of 1995, s 105.42.

42 *Australian Security Intelligence Organisation Act*, Act No 113 of 1979 as amended, Division 3.

43 *Ibid*, s 34T; *Australian Criminal Code Act*, Act No 12 of 1995 as amended, s 105.33. United Nations *Convention against Torture*, Can TS 1987 No 36.

44 *Ibid*, ss 105.5, 105.33A, and 105.39.

45 Government of Canada, "Backgrounder: Amending the Canadian Security Intelligence Service Act to Give CSIS the Mandate to Intervene to Disrupt Terror Plots While They Are in the Planning Stages" (30 January 2015), online: news.gc.ca/web/article-en.do?nid=926869.

46 CSIS, "Committee Note: Threat Diminishment: Hot Issues," released under CSIS ATIP 117-2015-35 [CSIS Committee Note].

47 Craig Forcese, "Bill C-51: Catching Up on the 'Catching Up with Our Allies' Justification for New CSIS Powers" (16 April 2015), online: craigforcese. squarespace.com/national-security-law-blog/2015/4/16/bill-c-51-catching-up-on-the-catching-up-with-our-allies-jus.html.

48 Joanne Levasseur, "Winnipeg Man Considered Radical Extremist by CSIS, His Father Says" *CBC News* (6 March 2015), online: www.cbc.ca/news/canada/manitoba/winnipeg-man-considered-radical-extremist-by-csis-his-father-says-1.2984074.

49 CSIS Committee Note, above note 46.

50 Colin Freeze, "Spy-Watchers Urge a Shorter Leash for CSIS" *Globe and Mail* (27 October 2010), online: www.theglobeandmail.com/news/politics/spy-watchers-urge-a-shorter-leash-for-csis/article1381179/. See also Levasseur, above note 48.

51 Security Intelligence Review Committee, "CSIS Use of Disruption to Counter National Security Threats" (SIRC Study 2009-05), File No 2800-150 (redacted version released under Access to Information).

52 *Ibid.*

53 *Canadian Security Intelligence Service Act*, RSC 1985, c C-23, s 12.1 [*CSIS Act*].

54 *Ibid*, s 2.

55 CSIS Committee Note, above note 46.

56 *Criminal Code*, s 83.01(b) (definition of "terrorist activity" includes serious interference with a critical infrastructure, but carves out protest so long as not associated with violence).

57 *CSIS Act*, above note 53, s 12.2.

58 *Ibid*, s 12.1.

59 *Ibid.*

60 *Ibid*, s 21.1.

61 Senate Standing Committee on National Security and Defence, "Evidence" (20 April 2015) (Chair: Daniel Lang), online: www.parl.gc.ca/content/sen/committee/412/SECD/52040-E.HTM.

62 Senate Standing Committee on National Security and Defence, "Issue 15 - Evidence" (30 March 2015), online: www.parl.gc.ca/content/sen/committee/412/SECD/15EV-52013-E.HTM.

63 Standing Committee on Public Safety and National Security, "Evidence" (31 March 2015) (Chair: Daryl Kramp), online: www.parl.gc.ca/HousePublications/Publication.aspx?DocId=7913958&Language=E&Mode=1&Parl=41&Ses=2.

64 *CSIS Act*, above note 53, s 12.1(4).

65 Standing Committee on Public Safety and National Security, above note 63, per Ted Falk, MP [emphasis added].

66 *Ibid*, Michael Duffy (Senior General Counsel, National Security Law, Department of Justice).

67 Security Intelligence Review Committee, "Annual Report 2006–07" at 20ff, online: www.sirc-csars.gc.ca/pdfs/ar_2006-2007-eng.pdf.

68 Remarks by Jim Judd, Director of CSIS, at the Global Futures Forum Conference in Vancouver (15 April 2008).

69 RCMP, Questions and Answers, Bill C-51, Q17 (Marked "Draft April 17 2015"), released via ATIP request A-2015-04006.

70 *Ibid* at Q18.

71 *Ibid* at Q20.

72 *Re Vancouver Sun*, 2004 SCC 43.

73 *CSIS Act*, above note 53, ss 12.1(2) and 21.1(2).

74 Senate Standing Committee on National Security and Defence, above note 62.

75 *CSIS Act*, above note 53, s 51(2).

76 *Ibid*, s 38(1.1).

77 See discussion in Craig Forcese, "Touching Torture with a Ten Foot Pole: The Legality of Canada's Approach to National Security Information Sharing with Human Rights-Abusing States" (2014) 52(1) *Osgoode Hall Law Journal* 263, online: http://digitalcommons.osgoode.yorku.ca/ohlj/vol52/iss1/7/; *R v Hape*, 2007 SCC 26 at para 90 [*Hape*]; *Canada (Justice) v Khadr*, 2008 SCC 28 at para 2.

78 *Amnesty International Canada v Canada (Canadian Forces)*, 2008 FCA 401; *Slahi v Canada (Minister of Justice)*, 2009 FCA 259

79 *Hape*, above note 77 at para 39.

80 RSC 1985, c 22 (4th Supp).

81 *R v Oakes*, [1986] 1 SCR 103.

82 2012 SCC 12 [*Doré*].

83 *Ibid* at para 57.

84 *Greater Vancouver Transportation Authority v Canadian Federation of Students - British Columbia Component*, 2009 SCC 3 at para 55.

85 *R v Morales*, [1992] 3 SCR 711 at para 28 (raising the question of whether a discretion tied to "public interest" was precise enough to meet the "prescribed by law" standard).

86 *O'Neill v Canada (AG)*, [2006] OJ No 4189 at para 87ff.

87 See discussion in Robert J Sharpe and Kent Roach, *The Charter of Rights and Freedoms*, 5th ed (Toronto: Irwin Law, 2013) at 66.

88 *Application under s 83.28 of the Criminal Code (Re)*, 2004 SCC 42.

89 *Ibid* at para 91.

90 *Canadian Civil Liberties Association et al v Attorney General of Canada* (Notice of Application) 25 July 2015 at para 18, online: https://ccla.org/cclanewsite/wp-content/uploads/2015/07/Notice-of-Application-Re-Bill-C-51-C1382903xA0E3A.pdf.

91 Jack Goldsmith, *The Terror Presidency: Law and Judgment inside the Bush Administration* (New York: WW Norton & Co, 2009).

CHAPTER NINE: PROSECUTE

1 *R v Khawaja* 2010 ONCA 862 at para 24, aff'd 2012 SCC 69.

2 RSC, 1985, c C-5.

3 *Canada (AG) v Khawaja*, 2007 FC 490 at para 50.

4 *Canada (AG) v Khawaja*, 2007 FCA 342 at para 12. See also *Canada (AG) v Khawaja*, 2007 FCA 388. For a fuller account of this pre-trial litigation, see Kent Roach, *The Unique Challenges of Terrorism Prosecutions: Towards a Workable Relation Between Intelligence and Evidence: Vol 4 of Research Papers of the Commission of Inquiry into the Investigation of Air India Flight 182* (Ottawa: Public Works, 2010) at 239–50.

5 *Khawaja v Canada*, [2007] SCCA No 610.

6   *R v Khawaja*, 2006 CanLII 63685 (ON SC).

7   *Khawaja v Her Majesty the Queen*, 2007 CanLII 11625 (SCC).

8   *R v Khawaja*, [2008] OJ No 4244 (SCJ).

9   *R v Khawaja*, [2009] OJ No 4279.

10 *R v Khawaja*, 2010 ONCA 862.

11 *R v Khawaja*, 2012 SCC 69. As noted in the preface, one of us (Roach) represented an intervenor in this case who unsuccessfully argued that part of the definition of terrorist activity violated the *Charter*.

12 *Criminal Code*, RSC 1985, c C-46, s 83.01.

13 *Ibid*, s 83.01, defining "terrorist group" and "entity."

14 *Ibid*, s 83.19.

15 *Ibid*, s 83.18.

16 *Ibid*, s 2, defining "terrorism offence."

17 *Ibid*, ss 83.2 and 83.27.

18 Richard Mosley, "Preventing Terrorism — Bill C-36: The *Anti-terrorism Act 2001*" in D Daubney et al, eds, *Terrorism, Law and Democracy: How Is Canada Changing following September 11?* (Montreal: Éditions Thémis, 2002) at 152.

19 Part of the opposition to Bill C-36, the 2001 *ATA*, revolved around the government's apparent discount of the ability to apply inchoate offences to apprehended acts of terrorism. In any event, compare Kent Roach, "The Dangers of a *Charter*-Proof and Crime-Based Approach to Terrorism" in Ronald Daniels, Patrick Macklem, & Kent Roach, eds, *The Security of Freedom: Essays on Canada's Anti-terrorism Bill* (Toronto: University of Toronto Press, 2001), with Kent Roach, "The Criminal Law and Terrorism" in Victor Ramraj et al, eds, *Global Anti-terrorism Law and Policy* (Cambridge: Cambridge University Press, 2005), and Kent Roach, "Counter-terrorism in and outside of Canada and the Anti-terrorism Act" (2012) 16 *Review of Constitutional Studies* 243.

20 *R v Khawaja*, 2012 SCC 69 at para 50.

21 *Ibid* at paras 46–47.

22 *Holder v Humanitarian Law Project*, 130 S Ct 2705 (2010).

23 *Criminal Code*, above note 12, s 83.03(b).

24 2012 SCC 69 at para 102.

25 *R v Thambaithurai*, 2011 BCCA 137 at para 22 [*Thambaithurai*].

26 *R v Malik and Bagri*, 2005 BCSC 350 [*Malik and Bagri*].

27 Canada, *Terrorism Prosecutions in Canada* (as of 16 March 2015), with the outcome updated by these authors to take into account more recently completed trials. (Internal government document on file with the authors.)

28 Andrew Lynch, Nicola McGarrity, & George Williams, *Inside Australia's Anti-terrorism Laws and Trials* (Sydney: NewSouth Publishing, 2015) at 92.

29 UK Home Office, "Operation of Police Powers under the Terrorism Act 2000 and Subsequent Legislation: Arrests, Outcomes and Stops and Searches, Quarterly Update to 31 December 2014" (25 June 2015), at Table A-13, showing total convictions of 452, and 41 "Northern Ireland related," online: www.gov.uk/government/publications/operation-of-police-powers-under-the-terrorism-act-2000-quarterly-update-to-december-2014/operation-of-police-powers-under-the-terrorism-act-2000-and-subsequent-legislation-arrests-outcomes-and-stops-and-searches-quarterly-update-to-31-d.

30 Center on Law and Security, New York University School of Law, "Terrorist Trial Report Case: September 11, 2001 – September 11, 2011" at 7, online: www. lawandsecurity.org/Portals/o/Documents/TTRC%20Ten%20Year%20Issue. pdf; note, however, that these numbers may include the statistical shortcoming identified in a subsequent US Justice Department audit, online: www. documentcloud.org/documents/791778-a1334.html.

31 Columbia Law School, Human Rights Watch, "Illusion of Justice: Human Rights Abuses in US Terrorism Prosecutions" (July 2014) at 201, online: www.hrw.org/ sites/default/files/reports/usterrorism0714_ForUpload_0_0_0.pdf.

32 Human Rights Watch, "Funding the 'Final War': LTTE Intimidation and Extortion in the Tamil Diaspora" (14 March 2006), online: www.hrw.org/ report/2006/03/14/funding-final-war/ltte-intimidation-and-extortion-tamil-diaspora.

33 Standing Senate Committee on Banking, Trade and Commerce, "Follow the Money: Is Canada Making Progress in Combatting Money Laundering and Terrorist Financing? Not Really" (March 2013), online: www.parl.gc.ca/Content/ SEN/Committee/411/BANC/rep/rep10mar13-e.pdf; Standing Senate Committee on National Security and Defence, *Countering the Terrorist Threat in Canada: An Interim Report* (July 2015), online: www.parl.gc.ca/Content/SEN/Committee/412/ secd/rep/rep18jul15-e.pdf.

34 *R v Bourque*, 2014 NBQB 237 at para 8.

35 *Ibid* at para 10.

36 Douglas Quan, "Justin Bourque: Terrorism Charges Were Once Pondered against Man Who Shot Dead Three Mounties" *O-Canada.com* (31 October 2014), online: o.canada.com/news/justin-bourque-terrorism-charges-were-once-pondered-against-man-who-shot-dead-three-mounties.

37 Allan Woods, "Shooting Suspect Well Known in Quebec Village" *Toronto Star* (5 September 2012), online: www.thestar.com/news/canada/2012/09/05/shooting_ suspect_wellknown_in_quebec_village.html.

38 Michelle Shephard, "Right-Wing Extremism a Greater Threat to North America" *Toronto Star* (28 June 2015), online: www.thestar.com/news/world/2015/06/28/ right-wing-extremism-a-greater-threat-in-north-america.html. The TSAS database is at www.extremism.ca.

39 "RBC Firebombing Arrests Made by Ottawa Police" *CBC News* (18 June 2010), online: www.cbc.ca/news/canada/ottawa/rbc-firebombing-arrests-made-by-ottawa-police-1.931220.

40 *Criminal Code*, above note 12, s 83.27.

41 "Alleged Halifax Shooting Plotters 'Were Prepared to Wreak Havoc and Mayhem'" *CBC News* (14 February 2015), online: www.cbc.ca/news/canada/ nova-scotia/alleged-halifax-shooting-plotters-were-prepared-to-wreak-havoc-and-mayhem-1.2957767.

42 Anna Mehler Paperny, "Halifax Plot: So What Is 'Terrorism,' Anyway?" *Global News* (14 February 2015), online: globalnews.ca/news/1830795/ halifax-plot-so-what-is-terrorism-anyway/.

43 Amanda Connolly, "MacKay Erred in Saying Terrorism Needs to Be 'Culturally Motivated,'" *iPolitics* (14 February 2015), online: ipolitics.ca/2015/02/14/ mackay-erred-in-saying-terrorism-must-be-culturally-motivated/.

44 Mohammad Fadel, "A Tale of Two Massacres: *Charlie Hebdo* and Utoya Island" in Edward Iacobucci & Stephen Toope, eds, *After the Paris Attacks: Responses in Canada, Europe and around the Globe* (Toronto: University of Toronto Press, 2015) at 32–33 (warning of the development of double standards in Canada with reference to Minister MacKay's comments and intelligence reports about the danger of terrorism in Canada from white supremacists).

45 Mitch Potter, "Moms Open Path for Kids in ISIS to Return" *Toronto Star* (4 June 2015).

46 Standing Senate Committee on National Security and Defence, above note 33.

47 *Ibid.*

48 *Malik and Bagri*, above note 26.

49 *R v Sher*, 2014 ONSC 4790.

50 *R v Hersi*, 2014 ONSC 1211.

51 *R v Hersi*, 2014 ONSC 1286 at para 18.

52 *R v Hersi*, 2014 ONSC 1217.

53 *R v Khawaja*, 2012 SCC 69.

54 *R v Hersi*, 2014 ONSC 1303.

55 *R v Hersi*, 2014 ONSC 2897 at para 5.

56 "Currently Listed Entities," online: Public Safety Canada www.publicsafety.gc.ca/cnt/ntnl-scrt/cntr-trrrsm/lstd-ntts/crrnt-lstd-ntts-eng.aspx#2009.

57 *R v Abdaheleem*, [2010] OJ No 5693 at para 71.

58 *R v N.Y.*, 2012 ONCA 745 at para 142.

59 *R v Barnes*, [1991] 1 SCR 449.

60 *R v Mack*, [1988] 2 SCR 903.

61 Columbia Law School, Human Rights Watch, above note 31.

62 *R v Hersi*, 2014 ONSC 4143 at para 19.

63 *Ibid* at para 34.

64 See Kent Roach, "Entrapment and Equality in Terrorism Prosecutions" (2011) 80 *Mississippi Law Journal* 1455.

65 *R v Hersi*, 2014 ONSC 4414 at para 63.

66 *Ibid* at para 44. Adrian Humphreys, "Canadian 'Terrorist Tourist' Mohamed Hersi Gets 10 Years in Jail for Planning to Join Islamic Terrorist Group in Somalia" *National Post* (24 July 2014), online: news.nationalpost.com/news/canada/canadian-terror-tourist-mohamed-hersi-gets-10-years-in-jail-for-planning-to-join-islamic-jihadist-group-in-somalia. See also Michelle Shephard, "The Case of the Big Talker Convicted of Terrorism" *Toronto Star* (23 June 2014), online: www.thestar.com/news/world/2014/06/23/the_case_of_the_big_talker_convicted_of_terrorism.html.

67 *R v Hersi*, 2014 ONSC 4414 at paras 37 and 45.

68 *Ibid* at para 84.

69 *R v Khawaja*, 2012 SCC 69 at para 124.

70 Humphreys, above note 66; see also Shephard, above note 66.

71 Commission of Inquiry into the Investigation of the Bombing of Air India Flight 182, *Air India Flight 182: A Canadian Tragedy: Vol 3, the Relationship between Intelligence and Evidence* (Ottawa: Public Works, 2010) [*Air India Inquiry Vol 3*].

72 Kent Roach, *September 11: Consequences for Canada* (Montreal: McGill-Queen's University Press, 2003) at 110; *R v Ahmad*, 2011 SCC 6 at para 34.

73 *R v Stinchcombe*, [1991] 3 SCR 326.

74 *R v O'Connor*, [1995] 4 SCR 411; *R v McNeil*, 2009 SCC 3.

75 *Air India Inquiry Vol 3*, above note 71 at 121.

76 Standing Senate Committee on National Security and Defence, "Issue 16-Evidence" (20 April 2015) (Chair: Daniel Lang), online: www.parl.gc.ca/content/sen/committee/412/SECD/16EV-52040-E.HTM.

77 *R v Ahmad*, 2009 CanLII 84776 (ON SC) at para 43.

78 *Air India Inquiry Vol 3*, above note 71 at 195.

79 *Ibid* at 91.

80 *Charkaoui v Canada*, 2008 SCC 38.

81 Hon. Bob Rae, *Lessons to be Learned* (Ottawa: Air India Review Secretariat, 2005) at 23.

82 *Air India Inquiry Vol 3*, above note 71 at 93.

83 Commission of Inquiry into the Investigation of the Bombing of Air India Flight 182, *Air India Flight 182: A Canadian Tragedy: Volume Two, Post Bombing* (Ottawa: Public Works, 2010) at 523 and 543; *Air India Inquiry Vol 3*, above note 71 at 152.

84 *Ibid* at 98.

85 Jim Bronskill & Murray Brewster, "Jeffrey Delisle Case: CSIS Secretly Watched Spy, Held File Back from the RCMP" *Toronto Star* (26 May 2013), online: www.thestar.com/news/canada/2013/05/26/jeffrey_delisle_case_csis_secretly_watched_spy_held_file_back_from_rcmp.html.

86 "CSIS and RCMP One Vision: An Operational Approach to Intelligence and Evidence" undated powerpoint presentation, Access to Information Request A-2014-224. The One Vision document contains only one reference to the overview of the Air India Commission's report and no reference to volume 3 of its report which was devoted to the relation between intelligence and evidence. It also contained frequent quotations from rulings of a Toronto 18 trial in *R v Ahmad*, 2009 CanLII 84776 (ON SC) [*Ahmad*], but omitted this case's important warning that while CSIS in that case would not be subject to disclosure under *R v Stinchcombe*, [1991] 3 SCR 326, it would still be subject to disclosure as a third party under *R v O'Connor*, [1995] 4 SCR 411. The *Ahmad* judge stated, "The standard of likely relevance to be met at the first stage of the O'Connor test is significant but not onerous (para 29). Once that test is met, the court will review the material and order it disclosed if it would have met the test for disclosure under *Stinchcombe* had it made its way into the Crown's file (para 42)": *Ahmad, ibid* at para 21.

87 *R v Ahmad*, 2009 CanLII 84776 (ON SC) at paras 37–40 and 43.

88 RCMP, Questions and Answers, Bill C-51, Q21 (Marked "Draft April 17 2015"), released via ATIP request A-2015-04006.

89 *R v Malik, Bagri and Reyat*, 2002 BCSC 864; *R v Malik and Bagri*, 2004 BCSC 554.

90 *R v Ahmad*, 2009 CanLII 84776 (ON SC) at paras 31 and 41–46.

91 The Victoria Canada day plot trial judge concluded that CSIS and the RCMP ran "in their essence, independent and separate investigations"; *R v Nuttall*, 2015 BCSC 1125 at para 44 [*Nuttall*]. A trial judge in another case adopted the conclusions from the Toronto 18 case that CSIS was a separate entity from the police for disclosure. *R v Alizadeh*, 2013 ONSC 5417 at para 14. CSIS was also treated as a third party not directly subject to *Stinchcombe* disclosure requirements in the VIA Rail plot case. *R v Jaser*, 2014 ONSC 6052 at para 5.

92   Standing Senate Committee on National Security and Defence, "Issue 15-Evidence" (2 April 2015) (Chair: Daniel Lang), online: www.parl.gc.ca/content/sen/committee/412/SECD/15EV-52037-E.HTM.

93   Standing Committee on National Security and Public Safety, *Evidence* (26 March 2015) (Chair: Daryl Kramp), online: www.parl.gc.ca/HousePublications/Publication.aspx?DocId=7898598.

94   *R v Mejid*, 2010 ONSC 5532 at para 96.

95   *R v Ul-Haque*, [2007] NWSC 1251 at para 62.

96   Inspector General of Intelligence and Security, "Report of Inquiry into the Actions Taken by ASIO in 2003 in Respect of Mr. Izhar Ul-Haque and Other Matters" (2008) at para 191.

97   Reg Whitaker, Gregory S Kealey, & Andrew Parnaby, *Secret Service: Political Policing in Canada: From the Fenians to Fortress America* (Toronto: University of Toronto Press, 2012) at 514.

98   *Criminal Code*, above note 12, s 2 as amended by SC 2015 c 20, s 15.

99   SC 2015 c 9.

100   *Canadian Security Intelligence Service Act*, RSC 1985, c C-23, s 18.1(4)(b) [*CSIS Act*].

101   *Nuttall*, above note 91 at para 2.

102   *Ibid*.

103   *Air India Inquiry Vol 3*, above note 71 at 139.

104   2014 SCC 37 at para 85.

105   *R v Khela*, (1998) 126 CCC (3d) 341 (QC CA).

106   *R v Parmar* (1987), 37 CCC (3d) 300, aff'd (1990) 53 CCC (3d) 489 (ON CA); Roach, above note 4 at 112.

107   Canadian Press, "Toronto 18 informant asked RCMP for $15M" *CBC News* (19 January 2010), online: www.cbc.ca/news/canada/toronto/toronto-18-informant-asked-rcmp-for-15m-1.928064.

108   *R v Named Person B*, 2013 SCC 9 at para 143 [*Named Person B*].

109   Canadian Press, above note 107.

110   SC 2013, c 29.

111   Kent Roach, "A Missed Opportunity to Reform Witness Protection" (2013) 59 *Constitutional Law Quarterly* 441.

112   *Air India Inquiry Vol 3*, above note 71 at 132.

113   Standing Committee on Public Safety and National Security, "Evidence" (24 November 2014) (Chair: Daryl Kramp), online: www.parl.gc.ca/HousePublications/Publication.aspx?DocId=6789939&Language=E&Mode=1&Parl=41&Ses=2.

114   *Named Person B*, above note 108.

115   *CSIS Act*, above note 100, s 2, defining "human source."

116   Above note 2.

117   *Air India Inquiry Vol 3*, above note 71 at 165–67.

118   See Kent Roach & Gary Trotter, "Miscarriages of Justice in the War against Terror" (2005) *109 Pennsylvania State Law Review* 967.

119   *R v Ribic*, 2004 CanLII 7091 (ON SC) at para 49.

120   *Air India Inquiry Vol 3*, above note 71 at ch 7.

121   *R v Ahmad*, 2011 SCC 6 at para 5 [*Ahmad*].

122 *Ibid* at para 34 [emphasis in original].

123 See, generally, Michael Code & Kent Roach, "The Role of the Independent Lawyer and Security Certificates" (2006) 52 *Criminal Law Quarterly* 85; *Ahmad*, above note 121 at para 49.

124 *R v Basi*, 2009 SCC 52.

125 *R v Jaser*, 2014 ONSC 6052.

126 *Nuttall*, above note 91 at para 2.

127 "Terrorism-Related Cases with Canadian Connections" *CBC News* (2 February 2015), online: www.cbc.ca/news/canada/recent-terrorism-related-cases-with-canadian-connections-1.1016842; Stewart Bell, "Mohamed Hersi Found Guilty of Attempting to Join Somali Terrorist Group Al-Shabab" *National Post* (30 May 2014), online: news.nationalpost.com/2014/05/30/mohamed-hersi-found-guilty-of-trying-to-join-somali-terrorist-group-al-shabab/?__federated=1.

128 *R v Gaya*, 2008 CanLII 24539 (ON SC) at para 187.

129 *R v St Cloud*, 2015 SCC 27.

130 The new maximum 1.5 day credit off of sentence for every day spent in pre-trial custody will be applied in most cases as a compensation for the fact that time in pre-trial custody does not count as time credited for eligibility for parole and remission. *R v Carvery*, 2014 SCC 27.

131 Megan O'Toole, "Toronto 18's Asad Ansari Sentenced to 6 Years 5 Months . . . Goes Free" *National Post* (4 October 2010), online: news.nationalpost.com/toronto/toronto-18s-asad-ansari-sentenced-to-6-5-years-goes-free.

132 Robert Diab, "Sentencing of Terrorism Offences after 9/11: A Comparative Review of Early Case Law" in Craig Forcese & Francois Crepeau, eds, *Terrorism, Law and Democracy: 10 Years after 9/11* (Montreal: Canadian Institute for the Administration of Justice, 2011) at 381.

133 *R v Khawaja*, 2012 SCC 69 at para 124. On this aspect of the discussion, see Robert Diab, "R v. Khawaja and the Fraught Question of Rehabilitation in Terrorism Sentencing" (2014) 39 *Queen's Law Journal* 587.

134 *Thambaithurai*, above note 25.

135 Stewart Bell, "As Convicted Terrorists Face Possible Release, Canada Faced with Growing Problem: How Do You Rehabilitate Them?" *National Post* (30 November 2012), online: news.nationalpost.com/news/canada/as-convicted-terrorists-face-possible-release-canada-faced-with-growing-problem-how-do-you-rehabilitate-them.

136 Canada, Integrated Terrorist Assessment Centre (ITAC), "Threat Assessment: Canada: Biannual Update on Terrorist and Extremist Threats (12-35-E)" (19 April 2012) at para 14.

137 Colin Freeze, "Terror-Wing Inmates Denounce Savagery" *Globe and Mail* (1 September 2011); Gary Dimmock, "Convicted Terrorist Scalded in Jail Attack" *National Post* (25 January 2012).

138 Jessica Hume, "Transfer to Provincial Jail Would Hinder Khadr's Rehabilitation: Warden" *Toronto Sun* (10 July 2014), online: www.torontosun.com/2014/07/10/transfer-to-provincial-jail-would-hinder-khadrs-rehabilitation-warden.

139 Alex Wilner & Brian Lee Crowley, "Preventing Prison Radicalization in Canada: More Needs to Be Done," online: The Macdonald-Laurier Institute www.macdonaldlaurier.ca/files/pdf/Wilner_Crowley_Prison_Radicalisation. pdf. See also Alex Wilner, "From Rehabilitation to Recruitment" *True North* (October 2010), online: www.macdonaldlaurier.ca/files/pdf/ FromRehabilitationToRecruitment.pdf.

CHAPTER TEN: DELETE

1   Translated by and quoted in William Tetley, *The October Crisis, 1970: An Insider's View* (Montreal: McGill-Queen's University Press, 2007) at 33–35.

2   *Public Order Regulations*, SOR/70-444, s 4.

3   Bill C-51, *An Act to enact the Security of Canada Information Sharing Act and the Secure Air Travel Act, to amend the Criminal Code, the Canadian Security Intelligence Service Act and the Immigration and Refugee Protection Act and to make related and consequential amendments to other Acts*, 2d Sess, 41st Parl, 2015 (assented to 18 June 2015), SC 2015, c 20.

4   *Criminal Code*, RSC 1985, c C-46, s 83.221.

5   *Ibid*, s 83.222–83.223.

6   Bill C-51, above note 3, s 31.

7   "Read Transcript of the Michael Zehaf-Bibeau Video" *Globe and Mail* (6 March 2015), online: www.theglobeandmail.com/news/politics/read-transcript-of-the-michael-zehaf-bibeau-video/article23329068/.

8   "Message of the Mujhaid 5" (8 December 2014), online: ringoffirenews.files. wordpress.com/2014/12/transcript.pdf. See also Stewart Bell, "ISIS Fighter from Ottawa Appears in Video Threatening Canada with Attacks 'Where It Hurts Most'" *National Post* (7 December 2014), online: news.nationalpost.com/news/world/israel-middle-east/john-maguire-an-isis-fighter-from-ottawa-appears-on-video-warning-canada-of-attacks-where-it-hurts-you-the-most.

9   Justice Canada, "Misconceptions about the New Offence of Advocating Terrorism Offences" (Undated document presented to Senate Standing Committee on National Security and Defence, 30 March 2015) [on file with authors].

10 Standing Senate Committee on National Security and Defence, "Evidence" (30 March 2015) (Chair: Daniel Lang).

11 See *Criminal Code*, above note 4, ss 83.18, 83.181, and 83.22.

12 *Requête n° 36109/03 du 2 octobre 2008* at paras 45–48, online: hudoc.echr.coe.int/ sites/eng/pages/search.aspx?i=001-88657.

13 Part I of the *Constitution Act, 1982*, being Schedule B to the *Canada Act 1982* (UK), 1982, c 11 [*Charter*].

14 Pierre Vallières, *White Niggers of America* (Toronto: McClelland and Stewart, 1971) at 266 and 268.

15 *R v Vallières*, [1970] 4 CCC 69 at 75 (Que CA). In a subsequent case, the Quebec Court of Appeal held 3:2 that evidence Vallières participated in the activities of the FLQ and wrote general political tracts was not sufficient to convict him of inciting the particular bombing: *R v Vallières* (1973), 15 CCC (2d) 241 (Que CA).

16 See *R v Namouh*, 2010 QCCQ 943 [*Namouh*].

17   See "Othman Ayed Hamdan Arrested, Facing Terrorism Charges" *CBC News* (10 July 2015), online: www.cbc.ca/news/canada/british-columbia/othman-ayed-hamdan-arrested-facing-terrorism-charges-1.3147663.

18   *Criminal Code*, above note 4, s 83.18.

19   See Bruce Campion-Smith & Michelle Shephard, "RCMP Charge Maguire and Two Others in Terror Investigation" *Toronto Star* (3 February 2015), online: www.thestar.com/news/canada/2015/02/03/rcmp-to-announce-terrorism-arrest-and-charges-at-3-pm.html.

20   See Jessica Stern & JM Berger, *ISIS: The State of Terror* (New York: Ecco/HarperCollins, 2015).

21   Quoted in Scott Shane & Ben Hubbard, "ISIS Displaying a Deft Command of Varied Media" *New York Times* (30 August 2014), online: www.nytimes.com/2014/08/31/world/middleeast/isis-displaying-a-deft-command-of-varied-media.html?_r=0.

22   See Senate Committee on National Security and Defence, *Countering the Terrorist Threat in Canada: An Interim Report* (2015) at 10.

23   *Criminal Code* (Cth), s 80.2C(3), as amended by *Counter-terrorism Legislation Amendment (Foreign Fighters) Act 2014*, No 116 of 2014.

24   Standing Committee on Public Safety and National Security, *Rights, Limits and Security: A Comprehensive Review of the Anti-terrorism Act* (Ottawa: Standing Committee on Public Safety and National Security, 2007) at 12 [*Rights, Limits and Security*].

25   Department of Justice Canada, *Criminalizing the Advocacy or Promotion of Terrorism Offences in General* (January 2015), online: news.gc.ca/web/article-en.do?nid=926049.

26   See *R v Vallières* (1973), 15 CCC (2d) 241 (Que CA).

27   See *Criminal Code*, above note 4, s 22.

28   *R v Hamilton*, 2005 SCC 47 at para 15.

29   See *Criminal Code*, above note 4, s 22.

30   See *ibid*, s 464.

31   See *R v Hersi*, 2014 ONSC 2897 [*Hersi*]. This case is discussed in Chapters 3 and 9.

32   See "Othman Ayed Hamdan Arrested, Facing Terrorism Charges" *CBC News* (10 July 2015), online: www.cbc.ca/news/canada/british-columbia/othman-ayed-hamdan-arrested-facing-terrorism-charges-1.3147663.

33   See *Criminal Code*, above note 4, s 59.

34   See *ibid*, s 264.1.

35   See *ibid*, s 319.

36   See *ibid*, s 318.

37   See *Mugesera v Canada*, 2005 SCC 40 at para 101.

38   See *Criminal Code*, above note 4, s 319.

39   See *ibid*, ss 318–19. The grounds were expanded in the *Protecting Canadians from Online Crime Act*, SC 2014, c 31, s 12.

40   The available terrorism offences are contained in the *Criminal Code*, above note 4, ss 83.02, 83.03, 83.04, 83.12, 83.18, 83.19, 83.191, 83.2, 83.201, 83.202, 83.21, 83.22, 83.23, and 83.231.

41   *Ibid*, s 83.01(b).

42   *Ibid*, s 83.03(a).

43 *Ibid*, s 83.22.

44 *Rights, Limits and Security*, above note 24.

45 *Criminal Code*, above note 4, s 83.21.

46 See *R v Khawaja*, 2012 SCC 69 at paras 50–51 [*Khawaja*].

47 *Namouh*, above note 16.

48 *Ibid* at para 10.

49 *Terrorism Act 2006* (UK), c 11, ss 1 & 2.

50 *Ibid*, s 20.

51 David Anderson, *Report on the Operation in 2010 of the Terrorism Act 2000 and of Part 1 of the Terrorism Act 2006* (July 2011) at para 10.7, online: www.gov.uk/government/uploads/system/uploads/attachment_data/file/243552/9780108510885.pdf.

52 See Tufyal Choudhury, "The *Terrorism Act 2006*: Discouraging Terrorism" in Ivan Hare & James Weinstein, eds, *Extreme Speed and Democracy* (Oxford: Oxford University Press, 2009) at 467.

53 *Terrorism Act 2006*, above note 49, s 3.

54 See Anderson, above note 51 at para 10.8.

55 See United Kingdom Home Office, "Operation of Police Powers under the *Terrorism Act 2000*: Data Tables, Financial Year Ending March 2014" (28 August 2014) at Table A.05a, online: www.gov.uk/government/statistics/operation-of-police-powers-under-the-terrorism-act-2000-data-tables-financial-year-ending-march-2014.

56 See *ibid* at Table A.08a.

57 See *ibid* at Table A.05a.

58 See *ibid* at Table A.08a.

59 See, for example, *R v Rahman*, [2008] EWCA Crim 1465; *R v Iqbal*, [2010] EWCA Crim 3215 (CA) [*Iqbal*].

60 See *Iqbal*, above note 59; *R v Gul*, [2014] 3 LRC 536 (UKSC) at para 2.

61 See *R v Brown*, [2011] EWCA Crim 2751.

62 See *R v Ahmad*, [2012] EWCA Crim 959; *Jobe v United Kingdom* (2011), 53 EHRR SE17 [*Jobe*].

63 See *Jobe*, above note 62 at para 11; *R v K*, [2008] 3 All ER 526 (CA).

64 See, in part, *R v Farooqi*, [2013] EWCA Crim 1649 at para 39.

65 Quoted in BBC News, "Bookseller Ahmed Faraz Jailed over Terror Offences" (13 December 2011), online: www.bbc.co.uk/news/uk-16171251.

66 *R v Faraz*, [2012] EWCA Crim 2820 at paras 8 and 47.

67 *Ibid* at para 57.

68 See above note 23.

69 *Criminal Code*, above note 4, s 83.221.

70 Justice Canada, above note 9.

71 See Neil Macdonald, "Ottawa Cites Hate Crime Laws When Asked about 'Zero Tolerance' for Israel Boycotters" *CBC News* (11 May 2015), online: www.cbc.ca/news/politics/ottawa-cites-hate-crime-laws-when-asked-about-its-zero-tolerance-for-israel-boycotters-1.3067497.

72 John Zimmerman, "Sayyid Qutb's Influence on the 11 September Attacks" (2004) 16:2 *Terrorism and Political Violence* 222 at 222.

73 *Ibid* at 234.

74 See *ibid* at 235.

75 See *ibid* at 244.

76 See *ibid* at 240–41.

77 Sayyid Qutb, *Milestones* (Cedar Rapids, IA: The Mother Mosque Foundation, 1981) at 55 (extract consulted only online).

78 *Ibid* at 63 and 72 (extract consulted only online) [emphasis added].

79 Frantz Fanon, *The Wretched of the Earth* (New York: Grove Press, 1968) at 37.

80 See *R v Keegstra*, [1990] 3 SCR 697 [*Keegstra*].

81 See Kady O'Malley & Kristen Everson, "Conservative Facebook Post on West Edmonton Mall 'Troubling,' Alberta MLA Says" *CBC News* (4 March 2015), online: www.cbc.ca/news/politics/conservative-facebook-post-on-west-edmonton-mall-threat-troubling-alberta-mla-says-1.2981167.

82 See Eric Blais, "Conservative Video Spreads ISIS Propaganda to Make Justin Trudeau Look Weak" *CBC News* (30 June 2015), online: www.cbc.ca/news/politics/conservative-video-spreads-isis-propaganda-to-make-justin-trudeau-look-weak-1.3133039.

83 See Kent Roach, "Terrorism" in Dubber & Hornle, eds, *The Oxford Companion to Criminal Law* (Oxford: Oxford University Press, 2014).

84 *Criminal Code*, above note 4, s 319(3).

85 *Ibid*, s 319(2).

86 Above note 46. As indicated in the Preface, one of us (Roach) represented the British Columbia Civil Liberties Association in this case.

87 *Ibid* at para 71.

88 *Suresh v Canada*, 2002 SCC 1 at para 108.

89 David Schneiderman, "What Lessons Have We Learned about Speech in the Aftermath of the Paris Attacks?" in Edward Iacobucci and Stephen J Toope, eds, *After the Paris Attacks: Responses in Canada, Europe and Around the Globe* (Toronto: University of Toronto Press, 2015) at 165.

90 *Khawaja*, above note 46 at para 70.

91 *Criminal Code*, above note 4, s 319(3)(b).

92 See *Keegstra*, above note 80.

93 See *R v Oakes*, [1986] 1 SCR 103.

94 See Sophia Moskalenko & Clark McCauley, "Measuring Political Mobilization: The Distinction between Activism and Radicalism" (2009) 21 *Terrorism and Political Violence* 239 at 240.

95 See Clark McCauley & Sophia Moskalenko, "Toward a Profile of Lone Wolf Terrorists: What Moves an Individual from Radical Opinion to Radical Action" (2014) 26 *Terrorism and Political Violence* 69 at 72.

96 See "Most British Muslims 'Oppose Muhammad Cartoons Reprisals'" *BBC News* (25 February 2015), online: www.bbc.com/news/uk-31293196.

97 McCauley & Moskalenko, above note 95 at 72.

98 See *R v Zundel*, [1992] 2 SCR 731.

99 For example, the Court recognized that while a ban on publishing opinion polls within seventy-two hours of an election may be the least restrictive means of preventing harms caused by inaccurate polls, the benefits achieved by the law were "marginal" compared to the "substantial" harms that the law caused to freedom of expression: *Thomson Newspapers v Canada*, [1998] 1 SCR 877 at para 129.

100 *Dagenais v CBC*, [1994] 3 SCR 835 at 887.

101 *Khawaja*, above note 46 at para 83.

102 Integrated Terrorist Assessment Centre, *Threat Assessment: Canada — Biannual Update on Terrorist and Extremist Threats* (10 April 2012, 12-35-E) at para 14.

103 *Criminal Code*, above note 4, ss 83.222–83.223.

104 *Criminal Code*, above note 4, s 320(8).

105 *Khawaja*, above note 46 at para 82.

106 *Criminal Code*, above note 4, ss 83.21–83.22.

107 "100,000 Terror postings deleted" *Yahoo News UK* (1 July 2015), online: uk.news.yahoo.com/100-000-net-terror-postings-deleted-195511020.html#m7loGdV.

108 Robert Hannigan, "The Web Is a Terrorist's Command-and-Control Network of Choice" *Financial Times* (3 November 2014), online: www.ft.com/cms/s/2/c89b6c58-6342-11e4-8a63-00144feabdco.html#axzz3hHj5UpaO.

109 See Jenna McLaughlan, "Twitter Is Not at War with ISIS: Here's Why" *Mother Jones* (18 November 2014), online: www.motherjones.com/politics/2014/11/twitter-isis-war-ban-speech.

110 See *R v Simmons*, [1988] 2 SCR 495.

111 Canada Border Services Agency, Memorandum D9-1-1, "Canada Border Services Agency's Policy on the Classification of Obscene Material" (26 October 2012), online: www.cbsa-asfc.gc.ca/publications/dm-md/d9/d9-1-1-eng.html. See also Canada Border Services Agency, Memorandum D9-1-15, "Canada Border Services Agency's Policy on the Classification of Hate Propaganda, Sedition and Treason" (14 February 2008), online: www.cbsa-asfc.gc.ca/publications/dm-md/d9/d9-1-15-eng.pdf. The latter memorandum quite broadly defines hate propaganda that can be seized (*ibid* at para 8). At the same time, it recognizes a variety of defences related to both seditious material and hate propaganda that would not be available for the new category of terrorist propaganda (*ibid* at paras 11 & 12).

112 *Little Sisters Book and Art Emporium v Canada (Minister of Justice)*, 2000 SCC 69, declaring that customs had violated the *Charter* but not striking the tariff down; *Little Sisters Book and Art Emporium v Canada (Commissioner of Customs and Revenue)*, 2007 SCC 2, denying the bookstore advance costs to litigate claims of continued discriminatory profiling by customs officials.

113 Commission of Inquiry into the Activities of Canadian Officials in relation to Maher Arar, *A New National Security Review Mechanism for the RCMP* (Ottawa: Supply and Services, 2006) at 573 (Recommendation 10).

114 2007 SCC 2.

115 See *Canadian Security Intelligence Service Act*, RSC 1985, c C-23, s 12.1(3) [*CSIS Act*].

116 *Ibid*, s 12.2.

117 See Ronald Deibert, "Who Knows What Evil Lurks in the Shadows" in Iacobucci & Toope, above note 89 at 198–200, on the Communications Security Establishment's offensive capabilities of disruption as revealed by the Edward Snowden leaks.

118 *CSIS Act*, above note 115, s 2.

119 (UK), c 6.

CHAPTER ELEVEN: OVERSIGHT

1   Royal Canadian Mounted Police, "RCMP Security Posture–Parliament Hill October 22, 2014: OPP Review and Recommendations" (March 2015) at 7 and 29, online: www.rcmp-grc.gc.ca/pubs/parl/opp-secur-eng.pdf.

2   House of Commons, "October 22, 2014: House of Commons Incident Response Summary" (3 June 2015) at 9, online: www.parl.gc.ca/about/house/newsroom/articles/2015-06-03-Summary-e.pdf.

3   Terry Millewski, "Ottawa Shooting: Federal Security Chiefs Warned Days before an Attack" *CBC News* (24 November 2014), online: www.cbc.ca/news/politics/ottawa-shooting-federal-security-chiefs-warned-days-before-attack-1.2847552; Stewart Bell, "Three Days before Ottawa Terror Attack, Alarm Bells Were Sounding, Intelligence Reports Show" *National Post* (1 March 2015), online: news.nationalpost.com/news/canada/security-forces-braced-for-terror-attacks-over-canadas-enhanced-profile-before-ottawa-shooting.

4   Joe Lofaro, "Police Services Board to Receive Internal Review on Parliament Hill Shooting" *Metro* (18 June 2015), online: metronews.ca/news/ottawa/1401486/police-services-board-to-receive-internal-review-on-parliament-hill-shooting/.

5   Adam Feibel, "Police Review of Oct 22 War Memorial Attack Finds Confusion, Communications Issues" *Ottawa Citizen* (21 May 2015), online: ottawacitizen.com/news/local-news/police-review-of-oct-22-shooting; "Ottawa Shooting Confusion Caused by Scale of Police Response" *CBC News* (21 May 2015), online: www.cbc.ca/news/canada/ottawa/ottawa-shooting-confusion-caused-by-scale-of-police-response-report-says-1.3081906.

6   Terry Millewski, "Attack on Parliament Exposed 'Systemic' Security Gaps, Says Ex-JTF-2 Commander" *CBC News* (19 November 2014), online: www.cbc.ca/news/politics/attack-on-parliament-exposed-systemic-security-gaps-says-ex-jtf2-commander-1.2840770.

7   Government of Australia and Government of New South Wales, *Martin Place Siege Joint Commonwealth and State Review* (Canberra: Commonwealth of Australia, State of New South Wales, 2015) at 59.

8   Commission of Inquiry into the Investigation of the Bombing of Air India Flight 182, *Air India Flight 182: A Canadian Tragedy, Volume One: Overview* (Ottawa: Public Works, 2010) at 141 [*Air India Volume One*].

9   Senate Standing Committee on National Security and Defence, "Issue 15 – Minutes of Proceedings" (2 April 2015) (Chair: Daniel Lang), online: www.parl.gc.ca/content/sen/committee/412/SECD/15MN-52037-E.HTM.

10 *House of Commons Debates*, 41st Parl, 2d Sess, No 218 (27 May 2015), online: www.parl.gc.ca/HousePublications/Publication.aspx?Doc=218&Language=E&Mode=1&Parl=41&Pub=Hansard&Ses=2.

11 *Debates of the Senate*, 41st Parl, 2d Sess, vol 149 (4 June 2015) (Hon Daniel Lang), online: www.parl.gc.ca/Content/Sen/Chamber/412/Debates/148db_2015-06-04-e.htm.

12 RCMP, Questions and Answers, Bill C-51, Q3 (Marked "Draft April 17 2015"), released via ATIP request A-2015-04006.

13 Jean Chrétien et al, "A Close Eye on Security Makes Canadians Safer" *Globe and Mail* (19 February 2015), online: www.theglobeandmail.com/globe-debate/a-close-eye-on-security-makes-canadians-safer/article23069152/.

14 For additional analysis of the distinction between efficacy- and propriety-based review, see Reg Whitaker & Stuart Farson, *Accountability in and for National Security* (Montreal: Institute for Research on Public Policy, 2009) at 15(9) IRPP Choices 1.

15 See discussion in Canada, Commission of Inquiry into the Actions of Canadian Officials in Relation to Maher Arar, *A New Review Mechanism for the RCMP's National Security Activities* (Ottawa: Public Works, 2006) at 456–58 [*Arar Inquiry*].

16 *Ibid* at 500.

17 Commission of Inquiry into the Investigation of the Bombing of Air India Flight 182, *Air India Flight 182: A Canadian Tragedy, Volume Three* (Ottawa: Public Works, 2010) at 43 [*Air India Volume Three*].

18 We are indebted to Mel Cappe, former clerk of the Privy Council, for this analogy in his comments on an earlier version of this chapter.

19 See, generally, Phillip Stenning, ed, *Accountability for Criminal Justice* (Toronto: University of Toronto Press, 1995).

20 For discussion of accountability gaps, including how public inquiries have had to be appointed with extraordinary jurisdiction to review the activities of all government officials in particular security areas, see Kent Roach, *The 9/11 Effect: Comparative Counter-terrorism* (Cambridge, New York: Cambridge University Press, 2011) at 455–59; Kent Roach, "Public Inquiries as an Attempt to Fill Accountability Gaps Left by Judicial and Legislative Review" in Fergal Francis Davis & Fiona de Londras, eds, *Critical Debates on Counter-terrorism Judicial Review* (Cambridge: Cambridge University Press, 2014) at 183ff.

21 Standing Senate Committee on National Security and Defence, "Evidence" (27 April 2015) (Chair: Daniel Lang), online: www.parl.gc.ca/content/sen/committee/412/SECD/52069-e.HTM.

22 Commission of Inquiry Concerning Certain Activities of the RCMP, *Freedom and Security under the Law* (Ottawa: Supply and Services, 1981) at 868.

23 Donald Savoie, *Governing from the Centre: The Concentration of Power in Canadian Politics* (Toronto: University of Toronto Press, 1999).

24 *Air India Volume One*, above note 8 at 116.

25 Commission of Inquiry Concerning Certain Activities of the RCMP, above note 22 at 873–75.

26 SI 2015-33, s 4, amending s 10 of the Passport Order SI/81-86.

27 *Canadian Security Intelligence Service Act*, RSC 1985, c C-23 [*CSIS Act*].

28 SC 2001, c 41 [*ATA*].

29 *Air India Volume Three*, above note 17 at ch 3.

30 Bill 59, *An act to enact the Act to prevent and combat hate speech*, 41st Legislature, 1st Sess, National Assembly of Québec.

31 Commission of Inquiry into the Investigation of the Bombing of Air India Flight 182, *Air India Flight 182: A Canadian Tragedy, Volume Five: Terrorism Financing* (Ottawa: Public Works, 2010) [*Air India Volume Five*].

32 *Ibid*.

33 Paul Heinbecker & Daniel Livermore, "Who Speaks for Canada, Spies or Diplomats?" *Globe and Mail* (29 June 2015), online: www.theglobeandmail.com/globe-debate/who-speaks-for-canada-spies-or-diplomats/article25142424/.

34 *Arar Inquiry*, above note 15 at 280.

35 Canadian Press, "Axing CSIS Watchdog 'Huge Loss,' Says Former Inspector General" *CBC News* (10 August 2012), online: www.cbc.ca/news/politics/axing-csis-watchdog-huge-loss-says-former-inspector-general-1.1143212.

36 Examples of the detailed reports that the Inspector General provided to the minister of public safety on matters such as the execution of warrants and foreign operations can be found online at http://cips.uottawa.ca/publication/thematic-series/csis_certificate_archive/.

37 SIRC, "Annual Report, 2013–14" at 19.

38 Privy Council Office, "Privy Council Secretariats," online: www.pco-bcp.gc.ca/index.asp?lang=eng&page=secretariats.

39 Privy Council Office, "Departmental Performance Report" (2014), online: www.pco-bcp.gc.ca/docs/information/publications/dpr-rmr/2013-2014/docs/dpr-rmr-eng.pdf.

40 CSIS, "Role of CSIS," online: www.csis.gc.ca/bts/role-en.php.

41 Standing Senate Committee on National Security and Defence, above note 21, citing Richard Fadden, current national security advisor for the prime minister.

42 *Air India Volume One*, above note 8 at 193. See also Senate, "Interim Report of the Special Senate Committee on Anti-terrorism" (March 2011) at 47, online: www.parl.gc.ca/content/sen/committee/403/anti/rep/rep03mar11-e.pdf, affirming the Air India Commission's recommendations.

43 *Ibid* at 24.

44 *Ibid* at 34–41. The Air India Commission recognized that the national security advisor "could work on co-ordination issues that are made more difficult by the fact that not all agencies . . . such as FINTRAC on one hand, and CSIS, the RCMP and CBSA, on the other, are within the same minister's portfolio": *Air India Volume Five*, above note 31 at 258.

45 *Air India Volume Three*, above note 17 at 29 and 31.

46 Commission of Inquiry into the Investigation of the Bombing of Air India Flight 182, *Action Plan* (Ottawa: Government of Canada, 2010) at 7.

47 SC 2015, c 20, s 2.

48 Standing Senate Committee on National Security and Defence, above note 21.

49 *Ibid*.

50 RCMP, Questions and Answers, above note 12, Q10.

51 Senate, above note 42 at 33 and 40.

52 RCMP, Questions and Answers, above note 12, Q17.

53 United Kingdom, "National Security Council," online: www.gov.uk/government/organisations/national-security/groups/national-security-council.

54 Andy Hayman, *The Terrorist Hunters* (London: Bantam Press, 2009).

55 David Omand, *Securing the State* (London: Hurst, 2010) at 40.

56 Standing Senate Committee on National Security and Defence, above note 21.

57 "Australia's First Counter-terrorism Co-ordinator Appointed" *SBS News* (25 May 2015), online: www.sbs.com.au/news/article/2015/05/25/australias-first-anti-terrorism-coordinator-appointed.

58 Government of Australia, *Review of Australia's Counter-terrorism Machinery* (Canberra: Australian Government, 2015) at 22 and 26.

59 Standing Senate Committee on National Security and Defence, above note 21.

60 50 US Code § 3091.

61 Standing Senate Committee on National Security and Defence, "Fourteenth Report" (27 May 2015) (Chair: Daniel Lang), online: www.parl.gc.ca/Content/SEN/Committee/412/secd/rep/rep14may15-e.htm.

62 Laura Payton, "C-51 Confusion Abounds as Tories Rush Anti-terrorism Bill to Committee" *CBC News* (20 February 2015), online: www.cbc.ca/news/politics/c-51-confusion-abounds-as-tories-rush-anti-terrorism-bill-to-committee-1.2963569.

63 *Arar Inquiry*, above note 15 at 491.

64 Since the Arar Commission report, the Supreme Court has made it easier for public interest groups to challenge legislation authorizing national security activities, and a group is now challenging the warrantless surveillance powers of CSE. Nevertheless, such groups would still face standing challenges in challenging executive action not supported by legislative authorization and through governmental claims of secrecy. The Canadians other than Maher Arar tortured in Syria, in part because of Canadian information sharing, are suing Canada, but their lawsuits have been delayed because of governmental claims of secrecy under s 38 of the *Canada Evidence Act*.

65 *Criminal Code*, RSC 1985, c C-46, s 83.3(2).

66 *Ibid*, s 810.011(1).

67 *Ibid*, s 83.3(7.1) & (7.2).

68 *CSIS Act*, above note 27, s 21(3.1) & (4).

69 *Ibid*, ss 12.1(3) and 21.1.

70 *Ibid*, s 12.2.

71 Federal Court, Andrew Baumberg, Media Relations, personal communication, February 2015.

72 *Ibid*.

73 *Canada (Minister of Citizenship) v Tobiass*, [1997] 3 SCR 391.

74 *Ibid*.

75 James K Hugessen, "Watching the Watchers: Democratic Oversight" in David Daubney et al, eds, *Terrorism, Law and Democracy: How Is Canada Changing following September 11?* (Montreal: Canadian Institute for the Administration of Justice, 2002) 381 at 384–85.

76 See, most famously and recently, *Re X*, 2014 FCA 249. Candour issues have also characterized several of the immigration "security certificate" cases. See, for example, *Almrei (Re)*, 2009 FC 1263.

77 *Charkaoui v Canada*, 2007 SCC 9.

78 Cristin Schmitz, "The Chief Justice Shows Where Line Is Drawn" *Lawyers Weekly* (3 July 2015), online: www.lawyersweekly.ca/articles/2417.

79 *Canada (AG) v Telbani*, 2014 CF 1050.

80 *Canada (Citizenship and Immigration) v Harkat*, 2014 SCC 37.

81 Privacy and Civil Liberties Oversight Board, "Report on the Telephone Records Program Conducted under Section 215 of the USA Patriot Act and on the Operations of the Foreign Intelligence Surveillance Court" (23 January 2014), online: www.pclob.gov/library/215-Report_on_the_Telephone_Records_Program.pdf; see also Privacy and Civil Liberties Oversight Board, "Report on the Surveillance Program Operated under s.702 of the Foreign Intelligence Surveillance Act" (2 July 2014) at 146, online: www.wired.com/wp-content/uploads/2014/07/PCLOB-Section-702-Report-PRE-RELEASE.pdf.

82   *USA Freedom Act*, HR 2048-14, s 401.

83   *Ibid*.

84   *Ibid*, s 402.

85   *R v Jaser*, 2014 ONSC 6052.

86   *Arar Inquiry*, above note 15 at 439.

87   *Re X*, 2013 FC 1275.

88   *Ibid* at paras 64–66.

89   *Re X*, 2014 FCA 249 at para 6ff.

90   *Re X*, above note 87 at paras 102ff.

91   *Ibid* at para 117.

92   Reg Whitaker, "Guerrilla Accountability" in Michael Geist, ed, *Law, Privacy and Surveillance in Canada in the Post-Snowden Era* (Ottawa: University of Ottawa Press, 2015) at 215.

93   *Re X*, above note 87 at para 117.

94   *Ibid* at para 110.

95   *CSIS Act*, above note 27, s 24.1 as amended by SC 2015, c 20. This provision requires the person who is authorized to execute the warrant — presumably someone in CSIS — to believe on reasonable grounds that the measure that person requests the other person to do is reasonable and proportional in the circumstances, but does not require that the judge who issued the warrant be informed of the additional assistance received in executing the warrant.

96   *Re X*, above note 87 at para 115.

97   *CSIS Act*, above note 27, s 22.3.

98   *Ibid*, s 24.1.

99   *Ibid*, s 21.1(5)(f).

100   *Ibid*, s 54(2).

101   *R v Jaser*, 2014 ONSC 6052 at para 36.

102   Pub L 95–511, 92 Stat 1783, 50 USC ch 36.

103   *USA Freedom Act*, above note 82, s 404.

104   *Re X*, above note 87 at para 117.

CHAPTER TWELVE: REVIEW

1   Bill C-51, *An Act to enact the Security of Canada Information Sharing Act and the Secure Air Travel Act, to amend the Criminal Code, the Canadian Security Intelligence Service Act and the Immigration and Refugee Protection Act and to make related and consequential amendments to other Acts*, 2d Sess, 41st Parl, 2015 (assented to 18 June 2015), SC 2015, c 20.

2   Quoted in Alex Boutilier, "Canada's Spy Review Body Struggling to Keep Tabs on Agencies" *Toronto Star* (1 April 2015), online: www.thestar.com/news/canada/2015/04/01/canadas-spy-review-bodies-struggling-to-keep-tabs-on-agencies.html; House of Commons, *Hansard* (5 May 2015), online: www.parl.gc.ca/HousePublications/Publication.aspx?Doc=207&Language=E&Mode=1&Parl=41&Pub=Hansard&Ses=2.

3   Quoted in Laura Payton, "C-51 Confusion Abounds as Tories Rush Anti-terrorism Bill to Committee" *CBC News* (20 February 2015), online: www.cbc.ca/news/politics/c-51-confusion-abounds-as-tories-rush-anti-terrorism-bill-to-committee-1.2963569.

4   See David Pugliese, "Government Knows Best, Says Conservative MP, No Need for More Oversight on Spy and Security Agencies" *Ottawa Citizen* (1 February 2015), online: ottawacitizen.com/news/national/defence-watch/government-knows-best-says-conservative-mpno-need-for-more-spy-and-security-agency-oversight; Aaron Wherry, "The Heart of Our Democracy in a Time of Terror" *Macleans* (5 February 2015), online: www.macleans.ca/politics/the-heart-of-our-democracy-in-time-terror/.

5   House of Commons, *Hansard* (19 February 2015) per Hon Peter Van Loan; Steven Chase, "Kenney Rejects Call to Increase Oversight of National-Security Agencies" *Globe and Mail* (22 February 2015), online: www.theglobeandmail.com/news/politics/kenney-spurns-call-to-increase-oversight-of-national-security-agencies/article23147599/; Tonda MacCharles, "Stephen Harper Rejects Calls for More Oversight of New Spy Powers" *Toronto Star* (19 February 2015), online: www.thestar.com/news/canada/2015/02/19/canada-faces-high-risk-of-terror-attack-jason-kenney-says.html.

6   See Parliament of Canada, "Standing Senate Committee on National Security and Defence" (30 March 2015), online: www.parl.gc.ca/content/sen/committee/412/SECD/15EV-52013-E.HTM.

7   Chrétien et al, "A Close Eye on Security Makes Canadians Safer" *Globe and Mail* (19 February 2015), online: www.theglobeandmail.com/globe-debate/a-close-eye-on-security-makes-canadians-safer/article23069152/. The letter was signed by The Right Honourable Jean Chrétien, prime minister of Canada 1993–2003, minister of justice 1980–82; The Right Honourable Joe Clark, prime minister of Canada 1979–80, minister of justice 1988–89; The Right Honourable Paul Martin, prime minister of Canada 2003–6; The Right Honourable John Turner, prime minister of Canada 1984, minister of justice 1968–72; The Honourable Louise Arbour, justice of the Supreme Court of Canada 1999–2004; The Honourable Michel Bastarache, justice of the Supreme Court of Canada 1997–2008; The Honourable Ian Binnie, justice of the Supreme Court of Canada 1998–2011; The Honourable Claire L'Heureux-Dubé, justice of the Supreme Court of Canada 1987–2002; The Honourable John Major, justice of the Supreme Court of Canada 1992–2005; The Honourable Irwin Cotler, minister of justice 2003–6; The Honourable Marc Lalonde, minister of justice 1978–79; The Honourable Anne McLellan, minister of justice 1997–2002, minister of public safety 2003–6; The Honourable Warren Allmand, solicitor general of Canada 1972–76; The Honourable Jean-Jacques Blais, solicitor general of Canada 1978–79; The Honourable Wayne Easter, solicitor general of Canada 2002–3; The Honourable Lawrence MacAulay, solicitor general of Canada 1998–2002; The Honourable Frances Lankin, SIRC member 2009–14; The Honourable Bob Rae, SIRC member 1998–2003; The Honourable Roy Romanow, SIRC member 2003–8; Chantal Bernier, acting privacy commissioner of Canada 2013–14; Shirley Heafey, chairperson, commission for public complaints against the RCMP 1997–2005; Jennifer Stoddart, privacy commissioner of Canada 2003–13.

8   Parliament, "The Standing Senate Committee on National Security and Defence" (9 December 2013), online: www.parl.gc.ca/content/sen/committee/412%5CSECD/51109-E.HTM.

9   Office of the Privacy Commissioner of Canada, *Checks and Controls: Reinforcing Privacy Protection and Oversight for the Canadian Intelligence Community in an Era of Cyber-Surveillance* (Ottawa: Ministry of Public Works and Government Services Canada, 2014).

10 Hugh Segal, "Freedom and Security: The Gordian Knot for Democracies" in Edward Iacobucci & Stephen Toope, eds, *After the Paris Attacks: Responses in Canada, Europe and around the Globe* (Toronto: University of Toronto Press, 2015) at 177.

11 SC 2013, c 18, ss 45.4–45.43.

12 See Barton Gellman & Laura Poitras, "U.S., British Intelligence Mining Data from Nine U.S. Internet Companies in Broad Secret Programs" *Washington Post* (7 June 2013), online: www.washingtonpost.com/investigations/us-intelligence-mining-data-from-nine-us-internet-companies-in-broad-secret-program/2013/06/06/3a0coda8-cebf-11e2-8845-d970ccb04497_story.html; Glenn Greenwald, "NSA Collecting Phone Records of Millions of Verizon Customers Daily" *Guardian* (6 June 2013), online: www.theguardian.com/world/2013/jun/06/nsa-phone-records-verizon-court-order.

13 See the reporting of CBC journalists Dave Seglins, Amber Hildrebandt, and Michael Pereira, for example "CSE Tracks Millions of Downloads Daily: Snowden Documents" *CBC News* (27 January 2015), online: www.cbc.ca/news/canada/cse-tracks-millions-of-downloads-daily-snowden-documents-1.2930120.

14 CSE Commissioner, *Statement by CSE Commissioner the Honourable Jean-Pierre Plouffe re: January 30 CBC Story* (31 January 2014), online: www.ocsec-bccst.gc.ca/media/pr/2014-01-31_e.php.

15 See Craig Forcese, "Law, Logarithms and Liberties: Legal Issues Arising from CSE's Metadata Program" in Michael Geist, ed, *Law, Privacy and Surveillance in Canada in the Post-Snowden Era* (Ottawa: University of Ottawa Press, 2015).

16 See, for example, Ronald Deibert, "Who Knows What Evil Lurks in the Shadows" in Iacobucci & Toope, above note 10 at 194–95.

17 See, for example, Reg Whitaker, "Guerilla Accountability" in Geist, above note 15.

18 See Nicholas MacDonald, "Parliamentarians and National Security in Canada" (2011) *Canadian Parliamentary Review* 33; Aiden Wills et al, *Parliamentary Oversight of Security and Intelligence Agencies in the European Union* (Brussels: European Parliament, 2011), online: issat.dcaf.ch/content/download/4148/36754/file/Parliamentary%20Oversight%20of%20Security%20and%20Intelligence%20Agencies%20in%20the%20European%20Union.pdf.

19 RSC 1985, c C-23 [*CSIS Act*].

20 See, for example, Douglas L Bland & Roy Rempel, "A Vigilant Parliament: Building Competence for Effective Parliamentary Oversight of National Defence and the Canadian Armed Forces" (2004) 5 *Institute for Research on Public Policy* 1.

21 Commission of Inquiry Concerning Certain Activities of the RCMP, *Freedom and Security under the Law* (Ottawa: Supply and Services Canada, 1981) at 902.

22 *Ibid* at 899.

23 *Report of the Special Senate Committee of the Senate on the Canadian Intelligence Service* (Ottawa: Senate of Canada, 1983) at 32.

24 For a discussion of the affair, see Heather MacIvor, "The Speaker's Ruling on Afghan Detainee Documents: The Last Hurrah for Parliamentary Privilege?" (2010) 19 *Constitutional Forum* 129.

25 Senate Standing Committee on National Security and Defence, *Countering the Terrorist Threat in Canada: An Interim Report* (July 2015) at 10, online: www.parl.gc.ca/Content/SEN/Committee/412/secd/rep/rep18jul15-e.pdf [*Countering the Terrorist Threat*].

26 Government of Canada, *A National Security Committee of Parliamentarians: A Consultation Paper to Help Inform the Creation of a Committee of Parliamentarians to Review National Security* (Ottawa: House of Commons, 2004); Government of Canada, *Securing an Open Society: Canada's National Security Policy* (Ottawa: Privy Council Office, 2004) at 19.

27 *Report of the Interim Committee of Parliamentarians on National Security* (October 2004), online: www.pco-bcp.gc.ca/docs/information/publications/aarchives/cpns-cpsn/cpns-cpsn-eng.pdf.

28 Bill C-81, *An Act to establish the National Security Committee of Parliamentarians*, 1st Sess, 38th Parl, 2004–2005.

29 *Ibid*, s 13.

30 *Justice and Security Act 2013* (UK), c 18, ss 1–4, Schedule 1.

31 See MacIvor, above note 24.

32 Parliamentarians possess freedom of speech, meaning that a parliamentarian cannot be held liable for what is said in Parliament, at least on the floor of the House: see *Re Ouellet* (1976), 67 DLR (3d) 73 at 86 (Que SC), aff'd 72 DLR (3d) 95 (Que CA), agreeing that "communications by a Member to another person outside the walls of the House are not covered by the privilege."

33 House of Commons Subcommittee on the Review of the *Anti-terrorism Act*, *Rights, Limits, Security: A Comprehensive Review of the* Anti-terrorism Act *and Related Issues* (Ottawa: Standing Committee on Public Safety and National Security, 2007) at 85.

34 Bill C-551, *An Act to establish the national security committee of Parliamentarians*, 41st Parl, 2d Sess, 2013.

35 Cabinet confidences are, in essence, the papers supporting or describing cabinet deliberations. For a definition of these papers, see *Canada Evidence Act*, RSC 1985, c C-5, s 37; *Access to Information Act*, RSC 1985, c A-1, s 69.

36 Bill S-220, *An Act to establish the intelligence and security committee of Parliament*, 41st Parl, 2d Sess, 2014.

37 Bill C-622, *CSEC Accountability and Transparency Act*, 41st Parl, 2d Sess, 2014. In the interest of transparency, one of us was consulted on the drafting of this bill but takes no credit for its content.

38 *House of Commons Debates*, 41st Parl, 2d Sess (30 October 2014), online: www.parl.gc.ca/HousePublications/Publication.aspx?Language=E&Mode=1&Parl=41&Ses=2&DocId=6751043.

39 Chrétien et al, above note 7.

40 See Tonda MacCharles, "Government Plans Four Amendments to Soften Anti-terror Bill C-51" *Toronto Star* (30 March 2015), online: www.thestar.com/news/canada/2015/03/30/government-plans-four-amendments-to-soften-anti-terror-bill-c-51.html.

41 Bill C-81, above note 28, s 13(a).

42 The full list of SIRC classified reports is available online: www.sirc-csars.gc.ca/opbapb/lsrlse-eng.html. The full list of CSE Commissioner classified reports is also available online: www.ocsec-bccst.gc.ca/ann-rpt/cr-rc_e.php.

43 Standing Senate Committee on National Security and Defence, "Fourteenth Report" (27 May 2015), online: www.parl.gc.ca/Content/SEN/Committee/412/secd/rep/rep14may15-e.htm.

44 See Richard E Matland & Donley T Studlar, "Determinants of Legislative Turnover: A Cross-national Analysis" (2004) 34 *British Journal of Political Science* 87, online: www.academia.edu/8407291/Richard_E._Matland_and_Donley_T._Studlar_Determinants_of_Legislative_Turnover_A_Cross-National_Analysis.

45 See Aaron Wherry, "Why MPs Come and Go in Ottawa" *Macleans* (19 January 2015), online: www.macleans.ca/politics/ottawa/what-to-do-with-all-the-new-in-the-house-of-commons/.

46 See Craig Forcese, "Fixing the Deficiencies of Parliament Review of Anti-terrorism Law: Lessons from the United Kingdom and Australia" (2008) 14:6 *IRPP Choices* 2, online: ssrn.com/abstract=1623472.

47 See *ibid*.

48 See Office of the Privacy Commissioner of Canada, above note 9.

49 SC 2015, c 20, s 2.

50 See, for example, James Keller, "BC Coroner Inquiry Called after CBSA Airport Detainee Death" *Canadian Press* (25 February 2014), online: metronews.ca/news/victoria/953041/b-c-coroner-inquest-called-after-cbsa-airport-detainee-death/.

51 Bill S-222, *An Act to amend the Canadian Border Service Act*, 41st Parl, 2d Sess, 2014.

52 See, for example, Colin Freeze, "Spy Agencies Try to Curb Watchdogs' Ties to Each Other" *Globe and Mail* (29 May 2014), online: www.theglobeandmail.com/news/national/spy-agencies-try-to-curb-watchdogs-ties-to-each-other/article18919190/#dashboard/follows/.

53 Commission of Inquiry into the Actions of Canadian Officials in relation to Maher Arar, *A New Review Mechanism for the RCMP's National Security Activities* (Ottawa: Public Works, 2006) at 582 [Arar Inquiry].

54 Chrétien et al, above note 7.

55 *Countering the Terrorist Threat*, above note 25.

56 Arar Inquiry, above note 53 at 425–26.

57 See *ibid*.

58 Stanley A Cohen, *Privacy, Crime and Terror: Legal Rights and Security in a Time of Peril* (Markham, ON: LexisNexis, 2005) at 561.

59 See *The Ottawa Principles on Anti-terrorism and Human Rights / Les Principes d'Ottawa relatifs à la lutte au terrorisme et aux droits de l'homme* (Ottawa: October 2006), Principle 9.3, online: aix1.uottawa.ca/~cforcese/hrat/principles.pdf.

60 Arar Inquiry, above note 53 at 502.

61 *Ibid*.

62 Peter Gill, "Symbolic or Real? The Impact of the Canadian Security Intelligence Review Committee, 1984–88" (1989) 4:3 *Intelligence and National Security* 550.

63 Reg Whitaker, "The Politics of Security Intelligence Policy-Making in Canada: II 1984–91" (1992) 7:2 *Intelligence and National Security* 53 at 59.

64 *Ibid* at 72.

65 Reg Whitaker, "The 'Bristow Affair': A Crisis of Accountability in Canadian Security Intelligence" (1996) 11:2 *Intelligence and National Security* 279 at 301.

66   Wesley Wark, "Our Security IQ Needs Testing" *Globe and Mail* (28 February 2002) A19.

67   Data produced by a search in ProQuest's Canadian Newsstand Major Dailies database using the keyword "SIRC."

68   In 1994, SIRC issued a report on a so-called agent provocateur associated with CSIS that galvanized substantial controversy, criticism, and press coverage: see, for example, Clayton Ruby, "SIRC's Intolerable 'Limit of the Tolerable'" *Toronto Star* (21 December 1994) A25.

69   Data produced by a search in ProQuest's Canadian Newsstand Major Dailies database using the keywords "commissioner" and "access to information."

70   Data produced by a search in ProQuest's Canadian Newsstand Major Dailies database using the keywords "privacy" and "Jennifer Stoddart."

71   Data produced by a search in ProQuest's Canadian Newsstand Major Dailies database using the keywords "SIRC" and "lapdog."

72   Andrew Mitrovica, "Canada's Spy Watchers Ring Alarm Many Years Too Late" *Toronto Star* (1 November 2010) A17. Mitrovica is probably the single most prolific critic of SIRC in the popular press. Other items authored by him include "Toothless Bark from Spy Watchdog" *Toronto Star* (1 November 2011) A19; "Casting Light on Our Spies" *Toronto Star* (15 November 2011) A23; "Same Old Torture Story" *Toronto Star* (13 February 2012) A15; "CSIS Freed from Final Shreds of Oversight" *Toronto Star* (1 March 2012) A19.

73   Craig Forcese, "Assessing Canada's Security Intelligence Review Committee: Some Preliminary Data" *National Security Law* (Blog) (22 May 2012), online: craigforcese.squarespace.com/national-security-law-blog/2012/5/22/assessing-canadas-security-intelligence-review-committee-som.html; Craig Forcese, "Accountability with a Dash of Context and a Pinch of Fire and Brimstone" (2014) 91 *Canadian Bar Review* 1, online: papers.ssrn.com/sol3/papers.cfm?abstract_id=2551295.

74   "List of SIRC Reviews under Section 54 of the *CSIS Act*" (10 November 2014), online: www.sirc-csars.gc.ca/opbapb/lsrlse-eng.html.

75   "Classified Reports" (20 August 2014), online: www.ocsec-bccst.gc.ca/ann-rpt/cr-rc_e.php.

76   Security Intelligence Review Committee, *Annual Report 2013–2014* at 34–35, online: www.sirc-csars.gc.ca/pdfs/ar_2013-2014-eng.pdf.

77   Forcese, above note 73.

78   See discussion in SIRC, *Annual Report, 2004–2005*, online: www.sirc-csars.gc.ca/anrran/2004-2005/sco3-eng.html#s2.

79   Data for these calculations were collected from the SIRC and CSIS annual reports available on these organizations' websites. SIRC annual reports report CSIS budgets throughout the 1980s and into the 1990s. The period for which data on CSIS budgets were available was 1985–2009. Calculations for CSIS spending for 2009–10 subtracted the $44 million spent on the new CSIS headquarters for that year and so can be regarded as capturing only spending on personnel and operations.

80   CSIS, *Annual Public Report, 2011–2013*, online: www.csis.gc.ca/pblctns/index-en.php?cat=01.

81   Treasury Board of Canada, "2015–16 Estimates," online: www.tbs-sct.gc.ca/ems-sgd/me-bpd/20152016/me-bpdtb-eng.asp.

82 Standing Senate Committee on National Security and Defence, *Evidence* (25 May 2015), online: www.parl.gc.ca/content/sen/committee/412/SECD/52146-E.HTM [*Evidence*].

83 *CSIS Act*, above note 19, s 39(2).

84 Arar Inquiry, above note 53 at 278.

85 *CSIS Act*, above note 19, s 37.

86 RSC 1985, c O-5.

87 SIRC, *Annual Report 2013–2014* at 27–28, online: www.sirc-csars.gc.ca/pdfs/ar_2013-2014-eng.pdf.

88 *Ibid* at 3.

89 *Ibid* at 7.

90 SIRC, *Annual Report 2006–2007* at 52, online: www.sirc-csars.gc.ca/pdfs/ar_2006-2007-eng.pdf.

91 SIRC, above note 87 at 12.

92 See *CSIS Act*, above note 19, s 53.

93 See *Thomson v Canada (Deputy Minister of Agriculture)*, [1992] 1 SCR 385.

94 Arar Inquiry, above note 53 at 280.

95 See *CSIS Act*, above note 19, s 30, as it then existed.

96 See *ibid*, s 31, as it then existed.

97 See *ibid*, s 33, as it then existed.

98 "Axing CSIS Watchdog 'Huge Loss,' Says Former Inspector General" *CBC News* (10 August 2012), online: www.cbc.ca/news/politics/axing-csis-watchdog-huge-loss-says-former-inspector-general-1.1143212.

99 *Ibid*.

100 *Ibid*.

101 *Ibid*.

102 Gill, above note 62 at 570.

103 SIRC, *Annual Report 2012–2013* at 10, online: www.sirc-csars.gc.ca/pdfs/ar_2012-2013-eng.pdf.

104 *Evidence*, above note 82.

105 Senate Standing Committee on National Security and Defence, *Evidence* (9 December 2013), online:www.parl.gc.ca/content/sen/committee/412%5CSECD/51109-E.HTM.

106 See *Abdelrazik v Canada (Minister of Foreign Affairs)*, 2009 FC 580.

107 SIRC, above note 103 at 27.

108 *Ibid* at 30.

109 SIRC, "CSIS's Role in Interviewing Afghan Detainees" (4 July 2011) at 4, online: www.sirc-csars.gc.ca/pdfs/criad_20110704-eng.pdf.

110 Standing Senate Committee on National Security and Defence, *Evidence* (23 April 2015), online: www.parl.gc.ca/content/sen/committee/412/SECD/16EV-52067-E.HTM.

111 House of Commons, Standing Committee on Public Safety and National Security, *Evidence* (26 November 2014), online: www.parl.gc.ca/HousePublications/Publication.aspx?DocId=6797879&Language=E&Mode=1&Parl=41&Ses=2.

112 *CSIS Act*, above note 19, s 22.3.

113 *Ibid*, s 24.1.

114 *Ibid*, s 38(1.1).

115 RSC 1985, c N-5, Part V.1.

116 See CSE Commissioner, *Annual Report 2013–2014*, at 13 and Annex C, online: www.ocsec-bccst.gc.ca/ann-rpt/2013-2014/ann-rpt_e.pdf; CSE Commissioner, *2014–2015 Report on Plans and Priorities*, online: www.ocsec-bccst.gc.ca/ finance/2014-2015/rpp/index_e.php.

117 Standing Senate Committee on National Security and Defence, above note 110.

118 CSE Commissioner, "Commissioner Plouffe's Letter to the Honourable Daryl Kramp" (6 March 2015), online: www.ocsec-bccst.gc.ca/media/pr/2015-03-06_e. php.

119 Above note 11.

120 Arar Inquiry, above note 53 at 491.

121 *Ibid* at 492.

122 *Ibid* at 549.

123 *Ibid* at 552–55.

124 *Royal Canadian Mounted Police Act*, RSC 1985, c R-10, s 45.34, as amended by SC 2013, c 18.

125 Civilian Review and Complaints Commission for the RCMP, "Report on Plans and Priorities 2015–2016" (2015), online: www.crcc-ccetp.gc.ca/pdf/rpp-2015-16-en.pdf.

126 Standing Senate Committee on National Security and Defence, above note 110.

127 See *R v Ahmad*, 2009 CanLII 84776 at paras 31 and 41–46 (Ont SCJ); *R v Alizadeh*, 2013 ONSC 5417 at para 14; *R v Nuttall*, 2015 BCSC 1125.

128 See Alex Boutilier, "RCMP Forced to Shuffle Cash, Staff to Meet Anti-terrorism Duties, Documents Show" *Toronto Star* (8 April 2015), online: www.thestar.com/ news/canada/2015/04/08/rcmp-forced-to-shuffle-cash-staff-to-meet-terrorism-duties-documents-show.html.

129 RSC 1985, c P-21, s 8.

130 Lisa Austin, "Anti-terrorism's Sleight-of-Hand: Bill C-51 and the Erosion of Privacy" in Iacobucci & Toope above note 10.

131 Daryl Kramp, "Bill C-51, the *Anti-terrorism Act, 2015:* Submission to the Standing Committee on Public Safety and National Security of the House of Commons" (5 March 2015), online: www.priv.gc.ca/parl/2015/parl_sub_150305_e.asp.

132 See Office of the Privacy Commissioner of Canada, above note 9.

133 Kramp, above note 131.

134 Standing Senate Committee on National Security and Defence, above note 110.

135 *Ibid*.

136 *Ibid*.

137 42 USC §2000e.

138 Privacy and Civil Liberties Oversight Board, *Report on the Telephone Records Program Conducted under Section 215 of the USA Patriot Act and on the Operations of the Foreign Intelligence Surveillance Court* (23 January 2014) at 4, online: www. pclob.gov/library/215-Report_on_the_Telephone_Records_Program.pdf.

139 HR 2048, ss 401–2.

140 *Counter-terrorism and Security Act 2015* (UK), c 6, s 46.

141 For a list of reports, see online: terrorismlegislationreviewer.independent.gov.uk.

142 Above note 30.

143 *Inspector-General of Intelligence and Security Act 1986*, Act No 101 of 1986, as amended.

144 See Inspector-General of Intelligence and Security, *Inquiry into the Actions of Australian Government Agencies in relation to the Arrest and Detention Overseas of Mr Mamdouh Habib from 2001 to 2005* (December 2011), online: www.igis.gov.au/sites/default/files/files/Inquiries/docs/habib-inquiry.pdf.

145 *Inspector-General of Intelligence and Security Act 1986*, above note 143.

146 *National Security Legislation Amendment Act*, No 127 of 2010, Schedule 9.

147 Arar Inquiry, above note 53 at 326.

148 Office of the Inspector-General of Intelligence and Security, "Annual Report for Year Ended June 30, 2014," online: www.igis.govt.nz/assets/FINAL-ANNUAL-REPORT-2013-14.pdf.

149 See MacCharles, above note 5.

150 See Greg Weston, "Other Spy Watchdogs Have Ties to the Oil Business" *CBC News* (10 January 2014), online: www.cbc.ca/news/politics/other-spy-watchdogs-have-ties-to-oil-business-1.2491093.

151 SIRC, above note 87.

152 See Privacy and Civil Liberties Oversight Board, *Report on the Surveillance Program Operated Pursuant to Section 702 of the* Foreign Intelligence Surveillance Act (2 July 2014) at 146, online: www.pclob.gov/library/702-Report.pdf.

153 *Federal Courts Act*, RSC 1985, c F-7, s18.3.

154 See *Canada (Information Commissioner) v Canada (AG)*, 2015 FC 405.

155 See *Secure Air Travel Act*, SC 2015, c 20, s 11 at ss 8 and 16(5).

156 *Charkaoui v Canada (Citizenship and Immigration)*, 2007 SCC 9.

157 *Canada (Citizenship and Immigration) v Harkat*, 2014 SCC 37.

CHAPTER THIRTEEN: DISSUADE

1 Except as otherwise noted, Clairmont's story quotes and summarizes Stewart Bell, "The Path to Extremism: RCMP Trying to Uncover Who Led a Canadian to Jihad" *National Post* (26 April 2014), online: news.nationalpost.com/news/canada/the-path-to-extremism-the-story-of-how-one-young-man-from-calgary-ended-up-dead-in-syria.

2 See Adrienne Arsenault, "Mother of Dead Canadian Jihadi Launches De-radicalization Effort" *CBC News* (9 September 2014), online: www.cbc.ca/news/canada/mother-of-dead-canadian-jihadi-launches-de-radicalization-effort-1.2759170.

3 See Radicalization Awareness Network, *Preventing Radicalization to Terrorism and Violent Extremism: Strengthening the EU's Response — RAN Collection: Approaches, Lessons Learned and Practices* (15 January 2014) at 80, online: ec.europa.eu/dgs/home-affairs/what-we-do/networks/radicalisation_awareness_network/ran-best-practices/docs/collection_of_approaches_lessons_learned_and_practices_en.pdf [*RAN Lessons Learned*].

4 See Arsenault, above note 2.

5 See "Hayat Canada Family Support," online: hayatcanada.webs.com/.

6   GIRDS: Mothers for Life Network, "We Mothers from Seven Countries . . ." (3 June 2015), posted on *GIRDS: Mothers for Life Network*, online: www.facebook.com/mothersandlife/posts/456073391222281.

7   Quoted in Mitch Potter, "Moms Using Social Media to Urge Offspring Lured by ISIS to Return Home" *Toronto Star* (3 June 2015), online: www.thestar.com/news/world/2015/06/03/moms-using-social-media-to-urge-offspring-lured-by-isis-to-come-home.html.

8   See Kent Roach, "Canadian Muslim Communities and Canadian National Security Policy" in Abdulkader H Sinno, ed, *Muslims in Western Politics* (Bloomington: Indiana University Press, 2009).

9   Quoted in Bruce Campion-Smith, "Prime Minister Stephen Harper Rejects 'Sociology' Talk in Wake of Terror Plots" *Toronto Star* (25 April 2013), online: www.thestar.com/news/canada/2013/04/25/prime_minister_stephen_harper_rejects_sociology_talk_in_wake_of_terror_plots.html.

10   Quoted in "Harper Says 'Islamism' Biggest Threat to Canada" *CBC News* (6 September 2011), online: www.cbc.ca/news/politics/harper-says-islamicism-biggest-threat-to-canada-1.1048280.

11   Richard Martin & Abbas Barzegar, *Islamism: Contested Perspectives on Political Islam* (Stanford: Stanford University Press, 2010).

12   Public Safety Canada documents define "Islamism" as "a politicized fom of Muslim faith that aims to implement Shari'ah (Islamic law) within an existing state or in the context of a pan-Islamic theocracy": Public Safety Canada, "Countering Violent Extremism: Strategies, Challenges and Lessons Learnt from Efforts to Tackle Radicalization in Europe" (Undated, marked "Draft"), Public Safety ATIP request A-2014-00202(2) at 000391.

13   See Lee Berthiaume, "John Baird Was Forced to Downplay Stephen Harper's 'Islamist Terrorism' Threat Comments, Documents Show" *National Post* (7 March 2013), online: news.nationalpost.com/news/canada/canadian-politics/john-baird-was-forced-to-downplay-stephen-harpers-islamist-terrorism-threat-comments-documents-show.

14   Quoted in Laura Payton, "Jihadists 'Declared War' on Those Who Disagree, Stephen Harper Says" *CBC News* (8 January 2015), online: www.cbc.ca/news/politics/jihadists-declared-war-on-those-who-disagree-stephen-harper-says-1.2894008.

15   Prime Minister of Canada, "PM Announces Anti-terrorism Measures to Protect Canadians" (30 January 2015), online: pm.gc.ca/eng/news/2015/01/30/pm-announces-anti-terrorism-measures-protect-canadians-0. Bill C-51, *An Act to enact the Security of Canada Information Sharing Act and the Secure Air Travel Act, to amend the Criminal Code, the Canadian Security Intelligence Service Act and the Immigration and Refugee Protection Act and to make related and consequential amendments to other Acts*, 2d Sess, 41st Parl, 2015 (assented to 18 June 2015), SC 2015, c 20.

16   Prime Minister of Canada, "PM Announces New Measures to Better Ensure the Security of Canadians" (4 June 2015), online: pm.gc.ca/eng/news/2015/06/04/pm-announces-new-measures-better-ensure-security-canadians-0.

17   Quoted in Laura Payton, "Muslim Groups 'Troubled' by Stephen Harper's Mosque Remark" *CBC News* (2 February 2015), online: www.cbc.ca/news/politics/muslim-groups-troubled-by-stephen-harper-s-mosque-remark-1.2940488.

18   *Ibid.*

19   Standing Committee on Public Safety and National Security, "Evidence" (12 March 2015) (Chair: Daryl Kramp), online: www.parl.gc.ca/HousePublications/ Publication.aspx?DocId=7881995&Language=E&Mode=1&Parl=41&Ses=2; Kristy Kirkup, "Bill C-51 Hearings: Diane Ablonczy's Questions to Muslim Group 'McCarthyesque'" *CBC News* (13 March 2015), online: www.cbc.ca/ news/politics/bill-c-51-hearings-diane-ablonczy-s-questions-to-muslim-group-mccarthyesque-1.2993531.

20   See Faisal Kutty, Naseer (Irfan) Syed, & Hussein Hamdani, "Attacks under the Guise of Parliamentary Privilege" *Canadian Lawyer* (23 March 2015), online: www.canadianlawyermag.com/5524/Attacks-under-the-guise-of-parliamentary-privilege.html.

21   Senate Standing Committee on National Security and Defence, *Countering the Terrorist Threat in Canada: An Interim Report* (Ottawa: Senate, July 2015) (Chair: Daniel Lang), online: www.parl.gc.ca/Content/SEN/Committee/412/secd/rep/ rep18jul15-e.pdf.

22   *Ibid* at vi (Recommendation 9).

23   Quoted in Vassy Kapelos, "Harper Government Won't Consider Controversial Suggestion to Certify Imams" *Global News* (9 July 2015), online: globalnews.ca/ news/2102318/harper-government-wont-consider-controversial-suggestion-to-certify-imams/.

24   Stephen Maher, "Fear Becomes a Political Game" *Vancouver Sun* (21 February 2015).

25   Quoted in Joan Bryden, "Stephen Harper's Anti-niqab Rhetoric Helps Terrorist Recruiters, Charles Taylor Says" *Toronto Star* (28 March 2015), online: www. thestar.com/news/canada/2015/03/28/stephen-harpers-anti-niqab-rhetoric-helps-terrorist-recruiters-charles-taylor-says.html.

26   Mary Allen, Statistics Canada, "Police-Reported Hate Crimes in Canada, 2013" (9 June 2015) *Juristat*, online: www.statcan.gc.ca/pub/85-002-x/2015001/article/14191-eng.htm.

27   Public Safety Canada, "Briefing Material for the Moroccan Government — Countering Terrorism and Violent Extremism in Canada" (Undated, but no earlier than 2013), Public Safety ATIP request A-2014-00202(2) at 000020.

28   The White House, Office of the Press Secretary, "Remarks by the President at the Summit on Countering Violent Extremism" (19 February 2015), online: www.whitehouse.gov/the-press-office/2015/02/19/remarks-president-summit-countering-violent-extremism-february-19-2015.

29   The White House, Office of the Press Secretary, "Remarks by the President in Closing of the Summit on Countering Violent Extremism" (18 February 2015), online: www.whitehouse.gov/the-press-office/2015/02/18/remarks-president-closing-summit-countering-violent-extremism.

30   Australian Prime Minister Tony Abbott, "Address to Australia's Regional Summit to Counter Violent Extremism, Sydney" (11 June 2015), online: www.pm.gov.au/ media/2015-06-11/address-australias-regional-summit-counter-violent-extremism-sydney-0.

31   Quoted in Jon Henley, "How Do You Deradicalise Returning Isis Fighters?" *Guardian* (12 November 2014), online: www.theguardian.com/world/2014/nov/12/ deradicalise-isis-fighters-jihadists-denmark-syria.

32   There are good reasons for this dearth of empirical research. There are obvious ethical difficulties in conducting such studies and evident logistical reasons why subjects of the studies may decline co-operation or misrepresent their views: see Anja Dalgaard-Nielsen, "Violent Radicalization in Europe: What We Know and What We Do Not Know" (2010) 33:9 *Studies in Conflict & Terrorism* 797 at 811.

33   See, for example, *ibid.*

34   Clark McCauley & Sophia Moskalenko, "Toward a Profile of Lone Wolf Terrorists: What Moves an Individual from Radical Opinion to Radical Action" (2014) 26 *Terrorism and Political Violence* 69 at 70.

35   *Ibid.*

36   *Ibid.*

37   *Ibid* at 71. Some of those data do suggest that in the United Kingdom in 2005 at least, the base tier of those Muslims who dispute every aspect of the al-Qaida-inspired discourse is smaller than the tier of those who believe that the West is engaged in a conflict with Islam.

38   *Ibid* at 73.

39   See Sophia Moskalenko & Clark McCauley, "Measuring Political Mobilization: The Distinction between Activism and Radicalism" (2009) 21 *Terrorism and Political Violence* 239 at 240.

40   Mitchell D Silber & Arvin Bhatt, *Radicalization in the West: The Homegrown Threat* (New York: New York City Police Department, 2007) at 10, online: www.nypdshield.org/public/SiteFiles/documents/NYPD_Report-Radicalization_in_the_West.pdf.

41   Quoted in John Knefel, "Everything You've Been Told about Radicalization Is Wrong" *Rolling Stone* (6 May 2013), online: www.rollingstone.com/politics/news/everything-youve-been-told-about-radicalization-is-wrong-20130506.

42   Quoted in Andrew Gilligan, "Hizb ut Tahrir Is Not a Gateway to Terrorism, Claims Whitehall Report" *Telegraph* (25 July 2010), online: www.telegraph.co.uk/journalists/andrew-gilligan/7908262/Hizb-ut-Tahrir-is-not-a-gateway-to-terrorism-claims-Whitehall-report.html.

43   McCauley & Moskalenko, above note 34 at 72.

44   See Moskalenko & McCauley, above note 39 at 240.

45   See McCauley & Moskalenko, above note 34 at 72.

46   Michael Noonan & Phyl Khalil, "North American Foreign Fighters" (2014/15) 1 *Journal of Deradicalization* 66 at 73.

47   Scott Flower & Deborah Birkett, "(Mis)Understanding Muslim Converts in Canada: A Critical Discussion of Muslim Converts in the Contexts of Security and Society" (July 2014) TSAS Working Paper Series, No 14-06, online: library.tsas.ca/media/TSASWP14-06_Flower-Birkett.pdf.

48   See Lorne Dawson, *Comprehending Cults: The Sociology of New Religious Movements* (Toronto: Oxford University Press Canada, 1998).

49   Lorne Dawson, "Trying to Make Sense of Home-Grown Terrorist Radicalization: The Case of the Toronto 18" in Paul Bramadat & Lorne Dawson, eds, *Religious Radicalization and Securitization in Canada and Beyond* (Toronto: University of Toronto Press, 2014) at location 1601 (Kindle ed).

50   Dalgaard-Nielsen, above note 32 at 805, citing Edwin Bakker, *Jihadi Terrorists in Europe* (The Hague: Netherlands Institute of International Relations Clingendael, December 2006).

51 Dalgaard-Nielsen, above note 32 at 805.

52 *Ibid* at 806, citing Petter Nesser's research: see Petter Nesser, "Jihad in Europe; Recruitment for Terrorist Cells in Europe" in Laila Bokhari et al, *Paths to Global Jihad: Radicalisation and Recruitment to Terror Networks* (Proceedings from a FFI Seminar, Oslo, 15 March 2006).

53 Dalgaard-Nielsen, above note 32 at 805.

54 *Ibid* at 806–7.

55 *Ibid* at 807, citing Marieke Slootman & Jean Tillie, *Processes of Radicalization: Why Some Amsterdam Muslims Become Radicals* (Amsterdam: Institute for Migrations and Ethnic Studies, University of Amsterdam, 2006).

56 Dalgaard-Nielsen, above note 32 at 807.

57 *Ibid.*

58 *Ibid.*

59 *Ibid.*

60 Mirra Noor Milla, Faturochman, & Djamaludin Ancok, "The Impact of Leader-Follower Interactions on the Radicalization of Terrorists: A Case Study of the Bali Bombers" (2013) 16:2 *Asian Journal of Social Psychology* 92 at 92.

61 *Ibid* at 99. For a discussion of charismatic authority in terrorist groups, see David C Hofmann & Lorne L Dawson, "The Neglected Role of Charismatic Authority in the Study of Terrorist Groups and Radicalization" (2014) 37:4 *Studies in Conflict & Terrorism* 348.

62 Francesca Bosco, "Terrorist Use of the Internet" in Uğur Gürbüz, ed, *Capacity Building in the Fight against Terrorism* (Amsterdam: IOS Press, 2013) at 40. See the analysis by Jialun Qin et al, "Analyzing Terror Campaigns on the Internet: Technical Sophistication, Content Richness, and Web Interactivity" (2007) 65:1 *International Journal of Human-Computer Studies* 71.

63 See, for example, David Benson, "Why the Internet Is Not Increasing Terrorism" (2014) 23:2 *Security Studies* 293 at 315ff. See also Craig Espeseth et al, "Terrorist Use of Communication Technology and Social Networks" in U Feyyaz Aydoğdu, ed, *Technological Dimensions of Defence against Terrorism* (Amsterdam: IOS Press, 2013) at 94.

64 Public Safety Canada, "Preventing Radicalization and Violent Extremism among Youths" (Undated), Public Safety ATIP request A-2014-00442.

65 Dalgaard-Nielsen, above note 32 at 808.

66 *Ibid* at 810.

67 For a summary, see Peter Neumann, "Options and Strategies for Countering Online Radicalization in the United States" (2013) 36:6 *Studies in Conflict & Terrorism* 431 at 435ff.

68 See, for example, Marc Sageman, *Leaderless Jihad: Terror Networks in the Twenty-First Century* (Philadelphia: University of Pennsylvania Press, 2008).

69 *Ibid.*

70 Bosco, above note 62 at 92.

71 Espeseth et al, above note 63 at 95.

72 Part I of the *Constitution Act, 1982*, being Schedule B to the *Canada Act 1982* (UK), 1982, c 11, s 2(b) [*Charter*].

73 International Centre for the Study of Radicalisation and Political Violence, *Countering Online Radicalisation: A Strategy for Action* (London: ICSR, 2009) at 17, online: cst.org.uk/docs/countering_online_radicalisation1.pdf.

74 Paul Bramadat, "The Public, the Political, and the Possible: Religion and Radicalization in Canada and Beyond" in Bramadat & Dawson, above note 49 at location 170 (Kindle ed).

75 John Horgan, "Individual Disengagement: A Psychological Analysis" in Tore Bjorgo & John Horgan, eds, *Leaving Terrorism Behind* (London: Routledge, 2009) at 27.

76 Dalgaard-Nielsen, above note 32 at 811.

77 See Kate Barrelle, "Pro-integration: Disengagement and Life after Extremism" (2015) 7 *Behavioural Sciences of Terrorism and Political Violence* 129.

78 Anja Dalgaard-Nielsen, "Promoting Exit from Violent Extremism: Themes and Approaches" (2013) 36:2 *Studies in Conflict & Terrorism* 99 at 110.

79 *Ibid.*

80 *Ibid.*

81 Neumann, above note 67 at 443.

82 Bosco, above note 62 at 45.

83 Froukje Demant & Beatrice de Graaf, "How to Counter Radical Narratives: Dutch Deradicalization Policy in the Case of Moluccan and Islamic Radicals" (2010) 33:5 *Studies in Conflict & Terrorism* 408 at 421.

84 See Andrew Zammit, *Australian Foreign Fighters: Risks and Responses* (Sydney: The Lowy Institute for International Policy, 2015) at 16.

85 Neumann, above note 67 at 444.

86 Attorney-General for Australia, "Communiqué: Ministerial Meeting, 12 June 2015, Sydney, Australia" (12 June 2015), online: www.attorneygeneral.gov.au/Mediareleases/Pages/2015/SecondQuarter/12-June-2015-Ministerial-Meeting-12-June-2015-Sydney-Australia.aspx.

87 *Ibid.*

88 See Neumann, above note 67 at 444.

89 See *ibid.*

90 Bosco, above note 62 at 45.

91 See *RAN Lessons Learned*, above note 3 at 86–87. One YouTube channel featuring animated shorts by a former extremist, Abdullah X, is supported by the Radicalization Awareness Network of the European Union and Google: Maura Conway & Clive Walker, "Countering Terrorism via the Internet" in Genevieve Lennon & Clive Walker, eds, *Routledge Handbook of Law and Terrorism* (London: Routledge, 2015) at 431.

92 Anthony Richards, "From Terrorism to 'Radicalization' to 'Extremism': Counterterrorism Imperative or Loss of Focus?" (2015) 91:2 *International Affairs* 371 at 380.

93 See András Sajó, ed, *Militant Democracy* (Utrecht, NL: Eleven International Publishing, 2004).

94 (UK), 2015 c 6, Part 5. Specified authorities are listed in Schedule 6 of this Act.

95 United Kingdom, Her Majesty's Government, *Channel Duty Guidance: Protecting Vulnerable People from Being Drawn into Terrorism — Statutory Guidance for Channel Panel Members and Partners of Local Panels* (London: HM Government, 2015) at 2, online: www.gov.uk/government/uploads/system/uploads/attachment_data/file/423550/Channel_Guidance_V.6.pdf.

96 *Ibid* at 5–7.

97 *Ibid.*

98 See, for example, West Midlands Counter Terrorism Unit, *Channel* (2013), online: www.west-midlands.police.uk/docs/keeping-you-safe/behind-the-badge/tackling-terrorism/DL-Channel%20lft_Channel-lft-DL_final.pdf.

99 Public Safety Canada, above note 12, at 000394.

100 United Kingdom, Her Majesty's Government, *Prevent Duty Guidance: For England and Wales* (London: HM Government, 2015) at 2, online: www.gov.uk/government/uploads/system/uploads/attachment_data/file/417943/Prevent_Duty_Guidance_England_Wales.pdf.

101 "PREVENT Will Have a Chilling Effect on Open Debate, Free Speech and Political Dissent" *Independent* (10 July 2015), online: www.independent.co.uk/voices/letters/prevent-will-have-a-chilling-effect-on-open-debate-free-speech-and-political-dissent-10381491.html.

102 Quoted in Matthew Weaver, "Expert on Cameron Strategy: 'People Are Drawn to Terrorism More Because of Identity Issues Than Ideology'" *Guardian* (20 July 2015), online: www.businessinsider.com/expert-on-cameron-strategy-people-are-drawn-to-terrorism-more-because-of-identity-issues-than-ideology-2015-7#ixzz3gXAyysaH.

103 Letter to the US Congress, organized by the Brennan Centre for Justice at NYU School of Law, "Re: H.R. 2899, Countering Violent Extremism Act of 2015" (10 July 2015), online: www.brennancenter.org/sites/default/files/analysis/071015%20Letter%20to%20H.%20Comm%20on%20Homeland%20Sec.%20Re.%20HR%202899%20%20.pdf.

104 Public Safety Canada, above note 12, at 000399.

105 See *RAN Lessons Learned*, above note 3 at 99.

106 Australian Government, "Living Safe Together," online: www.livingsafetogether.gov.au/partners/Pages/government.aspx.

107 Australian Government, *Working Together to Turn People Away from Violent Ideologies*, online: www.ag.gov.au/NationalSecurity/Counteringviolentextremism/Documents/Working-together-to-turn-people-away-from-violent-ideologies.pdf.

108 See, for example, Collaborative of Non-governmental and Governmental Stakeholders from the Greater Boston Region, *A Framework for Prevention and Intervention Strategies: Incorporating Violent Extremism into Violence Prevention Efforts* (Massachusetts: US Attorney's Office District of Massachusetts, February 2015), online: www.justice.gov/sites/default/files/usao-ma/pages/attachments/2015/02/18/framework.pdf.

109 *Debates of the Senate (Hansard)*, 41st Parl, 2d Sess, (28 May 2015) (Speaker: Hon Leo Housakos), online: www.parl.gc.ca/Content/Sen/Chamber/412/Debates/145db_2015-05-28-e.htm.

110 Public Safety Canada, *2014 Public Report on the Terrorist Threat to Canada* (Ottawa: PSC, 2014) at 35, online: www.publicsafety.gc.ca/cnt/rsrcs/pblctns/2014-pblc-rpr-trrrst-thrt/index-eng.aspx.

111 Memo for Assistant Deputy Minister, United States Department of State, "Re: Countering Violent Extremism Project in Canada" (Undated), Access request, Public Safety ATIP request A-2014-00202.

112 Bill 59, *An Act to enact the Act to prevent and combat hate speech and speech inciting violence and to amend various legislative provisions to better protect individuals*, 1st Sess, 41st Leg, (First reading 10 June 2015); Bill 62, *An Act to foster adherence to State religious neutrality and, in particular, to provide a framework for religious accommodation requests in certain bodies*, 1st Sess, 41st Leg, (First Reading 10 June 2015).

113 Canada, "Backgrounder: Countering Violent Extremism (CVE): Radicalization to Violence" (10 June 2014), Public Safety ATIP request A-2014-00202 at 00045.

114 Public Safety Canada, "Telling Stories: A New Approach to Community Engagement" (12 August 2014), Public Safety ATIP request A-2014-00202 at 00261.

115 Online: www.publicsafety.gc.ca/cnt/ntnl-scrt/cntr-trrrsm/cntrng-vlnt-xtrmsm/index-eng.aspx.

116 Public Safety Canada, "Memorandum to the Deputy Minister: Moving Forward on Countering Violent Extremism Program and Initiatives" (Undated), Public Safety ATIP request A-2014-00202(2) at 000283-84.

117 Edna Keeble, "The Cross-cultural Roundtable on Security as a Response to Radicalization: Personal Experiences and Academic Reflections" in Bramadat & Dawson, above note 49 at location 6466 (Kindle ed).

118 See Catherine Solymon, "Hero or Extremist? Tables Turned on Man Who Helped Canadian Government with Would-Be Jihadists" *National Post* (27 May 2015), online: news.nationalpost.com/news/canada/hero-or-extremist-tables-turn-on-man-who-helped-ottawa-with-would-be-jihadists.

119 Public Safety Canada, *Building Resilience against Terrorism: Canada's Counter-terrorism Strategy*, 2d ed (Ottawa: PSC, 2013) at 15.

120 Public Safety Canada, above note 110 at 34.

121 *Ibid.*

122 Canada, above note 113 [emphasis added].

123 Public Safety Canada, above note 27

124 Public Safety Canada, above note 110 at 35.

125 *Ibid* at 36.

126 *Ibid.*

127 Public Safety Canada, "Terms of Reference of the Cross-cultural Roundtable on Security" (2014), online: www.publicsafety.gc.ca/cnt/ntnl-scrt/crss-cltrl-rndtbl/trms-rfrnc-eng.aspx.

128 Canada, Special Senate Committee on Anti-terrorism, *Security, Freedom, and the Complex Terrorist Threat: Positive Steps Ahead* (Ottawa: Senate, 2011) (Chair: Hugh Segal) at 21, online: www.parl.gc.ca/content/sen/committee/403/anti/rep/rep03mar11-e.pdf.

129 Public Safety Canada, "Connecting with Canadian Communities: Cross-cultural Roundtable on Security," online: www.publicsafety.gc.ca/cnt/ntnl-scrt/crss-cltrl-rndtbl/index-eng.aspx.

130 Public Safety Canada, "Cross-cultural Roundtable on Security Meeting Summary — Radicalization Leading to Violence" (18–20 November 2011, Gatineau, Quebec), online: www.publicsafety.gc.ca/cnt/ntnl-scrt/crss-cltrl-rndtbl/smmr-2011-11-eng.aspx.

131 Cross-cultural Roundtable on Security Sub-group on Preventing and Countering Violent Extremism, *Final Report* (January 2014), Public Safety ATIP request A-2014-00202(2) at 000374.

132 *Ibid.*

133 Public Safety Canada, "Canada's Countering Violent Extremism Initiatives" (21 May 2014), Public Safety ATIP request A-2014-00202(2) at 000040.

134 Quoted in Adam Carter, "Hussein Hamdani Says Federal Election Politics behind His Suspension" *CBC News* (1 May 2015), online: www.cbc.ca/news/canada/hamilton/news/hussein-hamdani-says-federal-election-politics-behind-his-suspension-1.3056931.

135 Kutty, Syed, & Hamdani, above note 20.

136 Adam Carter, "Hamilton Lawyer Saved 10 Young People from Terror Extremism" *CBC News* (6 November 2015), online: www.cbc.ca/news/canada/hamilton/news/hamilton-lawyer-saved-10-young-people-from-terror-extremism-1.2825965.

137 See Jeff Green, "Hamilton's Muslim Community Praised at Whitehouse Anti-terror Summit" *CBC News* (21 February 2015), online: www.cbc.ca/news/canada/hamilton/news/hamilton-s-muslim-community-praised-at-whitehouse-anti-terror-summit-1.2966290.

138 Jeff Green, "Minister Blaney Denies Knowing about Muslim Lawyer's Liberal Support" *CBC News* (13 May 2015), online: www.cbc.ca/news/canada/hamilton/news/minister-blaney-denies-knowing-about-muslim-lawyer-s-liberal-support-1.3072480.

139 Public Safety Canada, above note 27 at 000021.

140 "About" (February 2015), online: Extreme Dialogue extremedialogue.org/about/.

141 See "Damian Clairmont's Grandfather Blames CSIS for Inaction" *CBC News* (16 January 2014), online: www.cbc.ca/news/canada/nova-scotia/damian-clairmont-s-grandfather-blames-csis-for-inaction-1.2499296.

142 Quoted in Colin Freeze, "Spy-Watchers Urge a Shorter Leash for CSIS" *Globe and Mail* (27 October 2010), online: www.theglobeandmail.com/news/politics/spy-watchers-urge-a-shorter-leash-for-csis/article1381179/.

143 CSIS, "Committee Note: Threat Diminishment: Hot Issues," released under CSIS ATIP 117-2015-35.

144 SIRC, "CSIS Use of Disruption to Counter National Security Threats" (SIRC Study May 2009), File No 2800-150 (redacted version released under Access to Information).

145 *Ibid.*

146 *Ibid.*

147 Security Intelligence Review Committee, *Annual Report 09/10: Time for Reflection — Taking the Measure of Security Intelligence* (Ottawa: Public Works and Government Services Canada, 2010) at 16, online: www.sirc-csars.gc.ca/pdfs/ar_2009-2010-eng.pdf.

148 RCMP, "Questions and Answers: Bill C-51, Q36" (marked "Draft April 17 2015"), released via ATIP request A-2015-04006.

149 Public Safety Canada, above note 110 at 37.

150 RCMP, above note 148.

151 *Ibid.*

152 Commission of Inquiry into the Activities of Canadian Officials in relation to Maher Arar, *Analysis and Recommendations* (Ottawa: Public Works, 2006) at 312–15.

153 See Dylan Robertson, "RCMP Poised to Roll Out Program to Prevent Radicalization" *Ottawa Citizen* (17 December 2014), online: ottawacitizen.com/news/politics/rcmp-poised-to-roll-out-program-to-prevent-radicalization; Dylan Robertson, "Delay of National Terrorism Intervention Strategy Prompts Local Upstarts" *Calgary Herald* (1 April 2015), online: calgaryherald.com/news/national/delay-of-national-terrorism-intervention-strategy-prompts-local-upstarts.

154 *Ibid.*

155 RCMP, "Questions and Answers: Bill C-51, Q42" (marked "Draft April 17 2015"), released via ATIP request A-2015-04006.

156 See Eugene Tan, "Singapore" in Kent Roach, ed, *Comparative Counter-terrorism Law* (Cambridge: Cambridge University Press, 2015) at 624, n 59.

157 Stewart Bell, "Ottawa Moves to Revoke Citizenship of Convicted Terrorist for the First Time since Controversial Law Took Effect" *National Post* (1 July 2015), online: news.nationalpost.com/news/ottawa-moves-to-revoke-citizenship-of-convicted-terrorist-for-first-time-since-controversial-law-took-effect.

158 See Chris Wodskou, "Privatizing the Prison Chaplain: A View from the Inside" *CBC News* (15 June 2014), online: www.cbc.ca/news/canada/privatizing-the-prison-chaplain-a-view-from-the-inside-1.2673301.

159 Office of the Correctional Investigator, "Annual Report of the Office of the Correctional Investigator 2012-2013" (2013) at 7, online: www.oci-bec.gc.ca/cnt/rpt/annrpt/annrpt20122013-eng.aspx.

160 Alex Wilner, *From Rehabilitation to Recruitment* (Ottawa: Macdonald-Laurier Institute for Public Policy, 2010) at 28.

161 See Jill Mahoney, "Government Cuts Non-Christian Prison Chaplains" *Globe and Mail* (5 October 2012), online: www.theglobeandmail.com/news/politics/government-cuts-non-christian-prison-chaplains/article4591355/.

162 See James Beckford & Ilona Cairns, "Muslim Prison Chaplains in Canada and Britain" (2015) 63 *The Sociological Review* 36 at 39 and 47.

163 "Hamilton Imam: Prison Chaplaincy Privatization a National Security Threat" *CBC News* (14 January 2015), online: www.cbc.ca/news/canada/hamilton/news/hamilton-imam-prison-chaplaincy-privatization-a-national-security-threat-1.2900484.

164 *Ibid.*

165 See Ian MacLeod, "Man Who Murdered Family in 'Honour Killing' Became a Jailhouse Religious Tyrant" *Ottawa Citizen* (5 May 2015), online: ottawacitizen.com/news/politics/man-who-murdered-family-became-jailhouse-religious-tyrant.

166 See Catherine Appleton & Clive Walker, "The Penology of Terrorism" in Lennon & Walker, above note 91 at 455–56. Professors Appleton and Walker do criticize the United Kingdom approach for paying little attention to rehabilitation.

167 See "Directors," online: Kairos Pneuma Chaplaincy Inc kpc-inc.ca/directors.html.

168 Public Safety Canada, above note 27 at 000024.

169 See Stewart Bell, "As Convicted Terrorists Face Possible Release, Canada Faced with Growing Problem: How Do You Rehabilitate Them?" *National Post* (30 November 2012), online: news.nationalpost.com/news/canada/as-convicted-terrorists-face-possible-release-canada-faced-with-growing-problem-how-do-you-rehabilitate-them.

170 See Mitch Potter, "Moms Open Path for Kids in ISIS to Return" *Toronto Star* (4 June 2015).

171 Quoted in Tracey McVeigh, "'Police Betrayed Me': Says Mother of Imprisoned British Jihadi" *Guardian* (6 December 2014), online: www.theguardian.com/world/2014/dec/06/yusuf-sarwar-mother-british-jihadist-police-betray-syria.

172 See Shadi Hamid & Daniel Byman, *Adversity and Opportunity* (The Hague: Clingendael Netherlands Institute of International Relations, 2015) at 25.

173 *Ibid* at 26.

174 Zammit, above note 84.

175 There do appear to be a few local programs: see Al Sunnah Foundation, online: www.alsunnahfoundation.org/about.html; Paradise Forever, online: thep4e.com/.

176 Clive Walker & Javaid Rehman, "Prevent Responses to Jihadi Terrorism" in Victor Ramraj et al, eds, *Global Anti-terrorism Law and Policy*, 2d ed (Cambridge: Cambridge University Press, 2012) at 242ff.

177 Global Counterterrorism Forum, "Good Practices on Community Engagement and Community-Oriented Policing as Tools to Counter Violent Extremism" (2013) at 2, online: www.thegctf.org/documents/10162/159885/13Aug09_EN_Good+Practices+on+Community+Engagement+and+Community-Oriented+Policing.pdf; Organization for Security and Co-operation in Europe, "Preventing Terrorism and Countering Violent Extremism and Radicalization That Lead to Terrorism: A Community-Policing Approach" (Vienna: OSCE, February 2014) at 90, online: www.osce.org/atu/111438?download=true.

178 Canada, Parliament, *House Debate* (31 March 2015).

179 Islamic Social Services Association, National Council of Canadian Muslims, & RCMP, *United against Terrorism: A Collaborative Effort towards a Secure, Inclusive and Just Canada* (Winnipeg: ISSA, NCCM, & RCMP, 2014), online: www.issaservices.com/issa/downloads/UAT-HANDBOOK-WEB-VERSION-SEPT-27-2014.pdf [*United*].

180 "Group Stunned RCMP Pulled Support from Anti-terrorism Handbook" *CBC News* (30 September 2014), online: www.cbc.ca/news/canada/manitoba/group-stunned-rcmp-pulled-support-from-anti-terrorism-handbook-1.2783234; "Muslim Group Proceeds with Libel Suit against Stephen Harper and Spokesman over 'Terrorist' Comment" *Toronto Star* (26 May 2014), online: www.thestar.com/news/canada/2014/05/26/muslim_group_to_proceed_with_libel_suit_against_stephen_harper_and_spokesman_over_terrorist_comment.html.

181 See Anna Mehler Paperny, "On Terror Rhetoric, Public Safety Minister Ignores RCMP and His Own Advisors" *Global News* (29 July 2015), online: globalnews.ca/news/2137578/on-terror-rhetoric-public-safety-minister-ignores-rcmp-and-his-own-advisors/.

182 Online: twitter.com/ThinkAgain_DOS/status/519853876833705984/photo/1. See Andrew McCarthy, "State Department Endorses Canadian Islamist Handbook That Describes Jihad as 'Noble'" *Washington Free Beacon* (8 October 2014), in RCMP ATIP request A-2014-07289 at 187 of 312.

183 *United*, above note 179 at 5.

184 *Ibid* at 8.

185 *Ibid* at 10.

186 *Ibid* at 17.

187 See Mark Juergensmeyer, "Christian Violence in America" (1998) 558 *Annals of the American Academy of Political and Social Science* 88.

188 See Public Safety Canada, above note 130.

189 RCMP, National Security Criminal Investigations, *Words Make Worlds: Terrorism and Language* (Ottawa: RCMP, 2009) at 2, online: https://shawglobalnews.files. wordpress.com/2015/07/ps64-98-2007-eng.pdf.

190 *United,* above note 179 at 6.

191 *Ibid* at 12.

192 *Ibid* at 16.

193 *Ibid* at 22.

194 *Ibid* at 26.

195 Douglas Quan, "RCMP Took Issue with 'Adversarial' Tone of Muslim Groups' Counter-radicalization Handbook" *Canada.com* (30 September 2014), online: o.canada.com/news/national/rcmp-took-issue-with-adversarial-tone-of-muslim-groups-counter-radicalization-handbook.

196 Email (29 September 2014) in Public Safety ATIP request A-2014-00315(2) p 186 of 394 in pdf.

197 Email (28 September 2014) in Public Safety ATIP request A-2014-07289 at 267 of 312 in pdf.

198 Email (29 September 2014) at 194–5 of 394 in pdf of Public Safety ATIP request A-2014-00315(2).

199 See Kirkup, above note 19.

200 Email, "Lines" (30 September 2014) in RCMP ATIP request A-2014-07289 at p 166 of 312 of pdf.

201 Royal Canadian Mounted Police, *Youth Online and at Risk: Radicalization Facilitated by the Internet* (Ottawa: RCMP, 2011) at 3, online: www.rcmp-grc. gc.ca/nsci-ecsn/rad/rad-eng.htm.

202 *Ibid* at 4.

203 *Ibid* at 12.

204 *Ibid* at 22.

205 "Preventing Radicalization and Violent Extremism among Youths" (Undated), Public Safety ATIP request A-2014-00442.

206 Bill 62, above note 112, s 9. See Giuseippe Valiante, "Quebec introduces action plan to combat violent radicalization" *Toronto Star* (11 June 2015); Les Perreaux, "Quebec crackdown on violent extremism re-opens secularism debate" *Globe and Mail* (11 June 2015); Catherine Solyom, "Muslim groups say they want to protect their youth from radicalization" *Montreal Gazette* (10 June 2015).

207 Bill 59, above note 112, s 1.

208 *Ibid,* s 9.

209 *Counter-terrorism and Security Act 2015,* above note 94, Part 5.

210 Authors' translation of « c'est que les parents puissent appeler dans un endroit, qu'ils puissent poser des questions. Il faut être capable de recommander les parents, les amis. Il faut être capable de mettre les bons intervenants en place, et pas seulement la police . . . . Ça fonctionne en France, en Belgique. Ces lignes confidentielles rassurent et incitent les gens à s'informer, mais aussi à signaler » : "Radicalisation : Quebec passé a l'action" *Radio Canada* (10 June 2015), online: ici.radio-canada.ca/nouvelles/politique/2015/06/10/004-radicalisation-neutralite-couillard-quebec-projets-lois.shtml.

211 Quoted in Jillian Kestler-D'Amours, "Quebec Muslims Question Montreal Plan for 'Anti-radicalization' Program" *Toronto Star* (11 June 2015), online: www.thestar.com/news/canada/2015/03/11/quebec-muslims-question-montreal-plan-for-anti-radicalization-program.html.

212 See Amy-Jane Gielen, "Supporting Families of Foreign Fighters" (2015) 2 *Journal for Deradicalization* 21 at 28, online: journals.sfu.ca/jd/index.php/jd/article/download/10/10.

213 *Ibid* at 24.

214 *Ibid* at 26.

215 Leslie MacKinnon, "Harper Slams Trudeau for Comments over the Boston Bombings" *CBC News* (17 April 2013), online: www.cbc.ca/news/politics/harper-slams-trudeau-for-comments-on-boston-bombings-1.1394586.

216 *Ibid*.

217 Janyce McGregor & Kady O'Malley, "Stephen Harper Makes His Case for New Powers to Combat Terrorism" *CBC News* (30 January 2015), online: www.cbc.ca/news/politics/stephen-harper-makes-his-case-for-new-powers-to-combat-terror-1.2937602.

CHAPTER FOURTEEN: CONCLUSION

1 *R v Ahmad*, 2011 SCC 6.

2 The former justice was quoted as stating that the minister of public safety "never read the report or that he was so stupid he didn't understand the report" in Don Butler, "Don't Rush the Enactment of New Anti-terror Laws, Former Judges Advise" *Ottawa Citizen* (29 October 2014), online: ottawacitizen.com/news/local-news/dont-rush-to-enact-new-anti-terror-laws-former-top-judges-advise-government.

3 Jean Chrétien et al, "A Close Eye on Security Makes Canadians Safer" *Globe and Mail* (19 February 2015), online: www.theglobeandmail.com/globe-debate/a-close-eye-on-security-makes-canadians-safer/article23069152/.

4 *Application under s. 83.28 of the Criminal Code (Re)*, 2004 SCC 42 at paras 7ff.

5 *Canada v Harkat*, 2014 SCC 37.

6 John Horgan, "Can Science Solve Terrorism? Q&A with Psychologist John Horgan" (2 March 2015), online: Scientific American blogs.scientificamerican.com/cross-check/can-science-solve-terrorism-q-amp-a-with-psychologist-john-horgan/.

7 *Public Committee against Torture in Israel v The State of Israel*, HCJ 5100/94 at para 39.

8 Jim Judd, Director of CSIS, Talking points for 2007 Raoul Wallenberg International Human Rights Symposium, *"How Should a Democracy Respond to Domestic Terrorist Threats"* (January 2007).

Index

Islam, 1, 2, 70–71, 84, 89, 102–3, 104,
106, 335, 338–39, 342, 348, 356,
449–50, 453, 456, 458, 459–60,
461, 464, 466, 467, 471, 473,
477–78, 484–85, 487. *See also*
Counter–violent extremism (CVE)
Islamic State of Iraq and Syria (ISIS), 1,
2, 8, 11, 12, 15, 17, 21, 23–25, 35,
37, 40, 54, 55, 59, 64, 65, 78, 81,
84–102, 104–6, 109, 113, 159–60,
164, 182, 190–91, 211, 213, 215,
218, 243, 278–79, 281, 282, 300,
324–30, 332, 340, 347, 348, 350,
352, 355–56, 375–76, 450, 452,
455–56, 462, 464, 471, 480,
482–84, 487–89, 491, 493, 501.
See also Couture-Rouleau, Martin;
Jihadism; Terrorist propaganda

Jaballah, Mahmoud, 206, 207
Jabarah, Mohammed, 73–74, 76,
256–57, 269, 499–500
James, Roxanne, 409, 411
Jihadism. See also Harper, Stephen
controversy over word, 89–90, 325
Cross-cultural Roundtable and,
509–10
government preoccupation with,
87–88, 90, 325, 337–38, 341, 347
ideology and, 89–90, 338–39
political rhetoric and, 86–88, 454
United against Terrorism and, 483–84
Justice, Department of, 184, 366, 368,
388
Justice, minister of, 2, 254, 366, 370, 425

Kanishka Project, 110, 475
Kenney, Jason, 136, 383, 399
Khadr, Omar, 74–76, 78, 108, 257, 269,
285, 312, 414, 499–500
Khawaja, Mohammed Momin, 271–74,
276, 277, 285, 289, 306, 308,
310–12, 317, 343, 347–48, 349

Law enforcement justification provision,
247, 255–56, 260–61, 514–15
"Less is more," 294–96, 297. *See also* One
Vision

Listing, terrorist, 25, 65, 76, 77–79, 96,
188, 189, 190–91, 382

MacKay, Peter
"cultural" requirement of terrorism, 2,
23, 280–81, 454
security review and, 43, 399, 407
speech offence and, 325, 337–38, 341
Mahjoub, Mohammed Zeki, 201–3,
205–7
May, Elizabeth, 249
Martin, Paul. *See* Prime ministers' letter
(February 2014) on review and
oversight
McDonald Commission
CSIS, proposals for, 39, 40–41, 43,
248, 366, 405, 496
parliamentary committee, 405–6, 411
RCMP illegality, 27, 39, 40–41, 230,
365, 405, 496
Security Intelligence Review Commission, 44, 405–6, 411
Mejid, Ayad, 178–80, 236–37, 269, 298
Metadata, 122, 125–29, 134–37, 440,
506, 519
Mobility rights. *See also* Bill-C-51 —
Anti-terrorism Act (2015), *Charter*
rights, violation of; *Charter of
Rights and Freedoms*, rights under;
Revocation, passport
CSIS threat disruption warrants, 255,
264
Murray, Joyce, 409, 411, 415
Muslim communities, 451–52, 454, 479,
481–82
government relationship with, 11, 12,
16, 341–42, 452, 454–55, 471,
473, 478, 482, 483, 489, 493. *See
also* Counter–violent extremism
(CVE)

National Council of Canadian Muslims,
455
Ablonczy, Diane and, 487
United against Terrorism, 483, 488
National Security Advisor
co-ordination and, 48, 374, 375, 380,
382, 508

About the Authors

Craig Forcese is an associate professor at the University of Ottawa's Faculty of Law (Common Law Section). He teaches Public International Law, Public Law and Legislation, Administrative Law, and National Security Law. Much of his present research and writing relates to national security and democratic accountability. He is the author of Irwin Law's *National Security Law: Canadian Practice in International Perspective* and a co-editor of *The Human Rights of Anti-terrorism*. He is also a co-author of *International Law: Doctrine, Practice, and Theory* and *The Laws of Government: The Legal Foundations of Canadian Democracy* and a co-editor of *Public Law: Cases, Materials, and Commentary*. Professor Forcese was vice-dean of the University of Ottawa's Common Law Section from 2011 to 2014. Before joining the faculty, he practised law with the Washington DC office of Hughes Hubbard & Reed LLP for two years, specializing in international trade and commercial law. He has a BA from McGill University, an MA from the Norman Paterson School of International Affairs, Carleton University, an LLB (summa cum laude) from the University of Ottawa, and an LLM from Yale University. Professor Forcese is a member in good standing of the bars of Ontario, New York, and the District of Columbia.

Kent Roach is Professor of Law and Prichard-Wilson Chair of Law and Public Policy at the University of Toronto's Faculty of Law. He was elected a Fellow of the Royal Society of Canada in 2002 and awarded a Pierre Trudeau Fellowship in 2013 for his academic and social contributions. He served on the research advisory committee of the Arar Commission from 2004 to 2006 and as research director (legal studies) of the Air India Commission from 2006 to 2010. He was the general reporter on counter-terrorism law for The XIXth International Congress of Comparative Law, which resulted in *Comparative Counter-terrorism Law* published in 2015. Other volumes edited by Professor Roach include *The Security of Freedom: Essays on Canada's Anti-terrorism Bill* and *Global Anti-terrorism Law and Policy*. He is the author of thirteen books including both *Criminal Law* and *The Charter of Rights and Freedoms* in Irwin's Essentials of Canadian Law series; *September 11: Consequences for Canada*, named one of the most important books of 2003 by the *Literary Review of Canada*; and *The 9/11 Effect: Comparative Counter-terrorism*, co-winner of the Mundell Medal in Law and Letters. He has frequently represented civil liberties and Aboriginal groups pro bono in litigation including in the *Khawaja* case at the Supreme Court of Canada.